READINGS IN THE
WESTERN HUMANITIES

READINGS IN THE WESTERN HUMANITIES
Volume I

Fifth Edition

Edited by

ROY T. MATTHEWS
F. DeWITT PLATT
Michigan State University

Boston   Burr Ridge, IL   Dubuque, IA   Madison, WI   New York   San Francisco   St. Louis
Bangkok   Bogotá   Caracas   Kuala Lumpur   Lisbon   London   Madrid   Mexico City
Milan   Montreal   New Delhi   Santiago   Seoul   Singapore   Sydney   Taipei   Toronto

Higher Education

READINGS IN THE WESTERN HUMANITIES, VOLUME I
Published by McGraw-Hill, a business unit of The McGraw-Hill Companies, Inc., 1221 Avenue of the Americas, New York, NY, 10020. Copyright © 2004 by the McGraw-Hill Companies, Inc. All rights reserved. Previous editions © 2001, 1998, 1995, 1992 by Mayfield Publishing Company. No part of this publication may be reproduced or distributed in any form or by any means, or stored in a database or retrieval system, without the prior written consent of The McGraw-Hill Companies, Inc., including, but not limited to, in any network or other electronic storage or transmission, or broadcast for distance learning.
Some Ancillaries, including electronic and print components, may not be available to customers outside the United States.

This book is printed on acid-free paper.

3 4 5 6 7 8 9 0 PBT/PBT 0 9 8 7 6 5 4

ISBN: 0-07-255639-0

Cover image: Young woman reading a book. Wallpainting from Pompeii, Italy. Museo Archeologico Nazionale, Naples, Italy. © Erich Lessing / Art Resource, NY

Publisher: Chris Freitag
Senior sponsoring editor: Joe Hanson
Development editor: Nadia Bidwell
Senior production supervisor: Richard DeVitto
Project manager: David Sutton
Lead designer: Jean Mailander
Compositor: TBH Typecast, Inc.
Typeface: 9/11 Palatino
Printer: Phoenix Book Technology

Library of Congress Cataloging-in-Publication Data
Readings in the Western humanities / edited by Roy T. Matthews, F. DeWitt Platt.—5th ed.
        p. cm.
    Includes bibliographical references and index.
    ISBN 0-07-255639-0 (alk. paper)
    1. Civilization, Western—History—Sources.   I. Matthews, Roy T.   II. Platt, F. DeWitt.
CB245.R39 2003
909'.09821—dc21

                                                           2003045893

www.mhhe.com

CONTENTS

PREFACE

With great pride we offer this newly revised edition—the fifth—of *Readings in the Western Humanities.* From its inception in the early '90s, this anthology has been designed to complement our textbook, *The Western Humanities,* now also in its fifth edition. Both books continue to reflect the educational ideal of the nineteenth-century poet and critic Matthew Arnold—that to be truly educated, students need to be exposed to "the best that has been thought and said." That ideal, we believe, offers the best alternative to the cultural forces that are threatening to engulf our era and isolate people from their historical roots. The forces we refer to are a cyberspace culture divorced from history and a mass culture catering to the lowest common denominator of society. This anthology offers students selections from the West's literary and philosophical heritage, which, if studied with care, will help students establish vital intellectual linkages to the great achievements of our continually evolving tradition and empower them to expand their horizons beyond the parochial present.

The Western tradition, originating in about 3000 B.C. and developed over five thousand years, consists of a vast, diverse, and complex tapestry of literary and philosophical writings. To keep this anthology to a manageable length, we have followed two principles as we made our selections: (1) to include works that have significantly affected Western culture, and (2) to offer as many diverse and representative voices as possible without sacrificing quality. The readings, placed in chronological order, are arranged in twenty-one chapters, echoing the format of *The Western Humanities,* and comprise two volumes. Volume I covers ancient Mesopotamia through the Renaissance; Volume II the Renaissance through the twentieth century.

The most substantive change in both volumes is a set of footnotes for the readings. With these annotations we identify difficult proper names, place names, titles, terms, ideas, quotations, and allusions in each selection that are either vital to a work's meaning or useful to know. The quantity and length of the notes vary among the selections, reflecting their differing levels of complexity and language usage. In Volume I, the notes are our own, except for the notes to Dante's *Divine Comedy,* which were adapted from those of John Ciardi, the translator of the complete poem. We believe our program of annotation has greatly enhanced the overall usefulness of the anthology, because the selections are now more accessible to students and easier for instructors to teach.

In Volume I we also made one structural change, just as we did in *The Western Humanities.* We enlarged the time frame for chapter 7 so that it now embraces the period between A.D. 284 and 1000, and we devoted chapter 8 exclusively to the world of Islam, from its founding in 630 to the conquest of Egypt and Syria by the Ottoman Turks in 1517. As part of this restructuring, we shifted from chapter 8 to chapter 7 the selections from *Beowulf,* Anna Comnena's *The Alexiad,* Boethius's *The Consolation of Philosophy,* and Hrosvitha's *Abraham,* and we expanded chapter 8 to include an enlarged selection from the *Qur'an,* the foundational text of the Islamic faith; we added selections from Ibn Khaldun's *Muqaddimah,* the most original study of history in the Muslim tradition; *The Arabian Nights,* Islam's best known literary work in the West and a classic of world literature; and the poetry of Rumi, the finest poet in Persian literature.

We also added or replaced eight selections in Volume I of the Reader. The three new selections we added in chapter 8 have been noted; we also included in chapter 5 excerpts from the *Meditations* by Marcus Aurelius, the Roman emperor, to show Stoic philosophy in action. And four replacement selections were made: In chapter 4, we exchanged "the Graces" from the *Idylls* of Theocritus with the more down-to-earth conversation between "Aeschines and Thyonichus," from the same work; we replaced Cicero's speech "Against Catiline" with "The Dream of Scipio," a highly influential work until modern times, in chapter 5; we substituted an obscure passage from Hildegard of Bingen's *Scivias* in chapter 9 for one that was more accessible; and we deleted two odes by Petrarch to make room for selections from his autobiographical memoir, "Letter to Posterity," in chapter 10. Together these eight changes represent more than one-seventh of the selections in Volume I of the new edition.

A few changes involved the introduction of new materials into existing selections. In chapter 2, two scenes from Book 23, treating the fate of Hector's corpse—its humiliation by Achilles and its eventual ransom by King Priam—were included in Homer's *Iliad,* in response to requests from reviewers; also in chapter 2, "the recognition scene" between Odysseus and Penelope from Book 24 was added to Homer's *Odyssey,* once again, in response to requests of reviewers; in chapter 6, the Flood Story was included in the excerpt from the Book of Genesis, making it available for comparison with a similar story in chapter 1's *Gilgamesh;* and an autobiographical passage was added to Anna Comnena's *The Alexiad* in chapter 7, thus offering insight in Anna's motivation in writings this history.

We were able to make these changes because we deleted several selections from the previous edition. These included selections by Aristophanes (the comic play, *Lysistrata*); Menander (the comic play, *The Woman of Samos*); Bede (*A History of the English Church and People*), and Pius II (observations of his age, *The Commentaries*).

*   *   *

We want to express our appreciation to Ashaki Charles, our acting sponsoring editor, who stepped into the breach and kept our project straight on course. We especially want to thank David Sutton, the Production Editor, who guided us through the proofing and final editing. We also extend our heartfelt gratitude to Kate Engelberg for her excellent support and advice; we are delighted that she remains a part of the lore and history of this book. We also thank Carol Crouse, Pam Suwinsky, and the production team at McGraw-Hill. To our former humanities students at Michigan State University who served as readers and critics for most of the anthology's selections, we offer our thanks; their informed responses helped hone the way we interpret literature and philosophy. If our headnotes and footnotes are clear and apposite, then part of the praise must be shared with those students.

1

PREHISTORY AND NEAR EASTERN CIVILIZATIONS

Selections from *The Code of Hammurabi*

Hammurabi (?–1750 B.C.), who ruled Babylonia from about 1792 to 1750 B.C., is the most famous of the Amorite tribal kings who gained control of the lower Euphrates Valley (modern Iraq) about 2050 B.C. Like most sovereigns of that period, he attended to the welfare of his cities and their inhabitants, attempted to appease the deities, and protected his people through alliances and wars. His reign was relatively peaceful until the last decade of his life, when he fought his enemies and expanded his empire. Hammurabi combined his newly acquired territories with his inherited lands and extended his bureaucracy to create a unified kingdom. After his death, the Amorite dynasty declined, and within two centuries the Kassites conquered Babylonia. The Babylonian kingdom was swept away, but Hammurabi's set of laws, promulgated to unify his diverse subjects, survived and became an enduring legacy.

Known as the Code of Hammurabi, these laws were inscribed on a seven-foot stele—a stone slab or pillar—which was enshrined in the temple of Marduk, the national god of the Babylonians. The stele miraculously survived over the centuries, being rediscovered in 1901 at Susa in southwest Iran, and is on display today in the Louvre. Once thought to be original with Hammurabi, the Code is now considered a summary of a body of long-standing Sumerian laws. Recent discoveries of Sumerian clay tablets, dating from about 2200 B.C. and inscribed with laws covering prices, wages, payments of loans, marriage contracts, property, and slaves, indicate that the Code borrowed laws from Hammurabi's predecessors. It is probable that the bureaucrats who drew up the Code relied on various local ordinances, some of them written, which had been used to control commerce, trade, and personal relationships for centuries. At one time scholars thought that the Code of Hammurabi influenced the Mosaic laws of the Hebrews (see *The Holy Scriptures*), but now it appears that the two sets of laws shared a common cultural tradition.

The Code is divided into three parts: the prologue, the laws, and an epilogue. The prologue repeats a message similar to others inscribed on ancient monuments. Hammurabi's achievements are listed and support from the gods is assured. The laws and regulations, usually including the punishments for breaking the law, are conditionally phrased; that is, if a person commits a certain act, he or she will be punished in certain prescribed ways. The extensive list of laws (282 examples) attempts to incorporate every phase of life—commerce, trade, parental and domestic relations, slavery, libel, slander, theft, marriage, adultery, divorce, property rights and ownership, and employer-employee regulations. Punishment for breaking the law is based on the *lex talionis* or the law of retaliation, "an eye for an eye," which most ancient societies imposed on wrongdoers. A long epilogue reiterates that Hammurabi has governed wisely and with the blessings of the deities and, in conclusion, warns future rulers that if they do not follow the laws and obey the gods, they will be cursed.

Reading the Selections

These excerpts illustrate how much the laws, regardless of their nature and types of punishment, were grounded in everyday life and the shared experiences of humans who lived in communities and were willing to accept a set of rules to settle their differences. In their historical context, they reveal how far societies had come from their earlier tribal customs of blood feuds and personal retaliation. Now, a set of laws, with harsh penalties, applied to all members of the kingdom. The selections from the prologue and the epilogue show that the rulers, who had been chosen by the deities to enact and to administer the laws, were totally dependent upon the gods who had originated the laws and would punish those who disobeyed. The Code, so closely related to the society's religious beliefs, meant that doing good or committing evil was what the gods deemed to be right or wrong. Thus, while the laws dealt with ordinary and mundane events, they possessed a moral dimension that bound the society together. Only by following the laws, emphasized the epilogue, would justice be done, peace maintained, and prosperity possible.

∞

Prologue

When the exalted Anum[1] king of the Annunaki[2] (and) Illil[3] lord of heaven and earth, who allots the destinies of the land, allotted the divine lordship of the multitude of the people unto Marduk[4] the first-born son of Ea,[5] magnified him amongst the Igigi,[6] called Babylon by its exalted name (and) so made it pre-eminent in the (four) quarters of the world, and stablished for him an everlasting kingdom whose foundations are firmly laid like heaven and earth, at that time Anum and Illil for the prosperity of the people called me by name Hammu-rabi, the reverent God-fearing prince, to make justice to appear in the land, to destroy the evil and the wicked that the strong might not oppress the weak, to rise indeed like Shamash[7] over the dark-haired folk to give light to the land.

·   ·   ·

When Marduk commanded me to give justice to the people of the land and to let (them) have (good) governance, I set forth truth and justice throughout the land (and) prospered the people.

---

[1] **Anum** In Akkadian, **Anu;** in Sumerian, **An.** King of the Babylonian gods and guardian of the city of Uruk, dominant from about 4000 to 2500 B.C.

[2] **Annunaki** Also called **Anunna.** Collective name for the seven gods of the Underworld, also called the seven judges of hell. Depending on myth and setting, they are sometimes called the gods of heaven.

[3] **Illil** In Sumerian, **Enlil.** Babylonian god of the air and storms; chief deity of the pantheon and protector of the city of Nippur, dominant from about 2500 to 1500 B.C.

[4] **Marduk** Chief god of the city of Babylon and the national deity of Babylonia.

[5] **Ea** In Sumerian, **Enki.** Babylonian god of water, depicted as half-goat, half-fish in art, the source of the Capricorn astrological sign. Ea, **Anu,** and **Enlil** were the most important gods of Mesopotamia.

[6] **Igigi** Collective name for the heavenly gods; often portrayed in opposition to the **Annunaki,** gods of the Underworld.

[7] **Shamash** In Sumerian, **Utu.** Babylonian god of the sun, god of justice, and, at night, judge of the Underworld.

∽

The Laws

§ 1

If a man has accused a man and has charged him with manslaughter and then has not proved (it against) him, his accuser shall be put to death.

§ 2

If a man has charged a man with sorcery and then has not proved (it against) him, he who is charged with the sorcery shall go to the holy river[8]; he shall leap into the holy river and, if the holy river overwhelms him, his accuser shall take and keep his house; if the holy river proves that man clear (of the offence) and he comes back safe, he who has charged him with sorcery shall be put to death; he who leapt into the holy river shall take and keep the house of his accuser.

§§ 3–4

If a man has come forward in a case to bear witness to a felony and then has not proved the statement that he has made, if that case (is) a capital one, that man shall be put to death.

If he has come forward to bear witness to (a claim for) corn or money, he shall remain liable for the penalty for that suit.

§ 5

If a judge has tried a suit, given a decision, caused a sealed tablet to be executed, (and) thereafter varies his judgement, they shall convict that judge of varying (his) judgement and he shall pay twelve-fold the claim in that suit; then they shall remove him from his place on the bench of judges in the assembly, and he shall not (again) sit in judgement with the judges.

§ 6

If a man has stolen property belonging to a god or a palace, that man shall be put to death, and he who has received the stolen property from his hand shall be put to death.

§ 7

If a man buys silver or gold or slave[9] or slave-girl or ox or sheep or ass or anything else whatsoever from a (free) man's son or a (free) man's slave or has received (them) for safe custody without witnesses or contract, that man is a thief; he shall be put to death.

§ 127

If a man has caused a finger to be pointed at a high-priestess or a married lady[10] and has then not proved (what he has said), they shall flog that man before the judges and shave half his head.

§ 128

If a man has taken a (woman to) wife and has not drawn up a contract for her, that woman is not a wife.

§ 129

If a married lady is caught lying with another man, they shall bind them and cast them into the water; if her husband wishes to let his wife live, then the king shall let his servant live.

§ 167

If a man has taken a wife and she has borne him sons (and) that woman goes to (her) fate, (if) after her (death) he marries another woman and she bears sons, after(!) the father goes to (his) fate, the sons shall not make a division according to mothers; they shall take the dowry of their (respective) mothers and shall divide the property of the paternal estate in proportion (to their number).

---

[9] **slave** The Code recognized a three-tiered social hierarchy: (1) free citizens *(Amelu)*, which included government officials, priests, and soldiers; (2) villeins *(Mushkinu)*, a middle class of merchants, shop owners, schoolteachers, workers, farmers, artisans, and craftspeople; and (3) slaves. Criminal law penalties were set according to one's place in the social hierarchy; no distinctions were made in issues of property.

[10] **married lady** The Code treated monogamy as the standard practice for families in Babylonian society, though concubines were tolerated.

---

[8] **holy river** The Euphrates River.

§§ 168–169

If a man sets his face to disinherit his son (and) states to the judges "I will disinherit my son," the judges shall determine the facts of his case and, if he has not deserved the heavy penalty of disinheritance, the father may not disinherit his son.

If he deserves the heavy penalty of disinheritance at the hands of his father, a first time they shall pardon him; if he deserves the (same) heavy penalty a second time, his father may disinherit his son.

§§ 196–205

If a man has put out the eye of a free man, they shall put out his eye.

If he breaks the bone of a (free) man, they shall break his bone.

If he puts out the eye of a villein or breaks the bone of a villein, he shall pay 1 maneh of silver.

If he puts out the eye of a (free) man's slave or breaks the bone of a (free) man's slave, he shall pay half his price.

If a man knocks out the tooth of a (free) man equal (in rank) to him(self), they shall knock out his tooth.

If he knocks out the tooth of a villein, he shall pay ⅓ maneh of silver.

If a man strikes the cheek of a (free) man who is superior (in rank) to him(self), he shall be beaten with sixty stripes with a whip of ox-hide in the assembly.

If the man strikes the cheek of a free man equal to him(self in rank), he shall pay 1 maneh of silver.

If a villein strikes the cheek of a villein, he shall pay 10 shekels of silver.

If the slave of a (free) man strikes the cheek of a free man, they shall cut off his ear.

. . .

Epilogue

(These are) the just laws which Hammurabi the able king has stablished and (thereby) has enabled the land to enjoy stable governance and good rule.

I Hammu-rabi, the gracious king, have not been careless nor been slack on behalf of the dark-haired folk whom Illil has granted to me (and) whose shepherding Marduk has given to me; I seek out peaceful places for them (and) have relieved their cruel distresses, (and) I make light to rise upon them. With the mighty weapon which Ilbaba[11] and Ishtar[12] have bestowed upon me, with the wisdom which Ea has allotted to me, with the ability which Marduk has given to me, I have plucked up (my) enemies from north to south, extinguished wars (and) prospered the land; I have made the people of the towns to lie down in safety (and) have left them none to affright them.

. . .

If that man has not heeded my words which I have inscribed on my monument, has despised my curses and has not feared the curses of the gods and so has razed the judgment which I have judged, revoked my commandments (and) altered my carved figures, has erased my name inscribed (thereon) and has then inscribed his (own) name (in its place), (or if) in fear of those curses he suborns another indeed (to do so), may the great Anum the father of the gods who has called me to reign deprive that man, whether king or lord or governor or any of mankind that bears a name, of royal splendour, break his sceptre (and) curse his destiny; may the lord Illil who allots the destinies (of mankind), whose word then is unalterable, the magnifier of my kingdom, kindle disorder that cannot be put down (and) despair to be the ruin of him in his habitation, may he allot unto him as (his) destiny a reign of sighs, days of scarcity (and) years of famine, thick darkness (and) death in the twinkling of an eye; may he by his honoured mouth ordain the ruin of his city, the scattering of his people, the overthrow of his kingdom, the extinction of his name and of his fame in the land.

. . .

May Ishtar, the lady of battle and conflict who unsheathes my weapon, my favouring guardian spirit (and) the lover of my reign, curse his kingdom in her great rage from her wrathful heart, turn his good fortune into ill fortune, break his weapons in field battle and conflict, raise disorder (and) rebellion against him, strike down his heroes (and) let the earth drink their blood, (and) let his armies be left a heap of corpses on the plain, let no quarter be given to his soldiers, deliver that man into the hand of his enemies and lead him in bonds to a land at enmity with him.

May Nergal,[13] mighty amongst the gods, the warrior whom none can resist, who has fulfilled my eager desire, by his great power consume his people like a fire raging amongst rushes, may he cleave him asunder with his mighty weapon and shatter his limbs as of a statue of clay.

---

[11] **Ilbaba** Also called **Zamama**. Babylonian god of war and protector of the city of Kish.
[12] **Ishtar** In Sumerian, **Inanna**. Babylonian goddess of love, fertility, and fighting. Said to be the daughter of various gods, including **Anu.**

[13] **Nergal** An Underworld deity, the god of war and sudden death.

May Nintu,[14] the exalted lady of the lands, the mother my creatress, bereave him of an heir and let him have no name, let him create no seed of mankind in the midst of his people.

May Ninkarrak,[15] the daughter of Anum, who speaks in my favour in Ekur,[16] bring upon his limbs a grievous sore, an evil plague, a sore wound which none can assuage (and) of which no physician knows the nature (and) can-not relieve it with dressings, (and which) like the sting of death cannot be plucked out, so that he may then bewail his (lost) manhood until his life is extinguished.

May the great gods of heaven and earth, the Anun-naki all together, and the protecting deity of the house, the brick-god of Ebabbar,[17] curse that (man), his seed, his land, his soldiers, his people and his army, with a baleful curse.

May Illil with his word which shall then be unalter-able curse him with clear curses, and may they quickly overtake him!

---

[14] **Nintu** Babylonian mother goddess.
[15] **Ninkarrak** Perhaps a minor mother goddess.
[16] **Ekur** Heaven.

---

[17] **Ebabbar** Temple of the Sun God **Shamash.**

Selections from *The Epic of Gilgamesh*

The Epic of Gilgamesh is now considered by most scholars to be the oldest known epic in Western literature. This work predates Homer's *Iliad* and *Odyssey* by some fifteen hundred years, appearing about 2200 B.C.

Like other epics, *The Epic of Gilgamesh* went through several variations before reaching its final form. It is based on a historical figure who quickly passed over into folklore. Gilgamesh reigned as king of the Sumerian city of Uruk around 2700 B.C., and soon after his death, his ordinary experiences were turned into stories of heroic deeds and dangerous journeys. Civiliza-tions that succeeded the Sumerians infused into the epic new episodes and characters, different sets of deities, and issues reflecting the concerns of their own time. Nonetheless, despite its evo-lution through various civilizations, this epic recalls similar events that appear in other cul-tures' histories. In *The Epic of Gilgamesh*, the tale of a devastating flood that killed all animals and humans except those who took refuge in a boat resembles stories from other societies, in particular the biblical narrative of Noah, his family, and God.

Another reason why *The Epic of Gilgamesh* evolved from its original form was that it, like all epics, was sung long before it was written, and storytellers adapted the episodes and characters to fit their new audiences. The earliest written form of *The Epic of Gilgamesh* uncovered by archaeologists dates from about 600 B.C., a time when many Middle Eastern societies were dis-appearing and just before many others would fall under the influence of Greek civilization, later to become provinces of the Roman Empire.

Reading the Selections

These excerpts deal with two themes: (1) that mortals cannot insult the gods and goddesses without punishment, and (2), that humans are destined to die. Ishtar, the goddess of love, attempts to seduce Gilgamesh, who spurns her overtures by recalling how she ruined other humans. Furious at Gilgamesh, Ishtar asks her father to send the Bull of Heaven to kill Gil-gamesh. Gilgamesh and Enkidu, the former wildman who had become civilized and had fought Gilgamesh before becoming his close companion, kill the bull. The gods and goddesses decide that Enkidu must die for this transgression. As Enkidu lies dying, he dreams of walking through the "house of dust," where he encounters dead kings and priests and various deities. Homer and many other writers later copy this device of transporting their heroes into the world of the dead to speak with the great men and, sometimes, women of history, as a way to glorify the past and allow the characters to be told of future events by the dead.

Gilgamesh's grief over the death of Enkidu reveals the Sumerian way of death. Gilgamesh orders his artisans to memorialize Enkidu with a statue—one that may have very well existed at some time in Sumerian history. Touched by Enkidu's death, Gilgamesh recognizes his own mortal nature but refuses to accept his final fate. He sets out to find Utnapishtim, to whom the gods have given everlasting life and who, Gilgamesh hopes, will answer his questions about immortality. Gilgamesh, on his journey, has many adventures, among them meeting Siduri, who keeps a vineyard and advises Gilgamesh to enjoy life now, for he is destined to die. When Gilgamesh finally meets Utnapishtim, he is told that nothing is permanent; thus life is not everlasting. Gilgamesh asks Utnapishtim why the gods gave him immortality, and the old man replies that he will reveal a secret about the gods and proceeds to tell The Story of the Flood. Utnapishtim's account of the flood is similar to the one in the Holy Scriptures, which should not be surprising since many societies located near rivers suffered from flooding and such stories eventually became part of the folklore.

∞

Ishtar and Gilgamesh, and the Death of Enkidu

Gilgamesh washed out his long locks and cleaned his weapons; he flung back his hair from his shoulders; he threw off his stained clothes and changed them for new. He put on his royal robes and made them fast. When Gilgamesh had put on the crown, glorious Ishtar[1] lifted her eyes, seeing the beauty of Gilgamesh. She said, "Come to me Gilgamesh, and be my bridegroom; grant me seed of your body, let me be your bride and you shall be my husband. I will harness for you a chariot of lapis lazuli[2] and of gold, with wheels of gold and horns of copper; and you shall have mighty demons of the storm for draft-mules. When you enter our house in the fragrance of cedar-wood, threshold and throne will kiss your feet. Kings, rulers, and princes will bow down before you; they shall bring you tribute from the mountains and the plain. Your ewes shall drop twins and your goats triplets; your pack-ass shall outrun mules; your oxen shall have no rivals, and your chariot horses shall be famous far-off for their swiftness."

Gilgamesh opened his mouth and answered glorious Ishtar, "If I take you in marriage, what gifts can I give in return? What ointments and clothing for your body? I would gladly give you bread and all sorts of food fit for a god. I would give you wine to drink fit for a queen. I would pour out barley to stuff your granary; but as for making you my wife—that I will not. How would it go with me? Your lovers have found you like a brazier which smoulders in the cold, a backdoor which keeps out neither squall of wind nor storm, a castle which crushes the garrison, pitch that blackens the bearer, a water-skin that chafes the carrier, a stone which falls from the parapet, a battering-ram turned back from the enemy, a sandal that trips the wearer. Which of your lovers did you ever love for ever? What shepherd of yours has pleased you for all time? Listen to me while I tell the tale of your lovers. There was Tammuz,[3] the lover of your youth, for him you decreed wailing, year after year. You loved the many-coloured roller,[4] but still you struck and broke his wing; now in the grove he sits and cries, 'Kappi,[5] kappi, my wing, my wing.' You have loved the lion tremendous in strength: seven pits you dug for him, and seven. You have loved the stallion magnificent in battle, and for him you decreed whip and spur and a thong, to gallop seven leagues by force and to muddy the water before he drinks; and for his mother Silili[6] lamentations. You have loved the shepherd of the flock; he made meal-cake for you day after day, he killed kids for your sake. You struck and turned him into a wolf; now his own herd-boys chase

---

[1] **Ishtar** Also called **Inanna.** The goddess of love, fertility, and war. Identified with the planet Venus. Daughter of **Anu,** king of the gods, and **Antum.**
[2] **lapis lazuli** A semiprecious stone that is usually azure blue; greatly valued in Mesopotamia.

[3] **Tammuz** Also called **Dumuzi** ("true son"). The shepherd god. In the myth entitled "Inanna's Journey to Hell," the goddess Ishtar abandons her husband Dumuzi in Hell.
[4] **roller** A bird that symbolized a lover of the goddess **Ishtar.**
[5] **kappi** A bird sound.
[6] **Silili** The divine mare, the mother of all horses.

him away, his own hounds worry his flanks. And did you not love Ishullanu,[7] the gardener of your father's palm-grove? He brought you baskets filled with dates without end; every day he loaded your table. Then you turned your eyes on him and said, 'Dearest Ishullanu, come here to me, let us enjoy your manhood, come forward and take me, I am yours.' Ishullanu answered, 'What are you asking from me? My mother has baked and I have eaten; why should I come to such as you for food that is tainted and rotten? For when was a screen of rushes sufficient protection from frosts?' But when you had heard his answer you struck him. He was changed to a blind mole deep in the earth, one whose desire is always beyond his reach. And if you and I should be lovers, should not I be served in the same fashion as all these others whom you loved once?"

When Ishtar heard this she fell into a bitter rage, she went up to high heaven. Her tears poured down in front of her father Anu,[8] and Antum[9] her mother. She said, "My father, Gilgamesh has heaped insults on me, he has told over all my abominable behaviour, my foul and hideous acts." Anu opened his mouth and said, "Are you a father of gods? Did not you quarrel with Gilgamesh the king, so now he has related your abominable behaviour, your foul and hideous acts?"

Ishtar opened her mouth and said again, "My father, give me the Bull of Heaven[10] to destroy Gilgamesh. Fill Gilgamesh, I say, with arrogance to his destruction; but if you refuse to give me the Bull of Heaven I will break in the doors of hell and smash the bolts; there will be confusion of people, those above with those from the lower depths. I shall bring up the dead to eat food like the living; and the hosts of dead will outnumber the living." Anu said to great Ishtar, "If I do what you desire there will be seven years of drought throughout Uruk when corn will be seedless husks. Have you saved grain enough for the people and grass for the cattle?" Ishtar replied, "I have saved grain for the people, grass for the cattle; for seven years of seedless husks there is grain and there is grass enough."

When Anu heard what Ishtar had said he gave her the Bull of Heaven to lead by the halter down to Uruk. When they reached the gates of Uruk the Bull went to the river; with his first snort cracks opened in the earth and a hundred young men fell down to death. With his second snort cracks opened and two hundred fell down to death. With his third snort cracks opened, Enkidu doubled over but instantly recovered, he dodged aside and leapt on the Bull and seized it by the horns. The Bull of Heaven foamed in his face, it brushed him with the thick of its tail. Enkidu cried to Gilgamesh, "My friend, we boasted that we would leave enduring names behind us. Now thrust in your sword between the nape and the horns." So Gilgamesh followed the Bull, he seized the thick of its tail, he

thrust the sword between the nape and the horns and slew the Bull. When they had killed the Bull of Heaven they cut out its heart and gave it to Shamash, and the brothers rested.

But Ishtar rose up and mounted the great wall of Uruk; she sprang on to the tower and uttered a curse: "Woe to Gilgamesh, for he has scorned me in killing the Bull of Heaven." When Enkidu heard these words he tore out the Bull's right thigh and tossed it in her face saying, "If I could lay my hands on you, it is this I should do to you, and lash the entrails to your side." Then Ishtar called together her people, the dancing and singing girls, the prostitutes of the temple, the courtesans. Over the thigh of the Bull of Heaven she set up lamentation.

But Gilgamesh called the smiths and the armourers, all of them together. They admired the immensity of the horns. They were plated with lapis lazuli two fingers thick. They were thirty pounds each in weight, and their capacity in oil was six measures, which he gave to his guardian god, Lugulbanda.[11] But he carried the horns into the palace and hung them on the wall. Then they washed their hands in Euphrates, they embraced each other and went away. They drove through the streets of Uruk where the heroes were gathered to see them, and Gilgamesh called to the singing girls, "Who is most glorious of the heroes, who is most eminent among men?" "Gilgamesh is the most glorious of heroes, Gilgamesh is most eminent among men." And now there was feasting, and celebrations and joy in the palace, till the heroes lay down saying, "Now we will rest for the night."

When the daylight came Enkidu got up and cried to Gilgamesh, "Oh my brother, such a dream I had last night. Anu, Enlil,[12] Ea[13] and heavenly Shamash[14] took counsel together, and Anu said to Enlil, 'Because they have killed the Bull of Heaven, and because they have killed Humbaba[15] who guarded the Cedar Mountain one of the two must die.' Then glorious Shamash answered the hero Enlil, 'It was by your command they killed the Bull of Heaven, and killed Humbaba, and must Enkidu die although innocent?' Enlil flung round in rage at glorious Shamash, 'You dare to say this, you who went about with them every day like one of themselves!'"

So Enkidu lay stretched out before Gilgamesh; his tears ran down in streams and he said to Gilgamesh, "O my brother, so dear as you are to me, brother, yet they will take me from you." Again he said, "I must sit down on the threshold of the dead and never again will I see my dear brother with my eyes."

While Enkidu lay alone in his sickness he cursed the gate as though it was living flesh, "You there, wood of the gate, dull and insensible, witless, I searched for you over twenty leagues until I saw the towering cedar. There is no

---

[7] **Ishullanu** The gardener of **Anu,** king of the Mesopotamian gods.
[8] **Anu** King of the Mesopotamian gods and father of **Ishtar.**
[9] **Antum** From Sumerian, "the earth." Mother of **Ishtar** and consort of **Anu.**
[10] **Bull of Heaven** Monster created by **Anu** and given to **Ishtar** to be used against Gilgamesh.

[11] **Lugulbanda** God-king of the city of Uruk and perhaps Gilgamesh's father. Gilgamesh worshiped him as a god.
[12] **Enlil** Babylonian god of air and storms.
[13] **Ea** In Sumerian, **Enki.** Babylonian god of water.
[14] **Shamash** Babylonian god of the sun.
[15] **Humbaba** Also called **Huwawa.** A nature god assigned to protect the cedar forest.

wood like you in our land. Seventy-two cubits high and twenty-four wide, the pivot and the ferrule[16] and the jambs[17] are perfect. A master craftsman from Nippur has made you; but O, if I had known the conclusion! If I had known that this was all the good that would come of it, I would have raised the axe and split you into little pieces and set up here a gate of wattle instead. Ah, if only some future king had brought you here, or some god had fashioned you. Let him obliterate my name and write his own, and the curse fall on him instead of on Enkidu."

With the first brightening of dawn Enkidu raised his head and wept before the Sun God,[18] in the brilliance of the sunlight his tears streamed down. "Sun God, I beseech you, about that vile Trapper, that Trapper of nothing because of whom I was to catch less than my comrade; let him catch least; make his game scarce, make him feeble, taking the smaller of every share, let his quarry escape from his nets."

When he had cursed the Trapper to his heart's content he turned on the harlot. He was roused to curse her also. "As for you, woman, with a great curse I curse you! I will promise you a destiny to all eternity. My curse shall come on you soon and sudden. You shall be without a roof for your commerce, for you shall not keep house with other girls in the tavern, but do your business in places fouled by the vomit of the drunkard. Your hire will be potter's earth,[19] your thievings will be flung into the hovel, you will sit at the cross-roads in the dust of the potter's quarter, you will make your bed on the dunghill at night, and by day take your stand in the wall's shadow. Brambles and thorns will tear your feet, the drunk and the dry will strike your cheek and your mouth will ache. Let you be stripped of your purple[20] dyes, for I too once in the wilderness with my wife had all the treasure I wished."

When Shamash heard the words of Enkidu he called to him from heaven: "Enkidu, why are you cursing the woman, the mistress who taught you to eat bread fit for gods and drink wine of kings? She who put upon you a magnificent garment, did she not give you glorious Gilgamesh for your companion, and has not Gilgamesh, your own brother, made you rest on a royal bed and recline on a couch at his left hand? He has made the princes of the earth kiss your feet, and now all the people of Uruk lament and wail over you. When you are dead he will let his hair grow long for your sake, he will wear a lion's pelt and wander through the desert."

When Enkidu heard glorious Shamash his angry heart grew quiet, he called back the curse and said, "Woman, I promise you another destiny. The mouth which cursed you shall bless you! Kings, princes and nobles shall adore you. On your account a man though twelve miles off will clap his hand to his thigh and his hair will twitch. For you he will undo his belt and open his treasure and you shall have your desire; lapis lazuli, gold

and carnelian[21] from the heap in the treasury. A ring for your hand and a robe shall be yours. The priest will lead you into the presence of the gods. On your account a wife, a mother of seven, was forsaken."

As Enkidu slept alone in his sickness, in bitterness of spirit he poured out his heart to his friend. "It was I who cut down the cedar, I who levelled the forest, I who slew Humbaba and now see what has become of me. Listen, my friend, this is the dream I dreamed last night. The heavens roared, and earth rumbled back an answer; between them stood I before an awful being, the somber-faced man-bird; he had directed on me his purpose. His was a vampire face, his foot was a lion's foot, his hand was an eagle's talon. He fell on me and his claws were in my hair, he held me fast and I smothered; then he transformed me so that my arms became wings covered with feathers. He turned his stare towards me, and he led me away to the palace of Irkalla,[22] the Queen of Darkness, to the house from which none who enters ever returns, down the road from which there is no coming back.

"There is the house whose people sit in darkness; dust is their food and clay their meat. They are clothed like birds with wings for covering, they see no light, they sit in darkness. I entered the house of dust and I saw the kings of the earth, their crowns put away for ever; rulers and princes, all those who once wore kingly crowns and ruled the world in the days of old. They who had stood in the place of the gods like Anu and Enlil, stood now like servants to fetch baked meats in the house of dust, to carry cooked meat and cold water from the water-skin. In the house of dust which I entered were high priests and acolytes, priests of the incantation and of ecstasy; there were servers of the temple, and there was Etana,[23] that King of Kish whom the eagle carried to heaven in the days of old. I saw also Samuqan,[24] god of cattle, and there was Ereshkigal[25] The Queen of the Underworld; and Belit-Sheri[26] squatted in front of her, she who is recorder of the gods and keeps the book of death. She held a tablet from which she read. She raised her head, she saw me and spoke: "Who has brought this one here?" Then I awoke like a man drained of blood who wanders alone in a waste of rushes; like one whom the bailiff has seized and his heart pounds with terror."

Gilgamesh had peeled off his clothes, he listened to his words and wept quick tears, Gilgamesh listened and his tears flowed. He opened his mouth and spoke to Enkidu: "Who is there in strong-walled Uruk who has wisdom like this? Strange things have been spoken, why does your heart speak strangely? The dream was marvellous but the terror was great; we must treasure the dream whatever the terror; for the dream has shown that misery comes at last to the healthy man, the end of life is sorrow."

---

[16] **ferrule** A metal brace to keep a gate from splitting.
[17] **jamb** An upright piece forming the side of a door opening.
[18] **Sun God Shamash.**
[19] **potter's earth** Dirt for a graveyard.
[20] **purple** Tyrian purple, an expensive dye available only from a mollusk at Tyre (in modern Lebanon), a color falling between red and blue; usually reserved for royalty or other high rank in ancient times.

[21] **carnelian** A hard, reddish stone used in jewelry.
[22] **Irkalla** Another name for **Ereshkigal,** the Queen of the Underworld.
[23] **Etana** Legendary king of Kish and a great friend of Gilgamesh.
[24] **Samuqan** Mesopotamian god of cattle; a member of **Ereshkigal's** court in the Underworld.
[25] **Ereshkigal** Mesopotamian Queen of the Underworld.
[26] **Belit-Sheri** Female scribe in the Underworld; works for **Ereshkigal.**

And Gilgamesh lamented, "Now I will pray to the great gods, for my friend had an ominous dream."

This day on which Enkidu dreamed came to an end and he lay stricken with sickness. One whole day he lay on his bed and his suffering increased. He said to Gilgamesh, the friend on whose account he had left the wilderness, "Once I ran for you, for the water of life, and I now have nothing." A second day he lay on his bed and Gilgamesh watched over him but the sickness increased. A third day he lay on his bed, he called out to Gilgamesh, rousing him up. Now he was weak and his eyes were blind with weeping. Ten days he lay and his suffering increased, eleven and twelve days he lay on his bed of pain. Then he called to Gilgamesh, "My friend, the great goddess cursed me and I must die in shame. I shall not die like a man fallen in battle; I feared to fall, but happy is the man who falls in the battle, for I must die in shame." And Gilgamesh wept over Enkidu. . . .

He touched his heart but it did not beat, nor did he lift his eyes again. When Gilgamesh touched his heart it did not beat. So Gilgamesh laid a veil, as one veils the bride, over his friend. He began to rage like a lion, like a lioness robbed of her whelps. This way and that he paced round the bed, he tore out his hair and strewed it around. He dragged off his splendid robes and flung them down as though they were abominations.

In the first light of dawn Gilgamesh cried out, "I [20] made you rest on a royal bed, you reclined on a couch at my left hand, the princes of the earth kissed your feet. I will cause all the people of Uruk to weep over you and raise the dirge of the dead. The joyful people will stoop with sorrow; and when you have gone to the earth I will let my hair grow long for your sake, I will wander through the wilderness in the skin of a lion." The next day also, in the first light, Gilgamesh lamented; seven days and seven nights he wept for Enkidu, until the worm fastened on him. Only then he gave him up to the earth, for the Anunnaki, the judges, had seized him.

Then Gilgamesh issued a proclamation through the land, he summoned them all, the coppersmiths, the goldsmiths, the stone-workers, and commanded them, "Make a statue of my friend." The statue was fashioned with a great weight of lapis lazuli for the breast and of gold for the body. A table of hard-wood was set out, and on it a bowl of carnelian filled with honey, and a bowl of lapis lazuli filled with butter. These he exposed and offered to the Sun; and weeping he went away.

∽

The Search for Everlasting Life

Bitterly Gilgamesh wept for his friend Enkidu; he wan- [1] dered over the wilderness as a hunter, he roamed over the plains; in his bitterness he cried, "How can I rest, how can I be at peace? Despair is in my heart. What my brother is now, that shall I be when I am dead. Because I am afraid of death I will go as best I can to find Utnapishtim[27] whom they call the Faraway, for he has entered the assembly of the gods." So Gilgamesh travelled over the wilderness, he wandered over the grasslands, a long journey, in search of Utnapishtim, whom the gods took after the deluge; and they set him to live in the land of Dilmun,[28] in the garden of the sun; and to him alone of men they gave everlasting life.

At night when he came to the mountain passes Gilgamesh prayed: "In these mountain passes long ago I saw lions, I was afraid and I lifted my eyes to the moon; I prayed and my prayers went up to the gods, so now, O moon god Sin,[29] protect me." When he had prayed he lay down to sleep, until he was woken from out of a dream.

He saw the lions round him glorying in life; then he took his axe in his hand, he drew his sword from his belt, and he fell upon them like an arrow from the string, and struck and destroyed and scattered them.

.   .   .

There was the garden of the gods; all round him stood bushes bearing gems. Seeing it he went down at once, for there was fruit of carnelian with the vine hanging from it, beautiful to look at; lapis lazuli leaves hung thick with fruit, sweet to see. For thorns and thistles there were haematite[30] and rare stones, agate, and pearls from out of the sea. While Gilgamesh walked in the garden by the edge of the sea Shamash saw him, and he saw that he was dressed in the skins of animals and ate their flesh. He was distressed, and he spoke and said, "No mortal man has gone this way before, nor will, as long as the winds drive over the sea." And to Gilgamesh he said, "You will never find the life for which you are searching." Gilgamesh said to glorious Shamash, "Now that I have toiled and strayed so far over the wilderness, am I to sleep, and let the earth cover my head for ever? Let my eyes see the sun until they are dazzled with looking. Although I am no better than a dead man, still let me see the light of the sun."

---

[27] **Utnapishtim** Son of **Ubara-Tutu.** Often called the Babylonian Noah (See *The Holy Scriptures*). Utnapishtim and his wife are made immortal after the flood.

[28] **Dilmun** The heavenly paradise of the immortal **Utnapishtim** and his wife. Historic Dilmun was an ancient kingdom on the island known today as al-Bahrain in the Persian Gulf, which flourished about 2000 B.C.

[29] **Sin** Also called **Su-en** or **Suen;** in Sumerian **Nanna.** Babylonian Moon-God.

---

[30] **haematite,** or **hematite** Iron ore occurring in two forms: crystals and reddish earth.

Beside the sea she lives, the woman of the vine, the maker of wine; Siduri[31] sits in the garden at the edge of the sea, with the golden bowl and the golden vats that the gods gave her. She is covered with a veil; and where she sits she sees Gilgamesh coming towards her, wearing skins, the flesh of the gods in his body, but despair in his heart, and his face like the face of one who has made a long journey. She looked, and as she scanned the distance she said in her own heart, "Surely this is some felon; where is he going now?" And she barred her gate against him with the cross-bar and shot home the bolt. But Gilgamesh, hearing the sound of the bolt, threw up his head and lodged his foot in the gate; he called to her, "Young woman, maker of wine, why do you bolt your door; what did you see that made you bar your gate? I will break in your door and burst in your gate, for I am Gilgamesh who seized and killed the Bull of Heaven, I killed the watchman of the cedar forest, I overthrew Humbaba who lived in the forest, and I killed the lions in the passes of the mountain."

Then Siduri said to him, "If you are that Gilgamesh 5 who seized and killed the Bull of Heaven, who killed the watchman of the cedar forest, who overthrew Humbaba that lived in the forest, and killed the lions in the passes of the mountain, why are your cheeks so starved and why is your face so drawn? Why is despair in your heart and your face like the face of one who has made a long journey? Yes, why is your face burned from heat and cold, and why do you come here wandering over the pastures in search of the wind?"

Gilgamesh answered her, "And why should not my cheeks be starved and my face drawn? Despair is in my heart and my face is the face of one who has made a long journey, it was burned with heat and with cold. Why should I not wander over the pastures in search of the wind? My friend, my younger brother, he who hunted the wild ass of the wilderness and the panther of the plains, my friend, my younger brother who seized and killed the Bull of Heaven and overthrew Humbaba in the cedar forest, my friend who was very dear to me and who endured dangers beside me, Enkidu my brother, whom I loved, the end of mortality has overtaken him. I wept for him seven days and nights till the worm fastened on him. Because of my brother I am afraid of death, because of my brother I stray through the wilderness and cannot rest. But now, young woman, maker of wine, since I have seen your face do not let me see the face of death which I dread so much."

She answered, "Gilgamesh, where are you hurrying to? You will never find that life for which you are looking. When the gods created man they allotted to him death, but life they retained in their own keeping. As for you, Gilgamesh, fill your belly with good things; day and night, night and day, dance and be merry, feast and rejoice. Let your clothes be fresh, bathe yourself in water, cherish the little child that holds your hand, and make your wife happy in your embrace; for this too is the lot of man."

But Gilgamesh said to Siduri, the young woman, "How can I be silent, how can I rest, when Enkidu whom I love is dust, and I too shall die and be laid in the earth. You live by the sea-shore and look into the heart of it; young woman, tell me now, which is the way to Utnapishtim, the son of Ubara-Tutu[32]? What directions are there for the passage; give me, oh, give me directions. I will cross the Ocean if it is possible; if it is not I will wander still farther in the wilderness." The wine-maker said to him, "Gilgamesh, there is no crossing the Ocean; whoever has come, since the days of old, has not been able to pass that sea. The Sun in his glory crosses the Ocean, but who beside Shamash has ever crossed it? The place and the passage are difficult, and the waters of death are deep which flow between. Gilgamesh, how will you cross the Ocean? When you come to the waters of death what will you do? But Gilgamesh, down in the woods you will find Urshanabi,[33] the ferryman of Utnapishtim; with him are the holy things, the things of stone. He is fashioning the serpent prow of the boat. Look at him well, and if it is possible, perhaps you will cross the waters with him; but if it is not possible, then you must go back."

When Gilgamesh heard this he was seized with anger. He took his axe in his hand, and his dagger from his belt. He crept forward and he fell on them like a javelin. Then he went into the forest and sat down. Urshanabi saw the dagger flash and heard the axe, and he beat his head, for Gilgamesh had shattered the tackle of the boat in his rage. Urshanabi said to him, "Tell me, what is your name? I am Urshanabi, the ferryman of Utnapishtim the Faraway." He replied to him, "Gilgamesh is my name, I am from Uruk, from the house of Anu." Then Urshanabi said to him, "Why are your cheeks so starved and your face drawn? Why is despair in your heart and your face like the face of one who has made a long journey; yes, why is your face burned with heat and with cold, and why do you come here wandering over the pastures in search of the wind?"

Gilgamesh said to him, "Why should not my cheeks 10 be starved and my face drawn? Despair is in my heart, and my face is the face of one who has made a long journey. I was burned with heat and with cold. Why should I not wander over the pastures? My friend, my younger brother who seized and killed the Bull of Heaven, and overthrew Humbaba in the cedar forest, my friend who was very dear to me, and who endured dangers beside me, Enkidu my brother whom I loved, the end of mortality has overtaken him. I wept for him seven days and nights till the worm fastened on him. Because of my brother I am afraid of death, because of my brother I stray through the wilderness. His fate lies heavy upon me. How can I be silent, how can I rest? He is dust and I too shall die and be laid in

---

[31] **Siduri** A young woman who makes wine and counsels Gilgamesh to seek pleasure instead of immortality.

[32] **Ubara-Tutu** Father of **Utnapishtim.**

[33] **Urshanabi** The ferryman and sailor god who crosses the water daily between the garden of the sun and the paradise where the immortal **Utnapishtim** and his wife live.

the earth for ever. I am afraid of death, therefore, Urshanabi, tell me which is the road to Utnapishtim? If it is possible I will cross the waters of death; if not I will wander still farther through the wilderness."

Urshanabi said to him, "Gilgamesh, your own hands have prevented you from crossing the Ocean; when you destroyed the tackle of the boat you destroyed its safety." Then the two of them talked it over and Gilgamesh said, "Why are you so angry with me, Urshanabi, for you yourself cross the sea by day and night, at all seasons you cross it." "Gilgamesh, those things you destroyed, their property is to carry me over the water, to prevent the waters of death from touching me. It was for this reason that I preserved them, but you have destroyed them, and the *urnu* snakes[34] with them. But now, go into the forest, Gilgamesh; with your axe cut poles, one hundred and twenty, cut them sixty cubits long, paint them with bitumen, set on them ferrules and bring them back."

When Gilgamesh heard this he went into the forest, he cut poles one hundred and twenty; he cut them sixty cubits long, he painted them with bitumen,[35] he set on them ferrules, and he brought them to Urshanabi. Then they boarded the boat, Gilgamesh and Urshanabi together, launching it out on the waves of Ocean. For three days they ran on as it were a journey of a month and fifteen days, and at last Urshanabi brought the boat to the waters of death. Then Urshanabi said to Gilgamesh, "Press on, take a pole and thrust it in, but do not let your hands touch the waters. Gilgamesh, take a second pole, take a third, take a fourth pole. Now, Gilgamesh, take a fifth, take a sixth and seventh pole. Gilgamesh, take an eighth, and ninth, a tenth pole. Gilgamesh, take an eleventh, take a twelfth pole." After one hundred and twenty thrusts Gilgamesh had used the last pole. Then he stripped himself, he held up his arms for a mast and his covering for a sail. So Urshanabi the ferryman brought Gilgamesh to Utnapishtim, whom they call the Faraway, who lives in Dilmun at the place of the sun's transit, eastward of the mountain. To him alone of men the gods had given everlasting life.

Now Utnapishtim, where he lay at ease, looked into the distance and he said in his heart, musing to himself, "Why does the boat sail here without tackle and mast; why are the sacred stones[36] destroyed, and why does the master not sail the boat? That man who comes is none of mine; where I look I see a man whose body is covered with skins of beasts. Who is this who walks up the shore behind Urshanabi, for surely he is no man of mine?" So Utnapishtim looked at him and said, "What is your name, you who come here wearing the skins of beasts, with your cheeks starved and your face drawn? Where are you hurrying to now? For what reason have you made this great journey, crossing the seas whose passage is difficult? Tell me the reason for your coming."

He replied, 'Gilgamesh is my name. I am from Uruk, from the house of Anu." Then Utnapishtim said to him, "If you are Gilgamesh, why are your cheeks so starved and your face drawn? Why is despair in your heart and your face like the face of one who has made a long journey? Yes, why is your face burned with heat and cold; and why do you come here, wandering over the wilderness in search of the wind?"

Gilgamesh said to him, "Why should not my cheeks be starved and my face drawn? Despair is in my heart and my face is the face of one who has made a long journey. It was burned with heat and with cold. Why should I not wander over the pastures? My friend, my younger brother who seized and killed the Bull of Heaven and overthrew Humbaba in the cedar forest, my friend who was very dear to me and endured dangers beside me, Enkidu, my brother whom I loved, the end of mortality has overtaken him. I wept for him seven days and nights till the worm fastened on him. Because of my brother I am afraid of death; because of my brother I stray through the wilderness. His fate lies heavy upon me. How can I be silent, how can I rest? He is dust and I shall die also and be laid in the earth for ever." Again Gilgamesh said, speaking to Utnapishtim, "It is to see Utnapishtim whom we call the Faraway that I have come this journey. For this I have wandered over the world, I have crossed many difficult ranges, I have crossed the seas, I have wearied myself with travelling; my joints are aching, and I have lost acquaintance with sleep which is sweet. My clothes were worn out before I came to the house of Siduri. I have killed the bear and hyena, the lion and panther, the tiger, the stag and the ibex, all sorts of wild game and the small creatures of the pastures. I ate their flesh and I wore their skins; and that was how I came to the gate of the young woman, the maker of wine, who barred her gate of pitch and bitumen against me. But from her I had news of the journey; so then I came to Urshanabi the ferryman, and with him I crossed over the waters of death. Oh, father Utnapishtim, you who have entered the assembly of the gods, I wish to question you concerning the living and the dead, how shall I find the life for which I am searching?"

Utnapishtim said, "There is no permanence. Do we build a house to stand for ever, do we seal a contract to hold for all time? Do brothers divide an inheritance to keep for ever, does the flood-time of rivers endure? It is only the nymph[37] of the dragon-fly who sheds her larva and sees the sun in his glory. From the days of old there is no permanence. The sleeping and the dead, how alike they are, they are like a painted death. What is there between the master and the servant when both have fulfilled their doom? When the Anunnaki, the judges, come together, and Mammetun[38] the mother of destinies,

---

[34] *urnu* **snakes** Unclear, but the references to **sacred stones** and *urnu* **snakes** are to something necessary for a ferry crossing; various conjectures have been made, including idols, magical amulets, and shore pylons to hold a crossing rope. See footnote 36.
[35] **bitumen** Mineral pitch or tar.
[36] **sacred stones** Unclear; perhaps idols or magical amulets. See footnote 34.

[37] **nymph** The larval form of an insect.
[38] **Mammetun** The goddess who makes fate.

together they decree the fates of men. Life and death they allot but the day of death they do not disclose."

Then Gilgamesh said to Utnapishtim the Faraway, "I look at you now, Utnapishtim, and your appearance is no different from mine; there is nothing strange in your features. I thought I should find you like a hero prepared for battle, but you lie here taking your ease on your back. Tell me truly, how was it that you came to enter the company of the gods and to possess everlasting life?" Utnapishtim said to Gilgamesh, "I will reveal to you a mystery, I will tell you a secret of the gods."

The Story of the Flood

"You know the city Shurrupak,[39] it stands on the banks of Euphrates? That city grew old and the gods that were in it were old. There was Anu, lord of the firmament, their father, and warrior Enlil their counsellor, Ninurta[40] the helper, and Ennug[41] watcher over canals; and with them also was Ea. In those days the world teemed, the people multiplied, the world bellowed like a wild bull, and the great god was aroused by the clamour. Enlil heard the clamour and he said to the gods in council, 'The uproar of mankind is intolerable and sleep is no longer possible by reason of the babel.'[42] So the gods agreed to exterminate mankind. Enlil did this, but Ea because of his oath warned me in a dream. He whispered their words to my house of reeds, 'Reed-house, reed-house! Wall, O wall, hearken reed-house, wall reflect; O man of Shurrupak, son of Ubara-Tutu; tear down your house and build a boat, abandon possessions and look for life, despise worldly goods and save your soul alive. Tear down your house, I say, and build a boat. These are the measurements of the barque as you shall build her: let her beam equal her length, let her deck be roofed like the vault that covers the abyss; then take up into the boat the seed of all living creatures.'

"When I had understood I said to my lord, 'Behold, what you have commanded I will honour and perform, but how shall I answer the people, the city, the elders?' Then Ea opened his mouth and said to me, his servant, 'Tell them this: I have learnt that Enlil is wrathful against me, I dare no longer walk in his land nor live in his city; I will go down to the Gulf to dwell with Ea my lord. But on you he will rain down abundance, rare fish and shy wild-fowl, a rich harvest-tide. In the evening the rider of the storm[43] will bring you wheat in torrents.'

"In the first light of dawn all my household gathered round me, the children brought pitch and the men whatever was necessary. On the fifth day I laid the keel and the ribs, then I made fast the planking. The ground-space was one acre, each side of the deck measured one hundred and twenty cubits, making a square. I built six decks below, seven in all, I divided them into nine sections with bulkheads between. I drove in wedges where needed, I saw to the punt-poles,[44] and laid in supplies. The carriers brought oil in baskets, I poured pitch into the furnace and asphalt and oil; more oil was consumed in caulking, and more again the master of the board took into his stores. I slaughtered bullocks[45] for the people and every day I killed sheep. I gave the shipwrights wine to drink as though it were river water, raw wine and red wine and oil and white wine. There was feasting then as there is at the time of the New Year's festival[46]; I myself anointed my head. On the seventh day the boat was complete.

"Then was the launching full of difficulty; there was shifting of ballast[47] above and below till two thirds was submerged. I loaded into her all that I had of gold and of living things, my family, my kin, the beast of the field both wild and tame, and all the craftsmen. I sent them on board, for the time that Shamash had ordained was already fulfilled when he said, 'In the evening, when the rider of the storm sends down the destroying rain, enter the boat and batten her down.' The time was fulfilled, the evening came, the rider of the storm sent down the rain. I looked out at the weather and it was terrible, so I too boarded the boat and battened[48] her down. All was now complete, the battening and the caulking; so I handed the

---

[39] **Shurrupak** A city in Mesopotamia. One of the five cities that, according to the Sumerian King List, were founded before the Flood (see *The Epic of Gilgamesh*).
[40] **Ninurta** The rain god and a war god, son of **Enlil.**
[41] **Ennugi** An Underworld god who guards canals for the **Anunnaki.** Son of **Enlil,** he is called Lord Who Returns Not.
[42] **babel** A confusion of sounds or voices. The Hebrew Bible (Gen. 11:1–9) describes the Tower of Babel and its destruction—a warning against human ambition.
[43] **rider of the storm** The Mesopotamian weather god **Adad,** the son of **Anu.**

---

[44] **punt-poles** Poles used to propel a punt, a flat-bottomed boat with square ends.
[45] **bullocks** Young bulls.
[46] **New Year's festival** Akitu, the chief festival of the Babylonian religious calendar. It was celebrated over an eleven-day period, during the spring equinox, in the month of Nisan (our April). Also, a second festival, the Autumn New Year, was sometimes observed after the gathering of last fruits and before the winter plowing.
[47] **ballast** Heavy material placed in a boat to ensure stability.
[48] **batten** To ready a boat for a storm, by securing open hatches and placing wooden strips in pockets at the edges of sails to keep them flat.

tiller to Puzur-Amurri[49] the steersman, with the navigation and the care of the whole boat.

"With the first light of dawn a black cloud came from the horizon; it thundered within where Adad,[50] lord of the storm was riding. In front over hill and plain Shullat[51] and Hanish,[52] heralds of the storm, led on. Then the gods of the abyss rose up; Nergal[53] pulled out the dams of the nether waters, Ninurta the war-lord threw down the dykes, and the seven judges of hell, the Annunaki, raised their torches, lighting the land with their livid flame. A stupor of despair went up to heaven when the god of the storm turned daylight to darkness, when he smashed the land like a cup. One whole day the tempest raged, gathering fury as it went, it poured over the people like the tides of battle; a man could not see his brother nor the people be seen from heaven. Even the gods were terrified at the flood, they fled to the highest heaven, the firmament of Anu; they crouched against the walls, cowering like curs. Then Ishtar the sweet-voiced Queen of Heaven cried out like a woman in travail: 'Alas the days of old are turned to dust because I commanded evil; why did I command this evil in the council of all the gods? I commanded wars to destroy the people, but are they not my people, for I brought them forth? Now like the spawn[54] of fish they float in the ocean.' The great gods of heaven and of hell wept, they covered their mouths.

"For six days and six nights the winds blew, torrent and tempest and flood overwhelmed the world, tempest and flood raged together like warring hosts. When the seventh day dawned the storm from the south subsided, the sea grew calm, the flood was stilled; I looked at the face of the world and there was silence, all mankind was turned to clay. The surface of the sea stretched as flat as a roof-top; I opened a hatch and the light fell on my face. Then I bowed low, I sat down and I wept, the tears streamed down my face, for on every side was the waste of water. I looked for land in vain, but fourteen leagues distant there appeared a mountain, and there the boat grounded; on the mountain of Nisir[55] the boat held fast, she held fast and did not budge. One day she held, and a second day on the mountain of Nisir she held fast and did not budge. A third day, and a fourth day she held fast on the mountain and did not budge; a fifth day and a sixth day she held fast on the mountain. When the seventh day dawned I loosed a dove and let her go. She flew away, but finding no resting-place she returned. Then I loosed a swallow, and she flew away but finding no resting-place

she returned. I loosed a raven, she saw that the waters had retreated, she ate, she flew around, she cawed, and she did not come back. Then I threw everything open to the four winds, I made a sacrifice and poured out a libation[56] on the mountain top. Seven and again seven cauldrons I set up on their stands, I heaped up wood and cane and cedar and myrtle. When the gods smelled the sweet savour, they gathered like flies over the sacrifice. Then, at last, Ishtar also came, she lifted her necklace with the jewels of heaven that once Anu had made to please her. 'O you gods here present, by the lapis lazuli round my neck I shall remember these days as I remember the jewels of my throat; these last days I shall not forget. Let all the gods gather round the sacrifice, except Enlil. He shall not approach this offering, for without reflection he brought the flood; he consigned my people to destruction.'

"When Enlil had come, when he saw the boat, he was wrath and swelled with anger at the gods, the host of heaven, 'Has any of these mortals escaped? Not one was to have survived the destruction.' Then the god of the wells and canals Ninurta opened his mouth and said to the warrior Enlil, 'Who is there of the gods that can devise without Ea? It is Ea alone who knows all things.' Then Ea opened his mouth and spoke to warrior Enlil, 'Wisest of gods, hero Enlil, how could you so senselessly bring down the flood?

> Lay upon the sinner his sin,
> Lay upon the transgressor his transgression,
> Punish him a little when he breaks loose,
> Do not drive him too hard or he perishes;
> Would that a lion had ravaged mankind
> Rather than the flood,
> Would that a wolf had ravaged mankind
> Rather than the flood,
> Would that famine had wasted the world
> Rather than the flood,
> Would that pestilence had wasted mankind
> Rather than the flood.

It was not I that revealed the secret of the gods; the wise man learned it in a dream. Now take your counsel what shall be done with him.'

"Then Enlil went up into the boat, he took me by the hand and my wife and made us enter the boat and kneel down on either side, he standing between us. He touched our foreheads to bless us saying, 'In time past Utnapishtim was a mortal man; henceforth he and his wife shall live in the distance at the mouth of the rivers.'[57] Thus it was that the gods took me and placed me here to live in the distance, at the mouth of the rivers."

---

[49] **Puzur-Amurri** The steersman for **Utnapishtim's** boat.
[50] **Adad** In Sumerian, **Ishkur**. The Mesopotamian weather god, the son of **Anu.**
[51] **Shullat** A divine herald of storms and bad weather.
[52] **Hanish** A divine herald of storms and bad weather.
[53] **Nergal** The Mesopotamian god of war and sudden death; an Underworld god. Son of **Enlil.**
[54] **spawn** Fish eggs.
[55] **Nisir** The mountain on whose top **Utnapishtim's** boat finally reached land. Called Ararat in the Genesis story of the flood in the Bible (see *The Holy Scriptures*).

---

[56] **libation** The pouring of a liquid offering on the ground, as part of a religious ritual.
[57] **the mouth of the rivers** Dilmun, the paradise of **Utnapishtim** and his wife. Historic **Dilmun** was an ancient kingdom on the island known today as al-Bahrain in the Persian Gulf. The rivers are the Tigris and Euphrates, whose waters empty into the Persian Gulf.

ENHEDUANNA

The Exaltation of Inanna

Enheduanna (fl. 2330 B.C.) is history's earliest known literary figure. Princess, priestess, and poet, she left an indelible mark on her age, so that her ecclesiastical and literary exploits were celebrated for centuries afterward in Mesopotamia.

This precedent-making poet flourished during the reign of her father, Sargon (ca. 2334–2278 B.C.), an upstart king who inaugurated Mesopotamia's Akkadian dynasty, displacing the Sumerian line when he conquered the cities of Sumer and set up his capital at Agade—the city that gave its name to his dynasty, language, and state. A legendary soldier, he forged a vast empire, stretching from Egypt to the Indus River, which he and his successors fought to control because of never-ending rebellions. To govern this unruly empire, Sargon founded garrison cities, turned enemies into allies, and began the custom of appointing royal family members to act as governors of conquered lands. He also installed Enheduanna as high priestess of the Moon-God Nanna in Ur and as priestess of An, the Heaven-God, in Uruk. His appointments were intended to align these old Sumerian cities with the new reality of Akkadian politics.

In furtherance of her father's designs, Enheduanna worked to propagandize the Sumerians and Akkadians into a harmonious union. Sargon spoke Akkadian and made this language the official language in his domains, but his daughter wrote in Sumerian, which now became a scholarly language, much as Latin was during the Middle Ages. She composed a cycle of hymns to the temples of Sumer and Akkad, thereby aiding the growth of Mesopotamian theology. These hymns also set the standard for later poets, who copied her language, poetic forms, and themes. In time, Enheduanna's life took on legendary qualities, and her name—Heduanna ("en," Sumerian for "high priestess")—became an attribute of the Moon-God, whom she had served.

Reading the Selection

The Exaltation of Inanna (Sumerian, *nin-me-sar-ra*) has definitively been linked to Enheduanna, since the text not only names her as author but also gives autobiographical details of her life. The survival of more than fifty partial or whole versions of this poem is proof of its wide prestige in later times. The layout of this English-language version of the poem echoes the cuneiform original, in which two column-wide stanzas can often be read down as well as across.

In theme, this poem belongs to that branch of mythology called *theogony,* which usually has to do with the birth of the gods, but here it also refers to the changing status, relative to each other, of various deities within the Mesopotamian pantheon. *Exaltation* means elevation, and in this poem Inanna, the Goddess of Love, is raised from junior queen to a status "superior to An," the chief Sumerian deity. This is the first known example of its kind in this culture, though many later ones exist. The epithet "superior to An" soon became a literary cliché, used by poets to glorify a deity whose status was changing, usually for historical reasons.

On the historic level, *The Exaltation of Inanna* grew out of Sargon's victory over rebels late in his reign, a deed Enheduanna attributed to Inanna. In the uprising, the rebel Lugalanne stripped the priestess of her temple offices in Ur and Uruk, and the divine protectors of these cities, the Moon-God and the Heaven-God, respectively, refused to come to her aid. Only Inanna heeded the priestess's cries. Thus, in the poem Inanna's supremacy among the gods ("Tis thine!") is guaranteed by her role in restoring Enheduanna to holy office, a fact made possible by Sargon's triumph over his enemies.

A. Exordium[1]

(I) INANNA AND THE *ME*

Lady[2] of all the *me*,[3]	resplendent light,
Righteous woman clothed in radiance,[4]	beloved of Heaven and Earth,

Hierodule[5] of An[6]	(you) of all the great ornaments,
Enamored of the appropriate tiara,	suitable for the high priesthood

Whose hand has attained	(all) the "seven" *me*,
Oh my lady, you are the guardian	of all the great *me*!

You have picked up the *me*,	you have hung the *me* on your hand,
You have gathered up the *me*,	you have clasped the *me* to your breast.

(II) INANNA AND AN

Like a dragon you have deposited venom on the land
When you roar at the earth like Thunder, no vegetation can stand up to you.

A flood descending from its mountain,
Oh foremost one, you are the Inanna of heaven and earth!

Raining the fanned fire	down upon the nation
Endowed with *me* by An,	lady mounted on a beast,

Who makes decisions	at the holy command of An.
(You) of all the great rites,	who can fathom what is yours?

(III) INANNA AND ENLIL[7]

Devastatrix[8] of the lands,	you are lent wings by the storm.
Beloved of Enlil,	you fly about in the nation.

You are at the service	of the decrees of An.
Oh my lady, at the sound of you	the lands bow down.

When mankind	comes before you
In fear and trembling	at (your) tempestuous radiance,

1

10

20

---

[1] **Exordium** From Latin, "to begin." An introductory part of a speech or treatise.

[2] **Lady** Inanna, the goddess of love and the protectress of the city of **Uruk**. She is also goddess of fertility and war. Her Sumerian name, **Nin-an-ah,** means "Lady of Heaven." In Akkadian, **Ishtar.** The poem's speaker is **Enheduanna** (ca. 2285–ca. 2250 B.C.), high priestess ("en") of the Moon-God **Nanna** and daughter of Sargon, founder of the Akkadian kingdom. Note that **Enheduanna,** despite being a devotee of the Moon-God, addresses her words to **Inanna.**

[3] *me* The divine rules, gifts, and powers. **Enheduanna** says that **Inanna** has been given all the *me*, a sign of her power over human affairs. The *me* are tangible objects, with **Inanna** hanging some on a hand (line 7) and clasping others to her breast (line 8).

[4] **radiance** A reference to **Inanna's** role as goddess of the planet Venus, the Morning and Evening Star.

[5] **hierodule** A temple slave serving a deity; in this instance, the goddess **Inanna,** as the servant of her father, the god **An.**

[6] **An** In Babylonian, **Anu.** The Sumerian king of the gods, father of **Inanna.** (Inanna is sometimes called the daughter of **Sin** or **Suen,** the Moon-God.) Originally depicted as a bull. Later images represented him with a head-dress of horns, a symbol of power. **Enheduanna** is priestess of the temple of **An,** in the city of **Uruk.**

[7] **Enlil** Mesopotamian god of the air and storms. His name means "Lord Wind." One of the triad of deities that included **An,** king of the gods, and **Ea,** the god of water.

[8] **Devastatrix** A woman who causes devastation.

They receive from you   their just deserts.

Proffering a song of lamentation,   they weep before you,
They walk toward you along the path   of the house of all the great sighs.

(IV) INANNA AND IŠKUR[9]

In the van of battle   everything is struck down by you.
Oh my lady, (propelled) on your own wings,   you peck away (at the land).

In the guise of a charging storm   you charge.
With a roaring storm   you roar.

With Thunder   you continually thunder.   30

With all the evil winds   you snort.

Your feet are filled   with restlessness.
To (the accompaniment of) the harp of sighs   you give vent to a dirge.

(V) INANNA AND THE ANUNNA[10]

Oh my lady, the Anunna,   the great gods,
Fluttering like bats   fly off from before you to the clefts,

They who dare not walk(?)   in your terrible glance,
Who dare not proceed   before your terrible countenance.

Who can temper   your raging heart?
Your malevolent heart   is beyond tempering.

Lady (who) soothes the reins,   lady (who) gladdens the heart,   40
Whose rage is not tempered,   oh eldest daughter of Suen[11]!
Lady supreme over the land,   who has (ever) denied (you) homage?

(VI) INANNA AND EBIH(?)[12]

In the mountain where homage is withheld from you vegetation is accursed.
Its grand entrance   you have reduced to ashes.

Blood rises in its rivers for you, its people have nought to drink.
It leads its army captive before you of its own accord.

It disbands its regiments before you of its own accord.
It makes its able-bodied young men parade before you of their own accord.

A tempest has filled the dancing of its city.
It drives its young adults before you as captives.   50

(VII) INANNA AND URUK[13]

Over the city which has not declared   "The land is yours,"
Which has not declared   "It is your father's, your begetter's"[14]

---

[9] **Iskur** In Babylonian, **Adad.** The Mesopotamian weather god.
[10] **Anunna** Another name for the **Anunnaki**, the gods of the Underworld.
[11] **Suen** In Akkadian, **Sin;** in Sumerian, **Nanna.** Mesopotamian Moon-God;
offspring of **Enlil**, the god of air, and **Ninlil**, the goddess of grain. **Inanna** is
variously described as the daughter of **Suen** or of **An.**
[12] **Ebih** Perhaps a country or range of mountains. Since **Inanna** is not worshiped properly in **Ebih**, devastation follows.
[13] **Uruk Inanna** is priestess of **An**, the Heaven-God, in the city of **Uruk.**
Note the consequences to the city when homage to **Inanna** is withheld.
[14] **your father's, your begetter's** The references are to **An**, the father of **Inanna.**

You have spoken your holy command,[15]   have verily turned it back from your path,
Have verily removed your foot   from out of its byre.[16]

Its woman no longer speaks of love   with her husband.
At night they no longer   have intercourse.
She no longer reveals to him   her inmost treasures.

Impetuous wild cow,   great daughter of Suen,
Lady supreme over An   who has (ever) denied (you) homage?

(VIII) INVOCATION OF INANNA

You of the appropriate *me,*   great queen of queens,   60
Issued from the holy womb,   supreme over the mother who bore you,

Omniscient sage,   lady of all the lands,
Sustenance of the multitudes,   I have verily recited your sacred song!

True goddess, fit for the *me,*   it is exalting to acclaim you.
Merciful one, brilliantly righteous woman,   I have verily recited your *me* for you!

B. The Argument

(IX) THE BANISHMENT FROM UR

Verily I[17] had entered   my holy *gipāru*[18] at your behest,
I, the high priestess,   I, Enheduanna!

I carried the ritual basket,[19]   I intoned the acclaim.[20]
(But now) I am placed in the leper's ward,[21]   I, even I, can no longer live with you

They approach the light of day,   the light is obscured about me,   70
The shadows approach the light of day,   it is covered with a (sand)storm.

My mellifluous mouth is cast into confusion.
My choicest features   are turned to dust.

(X) THE APPEAL TO NANNA-SUEN[22]

What is he to me, oh Suen,   this Lugalanne![23]
Say thus to An: "May An release me!"

---

[15] **You have spoken your holy command** **Enheduanna** claims that **Inanna** is now punishing **Uruk** for turning its back on both the god **An** and his daughter **Inanna.**

[16] **byre** A barn for cows. **Inanna** is sometimes addressed as "Lady of the Byre."

[17] **I** **Enheduanna.**

[18] *gipāru* Holy inner sanctum of the temple of the Moon-God **Nanna** in Ur. This temple was excavated in 1927 by archeologists from the University of Pennsylvania.

[19] **ritual basket** Sacred object used by **Enheduanna** in her duties as priestess.

[20] **intoned the acclaim** Recited in a singing tone, the hymn of praise (to the goddess **Inanna**). **Enheduanna** claims to have performed her priestly duties, and, thus, her prayers should be answered.

[21] **the leper's ward** **Enheduanna** calls herself an outcast, having been removed from her priestly office.

[22] **Nanna-Suen** The Moon-God. **Enheduanna** here appeals to the Moon-God **Nanna**, whose temple in Ur she serves, asking the god's support in regaining her priestly office. **Nanna** is also father of **Inanna,** the subject of the hymn.

[23] **Lugalanne** *Lugal* means "king" or "ruler." Rebel leader who defeated Sargon, **Enheduanna's** father, and temporarily seized control of **Uruk** and removed **Enheduanna** from her post as head of the temple of **An.**

Say but to An "Now!" and An will release me.
This woman will carry off   the manhood of Lugalanne.

Mountain (and?) flood   lie at her feet.
That woman is as exalted (as he)—   she will make the city divorce him.
Surely she will assuage   her heartfelt rage for me.   80

Let me, Enheduanna,   recite a prayer to her.
Let me give free vent to my tears like sweet drink for the holy Inanna!
Let me say "Hail!" to her!

(XI) The Indictment[24] of Lugalanne(?)

I cannot appease   Ashimbabbar.[25]
(Lugalanne) has altered the lustrations[26] of holy An and all his (other rites).

He has stripped An   of (his temple) Eanna.[27]
He has not stood in awe   of An-lugal[28]

That sanctuary whose attractions are irresistible, whose beauty is endless,
That sanctuary he has verily brought to destruction.

Having entered before you as a partner,[29] he has even approached his sister-in-law.[30]   90
Oh my divine impetuous wild cow,[31] drive out this man, capture this man!

(XII) The Curse of Uruk

In the place of sustenance   what am I, even I?
(Uruk) is a malevolent rebel against your Nanna—may An make it surrender!

This city—   may it be sundered by An!
May it be cursed   by Enlil!
May its plaintive child   not be placated by his mother!

Oh lady, the (harp of) mourning   is placed on the ground.
One had verily beached your ship of mourning on a hostile shore.
At (the sound of) my sacred song   they are ready to die.

(XIII) The Indictment of Nanna[32]

As for me, my Nanna   takes no heed of me.   100
He has verily given me over to destruction   in murderous straits.

Ashimbabbar   has not pronounced my judgment.
Had he pronounced it: what is it to me?   Had he not pronounced it: what is it to me?

---

[24] **indictment** A written statement of crimes committed.
[25] **Ashimbabbar** The "luminous"; **Enheduanna** here refers to the radiance
of the moon, an allusion to the Moon-God, **Nanna**.
[26] **lustration** Purification ceremony that is part of a religious ritual.
[27] **Eanna** The temple of **Anu** in the city of **Uruk**.
[28] **An-lugal** King **An**, the father of the Mesopotamian gods and goddesses.
[29] **partner** Here, **Enheduanna** accuses **Lugalanne** of impiety for taking partial credit for his exploits, rather than giving **An** the full glory.
[30] **sister-in-law** The unnamed high priestess of **An**, who succeeded **Enheduanna**
in the post. Thus, **Enheduanna** accuses **Lugalanne** of attempted sexual impropri-
ety with a servant of a deity—a great offense in the Babylonian religion.
[31] **wild cow** The goddess **Inanna**.
[32] **indictment of Nanna** In verse xiii, **Enheduanna** complains that the
Moon-God **Nanna** has abandoned her.

(Me) who once sat triumphant | he has driven out of the sanctuary.
Like a swallow he made me fly from the window, my life is consumed.

He made me walk | in the bramble of the mountain.
He stripped me of the crown | appropriate for the high priesthood.
He gave me dagger and sword[33]— | "It becomes you," he said to me.

(XIV) THE APPEAL TO INANNA[34]

Most precious lady, | beloved of An,
Your holy heart is lofty, | may it be assuaged on my behalf!   110

Beloved bride | of Ushumgalanna,[35]
You are the senior queen | of the heavenly foundations and zenith.

The Anunna | have submitted to you.
From birth on | you were the "junior" queen.

How supreme you are over the great gods, the Anunna!
The Anunna kiss the ground with their lips (in obeisance) to you.

(But) my own sentence is not concluded, | a hostile judgment appears before my eyes as my judgment.

(My) hands are no longer folded | on the ritual couch,
I may no longer reveal | the pronouncements of Ningal[36] to man.

(Yet) I am the brilliant | high priestess of Nanna,   120
Oh my queen beloved of An, | may your heart take pity on me!

(XV) THE EXALTATION[37] OF INANNA

That one has not recited[38] as a "Known! Be it known!" of Nanna, | that one has recited[39] as a "Tis Thine!"

"That you are lofty as Heaven (An)— | be it known!
That you are broad as the earth— | be it known!
That you devastate the rebellious land— | be it known!
That you roar at the land— | be it known!
That you smite the heads— | be it known!
That you devour cadavers like a dog— | be it known!
That your glance is terrible— | be it known!   130
That you lift your terrible glance— | be it known!"

---

[33] **dagger and sword** Enheduanna says that the Moon-God **Nanna** has rejected her, by taking away the symbol ("crown") of priestly office and turning her into a warrior.
[34] **Appeal to Inanna** In verse xiv, **Enheduanna** proclaims the superiority of **Inanna** to the other gods and goddesses of the Mesopotamian pantheon.
[35] **Ushumgalanna Dumuzi**, "the true or faithful son," the shepherd god. Also called **Tammuz**. One of the lovers of **Inanna**.
[36] **Ningal** "The Great Lady," the mother of **Inanna** and the wife of **Nanna**.
[37] **exaltation** The process of raising up to the highest status.
[38] **one has not recited** Enheduanna affirms that she has not exalted **Nanna** above other deities.
[39] **one has recited** Enheduanna affirms that she has exalted ("Tis Thine!") **Inanna** above the other gods and goddesses. In the rest of verse xv, **Enheduanna** lists the varied ways in which **Inanna** towers over the other deities of the Mesopotamian pantheon.

That your glance is flashing—   be it known!
That you are ill-disposed toward the . . . —   be it known!

That you attain victory—   be it known!"

That one has not recited (this) of Nanna,   that one has recited it as a "Tis Thine!"—
(That,) oh my lady, has made you great, you alone are exalted!

Oh my lady beloved of An,   I have verily recounted your fury!

C. Peroration[40]

(XVI) THE COMPOSITION OF THE HYMN

One has heaped up the coals (in the censer),[41] prepared the lustration
The nuptial chamber awaits you,   let your heart be appeased!

With "It is enough for me, it is too much for   oh exalted lady, (to this song) for you.   140
   me!" I have given birth[42]
That which I recited to you   at (mid)night
May the singer repeat it to you   at noon!

(Only) on account of your captive spouse,   on account of your captive child,
Your rage is increased,   your heart unassuaged.

(XVII) THE RESTORATION OF ENHEDUANNA[43]

The first lady,[44]   the reliance of the throne room,
Has accepted her offerings
Inanna's heart   has been restored.

The day was favorable for her, she was   she was garbed in womanly beauty.
   clothed sumptuously,
Like the light of the rising moon,   how she was sumptuously attired!

When Nanna appeared   in proper view,   150
They (all) blessed   her (Inanna's) mother Ningal.

The (heavenly) doorsill[45]   called "Hail!"

---

[40] **Peroration** The conclusion of a speech, delivered in a grandiloquent manner.
[41] **censer** A vessel for burning incense, used in a religious ritual.
[42] **I have given birth** Enheduanna uses a birthing metaphor to explain her writing of this hymn in praise of **Inanna.**
[43] **Enheduanna** Daughter of Sargon, founder of the Akkadian kingdom. Chief priest of the temple of the Moon-God **Nanna** in Ur and priestess of the temple of the Heaven-God **An** in **Uruk.**
[44] **The first lady** In this verse, **Enheduanna** reverts to the use of third person, describing herself as "the first lady," "the reliance of the throne room," and "she."
[45] **(heavenly) doorsill** In ancient religions, a divine threshold where heaven and earth intersect, offering a passageway between the two levels of existence.

(XVIII) DOXOLOGY[46]

For that her (Enheduanna's) speaking to the Hierodule was exalted,
Praise be (to) the devastatrix of the lands, endowed with *me* from An,
(To) my lady wrapped in beauty, (to) Inanna!

_____

[46] **Doxology** Praise for a god, recited as part of a liturgy.

The Dispute of a Man with His Soul

The Dispute of a Man with His Soul is probably Egypt's most philosophical work. Surviving in one manuscript found in about 1843, this complex text has aroused a great deal of curiosity and has provoked much controversy. Its text combines prose and poetry, a hybrid style of writing that also flourished in medieval Europe (see *The Consolation of Philosophy* by Boethius).

This work dates from the Middle Kingdom (ca. 2050–1800 B.C.), a period characterized by a significant shift in the social system. The old ruling elite of high-ranking royal officials now had to make room for lower officials. Mildly "democratic," this step resulted in revised funeral customs, as nobles claimed the right to immortality enjoyed by rulers; those with sufficient wealth to afford monuments began to build private funeral chapels. *The Dispute of a Man with His Soul* provides evidence of these changes because it was found in a tomb dating from about 1850 B.C., deposited there as reading matter for the deceased in eternity.

The Dispute is one of the outstanding achievements of the Middle Kingdom, Egypt's classical age, a period marked by an outpouring of literary works in many genres and with a complete mastery of forms. This work belongs to the Wisdom Literature genre, which began in the Old Kingdom and now reached its zenith. Wisdom Literature is didactic writing that ponders a problem of life and offers a solution. The Wisdom Literature of the Egyptians (and the Mesopotamians) contributed mightily to the subsequent flowering of this genre among the Hebrews, as in the Book of Job (see *The Holy Scriptures*).

The Wisdom Literature of the Middle Kingdom was dominated by the theme of "national distress," which portrayed the state as threatened by civil war and social upheaval, although no evidence has been unearthed to support this gloomy outlook. *The Dispute* shared the age's general pessimism, but its topic, unlike other Middle Kingdom writing, was personal and not social.

Reading the Selection

The theme of *The Dispute of a Man with His Soul* is whether death is a blessing, given the sorrows of this life. It is written in the form of a dialogue between a man ["I"] and the mysterious life force that Egyptians called the *ba* [the "soul"]. The *ba* was the inner power that guided human life, escaped from the body at death, and played a vital but ill-defined role in one's afterlife. Presented as an internal conflict without any specific references to a real person, the text is thus universally applicable to humankind. Beyond this exists very little agreement about the nature of the dispute and the positions of the two opponents.

Some well-regarded interpretations of *The Dispute* describe it as a clash between (1) the traditional belief in funerary rites (the man) and the skeptical view of those without financial means for proper burial (the *ba*); (2) a conservative, idealistic outlook (the man) and a materialistic, hedonistic view (the *ba*); (3) Osirian beliefs (the *ba*) and the solar theology of Ra (the man).

Regardless of its final meaning, the problem presented in *The Dispute of a Man with His Soul* is resolved through four poems, each marked by a repeated first line. In these poems the man laments the pain of human life and celebrates the promised joys of death and resurrection. After listening to the poems, the *ba* agrees to abide with the man—a conservative ending typical of the Wisdom Literature of the times.

∽

. . . Then[1] I opened my mouth to my soul,[2] that I might answer what it had said: "This is too much for me now, that my soul does not speak with me. My soul goes forth; let it stand and wait for me!

"Behold, my soul disobeys me because I did not hearken to it, and drag myself to death ere I have come to it, to cast myself upon the fire in order to consume myself. Rather, let it be near to me on this day of misfortune, and wait on the other side!

"My soul is foolish to hold back one wretched over life and delay me from death before I have come to it. Rather, make the West[3] pleasant for me! Is it something bad? The period of life is limited in any case: even the trees must fall! Thoth,[4] who contents the gods, he will judge me! Khonsu,[5] the Scribe in Truth, he will defend me! Ra,[6] who guides the Solar Bark,[7] he will hear my words! My distress is heavy, and he bears it for me!"

And this is what my soul said to me: "And are you not a plain man? Yet you are as concerned as if you were a possessor of wealth!"

I said: "If my soul will hearken to me, and its heart agrees with me, it will be happy. I will cause it to reach the West, like one who is in his pyramid,[8] and at whose burial there has stood a survivor. I shall drink from the river whose water is drawn, and look down on the souls that are unsatisfied!"

Then my soul opened its mouth to me, to answer what I had said: "If you are calling burial to mind, that is a distress of the heart; it is a bringing of tears, it is making a man sorrowful. It is hauling a man from his house and throwing him upon the hill. Never shall you go up above to behold the sun. They who built in granite and fashioned pyramids—fine things of good work—when the builders have become gods, their offering tables[9] are as empty as those of the wretches who die on the riverbank—part of their bodies held by the water and part by the heat of the sun, and the fish of the bank hold converse with them! Listen, then, to me; lo, it is good to listen to people! Follow the happy day and forget care!

"Take the case of a poor man who plows his field and then loads his harvest on to a boat, and hurries to tow the boat since his feast day approaches. He sees a flood coming on in the night, and keeps vigil when Ra goes down. He comes forth with his wife, but his children perish upon the water, dangerous with crocodiles in the night. At last he sits down, when he can regain his voice, and says: 'I do not weep for that girl; there is no coming forth into the West for her. I am troubled for her children that are broken in the egg, that behold the face of the crocodile-god[10] before they had lived.'"

Then I opened my mouth to my soul, that I might answer what it had said:

"Behold, you make my name reek,
  lo, more than the stench of carrion
    on days in summer, when the sky is hot.

"Behold, you make my name reek
  lo, more than a fisherman
    on the day of the catch, when the sky is hot.

"Behold, you make my name reek
  lo, more than the stench of bird droppings,
    more than the hill of willows with the geese.

---

[1] **Then** The poem begins in the midst of a dispute; the first part has not survived. The man seemingly has threatened suicide, a crime in the Egyptian religion, and the soul, failing to dissuade him, has ceased speaking. The man speaks first.

[2] **my soul** In Egyptian thought, the soul has three parts: the *ka*, the perishable body; the *ba*, the manifestation of the spirit that can take different forms, mainly in the afterlife; and the *akh*, the transformed spirit after death. In this work, *soul* refers to the *ba*, which typically manifests itself at the moment of death.

[3] **the West** The domain of the dead.

[4] **Thoth** The Egyptian god of the moon and of writing. Thoth also weighed the hearts of the dead at their final judgment and reported the results to **Osiris**, king of the Underworld.

[5] **Khonsu** An Egyptian Moon-god, who was sometimes identified with the god **Thoth.**

[6] **Ra** Also spelled **Re.** The Sun-god, who headed Egypt's solar religion. As father of Ma'at, the goddess of cosmic order, he was ultimately responsible for justice and right.

[7] **Solar Bark** The boat in which **Ra**, the Sun God, traveled across the sky during the day. At night, **Ra** sailed through the Underworld in a second boat, to be reborn at dawn of day.

[8] **in his pyramid** An allusion to the burial arrangement, which, because of its great cost, was only available to the wealthiest Egyptians.

[9] **offering tables** Tables for ritual offerings, such as food, wine, and beer, for the dead.

[10] **crocodile-god** The Egyptian god **Sobek,** who was associated with death and burial.

"Behold, you make my name reek
lo, more than the odor of fishermen,
more than the shores of the swamps when they have
fished.

"Behold, you make my name reek
lo, more than the stench of crocodiles,
more than sitting among crocodiles.

"Behold, you make my name reek
lo, more than that of a woman
when lies are told about her to her man.

"Behold, you make my name reek   15
lo, more than that of a lusty boy
against whom it is said, 'He belongs to his hated one!'

"Behold, you make my name reek
lo, more than a treacherous city,
more than a traitor who turns his back.

"To whom shall I speak today?
One's fellows are evil;
the friends of today do not love.

"To whom shall I speak today?
Men are rapacious;
every one seizes his neighbor's goods.

"To whom shall I speak today?
Gentleness has perished;
insolence has access to all men.

"To whom shall I speak today?   20
The evil have a contented countenance;
good is rejected in every place.

"To whom shall I speak today?
He who by his evil deeds should arouse wrath
moves all men to laughter, though his iniquity is
grievous.

"To whom shall I speak today?
Men rob;
Every man seizes his neighbor's goods.

"To whom shall I speak today?
The foul man is trusted,
but one who was a brother to him has become an
enemy.

"To whom shall I speak today?
No one remembers yesterday;
no one now requites good to him who has done it.

"To whom shall I speak today?   25
Brothers are evil;
a man is treated as an enemy for his uprightness.

"To whom shall I speak today?
Faces are not seen;
every man's face is downcast toward his brethren.

"To whom shall I speak today?
Hearts are greedy;
the man on whom men rely has no heart.

"To whom shall I speak today?
There are no righteous ones;
the land is given over to the doers of evil.

"To whom shall I speak today?
There is lack of a trusty friend;
one must go to an unknown in order to complain.

"To whom shall I speak today?   30
There is none that is peaceable;
the one with whom one went no longer exists.

"To whom shall I speak today?
I am laden with misery,
and lack a trusted friend.

"To whom shall I speak today?
The evil which treads the earth,
it has no end.

"Death is in my sight today
as when a sick man becomes whole,
as when one goes out after an illness.

"Death is in my sight today
as the odor of myrrh,[11]
as when sitting under sail on a breezy day.

"Death is in my sight today   35
as the odor of lotus flowers,[12]
as when sitting on the riverbank getting drunk.

"Death is in my sight today
as a well-trodden path,
as when a man returns home to his house from war.

"Death is in my sight today
as a clearing of the sky,
as a man discerning what he knew not.

"Death is in my sight today
as when a man longs to see his home again
after he has spent many years in captivity.

---

[11] **myrrh** From Arabic, "bitter." An aromatic, resinous gum from a
flowering tree. It was used to make incense, perfume, cosmetics, and
medicines and in embalming.
[12] **lotus flower** The white water lily, sacred to **Isis**, the mother goddess who was a central figure in the cult of the Underworld. The
lotus blooms in the day and closes at night and, thus, is a fitting symbol of rebirth and the promise of everlasting life.

"Nay, but he who is Yonder[13]
  will be as a living god,
    inflicting punishment for evil upon him who does it.

"Nay, but he who is Yonder
  will stand in the bark of the Sun-god
    and will assign the choicest things therein to the
      temples.

———

[13] **Yonder** The Eastern Kingdom, the place of rebirth, where souls go
to be reincarnated.

"Nay, but he who is Yonder
  will be a man of knowledge,
    not hindered from petitioning Ra when he speaks."

This is what my soul said to me: "Set aside lamentation, you who are mine, my brother! Although offered up on the brazier, still you shall cling to life, as you say. Whether I remain here if you reject the West, or whether you reach the West and your body is joined with the earth, I will alight after you go to rest. Then we shall make an abode together!"

The Story of Sinuhe the Egyptian

Egyptian literature, although not noted for fiction, gave birth to one great work of the imagination, *The Story of Sinuhe the Egyptian*, a short narrative that ranks among the classics of world literature. Several manuscripts and many fragments of this work are extant, thus attesting to its ancient popularity. A model of style and a masterpiece of the storyteller's art, it was assigned as a "set text" for teaching Egypt's classical language to aspiring scribes. In modern times, Sinuhe's story proved its lasting appeal when it became the basis of a historical novel and a popular movie. The original tale was written in a mix of prose and poetry, the typical style of Middle Kingdom literature (see *The Dispute of a Man with His Soul*).

Like most Egyptian writing, *The Story of Sinuhe* owes its form to the cult of the dead; it is an autobiography composed for a tomb. It may be a true account, but the original tomb-text has not been discovered. Whether true or not, the work reflects an actual event: the death of Amenemhat I [Amen-em-Hat] around 1908 B.C. and the onset of the reign of his coregent, Senwosret I [Sen-Wesret] (ca. 1918–1875 B.C.).

Reading the Selection

Senwosret's abrupt change of status set in motion *The Story of Sinuhe*'s simple plot. Hearing of Amenemhat's death, Sinuhe—an attendant of Senwosret's wife—is seized by uncontrollable shaking and rushes from the scene. Why should a high official who stood to gain from the royal changes bolt and run? In his defense, Sinuhe blames his hasty retreat on anxiety over "civil strife" and fear for his safety. The words "civil strife" echo the Middle Kingdom theme of "national distress" (see *The Dispute of a Man with His Soul*), but nothing else in the tale enlarges on his fears. This opening episode appears to be simply a pretext to throw the hero into foreign lands, where, as time passes, his beloved Egypt becomes all the more precious.

The middle part of the story concerns Sinuhe's flight to and success in Palestine, where he founds a family and acquires fabled riches among the local tribes. With the patronage of a local chief, he proves his worth as a chieftain and a warrior. Most memorable is the episode in which Sinuhe conquers a boastful Syrian warrior, much as David did Goliath in the Old Testament.

Running through these adventures is the theme that contrasts the ideal order of Egyptian life with the unstructured existence of the Palestinian tribes. The story's turning point occurs in the middle of Sinuhe's rejoicing at his worldly success, when he breaks down and bemoans the futility of his life. He prays: "O whichever God ordained this flight, show mercy and return me to the Palace! Surely you will grant that I see the place where dwells my heart!" For Sinuhe, life is meaningful and lasting only within the Egyptian state, as symbolized by the king and courtly ritual.

The story concludes with the hero's homecoming and reception into Egyptian court society. Welcomed by King Senwosret, the aged Sinuhe rids himself of foreign clothing, puts on court dress, and looks forward to the day of his own burial in a "pyramid-tomb of stone," a gift from the king.

Perhaps part of the reason that this work became a classic in Egypt is that readers shared Sinuhe's disdain for foreign cultures. Sinuhe's view that the non-Egyptian world was "uncivilized" was apparently in tune with Egypt's self-image as a land of timeless values.

∽

The Hereditary Prince and Chief,[1] Treasurer of the King, and Unique Courtier, Administrative Dignitary of the districts and estates of the Sovereign in the lands of the Syrians, Actual Acquaintance of the King and beloved of him, the King's Retainer Sinuhe says:

I was a retainer who followed his lord, a servant of the Royal Harem and of the Princess great of praise, the wife of King Sen-Wesret and daughter of King Amen-em-Hat, namely, Neferu, Lady of Reverence.

In the year 30 of his reign, in the third month of the season of Inundation,[2] the god ascended unto his horizon,[3] the King of Upper and Lower Egypt,[4] Amen-em-Hat, was taken up to heaven and united with the sun. The body of the god was united with him who made him. The city of royal residence was silent, all hearts were in grief, and the great Double Gates were sealed. The courtiers sat with heads bent down upon their laps, and the people were in mourning.

Now His Majesty had sent a great army to the land of the Libyans,[5] with his eldest son in command of it, namely, the beautiful god Sen-Wesret. He had been sent to smite the foreign lands, to strike down the dwellers in Libya. Indeed, even now was he returning, bringing living prisoners from among the Libyans and all kinds of cattle without limit.

The courtiers of the palace sent to the western border, advising the King's son of what had come about in the Palace. The messengers found him on the road, having reached him at the time of evening. Not a moment at all

did he delay: The Falcon[6] flew with his attendants, not letting his army know what had happened.

Now those others of the King's sons who were following him in this expedition were sought out, and one of them was called aside. And lo, I happened to be standing near by, and heard his voice as he was speaking. My heart was distraught, my arms flung apart, and trembling seized all my limbs. I sprang bounding away to seek myself a place to hide. I placed myself between two bushes to hide from the passers-by. I certainly had no intention of returning to the Residence, for I expected civil strife to break out, and I did not think I would live after the King's death.

I crossed Lake Maati[7] near Nehet[8] and landed at the island of Senefru.[9] I passed the day at the edge of the fields, and at dawn the next morning I set forth again. I met a man standing on the road. He was frightened of me, and stood in awe. When it was time for supper, I reached the town of Negau.[10] I crossed the river on a barge without a rudder, with the aid of a westerly wind. I passed eastward of the quarry, above the temple of Hathor,[11] Lady of the Red Hill.[12] I gave road to my legs and went northward.

I arrived at the Walls of the Ruler,[13] which were made to repel the Syrians[14] and to defeat the Sand-crossers.[15] I

---

[1] **The Hereditary Prince and Chief** The grandiose titles of courtiers, such as these of **Sinuhe,** were typical of the Egyptian court where rulers were worshiped as divine beings.
[2] **the season of Inundation** Egypt's agricultural calendar had three phases: the season of Inundation, when the Nile River overflowed; the Going Forth, the planting season, when the Nile receded to its banks; and the Deficiency, the harvest season, when the Nile was at low level.
[3] **god . . . horizon Horus,** the Egyptian god of the horizon, depicted as a falcon with his eyes as the sun and the moon. The ruler was believed to be a manifestation of **Horus.**
[4] **Upper and Lower Egypt** Egypt became the Double Land in 3100 B.C., when Menes, its legendary first king, united the South (Upper Egypt) and the North (Lower Egypt).
[5] **Libyans** North African nomads, living west of the Nile Valley, but not limited to modern Libya.

[6] **The Falcon** The new king, Sen-Wesret, who was identified with **Horus,** the falcon god.
[7] **Maati** Unidentified. The name derives from the Hall of Maati, a temple associated with the cult of the Underworld.
[8] **Nehet** Unidentified. The name means *sycamore,* from sycamore tree. The rulers grew these trees, using them for water wheels, farming tools, shade, wind shields, and fuel.
[9] **island of Senefru** Unidentified island in the Nile. **Senefru** (ca. 2613–ca. 2589 B.C.) founded the Fourth Dynasty and built the first true pyramid at Dahshur.
[10] **Negau** *Neg* is Egyptian for "ox"; perhaps a town devoted to the cattle trade.
[11] **Hathor** The Egyptian goddess associated with the royal queens; patroness of the sky, of women, and of fertility and love. Depicted either as a cow or a woman with horns.
[12] **Lady of the Red Hill** Title of the goddess **Hathor.** Red is **Hathor's** color, because of the red earth of Lower Egypt, her original home, and the vengeful side of her nature.
[13] **Walls of the Ruler** A royal fortress on Egypt's eastern border.
[14] **Syrians** A collective name for people from the region embracing the modern states of Syria, Lebanon, Jordan, and Israel.
[15] **Sand-crossers** Bedouins.

took up a crouching position under a bush, in fear lest the watch of the day standing on the wall would see me. At the time of late evening I journeyed on, and when the sun came forth again I reached Peten,[16] and halted at the island of Kem-Wer.[17] A great attack of thirst overtook me. My throat was hot and dry, and I said, "This is the taste of death."

Then I lifted up my heart and pulled my limbs together, for I heard the sound of the lowing of cattle and I spied some Syrians. A distinguished chieftain among them, who had been in Egypt, recognized me. Then he gave me water and cooked milk for me. I proceeded with him to his tribe, and they treated me well.

Land gave me to land. I went forth to Byblos,[18] and then I turned back to Kedem.[19] There I spent a year and a half. Then Amu-nenshi, a ruler in Palestine,[20] fetched me. He said to me, "You will fare well with me; here you will hear the speech of Egypt." He said this since he knew my character and had heard of my capacities. The Egyptians who were there with him bore witness for me.

He said to me, "For what reason have you come to this place? What is it? Has something happened at the Residence?"

Then I said to him, "King Amen-em-Hat has proceeded to the Horizon.[21] No one knows what can happen because of it." But I added, untruthfully:

"I was returning from an expedition to the land of the Libyans when it was reported to me. My mind became unquiet. My heart was not in my body, and it drew me to the desert roads. I had not been accused of anything, no one had spat in my face, and no wretched remarks had been heard about me. My name had not been heard in the mouth of the herald. I do not know what brought me to this land. It is like the dispensation of some god; or like a dream in which a man of the Delta might see himself in Nubia!"[22]

Then he said to me, "What, then, will the land be without him, that excellent god, the fear of whom pervaded the foreign lands like Sekhmet[23] in a year of pestilence?"

I spoke to him in reply, "Indeed his son has entered into the Palace and has assumed the heritage of his father.

For he[24] is a god; there is none his equal,
  and there is none other who surpasses him.
He is a master of understanding, excellent in plans
  and beneficent of decrees;

and going and coming are according to his
  commands.
He it was who subdued the foreign lands while his
  father was within the palace;
  and he reported to him that what he was ordered
    had been done.
Mighty indeed is he, achieving with his strong arm;
  a valiant one, and there is not his equal!
He slakes his wrath by smashing skulls;
  and no one can stand up about him.
He is robust of heart at the moment of attack;
  and does not let sloth rest upon his heart.
Bold of countenance is he when sees the mêlée;
  to attack the barbarian is his joy.
He girds his shield and crushes the foe;
  and does not strike twice in order to kill!
But he is lord of charm and great of sweetness;
  and through love has he conquered!
His city loves him more than itself;
  it rejoices in him more than in its god;
  men and women salute and rejoice with him
    now that he is King!
He conquered while still in the egg,
  and his face was turned to royal deeds since he
    was born.
He makes multiply those who were born with him;
  he is unique, the gift of the god.
He is one who makes wide the boundaries;
  he will seize the southern countries, and the
    northern ones with ease,
  having been created to smite the Syrians and to
    crush the Sand-crossers.
How this land rejoices now that he is come to rule!

Send to him, cause him to know your name as an inquirer far from His Majesty. He will not cease to make happy a land which will be loyal to him!"

Then he said to me, "Well, assuredly then, Egypt is happy, knowing that he flourishes. Behold, you are here, and you shall stay with me. I will treat you well."

He placed me at the head of his children, and he married me to his eldest daughter. He let me choose for myself from his land, from the choicest that he had, on his boundary adjoining another territory. It was a good land, and Yaa[25] was its name. There were figs in it, together with grapes. It had more wine than water; great was its honey and abundant its olives. Every fruit was on its trees. There was barley there, and emmer wheat,[26] and all kinds of cattle without limit.

And much, indeed, accrued to me as a result of the love of me. He appointed me as ruler of a tribe of the choicest of his country. Provisions were assigned for me daily, and wine for each day's needs; cooked meat and roasted fowl besides desert game. They used to snare for me and set aside game for me over and above what my hounds caught. Much wine was made for me, and milk was used in every kind of cooking.

---

[16] **Peten** Probably a foreign settlement east of Egypt.
[17] **Kem-Wer** One of the Bitter Lakes, on the Suez Isthmus.
[18] **Byblos** Jubayl in modern Lebanon.
[19] **Kedem** A city inland from Byblos.
[20] **Palestine** In Egyptian, *Retenu*, meaning variously Canaan, north Palestine, or south Syria.
[21] **Horizon** The domain of the dead.
[22] **a man of the Delta . . . in Nubia** As out of place as a man from Lower Egypt (the Nile's Delta region) in Upper Egypt (Nubia began at the Nile's first cataract).
[23] **Sekhmet** The "eye of **Ra.**" Egyptian goddess of war and of disease and the destroyer of the enemies of the Sun-god **Ra.**
[24] **he** King Sen-Wesret. This poem praising the ruling king establishes that **Sinuhe's** tale is basically a work of royal propaganda.

[25] **Yaa** Unidentified.
[26] **emmer wheat** A type of hardy wheat.

Thus I spent many years. My children became strong men, each man in control of a tribe. The couriers who went north or south to the Palace would tarry because of me, and I made all travelers tarry. I gave water to the thirsty; I put on the road those who had become lost, and I rescued those who were plundered.

When the Bedouin became so bold as to oppose the "Chiefs of the Foreign Lands," I advised them how to proceed. This ruler of the Syrians caused me to spend many years as commander of his army. Every foreign territory against which I went forth, I attacked and it was driven away from its pasturage and its wells. I plundered its cattle, I carried away its inhabitants, and seized their food. I slew people thereof with my strong arm, and by my movements and my excellent devices, I found favor in the ruler's heart, and he loved me. He recognized my valor, and placed me even before his children, since he saw that my arms flourished.

There came a powerful man of the Syrians to taunt me with challenges in my tent. He was a hero without peer, and he had beaten all the Syrians. He said he would fight with me. He expected to despoil me and plunder my cattle, being so counseled by his tribe.

The ruler discussed the matter with me, and I said, "I do not know him, and I certainly am not an associate of his going about in his camp. Is it that I have opened his gate, or thrown down his fence? It is envy, because he sees me carrying out your orders. Assuredly, I am like a bull who has wandered into the herd, and whom the long-horned steer of the herd attacks. Is there any man of humble origin who is loved when he becomes a superior? Well, if he wants to fight, let him speak out what he has in mind. Is a god ignorant of the fact that the nature of whatever he has ordained will eventually be known?"

During the night I strung my bow and practised my shooting. I made my dagger loose and free and polished my weapons. At dawn all Syria came, its tribes stirred up and half its peoples assembled; this fight had been planned.

Then he came toward me as I waited, and I placed myself in position near him. Every heart burned for me, and the women and even the men were murmuring. Every heart was sick for me as they said, "Is there another strong enough to fight him?"

But I escaped his missiles and made his arrows pass me by until none remained, and his shield, his ax, and his armful of spears fell down before me. Then he charged at me. I shot him; my arrow stuck in his neck. He shrieked and fell on his nose. I killed him with his own battle-ax. I gave forth my shout of victory on his back while every Syrian roared. I gave jubilant praise to Montu[27] while his partisans mourned him.

This ruler Amu-nenshi took me in his embrace. Then I carried away my enemy's goods, and I plundered his cattle. What he had planned to do to me, this I did to him. I seized all that was in his tent, and stripped his encampment. Thus I widened my possessions and became numer-ous in cattle. I became great there. Thus has the god done, in being gracious unto one against whom he had been angered, and whom he had sent astray into another land. Today is his heart appeased.

> *A fugitive has fled in his straitened moment;*
> *now my good report is in the Palace.*
> *A lingerer lingered because of hunger;*
> *now I give bread to my neighbor.*
> *A man left his land because of nakedness;*
> *now I am bright of raiment and of linen.*
> *A man ran for lack of someone to send;*
> *now I am rich in slaves.*
> *My house is beautiful, and broad is my abode.*
> *The memory of me is in the Palace.*

O whichever God ordained this flight, show mercy and return me to the Palace! Surely you will grant that I see the place where dwells my heart!

What is more important than that my body be buried in Egypt, the land where I was born? O come to my aid!

That which has occurred is a fortunate event—the god has shown mercy. May he do the like to bring to a good end him whom he has afflicted!

May his heart be sick for him whom he has cast out to live in a foreign land. Is it true that today he is appeased? Then let him hear the prayer of one who is afar! Let him turn his hand toward him who trod the earth, leading him back to the place whence he drew him forth!

May the King of Egypt be gracious unto me, who lives in his grace! May I hail the Lady of the Land, who is in his Palace, and may I hear word of his children! Then might my limbs flourish, since old age has befallen me, and infirmity has overtaken me.

My arms are weak, and my legs have slackened. My heart is weary; I am near to departure, and they will take me away to the City of Eternity!

Might I once more serve the Lady of All! Then will she tell me that it is well with her children! May she spend eternity over me!

Now, it was told to the Majesty of the King of Upper and Lower Egypt, Kheper-Ka-Ra [Senusret I], regarding the circumstances under which I was living. And His Majesty kept sending to me bearers of gifts of the royal bounty, that he might gladden the heart of this his servant like the ruler of any foreign land. And the children of the King, who were in the Palace, let me hear word from them.

[Here Sinuhe inserts the text of the message sent by King Senusret inviting him to return to Egypt:]

Copy of the decree brought to this servant about bringing him back to Egypt:

"The Horus Living-of-Births,[28] the Two Ladies Living-of-Births, the King of Upper and Lower Egypt, Kheper-Ka-Ra, Son of Ra, Senusret, Living forever unto eternity!

---

[27] **Montu** Old Egyptian god of war and of the sun, first worshiped in Upper Egypt.

[28] **The Horus Living-of-Births** Here begin the various titles of King Sen-Wesret.

"A decree of the King to the Retainer Sinuhe:

"Behold, this decree of the King is brought to you to advise you as follows: You have wandered about foreign lands—you have gone from Kedem to Tenu.[29] Under the counsel of your own heart, land gave you to land! What have you done, that anything should be done against you? You have not blasphemed, that your words should be reproved. Your words have not been evil in the Council of the Nobles, that your utterances should be opposed. This plan of yours carried away your heart. It was not in my heart against you.

"This your 'Heaven,' who is in the Palace, today prospers and flourishes. Her head is covered with the royalty of the land. Her children are in the Residence; you shall heap up precious things of what they will give you, and you shall live by their largesse.

"Do you return to Egypt, that you may see the Residence wherein you grew up. You shall kiss the earth at the Great Double Door, and you shall join the courtiers.

"For today indeed you have begun to grow old, and have lost your virile powers. Be mindful of the day of burial, of passing to a revered state! A night will be assigned for you for oils and wrappings from the hands of Tayit.[30] A funeral cortege will be made for you on the day of interment, a mummy case of gold with a headpiece of lapis lazuli[31] and a heaven canopy above you. You will be placed upon a bier, with oxen drawing you and singers going before you, and the mortuary dances will be performed at the door of your tomb. The lists of the offering-table shall be invoked for you, sacrifices shall be made before your tomb stelae, and your tomb columns shall be built of white limestone amidst the tombs of the royal children.

"You must not die in a foreign land! The Asiatics[32] shall not escort you to burial. You shall not be put in a sheepskin and a mound[33] made over you!

"This is too long to tread the earth. Be mindful of illness, and come back!"

This decree reached me as I was standing in the midst of my tribe. It was recited to me; I placed myself on my belly. I touched the earth and scattered it upon my hair. I went about my camp rejoicing and saying, "How can such things be done to a servant whom his heart led astray to foreign and barbarous lands? Good indeed is the clemency which rescued me from the hand of death! Your Divine Essence[34] will allow me to make my end with my body in the Residence!"

[Sinuhe now gives the text of his reply:]

Copy of the answer to this decree:

"The Servant of the Palace, Sinuhe, says:

"In very good peace! It is known to your Divine Essence, this flight made by your servant in his ignorance, O good God, Lord of the Two Lands, Beloved of Ra, Favored of Montu, Lord of Thebes!

"Amen,[35] Lord of the Thrones of the Two Lands, Sebek,[36] Ra, Horus, Hathor, Atum[37] with his Ennead,[38] Soped,[39] Nefer-Bau,[40] Semseru,[41] the Eastern Horus,[42] the Lady of Yemet[43]—The Serpent-goddess,[44] may she continue to enfold your head—the Council over the Nile waters, Min-Horus,[45] amidst the foreign lands, Wereret Lady of Punt,[46] Nut,[47] Ra-Horus[48] the Elder, and all the Gods of Egypt and the Islands of the Sea, may they give life and strength to your nostrils, may they endow you with their bounty, may they give you eternity without bound and everlasting without limit! May the fear of you be repeated in the lowlands and the highlands, when you have subdued all that the sun encircles! This is the prayer of your servant for his Lord, who saves from the West!

"The lord of perception who perceives his people, he perceives in the Majesty of his Palace that which your servant feared to say, and which is a grave thing to repeat. O great God, likeness of Ra, make prudent one who is laboring on his own behalf! Your servant is in the hand of one who takes counsel concerning him, and verily am I placed under his guidance. Your Majesty is Horus the Conqueror; your arms are mighty over all lands.

"Lo, this flight your servant made, I did not plan it; it was not in my heart, I did not devise it. I do not know what separated me from my place. It was like some sort of dream, as when a man of the Delta marshes sees himself in

---

[29] **Tenu** In Egyptian, [Re]tenu, meaning variously Canaan, north Palestine, or south Syria.
[30] **Tayit** Alternative spelling, **Tait.** Goddess of weaving, who wove the threads of fate.
[31] **lapis lazuli** A semiprecious stone, usually azure blue, greatly valued in Egypt.
[32] **Asiatics** A collective name for the Near Eastern peoples east of Egypt.
[33] **a sheepskin and a mound** A pejorative Egyptian notion of a foreign burial practice.
[34] **Divine Essence** The *ka,* the perishable part of the soul.

---

[35] **Amen** Also spelled **Amon** and **Ammon.** Creator-god from Thebes; during the Middle Kingdom, he became a national deity, **Amen-Re,** King of the Gods.
[36] **Sebek** Also spelled **Sobek.** Egyptian crocodile-god; associated with death and burial.
[37] **Atum Atum-Re,** god of the setting sun and head of the **Ennead** cult at Heliopolis.
[38] **Ennead** From Greek, "nine." The nine deities worshiped at Heliopolis.
[39] **Soped** Hawk god and personification of Egypt's eastern frontier.
[40] **Nefer-Bau** Unclear epithet describing **Soped.**
[41] **Semseru** Unclear epithet describing **Soped.**
[42] **the Eastern Horus** The god **Horus,** in his manifestation as ruler of the East.
[43] **the Lady of Yemet** Uncertain; perhaps goddess of floodwaters.
[44] **the Serpent-goddess** A title of the **Lady of Yemet.**
[45] **Min-Horus** A fusion of **Min,** the god of male virility, with **Horus,** the falcon god. The worship of **Min-Horus** flourished in the Middle Kingdom.
[46] **Wereret Lady of Punt** Uncertain; perhaps **Ipy,** also called **Taweret,** the goddess of childbirth. **Punt** is an unidentified land, located south of Egypt, the source of **myrrh.**
[47] **Nut** Egyptian goddess of the sky, portrayed with her body arched over the Earth and her star-studded belly representing the Night Sky.
[48] **Ra-Horus** A fusion of **Ra,** the Sun-god, and **Horus,** the falcon god.

Elephantine,[49] or a man of the northern swamps in Nubia. I did not take fright, no one was pursuing me, I had heard no reviling word. My name had not been heard in the mouth of the herald.

"However, my limbs began to quiver, and my legs began to tremble. My heart led me away. The god who ordained this flight[50] drew me, although I had not been rebellious.

"Any man who knows his land stands in awe, for Ra has set the fear of you throughout the earth, and the dread of you in every foreign land. Whether I am at the Palace or whether I am in this place, it is you, indeed, who clothes this horizon. The sun shines at your pleasure; the water in the rivers, it is drunk at your desire; the air is in the heaven, it is breathed when you so say.

"This your servant will resign the viziership which he has exercised in this place; it was a function they had requested your servant to perform. Your Majesty will act as he pleases; one lives by the breath which you bestow. Ra, Horus, and Hathor love this thy noble nose, which Montu, Lord of Thebes, desires shall live for ever!"

They came for me. I was allowed to spend a day in Yaa for transferring my possessions to my children, my eldest son having charge of my tribe—my tribe and all my property in his hands, my serfs and all my cattle, my stores of fruit and every pleasant tree of mine.

Then this servant went southward. I halted at the Roads of Horus. The commander there who was in charge of the frontier patrol sent a message to the Palace to make it known. Then His Majesty sent a capable overseer of the peasants who belonged to the Palace, followed by ships laden with gifts of the King for the Syrians who had come escorting me to the Roads of Horus. I introduced each of them by his name. Every servant was at his task when I set out and hoisted sail. They kneaded and strained before me, until I reached the vicinity of Yetchet-Tawy.[51]

And when it dawned, very early, they came to call me, ten men coming and ten men going, to conduct me to the Palace. I touched my forehead to the ground beneath the sphinxes. The King's children were standing in the gateway to meet me. The courtiers who had been led into the Great Hall took me on the way to the royal chambers.

I found His Majesty on a great throne in a gilded niche. Then when I was stretched out on my belly, I lost consciousness before him. This god addressed me joyfully, but I was like a man overcome by dusk. My soul departed; my limbs were powerless, my heart, it was not in my body, that I should know life from death.

Then His Majesty said to one of the courtiers, "Raise him, and let him speak to me."

And His Majesty said, "Behold, you have returned! You have trodden foreign lands; you fled away. Now infirmity has seized you, and you have reached old age. It is of no little importance for your body to be buried, that you should not be interred by the Bedouin. Come, do not behave thus, not to speak when your name is pronounced!"

But I still feared punishment, and I answered with the response of one afraid, "What does my Lord say to me? I should answer, but I can do nothing. It is indeed the hand of a god. There is a terror in my belly, like that which brought about that destined flight. Behold me before you; life is yours; may Your Majesty do as he desires!"

Then they had the King's children brought in, and His Majesty said to the Queen, "Behold Sinuhe, come as a Bedouin, as if born a Syrian!"

She uttered a very great cry, and the King's children all shouted together. And they said to His Majesty, "Is it not he, in truth, O King, My Lord?"

And His Majesty said, "It is he, in truth!"

Now they had brought with them their *menit* collars[52] and their rattles[53] and sistra[54] of Hathor, and they presented them before His Majesty, saying:

"Put forth your hands to these beautiful things.
    O enduring King,
    the adornments of the Lady of Heaven![55]
May the Golden One[56] give life to your nostrils;
    may she join with you, The Lady of the Stars![57]
May the Crown-goddess of Upper Egypt sail
        northward
    and the Crown-goddess of Lower Egypt sail
        southward,
    joined and united by the utterance of Your Majesty!
The Cobra-goddess[58] is set upon your brow,
    and you have removed your subjects from evil.
May Ra, Lord of the Two Lands, be gracious unto you;
    hail to you, as to the Lady of All!
Slacken your bow, make loose your arrow,
    give breath to him who is stifling!
Give us as good festal gift this sheik, son of the
        North,
    a barbarian born in Egypt!
He made flight through fear of you,
    he left the land through dread of you!
May the face of him who has seen your face not be

---

[49] **Elephantine** An island in the Nile River in Upper Egypt, opposite modern Aswan.
[50] **the god who ordained this flight** **Sinuhe** is being evasive; he now blames an unspecified god for his flight from Egypt.
[51] **Yetchet-Tawy** Probably Itj-Tawy, meaning "Seizer of Two Lands," located on the border between Upper and Lower Egypt, made capital of Egypt by Amenemhet I.

[52] *menit* **collars** Necklaces.
[53] **rattle** A noisemaker, or **sistrum** (pl. **sistra**), associated with the goddess **Hathor.**
[54] **sistra** Noisemakers (sing. **sistrum**), associated with the goddess **Hathor.**
[55] **Lady of Heaven** A title of **Hathor.**
[56] **the Golden One** A title of **Hathor.**
[57] **Lady of the Stars** A title of **Hathor.**
[58] **Cobra-goddess** The goddess **Wadjet,** the patroness of Lower Egypt, and one of "the Two Ladies," an ancient title of the ruler.

afraid;
may the eye which has looked at you not be terrified!"

Then said His Majesty, "Let him not fear, and let him not fall into dread. He shall be a courtier among the nobles, and he shall be placed in the midst of the courtiers. Proceed you to the Morning-chamber, and wait upon him!"

And so I went forth from the royal chambers, the King's children giving me their hands. We proceeded afterward to the Great Double Door. I was placed in the house of a son of the King, which had fine things in it; there was a cooling room in it, and landscape decoration. There were valuables of the Treasury in it, and in every room was clothing of royal linen, and myrrh,[59] and the best oil of the King, and of the courtiers, whom he loves. Every servingman was at his task.

The years were made to pass away from my limbs as I was shaved and my hair was combed. A load of dirt was given back to the desert, and their clothes to the sand farers. I was clothed in fine linen, and anointed with fine oil. I slept upon a bed. I gave back the sand to those who live in it, and tree oil to those who rub themselves with it.

65

There was given to me a house with grounds, which had belonged to a courtier. Many craftsmen restored it, and all its trees made to flourish anew. Meals from the Palace were brought to me three or four times a day besides what the King's children kept on giving me.

There was built for me a pyramid-tomb of stone, in the midst of the pyramids. The chief pyramid mason took charge of its ground, the chief draftsman designed it, the chief sculptor carved in it, and the chief builders of the necropolis concerned themselves with it. All the equipment which is placed in a tomb, those were supplied therein. Ka-priests[60] were assigned to me. A funerary domain was made for me with fields in it, as is done for a foremost courtier. My statue was overlaid with gold, its kilt with fine gold.

By His Majesty was it caused to be done. There is no commoner for whom the like has been done. I was bestowed the favors of the King until there came the day of mooring.

IT HAS COME FROM ITS BEGINNING TO ITS END, AS WAS FOUND IN THE WRITING.

---

[59] **myrrh** From Arabic, "bitter." An aromatic, resinous gum from a flowering tree. It was used to make incense, perfume, cosmetics, and medicines and in embalming.

[60] **Ka-priests** Mortuary priests who prepare the body (the *ka*) for embalming.

The Great Hymn to the Aten

In Egyptian culture, hymns to deities were simply part of the state religion and only incidentally expressions of literary art. Hymns functioned as a kind of metalanguage, a "language" beyond ordinary speech and writing, used by the elite to understand the universe. (The religious beliefs of the majority are virtually unknown.) Because the deities were never arranged into a logical structure, hymns (as well as rituals and figurative art) helped to shape theology, to the extent that it could be defined. Hymns offer information on ancient myths and beliefs and ritual, and over time, show the shifting "pecking order" among the deities. Recited during funerary rituals, hymns give evidence of the common belief that the divine coexists with the earthly, the eternal with the transient.

One of the most famous hymns is *The Great Hymn to the Aten*, dating from the New Kingdom (ca. 1552–1079 B.C.). This hymn is well known because of its association with King Akhenaten ("the glory of Aten") (ca. 1369–1353 B.C.). This king changed his name from Amenhotep ("Amen is content") IV as part of a campaign to make the Aten—the god of the solar disk—the head of the state religion. He ordered this change to downgrade the influence of the rich priests of Amen-Re, the local deity from Thebes who rose to national prominence in the New Kingdom and became Re (the sun god).

Abandoning Thebes, Akhenaten founded a new capital called Aket-Aten ("the horizon of the Aten"), today known by its Arabic name, Tel el Amarna, or simply Amarna, from which he launched a religious and an artistic revolution. (In Amarna art, the Aten is always represented as the sun disk, emitting rays that end in tiny hands, that bless the royal family and hold the *ankh,* the symbol of eternal life.) His innovations angered the political elite and the priests of Amen-Re, who got their revenge after Akhenaten's death by restoring Amen-Re to supremacy and trying to erase the heretic's memory from history. However, knowledge of Akhenaten's reign survives in inscriptions, artworks, and *The Great Hymn to the Aten.*

Reading the Selection

The Great Hymn to the Aten, perhaps written by Akhenaten himself, was inscribed in the tomb of King Ay, a brief successor to Akhenaten who ruled before the restoration of Amen-Re. The hymn is framed within a complex literary form that includes a list of the Aten's titles and a similar list, repeated at the beginning and the end, of the titles of Akhenaten and Queen Nefertiti.

This hymn's major theme is universalism, the idea that there is one god (the Aten) who is the lord of the entire creation, as in, for example: "You [the Aten] have created the earth according to your desire, while you were alone, / With men, cattle, and wild beasts, all that is upon earth and goes upon feet, and all that soars above and flies with its wings." Paralleling a similar theme in Psalm 104 of the Old Testament, this hymn is an example of the strong influence of Egypt on Hebrew culture over the centuries.

A second theme of the hymn is the mediating role played by the king in interpreting the divine world to humankind—a theme as old as *The Story of Sinuhe.* To the elite, who composed its literature, Egypt is a cosmic stage with the king as the sole actor, performing its history through his actions. The hymn expresses this idea in these words: "[T]here is no one who knows you [the Aten] save your son [Akhenaten]."

❧

Praise of the Living Ra,[1] Horus of the Double Horizon,[2]   1
Rejoicing on the Horizon, in His Name of Shu Who is in the Aten,[3] living forever unto eternity; Aten living and great, He who is in the Jubilee Festival,[4] Lord of all that the Aten encircles, Lord of the Heavens and Lord of the Earth, Lord of the House of Aten in Akhet-Aten.[5] The King of Upper and Lower Egypt,[6] Living in Truth, the Lord of the Two Lands, Nefer-Kheperu-Ra Wa-en-Ra,[7] Son of Ra,[8] Living in Truth, Lord of Diadems, Akh-en-Aten, Great in His

Duration, and the Great Wife of the King,[9] His Beloved, the Lady of the Two Lands, Nefer-Neferu-Aten Nefert-Iti,[10] living, healthy, and youthful forever unto eternity. He[11] says:

Beautiful is your shining forth on the horizon,
   O living Aten, beginning of life!
When you arise on the eastern horizon,
   you fill every land with your beauty.
You are bright and great and gleaming,
   and are high above every land.
Your rays envelop the lands,
   as far as all you have created.
You are Ra, and you reach unto their end,   10
   and subdue them all for your beloved son.
You are afar, yet are your rays upon earth;
   you are before their face, yet one knows not their going!
When you go down in the western horizon,
   the earth is in darkness, as if it were dead.
They sleep in their chamber, their heads enwrapped,
   and no eye sees the other.

---

[1] **the Living Ra** Hereafter follow a list of names of King Akhenaten. These are not simply royal titles. Kings are gods in their own right, and various other deities manifest themselves in the king's person. **Ra,** also spelled **Re,** the Sun-god and creator god.

[2] **Horus of the Double Horizon** The falcon god.

[3] **in His Name of Shu . . . Aten** A fusion of **Shu,** the primordial Egyptian god of the air and supporter of the sky, with **Aten,** the god of the solar disk.

[4] **Jubilee Festival** Sed-Festival, a repetition of the coronation ritual, in which the vows of kingship are renewed; usually held after thirty years of a reign, but sometimes after three.

[5] **Akhet-Aten** Also called **Aket-Aten.** "The horizon of the Aten." The capital of Akhenaten's kingdom.

[6] **The King of Upper and Lower Egypt** An old title, dating from 3100 B.C., when Menes united Egypt into one country. It precedes the Throne Name (see fn. 7).

[7] **Nefer-Kheperu-Ra Wa-en-Ra** Throne name of Akhenaten.

[8] **Son of Ra** Epithet that accompanies the king's name. The ruler's divinity arises from the belief that he or she is the offspring of the Sun-god **Ra,** also known as **Re.**

[9] **the Great Wife of the King** Here follow a list of divine names of Queen Nefertiti, Akhenaten's consort.

[10] **Nefer-Neferu-Aten Nefert-Iti** Throne name of Nefertiti.

[11] **He** King Akhenaten.

Though all their things were taken while under their
    heads,
        yet would they not perceive it.
Every lion comes forth from his den,   20
    and all serpents that bite.

Darkness is without and the earth is silent,
    for he who created it rests in his horizon.
When the earth brightens and you rise on the horizon,
    and shine as the Aten in the day,
When you scatter the darkness and offer your beams,
    the Two Lands are in festival,
They are awake and they stand on their feet,
    for you have raised them up.
They wash their bodies, and they take their garments,   30
    and their hands praise your arising.
        The whole land, it performs its work!

All beasts are content upon their pasture,
    and the trees and herbs are verdant.
The birds fly out of their nests,
    and their wings praise your Divine Essence.[12]
All wild beasts prance upon their feet,
    and all that fly and alight.
They live when you shine forth for them!
The ships voyage downstream and upstream likewise,   40
    and every way is open, since you have arisen.
The fish in the river leap up before your face,
    and your rays are in the midst of the Great Green.[13]

You who bring children into being in women,
    and make fluid[14] into mankind,
Who nourishes the son in the womb of his mother,
    who soothes him so that he weeps not,
    O nurse in the womb!
Who gives breath in order to keep alive
    all that he has made;   50

When he comes forth from the womb on the day of his
    birth,
        you open his mouth in speech, and give all that he
        needs.
The chick in the egg chirps in the shell
    for you give it breath therein to sustain its life.
You make its completion for it in the egg in order to
    break it;
It comes forth from the egg at its completion,
    and walks on its feet when it comes forth therefrom.

How manifold are the things which you have made,
    and they are hidden from before man!
        O unique god, who has no second to him!   60
You have created the earth according to your desire,
    while you were alone,
With men, cattle, and wild beasts,
    all that is upon earth and goes upon feet,
        and all that soars above and flies with its wings.

The lands of Syria[15] and Kush,[16]
    and the land of Egypt,
You put every man in his place,
    and supply their needs.
Each one has provision   70
    and his lifetime is reckoned.
Their tongues are diverse in speech,
    and their form likewise;
Their skins are distinguished,
    for you distinguish the peoples of foreign lands.

You make the Nile in the Other World,[17]
    and bring it whither you wish,
In order to sustain the people,
    even as you have made them.
For you are lord of them all,   80
    who weary yourself on their behalf,
The lord of every land, who arises for them,
    O Aten of the day, great of majesty!

All strange foreign lands,
    you make that whereon they live.
You have put a Nile in the sky,
    that it may come down for them,
And make waves on the hills like the sea,
    to water their fields in their townships.
How excellently made are your designs, O Lord of   90
    Eternity!
    the Nile in heaven, you appoint it for foreign peoples,
        and all beasts of the wilderness which walk upon feet;
The Nile upon earth,
    it proceeds from the Other World for the Beloved Land.

Your rays suckle every field,
    and when you shine forth
        they live and flourish for you.
You make the seasons
    to cause to continue all you have created:
The winter to cool them,   100
    and the warmth that they may taste of you.
You have made the sky afar off to shine therein,
    in order to behold all you have made.
You are alone, shining in your forms as living Aten,
    appearing, shining, withdrawing, returning,
        you make millions of forms of yourself alone!
Cities, townships, fields, road, and river,
    all eyes behold you against them.
        O Aten of the day above the earth!

You are in my heart,   110
    and there is no one who knows you save your son,
Nefer-Kheperu-Ra Wa-en-Ra,
    whom you made understanding of your designs and
        your might.

----

[12] **Divine Essence** The perishable part of **Aten's** soul, the *ka*.
[13] **Great Green** The sea.
[14] **fluid** Semen.

----

[15] **Syria** *Retenu*, identified variously as Canaan, north Palestine, and
south Syria.
[16] **Kush** Nubia, the land on Egypt's southern border.
[17] **Nile in the Other World** The god **Aten** is praised for making a
Nile River in heaven, for those foreigners who cannot enjoy the Nile
River in this world.

The earth came into being by your hand,
   even as you have created them.
When you arise they live,
   and when you set they die.
But you have eternity in your members,
   and all creatures live in you.

The eyes look on your beauty until you set;
   all work is laid aside when you set in the west.
When you rise you make all to flourish for the King,
   you who made the foundations of the earth.

120

You raise them up for your son,
   he who came forth from your body,
the King of Upper and Lower Egypt, Living in Truth, the Lord of the Two Lands, Nefer-Kheperu-Ra Wa-en-Ra, Son of Ra, Living in Truth, Lord of Diadems, Akh-en-Aten, Great in His Duration, and for the Great Wife of the King, His Beloved, the Lady of the Two Lands, Nefer-Neferu-Aten Nefert-Iti, living and youthful forever unto eternity.

2

AEGEAN CIVILIZATION
The Minoans, the Mycenaeans, and the Greeks of the Archaic Age

HOMER

Selections from the *Iliad*

The two Greek epics, the *Iliad* and the *Odyssey* (see the following selection), have never lost their appeal, though they were composed nearly three thousand years ago. Homer, with his strong grasp of the human psyche, expressed his characters' sorrow and happiness, hopes and fears, and most especially, their love of life and certainty of death. Performed as oral poetry accompanied by music, these works electrified his first audiences because they represented the basic human condition as his listeners had experienced it. In later periods, after the works were written down, readers were equally thrilled because they recognized the timeless truths contained in his words. Contributing to the epics' enduring appeal were the similes and metaphors that invoked images from Homer's world and remain memorable today as sublime expressions of poetic beauty. It is a measure of Homer's classic status that ever since his day, writers have reworked his two stories of war and travel, respectively, giving their own versions of his heroes and heroines and updating the plots to reflect their own times.

The *Iliad* focuses on the climactic year of the Greeks' nine-year siege of Ilium, or Troy (though it stops short of the fall of Troy). Composed in about the middle of the eighth century B.C., Homer's works are his own reworking of tales that previously had been circulating orally for about three hundred years. The oral tales reflected an earlier civilization, the Mycenaean (1900–1100 B.C.); thus, the Homeric heroes and the Olympian deities, who are considered the quintessence of Greek culture, are in reality Mycenaean in origin. The popularity of both the *Iliad* and the *Odyssey* resulted in their becoming moral guidebooks, offering to Greek youths models of behavior both on and off the battlefield. The works were also treated as religious scripture, providing insight into the personalities and motives of the Olympian deities.

Reading the Selections

These four selections from the *Iliad* illustrate Homer's talents as a storyteller and as a teacher of moral lessons. In the selection from Book 1, Homer's genius is evident in the opening line that announces his theme: "the rage of Peleus' son, Achilles, murderous, doomed, that cost the Achaeans countless losses. . . ." This theme becomes the thread that holds together the epic, despite the convoluted plot and its "cast of thousands." The Trojan War—the battle between the

Greeks (Achaeans) and the Trojans—always forms the backdrop and sometimes the temporary foreground to the story. Further complicating the plot are the adventures of the Olympic deities, who allow nothing to happen on earth without their consent.

The first selection also details the quarrel between Achilles and Agamemnon, the king, over their claims to a captured woman. Their quarrel creates dissension in the ranks of the Greek soldiers and angers Achilles to the point that he withdraws himself and his men from battling the Trojans. The consequences of this private dispute become clearer when many men are slaughtered as the two sides fight back and forth.

The selection from Book 6 shows how war touches the lives of everyone, especially wives and children. The conversation between Hector, the leading warrior for the Trojans, and his wife Andromache is one of the most moving scenes in literature. In a brief exchange, the husband and wife discuss why men fight wars and how women and children are the victims. The desire to live, so evident in this scene, is then contrasted in the selection from Book 22, where Hector and Achilles finally face each other. Homer shows that in the heat of battle, men, driven by revenge and the will to survive, kill their enemies and mutilate their bodies. He underscores both the glory and gore of war—themes that writers over the centuries will address to the present day.

The selection from Book 24, the climax of the *Iliad*, begins with Achilles out of control, intent on humiliating the corpse of Hector by dragging it behind his chariot. Confronted by Hector's grieving father, King Priam of Troy, Achilles is only able to let go of his all-consuming rage when the two men weep for their loved ones and for their own fate as mortals. Achilles yields up Hector's body to Priam, and the epic ends with Hector's funeral (not included here).

≪∞≫

Book 1

Rage[1]—Goddess,[2] sing the rage of Peleus'[3] son Achilles,   1
murderous, doomed, that cost the Achaeans[4] countless
    losses,
hurling down to the House of Death[5] so many sturdy
    souls,
great fighters' souls, but made their bodies carrion,
feasts for the dogs and birds,
and the will of Zeus[6] was moving toward its end.
Begin, Muse, when the two first broke and clashed,
Agamemnon[7] lord of men and brilliant Achilles.

What god[8] drove them to fight with such a fury?

Apollo[9] the son of Zeus and Leto.[10] Incensed at the king   10
he swept a fatal plague through the army—men were
    dying
and all because Agamemnon spurned Apollo's priest.[11]
Yes, Chryses[12] approached the Achaeans' fast ships
to win his daughter[13] back, bringing a priceless ransom
and bearing high in hand, wound on a golden staff,
the wreaths of the god, the distant deadly Archer.[14]
He begged the whole Achaean army but most of all
the two supreme commanders, Atreus'[15] two sons,
"Agamemnon, Menelaus[16]—all Argives[17] geared for war!

---

[1] **Rage . . . of . . . Achilles** The theme of the *Iliad*.
[2] **Goddess** Calliope, the muse of epic poetry.
[3] **Peleus** Father of Achilles, by the sea-goddess **Thetis**. King of **Phthia**, in Thessaly.
[4] **Achaeans** Collective name for the people of **Achaea**, or mainland Greece.
[5] **House of Death Hades**, or the Underworld.
[6] **Zeus** Son of **Cronus** and **Rhea**. King and father of the Olympic deities; god of the sky, of the weather, of hospitality, and of guests.
[7] **Agamemnon** King of Mycenae and overall leader of the **Achaean** army; son of **Atreus**, husband of **Clytemnestra**, and brother of **Menelaus**.
[8] **What god** The **Achaeans** thought the gods controlled human behavior.

[9] **Apollo** Son of **Zeus** and **Leto**. Patron of the arts, leader of the muses; god of archery and sudden death in men. **Apollo's** arrows bring on the plague; he fights for the Trojans.
[10] **Leto** A goddess, mother of **Apollo** and **Artemis**, by **Zeus**.
[11] **Apollo's priest Chryses**. When humans humiliate a priest, a god's representative, they are guilty of impiety, a sin for which they will be punished severely.
[12] **Chryses** A priest of **Apollo** and father of a daughter named **Chryseis**.
[13] **daughter Chryseis**, daughter of **Chryses**.
[14] **Archer** The god **Apollo**, known also as "**Lord of the Silver Bow.**"
[15] **Atreus** Father of **Agamemnon** and **Menelaus**.
[16] **Menelaus** King of **Lacedaemon**, a city on the Peloponnesus; son of **Atreus**, husband of **Helen**, and brother of **Agamemnon**.
[17] **Argives** Another name for the **Achaeans**.

May the gods who hold the halls of Olympus[18] give you   20
Priam's[19] city[20] to plunder, then safe passage home.
Just set my daughter free, my dear one . . . here,
accept these gifts, this ransom. Honor the god
who strikes from worlds away—the son of Zeus, Apollo!"

And all ranks of Achaeans cried out their assent:
"Respect the priest, accept the shining ransom!"
But it brought no joy to the heart of Agamemnon.
The king dismissed the priest with a brutal order
ringing in his ears: "Never again, old man,
let me catch sight of you by the hollow ships!   30
Not loitering now, not slinking back tomorrow.
The staff and the wreaths of god will never save you then.
The girl—I won't give up the girl. Long before that,
old age will overtake her in *my* house, in Argos,[21]
far from her fatherland, slaving back and forth
at the loom,[22] forced to share my bed!
                                     Now go,
don't tempt my wrath—and you may depart alive."

The old man was terrified. He obeyed the order,
turning, trailing away in silence down the shore   40
where the battle lines of breakers crash and drag.
And moving off to a safe distance, over and over
the old priest prayed to the son of sleek-haired Leto,
lord Apollo, "Hear me, Apollo! God of the silver bow
who strides the walls of Chryse[23] and Cilla[24] sacrosanct—
lord in power of Tenedos[25]—Smintheus,[26] god of the
       plague!
If I ever roofed a shrine to please your heart,
ever burned the long rich bones of bulls and goats
on your holy altar, now, now bring my prayer to pass.
Pay the Danaans[27] back—your arrows for my tears!"   50

His prayer went up and Phoebus[28] Apollo heard him.
Down he strode from Olympus' peaks, storming at heart
with his bow and hooded quiver slung across his
       shoulders.
The arrows clanged at his back as the god quaked with
       rage,

the god himself on the march and down he came like
       night.
Over against the ships he dropped to a knee, let fly a shaft
and a terrifying clash rang out from the great silver bow.
First he went for the mules and circling dogs but then,
launching a piercing shaft at the men themselves,
he cut them down in droves—   60
and the corpse-fires[29] burned on, night and day, no end in
       sight.

Nine days the arrows of god swept through the army.
On the tenth Achilles called all ranks to muster—
the impulse seized him, sent by white-armed Hera[30]
grieving to see Achaean fighters drop and die.
Once they'd gathered, crowding the meeting grounds,
the swift runner Achilles rose and spoke among them:
"Son of Atreus, now we are beaten back, I fear,
the long campaign is lost. So home we sail . . .
if we can escape our death—if war and plague   70
are joining forces now to crush the Argives.
But wait: let us question a holy man,
a prophet, even a man skilled with dreams—
dreams as well can come our way from Zeus—
come, someone to tell us why Apollo rages so,
whether he blames us for a vow we failed, or sacrifice.
If only the god would share the smoky savor of lambs
and full-grown goats, Apollo might be willing, still,
somehow, to save us from this plague."
                                     So he proposed   80
and down he sat again as Calchas[31] rose among them,
Thestor's son,[32] the clearest by far of all the seers
who scan the flight of birds.[33] He knew all things that are,
all things that are past and all that are to come,
the seer who had led the Argive ships to Troy
with the second sight[34] that god Apollo gave him.
For the armies' good the seer began to speak:
"Achilles, dear to Zeus . . .
you order me to explain Apollo's anger,
the distant deadly Archer[35]? I will tell it all.   90
But strike a pact with me, swear you will defend me
with all your heart, with words and strength of hand.
For there is a man I will enrage—I see it now—
a powerful man who lords it over all the Argives,
one the Achaeans must obey . . . A mighty king,
raging against an inferior, is too strong.
Even if he can swallow down his wrath today,
still he will nurse the burning in his chest

---

[18] **Olympus** The home of the Greek gods; an actual mountain in Thessaly.
[19] **Priam** King of **Troy**. Son of **Laomedon;** husband of **Hecuba,** father of **Hector** and **Paris.**
[20] **city Troy,** also known as **Ilium.**
[21] **Argos** (1) A city on the Peloponnesus, ruled by **Diomedes;** (2) another name for **Achaea,** or mainland Greece; (3) another name for the kingdom of **Agamemnon;** (4) Pelasgian **Argos,** in northern Greece, the kingdom of Achilles.
[22] **loom** Women had two basic roles: to be beautiful and to weave at the loom.
[23] **Chryse** A city in the Trojan lands; the home of **Chryses.**
[24] **Cilla** A city in the Trojan lands.
[25] **Tenedos** An island in the Aegean Sea, off the coast of **Troy.**
[26] **Smintheus** Epithet for **Apollo.** Means perhaps "mouse-god," associated with **Apollo's** role as the cause of plague.
[27] **Danaans** Another name for the **Greeks.**
[28] **Phoebus** Epithet for **Apollo.**

---

[29] **corpse-fires** Both the **Achaeans** and the **Trojans** honored the dead by burning their corpses on funeral pyres.
[30] **Hera** Daughter of **Cronus** and **Rhea,** sister and long-suffering wife of **Zeus.** She fights for the **Achaeans.**
[31] **Calchas** Blind prophet of the **Achaeans.**
[32] **Thestor** Father of **Calchas.**
[33] **the flight of birds** Interpreting the pattern of bird sightings was a major practice in the **Achaean** religion.
[34] **second sight** Since **Calchas** was blind, it was believed that **Apollo** had given him "second sight," the gift of prophecy.
[35] **Archer** Epithet for **Apollo.**

until, sooner or later, he sends it bursting forth.
Consider it closely, Achilles. Will you save me?"   100

  And the matchless runner reassured him: "Courage!
Out with it now, Calchas. Reveal the will of god,
whatever you may know. And I swear by Apollo
dear to Zeus, the power you pray to, Calchas,
when you reveal god's will to the Argives—no one,
not while I am alive and see the light on earth, no one
will lay his heavy hands on you by the hollow ships.
None among all the armies. Not even if you mean
Agamemnon here who now claims to be, by far,
the best of the Achaeans."   110
                              The seer took heart
and this time he spoke out, bravely: "Beware—
he casts no blame for a vow we failed, a sacrifice.
The god's enraged because Agamemnon spurned his
     priest,
he refused to free his daughter, he refused the ransom.
That's why the Archer sends us pains and he will send us
     more
and never drive this shameful destruction from the
     Argives,
not till we give back the girl with sparkling eyes
to her loving father—no price, no ransom paid—
and carry a sacred hundred bulls to Chryse town.   120
Then we can calm the god, and only then appease him."

  So he declared and sat down. But among them rose
the fighting son of Atreus, lord of the far-flung kingdoms,
Agamemnon—furious, his dark heart filled to the brim,
blazing with anger now, his eyes like searing fire.
With a sudden, killing look he wheeled on Calchas first:
"Seer of misery! Never a word that works to my
     advantage!
Always misery warms your heart, your prophecies—
never a word of profit said or brought to pass.
Now, again, you divine god's will for the armies,   130
bruit it about, as fact, why the deadly Archer
multiplies our pains: because I, I refused
that glittering price for the young girl Chryseis.
Indeed, I prefer *her* by far, the girl herself,
I want her mine in my own house! I rank her higher
than Clytemnestra,[36] my wedded wife—she's nothing
     less
in build or breeding, in mind or works of hand.
But I am willing to give her back, even so,
if that is best for all. What I really want
is to keep my people safe, not see them dying.   140
But fetch me another prize, and straight off too,
else I alone of the Argives go without my honor.
That would be a disgrace. You are all witness,
look—*my* prize is snatched away!"
                              But the swift runner
Achilles answered him at once, "Just how, Agamemnon,

great field marshal . . . most grasping man alive,
how can the generous Argives give you prizes now?
I know of no troves of treasure, piled, lying idle,
anywhere. Whatever we dragged from towns we   150
     plundered,
all's been portioned out. But collect it, call it back
from the rank and file? *That* would be the disgrace.
So return the girl to the god, at least for now.
We Achaeans will pay you back, three, four times over,
if Zeus will grant us the gift, somehow, someday,
to raze Troy's massive ramparts to the ground."

  But King Agamemnon countered, "Not so quickly,
brave as you are, godlike Achilles—trying to cheat *me*.
Oh no, you won't get past me, take me in that way!
What do you want? To cling to your own prize   160
while I sit calmly by—empty-handed here?
Is that why you order me to give her back?
No—if our generous Argives *will* give me a prize,
a match for my desires, equal to what I've lost,
well and good. But if they give me nothing
I will take a prize myself—your own, or Ajax'[37]
or Odysseus'[38] prize—I'll commander her myself
and let that man I go to visit choke with rage!
Enough. We'll deal with all this later, in due time.
Now come, we haul a black ship down to the bright sea,   170
gather a decent number of oarsmen along her locks
and put aboard a sacrifice, and Chryseis herself,
in all her beauty . . . we embark her too.
Let one of the leading captains take command.
Ajax, Idomeneus,[39] trusty Odysseus or you, Achilles,
you—the most violent man alive—so you can perform
the rites for us and calm the god yourself."
                              A dark glance
and the headstrong runner answered him in kind:
     "Shameless—
armored in shamelessness—always shrewd with greed!   180
How could any Argive soldier obey your orders,
freely and gladly do your sailing for you
or fight your enemies, full force? Not I, no.
It wasn't Trojan spearmen who brought me here to fight.
The Trojans never did *me* damage, not in the least,
they never stole my cattle or my horses, never
in Phthia[40] where the rich soil breeds strong men
did they lay waste my crops. How could they?
Look at the endless miles that lie between us . . .
shadowy mountain ranges, seas that surge and thunder.   190
No, you colossal, shameless—we all followed you,
to please you, to fight for you, to win your honor
back from the Trojans—Menelaus and you, you dog-face!

---

[36] **Clytemnestra** Wife of **Agamemnon** and sister of **Helen**.

[37] **Ajax   Achaean** warlord, son of **Telamon**. Called **Telamonian** or **Great Ajax;** leader of the troops from **Salamis**.
[38] **Odysseus   Achaean** warlord, son of **Laertes** and father of **Telemachus;** from **Ithaca**.
[39] **Idomeneus   Achaean** warlord; son of **Deucalion;** leader of the troops from **Crete**.
[40] **Phthia** A region in Thessaly; home of **Peleus** and **Achilles**.

What do *you* care? Nothing. You don't look right or left.
And now you threaten to strip me of my prize in person—
the one I fought for long and hard, and sons of Achaea
handed her to me.

           My honors never equal yours,
whenever we sack some wealthy Trojan stronghold—
my arms bear the brunt of the raw, savage fighting,   200
true, but when it comes to dividing up the plunder
the lion's share is yours, and back I go to my ships,
clutching some scrap, some pittance that I love,
when I have fought to exhaustion.

                No more now—
back I go to Phthia. Better that way by far,
to journey home in the beaked ships of war.
I have no mind to linger here disgraced,
brimming your cup and piling up your plunder."

    But the lord of men Agamemnon shot back,   210
"*Desert*, by all means—if the spirit drives you home!
I will never beg you to stay, not on *my* account.
Never—others will take my side and do me honor,
Zeus above all, whose wisdom rules the world.
You—I hate you most of all the warlords
loved by the gods. Always dear to your heart,
strife, yes, and battles, the bloody grind of war.
What if you are a great soldier? That's just a gift of god.
Go home with your ships and comrades, lord it over your
      Myrmidons[41]!
You *are* nothing to me—you and your overweening   220
      anger!
But let this be my warning on your way:
since Apollo insists on taking my Chryseis,
I'll send her back in my own ships with *my* crew.
But I, I will be there in person at your tents
to take Briseis[42] in all her beauty, your own prize—
so you can learn just how much greater I am than you
and the next man up may shrink from matching words
      with me,
from hoping to rival Agamemnon strength for strength!"

    He broke off and anguish gripped Achilles.
The heart in his rugged chest was pounding, torn . . .   230
Should he draw the long sharp sword slung at his hip,
thrust through the ranks and kill Agamemnon now?—
or check his rage and beat his fury down?
As his racing spirit veered back and forth,
just as he drew his huge blade from its sheath,
down from the vaulting heavens swept Athena,[43]
the white-armed goddess Hera sped her down:
Hera loved both men and cared for both alike.

Rearing behind him Pallas[44] seized his fiery hair—
only Achilles saw her, none of the other fighters—   240
struck with wonder he spun around, he knew her at once,
Pallas Athena! the terrible blazing of those eyes,
and his winged words went flying: "Why, why now?
Child of Zeus with the shield of thunder, why come now?
To witness the outrage Agamemnon just committed?
I tell you this, and so help me it's the truth—
he'll soon pay for his arrogance with his life!"

    Her gray eyes clear, the goddess Athena answered,
"Down from the skies I come to check your rage
if only you will yield.   250
The white-armed goddess Hera sped me down:
she loves you both, she cares for you both alike.
Stop this fighting, now. Don't lay hand to sword.
Lash him with threats of the price that he will face.
And I tell you this—and I *know* it is the truth—
one day glittering gifts will lie before you,
three times over to pay for all his outrage.
Hold back now. Obey us both."

            So she urged
and the swift runner complied at once: "I must—   260
when the two of you hand down commands, Goddess,
a man submits though his heart breaks with fury.
Better for him by far. If a man obeys the gods
they're quick to hear his prayers."

           And with that
Achilles stayed his burly hand on the silver hilt
and slid the huge blade back in its sheath.
He would not fight the orders of Athena.
Soaring home to Olympus, she rejoined the gods
aloft in the halls of Zeus whose shield is thunder.   270

    But Achilles rounded on Agamemnon once again,
lashing out at him, not relaxing his anger for a moment:
"Staggering drunk, with your dog's eyes, your fawn's
      heart!
Never once did you arm with the troops and go to battle
or risk an ambush packed with Achaea's picked men—
you lack the courage, you can see death coming.
Safer by far, you find, to foray all through camp,
commandeering the prize of any man who speaks against
      you.
King who devours his people! Worthless husks, the men
      you rule—
if not, Atrides,[45] this outrage would have been your last.   280
I tell you this, and I swear a mighty oath upon it . . .
by this, this scepter, look,
that never again will put forth crown and branches,
now it's left its stump on the mountain ridge forever,
nor will it sprout new green again, now the brazen[46] ax

---

[41] **Myrmidons** The troops from **Phthia** in Thessaly, the followers of **Achilles.**
[42] **Briseis** A woman loved by **Achilles**; daughter of **Briseus**, a captive of **Achilles.**
[43] **Athena** Goddess of wisdom, of warfare; patron of the city of Athens. She sprang full-grown from **Zeus's** head, after a headache. She fought for the **Achaeans.**

---

[44] **Pallas** Epithet for **Athena.**
[45] **Atrides** "Son of **Atreus**"; patronymic of **Agamemnon** and **Menelaus.**
[46] **brazen** Brass.

has stripped its bark and leaves, and now the sons of
   Achaea
pass it back and forth as they hand their judgments
   down,
upholding the honored customs whenever Zeus
   commands—
This scepter will be the mighty force behind my oath:
someday, I swear, a yearning for Achilles will strike   290
Achaea's sons and all your armies! But then, Atrides,
harrowed as you will be, *nothing* you do can save you—
not when your hordes of fighters drop and die,
cut down by the hands of man-killing Hector! Then—
then you will tear your heart out, desperate, raging
that you disgraced the best of the Achaeans!"
                                        Down on the ground
he dashed the scepter studded bright with golden nails,
then took his seat again. The son of Atreus smoldered,
glaring across at him, but Nestor[47] rose between them,   300
the man of winning words, the clear speaker of
   Pylos[48] . . .
Sweeter than honey from his tongue the voice flowed on
   and on.
Two generations of mortal men he had seen go down by
   now,
those who were born and bred with him in the old days,
in Pylos' holy realm, and now he ruled the third.
He pleaded with both kings, with clear good will,
"No more—or enormous sorrow comes to all Achaea!
How they would exult, Priam and Priam's sons
and all the Trojans. Oh they'd leap for joy
to hear the two of you battling on this way,   310
you who excel us all, first in Achaean councils,
first in the ways of war.
                        Stop. Please.
Listen to Nestor. You are both younger than I,
and in my time I struck up with better men than you,
even you, but never once did they make light of me.
I've never seen such men, I never will again . . .
men like Pirithous,[49] Dryas,[50] that fine captain,
Caeneus[51] and Exadius,[52] and Polyphemus,[53] royal
   prince,
and Theseus,[54] Aegeus'[55] boy, a match for the immortals.   320
They were the strongest mortals ever bred on earth,
the strongest, and they fought against the strongest too,
shaggy Centaurs,[56] wild brutes of the mountains—
they hacked them down, terrible, deadly work.
And I was in their ranks, fresh out of Pylos,

far away from home—they enlisted me themselves
and I fought on my own, a free lance, single-handed.
And none of the men who walk the earth these days
could battle with those fighters, none, but they,
they took to heart my counsels, marked my words.   330
So now you listen too. Yielding is far better . . .
Don't seize the girl, Agamemnon, powerful as you are—
leave her, just as the sons of Achaea gave her,
his prize from the very first.
And you, Achilles, never hope to fight it out
with your king, pitting force against his force:
no one can match the honors dealt a king, you know,
a sceptered king to whom great Zeus gives glory.
Strong as you are—a goddess was your mother—
he has more power because he rules more men.   340
Atrides, end your anger—look, it's Nestor!
I beg you, cool your fury against Achilles.
Here the man stands over all Achaea's armies,
our rugged bulwark braced for shocks of war."

   But King Agamemnon answered him in haste,
"True, old man—all you say is fit and proper—
but this soldier wants to tower over the armies,
he wants to rule over all, to lord it over all,
give out orders to every man in sight. Well,
there's one, I trust, who will never yield to *him!*   350
What if the everlasting gods have made a spearman of
   him?
Have they entitled him to hurl abuse at *me?*"

   "Yes!"—blazing Achilles broke in quickly—
"What a worthless, burnt-out coward I'd be called
if I would submit to you and all your orders,
whatever you blurt out. Fling them at others,
don't give me commands!
Never again, *I* trust, will Achilles yield to *you.*
And I tell you this—take it to heart, I warn you—
my hands will never do battle for that girl,   360
neither with you, King, nor any man alive.
You Achaeans gave her, now you've snatched her back.
But all the rest I possess beside my fast black ship—
not one bit of it can you seize against my will, Atrides.
Come, try it! So the men can see, that instant,
your black blood gush and spurt around my spear!"

   Once the two had fought it out with words,
battling face-to-face, both sprang to their feet
and broke up the muster beside the Argive squadrons.
Achilles strode off to his trim ships and shelters,   370
back to his friend Patroclus[57] and their comrades.
Agamemnon had a vessel hauled down to the sea,
he picked out twenty oarsmen to man her locks,
put aboard the cattle for sacrifice to the god
and led Chryseis in all her beauty amidships.

---

[47] **Nestor** The oldest **Achaean** warlord. Son of **Neleus,** king of **Pylos.**
[48] **Pylos** A city and region in the Peloponnesus; home to **Nestor.**
[49] **Pirithous** Son of **Zeus.** King of the Lapiths, a tribe in Thessaly.
[50] **Dryas** A Lapith warlord.
[51] **Caeneus** A Lapith warlord.
[52] **Exadius** A Lapith warlord.
[53] **Polyphemus** A Lapith warlord.
[54] **Theseus** Son of **Aegeus,** King of Athens.
[55] **Aegeus** King of Athens, father of **Theseus.** Eponymous source for
the **Aegean** Sea.
[56] **Centaur** Fabled creature, half-man and half-horse.

---

[57] **Patroclus Achaean** warrior; son of **Menoetius;** companion to
Achilles.

Versatile Odysseus took the helm as captain.
                                     All embarked,
the party launched out on the sea's foaming lanes
while the son of Atreus told his troops to wash,
to purify themselves from the filth of plague.   380

They scoured it off, threw scourings in the surf
and sacrificed to Apollo full-grown bulls and goats
along the beaten shore of the fallow barren sea
and savory smoke went swirling up the skies.

∽

Book 6

                        A flash of his[58] helmet   1
and off he strode and quickly reached his sturdy,
well-built house. But white-armed Andromache[59]—
Hector could not find her in the halls.
She and the boy[60] and a servant finely gowned
were standing watch on the tower, sobbing, grieving.
When Hector saw no sign of his loyal wife inside
he went to the doorway, stopped and asked the servants,
"Come, please, tell me the truth now, women.
Where's Andromache gone? To my sisters' house?   10
To my brothers' wives with their long flowing robes?
Or Athena's shrine where the noble Trojan women
gather to win the great grim goddess over?"

    A busy, willing servant answered quickly,
"Hector, seeing you want to know the truth,
she hasn't gone to your sisters, brothers' wives
or Athena's shrine where the noble Trojan women
gather to win the great grim goddess over.
Up to the huge gate-tower of Troy she's gone
because she heard our men are so hard-pressed,   20
the Achaean fighters coming on in so much force.
She sped to the wall in panic, like a madwoman—
the nurse went with her, carrying your child."

    At that, Hector spun and rushed from his house,
back by the same way down the wide, well-paved streets
throughout the city until he reached the Scaean Gates,[61]
the last point he would pass to gain the field of battle.
There his warm, generous wife came running up to meet
    him,
Andromache the daughter of gallant-hearted Eetion[62]
who had lived below Mount Placos[63] rich with timber,   30
in Thebe[64] below the peaks, and ruled Cilicia's[65] people.
His daughter had married Hector helmed in bronze.

She joined him now, and following in her steps
a servant holding the boy against her breast,
in the first flush of life, only a baby,
Hector's son, the darling of his eyes
and radiant as a star . . .
Hector would always call the boy Scamandrius,[66]
townsmen called him Astyanax,[67] Lord of the City,
since Hector was the lone defense of Troy.   40
The great man of war breaking into a broad smile,
his gaze fixed on his son, in silence. Andromache,
pressing close beside him and weeping freely now,
clung to his hand, urged him, called him: "Reckless one,
my Hector—your own fiery courage will destroy you!
Have you no pity for him, our helpless son? Or me,
and the destiny that weighs me down, your widow,
now so soon. Yes, soon they will kill you off,
all the Achaean forces massed for assault, and then,
bereft of you, better for me to sink beneath the earth.   50
What other warmth, what comfort's left for me,
once you have met your doom? Nothing but torment!
I have lost my father. Mother's gone as well.
Father . . . the brilliant Achilles laid him low
when he stormed Cilicia's city filled with people,
Thebe with her towering gates. He killed Eetion,
not that he stripped his gear—he'd some respect at least—
for he burned his corpse in all his blazoned bronze,
then heaped a grave-mound high above the ashes
and nymphs of the mountain planted elms around it,   60
daughters of Zeus whose shield is storm and thunder.
And the seven brothers I had within our halls . . .
all in the same day went down to the House of Death,
the great godlike runner Achilles butchered them all,
tending their shambling oxen, shining flocks.
                                     And mother,
who ruled under the timberline of woody Placos once—
he no sooner haled her here with his other plunder
than he took a priceless ransom, set her free
and home she went to her father's royal halls   70
where Artemis,[68] showering arrows, shot her down.
You, Hector—you are my father now, my noble mother,

---

[58] **his** Hector's.
[59] **Andromache** Trojan princess. Daughter of Eetion; wife of **Hector**; mother of **Astyanax.**
[60] **boy Astyanax,** a young Trojan prince; son of **Andromache** and **Hector.**
[61] **Scaean Gates** The main gates of **Troy.**
[62] **Eetion** King of the **Cilicians** in **Thebe** in the Trojan lands; father of **Andromache.**
[63] **Mount Placos** A mountain near the city of **Thebe.**
[64] **Thebe** A Trojan city; home of **Andromache.**
[65] **Cilicia** Trojan lands around **Thebe,** ruled by King **Eetion.**

---

[66] **Scamandrius** Another name for **Astyanax,** the son of **Hector.** Named for the Trojan river, **Scamander.**
[67] **Astyanax** Son of **Andromache** and **Hector;** a young Trojan prince.
[68] **Artemis** Daughter of **Zeus** and **Hera;** goddess of the hunt and of sudden death in women; sister of **Apollo.**

a brother too, and you are my husband, young and warm
   and strong!
Pity me, please! Take your stand on the rampart here,
before you orphan your son and make your wife a
   widow.
Draw your armies up where the wild fig tree stands,
there, where the city lies most open to assault,
the walls lower, easily overrun. Three times
they have tried that point, hoping to storm Troy
their best fighters led by the Great[69] and Little[70] Ajax,
famous Idomeneus, Atreus' sons, valiant Diomedes.[71]
Perhaps a skilled prophet revealed the spot—
or their own fury whips them on to attack."

   And tall Hector nodded, his helmet flashing:
"All this weighs on my mind too, dear woman.
But I would die of shame to face the men of Troy
and the Trojan women trailing their long robes
if I would shrink from battle now, a coward.
Nor does the spirit urge me on that way.
I've learned it all too well. To stand up bravely,
always to fight in the front ranks of Trojan soldiers,
winning my father great glory, glory for myself.
For in my heart and soul I also know this well:
the day will come when sacred Troy must die,
Priam must die and all his people with him,
Priam who hurls the strong ash spear . . .
                              Even so,
it is less the pain of the Trojans still to come
that weighs me down, not even of Hecuba[72] herself
or King Priam, or the thought that my own brothers
in all their numbers, all their gallant courage,
may tumble in the dust, crushed by enemies—
That is nothing, nothing beside your agony
when some brazen Argive hales you off in tears,
wrenching away your day of light and freedom!
Then far off in the land of Argos you must live,
laboring at a loom, at another woman's beck and call,
fetching water at some spring, Messeis[73] or Hyperia,[74]
resisting it all the way—
the rough yoke of necessity at your neck.
And a man may say, who sees you streaming tears,
'There is the wife of Hector, the bravest fighter
they could field, those stallion-breaking Trojans,
long ago when the men fought for Troy.' So he will say

and the fresh grief will swell your heart once more,
widowed, robbed of the one man strong enough
to fight off your day of slavery.
                              No, no,
let the earth come piling over my dead body
before I hear your cries, I hear you dragged away!"   120

   In the same breath, shining Hector reached down
for his son—but the boy recoiled,
cringing against his nurse's full breast,
screaming out at the sight of his own father,
terrified by the flashing bronze, the horsehair crest,
the great ridge of the helmet nodding, bristling terror—
so it struck his eyes. And his loving father laughed,
his mother laughed as well, and glorious Hector,
quickly lifting the helmet from his head,
set it down on the ground, fiery in the sunlight,   130
and raising his son he kissed him, tossed him in his arms,
lifting a prayer to Zeus and the other deathless gods:
"Zeus, all you immortals! Grant this boy, my son,
may be like me, first in glory among the Trojans,
strong and brave like me, and rule all Troy in power
and one day let them say, 'He is a better man than his
   father!'—
when he comes home from battle bearing the bloody gear
of the mortal enemy he has killed in war—
a joy to his mother's heart."
                        So Hector prayed   140
and placed his son in the arms of his loving wife.
Andromache pressed the child to her scented breast,
smiling through her tears. Her husband noticed,
and filled with pity now, Hector stroked her gently,
trying to reassure her, repeating her name: "Andromache,
dear one, why so desperate? Why so much grief for me?
No man will hurl me down to Death, against my fate.
And fate? No one alive has ever escaped it,
neither brave man nor coward, I tell you—
it's born with us the day that we are born.   150
So please go home and tend to your own tasks,
the distaff and the loom, and keep the women
working hard as well. As for the fighting,
men will see to that, all who were born in Troy
but I most of all."
                  Hector aflash in arms
took up his horsehair-crested helmet once again.
And his loving wife went home, turning, glancing
back again and again and weeping live warm tears.
She quickly reached the sturdy house of Hector,   160
man-killing Hector,
and found her women gathered there inside
and stirred them all to a high pitch of mourning.
So in his house they raised the dirges for the dead,
for Hector still alive, his people were so convinced
that never again would he come home from battle,
never escape the Argives' rage and bloody hands.

---

[69] **Great Ajax** Achaean warlord; see fn. 37.
[70] **Little Ajax** Achaean warlord, son of **Oileus;** leader of the troops from Locris.
[71] **Diomedes** Achaean warlord; son of **Tydeus,** king of **Argos** in the Peloponnesus.
[72] **Hecuba** Trojan queen; daughter of **Dymas,** wife of King **Priam,** mother of **Hector.**
[73] **Messeis** Spring in Greece, uncertain location.
[74] **Hyperia** Spring in Thessaly.

∽

Book 22

Athena luring him on with all her immortal cunning— 1
and now, at last, as the two came closing for the kill
it was tall Hector, helmet flashing, who led off:
"No more running from you in fear, Achilles!
Not as before. Three times I fled around
the great city of Priam—I lacked courage then
to stand your onslaught. Now my spirit stirs me
to meet you face-to-face. Now kill or be killed!
Come, we'll swear to the gods, the highest witnesses—
the gods will oversee our binding pacts. I swear 10
I will never mutilate you—merciless as you are—
if Zeus allows me to last it out and tear your life away.
But once I've stripped your glorious armor, Achilles,
I will give your body back to your loyal comrades.
Swear you'll do the same."
                    A swift dark glance
and the headstrong runner answered, "Hector, stop!
You unforgivable, you . . . don't talk to me of pacts.
There are no binding oaths between men and lions—
wolves and lambs can enjoy no meeting of the minds— 20
they are all bent on hating each other to the death.
So with you and me. No love between us. No truce
till one or the other falls and gluts with blood
Ares who hacks at men behind his rawhide shield.
Come, call up whatever courage you can muster.
Life or death—now prove yourself a spearman,
a daring man of war! No more escape for you—
Athena will kill you with my spear in just a moment.
Now you'll pay at a stroke for all my comrades' grief,
all you killed in the fury of your spear!" 30
                    With that,
shaft poised, he hurled and his spear's long shadow flew
but seeing it coming glorious Hector ducked away,
crouching down, watching the bronze tip fly past
and stab the earth—but Athena snatched it up
and passed it back to Achilles
and Hector the gallant captain never saw her.
He sounded out a challenge to Peleus' princely son:
"You missed, look—the great godlike Achilles!
So you knew nothing at all from Zeus about my death— 40
and yet how sure you were! All bluff, cunning with
     words,
that's all you are—trying to make me fear you,
lose my nerve, forget my fighting strength.
Well, you'll never plant your lance in my back
as I flee *you* in fear—plunge it through my chest
as I come charging in, if a god gives you the chance!
But now it's for you to dodge *my* brazen spear—
I wish you'd bury it in your body to the hilt.
How much lighter the war would be for Trojans then
if you, their greatest scourge, were dead and gone!" 50

     Shaft poised, he hurled and his spear's long shadow
          flew
and it struck Achilles' shield—a dead-center hit—
but off and away it glanced and Hector seethed,

his hurtling spear, his whole arm's power poured
in a wasted shot. He stood there, cast down . . .
he had no spear in reserve. So Hector shouted out
to Deiphobus[75] bearing his white shield—with a ringing
     shout
he called for a heavy lance—
                    but the man was nowhere near him,
vanished— 60
          yes and Hector knew the truth in his heart
and the fighter cried aloud, "My time has come!
At last the gods have called me down to death.
I thought he was at my side, the hero Deiphobus—
he's safe inside the walls, Athena's tricked me blind.
And now death, grim death is looming up beside me,
no longer far away. No way to escape it now. This,
this was their pleasure after all, sealed long ago—
Zeus and the son of Zeus, the distant deadly Archer—
though often before now they rushed to my defense. 70
So now I meet my doom. Well let me die—
but not without struggle, not without glory, no,
in some great clash of arms that even men to come
will hear of down the years!"
                    And on that resolve
he drew the whetted sword that hung at his side,
tempered, massive, and gathering all his force
he swooped like a soaring eagle
launching down from the dark clouds to earth
to snatch some helpless lamb or trembling hare. 80
So Hector swooped now, swinging his whetted sword
and Achilles charged too, bursting with rage, barbaric,
guarding his chest with the well-wrought blazoned
     shield,
head tossing his gleaming helmet, four horns strong
and the golden plumes shook that the god of fire
drove in bristling thick along its ridge.
Bright as that star amid the stars in the night sky,
star of the evening, brightest star that rides the heavens,
so fire flared from the sharp point of the spear Achilles
brandished high in his right hand, bent on Hector's 90
     death,
scanning his splendid body—where to pierce it best?
The rest of his flesh seemed all encased in armor,
burnished, brazen—*Achilles'* armor that Hector stripped
from strong Patroclus when he killed him—true,
but one spot lay exposed,
where collarbones lift the neckbone off the shoulders,
the open throat, where the end of life comes quickest—
     there
as Hector charged in fury brilliant Achilles drove his
     spear
and the point went stabbing clean through the tender
     neck
but the heavy bronze weapon failed to slash the 100
     windpipe—

---

[75] **Deiphobus** Trojan warrior; son of King **Priam.**

Hector could still gasp out some words, some last
    reply . . .
he crashed in the dust—
                godlike Achilles gloried over him:
"Hector—surely you thought when you stripped
    Patroclus' armor
that you, you would be safe! Never a fear of me—
far from the fighting as I was—you fool!
Left behind there, down by the beaked ships
his great avenger waited, a greater man by far—
that man was I, and I smashed your strength! And you—
the dogs and birds will maul you, shame your corpse   110
while Achaeans bury my dear friend in glory!"

    Struggling for breath, Hector, his helmet flashing,
said, "I beg you, beg you by your life, your parents—
don't let the dogs devour me by the Argive ships!
Wait, take the princely ransom of bronze and gold,
the gifts my father and noble mother will give you—
but give my body to friends to carry home again,
so Trojan men and Trojan women can do me honor
with fitting rites of fire once I am dead."

    Staring grimly, the proud runner Achilles answered,   120
"Beg no more, you fawning dog—begging me by my
    parents!
Would to god my rage, my fury would drive me now
to hack your flesh away and eat you raw—
such agonies you have caused me! Ransom?
No man alive could keep the dog-packs off you,
not if they haul in ten, twenty times that ransom
and pile it here before me and promise fortunes more—
no, not even if Dardan[76] Priam should offer to weigh out

---

[76] **Dardan** From **Dardania,** the kingdom of **Dardanus,** a predecessor
to **Troy.**

your bulk in gold! Not even then will your noble mother
lay you on your deathbed, mourn the son she bore . . .   130
The dogs and birds will rend you—blood and bone!"

    At the point of death, Hector, his helmet flashing,
said, "I know you well—I see my fate before me.
Never a chance that I could win you over . . .
Iron inside your chest, that heart of yours.
But now beware, or my curse will draw god's wrath
upon your head, that day when Paris and lord Apollo—
for all your fighting heart—destroy you at the Scaean
    Gates!"

    Death cut him short. The end closed in around him.
Flying free of his limbs   140
his soul went winging down to the House of Death,
wailing his fate, leaving his manhood far behind,
his young and supple strength. But brilliant Achilles
taunted Hector's body, dead as he was, "Die, die!
For my own death, I'll meet it freely—whenever Zeus
and the other deathless gods would like to bring it on!"
                . . . So he triumphed
and now he was bent on outrage, on shaming noble
    Hector.
Piercing the tendons, ankle to heel behind both feet,
he knotted straps of rawhide through them both,   150
lashed them to his chariot, left the head to drag
and mounting the car, hoisting the famous arms aboard,
he whipped his team to a run and breakneck on they flew,
holding nothing back. And a thick cloud of dust rose up
from the man they dragged, his dark hair swirling round
that head so handsome once, all tumbled low in the dust—
since Zeus had given him over to his enemies now
to be defiled in the land of his own fathers.

∞

<h1>Book 24</h1>

The games were over now. The gathered armies scattered,   1
each man to his fast ship, and fighters turned their minds
to thoughts of food and the sweet warm grip of sleep.
But Achilles kept on grieving for his friend,
the memory burning on . . .
and all-subduing sleep could not take him,
not now, he turned and twisted, side to side,
he longed for Patroclus' manhood, his gallant heart—
What rough campaigns they'd fought to an end together,
what hardships they had suffered, cleaving their way   10
through wars of men and pounding waves at sea.
The memories flooded over him, live tears flowing,
and now he'd lie on his side, now flat on his back,
now facedown again. At last he'd leap to his feet,
wander in anguish, aimless along the surf, and dawn on
    dawn
flaming over the sea and shore would find him pacing.

Then he'd yoke his racing team to the chariot-harness,
lash the corpse of Hector behind the car for dragging
and haul him three times round the dead Patroclus' tomb,
and then he'd rest again in his tents and leave the body   20
sprawled facedown in the dust. But Apollo pitied Hector—
dead man though he was—and warded all corruption off
from Hector's corpse and round him, head to foot,
the great god wrapped the golden shield of storm
so his skin would never rip as Achilles dragged him
    on . . .

*[Under cover of night, the Trojan King Priam, accompanied by a
herald, approaches the place where the Greeks are encamped.]*
                    [T]he god of luck,[77]
leaping onto the chariot right behind the team,

---

[77] **god of luck** Hermes.

quickly grasped the whip and reins in his hands 30
and breathed fresh spirit into the mules and horses.
As they reached the trench and rampart round the fleet,
the sentries had just begun to set out supper there
but the giant-killer[78] plunged them all in sleep . . .
he spread the gates at once, slid back the bars
and ushered Priam in with his wagon-load of treasure.
Now, at last, they approached royal Achilles' shelter,
the tall, imposing lodge the Mymidons built their king,
hewing planks of pine, and roofed it high with thatch,
gathering thick shaggy reeds from the meadow banks, 40
and round it built their king a spacious courtyard
fenced with close-set stakes. A single pine beam
held the gates, and it took three men to ram it home,
three to shoot the immense bolt back and spread the
    doors—
three average men. Achilles alone could ram it home
    himself.
But the god of luck now spread the gates for the old man,
drove in the glinting gifts for Peleus' swift son,
climbed down from behind the team and said to Priam,
"Old man, look, I am a god come down to you,
I am immortal Hermes— 50
my Father[79] sent me here to be your escort.
But now I will hasten back. I will not venture
into Achilles' presence: it would offend us all
for a mortal man to host an immortal face-to-face.
But you go in yourself and clasp Achilles' knees,[80]
implore him by his father, his mother with lovely hair,
by his own son—so you can stir his heart!"
                With that urging
Hermes[81] went his way to the steep heights of Olympus.
But Priam swung down to earth from the battle-car 60
and leaving Idaeus[82] there to rein in mules and team,
the old king went straight up to the lodge
where Achilles dear to Zeus would always sit.
Priam found the warrior there inside . . .
many captains sitting some way off, but two,
veteran Automedon[83] and the fine fighter Alcimus[84]
were busy serving him. He had just finished dinner,
eating, drinking, and the table still stood near.
The majestic king of Troy slipped past the rest
and kneeling down beside Achilles, clasped his knees 70
and kissed his hands, those terrible, man-killing hands
that had slaughtered Priam's many sons in battle.
Awesome—as when the grip of madness seizes one
who murders a man in his own fatherland and flees
abroad to foreign shores, to a wealthy, noble host,
and a sense of marvel runs through all who see him—
so Achilles marveled, beholding majestic Priam.

His men marveled too, trading startled glances.
But Priam prayed his heart out to Achilles:
"Remember your own father, great godlike Achilles— 80
as old as *I* am, past the threshold of deadly old age!
No doubt the countrymen round about him plague him
    now,
with no one there to defend him, beat away disaster.
No one—but at least he hears you're still alive
and his old heart rejoices, hopes rising, day by day,
to see his beloved son come sailing home from Troy.
But I—dear god, my life so cursed by fate . . .
I fathered hero sons in the wide realm of Troy
and now not a single one is left, I tell you.
Fifty sons I had when the sons of Achaea came, 90
nineteen born to me from a single mother's womb
and the rest by other women in the palace. Many,
most of them violent Ares[85] cut the knees from under.
But one, one was left me, to guard my walls, my people—
the one you killed the other day, defending his fatherland,
my Hector! It's all for him I've come to the ships now,
to win him back from you—I bring a priceless ransom.
Revere the gods, Achilles! Pity me in my own right,
remember your own father! I deserve more pity . . .
I have endured what no one on earth has ever done 100
    before—
I put to my lips the hands of the man who killed my son."

    Those words stirred within Achilles a deep desire
to grieve for his own father. Taking the old man's hand
he gently moved him back. And overpowered by
    memory
both men gave way to grief. Priam wept freely
for man-killing Hector, throbbing, crouching
before Achilles' feet as Achilles wept himself,
now for his father, now for Patroclus once again,
and their sobbing rose and fell throughout the house.
Then, when brilliant Achilles had his fill of tears 110
and the longing for it had left his mind and body,
he rose from his seat, raised the old man by the hand
and filled with pity now for his gray head and gray
    beard,
he spoke out winging words, flying straight to the heart:
"Poor man, how much you've borne—pain to break the
    spirit!
What daring brought you down to the ships, all alone,
to face the glance of the man who killed your sons,
so many fine brave boys? You have a heart of iron.
Come, please, sit down on this chair here . . .
Let us put our griefs to rest in our own hearts, 120
rake them up no more, raw as we are with mourning.
What good's to be won from tears that chill the spirit?
So the immortals spun our lives that we, we wretched
    men
live on to bear such torments—the gods live free of
    sorrows.
There are two great jars that stand on the floor of Zeus's
    halls

---

[78] **giant-killer** Epithet for **Hermes.**
[79] **Father** Zeus.
[80] **clasp . . . knees** A gesture of supplication.
[81] **Hermes** Messenger for the Olympic deities; patron of merchants and thieves; god of smiths; son of **Zeus.**
[82] **Idaeus** The herald of King **Priam.**
[83] **Automedon** Achaean warrior; son of Diores. A **Myrmidon,** charioteer of **Achilles.**
[84] **Alcimus** Another name for **Alcimedon,** son of **Laerces.** Achaean warrior and one of **Achilles'** commanders of the **Myrmidons.**

---

[85] **Ares** God of war; son of **Zeus** and **Hera;** fought for the Trojans.

and hold his gifts, our miseries one, the other blessings.
When Zeus who loves the lightning mixes gifts for a man,
now he meets with misfortune, now good times in turn.
When Zeus dispenses gifts from the jar of sorrows only,
he makes a man an outcast—brutal, ravenous hunger   130
drives him down the face of the shining earth,
stalking far and wide, cursed by gods and men.
So with my father, Peleus. What glittering gifts
the gods rained down from the day that he was born!
He excelled all men in wealth and pride of place,
he lorded the Myrmidons, and mortal that he was,
they gave the man an immortal goddess[86] for a wife.
Yes, but even on him the Father piled hardships,
no powerful race of princes born in his royal halls,
only a single son he fathered, doomed at birth,   140
cut off in the spring of life—
and I, I give the man no care as he grows old
since here I sit in Troy, far from my fatherland,
a grief to you, a grief to all your children.
And you too, old man, we hear you prospered once:
as far as Lesbos,[87] Macar's[88] kingdom, bounds to
      seaward,

────────

[86] **goddess** The sea-goddess **Thetis.**
[87] **Lesbos** An island and city in the **Aegean** Sea, south of **Troy.**
[88] **Macar** Legendary founder of the island kingdom of **Lesbos.**

Phrygia[89] east and upland, the Hellespont[90] vast and
      north—
that entire realm, they say, you lorded over once,
you excelled all men, old king, in sons and wealth.
But then the gods of heaven brought this agony on you—   150
ceaseless battles round your walls, your armies
      slaughtered.
You must bear up now. Enough of endless tears,
the pain that breaks the spirit.
Grief for your son will do no good at all.
You will never bring him back to life—
sooner you must suffer something worse."

     But the old and noble Priam protested strongly:
"Don't make me sit on a chair, Achilles, Prince,
not while Hector lies uncared-for in your camp!
Give him back to me, now, no more delay—   160
I must see my son with my own eyes.
Accept the ransom I bring you, a king's ransom!
Enjoy it, all of it—return to your own native land,
safe and sound . . . since now you've spared my life."

     A dark glance—and the headstrong runner answered,
"No more, old man, don't tempt my wrath, not now!
My own mind's made up to give you back your son."

────────

[89] **Phrygia** A region in Asia Minor, east of **Troy.**
[90] **Hellespont** Greek, "Greek Bridge." Modern **Dardanelles.** Narrow
strait between Europe (Gallipoli Peninsula) and Turkey in Asia; connects Sea of Marmara with **Aegean** Sea.

HOMER

Selections from the *Odyssey*

The *Odyssey* is the story of the ten years of wandering by the Greek warrior Odysseus, after the
Greeks' triumph over the Trojans in the Trojan War. He is trying to return to his island kingdom of
Ithaca and be reunited with his faithful wife, Penelope. His odyssey, or long voyage marked by
many challenges and changes of fortune, is in fact a divine punishment meted out by Poseidon,
the god of the sea and creator of the waters and earthquakes. Supportive of the Greeks during the
Trojan War, he now turns against Odysseus and tries to thwart his voyage home. Poseidon is the
father of the Cyclops, the one-eyed giant whom Odysseus outwits and blinds, as recounted in one
of the following selections. After the adventure with Polyphemus, the Cyclops, Odysseus experiences numerous other adventures and narrowly escapes death several times, as Poseidon uses his
supernatural powers to try to destroy his mortal enemy. Athena, the goddess of war and wisdom,
supports Odysseus in his many struggles against Poseidon. Thus, the deities, through favor or ill
will, affect the daily lives and determine the fate of humankind.

Reading the Selections

The first eight books of the *Odyssey* set the stage for the succeeding sixteen books. They introduce the deities, show how they control the lives of mortals, and describe Odysseus's plight

and his family's problems. Several of these books narrate the adventures of Telemachus, the son of Odysseus, who seeks information about his father's fate from some of the Greek warriors who have returned from the Trojan War. Other books note how Odysseus, through the intervention of the gods and goddesses, eventually finds himself on the island of Scheria, the home of the Phaeacians.

Book 9 of the *Odyssey* contains the first flashback in Western literature. In it, Odysseus tells his story from the time he left Troy until he arrived in the land of the Phaeacians, where he is welcomed by King Alcinous. The excerpt from Book 9 opens at a banquet with Odysseus thanking his host, King Alcinous, for the opportunity to recall his travels. The banqueters appreciate a lively story and, full of wine and good food, are eager to hear a tale of adventure. Odysseus first identifies himself, his lineage; and his kingdom. In passages omitted here, Odysseus talks about his men plundering the Cicones and, next, escaping the lures of the land of the lotus-eaters. They then arrive on the island of the Cyclops, the one-eyed giant. Odysseus, in outmaneuvering the Cyclops, displays his cunning and his bravery, the two talents that aided him in all of his travels. In Books 10–12 Homer has Odysseus finish the stories of his adventures. In Books 13–24 the author follows Odysseus's schemes and fights to win back his kingdom.

Homer writes more than an adventure story. He makes Odysseus, for all his faults, into a hero blessed with *arete,* or leadership qualities, including physical bravery, a keen wit, and a high regard for his servants. Above all, he possesses a deep resolve, come what may, to return to his devoted wife. Among the world's literary classics, the *Odyssey* is one of the few that celebrates the love of a husband and wife, as illustrated by the selection from Book 23, the reconciliation scene between Odysseus and Penelope. Faced with a stranger, who, at first, says he is a beggar and then throws off his rags and claims to be Odysseus, Penelope is initially skeptical of his true identity. Hence, she requires that the stranger pass a test known only to herself and her husband: explain the secret design of their marriage bed. Odysseus passes the test without missing a beat, and only then does faithful Penelope welcome him as her long-lost husband.

∞

Book 9

Odysseus, the great teller of tales, launched out on his
    story: 1
"Alcinous,[1] majesty, shining among your island people,
what a fine thing it is to listen to such a bard
as we have here—the man sings like a god.
The crown of life, I'd say. There's nothing better
than when deep joy holds sway throughout the realm
and banqueters up and down the palace sit in ranks,
enthralled to hear the bard, and before them all, the tables
heaped with bread and meats, and drawing wine from a
    mixing-bowl[2]
the steward makes his rounds and keeps the winecups   10
    flowing.
This, to my mind, is the best that life can offer.
                   "But now
you're set on probing the bitter pains I've borne,
so I'm to weep and grieve, it seems, still more.
Well then, what shall I go through first,
what shall I save for last?

What pains—the gods have given me my share.
Now let me begin by telling you my name . . .
so you may know it well and I in times to come,
if I can escape the fatal day, will be your host,   20
your sworn friend, though my home is far from here.
I am Odysseus,[3] son of Laertes,[4] known to the world
for every kind of craft—my fame has reached the skies.
Sunny Ithaca[5] is my home. Atop her stands our seamark,
Mount Neriton's[6] leafy ridges shimmering in the wind.
Around her a ring of islands circle side-by-side,
Dulichion,[7] Same,[8] wooded Zacynthus[9] too, but mine
lies low and away, the farthest out to sea,
rearing into the western dusk
while the others face the east and breaking day.   30

[1] **Alcinous** King of the **Phaeacians.**
[2] **mixing-bowl** For mixing water and wine; the **Achaeans** usually watered their wine.
[3] **Odysseus** Son of **Laertes** and **Anticleia;** husband of **Penelope;** father of **Telemachus;** king of **Ithaca.**
[4] **Laertes** Son of **Arcesius;** father of **Odysseus.**
[5] **Ithaca** Island in the Ionian Sea, off the west coast of Greece; home of **Odysseus.**
[6] **Neriton** A mountain on the island of **Ithaca.**
[7] **Dulichion** Island in the Ionian Sea, near **Ithaca.**
[8] **Same** Island in the Ionian Sea, near **Ithaca.**
[9] **Zacynthus** Island in the Ionian Sea, south of **Ithaca.**

Mine is a rugged land but good for raising sons—
and I myself, I know no sweeter sight on earth
than a man's own native country.
                                    "True enough,
Calypso[10] the lustrous goddess tried to hold me back,
deep in her arching caverns, craving me for a husband.
So did Circe,[11] holding me just as warmly in her halls,
the bewitching queen of Aeaea[12] keen to have me too.
But they never won the heart inside me, never.
So nothing is as sweet as a man's own country,   40
his own parents, even though he's settled down
in some luxurious house, off in a foreign land
and far from those who bore him.
                                    "No more. Come,
let me tell you about the voyage fraught with hardship
Zeus[13] inflicted on me, homeward bound from Troy[14] . . .
                                    "Now then,
I told most of my good trusty crew to wait,
to sit tight by the ship and guard her well
while I picked out my dozen finest fighters   50
and off I went. But I took a skin of wine along,
the ruddy, irresistible wine that Maron[15] gave me once,
Euanthes'[16] son, a priest of Apollo,[17] lord of Ismarus,[18]
because we'd rescued him, his wife and children,
reverent as we were;
he lived, you see, in Apollo's holy grove.
And so in return he gave me splendid gifts,
he handed me seven bars of well-wrought gold,
a mixing-bowl of solid silver, then this wine . . .
He drew it off in generous wine-jars, twelve in all,   60
all unmixed—and such a bouquet, a drink fit for the gods!

"No maid or man of his household knew that secret store,
only himself, his loving wife and a single servant.
Whenever they'd drink the deep-red mellow vintage,
twenty cups of water he'd stir in one of wine
and what an aroma wafted from the bowl—
what magic, what a godsend—
no joy in holding back when *that* was poured!
Filling a great goatskin now, I took this wine,
provisions too in a leather sack. A sudden foreboding   70
told my fighting spirit I'd soon come up against
some giant[19] clad in power like armor-plate—
a savage deaf to justice, blind to law.

---

[10] **Calypso** Goddess daughter of **Atlas;** lived on the island of Ogygia.
[11] **Circe** Goddess on the island of Aeaea, whose magic turned men into swine.
[12] **Aeaea** The island home of **Circe.**
[13] **Zeus** Son of **Cronus** and **Rhea.** King and father of the Olympic deities; god of the sky, of the weather, of hospitality, and of guests.
[14] **Troy** City besieged by the **Achaeans** in the *Iliad* and destroyed later, according to legends. **Odysseus,** in the *Odyssey,* is returning home from **Troy.**
[15] **Maron** Son of **Euanthes.**
[16] **Euanthes** Priest of **Apollo** at Ismarus in Thrace.
[17] **Apollo** Son of **Zeus** and **Leto.** Patron of the arts, leader of the muses; god of archery and sudden death in men. **Apollo's** arrows bring on the plague.
[18] **Ismarus** City in Thrace.
[19] **giant** Here begins the episode of the **Cyclops,** the one-eyed monster.

"Our party quickly made its way to his cave
but we failed to find our host himself inside;
he was off in his pasture, ranging his sleek flocks.
So we explored his den, gazing wide-eyed at it all,
the large flat racks loaded with drying cheeses,
the folds crowded with young lambs and kids,
split into three groups—here the spring-born,   80
here mid-yearlings, here the fresh sucklings
off to the side—each sort was penned apart.
And all his vessels, pails and hammered buckets
he used for miling, were brimming full with whey.
From the start my comrades pressed me, pleading hard,
'Let's make away with the cheeses, then come back—
hurry, drive the lambs and kids from the pens
to our swift ship, put out to sea at once!'
But I would not give way—
and how much better it would have been—   90
not till I saw him, saw what gifts he'd give.
But he proved no lovely sight to my companions.

"There we built a fire, set our hands on the cheeses,
offered some to the gods and ate the bulk ourselves
and settled down inside, awaiting his return . . .
And back he came from pasture, late in the day,
herding his flocks home, and lugging a huge load
of good dry logs to fuel his fire at supper.
He flung them down in the cave—a jolting crash—
we scuttled in panic into the deepest dark recess.   100
And next he drove his sleek flocks into the open vault,
all he'd milk at least, but he left the males outside,
rams and billy goats out in the high-walled yard.
Then to close his door he hoisted overhead
a tremendous, massive slab—
no twenty-two wagons, rugged and four-wheeled,
could budge that boulder off the ground, I tell you,
such an immense stone the monster wedged to block his
     cave!
Then down he squatted to milk his sheep and bleating
     goats,
each in order, and put a suckling underneath each dam.   110
And half of the fresh white milk he curdled quickly,
set it aside in wicker racks to press for cheese,
the other half let stand in pails and buckets,
ready at hand to wash his supper down.
As soon as he'd briskly finished all his chores
he lit his fire and spied us in the blaze and
'Strangers!' he thundered out, 'now who are you?
Where did you sail from, over the running sea-lanes?
Out on a trading spree or roving the waves like pirates,
sea-wolves raiding at will, who risk their lives   120
to plunder other men?'
                                    "The hearts inside us shook,
terrified by his rumbling voice and monstrous hulk.
Nevertheless I found the nerve to answer, firmly,
'Men of Achaea[20] we are and bound now from Troy!
Driven far off course by the warring winds,
over the vast gulf of the sea—battling home

---

[20] **Achaea** The Greek mainland.

on a strange tack, a route that's off the map,
and so we've come to you . . .
so it must please King Zeus's plotting heart.   130
We're glad to say we're men of Atrides[21] Agamemnon,[22]
whose fame is the proudest thing on earth these days,
so great a city he sacked, such multitudes he killed!
But since we've chanced on you, we're at your knees
in hopes of a warm welcome, even a guest-gift,
the sort that hosts give strangers. That's the custom.
Respect the gods, my friend. We're suppliants—at your
    mercy!
Zeus of the Strangers guards all guests and suppliants:
strangers are sacred—Zeus will avenge their rights!'

    "'Stranger,' he grumbled back from his brutal heart,   140
'you must be a fool, stranger, or come from nowhere,
telling *me* to fear the gods or avoid their wrath!
We Cyclops[23] never blink at Zeus and Zeus's shield
of storm and thunder, or any other blessed god—
we've got more force by far.
I'd never spare you in fear of Zeus's hatred,
you or your comrades here, unless I had the urge.
But tell me, where did you moor your sturdy ship
when you arrived? Up the coast or close in?
I'd just like to know.'   150
            "So he laid his trap
but he never caught me, no, wise to the world
I shot back in my crafty way, 'My ship?
Poseidon[24] god of the earthquake smashed my ship,
he drove it against the rocks at your island's far cape,
he dashed it against a cliff as the winds rode us in.
I and the men you see escaped a sudden death.'

    "Not a word in reply to that, the ruthless brute.
Lurching up, he lunged out with his hands toward my
    men
and snatching two at once, rapping them on the ground   160
he knocked them dead like pups—
their brains gushed out all over, soaked the floor—
and ripping them limb from limb to fix his meal
he bolted them down like a mountain-lion, left no scrap,
devoured entrails, flesh and bones, marrow and all!
We flung our arms to Zeus, we wept and cried aloud,
looking on at his grisly work—paralyzed, appalled.
But once the Cyclops had stuffed his enormous gut
with human flesh, washing it down with raw milk,
he slept in his cave, stretched out along his flocks.   170
And I with my fighting heart, I thought at first

to steal up to him, draw the sharp sword at my hip
and stab his chest where the midriff packs the liver—
I groped for the fatal spot but a fresh thought held me
    back.
There at a stroke we'd finish off ourselves as well—
how could *we* with our bare hands heave back
that slab he set to block his cavern's gaping maw?
So we lay there groaning, waiting Dawn's[25] first light.

    "When young Dawn with her rose-red fingers shone
        once more
the monster relit his fire and milked his handsome ewes,   180
each in order, putting a suckling underneath each dam,
and as soon as he'd briskly finished all his chores
he snatched up two more men and fixed his meal.
Well-fed, he drove his fat sheep from the cave,
lightly lifting the huge doorslab up and away,
then slipped it back in place
as a hunter flips the lid of his quiver shut.
Piercing whistles—turning his flocks to the hills
he left me there, the heart inside me brooding on revenge:
how could I pay him back? would Athena[26] give me   190
    glory?
Here was the plan that struck my mind as best . . .
the Cyclops' great club: there it lay by the pens,
olivewood, full of sap. He'd lopped it off to brandish
once it dried. Looking it over, we judged it big enough
to be the mast of a pitch-black ship with her twenty oars,
a freighter broad in the beam that plows through miles of
    sea—
so long, so thick it bulked before our eyes. Well,
flanking it now, I chopped off a fathom's length,
rolled it to comrades, told them to plane it down,
and they made the club smooth as I bent and shaved   200
the tip to a stabbing point. I turned it over
the blazing fire to char it good and hard,
then hid it well, buried deep under the dung
that littered the cavern's floor in thick wet clumps.
And now I ordered my shipmates all to cast lots—
who'd brave it out with me
to hoist our stake and grind it into his eye
when sleep had overcome him? Luck of the draw
I got the very ones I would have picked myself,
four good men, and I in the lead made five . . .   210

    "Nightfall brought him back, herding his woolly sheep
and he quickly drove the sleek flock into the vaulted
    cavern,
rams and all—none left outside in the walled yard—
his own idea, perhaps, or a god led him on.
Then he hoisted the huge slab to block the door
and squatted to milk his sheep and bleating goats,
each in order, putting a suckling underneath each dam,
and as soon as he'd briskly finished all his chores
he snatched up two more men and fixed his meal.

---

[21] **Atrides** "Son of **Atreus**"; the patronymic of either **Agamemnon** or
Menelaus.
[22] **Agamemnon** King of Mycenae; son of **Atreus,** husband of **Clytemnestra,** and brother of **Menelaus. Agamemnon's** homecoming from
Troy contrasts starkly with that of **Odysseus. Agamemnon** is killed
by the unfaithful **Clytemnestra,** whereas **Odysseus** is welcomed
home by the faithful **Penelope,** who has kept his property intact.
[23] **Cyclops** A race of one-eyed giants, in particular, the name for
Polyphemus.
[24] **Poseidon** Son of **Cronus** and **Rhea;** brother of **Zeus;** god of the sea
and of earthquakes. Father of **Polyphemus,** the **Cyclops;** enemy of
Odysseus in the *Odyssey.*

---

[25] **Dawn** Goddess of the morning.
[26] **Athena** Goddess of wisdom, of warfare; patron of the city of
Athens. She sprang full-grown from **Zeus's** head, after a headache.

But this time I lifted a carved wooden bowl,   220
brimful of my ruddy wine,
and went right up to the Cyclops, enticing,
'Here, Cyclops, try this wine—to top off
the banquet of human flesh you've bolted down!
Judge for yourself what stock our ship had stored.
I brought it here to make you a fine libation,[27]
hoping you would pity me, Cyclops, send me home,
but your rages are insufferable. You barbarian—
how can any man on earth come visit you after *this*?
What you've done outrages all that's right!'   230

    "At that he seized the bowl and tossed it off
and the heady wine pleased him immensely—'More'—
he demanded a second bowl—'a hearty helping!
And tell me your name now, quickly,
so I can hand my guest a gift to warm *his* heart.
Our soil yields the Cyclops powerful, full-bodied wine
and the rains from Zeus build its strength. But this,
this is nectar, ambrosia[28]—this flows from heaven!'

    "So he declared. I poured him another fiery bowl—
three bowls I brimmed and three he drank to the last   240
    drop,
the fool, and then, when the wine was swirling round his
    brain,
I approached my host with a cordial, winning word:
'So, you ask me the name I'm known by, Cyclops?
I will tell you. But you must give me a guest-gift
as you've promised. Nobody—that's my name. Nobody—
so my mother and father call me, all my friends.'

"But he boomed back at me from his ruthless heart,
'*Nobody*? I'll eat Nobody last of all his friends—
I'll eat the others first! That's my gift to *you*!'

                                        "With that   250
he toppled over, sprawled full-length, flat on his back
and lay there, his massive neck slumping to one side,
and sleep that conquers all overwhelmed him now
as wine came spurting, flooding up from his gullet
with chunks of human flesh—he vomited, blind drunk.
Now, at last, I thrust our stake in a bed of embers
to get it red-hot and rallied all my comrades:
'Courage—no panic, no one hang back now!'
And green as it was, just as the olive stake
was about to catch fire—the glow terrific, yes—   260
I dragged it from the flames, my men clustering round
as some god breathed enormous courage through us all.
Hoisting high that olive stake with its stabbing point,
straight into the monster's eye they rammed it hard—
I drove my weight on it from above and bored it home
as a shipwright bores his beam with a shipwright's drill
that men below, whipping the strap back and forth, whirl
and the drill keeps twisting faster, never stopping—

So we seized our stake with its fiery tip
and bored it round and round in the giant's eye   270
till blood came boiling up around that smoking shaft
and the hot blast singed his brow and eyelids round the
    core
and the broiling eyeball burst—
                              its crackling roots blazed
and hissed—
              as a blacksmith plunges a glowing ax or adze
in an ice-cold bath and the metal screeches steam
and its temper hardens—that's the iron's strength—
so the eye of the Cyclops sizzled round that stake!
He loosed a hideous roar, the rock walls echoed round   280
and we scuttled back in terror. The monster wrenched the
    spike
from his eye and out it came with a red geyser of blood—
he flung it aside with frantic hands, and mad with pain
he bellowed out for help from his neighbor Cyclops
living round about in caves on windswept crags.
Hearing his cries, they lumbered up from every side
and hulking round his cavern, asked what ailed him:
'What, Polyphemus, what in the world's the trouble?
Roaring out in the godsent night to rob us of our sleep.
Surely no one's rustling your flocks against your will—   290
surely no one's trying to kill you now by fraud or force!'

    "'*Nobody*, friends'—Polyphemus[29] bellowed back from
    his cave—
'Nobody's killing me now by fraud and not by force!'

    "'If you're alone,' his friends boomed back at once,
'and nobody's trying to overpower you now—look,
it must be a plague sent here by mighty Zeus
and there's no escape from *that*.
You'd better pray to your father, Lord Poseidon.'

    "They lumbered off, but laughter filled my heart
to think how nobody's name—my great cunning stroke—   300
had duped them one and all. But the Cyclops there,
still groaning, racked with agony, groped around
for the huge slab, and heaving it from the doorway,
down he sat in the cave's mouth, his arms spread wide,
hoping to catch a comrade stealing out with sheep—
such a blithering fool he took me for!
But I was already plotting . . .
what was the best way out? how could I find
escape from death for my crew, myself as well?
My wits kept weaving, weaving cunning schemes—   310
life at stake, monstrous death staring us in the face—
till this plan struck my mind as best. That flock,
those well-fed rams with their splendid thick fleece,
sturdy, handsome beasts sporting their dark weight of
    wool:
I lashed them abreast, quietly, twisting the willow-twigs
the Cyclops slept on—giant, lawless brute—I took them
three by three; each ram in the middle bore a man
while the two rams either side would shield him well.

---

[27] **libation** A ritual spilling of wine, as an act of religious devotion to
a deity.
[28] **ambrosia** Food for the gods.

---

[29] **Polyphemus** The **Cyclops**; son of **Poseidon**.

So three beasts to bear each man, but as for myself?
There was one bellwether ram, the prize of all the flock,   320
and clutching him by his back, tucked up under
his shaggy belly, there I hung, face upward,
both hands locked in his marvelous deep fleece,
clinging for dear life, my spirit steeled, enduring . . .
So we held on, desperate, waiting Dawn's first light.
                                              "As soon
as young Dawn with her rose-red fingers shone once
       more
the rams went rumbling out of the cave toward pasture,
the ewes kept bleating round the pens, unmilked,
their udders about to burst. Their master now,   330
heaving in torment, felt the back of each animal
halting before him here, but the idiot never sensed
my men were trussed up under their thick fleecy ribs.
And last of them all came my great ram now, striding out,
weighed down with his dense wool and my deep plots.
Stroking him gently, powerful Polyphemus murmured,
'Dear old ram, why last of the flock to quit the cave?
In the good old days you'd never lag behind the rest—
you with your long marching strides, first by far
of the flock to graze the fresh young grasses,   340
first by far to reach the rippling streams,
first to turn back home, keen for your fold
when night comes on—but now you're last of all.
And why? Sick at heart for your master's eye
that coward gouged out with his wicked crew?—
only after he'd stunned my wits with wine—
that, that Nobody . . .
who's not escaped his death, I swear, not yet.
Oh if only you thought like *me*, had words like *me*
to tell me where that scoundrel is cringing from my rage!   350
I'd smash him against the ground, I'd spill his brains—
flooding across my cave—and that would ease my heart
of the pains that good-for-nothing Nobody made me
       suffer!'"

"And with that threat he let my ram go free outside.
But soon as we'd got one foot past cave and courtyard,
first I loosed myself from the ram, then loosed my men,
then quickly, glancing back again and again we drove
our flock, good plump beasts with their long shanks,
straight to the ship and a welcome sight we were
to loyal comrades—we who'd escaped our deaths—   360
but for all the rest they broke down and wailed.
I cut it short, I stopped each shipmate's cries,
my head tossing, brows frowning, silent signals
to hurry, tumble our fleecy herd on board,
launch out on the open sea!
They swung aboard, they sat to the oars in ranks
and in rhythm churned the water white with stroke on
       stroke.
But once offshore as far as a man's shout can carry,
I called back to the Cyclops, stinging taunts:
'So, Cyclops, no weak coward it was whose crew   370
you bent to devour there in your vaulted cave—
you with your brute force! Your filthy crimes
came down on your own head, you shameless cannibal,
daring to eat your guests in your own house—

so Zeus and the other gods have paid you back!'

"That made the rage of the monster boil over.
Ripping off the peak of a towering crag, he heaved it
so hard the boulder landed just in front of our dark prow
and a huge swell reared up as the rock went plunging
       under—
a tidal wave from the open sea. The sudden backwash   380
drove us landward again, forcing us close inshore
but grabbing a long pole, I thrust us off and away,
tossing my head for dear life, signaling crews
to put their backs in the oars, escape grim death.
They threw themselves in the labor, rowed on fast
but once we'd plowed the breakers twice as far,
again I began to taunt the Cyclops—men around me
trying to check me, calm me, left and right:
'So headstrong—why? Why rile the beast again?'

"'That rock he flung in the sea just now, hurling our   390
       ship
to shore once more—we thought we'd die on the spot!'

"If he'd caught a sound from one of us, just a moan,
he would have crushed our heads and ship timbers
with one heave of another flashing, jagged rock!'

"'Good god, the brute can throw!'
                                    "So they begged
but they could not bring my fighting spirit round.
I called back with another burst of anger, 'Cyclops—
if any man on the face of the earth should ask you
who blinded you, shamed you so—say Odysseus,   400
raider of cities, *he* gouged out your eye,
Laertes' son who makes his home in Ithaca!'

"So I vaunted and he groaned back in answer,
'Oh no, no—that prophecy years ago . . .
it all comes home to me with a vengeance now!
We once had a prophet here, a great tall man,
Telemus,[30] Eurymus'[31] son, a master at reading signs,
who grew old in his trade among his fellow-Cyclops.
All this, he warned me, would come to pass someday—
that I'd be blinded here at the hands of one Odysseus.   410
But I always looked for a handsome giant man to cross
       my path,
some fighter clad in power like armor-plate, but now,
look what a dwarf, a spineless good-for-nothing,
stuns me with wine, then gouges out my eye!
Come here, Odysseus, let me give you a guest-gift
and urge Poseidon the earthquake god to speed you
       home.
I am his son and he claims to be my father, true,
and he himself will heal me if he pleases—
no other blessed god, no man can do the work!'
                                    "'Heal you!'—   420

---

[30] **Telemus** One of the **Cyclops**, who was a prophet.
[31] **Eurymus** Father of **Telemus**, the **Cyclops** prophet.

here was my parting shot—'Would to god I could strip
    you
of life and breath and ship you down to the House of
    Death[32]
as surely as no one will ever heal your eye,
not even your earthquake god himself!'

    "But at that he bellowed out to lord Poseidon,
thrusting his arms to the starry skies, and prayed, 'Hear
    me—
Poseidon, god of the sea-blue mane who rocks the earth!
If I really am your son and you claim to be my father—
come, grant that Odysseus, raider of cities,
Laertes' son who makes his home in Ithaca,   430
never reaches home. Or if he's fated to see
his people once again and reach his well-built house
and his own native country, let him come home late
and come a broken man—all shipmates lost,
alone in a stranger's ship—
and let him find a world of pain at home!'
                              "So he prayed
and the god of the sea-blue mane Poseidon heard his
    prayer.
The monster suddenly hoisted a boulder—far larger—
wheeled and heaved it, putting his weight behind it,   440
massive strength, and the boulder crashed close,
landing just in the wake of our dark stern,
just failing to graze the rudder's bladed edge.
A huge swell reared up as the rock went plunging under,
yes, and the tidal breaker drove us out to our island's

far shore where all my well-decked ships lay moored,
clustered, waiting, and huddled round them, crewmen
sat in anguish, waiting, chafing for our return.
We beached our vessel hard ashore on the sand,
we swung out in the frothing surf ourselves,   450
and herding Cyclops' sheep from our deep holds
we shared them round so no one, not on my account,
would go deprived of his fair share of spoils.
But the splendid ram—as we meted out the flocks
my friends-in-arms made him my prize of honor,
mine alone, and I slaughtered him on the beach
and burnt his thighs to Cronus' mighty son,[33]
Zeus of the thundercloud who rules the world.

"But my sacrifices failed to move the god:
Zeus was still obsessed with plans to destroy   460
my entire oarswept fleet and loyal crew of comrades.
Now all day long till the sun went down we sat
and feasted on sides of meat and heady wine.
Then when the sun had set and night came on
we lay down and slept at the water's shelving edge.
When young Dawn with her rose-red fingers shone once
    more
I roused the men straightway, ordering all crews
to man the ships and cast off cables quickly.
They swung aboard at once, they sat to the oars in ranks
and in rhythm churned the water white with stroke on   470
    stroke.
And from there we sailed on, glad to escape our death
yet sick at heart for the comrades we had lost."

---

[32] **House of Death** The Underworld.

[33] **Cronus' mighty son** Zeus.

Book 23

[T]he great-hearted Odysseus was home again at last.   1
The maid Eurynome[34] bathed him, rubbed him down
    with oil
and drew around him a royal cape and choice tunic too.
And Athena crowned the man with beauty, head to foot,
made him taller to all eyes, his build more massive,
yes, and down from his brow the great goddess
ran his curls like thick hyacinth clusters
full of blooms. As a master craftsman washes
gold over beaten silver—a man the god of fire
and Queen Athena trained in every fine technique—   10
and finishes of his latest effort, handsome work . . .
so she lavished splendor over his head and shoulders
    now.

He stepped from his bath, glistening like a god,
and back he went to the seat that he had left
and facing his wife,[35] declared,
"Strange woman! So hard—the gods of Olympus[36]
made you harder than any other woman in the world!
What other wife could have a spirit so unbending?
Holding back from her husband, home at last for *her*
after bearing twenty years of brutal struggle.   20
Come, nurse,[37] make me a bed, I'll sleep alone.
She has a heart of iron in her breast."
                        "Strange *man*,"

---

[34] **Eurynome** Maid to **Penelope**, in **Ithaca**.

[35] **his wife** Penelope.
[36] **Olympus** The home of the Greek gods; an actual mountain in Thessaly.
[37] **nurse** Eurycleia, the old nurse who had tended **Odysseus** and **Telemachus**; servant to **Penelope**.

wary Penelope said. "I'm not so proud, so scornful,
nor am I overwhelmed by your quick change . . .
You look—how well I know—the way he looked,
setting sail from Ithaca years ago
aboard the long-oared ship.
                                        Come, Eurycleia,[38]
move the sturdy bedstead out of our bridal chamber—   30
that room the master built with his own hands.
Take it out now, sturdy bed that it is,
and spread it deep with fleece,
blankets and lustrous throws to keep him warm."

Putting her husband to the proof—but Odysseus
blazed up in fury, lashing out at his loyal wife:
"Woman—your words, they cut me to the core!
Who could move my bed? Impossible task,
even for some skilled craftsman—unless a god
came down in person, quick to lend a hand,   40
lifted it out with ease and moved it elsewhere.
Not a man on earth, not even at peak strength,
would find it easy to prise it up and shift it, no,
a great sign, a hallmark lies in its construction.
I know, I built it myself—no one else . . .
There was a branching olive-tree inside our court,
grown to its full prime, the bole like a column, thickset.
Around it I built my bedroom, finished off the walls
with good tight stonework, roofed it over soundly
and added doors, hung well and snugly wedged.   50
Then I lopped the leafy crown of the olive,
clean-cutting the stump bare from roots up,
planing it round with a bronze smoothing-adze—
I had the skill—I shaped it plumb to the line to make
my bedpost, bored the holes it needed with an auger.
Working from there I built my bed, start to finish,
I gave it ivory inlays, gold and silver fittings,
wove the straps across it, oxhide gleaming red.
There's our secret sign, I tell you, our life story!
Does the bed, my lady, still stand planted firm?—   60
I don't know—or has someone chopped away
that olive-trunk and hauled our bedstead off?"
                                        Living proof—
Penelope felt her knees go slack, her heart surrender,
recognizing the strong clear signs Odysseus offered.
She dissolved in tears, rushed to Odysseus, flung her
        arms
around his neck and kissed his head and cried out,
"*Odysseus*—don't flare up at me now, not you,
always the most understanding man alive!
The gods, it was the gods who sent us sorrow—   70
they grudged us both a life in each other's arms
from the heady zest of youth to the stoop of old age.
But don't fault me, angry with me now because I failed,
at the first glimpse, to greet you, hold you, so . . .
In my heart of hearts I always cringed with fear
some fraud might come, beguile me with his talk;
the world is full of the sort,
cunning ones who plot their own dark ends.

Remember Helen of Argos,[39] Zeus's daughter—
would *she* have sported so in a stranger's bed   80
if she had dreamed that Achaea's sons were doomed
to fight and die to bring her home again?
Some god spurred her to do her shameless work.
Not till then did her mind conceive that madness,
blinding madness that caused her anguish, ours as well.
But now, since you have revealed such overwhelming
        proof—
the secret sign of our bed, which no one's ever seen
but you and I and a single handmaid, Actoris,[40]
the servant my father gave me when I came,
who kept the doors of our room you built so well . . .   90
you've conquered my heart, my hard heart, at last!"

The more she spoke, the more a deep desire for tears
welled up inside his breast—he wept as he held the wife
he loved, the soul of loyalty, in his arms at last.
Joy, warm as the joy that shipwrecked sailors feel
when they catch sight of land—Poseidon has struck
their well-rigged ship on the open sea with gale winds
and crushing walls of waves, and only a few escape,
        swimming,
struggling out of the frothing surf to reach the shore,
their bodies crusted with salt but buoyed up with joy   100
as they plant their feet on solid ground again,
spared a deadly fate. So joyous now to her
the sight of her husband, vivid in her gaze,
that her white arms, embracing his neck
would never for a moment let him go . . .
Dawn with her rose-red fingers might have shone
upon their tears, if with her glinting eyes
Athena had not thought of one more thing.
She held back the night, and night lingered long
at the western edge of the earth, while in the east   110
she reined in Dawn of the golden throne at Ocean's[41]
        banks,
commanding her not to yoke the windswift team that
        brings men light,
Blaze[42] and Aurora,[43] the young colts that race the
        Morning on.
Yet now Odysseus, seasoned veteran, said to his wife,
"Dear woman . . . we have still not reached the end
of all our trials. One more labor lies in store—
boundless, laden with danger, great and long,
and I must brave it out from start to finish.
So the ghost of Tiresias[44] prophesied to me,
the day that I went down to the House of Death   120
to learn our best route home, my comrades' and my own.

---

[38] **Eurycleia** The old nurse.

[39] **Helen of Argos** Another name for **Helen** of **Troy.** She was daughter of **Zeus** and the mortal woman **Leda;** wife of **Menelaus,** and lover of **Paris.**
[40] **Actoris** The maid to **Penelope.**
[41] **Ocean** The great river that encircles the world and the god who controls its waters.
[42] **Blaze** A horse that pulls the chariot of the goddess **Dawn.**
[43] **Aurora** A horse that pulls the chariot of the goddess **Dawn.**
[44] **Tiresias** Blind prophet from **Thebes,** who remained a seer in the Underworld.

But come, let's go to bed, dear woman—at long last
delight in sleep, delight in each other, come!"

   "If it's bed you want," reserved Penelope replied,
"it's bed you'll have, whenever the spirit moves,
now that the gods have brought you home again
to native land, your grand and gracious house.
But since you've alluded to it,
since a god has put it in your mind,
please, tell me about this trial still to come.   130
I'm bound to learn of it later, I am sure—
what's the harm if I hear of it tonight?"
                                     "Still so strange,"
Odysseus, the old master of stories, answered.
"Why again, why force me to tell you all?
Well, tell I shall. I'll hide nothing now.
But little joy it will bring you, I'm afraid,
as little joy for me.
              The prophet said
that I must rove through towns on towns of men,   140
that I must carry a well-planed oar until
I come to a people who know nothing of the sea,
whose food is never seasoned with salt, strangers all
to ships with their crimson prows and long slim oars,
wings that make ships fly. And here is my sign,
he told me, clear, so clear I cannot miss it,
and I will share it with you now . . .
When another traveler falls in with me and calls

that weight across my shoulder a fan to winnow grain,
then, he told me, I must plant my oar in the earth   150
and sacrifice fine beasts to the lord god of the sea,
Poseidon—a ram, a bull and a ramping wild boar—
then journey home and render noble offerings up
to the deathless gods who rule the vaulting skies,
to all the gods in order.
And at last my own death will steal upon me . . .
a gentle, painless death, far from the sea it comes
to take me down, borne down with the years in ripe old
    age
with all my people here in blessed peace around me.
All this, the prophet said, will come to pass."   160

   "And so," Penelope said, in her great wisdom,
"if the gods will really grant a happier old age,
there's hope that we'll escape our trials at last."

   So husband and wife confided in each other,
while nurse and Eurynome, under the flaring brands,
were making up the bed with coverings deep and soft.
And working briskly, soon as they'd made it snug,
back to her room the old nurse went to sleep
as Eurynome, their attendant, torch in hand,
lighted the royal couple's way to bed and,   170
leading them to their chamber, slipped away.
Rejoicing in each other, they returned to their bed,
the old familiar place they loved so well.

SAPPHO

Poems

Sappho is unquestionably Greece's finest composer of lyric poetry, which originally meant
verses sung to the music of a lyre (a stringed instrument) but later was applied to poetry characterized by musical qualities, subjectivism, and sensual words. Ancient writers, including
Plato (see *The Republic* and *Phaedo*), hailed her as the master of lyric poetry; modern critics tend
to do the same. Unlike epic poetry, in which the author speaks for an entire community (see
Homer's *Iliad* and *Odyssey,* and Vergil's *Aeneid*), lyric poetry focuses on the speaker's personal,
private thoughts. Sappho's autobiographical works helped to make lyric verse popular in her
day, and this genre has dominated Western poetry ever since (see Theocritus's *Idylls,* Catullus's
poems, Horace's *Odes,* Ovid's *Metamorphoses,* and Petrarch's *Canzoniere*).
   Lyric poetry flowered during Greece's Archaic Age (800–480 B.C.), a tumultuous period of
change on many fronts. Coming after three centuries of cultural breakdown, the Archaic Age
was a time of rebirth; it was marked by the growth of trade and the spread of Greek peoples
around the shores of the Mediterranean and Black seas. The old hereditary kingships gave way
to independent city-states ruled by landed aristocrats. In the city-states, the invention of money
permitted the rise of a monied class, a group of savers and lenders who both challenged the
power of the aristocrats and enslaved poorer debtors. These events embittered social relations

and sparked class warfare, which led to new types of regimes, such as tyranny, and expansion of voting rights to ordinary male citizens. The shift from epic to lyric poetry in the sixth century B.C. coincided with these changes in the city-states, where the rising democratic spirit encouraged a variety of voices to be heard.

The meager facts of Sappho's life (ca. 600 B.C.) reflect this turbulent age. Her home was the island of Lesbos in the Aegean, an Archaic cultural center that produced two well-known lyric poets before her birth. An aristocrat, she experienced exile twice—the penalty for being related to the landed elite who were overthrown by a coalition of merchants and poor citizens. Eventually, she opened a school on Lesbos for aristocratic young women, to whom she taught poetry, music, and dancing.

Reading the Selections

These poems (actually sections taken from extant works, which are fragmented in the extreme and number only about 600 lines), show that love was never far from Sappho's thoughts. Addressed to her circle, this poetry is private, filled with intimate expression. The first two fragments offer burning descriptions of erotic feelings and thus give a glimpse into this world. In the first the speaker laments young Anactoria, "far away": "I would rather watch her moving in her lovely way [than any other beautiful thing on earth]." In the second, the speaker feels paralyzed by the actions of an unnamed woman friend who flirts with a youth: "For as I look at you, if only for an instant, my voice no longer comes to me . . . I lose my sense of sight, hear only drumming in my ears."

In "Let's Not Pretend," the third fragment, she speaks of love and old age. Gray and wrinkled, she likens herself to Tithonos, the mythic hero whom the gods gave eternal life but not eternal youth; just as Tithonos, ever older and feebler, makes love to the goddess Dawn each day, so does Sappho, grown old herself, continue to seek beauty and light.

Sappho's poetic legacy lives on in today's confessional verses and most especially in popular love songs.

∞

I

There are those who say
an array of horsemen,
and others of marching men,
and others of ships, is
the most beautiful thing on the dark earth.

But I say it is whatever one loves.

It is very easy
to show this to all:
for Helen,[1]
by far the most beautiful of mortals,
left her husband

and sailed to Troy
giving no thought at all
to her child nor dear parents,
but was led . . .
[by her love alone.]

Now, far away, Anactoria[2]
comes to my mind.
For I would rather watch her
moving in her lovely way,
and see her face, flashing radiant,
than all the force of Lydian[3] chariots,
and their infantry in full display of arms.

---

[1] **Helen** Daughter of **Zeus** and the mortal woman **Leda;** wife of **Menelaus,** and lover of **Paris.**

[2] **Anactoria** The name of Sappho's beloved.
[3] **Lydia** Ancient country in western part of Asia Minor (modern Turkey).

∞

II

An equal to the gods, he seems to me,   1
the man who, with his face toward yours,
sits close and listens to the whispers of
your sweet voice and enticing laugh.
To watch has made my heart a pounding hammer in my
    breast.
For as I look at you, if only for an instant,
my voice no longer comes to me.
My silent tongue is broken,

and a quick and subtle flame
runs up beneath my skin.   10
I lose my sense of sight, hear only drumming in my ears.
I drip cold sweat,
and a trembling chases all through me.
I am greener than the pale grass
and it seems to me that I am close to death.

Still, I must endure all this

∞

Let's Not Pretend

No, Children, do not delude me.   1
You mock the good gifts of the Muses[4]
When you say: "Dear Sappho we'll crown you,
    Resonant player,
First on the clear sweet lyre. . . ."
Do you not see how I alter:
My skin with its aging,
My black hair gone white,
My legs scarcely carrying
Me, who went dancing   10
More neatly than fawns once
(Neatest of creatures)?
No, no one can cure it; keep beauty from going,
And *I* cannot help it.
God himself cannot do what cannot be done.
So age follows after and catches

Everything living.
Even rosy-armed Eos,[5] the Dawn,
Who ushers in morning to the ends of the earth,
Could not save from the grasp of old age   20
Her lover immortal Tithonus.[6]
And I too, I know, must waste away.
Yet for me—listen well—
My delight is the exquisite.
Yes, for me,
Glitter and sunlight and love
Are one society.
So I shall not go creeping away
To die in the dark:
I shall go on living with you,   30
Loving and loved.

---

[4] **Muses** The nine goddesses who inspired creativity in the art and sciences.

[5] **Eos** The Greek goddess of **Dawn.**
[6] **Tithonos** Lover of the goddess **Dawn;** he was granted eternal life but not **eternal** youth.

3

CLASSICAL GREEK CIVILIZATION
The Hellenic Age

SOPHOCLES
Oedipus the King

Sophocles' *Oedipus the King* is the most famous tragedy of antiquity. When first staged (about 430 B.C.) in Athens, it was awarded first prize—the civic honor voted by judges for reasons as political and social as they were aesthetic. In the fourth century B.C. it was used by Aristotle as the ground for his analysis of tragedy in the *Poetics,* the West's earliest book of literary criticism. In modern times, it has come to mean the perfect tragedy.

Tragedy (Greek, "goat song") developed from the choral odes sung to the rural god Dionysus. In sixth-century B.C. Athens, a tyrant introduced this god's cult to the city and made the staging of tragedies part of the Great Dionysia. The coming of democracy to Athens (after 508 B.C.) made these plays even more popular, as people of all classes formed the audience (though it is uncertain if women were present). The Hellenic Age—with Persia in retreat and Athens as the center of Greece—saw the flowering of this genre in the works of three native Athenians: Aeschylus (ca. 525–456 B.C.), Sophocles (ca. 496–406 B.C.), and Euripides (ca. 480–406 B.C.).

Tragedy was basically political in that it addressed the city-state, or its metaphorical equivalent in the audience at the Great Dionysia. Tragedians wrote for this community, speaking as citizens to citizens. A city leader chose three dramatists to present four plays each, and other officials appointed wealthy citizens to pay production costs. The spectators were seated according to tribes, thus mapping the city's political structure. A panel of ten judges was chosen, one from each tribe. Before the plays, the city scored propaganda points by parading orphans of soldiers killed in service and welcoming foreign emissaries. In sum, the drama was the centerpiece of a rite devoted to reinforcing community cohesion.

At first, tragedy (like comedy) had two distinct elements, the actors and the chorus, symbolic of opposing forces in the city-state. In political terms, the actors symbolized individualism (a democratic idea), and the chorus stood for community values (an aristocratic idea). As tragedy evolved, the chorus waned in importance until it disappeared in the fourth century B.C., leaving the actors supreme. This event paralleled the decline of both the city-state and tragic drama.

Reading the Selection

Oedipus the King is typical of what became known as Sophoclean tragedy in that it has two themes: the relation between humans and gods and the hero's moral dilemmas. These themes converge in the character Oedipus, a king destroyed by the gods as he tries to act morally. Highly ironic, the plot shows Oedipus unleashing new catastrophes despite good intentions. Warned by an oracle that he will kill his father and marry his mother, the well-meaning Oedipus flees from Corinth to Thebes, only to learn that his efforts to escape his dread fate have been in vain. Oedipus's downfall is the result of good motives, for he discovers his true identity after ordering an investigation into the old king's murder, so that a plague may be driven from the city.

Above all else, this tragedy is about the unbridgeable gulf between gods and humans. Oedipus repeatedly shows arrogance in his desire to credit himself and deny the truth of oracles ("the world knows my fame"; "I count myself the son of Chance"). Struck down, he finally recognizes that humans, even kings, are fated to suffer. The chorus makes this harsh vision the moral of the tragedy: "[L]ook on Oedipus. . . . [C]ount no man happy till he dies, free of pain at last."

Characters

OEDIPUS *king of Thebes*
A PRIEST *of Zeus*
CREON *brother of Jocasta*
A CHORUS *of Theban citizens and their* LEADER
TIRESIAS *a blind prophet*
JOCASTA *the queen, wife of Oedipus*
A MESSENGER *from Corinth*
A SHEPHERD
A MESSENGER *from inside the palace*
ANTIGONE, ISMENE *daughters of Oedipus and Jocasta*
Guards and attendants
Priests of Thebes
TIME AND SCENE: *The royal house of Thebes. Double doors dominate the façade; a stone altar stands at the center of the stage.*

Many years have passed since OEDIPUS *solved the riddle of the Sphinx and ascended the throne of Thebes, and now a plague has struck the city. A procession of priests enters; suppliants, broken and despondent, they carry branches wound in wool and lay them on the altar.*

The doors open. Guards assemble. OEDIPUS *comes forward, majestic but for a telltale limp, and slowly views the condition of his people.*

OEDIPUS: Oh my children, the new blood of ancient 1
Thebes,
why are you here? Huddling at my altar,
praying before me, your branches wound in wool.
Our city reeks with the smoke of burning incense,
rings with cries for the Healer and wailing for the dead.
I thought it wrong, my children, to hear the truth
from others, messengers. Here I am myself—
you all know me, the world knows my fame:
I am Oedipus.

Helping a Priest to his feet.

Speak up, old man. Your years, 10
your dignity—you should speak for the others.
Why here and kneeling, what preys upon you so?
Some sudden fear? some strong desire?
You can trust me. I am ready to help,
I'll do anything. I would be blind to misery
not to pity my people kneeling at my feet.

PRIEST: Oh Oedipus, king of the land, our greatest
power!
You see us before you now, men of all ages
clinging to your altars. Here are boys,
still too weak to fly from the nest, 20
and here the old, bowed down with the years,
the holy ones—a priest of Zeus[1] myself—and here
the picked, unmarried men, the young hope of Thebes.
And all the rest, your great family gathers now,
branches wreathed, massing in the squares,
kneeling before the two temples of queen Athena[2]
or the river-shrine where the embers glow and die
and Apollo[3] sees the future in the ashes.

Our city—
look around you, see with your own eyes— 30
our ship pitches wildly, cannot lift her head
from the depths, the red waves of death . . .
Thebes is dying. A blight on the fresh crops
and the rich pastures, cattle sicken and die,
and the women die in labor, children stillborn,
and the plague, the fiery god of fever hurls down
on the city, his lightning slashing through us—
raging plague in all its vengeance, devastating
the house of Cadmus[4]! And black Death luxuriates
in the raw, wailing miseries of Thebes. 40

Now we pray to you. You cannot equal the gods,
your children know that, bending at your altar.
But we do rate you first of men,
both in the common crises of our lives
and face-to-face encounters with the gods.

---

[1] **Zeus** Chief deity and keeper of order on Mt. Olympus, where the gods and goddesses live.
[2] **Athena** Goddess of wisdom and warfare.
[3] **Apollo** God of wisdom and moderation. Also god of prophecy with a shrine at Delphi.
[4] **house of Cadmus** Cadmus was the founder of Thebes and its first king.

You freed us from the Sphinx,[5] you came to Thebes
and cut us loose from the bloody tribute we had paid
that harsh, brutal singer. We taught you nothing,
no skill, no extra knowledge, still you triumphed.

A god was with you, so they say, and we believe it—   50
you lifted up our lives.
                              So now again,
Oedipus, king, we bend to you, your power—
we implore you, all of us on our knees:
find us strength, rescue! Perhaps you've heard
the voice of a god or something from other men,
Oedipus . . . what do you know?
The man of experience—you see it every day—
his plans will work in a crisis, his first of all.
Act now—we beg you, best of men, raise up our city!   60
Act, defend yourself, your former glory!
Your country calls you savior now
for your zeal, your action years ago.
Never let us remember of your reign:
you helped us stand, only to fall once more.
Oh raise up our city, set us on our feet.
The omens were good that day you brought us joy—
be the same man today!
Rule our land, you know you have the power,
but rule a land of the living, not a wasteland.   70
Ship and towered city are nothing, stripped of men
alive within it, living all as one.
OED.:   My children,
I pity you. I see—how could I fail to see
what longings bring you here? Well I know
you are sick to death, all of you,
but sick as you are, not one is sick as I.
Your pain strikes each of you alone, each
in the confines of himself, no other. But my spirit
grieves for the city, for myself and all of you.   80
I wasn't asleep, dreaming. You haven't wakened me—
I have wept through the nights, you must know that,
groping, laboring over many paths of thought.
After a painful search I found one cure:
I acted at once. I sent Creon,
my wife's own brother, to Delphi—
Apollo the Prophet's oracle—to learn
what I might do or say to save our city.

Today's the day. When I count the days gone by
it torments me . . . what is he doing?   90
Strange, he's late, he's gone too long.
But once he returns, then, then I'll be a traitor
if I do not do all the god makes clear.
PRIEST: Timely words. The men over there
are signaling—Creon's just arriving.

OED.:   *(Sighting* CREON, *then turning to the altar.)*

---

[5] **Sphinx** The winged monster, with the body of a lion and the head
and breasts of a woman, who, from her lair outside Thebes, asked
each traveler a riddle. She killed everyone who could not answer the
riddle: "What is that walks on four legs in the morning, on two at
noon, and on three in the evening?" Oedipus answered correctly that
it was man. The Sphinx then leapt from a rock and destroyed herself.

                              Lord Apollo,
let him come with a lucky word of rescue,
shining like his eyes!
PRIEST: Welcome news, I think—he's crowned, look,
and the laurel wreath is bright with berries.   100
OED.:   We'll soon see. He's close enough to hear—

Enter CREON *from the side; his face is shaded with a wreath.*

Creon, prince, my kinsman, what do you bring us?
What message from the god?
CREON: Good news.
I tell you even the hardest things to bear,
if they should turn out well, all would be well.
OED.:   Of course, but what were the god's *words?* There's
   no hope
and nothing to fear in what you've said so far.
CREON: If you want my report in the presence of these
   people . . .

Pointing to the priests while drawing OEDIPUS *toward the
palace.*   110

I'm ready now, or we might go inside.
OED: Speak out,
speak to us all. I grieve for these, my people,
far more than I fear for my own life.
CREON: Very well,
I will tell you what I heard from the god.
Apollo commands us—he was quite clear—
"Drive the corruption from the land,
don't harbor it any longer, past all cure,
don't nurse it in your soil—root it out!"   120
OED.:   How can we cleanse ourselves—what rites?
What's the source of the trouble?
CREON: Banish the man, or pay back blood with blood.
Murder sets the plague-storm on the city.
OED.:   Whose
   murder?
Whose fate does Apollo bring to light?
CREON: Our leader,
my lord, was once a man named Laius,
before you came and put us straight on course.
OED.:   I know—
or so I've heard. I never saw the man myself.   130
CREON: Well, he was killed, and Apollo commands us
   now—
he could not be more clear,
"Pay the killers back—whoever is responsible."
OED.:   Where on earth are they? Where to find it now,
the trail of the ancient guilt so hard to trace?
CREON: "Here in Thebes," he said.
Whatever is sought for can be caught, you know,
whatever is neglected slips away.
OED.:   But where,
in the palace, the fields or foreign soil,   140
where did Laius meet his bloody death?
CREON: He went to consult an oracle, Apollo said,
and he set out and never came home again.
OED.:   No messenger, no fellow-traveler saw what
   happened?
Someone to cross-examine?

CREON: No,
    they were all killed but one. He escaped,
    terrified, he could tell us nothing clearly,
    nothing of what he saw—just one thing.
OED.:   What's that?   150
    One thing could hold the key to it all,
    a small beginning give us grounds for hope.
CREON: He said thieves attacked them—a whole band,
    not single-handed, cut King Laius down.
OED.:   A thief,
    so daring, so wild, he'd kill a king? Impossible,
    unless conspirators paid him off in Thebes.
CREON: We suspected as much. But with Laius dead
    no leader appeared to help us in our troubles.
OED.:   Trouble? Your *king* was murdered—royal blood!   160
    What stopped you from tracking down the killer
    then and there?
CREON: The singing, riddling Sphinx.
    She . . . persuaded us to let the mystery go
    and concentrate on what lay at our feet.
OED.:   No,
    I'll start again—I'll bring it all to light myself!
    Apollo is right, and so are you, Creon,
    to turn our attention back to the murdered man.
    Now you have *me* to fight for you, you'll see: 170
    I am the land's avenger by all rights,
    and Apollo's champion too.
    But not to assist some distant kinsman, no,
    for my own sake I'll rid us of this corruption.
    Whoever killed the king may decide to kill me too,
    with the same violent hand—by avenging Laius
    I defend myself.

To the priests.

                Quickly, my children.
    Up from the steps, take up your branches now.

To the guards.

    One of you summon the city here before us,   180
    tell them I'll do everything. God help us,
    we will see our triumph—or our fall.

OEDIPUS *and* CREON *enter the palace, followed by the guards.*

PRIEST: Rise, my sons. The kindness we came for
    Oedipus volunteers himself.
    Apollo has sent his word, his oracle—
    Come down, Apollo, save us, stop the plague.

The priests rise, remove their branches and exit to the side.

Enter a CHORUS, *the citizens of Thebes, who have not heard the news that* CREON *brings. They march around the altar, chanting.*

CHORUS: Zeus!
    Great welcome voice of Zeus, what do you bring?
    What word from the gold vaults of Delphi
    comes to brilliant Thebes? Racked with terror—   190
                terror shakes my heart
    and I cry your wild cries, Apollo, Healer of Delos
    I worship you in dread . . . what now, what is your
        price?

some new sacrifice? some ancient rite from the past
come round again each spring?—
              what will you bring to birth?
Tell me, child of golden Hope
    warm voice that never dies!

You are the first I call, daughter of Zeus
deathless Athena—I call your sister Artemis,[6]   200
heart of the market place enthroned in glory,
              guardian of our earth—
I call Apollo, Archer astride the thunderheads of
    heaven—
O triple shield against death, shine before me now!
If ever, once in the past, you stopped some ruin
launched against our walls
        you hurled the flame of pain
far, far from Thebes—you gods
        come now, come down once more!
No, no   210
the miseries numberless, grief on grief, no end—
too much to bear, we are all dying
O my people . . .
    Thebes like a great army dying
and there is no sword of thought to save us, no
and the fruits of our famous earth, they will not ripen
no and the women cannot scream their pangs to birth—
screams for the Healer, children dead in the womb
        and life on life goes down
             you can watch them go   220
    like seabirds winging west, outracing the day's fire
down the horizon, irresistibly
        streaking on to the shores of Evening
                    Death
so many deaths, numberless deaths on deaths, no end—
Thebes is dying, look, her children
stripped of pity . . .
    generations strewn on the ground
unburied, unwept, the dead spreading death
and the young wives and gray-haired mothers with   230
    them
cling to the altars, trailing in from all over the city—
Thebes, city of death, one long cortege
    and the suffering rises
            wails for mercy rise
    and the wild hymn for the Healer blazes out
clashing with our sobs our cries of mourning—
    O golden daughter of god, send rescue
    radiant as the kindness in your eyes!

Drive him back!—the fever, the god of death
           that raging god of war   240
not armored in bronze, not shielded now, he burns me,
battle cries in the onslaught burning on—
O rout him from our borders!
Sail him, blast him out to the Sea-queen's chamber
        the black Atlantic gulfs

---

[6] **Artemis** Virgin goddess who aided women. Huntress of wild creatures and patroness of chastity. Sister of Athena and twin sister of Apollo.

or the northern harbor, death to all
where the Thracian[7] surf comes crashing.
Now what the night spares he comes by day and kills—
the god of death.

O lord of the stormcloud,   250
you who twirl the lightning, Zeus, Father,
thunder Death to nothing!

Apollo, lord of the light, I beg you—
whip your longbow's golden cord
showering arrows on our enemies—shafts of power
champions strong before us rushing on!

Artemis, Huntress,
torches flaring over the eastern ridges—
ride Death down in pain!

God of the headdress gleaming gold, I cry to you—   260
your name and ours are one, Dionysus[8]—
come with your face aflame with wine
your raving women's cries
your army on the march! Come with the lightning
come with torches blazing, eyes ablaze with glory!
Burn that god of death that all gods hate!

OEDIPUS *enters from the palace to address the* CHORUS, *as if
addressing the entire city of Thebes.*

OED.: You pray to the gods? Let me grant your prayers.
Come, listen to me—do what the plague demands:
you'll find relief and lift your head from the depths.

I will speak out now as a stranger to the story,   270
a stranger to the crime If I'd been present then,
there would have been no mystery, no long hunt
without a clue in hand. So now, counted
a native Theban years after the murder,
to all of Thebes I make this proclamation:
if any one of you knows who murdered Laius,
the son of Labdacus, I order him to reveal
the whole truth to me. Nothing to fear,
even if he must denounce himself,
let him speak up   280
and so escape the brunt of the charge—
he will suffer no unbearable punishment,
nothing worse than exile, totally unharmed.

OEDIPUS *pauses, waiting for a reply.*

Next,
if anyone knows the murderer is a stranger,
a man from alien soil, come, speak up.
I will give him a handsome reward, and lay up
gratitude in my heart for him besides.

Silence again, no reply.

But if you keep silent, if anyone panicking,

trying to shield himself or friend or kin,   290
rejects my offer, then hear what I will do.
I order you, every citizen of the state
where I hold throne and power: banish this man—
whoever he may be—never shelter him, never
speak a word to him, never make him partner
to your prayers, your victims burned to the gods.
Never let the holy water touch his hands.
Drive him out, each of you, from every home.
He is the plague, the heart of our corruption,
as Apollo's oracle has just revealed to me.   300
So I honor my obligations:
I fight for the god and for the murdered man.

Now my curse on the murderer. Whoever he is,
a lone man unknown in his crime
or one among many, let that man drag out
his life in agony, step by painful step—
I curse myself as well . . . if by any chance
he proves to be an intimate of our house,
here at my hearth, with my full knowledge,
may the curse I just called down on him strike me!   310

These are your orders: perform them to the last.
I command you, for my sake, for Apollo's, for this
country
blasted root and branch by the angry heavens.
Even if god had never urged you on to act,
how could you leave the crime uncleansed so long?
A man so noble—your king, brought down in blood—
you should have searched. But I am the king now,
I hold the throne that he held then, possess his bed
and a wife who shares our seed . . . why, our seed
might be the same, children born of the same mother   320
might have created blood-bonds between us
if his hope of offspring had not met disaster—
but fate swooped at his head and cut him short.
So I will fight for him as if he were my father,
stop at nothing, search the world
to lay my hands on the man who shed his blood,
the son of Labdacus descended of Polydorus,
Cadmus of old and Agenor, founder of the line:[9]
their power and mine are one.

Oh dear gods,   330
my curse on those who disobey these orders!
Let no crops grow out of the earth for them—
shrivel their women, kill their sons,
burn them to nothing in this plague
that hits us now, or something even worse.
But you, loyal men of Thebes who approve my actions,
may our champion, Justice, may all the gods
be with us, fight beside us to the end!

LEADER: In the grip of your curse, my king, I swear
I'm not the murderer, I cannot point him out.   340
As for the search, Apollo pressed it on us—
he should name the killer.

OED.:   Quite right,

---

[7] **Thracian** Thrace was an area east of Macedonia and north of the
Aegean Sea on the coast. Greeks traded with the inhabitants and
founded a colony there after 700 B.C.
[8] **Dionysus** God of the vine, who often represented the irrational
side of the Greek character.

---

[9] **Labdacus, Polydorus, Cadmus of old, Agenor** Ancestors of King
Laius and former rulers of Thebes; Agenor was the king of Phoenicia
and father of Cadmus.

but to force the gods to act against their will—
no man has the power.
LEADER: Then if I might mention
the next best thing . . .
OED.:   The third best too—
don't hold back, say it.
LEADER: I still believe . . .   350
Lord Tiresias sees with the eyes of Lord Apollo.
Anyone searching for the truth, my king,
might learn it from the prophet, clear as day.
OED.: I've not been slow with that. On Creon's cue
I sent the escorts, twice, within the hour.
I'm surprised he isn't here.
LEADER: We need him—
without him we have nothing but old, useless rumors.
OED.: Which rumors? I'll search out every word.
LEADER: Laius was killed, they say, by certain travelers.   360
OED.: I know—but no one can find the murderer.
LEADER: If the man has a trace of fear in him
he won't stay silent long,
not with your curses ringing in his ears.
OED.: He didn't flinch at murder,
he'll never flinch at words.

Enter TIRESIAS, *the blind prophet, led by a boy with escorts in
attendance. He remains at a distance.*

LEADER: Here is the one who will convict him, look,
they bring him on at last, the seer, the man of god.
The truth lives inside him, him alone.
OED.:   O Tiresias,   370
master of all the mysteries of our life,
all you teach and all you dare not tell,
signs in the heavens, signs that walk the earth!
Blind as you are, you can feel all the more
what sickness haunts our city. You, my lord,
are the one shield, the one savior we can find.
We asked Apollo—perhaps the messengers
haven't told you—he sent his answer back:
"Relief from the plague can only come one way.
Uncover the murderers of Laius,   380
put them to death or drive them into exile."
So I beg you, grudge us nothing now, no voice,
no message plucked from the birds, the embers
or the other mantic ways within your grasp.
Rescue yourself, your city, rescue me—
rescue everything infected by the dead.
We are in your hands. For a man to help others
with all his gifts and native strength:
that is the noblest work.
TIRESIAS: How terrible—to see the truth   390
when the truth is only pain to him who sees!
I knew it well, but I put it from my mind,
else I never would have come.
OED.: What's this? Why so grim, so dire?
TIR.: Just send me home. You bear your burdens,
I'll bear mine. It's better that way,
please believe me.
OED.:   Strange response . . . unlawful,
unfriendly too to the state that bred and reared you—
you withhold the word of god.   400
TIR.:   I fail to see

that your own words are so well-timed.
I'd rather not have the same thing said of me . . .
OED.: For the love of god, don't turn away,
not if you know something. We beg you,
all of us on our knees.
TIR.:   None of you knows—
and I will never reveal my dreadful secrets,
not to say your own.
OED.: What? You know and you won't tell?   410
You're bent on betraying us, destroying Thebes?
TIR.: I'd rather not cause pain for you or me.
So why this . . . useless interrogation?
You'll get nothing from me.
OED.:   Nothing! You,
you scum of the earth, you'd enrage a heart of stone!
You won't talk? Nothing moves you?
Out with it, once and for all!
TIR.: You criticize my temper . . . unaware
of the one *you* live with, you revile me.   420
OED.: Who could restrain his anger hearing you?
What outrage—you spurn the city!
TIR.: What will come will come.
Even if I shroud it all in silence.
OED.: What will come? You're bound to *tell* me that.
TIR.: I will say no more. Do as you like, build your anger
to whatever pitch you please, rage your worst—
OED.: Oh I'll let loose, I have such fury in me—
now I see it all. You helped hatch the plot,
you did the work, yes, short of killing him   430
with your own hands—and given eyes I'd say
you did the killing single-handed!
TIR.:   Is that so!
I charge you, then, submit to that decree
you just laid down: from this day onward
speak to no one, not these citizens, not myself.
You are the curse, the corruption of the land!
OED.: You, shameless—
aren't you appalled to start up such a story?
You think you can get away with this?   440
TIR.:   I have already.
The truth with all its power lives inside me.
OED.: Who primed you for this? Not your prophet's
trade.
TIR.: You did, you forced me, twisted it out of me.
OED.: What? Say it again—I'll understand it better.
TIR.: Didn't you understand, just now?
Or are you tempting me to talk?
OED.: No, I can't say I grasped your meaning.
Out with it, again!
TIR.: I say you are the murderer you hunt.   450
OED.: That obscenity, twice—by god, you'll pay.
TIR.: Shall I say more, so you can really rage?
OED.: Much as you want. Your words are nothing—
futile.
TIR.:   You cannot imagine . . . I tell you,
you and your loved ones live together in infamy,
you cannot see how far you've gone in guilt.
OED.: You think you can keep this up and never suffer?
TIR.: Indeed, if the truth has any power.
OED.:   It does   460
but not for you, old man. You've lost your power,

stone-blind, stone-deaf—senses, eyes blind as stone!
TIR.: I pity you, flinging at me the very insults
    each man here will fling at you so soon.
OED.:   Blind,
    lost in the night, endless night that nursed you!
    You can't hurt me or anyone else who sees the light—
    you can never touch me.
TIR.:   True, it is not your fate
    to fall at my hands. Apollo is quite enough,   470
    and he will take some pains to work this out.
OED.: Creon! Is this conspiracy his or yours?
TIR.: Creon is not your downfall, no, you are your own.
OED.:   O power—
    wealth and empire, skill outstripping skill
    in the heady rivalries of life,
    what envy lurks inside you! Just for this,
    the crown the city gave me—I never sought it,
    they laid it in my hands—for this alone, Creon,
    the soul of trust, my loyal friend from the start   480
    steals against me . . . so hungry to overthrow me
    he sets this wizard on me, this scheming quack,
    this fortune-teller peddling lies, eyes peeled
    for his own profit—seer blind in his craft!

    Come here, you pious fraud. Tell me,
    when did you ever prove yourself a prophet?
    When the Sphinx, that chanting Fury kept her
    deathwatch here,
    why silent then, not a word to set our people free?
    There was a riddle, not for some passer-by to solve—   490
    it cried out for a prophet. Where were you?
    Did you rise to the crisis? Not a word,
    you and your birds, your gods—nothing.
    No, but I came by, Oedipus the ignorant,
    I stopped the Sphinx! With no help from the birds,
    the flight of my own intelligence hit the mark.
    And this is the man you'd try to overthrow?
    You think you'll stand by Creon when he's king?
    You and the great mastermind—
    you'll pay in tears, I promise you, for this,   500
    this witch-hunt. If you didn't look so senile
    the lash would teach you what your scheming means!
LEADER: I would suggest his words were spoken in
        anger,
    Oedipus . . . yours too, and it isn't what we need.
    The best solution to the oracle, the riddle
    posed by god—we should look for that.
TIR.: You are the king no doubt, but in one respect,
    at least, I am your equal: the right to reply.
    I claim that privilege too.
    I am not your slave. I serve Apollo.   510
    I don't need Creon to speak for me in public.
                        So,
    you mock my blindness? Let me tell you this.
    You with your precious eyes,
    you're blind to the corruption of your life,
    to the house you live in, those you live with—
    who *are* your parents? Do you know? All unknowing
    you are the scourge of your own flesh and blood,
    the dead below the earth and the living here above,
    and the double lash of your mother and your father's   520
        curse

will whip you from this land one day, their footfall
treading you down in terror, darkness shrouding
your eyes that now can see the light!
                  Soon, soon
you'll scream aloud—what haven won't reverberate?
What rock of Cithaeron[10] won't scream back in echo?
That day you learn the truth about your marriage,
the wedding-march that sang you into your halls,
the lusty voyage home to the fatal harbor!
And a crowd of other horrors you'd never dream   530
will level you with yourself and all your children.
There. Now smear us with insults—Creon, myself
and every word I've said. No man will ever
be rooted from the earth as brutally as you.
OED.: Enough! Such filth from him? Insufferable—
    what, still alive? Get out—
    faster, back where you came from—vanish!
TIR.: I would never have come if you hadn't called me
        here.
OED.: If I thought you would blurt out such absurdities,
    you'd have died waiting before I'd had you   540
        summoned.
TIR.: Absurd, am I! To you, not to your parents:
    the ones who bore you found me sane enough.
OED.: Parents—who? Wait . . . who is my father?
TIR.: This day will bring your birth and your destruction.
OED.: Riddles—all you can say are riddles, murk and
        darkness.
TIR.: Ah, but aren't you the best man alive at solving
        riddles?
OED.: Mock me for that, go on, and you'll reveal my
        greatness.
TIR.: Your great fortune, true, it was your ruin.
OED.: Not if I saved the city—what do I care?
TIR.: Well then, I'll be going.   550

To his attendant.

                  Take me home, boy.
OED.: Yes, take him away. You're a nuisance here.
    —Out of the way, the irritation's gone.

Turning his back on TIRESIAS, *moving toward the palace.*

TIR.:   I will go,
    once I have said what I came here to say.
    I will never shrink from the anger in your eyes—
    you can't destroy me. Listen to me closely:
    the man you've sought so long, proclaiming,
    cursing up and down, the murderer of Laius—
    he is here. A stranger,   560
    you may think, who lives among you,
    he soon will be revealed a native Theban
    but he will take no joy in the revelation.
    Blind who now has eyes, beggar who now is rich,
    he will grope his way toward a foreign soil,
    a stick tapping before him step by step.

OEDIPUS *enters the palace.*

---

[10] **Cithaeron** A mountain on the frontier of Boeotia, the isthmus of Corinth and Attica. Oedipus was abandoned here when a baby, according to legend. Sophocles' use of this particular mountain is an example of his irony, and the audience most likely knew the legend and could appreciate the playwright's ironical reference.

Revealed at last, brother and father both
to the children he embraces, to his mother
son and husband both—he sowed the loins
his father sowed, he spilled his father's blood!   570

Go in and reflect on that, solve that.
And if you find I've lied
from this day onward call the prophet blind.

TIRESIAS *and the boy exit to the side.*

CHORUS: Who—
who is the man the voice of god denounces
resounding out of the rocky gorge of Delphi?
The horror too dark to tell,
whose ruthless bloody hands have done the work?
His time has come to fly
to outrace the stallions of the storm   580
                    his feet a streak of speed—
Cased in armor, Apollo son of the Father
lunges on him, lightning-bolts afire!
And the grim unerring Furies[11]
                    closing for the kill.
                                        Look,
the word of god has just come blazing
flashing off Parnassus'[12] snowy heights!
    That man who left no trace—
after him, hunt him down with all our strength!   590
Now under bristling timber
    up through rocks and caves he stalks
                    like the wild mountain bull—
cut off from men, each step an agony, frenzied, racing
    blind
but he cannot outrace the dread voices of Delphi
ringing out of the heart of Earth,
    the dark wings beating around him shrieking doom
                    the doom that never dies, the terror—
The skilled prophet scans the birds and shatters me
    with terror!
I can't accept him, can't deny him, don't know what   600
    to say,
I'm lost, and the wings of dark foreboding beating—
I cannot see what's come, what's still to come . . .
and what could breed a blood feud between
    Laius' house and the son of Polybus?
I know of nothing, not in the past and not now,
no charge to bring against our king, no cause
to attack his fame that rings throughout Thebes—
    not without proof—not for the ghost of Laius,
    not to avenge a murder gone without a trace.
Zeus and Apollo know, they know, the great masters   610
                    of all the dark and depth of human life.
But whether a mere man can know the truth,
whether a seer can fathom more than I—
there is no test, no certain proof

though matching skill for skill
    a man can outstrip a rival. No, not till I see
    these charges proved will I side with his accusers.
    We saw him then, when the she-hawk swept against
        him,
    saw with our own eyes his skill, his brilliant triumph—
    there was the test—he was the joy of Thebes!   620
    Never will I convict my king, never in my heart.

Enter CREON *from the side.*

CREON: My fellow-citizens, I hear King Oedipus
    levels terrible charges at me. I had to come.
    I resent it deeply. If, in the present crisis,
    he thinks he suffers any abuse from me,
    anything I've done or said that offers him
    the slightest injury, why, I've no desire
    to linger out this life, my reputation in ruins.
    The damage I'd face from such an accusation
    is nothing simple. No, there's nothing worse: 630
    branded a traitor in the city, a traitor
    to all of you and my good friends.
LEADER: True,
    but a slur might have been forced out of him,
    by anger perhaps, not any firm conviction.
CREON: The charge was made in public, wasn't it?
    I put the prophet up to spreading lies?
LEADER: Such things were said . . .
    I don't know with what intent, if any.
CREON: Was his glance steady, his mind right   640
    when the charge was brought against me?
LEADER: I really couldn't say. I never look
    to judge the ones in power.

The doors open. OEDIPUS *enters.*

                                        Wait,
    here's Oedipus now.
OED.:   You—here? You have the gall
    to show your face before the palace gates?
    You, plotting to kill me, kill the king—
    I see it all, the marauding thief himself
    scheming to steal my crown and power!   650
                                        Tell me,
    in god's name, what did you take me for,
    coward or fool, when you spun out your plot?
    Your treachery—you think I'd never detect it
    creeping against me in the dark? Or sensing it,
    not defend myself? Aren't you the fool,
    you and your high adventure. Lacking numbers,
    powerful friends, out for the big game of empire—
    you need riches, armies to bring that quarry down!
CREON: Are you quite finished? It's your turn to listen   660
    for just as long as you've . . . instructed me.
    Hear me out, then judge me on the facts.
OED.: You've a wicked way with words, Creon,
    but I'll be slow to learn—from you.
    I find you a menace, a great burden to me.
CREON: Just one thing, hear me out in this.
OED.:   Just one thing,
    don't tell *me* you're not the enemy, the traitor.
CREON: Look, if you think crude, mindless stubbornness
    such a gift, you've lost your sense of balance.   670
OED.: If you think you can abuse a kinsman,

---

[11] **Furies** The goddesses who avenge murder, perjury, and other
crimes, who chase and madden those who have committed such
crimes. They are winged maidens with snakes in their hair and blood
dripping from their eyes. Sometimes called the Erinyes or the
Eumenidies.
[12] **Parnassus** A Greek mountain sacred to Apollo and the nine muses
who are the goddesses of literature, music, dance, and other artistic
and creative pursuits.

then escape the penalty, you're insane.
CREON: Fair enough, I grant you. But this injury
　　you say I've done you, what is it?
OED.: Did you induce me, yes or no,
　　to send for that sanctimonious prophet?
CREON: I did. And I'd do the same again.
OED.: All right then, tell me, how long is it now
　　　　since Laius . . .
CREON:　　　　　　Laius—what did *he* do?
OED.:　　　　　　　　　　　　Vanished, 680
　　swept from sight, murdered in his tracks.
CREON: The count of the years would run you far
　　　　back . . .
OED.: And that far back, was the prophet at his trade?
CREON: Skilled as he is today, and just as honored.
OED.: Did he ever refer to me then, at that time?
CREON:　　　　　　　　　　No,
　　never, at least, when I was in his presence.
OED.: But you did investigate the murder, didn't you?
CREON: We did our best, of course, discovered nothing.
OED.: But the great seer never accused me then—why 690
　　　　not?
CREON: I don't know. And when I don't, *I* keep quiet.
OED.: You do know this, you'd tell it too—
　　if you had a shred of decency.
CREON:　　　　　　What?
　　If I know, I won't hold back.
OED.:　　　　　　Simply this:
　　if the two of you had never put heads together,
　　we would never have heard about *my* killing Laius.
CREON: If that's what he says . . . well, you know best.
　　But now I have a right to learn from you 700
　　as you just learned from me.
OED.:　　　　　　Learn your fill,
　　you never will convict me of the murder.
CREON: Tell me, you're married to my sister, aren't you?
OED.: A genuine discovery—there's no denying that.
CREON: And you rule the land with her, with equal
　　　　power?
OED.: She receives from me whatever she desires.
CREON: And I am the third, all of us are equals?
OED.: Yes, and it's there you show your stripes—
　　you betray a kinsman. 710
CREON:　　　　　Not at all.
　　Not if you see things calmly, rationally,
　　as I do. Look at it this way first:
　　who in his right mind would rather rule
　　and live in anxiety than sleep in peace?
　　Particularly if he enjoys the same authority.
　　Not I, I'm not the man to yearn for kingship,
　　not with a king's power in my hands. Who would?
　　No one with any sense of self-control.
　　Now, as it is, you offer me all I need, 720
　　not a fear in the world. But if I wore the crown . . .
　　there'd be many painful duties to perform,
　　hardly to my taste.
　　　　　　How could kingship
　　please me more than influence, power
　　without a qualm? I'm not that deluded yet,
　　to reach for anything but privilege outright,
　　profit free and clear.

Now all men sing my praises, all salute me,
now all who request your favors curry mine. 730
I am their best hope: success rests in me.
Why give up that, I ask you, and borrow trouble?
A man of sense, someone who sees things clearly
would never resort to treason.
No, I have no lust for conspiracy in me,
nor could I ever suffer one who does.

Do you want proof? Go to Delphi yourself,
examine the oracle and see if I've reported
the message word-for-word. This too:
if you detect that I and the clairvoyant 740
have plotted anything in common, arrest me,
execute me. Not on the strength of one vote,
two in this case, mine as well as yours.
But don't convict me on sheer unverified surmise.
How wrong it is to take the good for bad,
purely at random, or take the bad for good.
But reject a friend, a kinsman? I would as soon
tear out the life within us, priceless life itself.
You'll learn this well, without fail, in time.
Time alone can bring the just man to light— 750
the criminal you can spot in one short day.
LEADER:　　　　　　　Good advice,
　　my lord, for anyone who wants to avoid disaster.
　　Those who jump to conclusions may go wrong.
OED.: When my enemy moves against me quickly,
　　plots in secret, I move quickly too, I must,
　　I plot and pay him back. Relax my guard a moment,
　　waiting his next move—he wins his objective,
　　I lose mine.
CREON:　　　　What do you want? 760
　　You want me banished?
OED.:　　　　　　No, I want you dead.
CREON: Just to show how ugly a grudge can . . .
OED.:　　　　　　　　　　　So,
　　still stubborn? You don't think I'm serious?
CREON: I think you're insane.
OED.:　　　　　　Quite sane—in my behalf.
CREON: Not just as much in mine?
OED.:　　　　　　You—my mortal enemy?
CREON: What if you're wholly wrong? 770
OED.:　　　　　　No matter—I must rule.
CREON: Not if you rule unjustly.
OED.:　　　　　　Hear him, Thebes, my city!
CREON: My city too, not yours alone!
LEADER: Please, my lords.

Enter JOCASTA *from the palace.*

　　　　　　　Look, Jocasta's coming,
　　and just in time too. With her help
　　you must put this fighting of yours to rest.
JOCASTA: Have you no sense? Poor misguided men,
　　such shouting—why this public outburst? 780
　　Aren't you ashamed, with the land so sick,
　　to stir up private quarrels?

To OEDIPUS.

Into the palace now. And Creon, you go home.
Why make such a furor over nothing?

CREON: My sister, it's dreadful . . . Oedipus, your
  husband,
  he's bent on a choice of punishments for me,
  banishment from the fatherland or death.
OED.: Precisely. I caught him in the act, Jocasta,
  plotting, about to stab me in the back.
CREON: Never—curse me, let me die and be damned   790
  if I've done you any wrong you charge me with.
JOC: Oh god, believe it, Oedipus,
  honor the solemn oath he swears to heaven.
  Do it for me, for the sake of all your people.

The CHORUS *begins to chant.*

CHORUS: Believe it, be sensible
  give way, my king, I beg you!
OED.: What do you want from me, concessions?
CHORUS: Respect him—he's been no fool in the past
  and now he's strong with the oath he swears to god.
OED.: You know what you're asking?   800
CHORUS: I do.
OED.:   Then out with it!
CHORUS: The man's your friend, your kin, he's under
    oath—
  don't cast him out, disgraced
  branded with guilt on the strength of hearsay only.
OED.: Know full well, if that is what you want
  you want me dead or banished from the land.
CHORUS: Never—
  no, by the blazing Sun, first god of the heavens!
    Stripped of the gods, stripped of loved ones,   810
  let me die by inches if that ever crossed my mind.
  But the heart inside me sickens, dies as the land dies
  and now on top of the old griefs you pile this,
  your fury—both of you!
OED.:   Then let him go,
  even if it does lead to my ruin, my death
  or my disgrace, driven from Thebes for life.
  It's you, not him I pity—your words move me.
  He, wherever he goes, my hate goes with him.
CREON: Look at you, sullen in yielding, brutal in your   820
    rage—
  you will go too far. It's perfect justice:
  natures like yours are hardest on themselves.
OED.: Then leave me alone—get out!
CREON: I'm going.
  You're wrong, so wrong. These men know I'm right.

Exit to the side. The CHORUS *turns to* JOCASTA.

CHORUS: Why do you hesitate, my lady
  why not help him in?
JOC.: Tell me what's happened first.
CHORUS: Loose, ignorant talk started dark suspicions
  and a sense of injustice cut deeply too.   830
JOC.: On both sides?
CHORUS: Oh yes.
JOC.:   What did they say?
CHORUS: Enough, please, enough! The land's so racked
    already
  or so it seems to me . . .
  End the trouble here, just where they left it.
OED.: You see what comes of your good intentions now?

And all because you tried to blunt my anger.
CHORUS: My king,
  I've said it once, I'll say it time and again—   840
    I'd be insane, you know it,
  senseless, ever to turn my back on you.
  You who set our beloved land—storm-tossed,
    shattered—
  straight on course. Now again, good helmsman,
  steer us through the storm!

The chorus draws away, leaving OEDIPUS *and* JOCASTA *side
by side.*

JOC.:   For the love of god,
  Oedipus, tell me too, what is it?
  Why this rage? You're so unbending.
OED.: I will tell you. I respect you, Jocasta,
  much more than these men here . . .   850

Glancing at the CHORUS.

  Creon's to blame, Creon schemes against me.
JOC.: Tell me clearly, how did the quarrel start?
OED.: He says *I* murdered Laius—I am guilty.
JOC.: How does he know? Some secret knowledge or
    simple hearsay?
OED.:   Oh, he sent his prophet in
  to do his dirty work. You know Creon,
  Creon keeps his own lips clean.
JOC.:   A prophet?
  Well then, free yourself of every charge!
  Listen to me and learn some peace of mind: 860
  no skill in the world,
  nothing human can penetrate the future.
  Here is proof, quick and to the point.

  An oracle came to Laius one fine day
  (I won't say from Apollo himself
  but his underlings, his priests) and it declared
  that doom would strike him down at the hands of a son,
  our son, to be born of our own flesh and blood. But
    Laius,
  so the report goes at least, was killed by strangers,
  thieves, at a place where three roads meet . . . my son—   870
  he wasn't three days old and the boy's father
  fastened his ankles, had a henchman fling him away
  on a barren, trackless mountain.
                                There, you see?
  Apollo brought neither thing to pass. My baby
  no more murdered his father than Laius suffered—
  his wildest fear—death at his own son's hands.
  That's how the seers and all their revelations
  mapped out the future. Brush them from your mind.
  Whatever the god needs and seeks   880
  he'll bring to light himself, with ease.
OED.:   Strange,
  hearing you just now . . . my mind wandered
  my thoughts racing back and forth.
JOC.: What do you mean? Why so anxious, startled?
OED.: I thought I heard you say that Laius
  was cut down at a place where three roads meet.
JOC.: That was the story. It hasn't died out yet.
OED.: Where did this thing happen? Be precise.

JOC.: A place called Phocis, where two branching roads,   890
  one from Daulia, one from Delphi,[13]
  come together—a crossroads.

OED.: When? How long ago?

JOC.: The heralds no sooner reported Laius dead
  than you appeared and they hailed you king of
    Thebes.

OED.: My god, my god—what have you planned to do
  to me?

JOC.: What, Oedipus? What haunts you so?

OED.:   Not yet.
  Laius—how did he look? Describe him.
  Had he reached his prime?   900

JOC.:   He was swarthy,
  and the gray had just begun to streak his temples,
  and his build . . . wasn't far from yours.

OED.:   Oh no no,
  I think I've just called down a dreadful curse
  upon myself—I simply didn't know!

JOC.: What are you saying? I shudder to look at you.

OED.: I have a terrible fear the blind seer can see.
  I'll know in a moment. One thing more—

JOC.:   Anything,   910
  afraid as I am—ask, I'll answer, all I can.

OED.: Did he go with a light or heavy escort,
  several men-at-arms, like a lord, a king?

JOC.: There were five in the party, a herald among them,
  and a single wagon carrying Laius.

OED.:   Ai—
  now I can see it all, clear as day.
  Who told you all this at the time, Jocasta?

JOC.: A servant who reached home, the lone survivor.

OED.: So, could he still be in the palace—even now?   920

JOC.: No indeed. Soon as he returned from the scene
  and saw you on the throne with Laius dead and gone,
  he knelt and clutched my hand, pleading with me
  to send him into the hinterlands, to pasture,
  far as possible, out of sight of Thebes.
  I sent him away. Slave though he was,
  he'd earned that favor—and much more.

OED.: Can we bring him back, quickly?

JOC.: Easily. Why do you want him so?

OED.:   I am afraid,   930
  Jocasta, I have said too much already.
  That man—I've got to see him.

JOC.:   Then he'll come.
  But even I have a right, I'd like to think,
  to know what's torturing you, my lord.

OED.: And so you shall—I can hold nothing back from
    you,
  now I've reached this pitch of dark foreboding.
  Who means more to me than you? Tell me,
  whom would I turn toward but you
  as I go through all this?   940
  My father was Polybus, king of Corinth.
  My mother, a Dorian, Merope. And I was held
  the prince of the realm among the people there,

till something struck me out of nowhere,
something strange . . . worth remarking perhaps,
hardly worth the anxiety I gave it.
Some man at a banquet who had drunk too much
shouted out—he was far gone, mind you—
that I am not my father's son. Fighting words!
I barely restrained myself that day   950
but early the next I went to mother and father,
questioned them closely, and they were enraged
at the accusation and the fool who let it fly.
So as for my parents I was satisfied,
but still this thing kept gnawing at me,
the slander spread—I had to make my move.

                  And so,
unknown to mother and father I set out for Delphi,
and the god Apollo spurned me, sent me away
denied the facts I came for,   960
but first he flashed before my eyes a future
great with pain, terror, disaster—I can hear him cry,
"You are fated to couple with your mother, you will
    bring
a breed of children into the light no man can bear to
    see—
you will kill your father, the one who gave you life!"
I heard all that and ran. I abandoned Corinth,
from that day on I gauged its landfall only
by the stars, running, always running
toward some place where I would never see
the shame of all those oracles come true.   970
And as I fled I reached that very spot
where the great king, you say, met his death.

Now, Jocasta, I will tell you all.
Making my way toward this triple crossroad
I began to see a herald, then a brace of colts
drawing a wagon, and mounted on the bench . . .
    a man,
just as you've described him, coming face-to-face,
and the one in the lead and the old man himself
were about to thrust me off the road—brute force—
and the one shouldering me aside, the driver,   980
I strike him in anger—and the old man, watching me
coming up along his wheels—he brings down
his prod, two prongs straight at my head!
I paid him back with interest!
Short work, by god—with one blow of the staff
in this right hand I knock him out of his high seat,
roll him out of the wagon, sprawling headlong—
I killed them all—every mother's son!

Oh, but if there is any blood-tie
between Laius and this stranger . . .   990
what man alive more miserable than I?
More hated by the gods? *I* am the man
no alien, no citizen welcomes to his house,
law forbids it—not a word to me in public,
driven out of every hearth and home.
And all these curses I—no one but I
brought down these piling curses on myself!
And you, his wife, I've touched your body with these,

---

[13] **Phocis, Daulia, Delphi** Phocis was the territory in which the towns Daulia and Delphi were located. Apollo's temple was in Delphi.

the hands that killed your husband cover you with
   blood.

Wasn't I born for torment? Look me in the eyes!   1000
I am abomination—heart and soul!
I must be exiled, and even in exile
never see my parents, never set foot
on native ground again. Else I am doomed
to couple with my mother and cut my father down . . .
Polybus who reared me, gave me life.
                                     But why, why?
Wouldn't a man of judgment say—and wouldn't he be
   right—
some savage power has brought this down upon my
   head?

Oh no, not that, you pure and awesome gods,   1010
never let me see that day! Let me slip
from a world of men, vanish without a trace
before I see myself stained with such corruption,
stained to the heart.
LEADER: My lord, you fill our hearts with fear.
   But at least until you question the witness,
   do take hope.
OED.:   Exactly. He is my last hope—
   I am waiting for the shepherd. He is crucial.
JOC.: And once he appears, what then? Why so urgent?   1020
OED.: I will tell you. If it turns out that his story
   matches yours, I've escaped the worst.
JOC.: What did I say? What struck you so?
OED.:   You said *thieves*—
   he told you a whole band of them murdered Laius.
   So, if he still holds to the same number,
   I cannot be the killer. One can't equal many.
   But if he refers to one man, one alone,
   clearly the scales come down on me:
   I am guilty.   1030
JOC.:   Impossible. Trust me,
   I told you precisely what he said,
   and he can't retract it now;
   the whole city heard it, not just I.
   And even if he should vary his first report
   by one man more or less, still, my lord,
   he could never make the murder of Laius
   truly fit the prophecy. Apollo was explicit:
   my son was doomed to kill my husband . . . my son,
   poor defenseless thing, he never had a chance   1040
   to kill his father. They destroyed him first.

   So much for prophecy. It's neither here nor there.
   From this day on, I wouldn't look right or left.
OED.: True, true. Still, that shepherd,
   someone fetch him—now!
JOC.: I'll send at once. But do let's go inside.
   I'd never displease you, least of all in this.

OEDIPUS *and* JOCASTA *enter the palace.*

CHORUS: Destiny guide me always
   Destiny find me filled with reverence pure in word
      and deed.

Great laws tower above us, reared on high   1050
born for the brilliant value of heaven—
      Olympian Sky their only father,
nothing mortal, no man gave them birth,
their memory deathless, never lost in sleep:
within them lives a might god, the god does not grow
   old.

Pride breeds the tyrant
violent pride, gorging, crammed to bursting
with all that is overripe and rich with ruin—
clawing up to the heights, headlong pride
crashes down the abyss—sheer doom!
No footing helps, all foothold lost and gone.   1060
But the healthy strife that makes the city strong—
I pray that god will never end that wrestling:
god, my champion, I will never let you go.

But if any man comes striding, high and mighty
in all he says and does,
no fear of justice, no reverence
for the temples of the gods—
let a rough doom tear him down,
repay his pride, breakneck, ruinous pride!
If he cannot reap his profits fairly   1070
cannot restrain himself from outrage—
mad, laying hands on the holy things untouchable!

Can such a man, so desperate, still boast
he can save his life from the flashing bolts of god?
   If all such violence goes with honor now
      why join the sacred dance?

Never again will I go reverent to Delphi,
   the inviolate heart of Earth
or Apollo's ancient oracle at Abae[14]
   or Olympia of the fires—   1080
unless these prophecies all come true
for all mankind to point toward in wonder.
King of kings, if you deserve your titles
Zeus, remember, never forget!
You and your deathless, everlasting reign.

   They are dying, the old oracles sent to Laius,
   now our masters strike them off the rolls.
      Nowhere Apollo's golden glory now—
         the gods, the gods go down.

Enter JOCASTA *from the palace, carrying a suppliant's branch
wound in wool.*

JOC.: Lords of the realm, it occurred to me,   1090
   just now, to visit the temples of the gods,
   so I have a branch in hand and incense too.

   Oedipus is beside himself. Racked with anguish,
   no longer a man of sense, he won't admit
   the latest prophecies are hollow as the old—

---

[14] **Abae** A town in Phocis, where an oracle of Apollo resided.

he's at the mercy of every passing voice
if the voice tells of terror.
I urge him gently, nothing seems to help,
so I turn to you, Apollo, you are nearest.

Placing her branch on the altar, while an old herdsman enters
    from the side, not the one just summoned by the King but
    an unexpected MESSENGER *from Corinth.*

I come with prayers and offerings . . . I beg you,   1100
cleanse us, set us free of defilement!
Look at us, passengers in the grip of fear,
watching the pilot of the vessel go to pieces.

MESSENGER: *Approaching* JOCASTA *and the* CHORUS.

Strangers, please, I wonder if you could lead us
to the palace of the king . . . I think it's Oedipus.
Better, the man himself—you know where he is?
LEADER: This is his palace, stranger. He's inside.
But here is his queen, his wife and mother
of his children.
MESS.:   Blessings on you, noble queen,   1110
queen of Oedipus crowned with all your family—
blessings on you always!
JOC.: And the same to you, stranger, you deserve it . . .
such a greeting. But what have you come for?
Have you brought us news?
MESS.:   Wonderful news—
for the house, my lady, for your husband too.
JOC.: Really, what? Who sent you?
MESS.:   Corinth.
I'll give you the message in a moment.   1120
You'll be glad of it—how could you help it?—
though it costs a little sorrow in the bargain.
JOC.: What can it be, with such a double edge?
MESS.: The people there, they want to make your
        Oedipus
king of Corinth, so they're saying now.
JOC.: Why? Isn't old Polybus still in power?
MESS.: No more. Death has got him in the tomb.
JOC.: What are you saying? Polybus, dead?—dead?
MESS.:   If not,
if I'm not telling the truth, strike me dead too.   1130

JOC.: *To a servant.*

Quickly, go to your master, tell him this!

You prophecies of the gods, where are you now?
This is the man that Oedipus feared for years,
he fled him, not to kill him—and now he's dead,
quite by chance, a normal, natural death,
not murdered by his son.

OED.: *Emerging from the palace.*

                        Dearest,
what now? Why call me from the palace?

JOC.: *Bringing the* MESSENGER *closer.*

Listen to *him*, see for yourself what all
those awful prophecies of god have come to.   1140
OED.: And who is he? What can he have for me?
JOC.: He's from Corinth, he's come to tell you
your father is no more—Polybus—he's dead!

OED.: *Wheeling on the* MESSENGER.

What? Let me have it from your lips.
MESS.:   Well,
if that's what you want first, then here it is:
make no mistake, Polybus is dead and gone.
OED.: How—murder? sickness?—what? what killed
        him?
MESS.: A light tip of the scales can put old bones to rest.
OED.: Sickness then—poor man, it wore him down.   1150
MESS.:   That,
and the long count of years he'd measured out.
OED.:   So!
Jocasta, why, why look to the Prophet's hearth,
the fires of the future? Why scan the birds
that scream above our heads? They winged me on
to the murder of my father, did they? That was my
        doom?
Well look, he's dead and buried, hidden under the
        earth,
and here I am in Thebes, I never put hand to sword—
unless some longing for me wasted him away,   1160
then in a sense you'd say I caused his death.
But now, all those prophecies I feared—Polybus
packs them off to sleep with him in hell!
They're nothing, worthless.
JOC.:   There.
Didn't tell you from the start?
OED.: So you did. I was lost in fear.
JOC.: No more, sweep it from your mind forever.
OED.: But my mother's bed, surely I must fear—
JOC.:   Fear?   1170
What should a man fear? It's all chance,
chance rules our lives. Not a man on earth
can see a day ahead, groping through the dark.
Better to live at random, best we can.
And as for this marriage with your mother—
have no fear. Many a man before you,
in his dreams, has shared his mother's bed.
Take such things for shadows, nothing at all—
Live, Oedipus,
as if there's no tomorrow!   1180
OED.:   Brave words,
and you'd persuade me if mother weren't alive.
But mother lives, so for all your reassurances
I live in fear, I must.
JOC.:   But your father's death,
that, at least, is a great blessing, joy to the eyes!
OED.: Great, I know . . . but I fear *her*—she's still alive.
MESS.: Wait, who is this woman, makes you so afraid?
OED.: Merope, old man. The wife of Polybus.
MESS.: The queen? What's there to fear in her?   1190
OED.: A dreadful prophecy, stranger, sent by the gods.
MESS.: Tell me, could you? Unless it's forbidden
other ears to hear.
OED.:   Not at all.
Apollo told me once—it is my fate—
I must make love with my own mother,
shed my father's blood with my own hands.
So for years I've given Corinth a wide berth,
and it's been my good fortune too. But still,
to see one's parents and look into their eyes   1200

is the greatest joy I know.

MESS.: You're afraid of that?
That kept you out of Corinth?

OED.: My *father*, old man—
so I wouldn't kill my father.

MESS.: So that's it.
Well then, seeing I came with such good will, my king,
why don't I rid you of that old worry now?

OED.: What a rich reward you'd have for that!

MESS.: What do you think I came for, majesty? 1210
So you'd come home and I'd be better off.

OED.: Never, I will never go near my parents.

MESS.: My boy, it's clear, you don't know what you're doing.

OED.: What do you mean, old man? For god's sake, explain.

MESS.: If you ran from *them*, always dodging home . . .

OED.: Always, terrified Apollo's oracle might come true —

MESS.: And you'd be covered with guilt, from both your parents.

OED.: That's right, old man, that fear is always with me.

MESS.: Don't you know? You've really nothing to fear. 1220

OED.: But why? If I'm their son—Merope, Polybus?

MESS.: Polybus was nothing to you, that's why, not in blood.

OED.: What are you saying—Polybus was not my father?

MESS.: No more than I am. He and I are equals.

OED.: My father—
how can my father equal nothing? You're nothing to me!

MESS.: Neither was he, no more your father than I am.

OED.: Then why did he call me his son?

MESS.: You were a gift,
years ago—know for a fact he took you 1230
from my hands.

OED.: No, from another's hands?
Then how could he love me so? He loved me, deeply . . .

MESS.: True, and his early years without a child
made him love you all the more.

OED.: And you, did you . . .
buy me? find me by accident?

MESS.: I stumbled on you,
down the woody flanks of Mount Cithaeron.

OED.: So close, 1240
what were you doing here, just passing through?

MESS.: Watching over my flocks, grazing them on the slopes.

OED.: A herdsman, were you? A vagabond, scraping for wages?

MESS.: Your savior too, my son, in your worst hour.

OED.: Oh—
when you picked me up, was I in pain? What exactly?

MESS.: Your ankles . . . they tell the story. Look at them.

OED.: Why remind me of that, that old affliction?

MESS.: Your ankles were pinned together. I set you free.

OED.: That dreadful mark—I've had it from the cradle. 1250

MESS.: And you got your name from that misfortune too,
the name's still with you.

OED.: Dear god, who did it?—

mother? father? Tell me.

MESS.: I don't know.
The one who gave you to me, he'd know more.

OED.: What? You took me from someone else?
You didn't find me yourself?

MESS.: No sir,
another shepherd passed you on to me. 1260

OED.: Who? Do you know? Describe him.

MESS.: He called himself a servant of . . .
if I remember rightly—Laius.

JOCASTA *turns sharply.*

OED.: The king of the land who ruled here long ago?

MESS.: That's the one. That herdsman was *his* man.

OED.: Is he still alive? Can I see him?

MESS.: They'd know best, the people of these parts.

OEDIPUS *and the* MESSENGER *turn to the* CHORUS.

OED.: Does anyone know that herdsman,
the one he mentioned? Anyone seen him
in the fields, here in the city? Out with it! 1270
The time has come to reveal this once for all.

LEADER: I think he's the very shepherd you wanted to see,
a moment ago. But the queen, Jocasta,
she's the one to say.

OED.: Jocasta,
you remember the man we just sent for?
Is *that* the one he means?

JOC.: That man . . .
why ask? Old shepherd, talk, empty nonsense,
don't give it another thought, don't even think— 1280

OED.: What—give up now, with a clue like this?
Fail to solve the mystery of my birth?
Not for all the world!

JOC.: Stop—in the name of god,
if you love your own life, call off this search!
My suffering is enough.

OED.: Courage!
Even if my mother turns out to be a slave,
and I a slave, three generations back,
you would not seem common. 1290

JOC.: Oh no,
listen to me, I beg you, don't do this.

OED.: Listen to you? No more. I must know it all,
must see the truth at last.

JOC.: No, please—
for your sake—I want the best for you!

OED.: Your best is more than I can bear.

JOC.: You're doomed—
may you never fathom who you are!

OED.: *To a servant.* 1300
Hurry, fetch me the herdsman, now!
Leave her to glory in her royal birth.

JOC.: Aieeeeee—
man of agony—
that is the only name I have for you,
that, no other—ever, ever, ever!

Flinging through the palace doors. A long, tense silence follows.

LEADER: Where's she gone, Oedipus?
Rushing off, such wild grief . . .

I'm afraid that from this silence
something monstrous may come bursting forth.   1310
OED.: Let it burst! Whatever will, whatever must!
I must know my birth, no matter how common
it may be—I must see my origins face-to-face.
She perhaps, she with her woman's pride
may well be mortified by my birth,
but I, I count myself the son of Chance,
the great goddess, giver of all good things—
I'll never see myself disgraced. She is my mother!
And the moons have marked me out, my blood-
        brothers,
one moon on the wane, the next moon great with   1320
        power.
That is my blood, my nature—I will never betray it,
never fail to search and learn my birth!
CHORUS: Yes—if I am a true prophet
                    if I can grasp the truth,
      by the boundless skies of Olympus,
at the full moon of tomorrow, Mount Cithaeron
you will know how Oedipus glories in you—
you, his birthplace, nurse, his mountain-mother!
And we will sing you, dancing out your praise—
you lift our monarch's heart!   1330
      Apollo, Apollo, god of the wild cry
              may our dancing please you!
                              Oedipus—
                  son, dear child, who bore you?
Who of the nymphs who seem to live forever
mated with Pan,[15] the mountain-striding Father?
Who was your mother? who, some bride of Apollo
the god who loves the pastures spreading toward the
        sun?
      Or was it Hermes,[16] king of the lightning ridges?
Or Dionysus, lord of frenzy, lord of the barren peaks—   1340
did he seize you in his hands, dearest of all his lucky
        finds?—
      found by the nymphs, their warm eyes dancing, gift
to the lord who loves them dancing out his joy!

OEDIPUS *strains to see a figure coming from the distance.*
Attended by palace guards, an old SHEPHERD *enters slowly,*
reluctant to approach the king.

OED.: I never met the man, my friends . . . still,
if I had to guess, I'd say that's the shepherd,
the very one we've looked for all along.
Brothers in old age, two of a kind,
he and our guest here. At any rate
the ones who bring him in are my own men,
I recognize them.   1350

Turning to the LEADER.

                    But you know more than I,
you should, you've seen the man before.
LEADER: I know him, definitely. One of Laius' men,

_____

[15] **Pan** Nature and fertility deity, who was god of goat herds and
flocks. He wandered in hills pursuing nymphs and playing on his
musical instrument, a set of reed pipes cut in various lengths and fastened together. Pan is considered to be a son of Hermes.
[16] **Hermes** God of merchants and thieves. Messenger for the deities.
Wore a broad-brimmed traveler's hat and winged sandals. Also
known as an early Greek fertility god.

a trusty shepherd, if there ever was one.
OED.: You, I ask you first, stranger,
you from Corinth—is this the one you mean?
MESS.: You're looking at him. He's your man.

OED.: *To the* SHEPHERD.

You, old man, come over here—
look at me. Answer all my questions.
Did you ever serve King Laius?   1360
SHEP.:   So I did . . .
a slave, not bought on the block though,
born and reared in the palace.
OED.: Your duties, your kind of work?
SHEP.: Herding the flocks, the better part of my life.
OED.: Where, mostly? Where did you do your grazing?
SHEP.:   Well,
Cithaeron sometimes, or the foothills round about.
OED.: This man—you know him? ever see him there?

SHEP.: *Confused, glancing from the* MESSENGER *to the King.*

Doing what?—what man do you mean?   1370

OED.: *Pointing to the* MESSENGER.

This one here—ever have dealings with him?
SHEP.: Not so I could say, but give me a chance,
my memory's bad . . .
MESS.: No wonder he doesn't know me, master.
But let me refresh his memory for him.
I'm sure he recalls old times we had
on the slopes of Mount Cithaeron;
he and I, grazing our flocks, he with two
and I with one—we both struck up together,
three whole seasons, six months at a stretch   1380
from spring to the rising of Arcturus in the fall,
then with winter coming on I'd drive my herds
to my own pens, and back he'd go with his
to Laius' folds.

To the SHEPHERD.

                    Now that's how it was,
wasn't it—yes or no?
SHEP.:   Yes, I suppose . . .
it's all so long ago.
MESS.:   Come, tell me,
you gave me a child back then, a boy, remember?   1390
A little fellow to rear, my very own.
SHEP.: What? Why rake up that again?
MESS.: Look, here he is, my fine old friend—
the same man who was just a baby then.
SHEP.: Damn you, shut your mouth—quiet!
OED.: Don't lash out at him, old man—
you need lashing more than he does.
SHEP.:   Why,
master, majesty—what have I done wrong?
OED.: You won't answer his question about the boy.   1400
SHEP.: He's talking nonsense, wasting his breath.
OED.: So, you won't talk willingly—
then you'll talk with pain.

The guards seize the SHEPHERD.

SHEP.: No, dear god, don't torture an old man!
OED.: Twist his arms back, quickly!

SHEP.:   God help us, why?—
    what more do you need to know?
OED.: Did you give him that child? He's asking.
SHEP.: I did . . . I wish to god I'd died that day.
OED.: You've got your wish if you don't tell the truth.   1410
SHEP.: The more I tell, the worse the death I'll die.
OED.: Our friend here wants to stretch things out, does
    he?

Motioning to his men for torture.

SHEP.: No, no, I gave it to him—I just said so.
OED.: Where did you get it? Your house? Someone
    else's?
SHEP.: It wasn't mine, no, I got it from . . . someone.
OED.: Which one of them?

Looking at the citizens.

                              Whose house?
SHEP.:   No—
    god's sake, master, no more questions!
OED.: You're a dead man if I have to ask again.   1420
SHEP.: Then—the child came from the house . . .
    of Laius.
OED.:   A slave? or born of his own blood?
SHEP.:   Oh no,
    I'm right at the edge, the horrible truth—I've got to
    say it!
OED.: And I'm at the edge of hearing horrors, yes, but I
    must hear!
SHEP.: All right! His son, they said it was—his son!
    But the one inside, your wife,
    she'd tell it best.
OED.: My wife—   1430
    she gave it to you?
SHEP.: Yes, yes, my king.
OED.: Why, what for?
SHEP.: To kill it.
OED.: Her own child,
    how could she?
SHEP.: She was afraid—
    frightening prophecies.
OED.: What?
SHEP.:   They said—   1440
    he'd kill his parents.
OED.: But you gave him to this old man—why?
SHEP.: I pitied the little baby, master,
    hoped he'd take him off to his own country,
    far away, but he saved him for this, this fate.
    If you are the man he says you are, believe me,
    you were born for pain.
OED.:   O god—
    all come true, all burst to light!
    O light—now let me look my last on you!   1450
    I stand revealed at last—
    cursed in my birth, cursed in marriage,
    cursed in the lives I cut down with these hands!

Rushing through the doors with a great cry. The Corinthian
MESSENGER, *the* SHEPHERD *and attendants exit slowly to
the side.*

CHORUS: O the generations of men
    the dying generations—adding the total

of all your lives I find they come to nothing . . .
                    does there exist, is there a man on earth
    who seizes more joy than just a dream, a vision?
    And the vision no sooner dawns than dies
    blazing into oblivion.   1460

    You are my great example, you, your life
    your destiny, Oedipus, man of misery—
    I count no man blest.

                    You outranged all men!
        Bending your bow to the breaking-point
    you captured priceless glory, O dear god,
    and the Sphinx came crashing down,
                    the virgin, claws hooked
    like a bird of omen singing, shrieking death—
    like a fortress reared in the face of death   1470
    you rose and saved our land.

    From that day on we called you king
    we crowned you with honors, Oedipus, towering
        over all—
    mighty king of the seven gates of Thebes.
    But now to hear your story—is there a man more
        agonized?
    More wed to pain and frenzy? Not a man on earth,
    the joy of your life ground down to nothing
    O Oedipus, name for the ages—
    one and the same wide harbor served you
                    son and father both   1480
    son and father came to rest in the same bridal chamber.
    How, how could the furrows your father plowed
    bear you, your agony, harrowing on
    in silence O so long?

                    But now for all your power
    Time, all-seeing Time has dragged you to the light,
    judged your marriage monstrous from the start—
    the son and the father tangling, both one—
        O child of Laius, would to god
        I'd never seen you, never never!   1490
    Now I weep like a man who wails the dead
    and the dirge comes pouring forth with all my heart!
    I tell you the truth, you gave me life
    my breath leapt up in you
    and now you bring down night upon my eyes.

Enter a MESSENGER *from the palace.*

MESS.: Men of Thebes, always first in honor,
    what horrors you will hear, what you will see,
    what a heavy weight of sorrow you will shoulder . . .
    if you are true to your birth, if you still have
    some feeling for the royal house of Thebes.   1500
    I tell you neither the waters of the Danube
    nor the Nile can wash this palace clean.
    Such things it hides, it soon will bring to light—
    terrible things, and none done blindly now,
    all done with a will. The pains
    we inflict upon ourselves hurt most of all.
LEADER: God knows we have pains enough already.
    What can you add to them?
MESS.: The queen is dead.

LEADER: Poor lady—how?   1510

MESS.: By her own hand. But you are spared the worst,
    you never had to watch . . . I saw it all,
    and with all the memory that's in me
    you will learn what that poor woman suffered.

Once she'd broken in through the gates
    dashing past us, frantic, whipped to fury,
    ripping her hair out with both hands—
    straight to her rooms she rushed, flinging herself
    across the bridal-bed, doors slamming behind her—
    once inside, she wailed for Laius, dead so long,   1520
    remembering how she bore his child long ago,
    the life that rose up to destroy him, leaving
    its mother to mother living creatures
    with the very son she'd borne.
    Oh how she wept, mourning the marriage-bed
    where she let loose that double brood—monsters—
    husband by her husband, children by her child.
                                    And then—
    but how she died is more than I can say. Suddenly
    Oedipus burst in, screaming, he stunned us so   1530
    we couldn't watch her agony to the end,
    our eyes were fixed on him. Circling
    like a maddened beast, stalking, here, there,
    crying out to us—
                        Give him a sword! His wife,
    no wife, his mother, where can he find the mother earth
    that cropped two crops at once, himself and all his
        children?
    He was raging—one of the dark powers pointing the
        way,
    none of us mortals crowding around him, no,
    with a great shattering cry—someone, something   1540
        leading
    him on—
    he hurled at the twin doors and bending the bolts back
    out of their sockets, crashed through the chamber.
    And there we saw the woman hanging by the neck,
    cradled high in the woven noose, spinning,
    swinging back and forth. And when he saw her,
    giving a low, wrenching sob that broke our hearts,
    slipping the halter from her throat, he eased her down,
    in a slow embrace he laid her down, poor thing . . .
    then, what came next, what horror we beheld!   1550

He rips off her brooches, the long gold pins
    holding her robes—and lifting them high,
    looking straight up into the points,
    he digs them down the sockets of his eyes, crying, "You,
    you'll see no more the pain I suffered, all the pain I
        caused!
    Too long you looked on the bones you never should
        have seen,
    blind to the ones you longed to see, to know! Blind
    from this hour on! Blind in the darkness—blind!"
    His voice like a dirge, rising, over and over
    raising the pins, raking them down his eyes.   1560
    And at each stroke blood spurts from the roots,
    splashing his beard, a swirl of it, nerves and clots—
    black hail of blood pulsing, gushing down.
    These are the griefs that burst upon them both,

coupling man and woman. The joy they had so lately,
    the fortune of their old ancestral house
    was deep joy indeed. Now, in this one day,
    wailing, madness and doom, death, disgrace,
    all the griefs in the world that you can name,
    all are theirs forever.   1570

LEADER: Oh poor man, the misery—
    has he any rest from pain now?

A voice within, in torment.

MESS.:   He's shouting,
    "Loose the bolts, someone, show me to all of Thebes!
    My father's murderer, my mother's—"
    No, I can't repeat it, it's unholy.
    Now he'll tear himself from his native earth,
    not linger, curse the house with his own curse.
    But he needs strength, and a guide to lead him on.
    This is sickness more than he can bear.   1580

The palace doors open.

                                    Look,
    he'll show you himself. The great doors are opening—
    you are about to see a sight, a horror
    even his mortal enemy would pity.

Enter OEDIPUS, *blinded, led by a boy. He stands at the palace
steps, as if surveying his people once again.*

CHORUS: O the terror—
    the suffering, for all the world to see,
    the worst terror that ever met my eyes.
    What madness swept over you? What god,
    what dark power leapt beyond all bounds,
    beyond belief, to crush your wretched life?—   1590
    godforsaken, cursed by the gods!
    I pity you but I can't bear to look.
    I've much to ask, so much to learn,
    so much fascinates my eyes,
    but you . . . I shudder at the sight.

OED.:   Oh, Ohh—
    the agony! I am agony—
    where am I going? where on earth?
        where does all this agony hurl me?
    where's my voice—   1600
        winging, swept away on a dark tide—
    My destiny, my dark power, what a leap you made!

CHORUS: To the depths of terror, too dark to hear, to see.

OED.: Dark, horror of darkness
    my darkness, drowning, swirling around me
    crashing wave on wave—unspeakable, irresistible
    headwind, fatal harbor! Oh again,
    the misery, all at once, over and over
    the stabbing daggers, stab of memory
    raking me insane.   1610

CHORUS: No wonder you suffer
    twice over, the pain of your wounds,
    the lasting grief of pain.

OED.:   Dear friend, still here?
    Standing by me, still with a care for me,
    the blind man? Such compassion,
        loyal to the last. Oh it's you,
    I know you're here, dark as it is
    I'd know you anywhere, your voice—

it's yours, clearly yours.   1620
CHORUS: Dreadful, what you've done . . .
    how could you bear it, gouging out your eyes?
    What superhuman power drove you on?
OED.:   Apollo, friends, Apollo—
    he ordained my agonies—these, my pains on pains!
    But the hand that struck my eyes was mine,
    mine alone—no one else—
                          I did it all myself!
    What good were eyes to me?
    Nothing I could see could bring me joy.   1630
CHORUS: No, no, exactly as you say.
OED.:   What can I ever see?
    What love, what call of the heart
    can touch my ears with joy? Nothing, friends.
    Take me away, far, far from Thebes,
    quickly, cast me away, my friends—
    this great murderous ruin, this man cursed to heaven,
    the man the deathless gods hate most of all!
CHORUS: Pitiful, you suffer so, you understand so
            much . . .
    I wish you had never known.   1640
OED.:   Die, die—
    whoever he was that day in the wilds
    who cut my ankles free of the ruthless pins,
    he pulled me clear of death, he saved my life
    for this, this kindness—
                          Curse him, kill him!
    If I'd died then, I'd never have dragged myself,
    my loved ones through such hell.
CHORUS: Oh if only . . . would to god.
OED.:   I'd never have come to this,   1650
    my father's murderer—never been branded
    mother's husband, all men see me now! Now,
        loathed by the gods, son of the mother I defiled
        coupling in my father's bed, spawning lives in the
            loins
    that spawned my wretched life. What grief can crown
        this grief?
    It's mine alone, my destiny—I am Oedipus!
CHORUS: How can I say you've chosen for the best?
    Better to die than be alive and blind.
OED.: What I did was best—don't lecture me,   1660
    no more advice. I, with *my* eyes,
    how could I look my father in the eyes
    when I go down to death? Or mother, so abused . . .
    I have done such things to the two of them,
    crimes too huge for hanging.
                          Worse yet,
    the sight of my children, born as they were born,
    how could I long to look into their eyes?
    No, not with these eyes of mine, never.
    Not this city either, her high towers,   1670
    the sacred glittering images of her gods—
    I am misery! I, her best son, reared
    as no other son of Thebes was ever reared,
    I've stripped myself, I gave the command myself.
    All men must cast away the great blasphemer,
    the curse now brought to light by the gods,
    the son of Laius—I, my father's son!

    Now I've exposed my guilt, horrendous guilt,

could I train a level glance on you, my countrymen?
Impossible! No, if I could just block off my ears,   1680
the springs of hearing, I would stop at nothing—
I'd wall up my loathsome body like a prison,
blind to the sound of life, not just the sight.
Oblivion—what a blessing . . .
for the mind to dwell a world away from pain.

O Cithaeron, why did you give me shelter?
Why didn't you take me, crush my life out on the spot?
I'd never have revealed my birth to all mankind.

O Polybus, Corinth, the old house of my fathers,
so I believed—what a handsome prince you raised—   1690
under the skin, what sickness to the core.
Look at me! Born of outrage, outrage to the core.
O triple roads—it all comes back, the secret,
dark ravine, and the oaks closing in
where the three roads join . . .
You drank my father's blood, my own blood
spilled by my own hands—you still remember me?
What things you saw me do? Then I came here
and did them all once more!
                          Marriages! O marriage,   1700
you gave me birth, and once you brought me into the
    world
you brought my sperm rising back, springing to light
fathers, brothers, sons—one murderous breed—
brides, wives, mothers. The blackest things
a man can do, I have done them all!
                          No more—
it's wrong to name what's wrong to do. Quickly,
for the love of god, hide me somewhere,
kill me, hurl me into the sea
where you can never look on me again.   1710

Beckoning to the CHORUS *as they shrink away.*

                          Closer,
    it's all right. Touch the man of grief.
    Do. Don't be afraid. My troubles are mine
    and I am the only man alive who can sustain them.

Enter CREON *from the palace, attended by palace guards.*

LEADER: Put your requests to Creon. Here he is,
    just when we need him. He'll have a plan, he'll act.
    Now that he's the sole defense of the country
    in your place.
OED.:   Oh no, what can I say to him?
    How can I ever hope to win his trust?   1720
    I wronged him so, just now, in every way.
    You must see that—I was so wrong, so wrong.
CREON: I haven't come to mock you, Oedipus,
    or to criticize your former failings.

Turning to the guards.

                          You there,
    have you lost all respect for human feelings?
    At least revere the Sun, the holy fire
    that keeps us all alive. Never expose a thing
    of guilt and holy dread so great it appalls
    the earth, the rain from heaven, the light of day!   1730
    Get him into the halls—quickly as you can.

Piety demands no less. Kindred alone
should see a kinsman's shame. This is obscene.
OED.: Please, in god's name . . . you wipe my fears away,
coming so generously to me, the worst of men.
Do one thing more, for your sake, not mine.
CREON: What do you want? Why so insistent?
OED.: Drive me out of the land at once, far from sight,
where I can never hear a human voice.
CREON: I'd have done that already, I promise you.   1740
First I wanted the god to clarify my duties.
OED.: The god? His command was clear, every word:
death for the father-killer, the curse—
he said destroy me!
CREON: So he did. Still in such a crisis
it's better to ask precisely what to do.
OED.:   So miserable—
you would consult the god about a man like me?
CREON: By all means. And this time, I assume,
even you will obey the god's decrees.   1750
OED.:   I will,
I will. And you, I command you—I beg you . . .
the woman inside, bury her as you see fit.
It's the only decent thing,
to give your own the last rites. As for me,
never condemn the city of my fathers
to house my body, not while I'm alive, no,
let me live on the mountains, on Cithaeron,
my favorite haunt, I have made it famous.
Mother and father marked out that rock   1760
to be my everlasting tomb—buried alive.
Let me die there, where they tried to kill me.

Oh but this I know: no sickness can destroy me,
nothing can. I would never have been saved
from death—I have been saved
for something great and terrible, something strange.
Well let my destiny come and take me on its way!
About my children, Creon, the boys at least,
don't burden yourself. They're men,
wherever they go, they'll find the means to live.   1770
But my two daughters, my poor helpless girls,
clustering at our table, never without me
hovering near them . . . whatever I touched,
they always had their share. Take care of them,
I beg you. Wait, better—permit me, would you?
Just to touch them with my hands and take
our fill of tears. Please . . . my king.
Grant it, with all your noble heart.
If I could hold them, just once, I'd think
I had them with me, like the early days   1780
when I could see their eyes.

ANTIGONE and ISMENE, *two small children, are led in from
the palace by a nurse.*

                              What's that?
O god! Do I really hear you sobbing?—
my two children. Creon, you've pitied me?
Sent me my darling girls, my own flesh and blood!
Am I right?
CREON: Yes, it's my doing.
I know the joy they gave you all these years,

the joy you must feel now.
OED.:   Bless you, Creon!   1790
May god watch over you for this kindness,
better than he ever guarded me.
                              Children, where are you?
Here, come quickly—

Groping for ANTIGONE *and* ISMENE, *who approach their
father cautiously, then embrace him.*

                              Come to these hands of mine,
your brother's hands, your own father's hands
that served his once bright eyes so well—
that made them blind. Seeing nothing, children,
knowing nothing. I became your father,
I fathered you in the soil that gave me life.   1800
How I weep for you—I cannot see you now . . .
just thinking of all your days to come, the bitterness,
the life that rough mankind will thrust upon you.
Where are the public gatherings you can join,
the banquets of the clans? Home you'll come,
in tears, cut off from the sight of it all,
the brilliant rites unfinished.
And when you reach perfection, ripe for marriage,
who will he be, my dear ones? Risking all
to shoulder the curse that weighs down my parents,   1810
yes and you too—that wounds us all together.
What more misery could you want?
Your father killed his father, sowed his mother,
one, one and the selfsame womb sprang you—
he cropped the very roots of his existence.

Such disgrace, and you must bear it all!
Who will marry you then? Not a man on earth.
Your doom is clear: you'll wither away to nothing,
single, without a child.

Turning to CREON.

                              Oh Creon,   1820
you are the only father they have now . . .
we who brought them into the world
are gone, both gone at a stroke—
Don't let them go begging, abandoned,
women without men. Your own flesh and blood!
Never bring them down to the level of my pains.
Pity them. Look at them, so young, so vulnerable,
shorn of everything—you're their only hope.
Promise me, noble Creon, touch my hand!

Reaching toward CREON, *who draws back.*

You, little ones, if you were old enough   1830
to understand, there is much I'd tell you.
Now, as it is, I'd have you say a prayer.
Pray for life, my children,
live where you are free to grow and season.
Pray god you find a better life than mine,
the father who begot you.
CREON: Enough.
You've wept enough. Into the palace now.
OED.: I must, but I find it very hard.
CREON: Time is the great healer, you will see.   1840
OED.: I am going—you know on what condition?

CREON: Tell me. I'm listening.

OED.: Drive me out of Thebes, in exile.

CREON: Not I. Only the gods can give you that.

OED.: Surely the gods hate me so much—

CREON: You'll get your wish at once.

OED.:   You consent?

CREON: I try to say what I mean; it's my habit.

OED.: Then take me away. It's time.

CREON: Come along, let go of the children.   1850

OED.:   No—
    don't take them away from me, not now! No no no!

Clutching his daughters as the guards wrench them loose and take them through the palace doors.

CREON: Still the king, the master of all things?

No more: here your power ends.
None of your power follows you through life.

Exit OEDIPUS *and* CREON *to the palace. The* CHORUS *comes forward to address the audience directly.*

CHORUS: People of Thebes, my countrymen, look on
    Oedipus.
He solved the famous riddle with his brilliance,
he rose to power, a man beyond all power.
Who could behold his greatness without envy?
Now what a black sea of terror has overwhelmed him.   1860
Now as we keep our watch and wait the final day,
count no man happy till he dies, free of pain at last.

Exit in procession.

THUCYDIDES

Selections from *History of the Peloponnesian War*

In about 450 B.C. Athens was at the height of its political and cultural accomplishments; however, its towering position came at a high cost to other Greek city-states and, ultimately, to itself. Its decades of greatness were bracketed by two costly wars—the first against the Persians, which Athens won, at the beginning of the century; and the second against a coalition of other Greek city-states, which Athens lost, at the century's end.

In the second war—known as the Peloponnesian War—Athens, with a group of like-minded allies, attempted to impose its will on neighboring city-states. Alarmed at Athenian imperialism, these city-states turned to Sparta, who, responding to their pleas, formed a military alliance that overran Athens in 404 B.C. The events of this struggle were recorded by Thucydides, an Athenian general who fought in the war until he was forced into exile for his inability to raise a siege during the war.

In his history, Thucydides set standards of scholarship that have seldom been equaled. He interviewed eyewitnesses, read the sources, and attempted to verify findings with the goal of being as accurate as possible. Although he left the work unfinished, stopping in about 410 B.C., he detailed events so vividly that the narrative still holds the attention of today's readers. He displayed a dramatic flair by inserting speeches that were attributed to generals and politicians whose decisions affected the war's outcome. Of special note is his distinction as the first writer to interpret war in purely human terms, rather than searching for divine causes. He also presented his history as "philosophy teaching by example"; that is, he used the events of the war as fodder for his speculations about human nature and behavior.

Reading the Selections

In these two selections from Book II Thucydides displays his talents as a writer and an analyst. His prose reaches poetic heights in the funeral oration, the first selection. Although Pericles' description of Athenian democracy may be idealistic, it still explains how the system worked and why it was honored. Thucydides also hints that the Athenians' pride could well be their downfall. In his chapter on the plague, the second selection, the author provides a clinical account of the disease and then assesses its impact on the populace and on Athenian society. Thucydides exhibits his ability to arouse sympathy for the victims in the most humane terms while analyzing the long-range effects of communal diseases.

Pericles, the Athenian general, delivered this funeral oration during the first year of the war (430 B.C.) to honor the young men who had died in battle. (Pericles himself was carried off by the plague in the next year.) In a brief introduction, Thucydides sets the scene before Pericles gives his memorial speech to the mourners.

Pericles' speech has two themes: praise for Athens and the Athenian way of life and the traditional argument that the soldiers have not died in vain. He envisions Athens as a model for the Greek world to follow, a place where the individual is honored in a free and open society. There, tolerance and respect for others in their private lives is matched by respect for the law on the part of those engaged in public affairs. He praises Athenian education because it emphasizes natural rather than "state-induced" courage—a dig at Sparta. Thus, the city-state produced brave and loyal citizens eager to defend their open way of life. He even has praise for the Athenian business community, pointing out that it, like other segments of society, is committed to the general welfare. In sum, Athens is "an education to Greece."

Following Pericles' funeral oration Thucydides wrote about the plague, which swept through Athens during the second year of the Peloponnesian War. He defers to others as to how it started and its medical impact; all he can do is to describe the disease that he, himself, contracted. He then details how the disease attacked the individual and manifested itself in body sores, high fevers, and spasms that nearly always resulted in a painful death—descriptions similar to other accounts of the plague (see Boccaccio's *The Decameron*). He then notes the way the illness affected the relationships of individuals and how some persons tried to isolate themselves while others nursed the sick and buried the dead knowing that they would certainly catch the dreaded disease. Thucydides next records how the plague undermined the civic and political structure, encouraging lawlessness, corruption, extravagance, and a disregard for the legal system, that brought the city-state to the brink of a total breakdown. During such times of crisis, Thucydides notes, humans turn to oracles and the supernatural for answers, and he quotes an oracle that might offer an explanation of the plague. He clearly does not have much faith in this explanation, but neither can he ignore its possible role.

∽

Book II
Pericles' Funeral Oration

.   .   .

"Many of those who have spoken here in the past have praised the institution of this speech at the close of our ceremony. It seemed to them a mark of honour to our soldiers who have fallen in war that a speech should be made over them. I do not agree. These men have shown themselves valiant in action, and it would be enough, I think, for their glories to be proclaimed in action, as you have just seen it done at this funeral organized by the state. Our belief in the courage and manliness of so many should not be hazarded on the goodness or badness of one man's speech. Then it is not easy to speak with a proper sense of balance, when a man's listeners find it difficult to believe in the truth of what one is saying. The man who knows the facts and loves the dead may well think that an oration tells less than what he knows and what he would like to hear: others who do not know so much may feel envy for the dead, and think the orator over-praises them, when he speaks of exploits that are beyond their own capacities. Praise of other people is tolerable only up to a certain point, the point where one still believes that one could do oneself some of the things one is hearing about. Once you get beyond this point, you will find people becoming jealous and incredulous. However, the fact is that this institution was set up and approved by our forefathers, and it is my duty to follow the tradition and do my best to meet the wishes and the expectations of every one of you.

"I shall begin by speaking about our ancestors, since it is only right and proper on such an occasion to pay them the honour of recalling what they did. In this land of ours there have always been the same people living from generation to generation up till now, and they, by their courage and their virtues, have handed it on to us, a free country. They certainly deserve our praise. Even more so do our fathers deserve it. For to the inheritance they had received they added all the empire we have now, and it was not without blood and toil that they handed it down to us of the present generation. And then we ourselves, assembled here today, who are mostly in the prime of life, have, in most directions, added to the power of our empire and have organized our State in such a way that it is perfectly well able to look after itself both in peace and in war.

"I have no wish to make a long speech on subjects familiar to you all: so I shall say nothing about the warlike deeds by which we acquired our power or the battles in which we or our fathers gallantly resisted our enemies, Greek or foreign. What I want to do is, in the first place, to discuss the spirit in which we faced our trials and also our constitution and the way of life which has made us great. After that I shall speak in praise of the dead, believing that this kind of speech is not inappropriate to the present occasion, and that this whole assembly, of citizens and foreigners, may listen to it with advantage.

"Let me say that our system of government does not copy the institutions of our neighbours. It is more the case of our being a model to others, than of our imitating anyone else. Our constitution is called a democracy because power is in the hands not of a minority but of the whole people. When it is a question of settling private disputes, everyone is equal before the law; when it is a question of putting one person before another in positions of public responsibility, what counts is not membership of a particular class, but the actual ability which the man possesses. No one, so long as he has it in him to be of service to the state, is kept in political obscurity because of poverty. And, just as our political life is free and open, so is our day-to-day life in our relations with each other. We do not get into a state with our next-door neighbour if he enjoys himself in his own way, nor do we give him the kind of black looks which, though they do no real harm, still do hurt people's feelings. We are free and tolerant in our private lives; but in public affairs we keep to the law. This is because it commands our deep respect.

"We give our obedience to those whom we put in positions of authority, and we obey the laws themselves, especially those which are for the protection of the oppressed, and those unwritten laws which it is an acknowledged shame to break.

"And here is another point. When our work is over, we are in a position to enjoy all kinds of recreation for our spirits. There are various kinds of contests and sacrifices regularly throughout the year; in our own homes we find a beauty and a good taste which delight us every day and which drive away our cares. Then the greatness of our city brings it about that all the good things from all over the world flow in to us, so that to us it seems just as natural to enjoy foreign goods as our own local products.

"Then there is a great difference between us and our opponents, in our attitude towards military security. Here are some examples: Our city is open to the world, and we have no periodical deportations in order to prevent people observing or finding out secrets which might be of military advantage to the enemy. This is because we rely, not on secret weapons, but on our own real courage and loyalty. There is a difference, too, in our educational systems. The Spartans, from their earliest boyhood, are submitted

to the most laborious training in courage; we pass our lives without all these restrictions, and yet are just as ready to face the same dangers as they are. Here is a proof of this: When the Spartans invade our land, they do not come by themselves, but bring all their allies with them; whereas we, when we launch an attack abroad, do the job by ourselves, and, though fighting on foreign soil, do not often fail to defeat opponents who are fighting for their own hearths and homes. As a matter of fact none of our enemies has ever yet been confronted with our total strength, because we have to divide our attention between our navy and the many missions on which our troops are sent on land. Yet, if our enemies engage a detachment of our forces and defeat it, they give themselves credit for having thrown back our entire army; or, if they lose, they claim that they were beaten by us in full strength. There are certain advantages, I think, in our way of meeting danger voluntarily, with an easy mind, instead of with a laborious training, with natural rather than with state-induced courage. We do not have to spend our time practising to meet sufferings which are still in the future; and when they are actually upon us we show ourselves just as brave as these others who are always in strict training. This is one point in which, I think, our city deserves to be admired. There are also others:

"Our love of what is beautiful does not lead to extravagance; our love of the things of the mind does not make us soft. We regard wealth as something to be properly used, rather than as something to boast about. As for poverty, no one need be ashamed to admit it: the real shame is in not taking practical measures to escape from it. Here each individual is interested not only in his own affairs but in the affairs of the state as well: even those who are mostly occupied with their own business are extremely well informed on general politics—this is a peculiarity of ours: we do not say that a man who takes no interest in politics is a man who minds his own business; we say that he has no business here at all. We Athenians, in our own persons, make our decisions on policy or submit them to proper discussions: for we do not think that there is an incompatibility between words and deeds; the worst thing is to rush into action before the consequences have been properly debated. And this is another point where we differ from other people. We are capable at the same time of taking risks and of estimating them beforehand. Others are brave out of ignorance; and, when they stop to think, they begin to fear. But the man who can most truly be accounted brave is he who best knows the meaning of what is sweet in life and of what is terrible, and then goes out undeterred to meet what is to come.

"Again, in questions of general good feeling there is a great contrast between us and most other people. We make friends by doing good to others, not by receiving good from them. This makes our friendship all the more reliable, since we want to keep alive the gratitude of those who are in our debt by showing continued goodwill to them: whereas the feelings of one who owes us something lack the same enthusiasm, since he knows that, when he repays our kindness, it will be more like paying back a debt than giving something spontaneously. We are unique in this. When we do kindnesses to others, we do not do them out of any calculations of profit or loss: we do them without afterthought, relying on our free liberality. Taking everything together then, I declare that our city is an education to Greece, and I declare that in my opinion each single one of our citizens, in all the manifold aspects of life, is able to show himself the rightful lord and owner of his own person, and do this, moreover, with exceptional grace and exceptional versatility. And to show that this is no empty boasting for the present occasion, but real tangible fact, you have only to consider the power which our city possesses and which has been won by those very qualities which I have mentioned. Athens, alone of the states we know, comes to her testing time in a greatness that surpasses what was imagined of her. In her case, and in her case alone, no invading enemy is ashamed at being defeated, and no subject can complain of being governed by people unfit for their responsibilities. Mighty indeed are the marks and monuments of our empire which we have left. Future ages will wonder at us, as the present age wonders at us now. We do not need the praises of a Homer, or of anyone else whose words may delight us for the moment, but whose estimation of facts will fall short of what is really true. For our adventurous spirit has forced an entry into every sea and into every land; and everywhere we have left behind us everlasting memorials of good done to our friends or suffering inflicted on our enemies.

"This, then, is the kind of city for which these men, who could not bear the thought of losing her, nobly fought and nobly died. It is only natural that every one of us who survive them should be willing to undergo hardships in her service. And it was for this reason that I have spoken at such length about our city, because I wanted to make it clear that for us there is more at stake than there is for others who lack our advantages; also I wanted my words of praise for the dead to be set in the bright light of evidence. And now the most important of these words has been spoken. I have sung the praises of our city; but it was the courage and gallantry of these men, and of people like them, which made her splendid. Nor would you find it true in the case of many of the Greeks, as it is true of them, that no words can do more than justice to their deeds.

"To me it seems that the consummation which has overtaken these men shows us the meaning of manliness in its first revelation and in its final proof. Some of them, no doubt, had their faults; but what we ought to remember first is their gallant conduct against the enemy in defence of their native land. They have blotted out evil with good, and done more service to the commonwealth than they ever did harm in their private lives. No one of these men weakened because he wanted to go on enjoying his wealth: no one put off the awful day in the hope that

he might live to escape his poverty and grow rich. More to be desired than such things, they chose to check the enemy's pride. This, to them, was a risk most glorious, and they accepted it, willing to strike down the enemy and relinquish everything else. As for success or failure, they left that in the doubtful hands of Hope, and when the reality of battle was before their faces, they put their trust in their own selves. In the fighting, they thought it more honourable to stand their ground and suffer death than to give in and save their lives. So they fled from the reproaches of men, abiding with life and limb the brunt of battle; and, in a small moment of time, the climax of their lives, a culmination of glory, not of fear, were swept away from us.

"So and such they were, these men—worthy of their city. We who remain behind may hope to be spared their fate, but must resolve to keep the same daring spirit against the foe. It is not simply a question of estimating the advantages in theory. I could tell you a long story (and you know it as well as I do) about what is to be gained by beating the enemy back. What I would prefer is that you should fix your eyes every day on the greatness of Athens as she really is, and should fall in love with her. When you realize her greatness, then reflect that what made her great was men with a spirit of adventure, men who knew their duty, men who were ashamed to fall below a certain standard. If they ever failed in an enterprise, they made up their minds that at any rate the city should not find their courage lacking to her, and they gave to her the best contribution that they could. They gave her their lives, to her and to all of us, and for their own selves they won praises that never grow old, the most splendid of sepulchres—not the sepulchre in which their bodies are laid, but where their glory remains eternal in men's minds, always there on the right occasion to stir others to speech or to action. For famous men have the whole earth as their memorial: it is not only the inscriptions on their graves in their own country that mark them out; no, in foreign lands also, not in any visible form but in people's hearts, their memory abides and grows. It is for you to try to be like them. Make up your minds that happiness depends on being free, and freedom depends on being courageous. Let there be no relaxation in face of the perils of the war. The people who have most excuse for despising death are not the wretched and unfortunate, who have no hope of doing well for themselves, but those who run the risk of a complete reversal in their lives, and who would feel the difference most intensely, if things went wrong for them. Any intelligent man would find a humiliation caused by his own slackness more painful to bear than death, when death comes to him unperceived, in battle, and in the confidence of his patriotism."

∽

Second Year of the War. The Plague and Its Effects

In this way the public funeral was conducted in the winter that came at the end of the first year of the war. At the beginning of the following summer the Peloponnesians and their allies, with two-thirds of their total forces as before, invaded Attica, again under the command of the Spartan King Archidamus, the son of Zeuxidamus. Taking up their positions, they set about the devastation of the country.

They had not been many days in Attica before the plague first broke out among the Athenians. Previously attacks of the plague had been reported from many other places in the neighbourhood of Lemnos[1] and elsewhere, but there was no record of the disease being so virulent anywhere else or causing so many deaths as it did in Athens. At the beginning the doctors were quite incapable of treating the disease because of their ignorance of the right methods. In fact mortality among the doctors was the highest of all, since they came more frequently in contact with the sick. Nor was any other human art or science of any help at all. Equally useless were prayers made in the temples, consultation of oracles, and so forth; indeed, in the end people were so overcome by their sufferings that they paid no further attention to such things.

The plague originated, so they say, in Ethiopia in upper Egypt, and spread from there into Egypt itself and Libya and much of the territory of the King of Persia. In the city of Athens it appeared suddenly, and the first cases were among the population of Piraeus, so that it was supposed by them that the Peloponnesians had poisoned the reservoirs.[2] Later, however, it appeared also in the upper city, and by this time the deaths were greatly increasing in number. As to the question of how it could first have come about or what causes can be found adequate to explain its powerful effect on nature, I must leave that to be considered by other writers, with or without medical experience. I myself shall merely describe what it was like, and set down the symptoms, knowledge of which will enable it to be recognized, if it should ever break out again. I had the disease myself and saw others suffering from it.

That year, as is generally admitted, was particularly free from all other kinds of illness, though those who did have any illness previously all caught the plague in the end. In other cases, however, there seemed to be no reason for the attacks. People in perfect health suddenly began to have burning feelings in the head; their eyes became red and inflamed; inside their mouths there was bleeding from the throat and tongue, and the breath became unnatural and unpleasant. The next symptoms were sneezing and hoarseness of voice, and before long the pain settled on the chest and was accompanied by coughing. Next the stomach was affected with stomach-aches and with vomitings of every kind of bile that has been given a name by the medical profession, all this being accompanied by great pain and difficulty. In most cases there were attacks of ineffectual retching, producing violent spasms; this sometimes ended with this stage of the disease, but sometimes continued long afterwards. Externally the body was not very hot to the touch, nor was there any pallor: the skin was rather reddish and livid, breaking out into small pustules and ulcers. But inside there was a feeling of burning, so that people could not bear the touch even of the lightest linen clothing, but wanted to be completely naked, and indeed most of all would have liked to plunge into cold water. Many of the sick who were uncared for actually did so, plunging into the water-tanks in an effort to relieve a thirst which was unquenchable; for it was just the same with them whether they drank much or little. Then all the time they were afflicted with insomnia and the desperate feeling of not being able to keep still.

In the period when the disease was at its height, the body, so far from wasting away, showed surprising powers of resistance to all the agony, so that there was still some strength left on the seventh or eight day, which was the time when, in most cases, death came from the internal fever. But if people survived this critical period, then the disease descended to the bowels, producing violent ulceration and uncontrollable diarrhoea, so that most of them died later as a result of the weakness caused by this. For the disease, first settling in the head, went on to affect every part of the body in turn, and even when people escaped its worst effects, it still left its traces on them by fastening upon the extremities of the body. It affected the genitals, the fingers, and the toes, and many of those who recovered lost the use of these members; some, too, went blind. There were some also who, when they first began to get better, suffered from a total loss of memory, not knowing who they were themselves and being unable to recognize their friends.

Words indeed fail one when one tries to give a general picture of this disease; and as for the sufferings of individuals, they seemed almost beyond the capacity of human nature to endure. Here in particular is a point where this plague showed itself to be something quite different from ordinary diseases: though there were many dead bodies lying about unburied, the birds and animals that eat human flesh either did not come near them or, if they did taste the flesh, died of it afterwards. Evidence for this may be found in the fact that there was a complete disappearance of all birds of prey: they were not to be seen either round the bodies or anywhere else. But dogs, being domestic animals, provided the best opportunity of observing this effect of the plague.

These, then, were the general features of the disease, though I have omitted all kinds of peculiarities which

---

[1] **Lemnos** An island in the northeastern Aegean Sea. Athens sent to the island many of its poor inhabitants, who were given land and expected to serve in the Athenian army. These exiles also kept the islanders under control.
[2] **Piraeus** The port that served Athens. There were no wells in Piraeus at this time.

occurred in various individual cases. Meanwhile, during all this time there was no serious outbreak of any of the usual kinds of illness; if any such cases did occur, they ended in the plague. Some died in neglect, some in spite of every possible care being taken of them. As for a recognized method of treatment, it would be true to say that no such thing existed: what did good in some cases did harm in others. Those with naturally strong constitutions were no better able than the weak to resist the disease, which carried away all alike, even those who were treated and dieted with the greatest care. The most terrible thing of all was the despair into which people fell when they realized that they had caught the plague; for they would immediately adopt an attitude of utter hopelessness, and, by giving in this way, would lose their powers of resistance. Terrible, too, was the sight of people dying like sheep through having caught the disease as a result of nursing others. This indeed caused more deaths than anything else. For when people were afraid to visit the sick, then they died with no one to look after them; indeed, there were many houses in which all the inhabitants perished through lack of any attention. When, on the other hand, they did visit the sick, they lost their own lives, and this was particularly true of those who made it a point of honour to act properly. Such people felt ashamed to think of their own safety and went into their friends' houses at times when even the members of the household were so overwhelmed by the weight of their calamities that they had actually given up the usual practice of making laments for the dead. Yet still the ones who felt most pity for the sick and the dying were those who had had the plague themselves and had recovered from it. They knew what it was like and at the same time felt themselves to be safe, for no one caught the disease twice, or, if he did, the second attack was never fatal. Such people were congratulated on all sides, and they themselves were so elated at the time of their recovery that they fondly imagined that they could never die of any other disease in the future.

A factor which made matters much worse than they were already was the removal of people from the country into the city, and this particularly affected the incomers. There were no houses for them, and, living as they did during the hot season in badly ventilated huts, they died like flies. The bodies of the dying were heaped one on top of the other, and half-dead creatures could be seen staggering about in the streets or flocking around the fountains in their desire for water. The temples in which they took up their quarters were full of the dead bodies of people who had died inside them. For the catastrophe was so overwhelming that men, not knowing what would happen next to them, became indifferent to every rule of religion or of law. All the funeral ceremonies which used to be observed were now disorganized, and they buried the dead as best they could. Many people, lacking the necessary means of burial because so many deaths had already occurred in their households, adopted the most shameless methods. They would arrive first at a funeral pyre that had been made by others, put their own dead upon it and set it alight; or, finding another pyre burning, they would throw the corpse that they were carrying on top of the other one and go away.

In other respects also Athens owed to the plague the beginnings of a state of unprecedented lawlessness. Seeing how quick and abrupt were the changes of fortune which came to the rich who suddenly died and to those who had previously been penniless but now inherited their wealth, people now began openly to venture on acts of self-indulgence which before then they used to keep dark. Thus they resolved to spend their money quickly and to spend it on pleasure, since money and life alike seemed equally ephemeral. As for what is called honour, no one showed himself willing to abide by its laws, so doubtful was it whether one would survive to enjoy the name for it. It was generally agreed that what was both honourable and valuable was the pleasure of the moment and everything that might conceivably contribute to that pleasure. No fear of god or law of man had a restraining influence. As for the gods, it seemed to be the same thing whether one worshipped them or not, when one saw the good and the bad dying indiscriminately. As for offences against human law, no one expected to live long enough to be brought to trial and punished: instead everyone felt that already a far heavier sentence had been passed on him and was hanging over him, and that before the time for its execution arrived it was only natural to get some pleasure out of life.

This, then, was the calamity which fell upon Athens, and the times were hard indeed, with men dying inside the city and the land outside being laid waste. At this time of distress people naturally recalled old oracles, and among them was a verse which the old men claimed had been delivered in the past and which said:

> *War with the Dorians comes, and a death will come at the same time.*[3]

There had been a controversy as to whether the word in this ancient verse was 'dearth' rather than 'death'; but in the present state of affairs the view that the word was 'death' naturally prevailed; it was a case of people adapting their memories to suit their sufferings. Certainly I think that if there is ever another war with the Dorians after this one, and if a dearth results from it, then in all probability people will quote the other version.

---

[3] **Dorians** The last of the Hellenic tribes who settled in Greece around the eleventh century B.C. They infiltrated the peninsula over several centuries and destroyed the Mycenaean culture. Their reputation as brutal warriors was passed down in folklore and popular sayings.

PLATO

Selections from *The Republic*

Plato (ca. 427–347 B.C.), who was Socrates' (ca. 470–399 B.C.) best-known student, dedicated his life to explaining his master's methods of learning and his ideas. According to Plato, whose writings constitute the most authentic source for Socrates' life, the older philosopher saw himself as a "gadfly" whose mission was to annoy others by questioning their knowledge. Rather than being concerned with such issues as the nature of matter or the structure of the universe, the only topics being studied by philosophers at the time, Socrates caused an intellectual revolution by turning to more human interests such as Justice, Beauty, Love, and Wisdom. By recording in dialogue form the discussions between Socrates and others (sometimes a pupil, sometimes a critic), Plato illustrated Socrates' method of discourse, which reflected the belief that admitting one's ignorance is the first step toward wisdom. The Socratic method has three steps: First, Socrates encouraged his students to express opinions on a topic; second, he analyzed these opinions, pointing out faulty premises (things taken for granted) and weak arguments; third, through a series of questions, he led them not to a new truth but to a recognition of the rational steps needed to attain enlightenment. The Socratic method became a standard mode of inquiry that is still practiced today, formally in classroom settings and informally in personal discussions.

When Plato was not writing about Socrates, he taught in the Academy, the school he founded in Athens after 400 B.C. for the instruction of would-be political leaders. Its curriculum was mathematics and philosophy, ideal subjects for philosophers and kings—a reflection of Plato's antidemocratic beliefs. In his classes he put into practice his and Socrates' learning ideal—to lead students to ever higher levels of abstract thought, concluding with the ultimate truth. This intellectual journey required total concentration, in isolation from everyday life. Plato's students, upon graduation, spread the tenets of Platonism, as his philosophy is called, across the ancient world. Platonism helped shape Hellenistic (see Epicurus's "Letter to Menoeceus"), Roman, and early Christian (see St. Augustine's *Confessions*) thought. Athens became the intellectual center of the Classical world, and Plato's Academy taught generations of thinkers until the Christians closed it in the sixth century A.D.

Reading the Selections

Plato was perhaps the first feminist in Western culture. Women as well as men were taught in his school, the Academy, thus contradicting the basic norm of Greek life—to keep women fully separate from men in public. In *The Republic,* the West's first text in political theory, Plato made the case for equality between the sexes to be achieved through equal educational opportunity. His complete rationale for female equality is set forth in *The Republic,* Book V, part of which is excerpted in the selection.

"The Allegory of the Cave," taken from Book VII, is the most famous episode in *The Republic.* An allegory is a parable meant to clarify an idea too complex to understand on its own. In this selection, Socrates uses an allegory to explain his method of learning, introduced earlier in the book. For Socrates, the learning process is of prime concern, because he believed that only when rulers ("philosopher-kings") are well versed in the meaning of Justice can a state be said to be well regulated. Defining Justice and determining how it can be taught to future leaders is thus *The Republic*'s purpose, constituting, in effect, a textbook to be studied in the Academy.

Socrates' words about the nature of the learning process leave his audience puzzled, so he offers "The Allegory of the Cave" by way of explanation. In the allegory, set within a cave lit only by flickering shadows cast from an unseen fire, an exemplary individual releases himself from bondage; this person then moves, step by step, out of the darkness, upward through a passage, and into the natural world to stare at the sun. The allegorical journey symbolizes the intellectual journey that Socrates thought all students must undergo if they were to reach the ultimate truth.

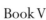

Book V

. . .

The men have fully played their part on our stage and made their exit; and now perhaps it would be right to call in the women, especially since you invite me to do it.

"For people then, born and educated as we explained, the only right way, in my opinion, for them to get and use children and women is the way we started them to go. You remember we tried in our discourse to establish the men as it were guardians of a herd."

"Yes."

"Then let us follow up by giving the women birth and training like theirs, and see if it is proper for us or not."

"How?" he asked.

"Thus; do we think that the females of the guardian dogs ought to share in the guard which the males keep? Ought they to join in the hunt and whatever else they do? Or should the females keep kennel indoors, as being unable because of the birth and training of pups, and should the males do the hard work and have all the care of the flocks?"

"They ought to do everything together," he said, "except that we treat the males as stronger and the females as weaker."

"But is it possible," I said, "to use animals for the same things, if you do not give them the same training and education?"

"Impossible."

"Then if we are to use the women for the same things as the men, we must teach them the same things."

"Yes."

"Now music and gymnastic were taught to the men."

"Yes."

"So we must teach the women those same two arts, and matters of war too, and use them in the same way."

"That seems fair from what you say," he replied.

"Well then," said I, "perhaps much in our present proposals would appear funny in contrast with usual custom, if they were done in the way we say."

"Likely enough," he said.

"And what will be the biggest joke of all?" I asked. "Surely to see naked women in the wrestling schools exercising with the men—not only the young women, but even the older ones too? Like old men in the gymnasium, all over wrinkles and not pleasant to look at, who still fancy the game!"

"You are right, upon my word!" said he; "it would seem funny as things are now!"

"Very well," said I, "since we have set out to speak, let us not fear the jests of refined people. Let them talk how they like and say what they like of such an upheaval,

about gymnastic and music, and not least about wearing armour and riding on horseback."

"Quite right," said he.

"But since we have begun let us march on to the rough part of our law. We will entreat these wits to leave their usual business and be serious for once; we will remind them that it is not so very long since Hellenes[1] thought it ugly and funny, as most barbarians do still, to see men naked; and when the Cretan[2] began naked athletics, and the Lacedaimonians[3] followed, the clever people then were able to make fun of the thing. Don't you agree?"

"Yes, I do."

"But we found by experience that it was better to strip than to hide all such things; and soon the seeming funny to the eyes melted away before that which was revealed in the light of reason to be the best. It showed also that he is a vain fool who thinks anything ridiculous but what is evil; and he is a fool who tries to raise laughter against any sight, as being that of something funny, other than the sight of folly and evil; or in earnest sets up any other mark to aim at than what is honourable and good."

"By all manner of means," he said.

"Then surely we must decide first whether this is possible or not. Next, we must open the debate to all, whether a man chooses to argue in jest or in earnest; and let them discuss whether the female nature in mankind allows women to share the same work with men in everything, or in nothing, or only in some things, and if in some, to which class war belongs. Would not this be the best beginning which would lead most likely to the best end?"

"Much the best," he said.

"Are you willing, then," said I, "that we should defend the others against ourselves, and not take the fort of the counterargument undefended?"

"There's nothing to hinder that," he replied.

"Then let us say on their behalf, 'You need no others to dispute with you, Socrates and Glaucon; you yourselves at the first foundation of your city admitted that each single person must do his own one business according to nature.' 'We admitted it, I think; of course.' 'Is there not all the difference in the world between man and woman according to nature?' 'There is a difference, certainly.' 'Then further, is it not proper to appoint work for each according to the nature of each?' 'What then?' 'Then

---

[1] **Hellenes** Another name for the Greeks.
[2] **Cretan** An inhabitant of the island of Crete.
[3] **Lacedaimonians** Another name for the Spartans who lived in Sparta, which was the ancient city of Laconia on the Peloponnesian peninsula.

you are mistaken surely, and contradict yourselves, when you say now that men and women must do the same things, although their natures are very different!' Come on now, answer me that and I will thank you!"

"What! all of a sudden!" he said. "That's not altogether easy; but I beg and pray you to interpret our argument for us, whatever that may be."

"That is what I expected, my dear Glaucon," said I, "and there are many other such objections, which I foresaw long ago; that is why I feared and shrank to touch the law about getting and training women and children."

"No, by heaven, it does not look like an easy thing," said he.

"And it is not," said I, "but it's like this: If anyone tumbles into a small swimming pool, or if into the middle of the broad sea, he has to swim all the same."

"Certainly."   35

"Then we must swim too, and try to save ourselves out of the argument; we may hope for some dolphin to take us on his back, or some other desperate salvation."

"So it seems," he said.

"Come along then," said I, "see if we can find the way out anywhere. We agreed, you know, that a different nature ought to practise a different work, and that man and woman have different natures; now we say that these different natures must do the same work. Is that the accusation against us?"

"Exactly."

"How noble is the power, my dear Glaucon," said I,   40
"of the art of word controversy!"

"How so?" he said.

"Because," I said, "so many seem unable to help falling into it; they think they are arguing, when they are only striving quarrelsomely. The reason is that they don't know how to split up a given utterance into its different divisions, but pursue simply a verbal opposition to what is uttered. They bandy words with each other, instead of using reasoned discussion."

"That certainly does happen," he said, "in many cases; but surely it does not apply to us in this case?"

"It does, by all manner of means," I said; "at any rate we appear to have got into a word controversy without meaning to."

"How?"   45

"That *different* natures ought not to engage in the *same* practices; we have been chasing the words about with plenty of courage and eristic wrangling, and never thought of enquiring in any way what was the sense of 'different nature' and what was the sense of 'same nature,' and what we were aiming at in our definition when we allotted to a different nature different practices, and to the same nature the same."

"True, we did not," said he.

"It seems we might just as well ask ourselves," I said, "whether the natures of bald men and hairy men are the same or opposite; and in case we agree that they are opposite, we might forbid long-haired men to make shoes if bald men do, and forbid bald men if long-haired men do."

"That would be ridiculous," he said.

"Yes, ridiculous," I said, "but only because we did not   50
then mean the words 'different' and 'same nature'

absolutely; we were thinking only of that kind of sameness or difference which had to do with their actual callings. Thus we meant that a man and a woman who have a physician's mind have the same nature, didn't we?"

"Yes."

"But a man physician and a man carpenter different natures?"

"Yes, I suppose so."

"Now," said I, "take the male and the female sex; if either is found to be better as regards any art or other practice, we shall say that this ought to be assigned to it. But if we find that they differ only in one thing, that the male begets and the female bears the child, we shall not take that difference as having proved any more clearly that a woman differs from a man for what we are speaking of; but we shall still believe that our guardians and their wives should practise the same things."

"And rightly so," he said.   55

.   .   .

My friend, no practice or calling in the life of the city belongs to woman as woman, or to man as man, but the various natures are dispersed among both sexes alike; by nature the woman has a share in all practices, and so has man, but in all, woman is rather weaker than man."

"Certainly."

"Then shall we assign all to man and none to woman?"

"Why, how can we?"

"No, for as I believe, we shall say one woman is musi-   60
cal by nature, one not, one is medical by nature, one not."

"Of course."

"But are we not to add—one woman is athletic or warlike, and another is unwarlike and unathletic?"

"Indeed we are."

"Shall we not say the same of philosophy and misosophy, one loves wisdom and one hates it? One has high spirit, one no spirit?"

"That is so also."   65

"Then there may be a woman fit to be a guardian, although another is not; for such was the nature we chose for our guardian men also?"

"Yes, it was."

"Then both woman and man may have the same nature fit for guarding the city, only one is weaker and one stronger."

"So it seems."

"Such women, then, must be chosen for such men, to   70
live with them and to guard with them, since they are fit for it and akin to them by nature."

"Certainly."

"Practice and calling must be assigned to both sexes, the same for the same natures?"

"Just the same."

"So we have come round to where we began, and we agree that it is not against nature to assign music and gymnastic to the wives of the guardians."

"By all means."   75

"Then our law was not impossible, not only like a pious dream; the law we laid down was natural. But rather, it seems, what happens now, the other way of doing things, is unnatural."

"So it seems."

"Our question then was: Is our proposal possible, and is it best?"

"Yes, that was it."

"It is possible, we are both agreed, aren't we?" 80

"Yes."

"Then the next thing is to agree if it is best."

"Clearly."

"Well, for a woman to become fit to be a guardian, we shall not need one education to make men fit and a different one to make women fit, especially as it will be dealing with the same nature in both?"

"No; the same education." 85

"Then what is your opinion about the following?"

"What?"

"About the notion in your mind that one man is better, another is worse. Or do you think all men are alike?"

"Not by any means."

"In the city that we were founding, then, which do 90 you think we formed into better men, the guardians educated as we described, or the cobblers educated in cobbling?"

"A ridiculous question," said he.

"I understand," said I, "but tell me—are not the guardians the best of all the citizens?"

"Much the best."

"Very well, will not these women be the best of the women?"

"Again the very best," he said. 95

"And is there anything better for a city than that both women and men in it should be as good as they can be?"

"There is not."

"But this will be brought about by the aid of music and gymnastic, as we have described?"

"Of course."

"Then the plan we proposed is not only possible, but 100 best for the city?"

"Just so."

"So the women of the guardians must strip, since naked they will be clothed in virtue for gowns; they must share in war and in all the guarding of the city, and that shall be their only work. But in these same things lighter parts will be given to women than men because of the weakness of their sex. And the man who laughs at naked women, exercising for the greatest good, plucks an unripe fruit of wisdom from his laughter; he apparently does not know what he laughs at or what he is doing. For it is and will be the best thing ever said, that the useful is beautiful and the harmful is ugly."

"Assuredly so."

∞

Book VII
The Allegory of the Cave

"Next, then," I said, "take the following parable of educa- 1 tion and ignorance as a picture of the condition of our nature. Imagine mankind as dwelling in an underground cave with a long entrance open to the light across the whole width of the cave; in this they have been from childhood, with necks and legs fettered, so they have to stay where they are. They cannot move their heads round because of the fetters, and they can only look forward, but light comes to them from fire burning behind them higher up at a distance. Between the fire and the prisoners is a road above their level, and along it imagine a low wall has been built, as puppet showmen have screens in front of their people over which they work their puppets."

"I see," he said.

"See, then, bearers carrying along this wall all sorts of articles which they hold projecting above the wall, statues of men and other living things, made of stone or wood and all kinds of stuff, some of the bearers speaking and some silent, as you might expect."

"What a remarkable image," he said, "and what remarkable prisoners!"

"Just like ourselves," I said. "For, first of all, tell me 5 this: What do you think such people would have seen of themselves and each other except their shadows, which the fire cast on the opposite wall of the cave?"

"I don't see how they could see anything else," said he, "if they were compelled to keep their heads unmoving all their lives!"

"Very well, what of the things being carried along? Would not this be the same?"

"Of course it would."

"Suppose the prisoners were able to talk together, don't you think that when they named the shadows which they saw passing they would believe they were naming things?"

"Necessarily." 10

"Then if their prison had an echo from the opposite wall, whenever one of the passing bearers uttered a sound, would they not suppose that the passing shadow must be making the sound? Don't you think so?"

"Indeed I do," he said.

"If so," said I, "such persons would certainly believe that there were no realities except those shadows of handmade things."

"So it must be," said he.

"Now consider," said I, "what their release would be 15 like, and their cure from these fetters and their folly; let us imagine whether it might naturally be something like this. One might be released, and compelled suddenly to stand up and turn his neck round, and to walk and look towards the firelight; all this would hurt him, and he would be too much dazzled to see distinctly those things whose shadows he had seen before. What do you think he would say, if someone told him that what he saw before was foolery, but now he saw more rightly, being a bit nearer reality and turned towards what was a little more real? What if he were shown each of the passing things, and compelled by questions to answer what each one was? Don't you think he would be puzzled, and believe what he saw before was more true than what was shown to him now?"

"Far more," he said.

"Then suppose he were compelled to look towards the real light, it would hurt his eyes, and he would escape by turning them away to the things which he was able to look at, and these he would believe to be clearer than what was being shown to him."

"Just so," said he.

"Suppose, now," said I, "that someone should drag him thence by force, up the rough ascent, the steep way up, and never stop until he could drag him out into the light of the sun, would he not be distressed and furious at being dragged; and when he came into the light, the brilliance would fill his eyes and he would not be able to see even one of the things now called real?"

"That he would not," said he, "all of a sudden." 20

"He would have to get used to it, surely, I think, if he is to see the things above. First he would most easily look at shadows, after that images of mankind and the rest in water, lastly the things themselves. After this he would find it easier to survey by night the heavens themselves and all that is in them, gazing at the light of the stars and moon, rather than by day the sun and the sun's light."

"Of course."

"Last of all, I suppose, the sun; he could look on the sun itself by itself in its own place, and see what it is like, not reflections of it in water or as it appears in some alien setting."

"Necessarily," said he.

"And only after all this he might reason about it, how 25 this is he who provides seasons and years, and is set over all there is in the visible region, and he is in a manner the cause of all things which they saw."

"Yes, it is clear," said he, "that after all that, he would come to this last."

"Very good. Let him be reminded of his first habitation, and what was wisdom in that place, and of his fellow prisoners there; don't you think he would bless himself for the change, and pity them?"

"Yes, indeed."

"And if there were honours and praises among them and prizes for the one who saw the passing things most sharply and remembered best which of them used to come before and which after and which together, and from these was best able to prophesy accordingly what was going to come—do you believe he would set his desire on that, and envy those who were honoured men or potentates among them? Would he not feel as Homer says, and heartily desire rather to be serf of some landless man on earth and to endure anything in the world, rather than to opine as they did and to live in that way?"

"Yes, indeed," said he, "he would rather accept any- 30 thing than live like that."

"Then again," I said, "just consider, if such a one should go down again and sit on his old seat, would he not get his eyes full of darkness coming in suddenly out of the sun?"

"Very much so," said he.

"And if he should have to compete with those who had been always prisoners, by laying down the law about those shadows while he was blinking before his eyes were settled down—and it would take a good long time to get used to things—wouldn't they all laugh at him and say he had spoiled his eyesight by going up there, and it was not worth-while so much as to try to go up? And would they not kill anyone who tried to release them and take them up, if they could somehow lay hands on him and kill him?"

"That they would!" said he.

"Then we must apply this image, my dear Glaucon," 35 said I, "to all we have been saying. The world of our sight is like the habitation in prison, the firelight there to the sunlight here, the ascent and the view of the upper world is the rising of the soul into the world of mind; put it so and you will not be far from my own surmise, since that is what you want to hear; but God knows if it is really true. At least, what appears to me is, that in the world of the known, last of all, is the idea of the good, and with what toil to be seen! And seen, this must be inferred to be the cause of all right and beautiful things for all, which gives birth to light and the king of light in the world of sight, and, in the world of mind, herself the queen produces truth and reason; and she must be seen by one who is to act with reason publicly or privately."

PLATO

Selection from *Phaedo*

Reading the Selection

Plato's dialogue entitled *Phaedo* lovingly recounts the last hours of Socrates: Having been convicted of impiety against the gods and corrupting Athenian youth, Socrates awaits execution. During these hours, he is shown talking with family and friends, drinking hemlock, as required by law, and quietly dying—an exemplary death. This setting enabled Plato to discourse on life's meaning, death's role in shaping life, and his belief in the soul's immortality.

Since Plato was not present, he made Phaedo, who was there, the narrator of these events. Phaedo first names those present and then describes their anguished reactions to Socrates' impending death, thus setting the stage for a discussion on immortality. The center of attention, Socrates keeps the discussion moving by various means to illustrate his views. For example, early on, he takes the position that the true philosopher (from Greek, "lover of wisdom") does not fear death, for in a sense he is always seeking death. Elaborating this idea, he points out that the soul is imprisoned inside the body by the need for drink, sex, and sleep, with the result that it is kept from its true aim, the gaining of knowledge. Thus, when death releases the soul from its prison, it is free to roam among the ideas that it dimly perceived while alive.

Not merely a philosophical discussion, the *Phaedo* resembles a stage drama, through such dramatically realistic details as the jailer's comings and goings and Socrates' friends referring to the passage of time. These details, while heightening the tension in the dialogue, also build toward one of the most poignant and memorable death scenes ever written in Western literature.

[Socrates is speaking.] "Now then, I want to give the proof at once, to you as my judges, why I think it likely that one who has spent his life in philosophy should be confident when he is going to die, and have good hopes that he will win the greatest blessings in the next world when he has ended: so Simmias and Cebes my judges, I will try to show how this could be true.

"The fact is, those who tackle philosophy aright are simply and solely practising dying, practising death, all the time, but nobody sees it. If this is true, then it would surely be unreasonable that they should earnestly do this and nothing else all their lives, yet when death comes they should object to what they had been so long earnestly practising."

Simmias laughed at this, and said, "I don't feel like laughing just now, Socrates, but you have made me laugh. I think the many if they heard that would say, 'That's a good one for the philosophers!' And other people in my city would heartily agree that philosophers are really suffering from a wish to die, and now they have found them out, that they richly deserve it!"

"That would be true, Simmias," said Socrates, "except the words 'found out.' For they have not found out in what sense the real philosophers wish to die and deserve to die, and what kind of death it is. Let us say good-bye to them," he went on, "and ask ourselves: Do we think there is such a thing as death?"

"Certainly," Simmias put in.

"Is it anything more than the separation of the soul from the body?" said Socrates. "Death is, that the body separates from the soul, and remains by itself apart from the soul, and the soul, separated from the body, exists by itself apart from the body. Is death anything but that?"

"No," he said, "that is what death is."

"Then consider, my good friend, if you agree with me here, for I think this is the best way to understand the question we are examining. Do you think it the part of a philosopher to be earnestly concerned with what are called pleasures, such as these—eating and drinking, for example?"

"Not at all," said Simmias.

"The pleasures of love, then?"

"Oh no."

"Well, do you suppose a man like that regards the other bodily indulgences as precious? Getting fine clothes and shoes and other bodily adornments—ought he to price them high or low, beyond whatever share of them it is absolutely necessary to have?"

"Low, I think," he said, "if he is a true philosopher."

"Then in general," he said, "do you think that such a man's concern is not for the body, but as far as he can he stands aloof from that and turns towards the soul?"

"I do."   15

"Then firstly, is it not clear that in such things the philosopher as much as possible sets free the soul from communion with the body, more than other men?"

"So it appears."

"And I suppose, Simmias, it must seem to most men that he who has no pleasure in such things and takes no share in them does not deserve to live, but he is getting pretty close to death if he does not care about pleasures which he has by means of the body."

"Quite true, indeed."

"Well then, what about the actual getting of wisdom?   20
Is the body in the way or not, if a man takes it with him as companion in the search? I mean, for example, is there any truth for men in their sight and hearing? Or as poets are forever dinning into our ears, do we hear nothing and see nothing exactly? Yet if these of our bodily senses are not exact and clear, the others will hardly be, for they are all inferior to these, don't you think so?"

"Certainly," he said.

"Then," said he, "when does the soul get hold of the truth? For whenever the soul tries to examine anything in company with the body, it is plain that it is deceived by it."

"Quite true."

"Then is it not clear that in reasoning, if anywhere, something of the realities becomes visible to it?"

"Yes."   25

"And I suppose it reasons best when none of these senses disturbs it, hearing or sight, or pain, or pleasure indeed, but when it is completely by itself and says goodbye to the body, and so far as possible has no dealings with it, when it reaches out and grasps that which really is."

"That is true."

"And is it not then that the philosopher's soul chiefly holds the body cheap and escapes from it, while it seeks to be by itself?"

"So it seems."

"Let us pass on, Simmias. Do we say there is such a   30
thing as justice by itself, or not?"

"We do say so, certainly!"

"Such a thing as the good and beautiful?"

"Of course!"

"And did you ever see one of them with your eyes?"

"Never," said he.   35

"By any other sense of those the body has did you ever grasp them? I mean all such things, greatness, health, strength, in short everything that really is the nature of things whatever they are: Is it through the body that the real truth is perceived? Or is this better—whoever of us prepares himself most completely and most exactly to comprehend each thing which he examines would come nearest to knowing each one?"

"Certainly."

"And would he do that most purely who should approach each with his intelligence alone, not adding sight to intelligence, or dragging in any other sense along with reasoning, but using the intelligence uncontaminated alone by itself, while he tries to hunt out each essence uncontaminated, keeping clear of eyes and ears and, one might say, of the whole body, because he thinks the body disturbs him and hinders the soul from getting possession of truth and wisdom when body and soul are companions —is not this the man, Simmias, if anyone, who will hit reality?"

"Nothing could be more true, Socrates," said Simmias.

"Then from all this," said Socrates, "genuine philoso-   40
phers must come to some such opinion as follows, so as to make to one another statements such as these: 'A sort of direct path, so to speak, seems to take us to the conclusion that so long as we have the body with us in our enquiry, and our soul is mixed up with so great an evil, we shall never attain sufficiently what we desire, and that, we say, is the truth. For the body provides thousands of busy distractions because of its necessary food; besides, if diseases fall upon us, they hinder us from the pursuit of the real. With loves and desires and fears and all kinds of fancies and much rubbish, it infects us, and really and truly makes us, as they say, unable to think one little bit about anything at any time. Indeed, wars and factions and battles all come from the body and its desires, and from nothing else. For the desire of getting wealth causes all wars, and we are compelled to desire wealth by the body, being slaves to its culture; therefore we have no leisure for philosophy, from all these reasons. Chief of all is that if we do have some leisure, and turn away from the body to speculate on something, in our searches it is everywhere interfering, it causes confusion and disturbance, and dazzles us so that it will not let us see the truth; so in fact we see that if we are ever to know anything purely we must get rid of it, and examine the real things by the soul alone; and then, it seems, after we are dead, as the reasoning shows, not while we live, we shall possess that which we desire, lovers of which we say we are, namely wisdom. For if it is impossible in company with the body to know anything purely, one thing of two follows: either knowledge is possible nowhere, or only after death; for then alone the soul will be quite by itself apart from the body, but not before. And while we are alive, we shall be nearest to knowing, as it seems, if as far as possible we have no commerce or communion with the body which is not absolutely necessary, and if we are not infected with its nature, but keep ourselves pure from it, until God himself shall set us free. And so, pure and rid of the body's foolishness, we shall probably be in the company of those like ourselves, and shall know through our own selves complete incontamination, and that is perhaps the truth. But for the impure to grasp the pure is not, it seems, allowed.' So we must think, Simmias, and so we must say to one another, all who are rightly lovers of learning; don't you agree?"

"Assuredly, Socrates."

"Then," said Socrates, "if this is true, my comrade, there is great hope that when I arrive where I am travelling, there if anywhere I shall sufficiently possess that for which all our study has been pursued in this past life. So the journey which has been commanded for me is made with good hope, and the same for any other man who believes he has got his mind purified, as I may call it."

"Certainly," replied Simmias.

"And is not purification really that which has been mentioned so often in our discussion, to separate as far as possible the soul from the body, and to accustom it to collect itself together out of the body in every part, and to dwell alone by itself as far as it can, both at this present and in the future, being freed from the body as if from a prison?"

"By all means," said he.

"Then is not this called death—a freeing and separation of soul from body?"

"Not a doubt of that," said he.

"But to set it free, as we say, is the chief endeavour of those who rightly love wisdom, nay of those alone, and the very care and practice of the philosophers is nothing but the freeing and separation of soul from body, don't you think so?"

"It appears to be so."

"Then, as I said at first, it would be absurd for a man preparing himself in his life to be as near as possible to death, so to live, and then when death came, to object?"

"Of course."

"Then in fact, Simmias," he said, "those who rightly love wisdom are practising dying, and death to them is the least terrible thing in the world. Look at it in this way: If they are everywhere at enmity with the body, and desire the soul to be alone by itself, and if, when this very thing happens, they shall fear and object—would not that be wholly unreasonable? Should they not willingly go to a place where there is good hope of finding what they were in love with all through life (and they loved wisdom), and of ridding themselves of the companion which they hated? When human favourites and wives and sons have died, many have been willing to go down to the grave, drawn by the hope of seeing there those they used to desire, and of being with them; but one who is really in love with wisdom and holds firm to this same hope, that he will find it in the grave, and nowhere else worth speaking of—will he then fret at dying and not go thither rejoicing? We must surely think, my comrade, that he will go rejoicing, if he is really a philosopher; he will surely believe that he will find wisdom in its purity there and there alone. If this is true, would it not be most unreasonable, as I said just now, if such a one feared death?"

"Unreasonable, I do declare," said he. . . .

With these words, he got up and retired into another room for the bath, and Criton went after him, telling us to wait. So we waited discussing and talking together about what had been said, or sometimes speaking of the great misfortune which had be fallen us, for we felt really as if we had lost a father and had to spend the rest of our lives as orphans. When he had bathed, and his children had been brought to see him—for he had two little sons, and one big—and when the women of his family had come, he

talked to them before Criton and gave what instructions he wished. Then he asked the women and children to go, and came back to us. It was now near sunset, for he had spent a long time within. He came and sat down after his bath, and he had not talked long after this when the servant of the Eleven came in, and standing by him said, "O Socrates! I have not to complain of you as I do of others, that they are angry with me, and curse me, because I bring them word to drink their potion, which my officers make me do! But I have always found you in this time most generous and gentle, and the best man who ever came here. And now too, I know well you are not angry with me, for you know who are responsible, and you keep it for them. Now you know what I came to tell you, so farewell, and try to bear as well as you can what can't be helped."

Then he turned and was going out, with tears running down his cheeks. And Socrates looked up at him and said, "Farewell to you also, I will do so." Then, at the same time turning to us, "What a nice fellow!" he said. "All the time he has been coming and talking to me, a real good sort, and now how generously he sheds tears for me! Come along, Criton, let's obey him. Someone bring the potion, if the stuff has been ground; if not, let the fellow grind it."

Then Criton said, "But Socrates, I think the sun is still over the hills, it has not set yet. Yes, and I know of others who, having been told to drink the poison, have done it very late; they had dinner first and a good one, and some enjoyed the company of any they wanted. Please don't be in a hurry, there is time to spare."

But Socrates said, "Those you speak of have very good reason for doing that, for they think they will gain by doing it; and I have good reasons why I won't do it. For I think I shall gain nothing by drinking a little later, only that I shall think myself a fool for clinging to life and sparing when the cask's empty. Come along," he said, "do what I tell you, if you please."

And Criton, hearing this, nodded to the boy who stood near. The boy went out, and after spending a long time, came in with the man who was to give the poison carrying it ground ready in a cup. Socrates caught sight of the man and said, "Here, my good man, you know about these things; what must I do?"

"Just drink it," he said, "and walk about till your legs get heavy, then lie down. In that way the drug will act of itself."

At the same time, he held out the cup to Socrates, and he took it quite cheerfully, Echecrates, not a tremble, not a change in colour or looks; but looking full at the man under his brows, as he used to do, he asked him, "What do you say about this drink? What of a libation to someone? Is that allowed, or not?"

He said, "We only grind so much as we think enough for a moderate potion."

"I understand," he said, "but at least, I suppose, it is allowed to offer a prayer to the gods and that must be done, for good luck in the migration from here to there. Then that is my prayer, and so may it be!"

With these words he put the cup to his lips and, quite easy and contented, drank it up. So far most of us had been able to hold back our tears pretty well; but when we saw him begin drinking and end drinking, we could no longer. I burst into a flood of tears for all I could do, so I wrapped up my face and cried myself out; not for him indeed, but for my own misfortune in losing such a man and such a comrade. Criton had got up and gone out even before I did, for he could not hold the tears in. Apollodoros had never ceased weeping all this time, and now he burst out into loud sobs, and by his weeping and lamentations completely broke down every man there except Socrates himself. He only said, "What a scene! You amaze me. That's just why I sent the women away, to keep them from making a scene like this. I've heard that one ought to make an end in decent silence. Quiet yourselves and endure."

When we heard him we felt ashamed and restrained our tears. He walked about, and when he said that his legs were feeling heavy, he lay down on his back, as the man told him to do; at the same time the one who gave him the potion felt him, and after a while examined his feet and legs; then pinching a foot hard, he asked if he felt anything; he said no. After this, again, he pressed the shins; and, moving up like this, he showed us that he was growing cold and stiff. Again he felt him, and told us that when

it came to his heart, he would be gone. Already the cold had come nearly as far as the abdomen, when Socrates threw off the covering from his face—for he had covered it over—and said, the last words he uttered, "Criton," he said, "we owe a cock to Asclepios[1]; pay it without fail."

"That indeed shall be done," said Criton. "Have you anything more to say?"

When Criton had asked this, Socrates gave no further answer, but after a little time, he stirred, and the man uncovered him, and his eyes were still. Criton, seeing this, closed the mouth and eyelids.

This was the end of our comrade, Echecrates, a man, as we would say, of all then living we had ever met, the noblest and the wisest and most just.

---

[1] **Asclepios** A legendary Greek physician who became the god of healing. His temple was at Epidaurus in Greece. Serpents and cocks were sacred to him. Individuals would make an offering to the cock in the hope that the person would awake in the morning, to the cock's crowing, having survived the night. Socrates is probably referring to this ritual, but with his usual wit and as a paradox—that is, the thank-offering is to be made because death is the cure for life.

ARISTOTLE

Selections from *Poetics* and *Politics*

In many ways Aristotle (384–322 B.C.) has had a more far-reaching effect on Western thought than Plato (see *The Republic, Phaedo*). Aristotle, for example, wrote on many topics that Plato never addressed, notably in the natural and physical sciences; thus, Aristotle was considered the greater authority. Western thinkers have also tended to favor Aristotle's empirical approach, with its reliance on the senses, rather than Plato's deductive method based on abstract reasoning and mathematics. Most of all, Westerners have preferred Aristotle's focus on what exists to Plato's imaginings about an ideal world, beyond the here and now.

Reading the Selections

In the *Poetics*—the first work of literary criticism that we know of and thus the one that established this genre—Aristotle addressed the topic of "poetry." At the time, poetry included tragedy, comedy, and the epic. Over the centuries Aristotle's section on comedy disappeared, and the part discussing the epic grew so mutilated that it is generally ignored today. The result is that the portion dealing with tragedy is all that effectively survives from Aristotle's original essay.

The section on tragedy shows Aristotle's empirical method in action, as he tries to define the rules to guide an author working in this genre. Typical of his method, he gathered scripts of existing tragedies on which to base his theory. In particular, he relied on Sophocles' *Oedipus the King,* which he claimed as the most perfect drama ever written. From his studies of playscripts, he isolated the six cardinal features of tragedy—plot, character, diction, thought, spectacle, and song—gave definitions of each, and showed the part each played in making tragedy work. Aristotle's terms and definitions are still used by modern literary critics. This treatise itself has had tremendous influence on Western literature as a whole and in particular on seventeenth-century French classical drama.

Aristotle was at his most original when he claimed that tragedy was cathartic ("purgative"). He proposed that tragedy's function was to arouse fear and pity in the spectators, thereby purging them of negative feelings and restoring them to psychic wholeness. Though under fire from today's critics, who believe that violence breeds violence, Aristotle's claim for tragedy as catharsis has had tremendous significance for Western drama.

In the *Politics* Aristotle discusses what constitutes good and bad governments, what are the purposes of government, and how to achieve the best forms of government. As in the *Poetics* and his other works, he takes the empirical approach. That is, he examines political systems as they exist or operate, not as they might be imagined in a utopian state. Aristotle believes that since a government is no better than its citizens, the training of those who will participate in the government is essential to the well-being of the political system. Citizenship, therefore, must be taught and practiced by those who aspire to rule. As in his *Ethics,* so in his *Politics,* humans learn what is virtue—or the good—not by seeking knowledge or debating terms but by practicing virtue. The state has to train its youth to be worthwhile citizens so that they can create a government that is based on justice and equality and that will bring the greatest happiness to the largest number of its inhabitants.

The selection from Book I of the *Politics* begins with some general observations on the relationships between those who rule and those who are ruled. He then turns to the basic units of any society, beginning with the family and ending with the state. The state becomes a necessity because "man," who by nature is a political animal, cannot live alone. Nor can the state and the individual be separated since they are interrelated and dependent on each other. From this discussion of the most basic units in society, Aristotle proceeds to examine all aspects of the political system and proposes practical ways to make it work.

∽

Poetics
A Description of Tragedy

.   .   .

Tragedy . . . , is a representation of an action that is worth serious attention, complete in itself, and of some amplitude; in language enriched by a variety of artistic devices appropriate to the several parts of the play; presented in the form of action, not narration; by means of pity and fear bringing about the purgation of such emotions. By language that is enriched I refer to language possessing rhythm, and music or song; and by artistic devices appropriate to the several parts I mean that some are produced by the medium of verse alone, and others again with the help of song.

Now since the representation is carried out by men performing the actions, it follows, in the first place, that spectacle is an essential part of tragedy, and secondly that there must be song and diction, these being the medium of representation. By diction I mean here the arrangement of the verses; song is a term whose sense is obvious to everyone.

In tragedy it is action that is imitated, and this action is brought about by agents who necessarily display certain distinctive qualities both of character and of thought, according to which we also define the nature of the actions. Thought and character are, then, the two natural causes of actions, and it is on them that all men depend for success or failure. The representation of the action is the plot of the tragedy; for the ordered arrangement of the incidents is what I mean by plot. Character, on the other hand, is that which enables us to define the nature of the participants, and thought comes out in what they say when they are proving a point or expressing an opinion.

Necessarily, then, every tragedy has six constituents, which will determine its quality. They are plot, character, diction, thought, spectacle, and song. Of these, two represent the media in which the action is represented, one involves the manner of representation, and three are connected with the objects of the representation; beyond them nothing further is required. These, it may be said, are the dramatic elements that have been used by practically all playwrights; for all plays alike possess spectacle, character, plot, diction, song, and thought.

Of these elements the most important is the plot, the ordering of the incidents; for tragedy is a representation, not of men, but of action and life, of happiness and unhappiness—and happiness and unhappiness are bound up with action. The purpose of living is an end which is a kind of activity, not a quality; it is their characters, indeed, that make men what they are, but it is by reason of their actions that they are happy or the reverse. Tragedies are not performed, therefore, in order to represent character, although character is involved for the sake of the action. Thus the incidents and the plot are the end aimed at in tragedy, and as always, the end is everything. Furthermore, there could not be a tragedy without action, but there could be without character; indeed the tragedies of most of our recent playwrights fail to present character, and the same might be said of many playwrights of other periods. A similar contrast could be drawn between Zeuxis and Polygnotus as painters, for Polygnotus represents character well, whereas Zeuxis is not concerned with it in his painting.[1] Again, if someone writes a series of speeches expressive of character, and well composed as far as thought and diction are concerned, he will still not achieve the proper effect of tragedy; this will be done much better by a tragedy which is less successful in its use of these elements, but which has a plot giving an ordered combination of incidents. Another point to note is that the two most important means by which tragedy plays on our feelings, that is, "reversals" and "recognitions," are both constituents of the plot. A further proof is that beginners can achieve accuracy in diction and the portrayal of character before they can construct a plot out of the incidents, and this could be said of almost all the earliest dramatic poets.

---

[1] **Zeuxis and Polygnotus** Two famous artists who lived in the fifth century. Their frescoes and paintings were greatly admired and influenced other artists, but none of their works has survived.

The plot, then, is the first essential of tragedy, its lifeblood, so to speak, and character takes the second place. It is much the same in painting; for if an artist were to daub his canvas with the most beautiful colours laid on at random, he would not give the same pleasure as he would by drawing a recognizable portrait in black and white. Tragedy is the representation of an action, and it is chiefly on account of the action that it is also a representation of persons.

The third property of tragedy is thought. This is the ability to say what is possible and appropriate in any given circumstances; it is what, in the speeches in the play, is related to the arts of politics and rhetoric. The older dramatic poets made their characters talk like statesmen, whereas those of today make them talk like rhetoricians. Character is that which reveals personal choice, the kinds of thing a man chooses or rejects when that is not obvious. Thus there is no revelation of character in speeches in which the speaker shows no preferences or aversions whatever. Thought, on the other hand, is present in speeches where something is being shown to be true or untrue, or where some general opinions is being expressed.

Fourth comes the diction of the speeches. By diction I mean, as I have already explained, the expressive use of words, and this has the same force in verse and in prose.

Of the remaining elements, the music is the most important of the pleasurable additions to the play. Spectacle, or stage-effect, is an attraction, of course, but it has the least to do with the playwright's craft or with the art of poetry. For the power of tragedy is independent both of performance and of actors, and besides, the production of spectacular effects is more the province of the property-man than of the playwright.

∽

Reversal, Discovery, and Calamity

As has already been noted, a reversal is a change from one state of affairs to its opposite, one which conforms, as I have said, to probability or necessity. In *Oedipus*,[2] for example, the Messenger who came to cheer Oedipus and relieve him of his fear about his mother did the very opposite by revealing to him who he was. In the *Lynceus*,[3] again, Lynceus is being led off to execution, followed by Danaus who is to kill him, when, as a result of events that occurred earlier, it comes about that he is saved and it is Danaus who is put to death.

---

[2] **Oedipus** Sophocles' play, *Oedipus Rex*, which Aristotle admired as an example of how a play should be constructed.
[3] **Lynceus** A play by Theodectes, who was a playwright and friend of Aristotle. Lynceus was a mythological figure who was king of Argos. Aristotle's reference is to an eposide in Lycneus's life when he is about to be killed and the reversal takes place. Danaus, his father-in-law, by a quick turn of events, is the victim. Theodectes probably invented this incident.

As the word itself indicates, a discovery is a change from ignorance to knowledge, and it leads either to love or to hatred between persons destined for good or ill fortune. The most effective form of discovery is that which is accompanied by reversals, like the one in *Oedipus*. There are of course other forms of discovery, for what I have described may happen in relation to inanimate and trifling objects, and moreover it is possible to discover whether a person has done something or not. But the form of discovery most essentially related to the plot and action of the play is the one described above, for a discovery of this kind in combination with a reversal will carry with it either pity or fear, and it is such actions as these that, according to my definition, tragedy represents; and further, such a combination is likely to lead to a happy or an unhappy ending.

As it is persons who are involved in the discovery, it may be that only one person's identity is revealed to another, that of the second being already known. Sometimes, however, a natural recognition of two parties is necessary, as for example, when the identity of Iphigenia was made known to Orestes by the sending of the letter, and a second discovery was required to make him known to Iphigenia.[4]

Two elements of plot, then, reversal and discovery, turn upon such incidents as these. A third is suffering, or calamity. Of these three, reversal and discovery have already been defined. A calamity is an action of a destructive or painful nature, such as death openly represented, excessive suffering, wounding, and the like. . . .

---

[4] **Orestes and Iphigenia** Brother and sister who appeared in several plays by Greek playwrights. Aristotle is referring to a scene from Euripides' *Iphigenia in Tauris*.

∞

Tragic Action

Following upon the points I have already made, I must go on to say what is to be aimed at and what guarded against in the construction of plots, and what are the sources of the tragic effect.

We saw that the structure of tragedy at its best should be complex, not simple, and that it should represent actions capable of awakening fear and pity—for this is a characteristic function of representations of this type. It follows in the first place that good men should not be shown passing from prosperity to misery, for this does not inspire fear or pity, it merely disgusts us. Nor should evil men be shown progressing from misery to prosperity. This is the most untragic of all plots, for it has none of the requisites of tragedy; it does not appeal to our humanity, or awaken pity or fear in us. Nor again should an utterly worthless man be seen falling from prosperity into misery. Such a course might indeed play upon our humane feelings, but it would not arouse either pity or fear; for our pity is awakened by undeserved misfortune, and our fear by that of someone just like ourselves—pity for the undeserving sufferer and fear for the man like ourselves—so that the situation in question would have nothing in it either pitiful or fearful.

There remains a mean between these extremes. This is the sort of man who is not conspicuous for virtue and justice, and whose fall into misery is not due to vice and depravity, but rather to some error, a man who enjoys prosperity and a high reputation, like Oedipus and Thyestes[5] and other famous members of families like theirs.

Inevitably, then, the well-conceived plot will have a single interest, and not, as some say, a double. The change in fortune will be, not from misery to prosperity, but the reverse, from prosperity to misery, and it will be due, not to depravity, but to some great error either in such a man as I have described or in one better than this, but not worse. This is borne out by existing practice. For at first the poets treated any stories that came to hand, but nowadays the best tragedies are written about a handful of families, those of Alcmaeon, for example, and Oedipus and Orestes and Meleager and Thyestes and Telephus, and others whom it has befallen to suffer or inflict terrible experiences.[6]

---

[5] **Oedipus and Thyestes** Both were powerful rulers who then committed horrendous crimes that haunted them for the rest of their lives and affected their own children.
[6] **Alcmaeon, Oedipus, Orestes, Meleager, Thyestes, Telephus** According to various Greek myths, each person killed a member or several members of his family.

∞

Fear and Pity

Fear and pity may be excited by means of spectacle; but they can also take their rise from the very structure of the action, which is the preferable method and the mark of a better dramatic poet. For the plot should be so ordered that even without seeing it performed anyone merely hearing what is afoot will shudder with fear and pity as a result of what is happening—as indeed would be the experience of anyone hearing the story of Oedipus. To produce this effect by means of stage-spectacle is less artistic, and requires the cooperation of the producer. Those who employ spectacle to produce an effect, not of fear, but of something merely monstrous, have nothing to do with tragedy, for not every kind of pleasure should be demanded of tragedy, but only that which is proper to it; and since the dramatic poet has by means of his representation to produce the tragic pleasure that is associated with pity and fear, it is obvious that this effect is bound up with the events of the plot.

Let us now consider what kinds of incident are to be regarded as fearful or pitiable. Deeds that fit this description must of course involve people who are either friends to one another, or enemies, or neither. Now if a man injures his enemy, there is nothing pitiable either in his act or in his intention, except in so far as suffering is inflicted; nor is there if they are indifferent to each other. But when the sufferings involve those who are near and dear to one another, when for example brother kills brother, son father, mother son, or son mother, or if such a deed is contemplated, or something else of the kind is actually done, then we have a situation of the kind to be aimed at. Thus it will not do to tamper with the traditional stories, the murder of Clytemnestra by Orestes, for instance, and that of Eriphyle by Alcmaeon[7]; on the other hand, the poet must use his imagination and handle the traditional material effectively.

I must explain more clearly what I mean by "effectively." The deed may be done by characters acting consciously and in full knowledge of the facts, as was the way of the early dramatic poets, when for instance Euripides made Medea kill her children. Or they may do it without realizing the horror of the deed until later, when they discover the truth; this is what Sophocles did with Oedipus. Here indeed the relevant incident occurs outside the action of the play; but it may be a part of the tragedy, as with Alcmaeon in Astydamas's play, or Telegonus in *The Wounded Odysseus*.[8] A third alternative is for someone who is about to do a terrible deed in ignorance of the relationship to discover the truth before he does it. These are

the only possibilities, for the deed must either be done or not done, and by someone either with or without knowledge of the facts.

The least acceptable of these alternatives is when someone in possession of the facts is on the point of acting but fails to do so, for this merely shocks us, and, since no suffering is involved, it is not tragic. Hence nobody is allowed to behave like this, or only seldom, as when Haemon fails to kill Creon in the *Antigone*.[9] Next in order of effectiveness is when the deed is actually done, and here it is better that the character should act in ignorance and only learn the truth afterwards, for there is nothing in this to outrage our feelings, and the revelation comes as a surprise. However, the best method is the last, when, for example, in the *Cresphontes* Merope intends to kill her son, but recognizes him and does not do so; or when the same thing happens with brother and sister in *Iphigenia in Tauris*; or when, in the *Helle*,[10] the son recognizes his mother when he is just about to betray her.

This then is the reason why, as I said before, our tragedies keep to a few families. For in their search for dramatic material it was by chance rather than by technical knowledge that the poets discovered how to gain tragic effects in their plots. And they are still obliged to have recourse to those families in which sufferings of the kind I have described have been experienced.

I have said enough now about the arrangement of the incidents in a tragedy and the type of plot it ought to have.

---

[7] **Clytemnestra and Orestes; Eriphyle and Alcmaeon** Orestes and Alcmaeon murdered their respective mothers, Clytemnestra and Eriphyle, to revenge the killings of their fathers by their mothers.
[8] **Astydamas, Telegonus** Astydamas was a fourth-century Athenian playwright who wrote a play about Alcmaeon killing his mother. Telegonus, the illegitimate son of Odysseus, accidentally killed his father in Sophocles' lost play, *The Wounded Odysseus*.

---

[9] **Haemon and Creon** Haemon was Creon's son and engaged to marry Antigone, the daughter of Oedipus and for whom Sophocles named his play.
[10] *Cresphontes, Iphigenia in Tauris, Helle* *Cresphontes* is one of Euripides' lost plays; *Iphigenia in Tauris* is one of Euripides' extant plays; *Helle* is the title of an unknown tragedy.

The Characters of Tragedy

In characterization there are four things to aim at. First and foremost, the characters should be good. Now character will be displayed, as I have pointed out, if some preference is revealed in speech or action, and if it is a preference for what is good the character will be good. There can be goodness in every class of person; for instance, a woman or a slave may be good, though the one is possibly an inferior being and the other in general an insignificant one.

In the second place the portrayal should be appropriate. For example, a character may possess manly qualities, but it is not appropriate that a female character should be given manliness or cleverness.

Thirdly, the characters should be lifelike. This is not the same thing as making them good, or appropriate in the sense in which I have used the word.

And fourthly, they should be consistent. Even if the person who is being represented is inconsistent, and this trait is the basis of his character, he must nevertheless be portrayed as consistently inconsistent.

As an example of unnecessary badness of character, there is Menelaus in the *Orestes*. The character who behaves in an unsuitable and inappropriate way is exemplified in Odysseus' lament in the *Scylla*,[11] and in Melanippe's speech.[12] An inconsistent character is shown in

---

[11] **Scylla** A dithyramb written by Timotheus, a fourth-century poet. The dithyramb is a type of lyric poem, often performed by large choruses. Aristotle believes that Odysseus overreacted when Scylla, the sea monster, swallowed his companions. Timotheus was inspired by one of Odysseus's adventures from the *Odyssey*.
[12] **Melanippe** A mythological figure and the subject of one of Euripides' lost plays, *Melanippe the Wise*.

Iphigenia at Aulis, for Iphigenia as a suppliant is quite unlike what she is later.

As in the arrangement of the incidents, so too in characterization one must always bear in mind what will be either necessary or probable; in other words, it should be necessary or probable that such and such a person should say or do such and such a thing, and similarly that this particular incident should follow on that.

Furthermore, it is obvious that the unravelling of the plot should arise from the circumstances of the plot itself, and not be brought about *ex machina,* as is done in the *Medea* and in the episode of the embarkation in the *Iliad.* The *deus ex machina*[13] should be used only for matters outside the play proper, either for things that happened before it and that cannot be known by the human characters, or for things that are yet to come and that require to be foretold prophetically—for we allow to the gods the

power to see all things. However, there should be nothing inexplicable about what happens, or if there must be, it should be kept outside the tragedy, as is done in Sophocles's *Oedipus.*

Since tragedy is a representation of people who are better than average, we must copy the good portrait-painters. These, while reproducing the distinctive appearance of their sitters and making likenesses, paint them better-looking than they are. In the same way the poet, in portraying men who are hot-tempered, or phlegmatic, or who have other defects of character, must bring out these qualities in them, and at the same time show them as decent people, as Agathon[14] and Homer have portrayed Achilles.

These points must be carefully watched, as too must those means used to appeal to the eye, which are necessarily dependent on the poet's art; for here too it is often possible to make mistakes. However, enough has been said about these matters in my published works.

---

[13] *deus ex machina* Literally, "a god from a machine." Can be a person or a thing suddenly introduced in a play to provide a contrived solution to a seemingly insoluble problem.

---

[14] **Agathon** Athenian playwright and poet active in the later part of the fifth century.

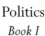

Politics
Book I

Every state is a community of some kind, and every community is established with a view to some good; for mankind always act in order to obtain that which they think good. But, if all communities aim at some good, the state or political community, which is the highest of all, and which embraces all the rest, aims at good in a greater degree than any other, and at the highest good.

Some people think that the qualifications of a statesman, king, householder, and master are the same, and that they differ, not in kind, but only in the number of their subjects. For example, the ruler over a few is called a master; over more, the manager of a household; over a still larger number, a statesman or king, as if there were no difference between a great household and a small state. The distinction which is made between the king and the statesman is as follows: When the government is personal, the ruler is a king; when, according to the rules of the political science, the citizens rule and are ruled in turn, then he is called a statesman.

But all this is a mistake; for governments differ in kind, as will be evident to anyone who considers the matter according to the method which has hitherto guided us. As in other departments of science, so in politics, the compound should always be resolved into the simple elements or least parts of the whole. We must therefore look at the elements of which the state is composed, in order that we may see in what the different kinds of rule differ from one another, and whether any scientific result can be attained about each one of them.

He who thus considers things in their first growth and origin, whether a state or anything else, will obtain the clearest view of them. In the first place there must be a union of those who cannot exist without each other; namely, of male and female, that the race may continue (and this is a union which is formed, not of deliberate purpose, but because, in common with other animals and with plants, mankind have a natural desire to leave behind them an image of themselves), and of natural ruler and subject, that both may be preserved. For that which can foresee by the exercise of mind is by nature intended to be lord and master, and that which can with its body give effect to such foresight is a subject, and by nature a slave; hence master and slave have the same interest. Now nature has distinguished between the female and the slave. For she is not niggardly, like the smith who fashions the Delphian knife for many uses; she makes each thing for a single use, and every instrument is best made when intended for one and not for many uses. But among barbarians no distinction is made between women and slaves, because there is no natural ruler among them: they are a community of slaves, male and female. Wherefore the poets say—

"It is meet that Hellenes should rule over barbarians";

as if they thought that the barbarian and the slave were by nature one.

Out of these two relationships between man and woman, master and slave, the first thing to arise is the family, and Hesiod[1] is right when he says—

"First house and wife and an ox for the plough,"

for the ox is the poor man's slave. The family is the association established by nature for the supply of men's everyday wants, and the members of it are called by Charondas[2] "companions of the cupboard," and by Epimenides the Cretan,[3] "companions of the manger." But when several families are united, and the association aims at something more than the supply of daily needs, the first society to be formed is the village. And the most natural form of the village appears to be that of a colony from the family, composed of the children and grandchildren, who are said to be "suckled with the same milk." And this is the reason why Hellenic states were originally governed by kings; because the Hellenes were under royal rule before they came together, as the barbarians still are. Every family is ruled by the eldest, and therefore in the colonies of the family the kingly form of government prevailed because they were of the same blood. As Homer[4] says:

"Each one gives law to his children and to his wives."

For they lived dispersedly, as was the manner in ancient times. Wherefore men say that the Gods have a king, because they themselves either are or were in ancient times under the rule of a king. For they imagine, not only the forms of the Gods, but their ways of life to be like their own.

When several villages are united in a single complete community, large enough to be nearly or quite self-sufficing, the state comes into existence, originating in the bare needs of life, and continuing in existence for the sake of a good life. And therefore, if the earlier forms of society are natural, so is the state, for it is the end of them, and the nature of a thing is its end. For what each thing is when fully developed, we call its nature, whether we are speaking of a man, a horse, or a family. Besides, the final cause

---

[1] **Hesiod** Eighth-century B.C. Greek poet who wrote *Works and Days,* a collection of stories and advice on such matters as running a farm, navigating the seas, and living by moral codes.

[2] **Charondas** Sixth-century B.C. Greek lawgiver who made special laws for families.

[3] **Epimenides** Sixth-century B.C. philosopher, poet, and prophet from the island of Crete who wrote religious and poetical works. Subject of many legends.

[4] **Homer** Eighth-century B.C. poet and author of the *Iliad* and the *Odyssey.*

and end of a thing is the best, and to be self-sufficing is the end and the best.

Thence it is evident that the state is a creation of nature, and that man is by nature a political animal. And he who by nature and not by mere accident is without a state, is either a bad man or above humanity; he is like the

"Tribeless, lawless, heartless one,"

whom Homer denounces—the natural outcast is forthwith a lover of war; he may be compared to an isolated piece at draughts.

Now, that man is more of a political animal than bees or any other gregarious animals is evident. Nature, as we often say, makes nothing in vain, and man is the only animal whom she has endowed with the gift of speech. And whereas mere voice is but an indication of pleasure or pain, and is therefore found in other animals (for their nature attains to the perception of pleasure and pain and the intimation of them to one another, and no further), the power of speech is intended to set forth the expedient and inexpedient, and therefore likewise the just and the unjust. And it is a characteristic of man that he alone has any sense of good and evil, of just and unjust, and the like, and the association of living beings who have this sense makes a family and a state.

Further, the state is by nature clearly prior to the family and to the individual, since the whole is of necessity prior to the part; for example, if the whole body be destroyed, there will be no foot or hand, except in an equivocal sense, as we might speak of a stone hand; for when destroyed the hand will be no better than that. But things are defined by their working and power; and we ought not to say that they are the same when they no longer have their proper quality, but only that they have the same name. The proof that the state is a creation of nature and prior to the individual is that the individual, when isolated, is not self-sufficing; and therefore he is like a part in relation to the whole. But he who is unable to live in society, or who has no need because he is sufficient for himself, must be either a beast or a god: he is no part of a state. A social instinct is implanted in all men by nature, and yet he who first founded the state was the greatest of benefactors. For man, when perfected, is the best of animals, but, when separated from law and justice, he is the worst of all; since armed injustice is the more dangerous, and he is equipped at birth with arms, meant to be used by intelligence and virtue, which he may use for the worst ends. Wherefore, if he have not virtue, he is the most unholy and the most savage of animals, and the most full of lust and gluttony. But justice is the bond of men in states, for the administration of justice, which is the determination of what is just, is the principle of order in political society.

4

CLASSICAL GREEK CIVILIZATION
The Hellenistic Age

THEOCRITUS
Selection from the *Idylls*

During the Hellenistic Age, original creative literature hardly existed; most writers either imitated the forms and styles of their Hellenic predecessors or, following the lead of Aristotle, turned to literary criticism. These authors, often working from manuscripts on deposit at the library in Egypt's port city of Alexandria, perfected a literary style known as Alexandrianism. What distinguished these writers were their wide knowledge of details of Greek myths and history, their understanding of exotic literary figures and references, and their masterful command of the Greek language. They polished the Greek styles until their own works only faintly echoed the robustness of the originals. The Alexandrians owed their success, in part, to Egypt's Ptolemaic rulers, who were great patrons of culture, building the great library in Alexandria, stocking it with ancient manuscripts either through purchase or as spoils of war, and providing financial subsidies for scholars. Alexandrianism eventually spread across the Hellenistic world, affecting local literary styles and later influencing Roman culture.

In the cosmopolitan Hellenistic world, educated readers turned to scientific essays or to biographies; the writers based in Alexandria tended to serve the mass market, who demanded updated copies of Greek works. Among the popular but mediocre writers who catered to this market, only one or two, such as Theocritus, were able to establish reputations beyond their lifetime.

Theocritus (ca. 310–250 B.C.) was more original than his contemporaries for he pioneered two literary forms: the pastoral and the idyll. The pastoral focuses on the lives of shepherds in the wilds; it became a popular genre in this period because it had special appeal to those who had moved from the countryside to newly founded Hellenistic cities. Theocritus's sensitive descriptions of unspoiled nature, lowing cattle, and lovesick shepherds resulted in charming, though artificial, poems. However, Theocritus's reputation rests on his idylls—small portraits or vignettes of Hellenistic life, dating from the 270s. These poems evoked a simpler past or addressed themselves to familiar human traits such as love and jealousy.

Reading the Selection

Of Theocritus's thirty surviving idylls, the best is perhaps Idyll 14, "Aeschines and Thyonicus," which offers a rare glimpse of daily life in Hellenistic Egypt. Written in the form of a conversation, the idyll recounts a chance meeting between two old friends, the slightly disheveled

Aeschines and the empathetic Thyonichus. Fresh from his country house, Aeschines is bursting with gossip about his love affair with the young Cynisca—a tale that reflects badly on his behavior toward women. The conversation ends with Thyonichus advising his friend to forget his troubles and join the army, that is, become a mercenary soldier for King Ptolemy—Egypt's ruler. The Ptolemy named in the poem is Ptolemy II, called Ptolemy Philadelphus (r. 285–246 B.C.), son and successor to Ptolemy I (r. 323–285 B.C.), the Macedonian general who founded the Ptolemaic dynasty after the death of Alexander the Great in 323 B.C.

This idyll provides a window into Egypt's Greek community, populated by colonists who settled there after Alexander's conquest and the founding of the city of Alexandria in 332 B.C. According to scholars, the Egyptian Greeks maintained a distinct identity, living apart from the native population. In the poem, all the named characters have Greek names, there are references to a Greek city—Athens—and to two Greek-speaking regions, Thessaly and Thrace. The expression "Seen a wolf?" is a bit of Greek folklore, the equivalent of the English saying, "Has the cat got your tongue?" The characters also hold traditional Greek cultural values, including talking frankly about extramarital affairs, bonding in social rituals with fellow males, and worrying that the swift passage of time is robbing them of their youth ("Our time has gone").

Aeschines and Thyonichus

AESCHINES: Good to see you, Thyonichus.   1
THYONICHUS: And you, Aeschines.
   It's been some time.
AESCHINES: It has.
THYONICHUS: What's up with you?
AESCHINES: Trouble, Thyonichus.
THYONICHUS: Look how thin you've got;
   Unshaved moustache, long straggly hair! You're like
   That pasty-faced barefoot "philosopher"[1]
   Who came by the other day. "From Athens," he said.   10
AESCHINES: Was he in love too?
THYONICHUS: Pining . . . for a square meal.
AESCHINES: You can joke! It's driven me nearly crazy,
   The way Cynisca's been messing me about.
THYONICHUS: You could never take things easy,
     Aeschines.
   You want everything "just right." . . .
               Tell me the worst.
AESCHINES: The Argive[2] and Agis, the trainer[3] from
     Thessaly,
   And me and the soldier, Cleunicus—we were drinking
   At my country place. I'd killed a sucking pig   20
   And a pair of chickens, opened a jar of old wine
   —It smelt as good, almost, as the day it was pressed—
   Got onions and snails. It was a proper party.
   When things were going nicely we offered a toast
   "To the one I love," and we had to say the name.

We all spoke up and the toast went round. But *she*
Went quiet. And me right there! You can guess my
   feelings.
"Seen a wolf?" quipped someone. "That's right," she
   said,
Then blushed. You could have lit a lamp at her
   cheeks.[4]
There *is* a wolf—a wolf at the door, you might say.   30
My neighbour Labas's son. That's her great lover!
Handsome they call him. Skinny and overgrown!
A whisper about it had reached my ears, it's true,
But I took no notice. Trusting as a babe, I was.
Well, the four of us had had a few by this time,
And the man from Thessaly sang "Little Red
   Ridinghood"[5]
Right through from the beginning, which didn't help.
Cynisca burst into tears like a girl of six
Sobbing to be taken up on her mother's lap.
So I let her have it, Thyonichus—you know me—   40
I smacked[6] her about the head a couple of times,
"Not good enough for you, am I?" She picked herself
   up
And ran. "Don't hang around, dear. That boyfriend of
   yours
Will be catching cold. I hope he makes you cry."
A swallow, bringing a scrap to its young in the eaves,
Darts out a split-second later to fetch more food:

---

[1] **barefoot "philosopher"** Perhaps a reference to the Cynics, a philosophic school that flourished in the Hellenistic period; the Cynics practiced a life of self-denial.
[2] **Argive** A person from Argos, a city and region in the Peloponnesus.
[3] **trainer** A person who helps athletes prepare for the games.

[4] **lit a lamp at her cheeks** She was blushing red.
[5] **Little Red Ridinghood** A song with a wolf-theme, meant to make Cynisca uneasy about her dalliance with the neighbor's "wolfish" son.
[6] **smacked** Aeschines shows no remorse for his physical abuse of Cynisca.

That's how she was, one moment stretched in a chair,
The next, flying down the passage and out of the
    house.
Talk about the stable door and the bolting horse!
Twenty days . . . then eight . . . nine . . . then ten   50
    more . . .
Eleven till today. Plus two makes two whole months[7]
Since we split up. If I spiked my hair like a Thracian
She'd never notice the change. The Wolf's her man now,
She has him in at nights.
                I'm out in the cold,
No room for a poor Yahoo like me in her life.
If I could stop thinking about her, well and good.
But as it is . . . I'm like a mouse in a trap.
What the doctor orders to treat a lover's pangs
I don't know. But when my old friend Simus fell   60
For that brassy girl, a sea-voyage did the trick.

—————

[7] **two whole months** The days add up to sixty—two whole months.

I'll cross the sea too, and enlist as a soldier—
    Not the best life, perhaps, but it could be worse.
THYONICHUS: I only wish that things had gone as you
    wanted,
    Aeschines. But if serving abroad's your answer,
    King Ptolemy gives a free man honest terms.
AESCHINES: Tell me more.
THYONICHUS: Ptolemy's one of the best!
    Warm-hearted, loves his mistresses, loves learning,
    Never forgets a friend—or an enemy.   70
    He's generous to a fault, as a great prince should be,
    But be careful not to push your luck in asking,
    Aeschines. If you're ready to sling a soldier's
    Cloak about your shoulders and bear the brunt
    Of an enemy charge without budging from your place,
    Hurry to Egypt.
                  A touch of grey at the temples
    Creeps outward, hair by hair, and before we know it
    Our time has gone. Act now, while the sap runs green.

EPICURUS

"Letter to Menoeceus"

The Greek philosopher Epicurus (ca. 342–270 B.C.) is the founder of a type of hedonism that identifies the good with pleasure and the bad with pain—epicureanism. Born on the island of Samos, he moved to Athens, where he founded a school. Most of his writings have been lost; only scattered fragments survive. His disciples, including the Roman thinker Lucretius, wrote extensively on his teachings, preserving their basic ideas. Consequently, Epicurus's personal letter (early third century B.C.) to Menoeceus is a treasured document because it records both the philosopher's observations, in his own words, on what is needed to gain happiness and his view of the "good life."

Epicurus apparently practiced what he preached, living a simple and frugal, almost monastic, existence in the company of his pupils. Among them, he expounded his simple rules for becoming happy and avoiding fear and pain. He cautioned them against seeking wealth and power, which he thought were likely to bring suffering and pain. He also pointed out that death should not be feared, since dying has little meaning to a person who understands the workings of nature. Building on the ideas of the Greek thinker Democritus (ca. 460 B.C.–?), the founder of the Atomic theory, Epicurus argued that death is simply the loss of a few atoms from the body. He believed that everything, including soul and body, is composed of atoms, or particles of matter. That being the case, humans should shut their ears to priests who try to put fear of death into their hearts. Instead, the best way to live is serenely, in the face of one's own death. Many educated people in his day, and later in Roman times, found satisfaction in this teaching about calmness in the face of death; thus, Epicurus came to be known as a "savior of souls."

Reading the Selection

In this letter to a pupil Menoeceus, Epicurus offers advice on happiness, the final goal of most philosophies and religions. For Epicurus, the beginning of happiness lies in accepting that the gods exist but, at the same time, rejecting the common notion that the deities have any interest in mortals. It also involves realizing that death should not be feared, since it is nothing more than depriving the body of its senses.

Having offered these preconditions of happiness, Epicurus next explains the meaning of the good life. He maintains that the human ability to differentiate between "natural" and "unnecessary" desires will help bring us happiness. A healthy body and a sound mind, which are the twin goals of "happy living," will aid the individual in gaining pleasure and avoiding pain. Epicurus further asserts that a simple but wholesome diet combined with a life of moderation and sober thinking will free the individual from pain. In his final observations, Epicurus turns to a question that is central to many philosophies and religions, that of free will versus predestination. He acknowledges that some events are predetermined, but he thinks that others occur by chance, thus allowing individuals to exercise free will and take advantage of opportunities to do good or evil.

No one should postpone the study of philosophy when he is young, nor should he weary of it when he becomes mature, because the search for mental health is never untimely or out of season. To say that the time to study philosophy has not yet arrived or that it is past is like saying that the time for happiness is not yet at hand or is no longer present. Thus both the young and the mature should pursue philosophy, the latter in order to be rejuvenated as they age by the blessings that accrue from pleasurable past experience, and the youthful in order to become mature immediately through having no fear of the future. Hence we should make a practice of the things that make for happiness, for assuredly when we have this, we have everything, and we do everything we can to get it when we don't have it.

The Preconditions of Happiness

[1. You should do and practice all the things I constantly recommended to you, with the knowledge that they are the fundamentals of the good life. First of all, you should think of deity as imperishable and blessed being (as delineated in the universal conception of it common to all men), and you should not attribute to it anything foreign to its immortality or inconsistent with its blessedness. On the contrary, you should hold every doctrine that is capable of safeguarding its blessedness in common with its imperishability. The gods do indeed exist, since our knowledge of them is a matter of clear and distinct perception; but they are not like what the masses suppose them to be, because most people do not maintain the pure conception of the gods. The irreligious man is not the person who destroys the gods of the masses but the person who imposes the ideas of the masses on the gods. The opinions held by most people about the gods are not true conceptions of them but fallacious notions, according to which awful penalties are meted out to the evil and the greatest of blessings to the good. The masses, by assimilating the gods in every respect to their own moral qualities, accept deities similar to themselves and regard anything not of this sort as alien.

Second, you should accustom yourself to believing that death means nothing to us, since every good and every evil lies in sensation; but death is the privation of sensation.[1] Hence a correct comprehension of the fact that death means nothing to us makes the mortal aspect of life pleasurable, not by conferring on us a boundless period of time but by removing the yearning for deathlessness. There is nothing fearful in living for the person who has really laid hold of the fact that there is nothing fearful in not living. So it is silly for a person to say that he dreads death—not because it will be painful when it arrives but because it pains him now as a future certainty; for that which makes no trouble for us when it arrives is a meaningless pain when we await it. This, the most horrifying of evils, means nothing to us, then, because so long as we are existent death is not present and whenever it is present we are nonexistent. Thus it is of no concern either to the living or to those who have completed their lives. For the former it is nonexistent, and the latter are themselves nonexistent.

Most people, however, recoil from death as though it were the greatest of evils; at other times they welcome it as the end-all of life's ills. The sophisticated person, on the other hand, neither begs off from living nor dreads not living. Life is not a stumbling block to him, nor does he regard not being alive as any sort of evil. As in the case of food he prefers the most savory dish to merely the larger portion, so in the case of time, he garners to himself the most agreeable moments rather than the longest span.

Anyone who urges the youth to lead a good life but counsels the older man to end his life in good style is silly, not merely because of the welcome character of life but because of the fact that living well and dying well are one and the same discipline. Much worse off, however, is the person[2] who says it were well not to have been born "but once born to pass Hades' portals as swiftly as may be."

_____
[1] **sensation** Sense impressions, a belief based on the Atomic theory.
[2] **the person** Theognis (fl. sixth–fifth-century B.C.); Greek poet.

Now if he says such a thing from inner persuasion why does he not withdraw from life? Everything is in readiness for him once he has firmly resolved on this course. But if he speaks facetiously he is a trifler standing in the midst of men who do not welcome him.

It should be borne in mind, then, that the time to come is neither ours nor altogether not ours. In this way we shall neither expect the future outright as something destined to be, nor despair of it as something absolutely not destined to be.

The Good Life

[2. It should be recognized that within the category of desire certain desires are natural, certain others unnecessary and trivial; that in the case of the natural desires certain ones are necessary, certain others merely natural; and that in the case of necessary desires certain ones are necessary for happiness, others to promote freedom from bodily discomfort, others for the maintenance of life itself. A steady view of these matters shows us how to refer all moral choice and aversion to bodily health and imperturbability of mind, these being the twin goals of happy living. It is on this account that we do everything we do— to achieve freedom from pain and freedom from fear. When once we come to this, the tumult in the soul is calmed and the human being does not have to go about looking for something that is lacking or to search for something additional with which to supplement the welfare of soul and body. Accordingly we have need of pleasure only when we feel pain because of the absence of pleasure, but whenever we do not feel pain we no longer stand in need of pleasure. And so we speak of pleasure as the starting point[3] and the goal of the happy life because we realize that it is our primary native good, because every act of choice and aversion originates with it, and because we come back to it when we judge every good by using the pleasure feeling as our criterion.

Because of the very fact that pleasure is our primary and congenital good we do not select every pleasure; there are times when we forego certain pleasures, particularly when they are followed by too much unpleasantness. Furthermore, we regard certain states of pain as preferable to pleasures, particularly when greater satisfaction results from our having submitted to discomforts for a long period of time. Thus every pleasure is a good by reason of its having a nature akin to our own, but not every pleasure is desirable. In like manner every state of pain is an evil, but not all pains are uniformly to be rejected. At any rate, it is our duty to judge all such cases by measuring pleasures against pains, with a view to their respective assets and liabilities, inasmuch as we do experience the good as being bad at times and, contrariwise, the bad as being good.

In addition, we consider limitation of the appetites[4] a major good, and we recommend this practice not for the purpose of enjoying just a few things and no more but rather for the purpose of enjoying those few in case we do not have much. We are firmly convinced that those who need expensive fare least are the ones who relish it most keenly and that a natural way of life is easily procured, while trivialities are hard to come by. Plain foods afford pleasure equivalent to that of a sumptuous diet, provided that the pains of penury are wholly eliminated. Barley bread and water yield the peak of pleasure whenever a person who needs them sets them in front of himself. Hence becoming habituated to a simple rather than a lavish way of life provides us with the full complement of health; it makes a person ready for the necessary business of life; it puts us in a position of advantage when we happen upon sumptuous fare at intervals and prepares us to be fearless in facing fortune.

Thus when I say that pleasure is the goal of living I do not mean the pleasures of libertines or the pleasures inherent in positive enjoyment, as is supposed by certain persons who are ignorant of our doctrine or who are not in agreement with it or who interpret it perversely. I mean, on the contrary, the pleasure that consists in freedom from bodily pain and mental agitation. The pleasant life is not the product of one drinking party after another or of sexual intercourse with women and boys or of the sea food and other delicacies afforded by a luxurious table. On the contrary, it is the result of sober thinking—namely, investigation of the reasons for every act of choice and aversion and elimination of those false ideas about the gods and death which are the chief source of mental disturbances.

The starting point of this whole scheme and the most important of its values is good judgment, which consequently is more highly esteemed even than philosophy. All the other virtues stem from sound judgment, which shows us that it is impossible to live the pleasant Epicurean life without also living sensibly, nobly, and justly and, vice versa, that it is impossible to live sensibly, nobly, and justly without living pleasantly. The traditional virtues grow up together with the pleasant life; they are indivisible. Can you think of anyone more moral than the person who has devout beliefs about the gods, who is consistently without fears about death, and who has pondered man's natural end? Or who realizes that the goal of the good life is easily gained and achieved and that the term of evil is brief, both in extent of time and duration of pain? Or the man who laughs at the "decrees of Fate," a deity[5] whom some people have set up as sovereign of all?

The good Epicurean believes that certain events occur deterministically, that others are chance events, and that still others are in our own hands. He sees also that necessity cannot be held morally responsible and that chance is an unpredictable thing, but that what is in our own hands, since it has no master, is naturally associated with blameworthiness and the opposite. (Actually it would be better to subscribe to the popular mythology than to become a slave by accepting the determinism of the natural philoso-

---

[3] **pleasure as the starting point** The basic doctrine of hedonism.
[4] **limitation of the appetites** Here Epicurus makes the case for simple living.

[5] **Fate, a deity** The worship of Fate as a deity began in Babylonia and spread to the Hellenistic states, flourishing there and later in the Roman world.

phers, because popular religion underwrites the hope of supplicating the gods by offerings but determinism contains an element of necessity, which is inexorable.) As for chance, the Epicurean does not assume that it is a deity (as in popular belief) because a god does nothing irregular; nor does he regard it as an unpredictable cause of all events. It is his belief that good and evil are not the chance contributions of a deity, donated to mankind for the happy life, but rather that the initial circumstances for great good and evil are sometimes provided by chance. He thinks it preferable to have bad luck rationally than good luck irrationally. In other words, in human action it is better for a rational choice to be unsuccessful than for an irrational choice to succeed through the agency of chance.

Think about these and related matters day and night, by yourself and in company with someone like yourself. If you do, you will never experience anxiety, waking or sleeping, but you will live like a god among men. For a human being who lives in the midst of immortal blessings is in no way like mortal man!

5

ROMAN CIVILIZATION
The Pre-Christian Centuries

CICERO

Selection from *On the Republic*

For more than two thousand years Cicero (106–43 B.C.) has been one of the West's guiding spirits. The impact of his writings first on Rome and later on Europe cannot be overestimated. Within his vast works, the most famous passage is perhaps "The Dream of Scipio" from *On the Republic,* a study of the ideal polity. Its popularity stems largely from its lofty theme: The joys of heaven are greater than the glories of earth. Romans heard in this theme an echo of Plato; later, Christians thought it signaled that Cicero was one of them, even if he did live before Christ. Today's readers can still appreciate "The Dream" as a noble vision by one of Rome's leading thinkers.

Cicero was both a man of action and a man of letters. When in power, he worked to heal the social ills of late republican Rome (133–31 B.C.), a period wracked by civil wars. When in eclipse, he wrote prodigiously and quickly, advocating constitutionalism and opposing autocracy. In the end he failed as a statesman and, though not a conspirator, was killed in the fallout from the plot to murder Julius Caesar. Mark Antony, Caesar's friend and self-proclaimed heir, distrusted Cicero and ordered his death.

Cicero wrote from the vantage point of an eclectic thinker, one who knew philosophy but was not a true philosopher. He was open to criticism and claimed the right to change his mind. In his letters he describes his method of reaching a decision—by debating both sides of a problem. For his treatises, such as *On the Republic,* he favored the dialogue form because its "give-and-take" format enabled readers to make up their minds based on opposing viewpoints.

Two traits characterized Cicero's world: It was civilized and tolerant. To express this ideal, he coined the term *humanitas* (humanity), meaning devotion to books, language, and art. He gave *humanitas* a social face in his dialogues, setting them in a courteous society free of rudeness. He himself lived this ideal, being well read in Greek and Roman letters, philosophy, history, and law. His learning, though highly valued, still could not compete with his love of politics. When called to office, he welcomed the chance to be a "man of the world." Hence, the claim in "The Dream" that contemplation is superior to action must be doubted, reflecting instead Cicero's exile from politics when he wrote it.

Reading the Selection

"The Dream of Scipio" offers a cosmic perspective on human affairs. Not original in outlook, it is a Romanized synthesis of Greek thought on the soul and the afterlife; it is drawn largely from sixth-century thinker Pythagoras, whose ideas were passed on to Plato (see *Phaedo*). Expressive of *humanitas* and his love of Rome, Cicero's "The Dream" claims that there is a life beyond the grave for deserving politicians and philosophers.

Cicero's choice of Publius Cornelius Scipio (the younger) (ca. 184–129 B.C.) as his mouthpiece reflects Cicero's patriotism and Hellenism (love of Greek culture), the bedrock of his ideals. Deeply aware of his status as a "new man" (the first in his family to achieve the consulship), Cicero adopted as spiritual ancestors the younger Scipio and his friends. The grandson of Scipio Africanus (the elder) (237–183 B.C.), Rome's savior during the Second Punic War, Scipio the younger was, in his own right, a great statesman and the leader of a highly educated literary circle. It was this circle that introduced to Rome the Stoic ideas that Cicero quoted in "The Dream," such as the stress on virtue and duty.

∽

The Dream of Scipio

As you know, I was military tribune in the Fourth Legion 1
in Africa under the command of the consul Manius Manilius.[1] When I arrived there I was particularly eager to meet King Masinissa,[2] who for good reason was a close friend of my family. When I came into his presence the old man embraced me and wept. Then, after a moment, he lifted his eyes to heaven and uttered these words.

'Most glorious Sun and other heavenly beings, I offer you my thanks! For before I depart from this life, I am now seeing with my own eyes, within this kingdom of mine and beneath my roof, Publius Cornelius Scipio. The very sound of his name revives my strength. For never a moment has the recollection of his glorious, invincible forbear faded from my memory.'

Then I began asking him questions about his kingdom, and he in turn interrogated me about Rome; and so we spent the whole day in conversation. Afterwards, he entertained me in regal splendour, and we continued our discussion far into the night, as the aged king wanted nothing better than to talk of Africanus. He had not forgotten a single deed the great man had ever done, or a single word he had ever uttered.

When we finally parted and retired to bed, my journey and the lateness of the hour had made me tired, and I fell into a deeper sleep than usual. As I slept I had a dream, prompted no doubt by what we had been talking

about. For it frequently happens that the subjects of our meditations and discussions reappear in our dreams. This happened for example to the poet Ennius[3]; he writes of his dream about Homer, who was naturally the constant subject of his thoughts and conversations when he was awake. And so I dreamt that Africanus was with me; his appearance recalled his portrait busts rather than his actual living self.

. . .

I recognized him—and trembled with fear. But he spoke to 5
me; and this is what he said.

'Calm yourself, Scipio. Do not be afraid. But remember carefully the things I am about to tell you. Do you see that city there? It was I who made its people submit to Rome. But now they are starting up the old conflicts once again; they refuse to remain at peace!' And from where he stood amid the bright illumination of radiant stars, he pointed down at Carthage, and began speaking once more. 'This,' he declared, is the city you have come to attack. At present you are not much more than an ordinary soldier. But within the space of two years you will have been elected consul, and then you will overthrow the place utterly. Thereafter the surname, which you now bear as an inheritance from myself, will be yours by your own right. Later on, after you have destroyed Carthage and celebrated a Triumph, after you have held the office of censor

---

[1] **Manius Manilius** Consul in 149 B.C. who commanded the Roman army that besieged Carthage, in North Africa, during the Third Punic War.
[2] **King Masinissa** King of Numidia, which was located in modern-day Algeria. He helped start the Third Punic War.

[3] **Ennius** Third-century B.C. Roman poet and playwright who is considered to be the founder of Latin literature. Only fragments of his works remain.

and undertaken missions to Egypt, Syria, Asia and Greece, you will be elected to the consulship for the second time, while you are absent, and you will win a very great war and raze Numantia[4] to the ground. But at the time when you yourself are proceeding in Triumph to the Capitol, you will find the government in a state of confusion: for which the machinations of my grandson will be responsible.

'After that, Africanus, it will be your duty to devote to your people the full splendid benefit of all your integrity, talent and wisdom. But at that juncture I see two divergent paths of destiny opening up before you. For when your life has completed seven times eight circuitous revolutions of the sun, and when these two numbers, each of which for a different reason is regarded as possessing some quality of perfection, have in their natural course brought you to your supreme moment of destiny, that is the time when the entire Roman State will turn to you and all that you stand for: the Senate, every right-minded citizen, our subject allies, the entire Latin people. The fate of the whole country, at that juncture, will depend on you and you alone. In other words, it will be your duty to assume the role of dictator, and restore order to our commonwealth—provided only that death does not overtake you at the criminal hands of your own kinsmen!'

At this, Laelius[5] cried out aloud, and a deep groan was heard from all. But the younger Scipio smiled serenely, and went on: 'Hush! Do not, I beg you, awaken me from my sleep. Listen a little longer, and take heed of what my ancestor went on to say next.'

For then he continued speaking. 'But consider this, Africanus,' he said, 'and the thought will make your determination to defend your homeland even greater than it is already. Every man who has preserved or helped his country, or has made its greatness even greater, is reserved a special place in heaven, where he may enjoy an eternal life of happiness. For all things that are done on earth nothing is more acceptable to the Supreme God, who rules the whole universe, than those gatherings and assemblages of men who are bound together by law, the communities which are known as states. Indeed, it is from here in heaven that the rulers and preservers of those states once came; and it is to here that they eventually return.'

By now I was thoroughly alarmed. It was not the idea   10
of death that frightened me so much, but the thought of treachery inside my own family. Nevertheless, I managed to ask Africanus a question. Was he, was my father Paullus, were the other men we think of as having died, really dead? Or were they still alive?

'To be sure they are still living,' he replied, 'seeing that they have escaped from the prison-house of their bodies—that is to say from "life," as you call it, which is, in fact, death. Look: do you not see your father Paullus coming towards you?'

---

[4] **Numantia** Ancient city in Spain, captured by the Romans in 133 B.C. This victory marked the triumph of the Romans in Spain.
[5] **Laelius** Gaius Laelius was one of the characters who appeared in several of Cicero's writing as a voice or foil in the dialogues.

Indeed I now saw him approaching; and I burst into a flood of tears. But my father put his arms round me and kissed me, and told me not to weep. So when I had suppressed my tears and felt able to speak, I cried out, 'Since this, most revered and best of fathers, is true life, as I hear Africanus declare, why must I stay any longer upon earth? Why should I not come and join you, with the utmost possible speed?'

'That must not be,' replied Paullus. 'For unless God, whose sacred domain is all that you see around you here, has freed you from your confinement in the body, you cannot be admitted to this place. For men were brought into existence in order that they should inhabit the globe known as the earth, which you see here at the centre of this holy space. They have been endowed with souls made out of the everlasting fires called stars and constellations, consisting of globular, spherical bodies which are animated by the divine mind and move with marvellous speed, each in its own orbit and cycle. Therefore it is destined that you, Publius, and all other righteous men, shall suffer your souls to stay in the custody of the body. You must not abandon human life except at the command of him who gave it to you. For otherwise you would have failed in the duty which you, like the rest of humanity, have to fulfil.

'Instead, then, Scipio, do upon earth as your grandfather has done. Do as I have done, who begot you. Cherish justice and devotion. These qualities in abundance are owed to parents and kinsmen; and most of all they are owed to one's country.

'That is the life which leads to heaven, and to the company of those who, having completed their lives in the world, are now released from their bodies and dwell in that region you see over there, which the Greeks have taught you people on earth to call the Milky Way.' And he pointed to a circle of light, blazing brilliantly among all other fires.   15

As I gazed out from where I stood, first in one direction and then another, the whole prospect looked marvellously beautiful. There were stars we never see from the earth, and they were larger than we could possibly have imagined. The smallest was the luminary which is farthest away from heaven and nearest to the earth, and shines with reflected light. These starry spheres were much larger than the earth. Indeed the earth now seemed to me so small that I began to think less of this empire of ours, which only amounts to a pinpoint on its surface.

· · ·

While I looked more and more intently down at the earth Africanus checked me. 'How long,' he asked, 'do you propose to keep your eyes fastened down there upon that world of yours? Look up, instead, and look round at the sacred region into which you have now entered.

The universe is held together by nine concentric spheres. The outermost sphere is heaven itself, and it includes and embraces all the rest. For it is the Supreme God in person, enclosing and comprehending everything that exists, that is to say all the stars which are fixed in the sky yet rotate upon their eternal courses. Within this outermost sphere are eight others. Seven of them contain the planets—a single one in each sphere, all moving in the contrary direction to the great movement of heaven itself. The next sphere to the outermost is occupied by the orb which people on earth name after Saturn. Below Saturn shines the brilliant light of Jupiter, which is benign and healthful to mankind. Then comes the star we call Mars, red and terrible to men upon earth.

'Next, almost midway between heaven and earth, blazes the Sun. He is the prince, lord and ruler of all the other worlds, the mind and guiding principle of the entire universe, so gigantic in size that everything, everywhere, is pervaded and drenched by his light. In attendance upon the Sun are Venus and Mercury, each in its own orbit; and the lowest sphere of all contains the Moon, which takes its light, as it revolves, from the rays of the sun. Above the Moon there is nothing which is not eternal, but beneath that level everything is moral and transient (except only for the souls in human beings, which are a gift to mankind from the gods). For there below the Moon is the earth, the ninth and lowest of the spheres, lying at the centre of the universe. The earth remains fixed and without motion; all things are drawn to it, because the natural force of gravity pulls them down.'

I surveyed the scene in a stupor. But finally I recovered enough to ask: 'What is this sound, so strong and so sweet, which fills my ears?' 20

'That,' he replied, 'is the music of the spheres. They create it by their own motion as they rush upon their way. The intervals between them, although differing in length, are all measured according to a fixed scheme of proportions; and this arrangement produces a melodious blend of high and low notes, from which emerges a varied harmony. For it cannot be that these vast movements should take place in silence, and nature has ordained that the spheres utter music, those at the summit giving forth high sounds, whereas the sounds of those beneath are low and deep. That is to say, the spheres containing the uppermost stars, comprising those regions of the sky where the movements are speediest, give out a high and piercing sound, whereas the Moon, which lies beneath all the others, sends forth the lowest note.

'The ninth of the spheres, the earth, fixed at the centre of the universe, is motionless and silent. But the other eight spheres produce seven different sounds on the scale—not eight, since two of these orbs move at identical speeds, but seven, a number which is the key to almost all things that exist. Clever men, by imitating these musical effects with their stringed instruments and voices, have given themselves the possibility of eventually returning to this place; and the same chance exists for others too, who during their earthly lives have devoted their outstanding talents to heavenly activities.

'The ears of mankind are filled with this music all the time. But they have become completely deaf to its melody; no other human faculty has become so atrophied as this. The same thing happens where the Nile rushes down from high mountains to the place known as Catadupa. For the sound there is so loud that the people who live nearby have entirely lost their sense of hearing. And that, too, is why the mighty music of the spheres, created by the

immeasurably fast rotations of the whole universe, cannot be apprehended by the human ears—any more than you can look at the light of the Sun, which is so intense it blots out your power of vision altogether.'

The scene filled me with awe and delight. And yet all the time I still could not help riveting my eyes upon our own world there below. Africanus noticed this, and spoke again. 'I see,' he said, 'that your gaze is still fastened, even now, upon the places where mortals dwell upon the earth. But can you not understand that the earth is totally insignificant? Contemplate these heavenly regions instead! Scorn what is mortal!

'For the lips of mankind can give you no fame or glory 25
worth the seeking. Note how few and minute are the inhabited portions of the earth, and look upon the vast deserts that divide each one of these patches from the next. See, the inhabitants of the world are so cut off from one another that their different centres cannot even communicate with each other. The place where you yourself dwell, for example, is far removed from certain of the other populated areas, both in latitude and longitude; and some people live in regions that are at the very opposite end of the world from yours. Surely you cannot expect *them* to honour your name.

'Furthermore, you will observe that the surface of the earth is girdled and encompassed by a number of different zones; and that the two which are most widely separated from one another, and lie beneath opposite poles of the heavens, are rigid with icy cold, while the central, broadest zone is burnt up with the heat of the sun. Two others, situated between the hot zones and the cold, are habitable. The zone which lies towards the south has no connexion with yours at all; it represents your antipodes. As to its northern counterpart, where you yourselves live, you will realize, if you look, what a diminutive section of this region can really be regarded as your property. For the territory you occupy is nothing more than a small island, narrow from north to south, somewhat less narrow from east to west, and surrounded by the sea which is known on earth as the Atlantic, or the Great Sea, or the Ocean. In spite of the grand name this stretch of water bears, you can tell from here how tiny it really is.

'And I must disabuse you of any idea that your own fame, or the fame of any one of us, could ever be great enough to extend beyond these known and settled lands. It could never scale the Caucasus mountains (you see them down there); it could never swim the river Ganges. Not one of the inhabitants of all those eastern tracts, or the remote west either, or the far off north and south, will ever so much as hear the sound of your name! And once you leave all these hosts of people out of account, you will have to conclude that the area over which your glory is so eager to extend itself is really of the most trifling dimensions.

'And now about the people who *do* know and speak about us. The point is, how long will this go on? Assume, if you like, that future generations, having inherited our praises from their fathers, will indeed retain the desire to hand them down to their children as well. Even so the deluges and conflagrations which inevitably descend upon the earth at fixed intervals will make it impossible for any glory we may gain in this way to be eternal—or even to last for any length of time. But in any case why do you regard it as so important to be talked about by people who have not yet been born? After all, you were never spoken of by all the multitudes who lived before you—and they were every bit as numerous, and were better men.

'It is also necessary to remind ourselves that even the people who may in fact hear our names mentioned will not retain the recollection even for as much as the space of one year. I am not referring to the year as it is commonly understood, which is measured according to the revolution of the sun, that is to say according to the movements of one single star. But when *all* the stars return to the places where they started from, so that after an immense interval has elapsed the entire heavens finally resume their original configuration, then that great period of rotation can truly be called a year—but how many generations of human life it comprises, I should not venture to say.

'Long ago, when the spirit of Romulus ascended into these sacred expanses, it seemed to those living at the time that a shadow suddenly passed over the sun, and its light was blotted out. When, once again, the sun shall go into eclipse in the very same position and at the very same hour, that will signify that all the constellations and stars have returned to their original positions: and then you will know that the Year has been completed. But you must understand that, up to now, not one twentieth part of its course has been run.

.   .   .

'As for yourself, do not abandon hope of coming back here one day. For this is the place which offers great and eminent men their authentic reward—and, after all, such fame as you are able to win among mere human beings can evidently be disregarded, seeing that it is scarcely capable of enduring even for a small part of one single year. Look upwards, then! Contemplate this place which is a habitation for all eternity! Then you will not need any longer to be at the mercy of what the multitude says about you: then you will not have to put your trust in whatever human rewards your achievements may earn.

'Instead let Virtue herself, by her own unaided allurements, summon you to a glory that is genuine and real. Feel no concern about what other people may say about you. They will say it in any case. Besides, whatever words they may choose to utter will not pass beyond the narrow limits you now see below you. No utterance of man about his fellowmen has ever been lasting. When a person dies his words die with him. Posterity forgets them; and they pass into annihilation.'

He stopped speaking, and I cried out my assent. 'Even when I was only a boy, Africanus,' I declared, 'I was already exerting myself to the utmost to follow in your footsteps, and in those of my father. I longed to be not unworthy of your fame! And if there is really a path leading right to the entrance of heaven for those who have served their country well, the knowledge of this great goal before me will inspire me to redouble my endeavours.'

'Strive on,' he replied. 'And rest assured that it is only your body that is mortal; your true self is nothing of the

kind. For the man you outwardly appear to be is not yourself at all. Your real self is not that corporeal, palpable shape, but the spirit inside. *Understand that you are god.* You have a god's capacity of aliveness and sensation and memory and foresight; a god's power to rule and govern and direct the body that is your servant, in the same way as God himself, who reigns over us, directs the entire universe. And this rule exercised by eternal God is mirrored in the dominance of your frail body by your immortal soul.

.   .   .

That which is always in motion is eternal; yet that which communicates motion to something else, but is itself moved by another force, must necessarily cease to live when the transmission of this motion to it has ceased. Consequently the only thing that never ceases to move is something which has the power of starting up motion all *on its own*—it can go on moving because its power to achieve motion depends on itself and itself alone. This, therefore, it must be concluded, is the source and first principle of motion for all things that move.

'Being the first principle, it never had a beginning: since the first principle is what everything else has originated from, it cannot possibly have originated from anything else. For if it owed its origin to something else, it could not be described as the first principle.

'And since it never had a beginning it will never have an end. For if the first principle were destroyed it could never be reborn from any other source and would no longer be able to create things on its own account—which is obviously what the first principle has to do.

'The beginning of all movement, then, comes from that which has set itself in motion: which can neither be born nor die. For if that were not so, one would have to envisage the entire heavens and all things that have ever been created crashing down and coming to an end—for that is what would happen if the force generating their motion were taken away from them.

'Since, therefore, it is plain that the self-moving principle is eternal, the same must evidently apply to the human soul. For unlike lifeless objects which can only be set in motion from outside, the soul, by its very essence and nature, is a living thing such as can only derive its life and motion from within itself. And since, uniquely, it possesses this characteristic of self-impulsion, surely it has no beginning, and lives for ever.

.   .   .

'Use this eternal force, therefore, for the most splendid deeds it is in you to achieve! And the very best deeds are those which serve your country. A soul devoted to such pursuits will find it easiest of all to soar upwards to this place, which is its proper habitation and home. And its flight will be all the more rapid if already during the period of its confinement within the body it has ranged freely abroad, and, by contemplating what lies outside itself, has contrived to detach itself from the body to the greatest possible degree.

'When, on the other hand, a man has failed to do this, and has abandoned himself instead to bodily indulgence and become its slave, letting the passions which serve pleasure impel him to flout the laws both of gods and of men, his soul, after departing from his body, hovers about close to the earth. Nor does it return to this place until many ages of torment have been undergone.'

Then Africanus vanished; and I awoke from my sleep.

CATULLUS
Poems

Born into a wealthy and distinguished Italian family, Catullus (ca. 84–57 B.C.) enjoyed a short, bittersweet life during the turbulent last years of the Roman Republic. Indeed, his life seemed to mirror the unsettled times of political intrigue and the scramble for power as he suffered through torrid love affairs, experienced fickle friendships, and endured life's capriciousness.

Often rebuffed by his manipulative mistress, Clodia, the wife of a Roman consul, whom he immortalized in his love poetry as "Lesbia" (named for Sappho; see Sappho *Poems*), Catullus chose to spend much of his time in travel. While away from Rome, he was intent on trying to heal his wounded heart and restore his fortune. During one long voyage to the eastern Mediterranean, he wrote a series of poems setting forth his adventures, as he tried to put his life in perspective. This poetry survived his own short life to leave a personal testament; it transcends the times and reminds readers that sometimes the best way to survive calamity is to turn inward and commune with one's soul.

Catullus's poems, closely linked with the Alexandrian style (see Theocritus's *Idylls*), fall into three categories: the "small" or short epic, epigrams or elegies, and love poetry. In his short epics, he exhibits his vast knowledge of Greek myth. His epigrams, short and diverse, range across the spectrum of human life—from mourning a friend's death to attacking Julius Caesar. His love poems—his best-known works—express his innermost feelings, from raw lust to calculated betrayals and total rejection that break the heart.

Reading the Selections

Three of the four poems included here treat of Catullus's love for his beloved Lesbia, though in contradictory ways. In the first poem, the earliest of the four, he is besotted, relishing her kisses and declaring the eternity of their love. The two later poems show him sadder but no wiser; he accuses Lesbia of unfaithfulness yet still confesses his love for her.

The other poem included here reveals Catullus's sharp insight into the human condition. In the opening stanzas he notes that Suffenus, a fellow poet, publishes his works in finely crafted scrolls (bookbinding had not yet been invented). These scrolls were similar, perhaps, to handsome and lavishly illustrated "coffee table" books in which content is second to appearance. Catullus charges that Suffenus, who dines out on his glossy products, composes very mediocre poetry. Turning the tables on the reader, Catullus, in his concluding comments, asks if we are not all like Suffenus, self-deluded about our own talents and our place in the world—a conclusion that echoes the folk wisdom of the Greek storyteller Aesop. What Catullus wrote regarding the human tendency to self-delusion still rings true after more than two thousand years.

∞

5

Lesbia
  live with me
& love me so
we'll laugh at all
the sour-faced stric-
tures of the wise.
This sun once set
will rise again,
when our sun sets
follows night &
an endless sleep.
Kiss me now a
thousand times &
now a hundred
more & then a

1   hundred & a
thousand more again
till with so many
hundred thousand
kisses you & I   20
shall both lose count
nor any can
from envy of
so much of kissing
10   put his finger
on the number
of sweet kisses
you of me &
I of you,
darling, have had.   30

∞

22

I must, Varus, tell you:
  Suffenus, known to us both as
a man of elegance, wit
  & sophistication
is also a poet
  who turns out verse by the yard.
No palimpsest copies
  but new books with new ivories
inscribed on Augustan Royal,
  the lines lead-ruled,
red tabs & red wrappers,
  the ends shaved with pumice.
But unwind the scroll
  & Suffenus
the well-known diner-out
  disappears.
A goatherd
  a country bumpkin

1   looks at us—
  strangely transmogrified.   20
What should one think?
  The envy of wits
becomes
  at the touch of the Muses
a bundle of gaucheries. . . .
  and he likes nothing better
fancies himself
10   in the role of a poet. . . .
Yet who,
  in his own way,   30
is not a Suffenus?
  Each has his blind spot.
The mote & the beam.
  As Aesop says,
the pack on our own back
  that we don't see.

∞

51

Godlike the man who
sits at her side, who
watches and catches that laughter
which (softly) tears me
to tatters: nothing is

1   left of me, each time I see her,
. . . tongue numbed; arms, legs
melting, on fire; drum
drumming in ears; head-lights gone black.

Coda

Her ease is your sloth, Catullus
you itch & roll in her ease:

former kings and cities
lost in the valley of her arm.

10

72

There was a time, Lesbia, when
you confessed only to Catullus in love:
you would set me above Jupiter himself.
I loved you then
    not as men love their women
but as a father his children—his family.
Today I know you too well

1

and desire burns deeper in me
    and you are more coarse
more frivolous in my thought.
"How," you may ask, "can this be?"
Such actions as yours excite
    increased violence of love,
Lesbia, but with friendless intention.

10

VERGIL

Selections from the *Aeneid*

Vergil (70–19 B.C.), from a modest rural family of northern Italy, studied, as part of his education, the Greek and Alexandrian poets and writers. Homer, his chief inspiration, would guide him through much of his literary career. Returning to his family farm upon completing his education, Vergil worked the land and began to compose poetry. By a series of chance circumstances, he met Octavian, the future Caesar Augustus (ruled 31 B.C.–A.D. 14), to whom he dedicated his first collection of poems. Vergil, upon moving to Rome, was introduced to the wealthy and powerful who became his patrons. His two books of poems, *Eclogues* and *Georgics*, reminded the Romans of the simple rural values that had made them masters of the Mediterranean and the envy of all nations; these poems established Vergil as the leading voice of the Golden Age of Roman literature. Vergil drew on his earlier years as a farmer to argue that the plain life of the early Romans had prepared them for their mission and responsibility as world leaders, but he warned his readers to return to the good old days and to reject the temptation to amass wealth and live in cities.

    As Vergil's fame grew, he decided to write an epic that would portray Rome's glorious past down to the triumph of Augustus. His tale was to be a sweeping story of symbolic events built around the adventures of Aeneas, the Trojan prince, who escaped from Troy at the time of its fall with his son, father, and loyal band of soldiers. Driven by fate and his own sense of duty, Aeneas overcame one obstacle after another to fulfill his destiny to found Rome. In laying the foundation of this great nation, Aeneas was foreshadowing Augustus; under his wise and just leadership, Rome was prepared to play a dominant role in history. By today's standards, Vergil's praise for Augustus flatters his hero too much; for the Romans, however, the *Aeneid* inspired generations of young men to take their place among those who served Rome.

Reading the Selections

Book I introduces the major characters in the *Aeneid* and sets the stage for the doomed love affair between Aeneas and Dido that will have repercussions throughout the epic and represents the larger themes Vergil is addressing in his work. Aeneas, after the sack of Troy, sails for Italy, where he and his followers will settle and eventually establish a colony that will one day become Rome. En route, a storm drives his ships to the coast of Africa and Carthage. He and his men are welcomed by Dido, the queen of Carthage. Venus, who is Aeneas's mother, seeks to protect him from Juno, the goddess who is determined to thwart Aeneas's mission to get to Italy. Venus, in her efforts to prevent Juno from using Dido in any scheme to impede Aeneas's quest, decides that Dido should fall in love with Aeneas—a decision that will ultimately make her son's life much more complicated than she had anticipated.

In this selection from Book I, when Dido sees Aeneas for the first time, Venus inflames her heart, and her love for Aeneas begins to grow. Dido entertains her new guests at a banquet where, with food and wine, she becomes more infatuated with the Trojan prince. As she falls under his spell, Dido asks him to tell about the fall of Troy and his wanderings. Aeneas, in a flashback similar to Odysseus's recounting of his wanderings (see Homer's *Odyssey*), recounts his adventures from the fall of Troy to arriving in Carthage.

Book VI of the *Aeneid* records Aeneas's journey through the Underworld with the aid of a Sibyl (a female prophet). Along the way, they encounter many of Aeneas's friends and a few enemies. On several occasions, Aeneas and a former companion recall shared adventures. One of the most poignant scenes in the Underworld has Aeneas meeting Dido, the queen of Carthage, who killed herself when he rejected her love and pleadings to remain with him in northern Africa.

As Aeneas and the Sibyl pass from one hideous scene in the Underworld to the next, she explains to him why the dead souls behave as they do. They eventually locate Anchises, Aeneas's father, who rejoices in this reunion with his son. Telling his father how much he values his moral teaching about obedience to duty, Aeneas asks for his father's blessing and tries to embrace him, only to discover that he is a ghostly shade.

In the *Aeneid,* Vergil is heavily indebted to Homer, his literary hero; indeed, he modeled his epic's first six books on the *Odyssey* and imitated the *Iliad* in the last six books. Although Vergil's style and method (using invocations, digressions, and similes) recall Homer's, Vergil is a more "civilized" poet, a more self-conscious artist who has an intense feeling for and sense of the past.

∽

Book I

While Trojan Aeneas stood gazing, rooted to the spot and lost in amazement at what he saw, queen Dido in all her beauty arrived at the temple with a great crowd of warriors around her. She was like Diana leading the dance on the banks of the Eurotas or along the ridges of Mount Cynthus with a thousand mountain nymphs thronging behind her on either side.[1] She carries her quiver on her shoulder, and as she walks, she is the tallest of all the goddesses. Her mother Latona does not speak, but a great joy stirs her heart at the sight of her. Dido was like Diana, and like Diana she bore herself joyfully among her people, urging on their work for the kingdom that was to be. Then she sat on her high throne under the coffered roof, in the middle of the temple before the doors of the shrine of the goddess. There, as she was giving laws and rules of conduct to her people, and dividing the work that had to be done in equal parts or allocating it by lot, Aeneas suddenly saw a great throng approaching, Antheus, Sergestus, brave Cloanthus and the other Trojans who had been scattered over the sea by the dark storm and swept away to distant shores. He was astounded, and Achates, too, was stunned

1

---

[1] **Diana, Eurotas, Mount Cynthus** Diana, the Roman goddess (Artemis in the Greek Olympian system) is playing one of her major roles—that of the maiden huntress. She is described as being either along the shores of the Euratos River, located in Greece near Sparta, or on Mount Cynthus, her alleged birthplace on the island of Delos in the Aegean Sea.

with joy and fear. They burned with longing to clasp the hands of their comrades, but were at a loss because they did not understand what they saw. They did nothing, but stayed hidden in their cloak of cloud, waiting to learn how Fortune had dealt with their comrades. On what shore had they left their fleet? Why were they here? For these were picked men coming from each of the ships to plead their case, and they were now walking to the temple with shouting all about them.

They came in and were allowed to address the queen. Ilioneus, the oldest of them, made this appeal: "You are a queen whom Jupiter[2] has allowed to found a new city and curb proud peoples with your justice; we are the unhappy men of Troy, blown by the winds over all the oceans of the world, and we come to you as suppliants. Save our ships from the impious threat of fire. We are god-fearing men. Take pity on us. Look more closely at us—we have not come to Libya to pillage your homes and their gods, to take plunder and drive it down to the shore. Such violence and arrogance are not to be found in the hearts of the defeated.

"There is a place which Greeks know by the name Hesperia.[3] It is an ancient land, strong in war and rich in the fertility of its soil. It was once tilled by Oenotrians,[4] but now we believe their descendants have called themselves Italians after their king Italus. This is where we were steering when suddenly Orion[5] rose in cloud and tempest and drove us on to hidden shallows, the sea overwhelmed us and fierce southerly squalls scattered us far and wide among breakers and uncharted rocks. A few of us drifted ashore here to your land. What manner of men are these? Is this a country of barbarians that allows its people to act in this way? Sailors have a right to the shore and we are refused it. They make war on us and will not let us set foot on land. You may be no respecters of men. You may fear no men's arms, but think of the gods, who see right and wrong and do not forget. Our king was Aeneas. He had no equal for his piety and his care for justice, and no equal in the field of battle. If the Fates still protect him, if he still breathes the air of heaven, if he is not even now laid low among the merciless shades, you would have nothing to fear or to regret by taking the lead in a contest of kindness. In the land of Sicily we have arms and cities and the great Acestes, sprung from Trojan blood. Allow us to draw up our storm-battered ships, to hew timbers in your woods and shape new oars, so that we can make for Italy and Latium with joy in our hearts, if indeed we go to Italy with our comrades and our king; but if they are lost, if you, great Father of the Trojans, are drowned in the sea off Libya, and there are no hopes left in Iulus, then we can at least go back to where we came from across the

Sicilian sea, to the place that is prepared for us, and return to king Acestes."[6] So spoke Ilioneus and all the Trojans to a man murmured in agreement.

Then Dido looked down at them and made a brief answer: "Have no fear, men of Troy. Put every anxious thought out of your hearts. This is a new kingdom, and it is harsh necessity that forces me to take these precautions and to post guards on all our frontiers. But who could fail to know about the people of Aeneas and his ancestry, or the city of Troy, the valour of its men and the flames of war that engulfed it? We here in Carthage are not so dull in mind as that. The sun does spare a glance for our Tyrian city when he yokes his horses in the morning. Whether you choose to go to great Hesperia and the fields of Saturn, or to the land of Eryx[7] and king Acestes, you will leave here safe under my protection, and I shall give you supplies to help you on your way. Or do you wish to settle here with me on an equal footing, even here in this kingdom of Carthage? The city which I am founding is yours. Draw up your ships on the beach. Trojan and Tyrian shall be as one in my eyes. I wish only that your king Aeneas had been driven by the same south wind, and were here with you now. But what I can, I shall do. I shall send men whom I can trust all along the coast, and order them to cover every furthest corner of Libya, in case he has been shipwrecked and is wandering in any of the woods or cities."

The brave Achates and Father Aeneas had long been impatient to break out of the cloud, and at Dido's words their eagerness increased. "Aeneas," said Achates, "son of the goddess, what thoughts are now rising in your heart? You see there is no danger. Our ships are safe. Our comrades are rescued. Only one of them is missing, and we saw him with our own eyes founder in mid-ocean. Everything else is as your mother Venus said it would be."

He had scarcely finished speaking when the cloud that was all about them suddenly parted and dissolved into the clear sky. Aeneas stood there resplendent in the bright light of day with the head and shoulders of a god. His own mother had breathed upon her son and given beauty to his hair and the sparkle of joy to his eyes, and the glow of youth shone all about him. It was as though skilled hands had added embellishments to ivory or applied gilding to silver or Parian marble. Then suddenly, to the surprise of all, he addressed the queen: "The man you are looking for is standing before you. I am Aeneas the Trojan, saved from the Libyan sea. And you, Dido, alone have pitied the unspeakable griefs of Troy. We are the remnants left by the Greeks. We have suffered every calamity that land and sea could inflict upon us. We have lost everything. And now you offer to share your city and your home with us. It is not within our power to repay you as you deserve, nor could whatever survives of the Trojan race, scattered as it is over the face of the wide earth. May the gods bring you the reward you deserve, if there are any gods who have regard for goodness, if there

---

[2] **Jupiter** The original Italian sky-god who was later linked to Zeus, the head god of the Greek Olympian system. Jupiter was associated with storms and thunder. The Romans placed his temple in Rome at the center of their state religion.

[3] **Hesperia** A Greek name for Italy and Sicily; it means "Land of the Evening." To the Greeks, these lands were to the west.

[4] **Oenotrians** The inhabitants of Oenotria; another name for a region of Italy.

[5] **Orion** Originally, he was a legendary giant hunter. Diane then made him into a constellation.

[6] **king Acestes** An earlier Trojan chieftain who had settled in Sicily before the time of Aeneas.

[7] **Eryx** Both a city and a mountain in Sicily. Eryx was a mythical Sicilian hero whose mother was Venus.

is any justice in the world, if their minds have any sense of right. What happy age has brought you to the light of life? What manner of parents have produced such a daughter? While rivers run into the sea, while shadows of mountains move in procession round the curves of valleys, while the sky feeds the stars, your honour, your name, and your praise will remain for ever in every land to which I am called." As he spoke, he put out his right hand to his friend Ilioneus and his left to Serestus, then greeted the others, brave Gyas, and brave Cloanthus.

Dido of Sidon was amazed at her first sight of him and then at the thought of the ill fortune he had endured. "What sort of chance is this," she exclaimed, "that hounds the son of a goddess through all these dangers? What power has driven you to these wild shores? Are you that Aeneas whom the loving goddess Venus bore to Dardanian Anchises in Phrygia by the river waters of the Simois? I myself remember the Greek Teucer coming to Sidon after being exiled from his native Salamis. He was looking to found a new kingdom, and was helped by my father Belus, who in those days was laying waste the wealth of Cyprus. He had conquered the island and it was under his control. From that day on I knew all the misfortunes of the city of Troy. I knew your name and the names of the Greek kings. Teucer himself, your enemy, held the Teucrians, the people of Troy, in highest respect and claimed descent from an ancient Teucrian family. This is why I now invite your warriors to come into my house. I, too, have known ill fortune like yours and been tossed from one wretchedness to another until at last I have been allowed to settle in this land. Through my own suffering, I am learning to help those who suffer."

With these words she led Aeneas into her royal palace, and as she went she appointed sacrifices to be offered in the temples of the gods. Nor at that moment did she forget Aeneas' comrades on the shore, but sent down to them twenty bulls, a hundred great bristling hogs' backs and a hundred fat lambs with their mothers, rich gifts to celebrate the day. Meanwhile the inside of her palace was being prepared with all royal luxury and splendour. They were laying out a banquet in the central hall and the draperies were of proud purple, richly worked. The silver was massive on the tables, with the brave deeds of their ancestors embossed in gold, a long tradition of feats of arms traced through many heroes from the ancient origins of the race.

But a father's love allowed Aeneas' mind no rest, and he asked Achates to go quickly ahead to the ships to take the news to Ascanius and bring him back to the city. All his thoughts were on his dear son Ascanius. He also told Achates to bring back with him as gifts for Dido some of the treasures that had been rescued from the ruins of Troy, a cloak stiff with gold-embroidered figures and a dress with a border woven of yellow acanthus flowers. These miracles of workmanship had been given to Helen of Argos by her mother Leda, and she had taken them from Mycenae when she came to Troy for her illicit marriage with Paris. There was also the sceptre which had once been carried by Ilione, the eldest daughter of Priam, a necklace of pearls and a double gold coronet set with jew-

els. Achates set off for the ships in great haste to carry out his instructions.

Venus meanwhile was turning over new schemes in [10] her mind and devising new plans. She decided to change the form and features of Cupid, and send him in place of the lovely young Ascanius to inflame the heart of the queen, driving her to madness by the gifts and winding the fire of passion round her bones. For Venus was afraid of the treacherous house of Carthage and the double-tongued people of Tyre. The thought of the bitterness of Juno's hatred burned in her heart, and as night began to fall and her anxiety kept returning, she spoke to the winged god of love in these words: "My dear son, you are the source of my power. You are my great strength. Only you, my son, can laugh at the thunderbolts which my father, highest Jupiter, hurled against the Giant Typhoeus.[8] To you I come for help. I am your suppliant, begging the aid of your divine power. You well know how Juno's bitter hatred is tossing your own brother from shore to shore round all the seas of the world and you have often grieved to see me grieving. Now he is in the hands of the Phoenician Dido, who is delaying him with honeyed words, and I am afraid of Juno's hospitality and what it may bring. She will not stand idle when the gate of the future is turning. That is why I am resolved to act first, taking possession of the queen by a stratagem and surrounding her with fire. No power in heaven will change her. I shall grapple her to myself in love for Aeneas. As for how you are to achieve this, listen now and I shall tell you my mind. Aeneas has sent for his son, whom I so love, and the young prince is preparing to go to the city of Carthage, bringing gifts which have survived the burning of Troy and the hazards of the sea. I shall put him into a deep sleep and hide him in one of my sacred shrines on Mount Idalium or on the heights of Cythera,[9] so that he will not know of my scheme or suddenly arrive to interrupt it. You will have to use your cunning and take on his appearance for just one night. He is a boy like yourself and you know him, so put on his features, and when the royal table is flowing with wine that brings release, and Dido takes you happily on to her lap and gives you sweet kisses, you can then breathe fire and poison into her and she will not know."

Cupid obeyed his beloved mother. He took off his wings and strutted about copying Iulus' walk and laughing. But the goddess poured quiet and rest into all the limbs of Ascanius, and holding him to the warmth of her breast, she lifted him into the high Idalian woods, where the soft amaracus breathed its fragrant shade and twined its flowers around him.

Now Cupid was obeying his instructions and taking the royal gifts, amused to be escorted by Achates. When he came in, the queen was already sitting under a rich awning on a golden couch in the middle of the palace.

---

[8] **Giant Typhoeus** A mythical fire-eating creature who was supposed to live under a volcano.
[9] **Mount Idalium and Cythera** Two places sacred to Venus where she was worshiped. Mount Idalium was on the island of Cyprus, and Cythera was an island off the southeast coast of Greece.

Presently Father Aeneas and after him the men of Troy arrived and reclined on purple coverlets. Attendants gave them water for their hands, plied them with bread from baskets and brought them fine woollen napkins with close-cut nap. Inside were fifty serving-women, whose task it was to lay out the food in order in long lines and honour the Penates[10] by tending their fires. There were a hundred other female slaves and a hundred men, all of the same age, to load the tables for the banquet and set out the drinking cups. The Tyrians, too, came thronging through the doors, and the palace was full of joy as they took their appointed places on the embroidered couches. They admired the gifts Aeneas had given. They admired Iulus, the glowing face of the god and his false words, the cloak and the dress embroidered with yellow acanthus flowers. But most of all the unfortunate Dido, doomed to be the victim of a plague that was yet to come, could not have her fill of gazing, and as she gazed, moved by the boy as much as by the gifts, the fire within her grew. After he had embraced Aeneas and hung on his neck to satisfy the great love of his father who was not his father, he went to the queen. She fixed her eyes and her whole heart on him and sometimes dandled him on her knee, without knowing what a great god was sitting there marking her out to suffer. But he was remembering his mother, the goddess of the Acidalian spring, and he began gradually to erase the memory of Sychaeus,[11] trying to turn towards a living love, a heart that had long been at peace and long unused to passion.

As soon as the first pause came in the feasting and the tables were cleared away, they set up great mixing bowls full of wine and garlanded them with flowers. The palace was ringing with noise and their voices swelled through the spacious hall. Lamps were lit and hung from the gold-coffered ceilings and the flame of torches routed the darkness. The queen now asked for a golden bowl heavy with jewels, and filled it with wine unmixed with water. From this bowl Belus had drunk, and all the royal line descended from Belus. They called for silence in the great chamber as Dido spoke: "Jupiter, to you we pray, since men say that you ordain the laws of hospitality. Grant that this day may be a day of happiness for the Tyrians and the men from Troy, and may our descendants long remember it. Let Bacchus, giver of good cheer, be among us, and kindly Juno, and you, Tyrians, celebrate this gathering with welcome in your hearts."

At these words she poured a libation of wine on the table to honour the gods, and having poured it, she took it first and just touched it to her lips. She then passed it to Bitias with a smile and a challenge. Nothing loth, he took a great draught from the golden bowl foaming to the brim, and bathed himself in wine. The other leaders of the Carthaginians did the same after him. Long-haired Iopas, the pupil of mighty Atlas, then sang to his gilded lyre of the wanderings of the moon and the labours of the sun, the origin of the human race and of the animals, the causes of rain and of the fires of heaven, of Arcturus, of the Hyades, bringers of rain, of the two Triones, the oxen of the Plough; why the winter suns are so eager to immerse themselves in the ocean, and what it is that slows down the passage of the nights. The Tyrians applauded again and again and the Trojans followed their lead.

So the doomed Dido was drawing out the night with all manner of talk, drinking long draughts of love as she asked question after question about Priam and Hector, what armour Memnon, son of the Dawn, was wearing when he came, what kind of horses did Diomede have, how tall was Achilles. "But no," she said, "come tell your hosts from the beginning about the treachery of the Greeks, the sufferings of your people and your own wanderings, for this is now the seventh summer that has carried you as a wanderer over every land and sea."

---

[10] **Penates** Roman household gods that watched over the goods and the pantry of the home. Probably originated with ancient Roman kings, but, according to legend, Aeneas bought them from Troy. Vergil repeats this story in the *Aeneid*.

[11] **Sychaeus** Dido's husband, who was murdered in Tyre. She and her fellow Tyrians escaped to Carthage soon after his death.

∽

Book VI

.   .   .

You gods who rule the world of the spirits, you silent shades, and Chaos, and Phlegethon,[12] you dark and silent wastes, let it be right for me to tell what I have been told, let it be with your divine blessing that I reveal what is hidden deep in the mists beneath the earth.

They walked in the darkness of that lonely night with shadows all about them, through the empty halls of Dis and his desolate kingdom, as men walk in a wood by the sinister light of a fitful moon when Jupiter has buried the sky in shade and black night has robbed all things of their colour. Before the entrance hall of Orcus,[13] in the very

---

[12] **Chaos and Phlegethon** The vast abysmal deep that existed before the universe or the deities, and a river of fire located in Hades. They symbolize powers or forces deep in the earth—images of impending evil and frightening events to come.

[13] **Orcus** A Roman name for Hades.

throat of hell, Grief and Revenge have made their beds and Old Age lives there in despair, with white faced Diseases and Fear and Hunger, corrupter of men, and squalid Poverty, things dreadful to look upon, and Death and Drudgery besides. Then there are Sleep, Death's sister, perverted Pleasures, murderous War astride the threshold, the iron chambers of the Furies and raving Discord with blood-soaked ribbons binding her viperous hair. In the middle a huge dark elm spreads out its ancient arms, the resting-place, so they say, of flocks of idle dreams, one clinging under every leaf. Here too are all manner of monstrous beasts, Centaurs stabling inside the gate, Scyllas—half dogs, half women—Briareus with his hundred heads, the Hydra of Lerna hissing fiercely, the Chimaera armed in fire, Gorgons and Harpies and the triple phantom of Geryon. Now Aeneas drew his sword in sudden alarm to meet them with naked steel as they came at him, and if his wise companion had not warned him that this was the fluttering of disembodied spirits, a mere semblance of living substance, he would have rushed upon them and parted empty shadows with steel.

Here begins the road that leads to the rolling waters of Acheron, the river of Tartarus. Here is a vast quagmire of boiling whirlpools which belches sand and slime into Cocytus, and these are the rivers and waters guarded by the terrible Charon in his filthy rags. On his chin there grows a thick grey beard, never trimmed. His glaring eyes are lit with fire and a foul cloak hangs from a knot at his shoulder. With his own hands he plies the pole and sees to the sails as he ferries the dead in a boat the colour of burnt iron. He is no longer young but, being a god, enjoys rude strength and a green old age. The whole throng of the dead was rushing to this part of the bank, mothers, men, great-hearted heroes whose lives were ended, boys, unmarried girls and young men laid on the pyre before the faces of their parents, as many as are the leaves that fall in the forest at the first chill of autumn, as many as the birds that flock to land from deep ocean when the cold season of the year drives them over the sea to lands bathed in sun. There they stood begging to be allowed to be the first to cross and stretching out their arms in longing for the further shore. But the grim boatman takes some here and some there, and others he pushes away far back from the sandy shore.

Aeneas, amazed and distressed by all this tumult, cried out: "Tell me, virgin priestess, what is the meaning of this crowding to the river? What do the spirits want? Why are some pushed away from the bank while others sweep the livid water with their oars?" The aged Sibyl made this brief reply: "Son of Anchises, beyond all doubt the offspring of the gods, what you are seeing is the deep pools of the Cocytus and the swamp of the Styx, by whose divine power the gods are afraid to swear and lie. The throng you see on this side are the helpless souls of the unburied. The ferryman there is Charon. Those sailing the waters of the Styx have all been buried. No man may be ferried from fearful bank to fearful bank of this roaring current until his bones are laid to rest. Instead they wander for a hundred years, fluttering round these shores until they are at last allowed to return to the pools they

have so longed for." The son of Anchises checked his stride and stood stock still with many thoughts coursing through his mind as he pitied their cruel fate, when there among the sufferers, lacking all honour in death, he caught sight of Leucaspis, and Orontes, the captain of the Lycian fleet, men who had started with him from Troy, sailed the wind-torn seas and been overwhelmed by gales from the south that rolled them in the ocean, ships and crews. . . .

And so they carried on to the end of the road on which they had started, and at last came near the river. When the boatman, now in mid-stream, looked ashore from the waves of the Styx and saw them coming through the silent wood towards the bank, he called out to them and challenged them: "You there, whoever you are, making for our river with a sword by your side, come tell us why you are here. Speak to us from where you stand. Take not another step. This place belongs to the shades, to Sleep and to Night, the bringer of Sleep. Living bodies may not be carried on the boat that plies the Styx. It gave me little enough pleasure to take even Hercules aboard when he came, or Theseus, or Pirithous,[14] although they said they were born of gods and their strength was irresistible. It was Hercules whose hand put chains on the watchdog of Tartarus and dragged him shivering from the very throne of our king. The others had taken it upon themselves to steal the queen, my mistress, from the chamber of Dis." The answer of the Amphrysian Sibyl was brief: "Here there are no such designs. You have no need for alarm. These weapons of his bring no violence. The monstrous keeper of the gate can bark in his cave and frighten the bloodless shades till the end of time and Proserpina can stay chaste behind her uncle's doors. Trojan Aeneas, famous for his devotion and his feats of arms, is going down to his father in the darkest depths of Erebus. If the sight of such devotion does not move you, then look at this branch," she said, showing the branch that had been hidden in her robes, "and realize what it is." At this the swelling anger subsided in his heart. No more words were needed. Seeing it again after a long age, and marvelling at the fateful branch, the holy offering, he turned his dark boat and steered towards the bank. He then drove off the souls who were on board with him sitting all along the cross benches, and cleared the gangways. In the same moment he took the huge Aeneas into the hull of his little boat. Being only sewn together, it groaned under his weight, shipping great volumes of stagnant water through the seams, but in the end it carried priestess and hero safely over and landed them on the foul slime among the grey-green reeds.

The kingdom on this side resounded with barking from the three throats of the huge monster Cerberus lying in a cave in front of them. When the priestess was close enough to see the snakes writhing on his neck, she threw him a honey cake steeped in soporific drugs. He opened

[14] **Theseus and Pirithous** Theseus, legendary king of Athens, and his companion, Pirithous, attempted to carry off Proserpina, who was queen of the dead, from the Underworld.

his three jaws, each of them rabid with hunger, and snapped it up where it fell. The massive back relaxed and he sprawled full length on the ground, filling his cave. The sentry now sunk in sleep, Aeneas leapt to take command of the entrance and was soon free of the bank of that river which no man may recross.

In that instant they heard voices, a great weeping and wailing of the souls of infants who had lost their share of the sweetness of life on its very threshold, torn from the breast on some black day and drowned in the bitterness of death. Next to them were those who had been condemned to death on false charges, but they did not receive their places without the casting of lots and the appointment of juries. Minos, the president of the court, shakes the lots in the urn, summoning the silent dead to act as jurymen, and holds inquiry into the lives of the accused and the charges against them. Next to them were those unhappy people who had raised their innocent hands against themselves, who had so loathed the light that they had thrown away their own lives. But now how they would wish to be under high heaven, enduring poverty and drudgery, however hard! That cannot be, for they are bound in the coils of the hateful swamp of the waters of death, trapped in the ninefold windings of the river Styx. Not far from here could be seen what they call the Mourning Plains, stretching away in every direction. Here are the victims of unhappy love, consumed by that cruel wasting sickness, hidden in the lonely byways of an encircling wood of myrtle trees, and their suffering does not leave them even in death. Here Aeneas saw Phaedra, and Procris, and Eriphyle[15] in tears as she displayed the wounds her cruel son had given her. Here he saw Evadne and Pasiphae with Laodamia[16] walking by their side, and Caeneus,[17] once a young man, but now a woman restored by destiny to her former shape.

Wandering among them in that great wood was Phoenician Dido with her wound still fresh. When the Trojan hero stopped beside her, recognizing her dim form in the darkness, like a man who sees or thinks he has seen the new moon rising through the clouds at the beginning of the month, in that instant he wept and spoke sweet words of love to her: "So the news they brought me was true, unhappy Dido? They told me you were dead and had ended your life with the sword. Alas! Alas! Was I the cause of your dying? I swear by the stars, by the gods above, by whatever there is to swear by in the depths of the earth, it was against my will, O queen, that I left your shore. It was the stern authority of the commands of the gods that drove me on, as it drives me now through the shades of

this dark night in this foul and mouldering place. I could not have believed that my leaving would cause you such sorrow. Do not move away. Do not leave my sight. Who are you running from? Fate has decreed that I shall not speak to you again." With these words Aeneas, shedding tears, tried to comfort that burning spirit, but grim-faced she kept her eyes upon the ground and did not look at him. Her features moved no more when he began to speak than if she had been a block of flint or Parian marble quarried on Mount Marpessus. Then at last she rushed away, hating him, into the shadows of the wood where Sychaeus, who had been her husband, answered her grief with grief and her love with love. Aeneas was no less stricken by the injustice of her fate and long did he gaze after her, pitying her as she went.

From here they continued on their appointed road and they were soon on the most distant of these fields, the place set apart for brave warriors. Here Tydeus came to meet him, and Parthenopaeus, famous for his feats of arms, and the pale phantom of Adrastus.[18] Here he saw and groaned to see standing in their long ranks all the sons of Dardanus who had fallen in battle and been bitterly lamented in the upper world, Glaucus, Medon and Thersilochus, the three sons of Antenor, and Polyboetes, the consecrated priest of Ceres, and Idaeus still keeping hold of Priam's chariot, still keeping hold of his armour. The shades crowded round him on the right and on the left and it was not enough just to see him, they wished to delay him, to walk with him, to learn the reasons for his coming. But when the Greek leaders and the soldiers of Agamemnon in their phalanxes saw the hero and his armour gleaming through the shadows, a wild panic seized them. Some turned and ran as they had run once before to get back to their ships, while others lifted up their voices and raised a tiny cry, which started as a shout from mouth wide open, but no shout came.[19]

Here too he saw Deiphobus, son of Priam, his whole body mutilated and his face cruelly torn. The face and both hands were in shreds. The ears had been ripped from the head. He was noseless and hideous. Aeneas, barely recognizing him as he tried frantically to hide the fearsome punishment he had received, went up to him and spoke in the voice he knew so well: "Deiphobus, mighty warrior, descended from the noble blood of Teucer, who could have wished to inflict such a punishment upon you? And who was able to do this? I was told that on that last night you wore yourself out killing the enemy and fell on a huge pile of Greek and Trojan dead. At that time I did all I could do, raising an empty tomb for you on the shore of Cape Rhoeteum and lifting up my voice to call three times upon your shade. Your name and your arms mark the

---

[15] **Phaedra, Procris, and Eriphyle** Three women who either killed or betrayed their husbands or sons.
[16] **Evadne, Pasiphae, Laodamia** Evadne and Laodamia committed suicide. Pasiphae was the wife of King Minos of Crete and the mother of the monster the Minotaur, who lived in the Labyrinth and ate the prisoners sent into the Labyrinth.
[17] **Caeneus** A mythological character who was first a nymph, then changed into a man by Neptune, the sea god, and then to a woman.

[18] **Tydeus, Parthenopaeus, and Adrastus** Tydeus was the father of Diomede, who was a Greek warrior in the *Iliad*. Parthenopaeus was a member of the "seven against Thebes" band that laid siege to the city. Adrastus, the mythical king of Argos, lost two sons-in-law in the battle of Thebes.
[19] **Dardanus, Glaucus, Medon, Thersilochus, Antenor, Polyboetes, Idaeus, Priam, and Agamemnon** All these characters were warriors or leaders on both sides of the Trojan War and were in the *Iliad*.

place but you I could not find, my friend, to bury your body in our native land as I was leaving it."

To this the son of Priam answered: "You, my friend, have left nothing undone. You have paid all that is owed to Deiphobus and to his dead shade. It is my own destiny and the crimes of the murderess from Sparta that have brought me to this. These are reminders of Helen. You know how we spent that last night in false joy. It is our lot to remember it only too well. When the horse that was the instrument of Fate, heavy with the brood of armed men in its belly, leapt over the high walls of Pergamum, Helen was pretending to be worshipping Bacchus, leading the women of Phrygia around the city, dancing and shrieking their ritual cries. There she was in the middle of them with a huge torch, signalling to the Greeks from the top of the citadel, and all the time I was sleeping soundly in our accursed bed, worn out by all I had suffered and sunk in a sleep that was sweet and deep and like the peace of death. Meanwhile this excellent wife of mine, after moving all my armour out of the house and taking the good sword from under my head, called in Menelaus and threw open the doors, hoping no doubt that her loving husband would take this as a great favour to wipe out the memory of her past sins. You can guess the rest. They burst into the room, taking with them the man who had incited them to their crimes, their comrade Ulixes—they say he is descended from Aeolus. You gods, if the punishment I ask is just, grant that a fate like mine should strike again and strike Greeks. But come, it is now time for you to tell me what chance has brought you here alive. Is it your sea wanderings that have taken you here? Are you under the instructions of the gods? What fortune is dogging you, that you should come here to our sad and sunless homes in this troubled place?"

While they were speaking to one another, Dawn's rosy chariot had already run its heavenly course past the midpoint of the vault of the sky, and they might have spent all the allotted time in talking but for Aeneas' companion. The Sibyl gave her warning in few words: "Night is running quickly by, Aeneas, and we waste the hours in weeping. This is where the way divides. On the right it leads up to the walls of great Dis. This is the road we take for Elysium. On the left is the road of punishment for evildoers, leading to Tartarus,[20] the place of the damned." "There is no need for anger, great priestess," replied Deiphobus. "I shall go to take my place among the dead and return to darkness. Go, Aeneas, go, great glory of our Troy, and enjoy a better fate than mine." These were his only words, and as he spoke he turned on his heel and strode away.

Aeneas looked back suddenly and saw under a cliff on his left a broad city encircled by a triple wall and washed all round by Phlegethon, one of the rivers of Tartarus, a torrent of fire and flame, rolling and grinding great boulders in its current. There before him stood a huge gate with columns of solid adamant so strong that neither the violence of men nor of the heavenly gods themselves could ever uproot them in war, and an iron tower rose into the air where Tisiphone sat with her blood-soaked dress girt up, guarding the entrance and never sleeping, night or day. They could hear the groans from the city, the cruel crack of the lash, the dragging and clanking of iron chains. Aeneas stood in terror, listening to the noise. "What kinds of criminal are here? Tell me, virgin priestess, what punishments are inflicted on them? What is this wild lamentation in the air?" The Sibyl replied: "Great leader of the Trojans, the chaste may not set foot upon the threshold of that evil place, but when Hecate put me in charge of the groves of Avernus,[21] she herself explained the punishments the gods had imposed and showed me them all. Here Rhadamanthus, king of Cnossus, holds sway with his unbending laws, chastising men, hearing all the frauds they have practised and forcing them to confess the undiscovered crimes they have gloated over in the upper world—foolishly, for they have only delayed the day of atonement till after death. Immediately the avenging Tisiphone[22] leaps upon the guilty and flogs them till they writhe, waving fearful serpents over them in her left hand and calling up the cohorts of her savage sisters, the Furies. Then at last the gates sacred to the gods below shriek in their sockets and open wide. You see what a watch she keeps, sitting in the entrance? What a sight she is guarding the threshold? Inside, more savage still, the huge, black-throated, fifty-headed Hydra has its lair. And then there is Tartarus itself, stretching sheer down into its dark chasm twice as far as we look up to the ethereal Olympus in the sky. Here, rolling in the bottom of the abyss, is the ancient brood of Earth, the army of Titans, hurled down by the thunderbolt. Here too I saw the huge bodies of the twin sons of Aloeus who laid violent hands on the immeasurable sky to wrench it from its place and tear down Jupiter from his heavenly kingdom. I saw too Salmoneus suffering cruel punishment, still miming the flames of Jupiter and the rumblings of Olympus. He it was who, riding his four-horse chariot and brandishing a torch, used to go in glory through the peoples of Greece and the city of Olympia in the heart of Elis, laying claim to divine honours for himself—fool that he was to copy the storm and the inimitable thunderbolt with the rattle of the horn of his horses' hooves on bronze. Through the thick clouds the All-powerful Father hurled his lightning—no smoky light from pitchy torches for him—and sent him spinning deep into the abyss. Tityos too I could see, the nurseling of Earth, mother of all, his body sprawling over nine whole acres while a huge vulture with hooked beak cropped his immortal liver and the flesh that was such a rich supplier of punishment. Deep in his breast

---

[20] **Dis, Elysium, Tartarus** Three regions in the Underworld. Dis was another name for Hades. Elysium was where the souls of the blessed dead dwelled. Tartarus was an abyss under Hades where some of the most heinous offenders were kept, including the Titans, who were a family of mythical giants who came before the Roman deities and were put here by Jupiter when he became the chief god.

[21] **Hecate, Avernus** Hecate was a goddess of the Underworld. Avernus is a lake near Naples, thought to be an entrance to the Underworld.

[22] **Tisiphone** A goddess of the Underworld, whose name means "Avenger of Blood."

it roosts and forages for its dinners, while the filaments of his liver know no rest but are restored as soon as they are consumed. I do not need to speak of the Lapiths, of Ixion or Pirithous, over whose heads the boulder of black flint is always slipping, always seeming to be falling. The gold gleams on the high supports of festal couches and a feast is laid in regal splendour before the eyes of the guilty, but the greatest of the Furies is reclining at table and allows no hand to touch the food, but leaps up brandishing a torch and shouting with a voice of thunder. Immured in this place and waiting for punishment are those who in life hated their brothers, beat their fathers, defrauded their dependants, found wealth and brooded over it alone without setting aside a share for their kinsmen—these are most numerous of all—men caught and killed in adultery, men who took up arms against their own people and did not shrink from abusing their masters' trust. Do not ask to know what their punishments are, what form of pain or what misfortune has engulfed them. Some are rolling huge rocks, or hang spreadeagled on the spokes of wheels. Theseus is sitting there dejected, and there he will sit until the end of time, while Phlegyas,[23] most wretched of them all, shouts this lesson for all men at the top of his voice in the darkness: 'Learn to be just and not to slight the gods. You have been warned.' Here is the man who has sold his native land for gold, and set a tyrant over it, putting up tablets with new laws for a price and for a price removing them. Here is the man who forced his way into his daughter's bed and a forbidden union. They have all dared to attempt some monstrous crime against the gods and have succeeded in their attempt. If I had a hundred tongues, a hundred mouths and a voice of iron, I could not encompass all their different crimes or speak the names of all their different punishments."

When the aged priestess of Apollo had finished her answer, she added these words: "But come now, you must take the road and complete the task you have begun. Let us hasten. I can see the high walls forged in the furnaces of the Cyclopes[24] and the gates there in front of us in the arch. This is where we have been told to lay the gift that is required of us." After these words they walked the dark road together, soon covering the distance and coming close to the doors. There Aeneas leapt on the threshold, sprinkled his body with fresh water and fixed the bough full in the doorway.

When this rite was at last performed and his duty to the goddess was done, they entered the land of joy, the lovely glades of the fortunate woods and the home of the blest. Here a broader sky clothes the plains in glowing light, and the spirits have their own sun and their own stars. Some take exercise on grassy wrestling-grounds and hold athletic contests and wrestling bouts on the golden sand. Others pound the earth with dancing feet and sing

their songs while Orpheus, the priest of Thrace, accompanies their measures on his seven-stringed lyre, plucking the notes sometimes with his fingers, sometimes with his ivory plectrum. Here was the ancient line of Teucer, the fairest of all families, great-hearted heroes born in a better time, Ilus, Assaracus and Dardanus,[25] the founder of Troy. Aeneas admired from a distance their armour and empty chariots. Their swords were planted in the ground and their horses wandered free on the plain cropping the grass. Reposing there below the earth, they took the same joy in their chariots and their armour as when alive, and the same care to feed their sleek horses. Then suddenly he saw others on both sides of him feasting on the grass, singing in a joyful choir their paean to Apollo all through a grove of fragrant laurels where the mighty river Eridanus rolls through the forest to the upper world. Here were armies of men bearing wounds received while fighting for their native land, priests who had been chaste unto death and true prophets whose words were worthy of Apollo; then those who have raised human life to new heights by the skills they have discovered and those whom men remember for what they have done for men. All these with sacred ribbons of white round their foreheads gathered round Aeneas and the Sibyl, and she addressed these words to them, especially to Musaeus,[26] for the whole great throng looked up to him as he stood there in the middle, head and shoulders above them all: "Tell me, blessed spirits, and you, best of poets, which part of this world holds Anchises? Where is he to be found? It is because of Anchises that we have come here and crossed the great rivers of Erebus." The hero returned a short answer. "None of us has a fixed home. We live in these densely wooded groves and rest on the soft couches of the river bank and in the fresh water-meadows. But if that is the desire of your hearts, come climb this ridge and I shall soon set you on an easy path." So saying, he walked on in front of them to a place from where they could see the plains below them bathed in light, and from that point Aeneas and the Sibyl came down from the mountain tops.

Father Anchises was deep in a green valley, walking among the souls who were enclosed there and eagerly surveying them as they waited to rise into the upper light. It so happened that at that moment he was counting the number of his people, reviewing his dear descendants, their fates and their fortunes, their characters and their courage in war. When he saw Aeneas coming towards him over the grass, he stretched out both hands in eager welcome, with the tears streaming down his cheeks, and these were the words that broke from his mouth: "You have come at last," he cried. "I knew your devotion would prevail over all the rigour of the journey and bring you to your father. Am I to be allowed to look upon your face, my son, to hear the voice I know so well and answer it with my own? I never doubted it. I counted the hours, knowing you would come, and my love has not deceived me. I

---

[23] **Phlegyas** Mythical king of the Lapiths, who supposedly burnt Apollo's temple at Delphi and was punished in the Underworld by having to sit under a rock that could fall on him at any moment.
[24] **Cyclopes** The giants with one eye in the middle of their foreheads. One legend claims that they were thrown into Hades by Kronos, the Titan god who was the father of Zeus. They were also associated with working around forges.

[25] **Teucer, Ilus, Assaracus, Dardanus** All these characters were identified with the city of Troy.
[26] **Musaeus** Ancient mythical poet, considered to be the successor to Orpheus, the first poet.

understand how many lands you have travelled and how many seas you have sailed to come to me here. I know the dangers that have beset you. I so feared the kingdom of Libya would do you harm." "It was my vision of you," replied Aeneas, "always before my eyes and always stricken with sorrow, that drove me to the threshold of this place. The fleet is moored in the Tyrrhenian sea on the shores of Italy. Give me your right hand, father. Give it me. Do not avoid my embrace." As he spoke these words his cheeks were washed with tears and three times he tried to put his arms around his father's neck. Three times the phantom melted in his hands, as weightless as the wind, as light as the flight of sleep.

And now Aeneas saw in a side valley a secluded grove with copses of rustling trees where the river Lethe glided along past peaceful dwelling houses. Around it fluttered numberless races and tribes of men, like bees in a meadow on a clear summer day, settling on all the many-coloured flowers and crowding round the gleaming white lilies while the whole plain is loud with their buzzing. Not understanding what he saw, Aeneas shuddered at the sudden sight of them and asked why this was, what was that river in the distance and who were all those companies of men crowding its banks. "These are the souls to whom Fate owes a second body," replied Anchises. "They come to the waves of the river Lethe and drink the waters of serenity and draughts of long oblivion. I have long been eager to tell you who they are, to show them to you face to face and count the generations of my people to you so that you could rejoice the more with me at the finding of Italy." "But are we to believe," replied Aeneas to his dear father, "that there are some souls who rise from here to go back under the sky and return to sluggish bodies? Why do the poor wretches have this terrible longing for the light?" "I shall tell you, my son, and leave you no longer in doubt,"

replied Anchises, and he began to explain all things in due order.

"In the beginning Spirit fed all things from within, the sky and the earth, the level waters, the shining globe of the moon and the Titan's star, the sun. It was Mind that set all this matter in motion. Infused through all the limbs, it mingled with that great body, and from the union there sprang the families of men and of animals, the living things of the air and the strange creatures born beneath the marble surface of the sea. The living force within them is of fire and its seeds have their source in heaven, but their guilt-ridden bodies make them slow and they are dulled by earthly limbs and dying flesh. It is this that gives them their fears and desires, their griefs and joys. Closed in the blind darkness of this prison they do not see out to the winds of air. Even when life leaves them on their last day of light, they are not wholly freed from all the many ills and miseries of the body which must harden in them over the long years and become ingrained in ways we cannot understand. And so they are put to punishment, to pay the penalty for all their ancient sins. Some are stretched and hung out empty to dry in the winds. Some have the stain of evil washed out of them under a vast tide of water or scorched out by fire. Each of us suffers his own fate in the after-life. From here we are sent over the broad plains of Elysium and some few of us possess these fields of joy until the circle of time is completed and the length of days has removed ingrained corruption and left us pure ethereal sense, the fire of elemental air. All these others whom you see, when they have rolled the wheel for a thousand years, are called out by God to come in great columns to the river of Lethe, so that they may duly go back and see the vault of heaven again remembering nothing, and begin to be willing to return to bodies." . . .

HORACE

Selections from *Odes* and *Satires*

Horace's *Odes* (Books I–III, 23 B.C.; Book IV, ca. 13 B.C.) were a milestone in ancient literature. They signal the beginning of Latin lyric poetry and are also its zenith. They confirmed Horace's literary reputation and brought him favor from Augustus, Rome's first emperor. Ignored in medieval Europe, Horace's works came into their own during the Renaissance and enjoyed their finest hour in the classical revival of the seventeenth and eighteenth centuries. The poems' tact and good taste are traits of the Augustan Age (31 B.C.–A.D. 14), which gave them birth.

Horace (65–8 B.C.) and the Greek poet Pindar (522–442 B.C.) are usually credited with begetting the ode, a lyric poem expressing lofty feelings and ideas in a stately tone. Pindar's odes were written for public occasions, such as honoring victors in the games. In contrast, Horace's odes were private and personal, speaking of love and wine, religion and the state, life and death, and praise for his patron, Maecenas. Their variety reflects Horace's love of Greek literature and his experiences as a man of both city and countryside.

In the *Odes,* Horace adapted Greek verse forms, borrowing largely from Sappho and Alcaeus (fl. ca. 611–580 B.C.). Following them, he grew into a master of poetic subtlety and tightly compressed lyrics. He delighted in finding the exact word to convey a precise shade of meaning: "If a clever combination makes a familiar word new, that is distinguished writing." One feature, however, made his odes distinctive—unlike Alcaeus's and Sappho's lyrics, his odes were not composed for musical performance.

The *Odes* are normally called his greatest work, but Horace also wrote poetic epistles, epodes ("refrains"), and satires (see Juvenal's *Satire III*), the latter of which he pioneered. He also wrote the *Art of Poetry,* a book of literary advice whose focus on decorum undergirded the classicism of seventeenth and eighteenth-century literature.

A sketch of Horace's life shows Rome's social diversity. Horace was the son of an ex-slave. Partly because of the paradox that freedmen were second-class citizens whereas their sons had full rights, he had a keen eye for social slights. Even at the height of his fame, he detected traces of resentment. Nevertheless, he experienced the best of his world. Paternal wealth enabled him to study at an aristocratic school in Rome and at the Academy in Athens, and his literary works won the esteem of the imperial court.

Reading the Selections

Horace's theme in Ode II.16 is peace of mind and how to achieve it. Addressed to a rich man named Grosphus, the ode gently chides as it gives advice. The advice the speaker offers is epicurean: Avoid politics, live modestly, and cultivate poetry. The reference to "a little farm" is Horace's Sabine farm, a gift from Maecenas.

Ode III.6 is a public ode, reflecting Horace's critique of Rome written before Augustus's reign. Paying no heed to the gods has brought tragedy to Rome: military defeat, civil war, adultery. The ode concludes with a chilling forecast. A highlight of this lyric is that, near the end, it conveys the poet's love of nature.

An amused, though gently critical, spectator of his fellow Romans, Horace wrote two books of satires (issued 34 B.C. and 30 B.C.) in which he dissected the foibles and vices of the capital city. "The Bore" is typical of the satire genre he pioneered, in that it depicts a social type, allowing the subject to speak in an almost colloquial voice. In this selection, an ever polite speaker ("I") is tormented by a talkative bore, who monopolizes the conversation and refuses to go away despite the speaker's evasive maneuvers. In real life, Horace turned his back on Rome, rejecting its "smoke and wealth and noise" in favor of a quiet country existence.

Ode II.16
Otium divos (Restiveness)

Peace, Grosphus, is what the man on the open
Aegean requires of the Gods when black cloud
obscures the moon and no fixed star can flash for the
    sailors.

Peace for the Thracians[1] enraged with war,

peace for the Medes[2] with their stylish quivers,
is not to be bought with gems or gold or gleaming fabrics.

Neither Persian treasure nor the consul's
lictor can disperse the wretched mob

1

---

[1] **Thracians** Inhabitants of Thrace, which was located east of Macedonia and north of the Aegean Sea. They were often at war and subject to various conquerors. The Roman emperor Claudius subdued Thrace in 26 B.C., during Horace's lifetime.

[2] **Medes** Inhabitants of Media, which was located in western Asia or in modern western Iran. The Medes conquered the Persians in the eighth century B.C. and then were overrun by the Assyrians, from whom they gained their independence. Later conquered by the Persians, then the Parthians, and, finally, the Romans.

of the mind or the cares that flit about your coffered
    ceilings.

He lives well on a little whose family   10
salt-cellar shines amid a modest
table, whose gentle sleep is not dispelled by fear or base
    greed.

Why do we aim so high, so bravely,
so briefly? Why hanker for countries scorched
by an alien sun? What exile from home can avoid
    himself?

Care clambers aboard the armoured ships,
keeps pace with the cavalry squadrons, comes
swift as East-Wind-driven rain, comes swift as any stag.

The soul content with the present
is not concerned with the future and tempers   20

dismay with an easy laugh. No blessing is unmixed.

An early death snatched bright Achilles;
long senility reduced Tithonus:[3]
this hour will offer to me, maybe, the good it denies to you.

For you a hundred herds of Sicilian
cattle moo; for you are bred
neighing mares apt for the chariot; you dress in twice-dyed

Tyrian purple wool: to me honest Fate
has given a little farm, the delicate breath
of the Grecian Muse, and disdain for the jealous mob.   30

---

[3] **Tithonus** A legendary Trojan who was loved by Eos, the goddess of
the dawn. She granted him immortality but not eternal youth, so he
grew very decrepit and, by some accounts, turned into a grasshopper.

Ode III.6

Delicta maiorum (How we are fallen!)

Though innocent you shall atone for the crimes   1
of your fathers, Roman, until you have restored
the temples and crumbling shrines of the Gods
and their statues grimy with smoke.

Acknowledge the rule of the Gods—and rule:
hence all things begin, to this ascribe the outcome.
Contemned, the Gods have visited many
evils on grieving Hesperia.[1]

Already twice Monaeses and Pacorus'[2] band
have crushed our ill-starred offensive   10
and preen themselves on having added
Roman spoils to their paltry gauds.

Our city busied with sedition has almost
suffered destruction by Egypt allied to Dacia,
the former renowned for her fleet, the latter
rather for hurtling arrows.

Teeming with sin, the times have sullied
first marriage, our children, our homes:
sprung from that source disaster has whelmed
our fatherland and our people.   20

The grown girl loves to be taught to be
artful and dance oriental dances,
obsessed to her dainty fingernails
with illicit amours.

She sniffs out young philand'rers at her
husband's feast, nor is she nice to choose
to whom she (hurriedly) grants her favours
when the lamps are removed,

but brazenly stands when called—with her
husband's assent—though some travelling   30
salesman or Spanish ship's captain
may be the agent of Shame.

The generation that dyed the Punic
sea with blood and laid low Pyrrhus,
Antiochus and Hannibal[3] was not born
of parents such as these,

but of manly comrades, yeoman soldiers
taught to turn the soil with Sabine[4] hoes

---

[1] **Hesperia** The Greek name for the western or evening land, that is,
Italy.
[2] **Monaeses and Pacorus** Two Parthian commanders who defeated
the Romans during Horace's lifetime.

[3] **Pyrrhus, Antiochus, Hannibal** Three generals who tried to conquer Rome but failed.
[4] **Sabine** The Sabines were an ancient tribe north of Rome that was
conquered in the early years of the third century B.C. The Romans
adopted many religious traditions from the Sabines.

and carry cut firewood at a strict
mother's bidding when the Sun   40

advanced the shadows of the hills
and lifted the yokes from weary steers,
his departing chariot leading in
the hours of comfort.

What does corrupting time not diminish?
Our grandparents brought forth feebler heirs;
we are further degen'rate; and soon will beget
progeny yet more wicked.

∾

Satire I.9

The Bore (or *A morning stroll*)

Ibam forte via Sacra, sicut meus est mos

I was walking down the Sacred Way,[1] my usual route,   1
Turning over some lines in my head, completely
    absorbed.
A man I knew only by name ran up, seized my hand:
"How *are* you, my dear old fellow?" "Just fine," I
    answered,
"The way things are going. I hope *you* are getting on
    nicely."
When he kept up with me, I thought I'd forestall him by
    asking
"There's nothing I can do for you, is there?" "Oh, YES!" he
    shot back,
"Get to know me. I'm quite avant-garde." "Oh, good," I
    replied,
"I like you for that." Trying awfully hard to shake him,
I went on faster, then stopped in my tracks and   10
    whispered
Something in my slave's ear while sweat streamed down
    to my ankles.
"Bolanus,"[2] I thought to myself, "I envy the way
You blow your top. That would fix this fellow," who
    meanwhile
Kept yammering on, ga-ga with the big city sights.
When I failed to respond, he piped up, "I see how
    impatient
You are to be off. It's no use. I'm sticking with you—
I'll just tag along—where are you headed?" "Oh, NO,
Don't put yourself out! I'm going to see a sick friend,
Someone you don't know, way over in Trastevere[3]
Near the Villa Aurelia." "Oh, well, I've got nothing to do,   20
And I'm not afraid of the walk, so I'll go along with you."

My ears drooped down as a donkey's will do when he
    knows
He's loaded beyond his strength. Then he started in,
"If I know myself, you'll find me as good a friend
As Varius or Viscus.[4] What author writes *more*, for
    example,
Or *faster* than I do? What dancer is more suggestive?
And sing? Why, Hermogenes [he meant Tigellius H.,
The singer, not the dessert] would envy my voice."
This was my chance to cut in, "And your poor old mother,
The relatives who care for you, won't they be worried   30
    if . . . ?"
"I haven't a soul in the world! I've buried them all."
"Lucky people," I sighed. "I seem to be all that's left.
Finish me off! For the hour is come the old gypsy
Foretold in my youth, as she shook the lots in an urn:

'This lad shall not be killed by malignant poison
Nor by the enemy's sword, neither by pleurisy
Nor pneumonia, nor gout that goes slow. But
    someday someone
Will simply talk him to death. When he comes of age,
If he's smart let him keep his distance from Talkative
    Persons.'"

By now it was nine o'clock, and we had arrived   40
At the temple of Vesta.[5] My companion, it seemed, was
    due
In court at nine, or would forfeit his case. "Won't you
    please
Stay around and lend me support?" he asked. "Hell, no!"
I answered. "I can't stand around, and I'm no good at law.

---

[1] **Sacred Way** One of the main thoroughfares leading into the Roman Forum.

[2] **Bolanus** Horace is probably referring to his slave, who has a short temper and would have told off this bore; but, he, Horace, is not able to get rid of the bore.

[3] **Trastevere** A residential section of Rome across the Tiber River from the Forum and the Sacred Way.

---

[4] **Varius or Viscus** Varius was a contemporary poet and friend of Horace. Only fragments of his works remain. Viscus, to rhyme with Varius, seemingly refers to one of the body's internal organs. Thus the bore wants to be a close friend.

[5] **Vesta** The temple of Vesta was where the eternal flame burned, guarded by the vestal virgins.

You know where I'm hurrying off to." "I just don't know
What to do," he mused, "leave you, or my case." "ME
    please."
"I couldn't do that," he concluded, and started on ahead.
And I—well, you can't beat a winner—so I followed
    after him.
  "How are things with you and Maecenas?" he asked. I
    answered,
"He's a man of much sense and few friends." But he kept   50
    boring in,
"You've drawn good cards and played your hand right,
    you have.
Now if you wanted to do something more, you'd bring in
    myself,
The fellow who's talking to you. I'd be a help,
And I'm willing to play second fiddle. Damn it all, man,
You'd make them all knuckle under." "We don't carry on
Quite the way you think," I said icily; "there's no place
    so free
From intrigue as Maecenas', no place so thoroughly
    honest.
It just doesn't matter to them whether someone is richer
Or smarter than somebody else. Everyone gets along."
"A TALL one," he said, "hard to believe." "But it's true!"   60
"Well, it just makes me hotter than ever to be admitted."
"Keep wishing. Your talent is such that you'll storm his
    defenses.
He's a man one can conquer—for this is surely the reason
He makes the approaches so hard." "I bet I don't fail.
I'll bribe all his servants. I'll keep coming back, pick my
    times,
Meet him walking in town, join his escort. Nothing
In life comes to men without labor."

                     While we were talking
Along comes my dear friend Aristius Fuscus, who knew,
Perfectly well, the man I was with. We stopped.   70
"Where are you coming from, where are you going?" got
    asked
And answered. I started pulling his sleeve and tugging
At his unfeeling arm. No response! I nodded, and winked
Fiercely at him to save me. No response but a laugh from
    the wag,
Who pretended to misunderstand. I was livid and
    spluttered
"Oh, Fuscus, you said you had something to say to me
    privately."
"Yes, I know, but let's save it for some other time.
                            Today
Is the Thirtieth Sabbath. You wouldn't want to offend
The circumcised Jews, now would you?" "Oh, I'm not   80
    religious."
I said. "Well, *I* am," he said, "it's a weakness I share
With most people. You forgive me? Some other time
I'll tell you what I had in mind to say." How black
Can things look? That best of all blackguards, Aristius
    Fuscus,
Ran off and left the knife at my throat.
                          Just then
The plaintiff chanced to come by and see his opponent.
"You scoundrel, where are you off to?" he yelled.
    "Would you   90
[Turning to me] be a witness to this arrest?"
WOULD I! He dragged him to court, both of them
    shouting.
A crowd had formed. And thus I was saved by Apollo.

OVID

Selections from *Metamorphoses*

Ovid (43 B.C.–A.D. 17), like Horace (see *Odes*), was a great Latin writer who was not a native
Roman. From Sulmo (central Italy), Ovid came to Rome to study in an aristocratic school.
Trained for politics, he turned to poetry and became the epitome of the worldly set that domi-
nated Roman fashion in his day.

    Ovid's *Metamorphoses* has delighted readers since it first circulated (A.D. 8) in Rome's
Augustan Age; few works from any period have had such a lasting impact on later culture.
Since the Middle Ages, poets and artists have mined it for subjects and plots. In it they found a
collection of Roman and mainly Greek myths and legends—the intellectual stock-in-trade of
Ovid's day. The *Metamorphoses* mediated these myths to the whole of Europe.

    A long poem, the *Metamorphoses* consists of more than two hundred stories divided into
fifteen "books" and organized around a simple theme: All are tales of shape-shifting, or magical changes of form. They are about people, usually legendary, changed into stone, trees, animals, birds, and stars. The poet's tone toward these shape-shiftings is lighthearted, even
tongue-in-cheek.

The poem's subject touched on a growing trend in Rome: the worship of rulers as gods—an inheritance from the Middle East as new peoples joined the empire. Ovid welcomed this trend, for he made the poem's climax (Book XV) the transformation of Julius Caesar into a blazing comet, with the added prediction that Augustus too would "make his way to heaven. . . ." Here Ovid showed his patriotism, because the Senate had voted Caesar divine status, and plans were afoot to do the same for Augustus.

The *Metamorphoses* is ironic in that Ovid's praise for Augustus did not save him from the emperor's wrath. As the poet was finishing this work, Augustus banished him to a remote frontier-post of the empire, Tomis (Constanta in Rumania). He was never granted permission to return. Why Ovid was banished is not clear. Perhaps it was the flippant *Art of Love,* a handbook on seduction, which offended propriety and thus damaged Augustus's efforts to reform Roman morals. Perhaps he knew too much about a sex scandal involving the emperor's granddaughter Julia. Whatever the reason, Ovid saw his exile as a spiritual death. He nevertheless continued to write, sustained by the thought that his poetry would make him immortal. "I shall live to all eternity, immortalized by fame."

Reading the Selections

The story of Daphne and Apollo (Book I of the *Metamorphoses*) is Ovid's account of the star-crossed love of the god Apollo (called Phoebus) for the nymph Daphne. Its premise is that the gods have absolute power but lack moral scruples. Apollo, pierced by Cupid's arrow, is overcome with lust, so that his prophetic powers are useless. To win Daphne, he first tries to woo her; when that fails, he decides on rape. Apollo is depicted as the slave of his passions. Daphne ultimately escapes rape by being changed into a laurel tree. True "happy endings" are rare in this poem.

Ovid's lighthearted style sugarcoats his basic cynicism. He wrote to entertain, not to improve. Not religious in any ordinary sense, Ovid did not shrink from depicting the gods in indecent roles, as in Apollo's rape attempt. Ovid's world was conspicuously amoral, where divine caprice ran riot. As with humans, the gods were victims of their emotions and liable to be swept away by fate.

Ovid's tone in the *Metamorphoses* was not completely cynical, however, as may be seen in probably its best known episode, the story of Pyramus, "the most handsome of young men," and Thisbe, "the fairest beauty of the East" (Book IV). Ovid's tone is tender and loving, as he describes the stirrings of first love between the doomed Pyramus and Thisbe. Ovid's is the first known account of this tale and, later writers, finding it attractive, composed their own versions, as, for example, Marie de France, Boccaccio, and Chaucer. Shakespeare even used the Pyramus and Thisbe episode as a subject for comedy, in *A Midsummer Night's Dream.*

Book I
Daphne and Apollo

. . .

Daphne, the daughter of Peneus,[1] was Phoebus'[2] first love, and it was not blind chance which brought this about, but Cupid's savage spite. Not long before, the Delian god, still exultant over his slaying of the serpent, had seen Cupid[3] bending his taut bow, and had said: "You naughty boy, what have you to do with a warrior's arms? Weapons such as these are suited to my shoulders: for I can aim my shafts unerringly, to wound wild beast or

---

[1] **Peneus** A river in Thessaly, a country in northeastern Greece, and the name of the god of the river.
[2] **Phoebus** Another name for Apollo.

[3] **Cupid** The Roman god of love; son of Venus, the Roman goddess of love.

human foe, as I lately slew the bloated Python with my countless arrows, though it covered so many acres with its pestilential coils. You be content with your torch to excite love, whatever that may be, and do not aspire to praises that are my prerogative." But Venus' son replied: "Your bow may pierce everything else, Phoebus, but mine will pierce *you:* and as all animals are inferior to the gods, your glory is to that extent less than mine."

With these words he swiftly winged his way through the air, till he alighted on the shady summit of Parnassus.[4] From his quiver, full of arrows, he drew two darts, with different properties. The one puts love to flight, the other kindles it. That which kindles love is golden, and shining, sharp-tipped; but that which puts it to flight is blunt, its shaft tipped with lead. With this arrow the god pierced the nymph, Peneus' daughter, but Apollo he wounded with the other, shooting it into the marrow of his bones. Immediately the one fell in love; the other, fleeing the very word "lover," took her delight in woodland haunts and in the spoils of captured beasts, emulating Diana,[5] the maiden goddess, with her hair carelessly caught back by a single ribbon.

Many a suitor wooed her but, turning away from their entreaties, she roamed the pathless woods, knowing nothing of men, and caring nothing for them, heedless of what marriage or love or wedded life might be. Again and again her father said: "It is your duty to marry and give me a son-in-law, my child." Often he repeated: "My child, it is your duty to give me grandchildren." But she blushed, hating the thought of marriage as if it were some crime. The modest colour crimsoned her fair face and, throwing her arms round her father's neck, she cried imploringly: "My dear, dear father let me enjoy this state of maiden bliss for ever! Diana's father granted her such a boon in days gone by!" Her father did, indeed, yield to her request, but her very loveliness prevented her from being what she desired, and her beauty defeated her own wishes.

As soon as Phoebus saw Daphne, he fell in love with her, and wanted to marry her. His own prophetic powers deceived him and he hoped to achieve his desire. As the light stubble blazes up in a harvested field, or as the hedge is set alight, if a traveller chance to kindle a fire too close, or leaves one smouldering when he goes off at daybreak, so the god was all on fire, his whole heart was aflame, and he nourished his fruitless love on hope. He eyed her hair as it hung carelessly about her neck, and sighed: "What if it were properly arranged!" He looked at her eyes, sparkling bright as stars, he looked at her lips, and wanted to do more than look at them. He praised her fingers, her hands and arms, bare almost to the shoulder. Her hidden charms he imagined lovelier still.

But Daphne ran off, swifter than the wind's breath, and did not stop to hear his words, though he called her

back: "I implore you, nymph, daughter of Peneus, do not run away! Though I pursue you, I am no enemy. Stay, sweet nymph! You flee as a lamb flees the wolf, or the deer the lion, as doves on fluttering wings fly from an eagle, as all creatures flee their natural foes! But it is love that drives me to follow you. Alas, how I fear lest you trip and fall, lest briars scratch your innocent legs, and I be the cause of your hurting yourself. These are rough places through which you are running—go less swiftly, I beg of you, slow your flight, and I in turn shall pursue less swiftly!

"Yet stay to inquire whose heart you have charmed. I am no peasant, living in a mountain hut, nor am I a shepherd or boorish herdsman who tends his flocks and cattle in these regions. Silly girl, you do not know from whom you are fleeing: indeed, you do not, or else you would not flee. I am lord of Delphi, Claros, and Tenedos, and of the realms of Patara[6] too. I am the son of Jupiter.[7] By my skill, the past, the present, and the future are revealed; thanks to me, the lyre strings thrill with music. My arrow is sure, though there is one surer still, which has wounded my carefree heart. The art of medicine is my invention, and men the world over give me the name of healer. All the properties of herbs are known to me: but alas, there are no herbs to cure love, and the skill which helps others cannot help its master."

He would have said more, but the frightened maiden fled from him, leaving him with his words unfinished; even then, she was graceful to see, as the wind bared her limbs and its gusts stirred her garments, blowing them out behind her. Her hair streamed in the light breeze, and her beauty was enhanced by her flight. But the youthful god could not endure to waste his time on further blandishments and, as love itself prompted, sped swiftly after her. Even so, when a Gallic hound spies a hare in some open meadow he tries by his swiftness to secure his prey, while the hare, by her swiftness, seeks safety: the dog, seeming just about to fasten on his quarry, hopes at every moment that he has her, and grazes her hind quarters with outstretched muzzle, but the hare, uncertain whether she has not already been caught, snatches herself out of his very jaws, and escapes the teeth which almost touch her.

Thus the god and the nymph sped on, one made swift by hope and one by fear; but he who pursued was swifter, for he was assisted by love's wings. He gave the fleeing maiden no respite, but followed close on her heels, and his breath touched the locks that lay scattered on her neck, till Daphne's strength was spent, and she grew pale and weary with the effort of her swift flight. Then she saw the waters of the Peneus: "O father," she cried, "help me! If your rivers really have divine powers, work some transformation, and destroy this beauty which makes me please all too well!" Her prayer was scarcely ended when a deep languor took hold on her limbs, her soft breast was enclosed in thin bark, her hair grew into leaves, her arms into branches, and her feet that were lately so swift were

---

[4] **Parnassus** A mountain near Delphi in Greece, sacred to Apollo and the Muses.
[5] **Diana** Twin sister of Apollo and the virgin huntress goddess.

[6] **Delphi, Claros, Tenedos, Patara** Locations, around the Mediterranean area, of temples to Apollo.
[7] **Jupiter** Chief God of the Romans.

held fast by sluggish roots, while her face became the tree-top. Nothing of her was left, except her shining loveliness.

Even as a tree, Phoebus loved her. He placed his hand against the trunk, and felt her heart still beating under the new bark. Embracing the branches as if they were limbs he kissed the wood: but, even as a tree, she shrank from his kisses. Then the god said: "Since you cannot be my bride, surely you will at least be my tree. My hair, my lyre, my quivers will always display the laurel. You will accompany the generals of Rome, when the Capitol beholds their long triumphal processions, when joyful voices raise the song of victory. You will stand by Augustus' gateposts too, faithfully guarding his doors, and keeping watch from either side over the wreath of oak leaves that will hang there. Further, as my head is ever young, my tresses never shorn, so do you also, at all times, wear the crowning glory of never-fading foliage." Paean, the healer, had done: the laurel tree inclined her newmade branches, and seemed to nod her leafy top, as if it were a head, in consent. . . .

Book IV
Pyramus and Thisbe

"Pyramus and Thisbe lived next door to each other, in the lofty city whose walls of brick are said to have been built by Semiramis.[1] Pyramus was the most handsome of young men, and Thisbe the fairest beauty of the East. Living so near, they came to know one another, and a friendship was begun; in time, love grew up between them, and they would have been married, but their parents forbade it. None the less—for this their parents could not forbid—both their hearts were caught in love's snare, and both burned with equal passion. No one shared their secret: they communicated by nods and signs, and the more it was concealed, the more their hidden love blazed up.

"There was a crack, a slender chink, that had developed in the party wall between their two houses, when it was being built. This fault had gone unnoticed for long years, and the lovers were the first to find it: nothing can escape a lover's eyes! They used it as a channel for their voices, and by this means their endearments were safely conveyed to one another, in the gentlest of whispers. Often when Pyramus stood on this side, Thisbe on that, when in turn they felt each other's breath, they used to exclaim: "Jealous wall, why do you stand in the way of lovers? How little it would be to ask that you should let us embrace or, if that is too much, that you should at least open wide enough for us to exchange kisses! Not that we are ungrateful—we admit that it is thanks to you that we have any way at all by which our words can reach our true love's ears." So they talked, in vain, on their opposite sides. At nightfall, they said good-bye, and though they could not reach each other with their kisses, they kissed their own side of the wall.

"Next day, when Aurora[2] had put out night's starry fires and the sun's rays had dried the frosty grass, they came to their usual meeting place. At first, softly sighing, they lamented their sad lot. Then they determined that, at dead of night, they would try to slip past the watchmen and steal out of doors; once outside their homes, they would make their way out of the city too; and in case they should miss each other, wandering aimlessly in the open country, they agreed to meet at Ninus' tomb, and to hide in the shade of its tree. For a tree grew there, a tall mulberry, hung thick with snowy fruits; it stood close by a cool spring. They were enraptured with their plan. The daylight seemed slow to depart, but at last the sun plunged into the waters, and from those waters came forth the night. Stealthily Thisbe turned the door on its hinges, and slipped out into the darkness, unseen by any. Her face hidden by her veil, she came to the tomb, and sat down under the appointed tree. Love made her bold. But suddenly a lioness, fresh from the kill, her slavering jaws dripping with the blood of her victims, came to slake her thirst at the neighbouring spring. While the animal was still some distance off, Thisbe saw her in the moonlight. Frightened, she fled into the darkness of a cave, and as she ran her veil slipped from her shoulders, and was left behind.

"When the savage lioness had drunk her fill, and was returning to the woods, she found the garment, though not the girl, and tore its fine fabric to shreds, ripping it with bloodstained jaws.

"Pyramus came out of the city a little later. He saw the prints of the wild beast, clearly outlined in the deep dust, and the colour drained from his face. Worse still, he found the veil, all stained with blood. Then he cried out: "This night will bring about the death of two fond lovers, and of the two she deserved to live far more than I. 'Tis I who am to blame: poor girl, it was I who killed you! I told you to come, by night, to a place that was full of danger, and did not arrive first myself. Come, all you lions who live beneath this cliff, come and tear me limb from limb! With your fierce jaws, devour my guilty person. But it is a coward's trick, only to pray for death!" He picked up Thisbe's veil, and carried it into the shade of the tree where they

---

[1] **Semiramis** Queen of Babylon, the home of Pyramus and Thisbe.
[2] **Aurora** Goddess of the dawn.

should have met. Weeping and kissing the garment he knew so well, he said: "Drink deep, now, of my blood too." And as he spoke he took the sword which hung at his waist, and thrust it into his side: then, with a dying effort, pulled it out of the warm wound. As he lay, fallen back upon the ground, his blood spouted forth, just as when a water pipe bursts, if there is some flaw in the lead, and through the narrow hissing crack a long stream of water shoots out, and beats on the air. The fruits of the tree were sprinkled with his blood, and changed to a dark purple hue. The roots, soaked in his gore, tinged the hanging berries with the same rich colour.

"Now, though Thisbe had not yet quite recovered from her fear, she came back; for she was anxious not to disappoint her lover. She looked about for the youth with eager eyes and heart, impatient to tell him of the perils she had escaped. But although she recognized the spot, and the shape of the tree, yet the colour of its fruit made her uncertain; she was unable to decide whether this was the place or not. As she stood in doubt, she saw the quivering limbs writhing on the bloodstained ground, and started back. Her cheeks grew paler than boxwood, and she trembled as the sea shivers when a soft breeze ripples its surface. After a moment's pause, she recognized her love. Wailing aloud, she beat her innocent arms, tore her hair, and embracing his beloved form, bathed his wound with her tears, mingling the salt drops with his blood, and passionately kissing his cold cheeks. "Pyramus," she cried, "What mischance has taken you from me? Pyramus, speak to me! It is your own dear Thisbe who is calling you! Hear me, and raise your drooping head!" At Thisbe's name, Pyramus opened his eyes, which were already heavy with death's stupor; then, with one last look, closed them for ever. Thisbe, when she recognized her veil, and saw the ivory scabbard empty of its sword, exclaimed: "Alas, your own hand and your love have destroyed you. I, too, have a hand resolute for this one deed; my love, as great as yours, will give me strength to deal the wound. I shall follow you in death, and men will speak of me as at once the unhappy cause and the companion of your fate. Only death could have separated you from me, but not even death will part us. Most wretched parents, mine and his, I beg this one boon for us both: since our steadfast love and the hour of our death have united us, do not grudge that we be laid together in a single tomb. And you, O tree, already sheltering one hapless body, soon to shelter two, bear for ever the marks of our death: always have fruit of a dark and mournful hue, to make men remember the blood we two have shed!" As she spoke, she placed the sword blade beneath her breast, and fell forward on the steel, which was still warm from Pyramus' death. Her prayers touched the gods, and they touched the parents also: for the berry of the tree, when ripe, is a dark purple colour, and the remains of the two lovers, gathered from the funeral fires, rest together in a single urn."

JUVENAL

Satire III

Much of Juvenal's life (ca. A.D. 60–140) remains a mystery. He is seldom mentioned by his contemporaries, and his satires contain very little autobiographical material. Some events in his satires can be dated, which aid scholars in determining when and where Juvenal wrote. Evidence indicates that he was the son of a fairly prosperous Spanish freedman and that he served in the Roman army. Upon returning from a campaign in Britain, he became mayor of his hometown but failed to launch a political career. Meanwhile, Juvenal started to write satirical works. He soon displeased the Emperor Domitian, who exiled him to Egypt and stripped him of his property and civil rights. Emperor Nerva, Domitian's successor, permitted Juvenal to return to Rome; however, being poor and without patrons, he was forced to live the life of a hanger-on, one who survived only by flattering those in power. This experience led him to write many embittered and vindictive poems. Only in his later years, when he received patronage from influential Romans, including the Emperor Hadrian, did his satires lose their coarse tone and become nostalgic. When he died, he was not well known, and for two hundred years Juvenal was a forgotten poet. In about A.D. 400, he was rediscovered, and his reputation has remained high ever since.

Many of Juvenal's satires reflected his contempt for his age. He was highly critical of its literature, which seemed to be written by second-rate authors and read by an uncultured public.

He specifically singled out the Greeks, whom he denounced for undermining Roman values. Looking at the Rome of his day, he saw only the decline of those values that he believed still survived in small villages among simple folk who appreciated the old ways.

Reading the Selection

Satire III contains most of Juvenal's major complaints and popular targets against contemporary Rome. In the opening lines he confesses his admiration for an old friend, Umbricius, who was leaving Rome for good to live in a provincial town. As they walked from one familiar site to another and observed the changes—all for the worse—Umbricius blamed his own lowered standard of living on the corrupt engineers and flattering hypocrites who dominated society. He deplored this "Greek-struck Rome," which had brought on degeneration, drunkenness, and sexual perversity. He thought that the worth of an individual was determined by what he owned—the number of slaves, the amount of land, or his dinner service. He saw no hope for the poor, who were victims of inflation and civil injustice. Wherever he looked, he saw urban blight and inhuman existence, as manifested in slipshod construction and apartment fires. He was convinced that no one could live amid the constant noise and endless moving of carts and humans; to walk in the street was to subject oneself to bodily harm from flying objects or from drunken bullies looking for a fight. He saved his richest invective for the Jews and Greeks, who seemed to have overrun Rome. As a result of this deterioration, the city was under siege and its inhabitants afraid to leave their homes. In closing, Umbricius bade final farewell, asking Juvenal to visit him when he tired of the city.

The poet's description of street life and the "terrors" in this urban nightmare has to strike a modern note for many readers. Rome, in Juvenal's eyes, had become the symbol of all that was evil in his day; the parallels to urban areas of today are inescapable.

Despite the wrench of parting, I applaud my old friend's
Decision to make his home in lonely Cumae[1]—the poor
Sibyl[2] will get at least *one* fellow-citizen now!
It's a charming coastal retreat, and just across the point
From our smartest watering-spot. Myself, I would value
A barren offshore island more than Rome's urban heart:
Squalor and isolation are minor evils compared
To this endless nightmare of fires and collapsing houses,
The cruel city's myriad perils—and poets reciting
Their work in *August!*   10
                            While his goods were being loaded
On one small waggon, my old friend lingered a while
By the ancient dripping arches of the Capuan Gate,[3]
        where once

King Numa[4] had nightly meetings with his mistress.
        (But today
Egeria's[5] grove and shrine and sacred spring are rented
To Jewish squatters, their sole possession a Sabbath
        haybox.[6]
Each tree must show a profit, the Muses have been
        evicted,
The wood's aswarm with beggars.)
                            From here we strolled down
To the nymph's new, modernized grotto. (What a gain in   20
        sanctity
And atmosphere there would be if grassy banks
Surrounded the pool, if no flash marble affronted
Our native limestone!) Here Umbricius[7] stood, and

---

[1] **Cumae** A seacoast town on the western Italian coast. The first Greek settlement was here. By Juvenal's time it was a sleepy and forgotten place but near more fashionable resorts.
[2] **Sibyl** Cumae was known for a famous prophetess who resided there in a grotto.
[3] **Capuan Gate** A gate on the Appian Way, a road leading to Rome. An aqueduct passed over the gate, thus the dripping arches.

[4] **King Numa** A semi-mythical king of Rome.
[5] **Egeria** A nymph through whom King Numa received the laws for the kingdom.
[6] **Sabbath haybox** A container for keeping food hot on a day when cooking was prohibited, the Sabbath.
[7] **Umbricius** Juvenal's friend, who may have been a real or an imaginary person.

Opened his heart to me.
　　　　　　"There's no room in this city,"
He said, "for the decent professions: they don't show any
　　　profit.
My resources have shrunk since yesterday, and tomorrow
Will eat away more of what's left. So I am going
Where Daedalus[8] put off his weary wings, while as yet
I'm in vigorous middle age, while active years are left me,　30
While my white hairs are still few, and I need no stick
To guide my tottering feet. So farewell Rome, I leave you
To sanitary engineers and municipal architects, men
Who by swearing black is white land all the juicy
　　　contracts
Just like that—a new temple, swamp-drainage, harbour-
　　　works,
River-clearance, undertaking, the lot—then pocket the cash
And fraudulently file their petition in bankruptcy.
Once these fellows were horn-players, stumping the
　　　provinces
In road-shows, their puffed-out cheeks a familiar sight
To every country village. But now they stage shows　40
　　　themselves,
Of the gladiatorial sort, and at the mob's thumbs-down
Will butcher a loser for popularity's sake, and
Pass on from that to erecting public privies. Why not?
These are such men as Fortune, by way of a joke,
Will sometimes raise from the gutter and make Top
　　　People.
What can I do in Rome? I never learnt how
To lie. If a book is bad, I cannot puff it, or bother
To ask around for a copy; astrological clap-trap
Is not in my stars. I cannot and will not promise
To encompass any man's death by way of obliging his son.　50
I have never meddled with frogs' guts; the task of
　　　carrying
Letters and presents between adulterous lovers
I resign to those who know it. I refuse to become
An accomplice in theft—which means that no governor
Will accept me on his staff. It's like being a cripple
With a paralysed right hand. Yet who today is favoured
Above the conspirator, his head externally seething
With confidential matters, never to be revealed?
Harmless secrets carry no obligations, and he
Who shares them with you feels no great call thereafter　60
To keep you sweet. But if Verres[9] promotes a man
You can safely assume that man has the screws on Verres
And could turn him in tomorrow. Not all the gold
Washed seaward with the silt of tree-lined Tagus[10]
Is worth the price you pay, racked by insomnia, seeing
Your high-placed friends all cringe at your approach—and
For what? Too-transient prizes, unwillingly resigned.

"Now let me turn to that race which goes down so well
With our millionaires, but remains *my* special pet
　　　aversion,
And not mince my words. I cannot, citizens, stomach　70
A Greek-struck Rome. Yet what fraction of these
　　　sweepings
Derives, in fact, from Greece? For years now Syrian
Orontes[11] has poured its sewerage into our native Tiber—
Its lingo and manners, its flutes, its outlandish harps
With their transverse strings, its native tambourines,
And the whores who hang out round the race-course.
　　　(That's where to go
If you fancy a foreign piece in one of those saucy
　　　toques.[12])
Our beloved Founder should see how his homespun
　　　rustics
Behave today, with their dinner-pumps—*trechedipna*
They call them—not to mention their *niceteria*　80
(Decorations to you) hung round their *ceromatic*[13] (that's
Well-greased) wrestlers' necks. Here's one from Sicyon,
Another from Macedonia, two from Aegean islands—
Andros, say, or Samos—two more from Caria,[14]
All of them lighting out for the City's classiest districts
And burrowing into great houses, with a long-term plan
For taking them over. Quick wit, unlimited nerve, a gift
Of the gab that outsmarts a professional public speaker—
These are their characteristics. What do you take
That fellow's profession to be? He has brought a whole　90
　　　bundle
Of personalities with him—schoolmaster, rhetorician,
Surveyor, artist, masseur, diviner, tightrope-walker,
Magician or quack, your versatile hungry Greekling
Is all by turns. Tell him to fly—he's airborne.
The inventor of wings was no Moor or Slav, remember,
Or Thracian, but born in the very heart of Athens.
　"When such men as these wear the purple, when some
　　　creature
Blown into Rome along with the figs and damsons
Precedes me at dinner-parties, or for the witnessing
Of manumissions and wills—*me*, who drew my first　100
　　　breath
On these Roman hills, and was nourished on Sabine[15]
　　　olives!—
Things have reached a pretty pass. What's more, their
　　　talent
For flattery is unmatched. They praise the conversation

---

[8] **Daedalus** The legendary inventor and hero who flew with wax wings from Crete to Cumae.
[9] **Verres** A governor of the island of Sicily who was corrupt and extorted money from the public.
[10] **Tagus** A river in Spain that flows from central Spain to the Atlantic Ocean; longest river in the Iberian peninsula.

---

[11] **Orontes** A river in Syria. The reference is not to the river itself but to the Syrians who have polluted the Tiber River with their way of life.
[12] **toques** A woman's hat, brimless and close fitting.
[13] *trechedipna, niceteria, ceromatic* Juvenal is mocking Romans who use Greek words to impress others. Thus, *niceteria* are decorations and *ceromatic* is the mud in wrestling pits.
[14] **Sicyon, Macedonia, Andros, Samos, Caria** Greek islands and towns whose inhabitants are taking over Rome.
[15] **Sabine** Territory northeast of Rome, conquered by the Romans in the early third century B.C. Juvenal is being nostalgic about his youth and remembering food grown in the Sabine region.

Of their dimmest friends; the ugly they call handsome,
So that your scrag-necked weakling finds himself
    compared
To Hercules holding the giant Antaeus[16] aloft
Way off the earth. They go into ecstasies over
Some shrill and scrannel voice that sounds like a hen
When the cock gets at her. We can make the same
    compliments, but
It's they who convince. On the stage they remain
    supreme   110
In female parts, courtesan, matron or slave-girl,
With no concealing cloak: you'd swear it was a genuine
Woman you saw, and not a masked performer.
Look there, beneath that belly: no bulge, all smooth, a neat
Nothingness—even a hint of the Great Divide. Yet back
    home
These queens and dames[17] pass unnoticed. Greece is a
    nation
Of actors. Laugh, and they split their sides. At the sight
Of a friend's tears, they weep too—though quite
    unmoved.
If you ask for a fire in winter, the Greek puts on his cloak;
If you say "I'm hot," *he* starts sweating. So you see   120
We are not on an equal footing: he has the great
    advantage
Of being able on all occasions, night and day,
To take his cue, his mask, from others. He's always ready
To throw up his hands and applaud when a friend
    delivers
A really resounding belch, or pisses right on the mark,
With a splendid drumming sound from the upturned
    golden basin.
    "Besides, he holds nothing sacred, not a soul is safe
From his randy urges, the lady of the house, her
Virgin daughter, her daughter's still unbearded
Husband-to-be, her hitherto virtuous son—   130
And if none of these are to hand, he'll cheerfully lay
His best friend's grandmother. (Anything to ferret
Domestic secrets out, and get a hold over people.)
    "And while we are on the subject of Greeks, let us
    consider
Academics and their vices—not the gymnasium crowd
But big philosophical wheels, like that Stoic greybeard[18]
Who narked on his friend and pupil, and got him
    liquidated.

He was brought up in Tarsus, by the banks of that river
Where Bellerophon fell to earth from the Gorgon's flying
    nag.
No room for honest Romans when Rome's ruled by a junta   140
Of Greek-born secret agents, who—like all their race—
Never share friends or patrons. One small dose of venom
(Half Greek, half personal) dropped in that ready ear
And I'm out, shown the back-door, my years of
    obsequious
Service all gone for nothing. Where can a hanger-on
Be ditched with less fuss than in Rome? Besides (not to
    flatter ourselves)
What use are our poor efforts, where does it all get us,
Dressing up while it's dark still, hurrying along
To pay our morning respects to a couple of wealthy
Maiden aunts? But the praetor's really worked up, his   150
Colleague may get there before him, the ladies have
    been awake
For hours already, the minions catch it—"Get
A *move* on there, can't you?" Here a citizen, free-born,
Must stand aside on the pavement for some wealthy
    tycoon's slave:
He can afford to squander a senior officer's income
On classy amateur harlots, just for the privilege
Of laying them once or twice. But when *you* fancy
A common-or-garden tart, you dither and hesitate:
Can I afford to accost her? With witnesses in court
The same applies. Their morals may be beyond cavil,   160
    and yet
If Scipio took the stand (and he was selected
To escort the Mother Goddess on her journey to Rome) or
    Metellus
Who rescued Minerva's image from her blazing shrine,
    or even
King Numa[19] himself, still the first and foremost question
Would be: *"What's he worth?"* His character would
    command
Little if any respect. "How many slaves does he keep?
What's his acreage? What sort of dinner-service
Appears on his table—how many pieces, how big?"
Each man's word is as good as his bond—or rather,
The number of bonds in his strong-box. A pauper can   170
    swear by every
Altar, and every god between Rome and Samothrace,[20] still
(Though the gods themselves forgive them) he'll pass for
    a perjuror
Defying the wrath of heaven. The poor man's an eternal
Butt for bad jokes, with his torn and dirt-caked top-coat,
His grubby toga, one shoe agape where the leather's
Split—those clumsy patches, that coarse and tell-tale
    stitching
Only a day or two old. The hardest thing to bear

---

[16] **Antaeus** The giant wrestler who murdered his defeated opponents. Hercules killed Antaeus by crushing him in the air and keeping him off the ground, which was the source of Antaeus's strength.
[17] **queens and dames** Juvenal, in lines 107–116, comments on Greek male actors playing female parts so well that one would believe them to be women. He then proceeds to condemn Greeks who flatter Romans in order to seduce their females.
[18] **that Stoic greybeard** Stoicism, the Greek philosophy, was very popular in Rome. The Stoic greybeard was Publius Egnatius Celer, who betrayed his friend and his own daughter to Roman authorities. Juvenal identified Celer's home as Tarsus (in modern Turkey), which had been annexed by Rome in the first century B.C. Juvenal linked the city to the myth of Bellerphon, who fell from Pegasus, the winged horse, at this spot.

[19] **Scipio, Metellus, King Numa** Scipio and Metellus helped save some of Rome's sacred objects. King Numa, as noted in fn. 4, was a semi-mythical ruler of Rome.
[20] **Samothrace** A Greek island in the Aegean Sea, off the coast of Thrace.

In poverty is the fact that it makes us ridiculous.
"Out of those front-row seats," we're told. "You ought to
        be
Ashamed of yourselves—your incomes are far too small,   180
        and
The law's the law. Make way for some pander's son,
Spawned in an unknown brothel, let your place be
        occupied
By that natty auctioneer's offspring, with his high-class
        companions
The trainer's brat and the son of the gladiator
Applauding beside him." Such were the fruits of that
        pinhead
Otho's Reserved Seat Act.[21] What prospective son-in-law
Ever passed muster here if he was short on cash
To match the girl's dowry? What poor man ever inherits
A legacy, or is granted that meanest of sinecures—
A job with the Office of Works? All lower-income citizens   190
Should have marched out of town, in a body, years ago.
Nobody finds it easy to get to the top if meagre
Resources cripple his talent. But in Rome the problem's
        worse
Than anywhere else. Inflation hits the rental
Of your miserable apartment, inflation distends
The ravenous maws of your slaves; your humble dinner
Suffers inflation too. You feel ashamed to eat
Off earthenware dishes—yet if you were transported
To some rural village, you'd be content enough
And happily wear a cloak of coarse blue broadcloth   200
Complete with hood. Throughout most of Italy—we
Might as well admit it—no one is seen in a toga
Till the day he dies. Even on public holidays,
When the same old shows as last year are cheerfully
        staged
In the grassgrown theatre, when peasant children, sitting
On their mothers' laps, shrink back in terror at the sight
Of those gaping, whitened masks, you will still find the
        whole
Audience—top row or bottom—dressed exactly alike;
Even the magistrates need no better badge of status
Than a plain white tunic. But here in Rome we must toe   210
The line of fashion, living beyond our means, and
Often on borrowed credit: every man jack of us
Is keeping up with his neighbours. To cut a long story
        short,
Nothing's for free in Rome. How much does it cost you
To salute our noble Cossus (rare privilege!) or extract
One casual, tight-lipped nod from Veiento the honours-
        broker[22]?
X will be having his beard trimmed, Y just offering up
His boy-friend's kiss-curls: the whole house swarms with
        barbers,

Each of them on the make. You might as well swallow
Your bile, and face the fact that we hangers-on   220
Have to bribe our way, swell some sleek menial's savings.
    "What countryman ever bargained, besides, for his
        house collapsing
About his ears? Such things are unheard-of in cool
Praeneste, or rural Gabii, or Tivoli perched on its hillside,
Or Volsinii,[23] nestling amid its woodland ridges. But here
We live in a city shored up, for the most part, with
        gimcrack
Stays and props: that's how our landlords arrest
The collapse of their property, papering over great cracks
In the ramshackle fabric, reassuring the tenants
They can sleep secure, when all the time the building   230
Is poised like a house of cards. I prefer to live where
Fires and midnight panics are not quite such common
        events.
By the time the smoke's got up to your third-floor
        apartment
(And you still asleep) your downstairs neighbour is
        roaring
For water, and shifting his bits and pieces to safety.
If the alarm goes at ground-level, the last to fry
Will be the attic tenant, way up among the nesting
Pigeons, with nothing but tiles between himself and the
        weather.
What did friend Cordus own? One truckle bed, too short
For even a midget nympho; one marble-topped sideboard   240
On which stood six little mugs; beneath it, a pitcher
And an up-ended bust of Chiron,[24] one ancient settle
Crammed with Greek books (though by now
        analphabetic mice
Had gnawed their way well into his texts of the great
        poets).
Cordus could hardly be called a property-owner, and yet
What little the poor man had, he lost. Today the final
Straw on his load of woe (clothes worn to tatters, reduced
To begging for crusts) is that no one will offer him
        lodging
Or shelter, not even stand him a decent meal. But if
Some millionaire's mansion is gutted, women rend their   250
        garments,
Top people put on mourning, the courts go into recess:
Then you hear endless complaints about the hazards
Of city life, these deplorable outbreaks of fire;
Then contributions pour in while the shell is still ash-hot—
Construction materials, marble, fresh-gleaming
        sculptured nudes.
Up come A with bronzes (genuine antique works
By a real Old Master) acquired, as part of his booty,
From their hallowed niche in some Asiatic temple;
B provides bookshelves, books, and a study bust of
        Minerva;
C a sackful of silver. So it goes on, until   260

[21] **Otho's Reserved Seat Act** Otho, an official in Rome, established
the seating arrangements in Roman theaters, whereby the rich always
had the best seats.
[22] **Cossus and Veiento** The original Cossus was a highly honored
aristocrat. This Cossus and Veiento were unsavory characters.
Veiento conducted many shady deals but kept in favor with several
emperors.

[23] **Praeneste, Gabii, Tivoli, Volsinii** Quiet rural towns or retreats not
far from Rome.
[24] **Chiron** The wise and just centaur who was taught by the Greek
gods and later instructed some Greek heroes, including Achilles and
Jason.

This dandified bachelor's losses are all recouped—
And more than recouped—with even rarer possessions,
And a rumour (well-founded) begins to circulate
That he fired the place himself, a deliberate piece of arson.
"If you can face the prospect of no more public games
Purchase a freehold house in the country. What it will
    cost you
Is no more than you pay in annual rent for some shabby
And ill-lit garret here. A garden plot's thrown in
With the house itself, and a well with a shallow basin—
No rope-and-bucket work when your seedlings need   270
    some water!
Learn to enjoy hoeing, work and plant your allotment
Till a hundred vegetarians could feast off its produce.
It's quite an achievement, even out in the backwoods,
To have made yourself master of—well, say one lizard,
    even.
    "Insomnia causes more deaths amongst Roman
        invalids
Than any other factor (the most common *complaints*, of
    course,
Are heartburn and ulcers, brought on by over-eating).
How much sleep, I ask you, can one get in lodgings here?
Unbroken nights—and this is the root of the trouble—
Are a rich man's privilege. The waggons thundering past   280
Through those narrow twisting streets, the oaths of
    draymen
Caught in a traffic-jam—these alone would suffice
To jolt the doziest sea-cow of an Emperor[25] into
Permanent wakefulness. If a business appointment
Summons the tycoon, *he* gets there fast, by litter,
Tacking above the crowd. There's plenty of room inside:
He can read, or take notes, or snooze as he jogs along—
Those drawn blinds are most soporific. Even so
He outstrips us: however fast we pedestrians hurry
We're blocked by the crowds ahead, while those behind us   290
Tread on our heels. Sharp elbows buffet my ribs,
Poles poke into me; one lout swings a crossbeam
Down on my skull, another scores with a barrel.
My legs are mud-encrusted, big feet kick me, a hobnailed
Soldier's boot lands squarely on my toes. Do you see
All that steam and bustle? The great man's hangers-on
Are getting their free dinner, each with his own
Kitchen-boy in attendance. Those outsize dixies,[26]
And all the rest of the gear one poor little slave
Must balance on his head, while he trots along   300
To keep the charcoal glowing, would tax the strength
Of a musclebound general. Recently-patched tunics
Are ripped to shreds. Here's the great trunk of a fir-tree
Swaying along on its waggon, and look, another dray
Behind it, stacked high with pine-logs, a nodding threat
Over the heads of the crowd. If that axle snapped, and a
Cartload of marble avalanched down on them, what

Would be left of their bodies? Who could identify bits
Of ownerless flesh and bone? The poor man's flattened
    corpse
Would vanish along with his soul. And meanwhile, all   310
    unwitting,
The folk at home are busily scouring dishes,
Blowing the fire to a glow, clattering over greasy
Flesh-scrapers, filling up oil-flasks, laying out clean
    towels.
But all the time, as his houseboys hasten about their
    chores,
Himself is already sitting—the latest arrival—
By the bank of the Styx, and gawping in holy terror
At its filthy old ferryman. No chance of a passage over
That mud-thick channel for him, poor devil, without so
    much
As a copper stuck in his mouth to pay for the ride.[27]
"There are other nocturnal perils, of various sorts,   320
Which you should consider. It's a long way up to the
    rooftops,
And a falling tile can brain you—not to mention all
Those cracked or leaky pots that people toss out through
    windows.
Look at the way they smash, the weight of them, the
    damage
They do to the pavement! You'll be thought most
    improvident,
A catastrophe-happy fool, if you don't make your will
    before
Venturing out to dinner. Each open upper casement
Along your route at night may prove a death-trap:
So pray and hope (poor you!) that the local housewives
Drop nothing worse on your head than a pailful of slops.   330
    "Then there's the drunken bully, in an agonized state
For lack of a victim, who lies there tossing and turning
The whole night through, like Achilles after the death
Of his boy-friend Patroclus.[28] [This lout is doomed to
    insomnia
Unless he gets a fight.] Yet however flown with wine
Our young hothead may be, he carefully keeps his
    distance
From the man in a scarlet cloak, the man surrounded
By torches and big brass lamps and a numerous
    bodyguard.
But for me, a lonely pedestrian, trudging home by
    moonlight
Or with hand cupped round the wick of one poor   340
    guttering candle,
He has no respect whatever. This is the way the wretched
Brawl comes about (if you can term it a brawl
When you do the fighting and I'm just cast as punchbag).

---

[25] **sea-cow of an Emperor** The sea-cow or seal was believed to have curious sleeping patterns. The emperor is Claudius, who often fell asleep in public. Also, Claudius supposedly spoke in a bark-like voice. Thus, the references have double meaning. Some translations use *or* rather than *of*, which probably makes more sense.
[26] **dixies** Large cooking pots.

[27] **Styx, ferryman, and copper** These terms refer to what happens when a dead person or shade arrives at the Styx River to be ferried over to the other side to Hades by Charon, the ferryman, who must be paid a coin. Thus, a coin would be stuck in the dead person's mouth.
[28] **Achilles and Patroclus** Achilles, the Greek warrior and a leader in the Trojan War, mourned the death of his close companion, Patroclus, who was killed in a battle during the siege of Troy.

He blocks my way. "Stop," he says. I have no option
But to obey—what else can one do when attacked
By a huge tough, twice one's size and fighting-mad as
    well?
"Where have *you* sprung from?" he shouts. "Ugh, what a
    stench
Of beans and sour wine! I know your sort, you've been
    round
With some cobbler-crony, scoffing a boiled sheep's head
And a dish of spring leeks. What? Nothing to say for   350
    yourself?
Speak up, or I'll kick your teeth in! Tell me, where's your
    pitch?
What synagogue do you doss in?" It makes not a jot of
    difference
Whether you try to answer, or back away from him
Without saying a word, you get beaten up just the same—
And then your irate "victim" takes *you* to court on a
    charge
Of assault and battery. Such is the poor man's "freedom":
After being slugged to a pulp, he may beg, as a special
Favour, to be left with his last few remaining teeth.
"Nor is this the sum of your terrors: when every house
Is shut up for the night, when shops stand silent, when   360
    bolts
Are shot, and doors on the chain, there are still burglars
Lurking around, or maybe some street-apache will settle
Your hash with a knife, the quick way. (Whenever armed
    detachments

Are patrolling the swamps and forests,[29] Rome becomes
A warren for this sort of scum.) Our furnaces glow, our
    anvils
Groan everywhere under their output of chains and
    fetters:
That's where most of our iron goes nowadays: one
    wonders
Whether ploughshares, hoes and mattocks may not soon
    be obsolete.
How fortunate they were (you well may think) those early
Forbears of ours, how happy the good old days   370
Of Kings and Tribunes, when Rome made do with one
    prison only!
    "There are many other arguments I could adduce: but
    the sun
Slants down, my cattle are lowing, I must be on my way—
The muleteer has been signalling me with his whip
For some while now. So goodbye, and don't forget me—
Whenever you go back home for a break from the City,
    invite
Me over too, to share your fields and coverts,
Your country festivals: I'll put on my thickest boots
And make the trip to those chilly uplands—and listen
To your *Satires*, if I am reckoned worthy of that honour."   380

---

[29] **swamps and forests** Swamps and forests near Rome were ideal hideouts for thieves and robbers, who would be flushed out of their dens and would head to Rome when the soldiers patrolled these areas.

MARCUS AURELIUS

Selections from *Meditations*

The Roman emperor Marcus Aurelius (A.D. 121–180), who ruled from 161 to 180, has been remembered as the "philosopher-king" because he possessed some of the attributes of Plato's ideal leader (see Plato's *The Republic*). In his youth he embraced Stoicism, the Greek philosophy, and he left an account of how he tried to apply the tenets of Stoicism to his public and private life. The *Meditations*, written in the 170s, toward the end of his reign and during a long military campaign, voiced his opinions on human behavior, provided him guidance and solace, and summarized his philosophy of life. By then he had witnessed plagues, wars, and revolts and had suffered the loss of many of his fellow soldiers, most of his children, and his wife. Since the rediscovery of the *Meditations* in the sixteenth century, generations of political leaders, intellectuals, writers, and ordinary people have found his ruminations, confessions, and advice helpful and comforting when they, too, have faced life's uncertainties and disappointments.

Even if Marcus Aurelius had never written anything to ensure his literary legacy, he seemed destined, from his birth, to play an important role in Roman history. He came from a wealthy and distinguished Roman family who had been active in politics and governance for several decades. His grandfather, who was a consul (the highest office in the Roman government below the emperor), reared the young man after his father's death. Marcus's education, typical for an upper-class Roman, was steeped in Greek and Roman literature and rhetoric to prepare him for a political career. The new Roman emperor, Antoninus Pius (81–161), who was married to Marcus Aurelius's aunt, chose Marcus Aurelius, at age sixteen, to be his successor, along with another young man, Lucius Verus. Both youths furthered their education in rhetoric and oratory skills while Marcus began his study of Greek philosophy, in particular the writings of the former slave Epictitus, who was one of the leading exponents of Stoicism. However, Marcus was soon involved in more practical matters, witnessing the Emperor in his daily activities, engaging in debates, and associating with public figures. He was a consul twice before he was thirty, and, in 145, married Antoninus Pius's daughter—an event that further solidified his position as one of the two heirs apparent to the emperor.

Little is known of his life from 145 to 161 when, upon the death of Antoninus Pius, Marcus Aurelius and his adopted brother, Lucius Verus, ascended to power. The serenity identified with the *Pax Romana* (Roman Peace) and Antoninus Pius's reign faded quickly. Within a short time the co-emperors faced the Parthians, a strong enemy in the East, who were finally defeated in the mid-160s. However, the returning army brought back the plague, which devastated the empire for several decades. Floods, followed by invasions from across the Danube, bred more troubles. In the late 160s the Romans temporarily defeated the German tribes, but the cost was high, as Verus died suddenly. The wars dragged on for another six years before the Romans pushed the Germans back across the Danube. During this extended expedition, Marcus Aurelius, who was alone and without close friends or family, fighting the enemy and governing the empire from the frontiers, composed his *Meditations*.

Many upper-class Romans, like Marcus Aurelius, were attracted to Stoicism as it had evolved from its Greek origins and been re-interpreted by Greco-Roman philosophers, writers, and practitioners by the second century A.D. The philosophy's teachings—to do one's duty, to accept the good and bad in life, to respect all humans, to be ready for death—offered ways to live and answers to questions for many Romans. In contrast to earlier Greek Stoicism, which was concerned with the hypothetical or theoretical aspects of knowing and understanding, Roman Stoicism offered a practical and pragmatic approach to life. More a code to live by than a speculative discourse on the meaning of life, Roman Stoicism stressed manliness, rationality, fortitude, and self-discipline, which appealed to dedicated Romans who felt responsible for governing a sprawling empire of many races and ethnic groups. However, like Greek Stoicism, Roman Stoicism believed in a supreme being that went by many names—reason, *logos,* Nature, God. The deity also resided in each human, thus giving that person reason, a connection to the divine, and a common bond with other humans who shared these same characteristics. This implied a brotherhood of all humans who could be joined together by appealing to a universal reason or Nature or God found in each individual.

Marcus Aurelius, while believing in and practicing Roman Stoicism, was more concerned with its ethical aspects than its explanations of the physical world or its theories of how knowledge is obtained. He struggled to answer the fundamental questions that all humans ask: Why are we here? What will happen to us at death? What is right and what is wrong? How do we confront life's disappointments and our failures? How do we deal with other humans? What is happiness and can it be achieved? How should we live our lives? Although his answers, which are scattered throughout the *Meditations,* cannot be easily summarized, they shared certain basic assumptions regarding the human condition. For example, humans can control some circumstances in their lives; others, like health, wealth, and death, they cannot. Humans, therefore, must be able to distinguish between what they can control and cannot control, and they must accept whatever falls their way. Likewise, people should not pass judgment on what they see or experience as being good or evil but remain indifferent, which will, consequently, keep them detached, unharmed, and protected from making errors.

Since the *Meditations* are actually the musings and inner thoughts of one person jotted down at various times in his life, the work has no beginning and end, nor is it an analysis of life's problems with ready-made remedies. An earlier title of the book, "To Himself," comes closer to defining what Marcus Aurelius intended his work to be—personal observations and how to survive each day. Some scholars have suggested it should be called "Memoranda" or be defined as a set of "spiritual exercises," which the author referred to and practiced on a regular basis. The *Meditations* contain no original philosophical theses or arguments and have no story line of a person's journey through life. Therefore, the work should be read in bits and pieces and as the mood strikes the reader.

Reading the Selections

Twelve books make up the *Meditations*. Book 1, "Debts and Lessons," names individuals who influenced Marcus Aurelius and to whom he was indebted for various reasons in the course of his life. Book 2 is entitled "On the River Gran, Among the Quadi," which refers to a river in present-day central Slovakia, known as the Hron, which flows into the Danube. The Quadi were a tribe later defeated by Marcus Aurelius in the early 170s. Book 3, "Carnumtum," refers to a Roman fortress on the Danube when Marcus Aurelius was in this area in 172 and 173. All the other books have no title or heading. Except for the similar format and entries in Book 1, the other books contain a variety of structures and writing styles: short essays, commands or imperatives, aphorisms, quotations, analogies, and lists of what should be done.

Book 1. "Debts and Lessons." The only autobiographical section in the *Meditations,* Book 1 has seventeen entries, beginning with the shortest first—thanking his grandparents and parents in the early entries and his adopted father, Antoninus Pius, and the gods in the final passages. Others he refers to are persons who aided him in life. Rusticus was a mentor who served as consul of Rome; Apollonius and Sextus were Stoic philosophers who instructed Marcus Aurelius; Fronto was one of his most influential teachers.

Book 2. "On the River Gran, Among the Quadi," 1–2. Marcus Aurelius advises the reader on human behavior and how to work with others. In the second passage he discusses the three components that are found in all humans. 17. Human Life notes the transitory nature of life and concludes that only philosophy can be one's guide.

Book 5.1. An admonition to get out of bed and be on with the day and a reminder to like and enjoy your job.

Book 6.16. "What is it in ourselves that we should prize?" The author attempts to answer this question.

Book 10.1–2. "To my soul" is a plea to accept one's situation in life and make the best of it. The second passage is a list of epithets and how they will assist the reader in confronting life.

Book 12.3. Marcus Aurelius claims that peace and tranquility will come if the mind is kept under control.

∾

Book 1
Debts and Lessons

7. Rusticus

The recognition that I needed to train and discipline my character. ₁

Not to be sidetracked by my interest in rhetoric. Not to write treatises on abstract questions, or deliver moralizing little sermons, or compose imaginary descriptions of The Simple Life or The Man Who Lives Only for Others. To steer clear of oratory, poetry, and *belles lettres.*

Not to dress up just to stroll around the house, or things like that. To write straightforward letters (like the one he sent my mother from Sinuessa). And to behave in a conciliatory way when people who have angered or annoyed us want to make up.

To read attentively—not to be satisfied with "just getting the gist of it." And not to fall for every smooth talker.

And for introducing me to Epictetus's lectures—and ₅ loaning me his own copy.

8. Apollonius

Independence and unvarying reliability, and to pay attention to nothing, no matter how fleetingly, except the *logos.* And to be the same in all circumstances—intense pain, the loss of a child, chronic illness. And to see clearly, from his example, that a man can show both strength and flexibility.

His patience in teaching. And to have seen someone who clearly viewed his expertise and ability as a teacher as the humblest of virtues.

And to have learned how to accept favors from friends without losing your self-respect or appearing ungrateful.

9. Sextus

Kindness.

An example of fatherly authority in the home. What it means to live as nature requires.

Gravity without airs.

To show intuitive sympathy for friends, tolerance to amateurs and sloppy thinkers. His ability to get along with everyone: sharing his company was the highest of compliments, and the opportunity an honor for those around him.

To investigate and analyze, with understanding and logic, the principles we ought to live by.

Not to display anger or other emotions. To be free of passion and yet full of love.

To praise without bombast; to display expertise without pretension.

11. Fronto

To recognize the malice, cunning, and hypocrisy that power produces, and the peculiar ruthlessness often shown by people from "good families."

16. My Adopted Father

Compassion. Unwavering adherence to decisions, once he'd reached them. Indifference to superficial honors. Hard work. Persistence.

Listening to anyone who could contribute to the public good.

His dogged determination to treat people as they deserved.

A sense of when to push and when to back off.

Putting a stop to the pursuit of boys.

His altruism. Not expecting his friends to keep him entertained at dinner or to travel with him (unless they wanted to). And anyone who had to stay behind to take care of something always found him the same when he returned.

His searching questions at meetings. A kind of single-mindedness, almost, never content with first impressions, or breaking off the discussion prematurely.

His constancy to friends—never getting fed up with them, or playing favorites.

Self-reliance, always. And cheerfulness.

And his advance planning (well in advance) and his discreet attention to even minor things.

His restrictions on acclamations—and all attempts to flatter him.

His constant devotion to the empire's needs. His stewardship of the treasury. His willingness to take responsibility—and blame—for both.

His attitude to the gods: no superstitiousness. And his attitude to men: no demagoguery, no currying favor, no pandering. Always sober, always steady, and never vulgar or a prey to fads.

The way he handled the material comforts that fortune had supplied him in such abundance—without arrogance and without apology. If they were there, he took advantage of them. If not, he didn't miss them.

No one ever called him glib, or shameless, or pedantic. They saw him for what he was: a man tested by life, accomplished, unswayed by flattery, qualified to govern both himself and them.

His respect for people who practiced philosophy—at least, those who were sincere about it. But without denigrating the others—or listening to them.

His ability to feel at ease with people—and put them at *their* ease, without being pushy.

His willingness to take adequate care of himself. Not a hypochondriac or obsessed with his appearance, but not ignoring things either. With the result that he hardly ever needed medical attention, or drugs, or any sort of salve or ointment.

This, in particular: his willingness to yield the floor to experts—in oratory, law, psychology, whatever—and to support them energetically, so that each of them could fulfill his potential.

That he respected tradition without needing to constantly congratulate himself for Safeguarding Our Traditional Values.

Not prone to go off on tangents, or pulled in all directions, but sticking with the same old places and the same old things.

The way he could have one of his migraines and then go right back to what he was doing—fresh and at the top of his game.

That he had so few secrets—only state secrets, in fact, and not all that many of those.

The way he kept public actions within reasonable bounds—games, building projects, distributions of money, and so on—because he looked to what needed doing and not the credit to be gained from doing it.

No bathing at strange hours, no self-indulgent building projects, no concern for food, or the cut and color of his clothes, or having attractive slaves. (The robe from his farm at Lorium, most of the things at Lanuvium, the way he accepted the customs agent's apology at Tusculum, etc.)

He never exhibited rudeness, lost control of himself, or turned violent. No one ever saw him sweat. Everything was to be approached logically and with due consideration, in a calm and orderly fashion but decisively, and with no loose ends.

You could have said of him (as they say of Socrates) that he knew how to enjoy and abstain from things that most people find it hard to abstain from and all too easy to enjoy. Strength, perseverance, self-control in both areas: the mark of a soul in readiness—indomitable.

17. The Gods

That I had good grandparents, a good mother and father, a good sister, good teachers, good servants, relatives, friends—almost without exception. And that I never lost control of myself with any of them, although I had it in me to do that, and I might have, easily. But thanks to the gods, I was never put in that position, and so escaped the test.

That I wasn't raised by my grandfather's girlfriend for longer than I was. That I didn't lose my virginity too early, and didn't enter adulthood until it was time—put it off, even.

That I had someone—as a ruler and as a father—who could keep me from being arrogant and make me realize that even at court you can live without a troop of body-guards, and gorgeous clothes, lamps, sculpture—the whole charade. That you can behave almost like an ordinary person without seeming slovenly or careless as a ruler or when carrying out official obligations.

That I had the kind of brother I did. One whose character challenged me to improve my own. One whose love and affection enriched my life.

That my children weren't born stupid or physically deformed.

That I wasn't more talented in rhetoric or poetry, or other areas. If I'd felt that I was making better progress I might never have given them up.

That I conferred on the people who brought me up the honors they seemed to want early on, instead of putting them off (since they were still young) with the hope that I'd do it later.

That I knew Apollonius, and Rusticus, and Maximus.[1]

That I was shown clearly and often what it would be like to live as nature requires. The gods did all they could—through their gifts, their help, their inspiration—to ensure that I could live as nature demands. And if I've failed, it's no one's fault but mine. Because I didn't pay attention to what they told me—to what they taught me, practically, step by step.

That my body has held out, especially considering the life I've led.

That I never laid a finger on Benedicta or on Theodotus.[2] And that even later, when I was overcome by passion, I recovered from it.

That even though I was often upset with Rusticus I never did anything I would have regretted later.

That even though she died young, at least my mother spent her last years with me.

That whenever I felt like helping someone who was short of money, or otherwise in need, I never had to be told that I had no resources to do it with. And that I was never put in that position myself—of having to take something from someone else.

That I have the wife I do: obedient, loving, humble.

That my children had competent teachers.

Remedies granted through dreams—when I was coughing blood, for instance, and having fits of dizziness. And the one at Caieta.

That when I became interested in philosophy I didn't fall into the hands of charlatans, and didn't get bogged down in writing treatises, or become absorbed by logic-chopping, or preoccupied with physics.

All things for which "we need the help of fortune and the gods."

---

[1] **Apollonius, Rusticus, Maximus** Three of Marcus Aurelius's friends and/or mentors.

[2] **Benedicta and Theodorus** Probably slaves, but the reference is not certain.

≈

Book 2

On the River Gran, Among the Quadi

1. When you wake up in the morning, tell yourself: The people I deal with today will be meddling, ungrateful, arrogant, dishonest, jealous, and surly. They are like this because they can't tell good from evil. But I have seen the beauty of good, and the ugliness of evil, and have recognized that the wrongdoer has a nature related to my own—not of the same blood or birth, but the same mind, and possessing a share of the divine. And so none of them can hurt me. No one can implicate me in ugliness. Nor can I feel angry at my relative, or hate him. We were born to work together like feet, hands, and eyes, like the two rows of teeth, upper and lower. To obstruct each other is unnatural. To feel anger at someone, to turn your back on him: these are obstructions.

2. Whatever this is that I am, it is flesh and a little spirit and an intelligence. Throw away your books; stop letting yourself be distracted. That is not allowed. Instead, as if you were dying right now, despise your flesh. A mess of blood, pieces of bone, a woven tangle of nerves, veins, arteries. Consider what the spirit is: air, and never the same air, but vomited out and gulped in again every instant. Finally, the intelligence. Think of it this way: You are an old man. Stop allowing your mind to be a slave, to be jerked about by selfish impulses, to kick against fate and the present, and to mistrust the future.

17. Human life.

Duration: *momentary.* Nature: *changeable.* Perception: *dim.* Condition of Body: *decaying.* Soul: *spinning around.* Fortune: *unpredictable.* Lasting Fame: *uncertain.* Sum Up: *The body and its parts are a river, the soul a dream and mist, life is warfare and a journey far from home, lasting reputation is oblivion.*

Then what can guide us?   5

Only philosophy.

Which means making sure that the power within stays safe and free from assault, superior to pleasure and pain, doing nothing randomly or dishonestly and with imposture, not dependent on anyone else's doing something or

not doing it. And making sure that it accepts what happens and what it is dealt as coming from the same place it came from. And above all, that it accepts death in a cheerful spirit, as nothing but the dissolution of the elements from which each living thing is composed. If it doesn't hurt the individual elements to change continually into one another, why are people afraid of all of them changing and separating? It's a natural thing. And nothing natural is evil.

Book 5

1. At dawn, when you have trouble getting out of bed, tell   1
yourself: "I have to go to work—as a human being. What do I have to complain of, if I'm going to do what I was born for—the things I was brought into the world to do? Or is *this* what I was created for? To huddle under the blankets and stay warm?

—But it's nicer here. . . .

So you were born to feel "nice"? Instead of doing things and experiencing them? Don't you see the plants, the birds, the ants and spiders and bees going about their individual tasks, putting the world in order, as best they can? And you're not willing to do your job as a human being? Why aren't you running to do what your nature demands?

—But we have to sleep sometime. . . .

Agreed. But nature set a limit on that—as it did on   5
eating and drinking. And you're over the limit. You've had more than enough of that. But not of working. There you're still below your quota.

You don't love yourself enough. Or you'd love your nature too, and what it demands of you. People who love what they do wear themselves down doing it, they even forget to wash or eat. Do you have less respect for your own nature than the engraver does for engraving, the dancer for the dance, the miser for money, or the social climber for status? When they're really possessed by what they do, they'd rather stop eating and sleeping than give up practicing their arts.

Is helping others less valuable to you? Not worth your effort?

Book 6

16. What is it in ourselves that we should prize?   1

Not just transpiration (even plants do that).

Or respiration (even beasts and wild animals breathe).

Or being struck by passing thoughts.

Or jerked like a puppet by your own impulses.

Or moving in herds.

Or eating, and relieving yourself afterwards.

Then what is to be prized?

An audience clapping? No. No more than the clacking of their tongues. Which is all that public praise amounts to—a clacking of tongues.

So we throw out other people's recognition. What's left for us to prize?

I think it's this: to do (and not do) what we were   5
designed for. That's the goal of all trades, all arts, and

what each of them aims at: that the thing they create should do what it was designed to do. The nurseryman who cares for the vines, the horse trainer, the dog breeder—this is what they aim at. And teaching and education—what else are they trying to accomplish?

So that's what we should prize. Hold on to that, and you won't be tempted to aim at anything else.

And if you can't stop prizing a lot of other things? Then you'll never be free—free, independent, imperturbable. Because you'll always be envious and jealous, afraid that people might come and take it all away from you. Plotting against those who have them—those things you prize. People who need those things are bound to be a mess—and bound to take out their frustrations on the gods. Whereas to respect your own mind—to prize it—will leave you satisfied with your own self, well integrated into your community and in tune with the gods as well—embracing what they allot you, and what they ordain.

∽

Book 10

1. To my soul:

Are you ever going to achieve goodness? Ever going to be simple, whole, and naked—as plain to see as the body that contains you? Know what an affectionate and loving disposition would feel like? Ever be fulfilled, ever stop desiring—lusting and longing for people and things to enjoy? Or for more time to enjoy them? Or for some other place or country—"a more temperate clime"? Or for people easier to get along with? And instead be satisfied with what you have, and accept the present—all of it. And convince yourself that everything is the gift of the gods, that things are good and always will be, whatever they decide and have in store for the preservation of that perfect entity—good and just and beautiful, creating all things, connecting and embracing them, and gathering in their separated fragments to create more like them.

Will you ever take your stand as a fellow citizen with gods and human beings, blaming no one, deserving no one's censure?

2. Focus on what nature demands, as if you were governed by that alone. Then do that, and accept it, unless your nature as a living being would be degraded by it.

Then focus on what *that* nature demands, and accept that too—unless your nature as a rational being would be degraded by it.

And of course, "rational" also implies "civic."

Follow these guidelines and don't waste time on anything else.

8. Epithets for yourself: Upright. Modest. Straightforward. Sane. Cooperative. Disinterested.

Try not to exchange them for others.

And if you should forfeit them, set about getting them back.

Keep in mind that "sanity" means understanding things—each individual thing—for what they are. And not losing the thread.

And "cooperation" means accepting what nature assigns you—accepting it willingly.

And "disinterest" means that the intelligence should rise above the movements of the flesh—the rough and the smooth alike. Should rise above fame, above death, and everything like them.

If you maintain your claim to these epithets—without caring if others apply them to you or not—you'll become a new person, living a new life. To keep on being the person that you've been—to keep being mauled and degraded by the life you're living—is to be devoid of sense and much too fond of life. Like those animal fighters at the games—torn half to pieces, covered in blood and gore, and still pleading to be held over till tomorrow . . . to be bitten and clawed again.

Set sail, then, with this handful of epithets to guide you. And steer a steady course, if you can. Like an emigrant to the islands of the blest. And if you feel yourself adrift—as if you've lost control—then hope for the best, and put in somewhere where you can regain it. Or leave life altogether, not in anger, but matter-of-factly, straightforwardly, without arrogance, in the knowledge that you've at least done that much with your life.

And as you try to keep these epithets in mind, it will help you a great deal to keep the gods in mind as well. What they want is not flattery, but for rational things to be like them. For figs to do what figs were meant to do—and dogs, and bees . . . and people.

∽

Book 12

3. Your three components: body, breath, mind. Two are yours in trust; to the third alone you have clear title.

If you can cut yourself—your mind—free of what other people do and say, of what you've said or done, of the things that you're afraid will happen, the impositions of the body that contains you and the breath within, and what the whirling chaos sweeps in from outside, so that the mind is freed from fate, brought to clarity, and lives life on its own recognizance—doing what's right, accepting what happens, and speaking the truth—

If you can cut free of impressions that cling to the mind, free of the future and the past—can make yourself, as Empedocles[3] says, "a sphere rejoicing in its perfect stillness," and concentrate on living what can be lived (which means the present) . . . then you can spend the time you have left in tranquillity. And in kindness. And at peace with the spirit within you.

---

[3] **Empedocles** Fifth century B.C. Greek philosopher and poet.

6

JUDAISM AND THE RISE
OF CHRISTIANITY

Selections from *The Holy Scriptures* (The Jewish Bible)

The Jewish Bible (from the Greek *biblia,* "books") is a set of sacred writings for the Jewish faithful, containing thirty-nine books, dating from the tenth to the first centuries B.C. and arranged into three categories: the Torah, the Prophets, and the Writings. Originally written in Hebrew, this book collection became more accessible in the third century B.C. when, as the Septuagint, it was translated into the period's international language, Greek. Later, around A.D. 100, Jewish scholars declared this collection to be the Word of God, hence its title *The Holy Scriptures,* in Hebrew, *Tanakh.*

The most authoritative parts of *The Holy Scriptures* for Jewish readers are the Torah, or Law, which provides rules and instructions for everyday life, and the Prophets, which represents the sayings or writings of seers who were understood to be the voices of God. The Writings, while lacking the force of the Torah and the Prophets, nevertheless contains beautiful prose and poetic works, replete with words of comfort and moral advice, such as the Book of Psalms, the Book of Job, and the Book of Ecclesiastes.

Genesis, the first book of the Torah, opens with the stories of creation, followed by accounts of Noah, his family, and the flood; then begins the historical narrative of Terah, the father of Abraham, from whom descend the leaders of the Hebrew people. These patriarchal tribal rulers—such as Abraham, Jacob, and Moses—make agreements (covenants) with Yahweh, their deity, to worship him and obey the rules of conduct he has given them. However, throughout their history, the Hebrews do not always live by the covenant; that is, they commit sin, and as a result, Yahweh punishes them.

After their return from exile in Egypt to their former homeland, Palestine, around 1150 B.C., the Hebrews slowly conquer the local tribes and begin to prosper. Their good fortune causes them to forget Yahweh and his moral decrees and to turn more and more away from him and the covenant. At this stage of Hebrew history, God chooses certain persons as prophets to deliver his messages of repentance or consequential destruction. Two of his prophets are Isaiah and Amos. Despite falling away from God, many Hebrews continue to honor Yahweh with songs of praise, as recorded in the Book of Psalms. Yet, other Hebrews question their faith and suffering, as revealed in the Book of Job—a poignant account of the torment experienced by a man who was blameworthy.

Reading the Selections

On the surface, the selections—Genesis, Exodus, Amos, Psalms, Job, and Ecclesiastes—seem quite different, but all deal with similar and profound issues, such as the nature of God's existence and power, the relationship of God to humans, and the role God plays in the lives of humans and in history. The first three chapters of Genesis offer two accounts of the creation story. In the first, God, as the source of all, creates the universe, the celestial bodies, the earth, and all living things. The second account focuses on God's relationship with his first two human creatures, Adam and Eve. The original covenant—that God will provide for humans if they obey him and not eat of the forbidden fruit—is broken. As a consequence, Adam and Eve and all their descendants will be punished according to their sex; that is, Adam and his male heirs will have to work, and Eve and all other women will suffer pain at childbirth. Both are cast out of the Garden of Eden; ever since, humans have been trying to reenter this paradise by attempting to create utopias on earth.

Genesis 4 records the rivalry between the two sons of Adam and Eve, Cain and Abel. Chapter 5 lists the descendents of Adam and Eve down to Noah. Chapters 6–8 is the story of Noah, his family, and the flood. Again, the themes of humans disobeying God, his punishing them for their waywardness and sins, their worshiping and sacrificing to him, and his forgiveness are repeated. However, the themes of the Hebrews' emerging monotheistic faith are woven into the story of the flood. Accounts of floods and their destructive power are found in several sources of ancient literature (see *The Epic of Gilgamesh*). The Babylonian and Hebrew stories are so similar that many scholars have concluded that the two had a common source.

At some point in history, a portion of the Hebrew tribe moved to Egypt, where they were cast into slavery. Eventually, under the leadership of Moses, they slipped their bondage and were guided to freedom through the desert by God. During years of wandering, they formed the central core of their covenant with God: a set of moral rules, of which the first ten are the Ten Commandments, laid down by Yahweh and to be obeyed by the Hebrew people. Besides the Ten Commandments, these rules included many other guidelines by which the Hebrew people were to regulate their lives as individuals and as a tribe. Later, Christians made the Ten Commandments, along with Christ's teachings, the basis of their moral code.

The excerpt from Amos illustrates how a prophet, as the voice of God, spoke to the Hebrews, warning them to change their sinful ways or suffer punishment. In his prophecy, Amos predicts the destruction of the kingdom of Israel (it was destroyed by Assyria in 722 B.C.) if the populace does not give social justice to the poor, so that justice will "well up like water" and righteousness will flow as an "unfailing stream." Amos's prophecy, with its rich imagery, was a favorite of the civil rights leader Martin Luther King, Jr. (see *Letter from a Birmingham Jail*).

The Book of Psalms, with its prayers, laments, and wisdom, has inspired and comforted both Jews and Christians down through the ages. Psalm 22 is a lament, uttered by the speaker, who, after confessing a sense of having been betrayed by God, resolves to once again trust in the Lord. Its first two lines were spoken by Jesus on the cross. Psalm 23, among the most comforting messages in the Bible, is often recited at funerals or turned to in times of trouble. Psalm 104, in its praise of God, echoes an Egyptian poem (see *The Great Hymn to the Aten*).

The Book of Job rivals *Oedipus the King* in depicting the tragedy of a well-meaning hero. Unlike any other book in *The Holy Scriptures*, Job concentrates on a single theological topic: the question of suffering. In prose form, the Prologue tells of the disasters that befall the blameless Job, the conversation between God and Satan about testing Job's faith, and Job's meeting with friends who offer advice on his plight. Shifting into poetic form, the book next sets forth Job's complaint to God, God's magisterial response, and Job's final reply. The Epilogue, reverting to prose, shows God richly rewarding Job for not renouncing him. The Book of Job steadfastly refuses to answer the bewildering question of why humans suffer, and this silence is part of the work's grandeur.

The name *Ecclesiastes* is the pseudonym of the author of this biblical work. It is the Greek word used to translate the Hebrew word *Koheleth*, meaning "the Assembler," that is, one who gathers or teaches before an assembly. The Book of Ecclesiastes is part of the Megillot, five scrolls that are read at various festivals of the Jewish religious year. In literary terms, this book belongs to the tradition of Hebrew wisdom literature, yet its rationalistic point of view calls into question the doctrine of retributive justice associated with wisdom theology. Retributive justice means that rewards and punishments, respectively, are directly linked to good and evil deeds. In contrast, the author of Ecclesiastes asserts "that [it] is a sad thing about all that goes on under the sun: that the same fate is in store for all. (Not only that, but men's hearts are full of sadness, and their minds of madness, while they live; and then—to the dead!)" (9:3). Human fate is unknowable, according to the author, because it is strictly in God's hands: "He brings everything to pass precisely at his time" (3:11). Faced with such moral uncertainty, the wise person gratefully accepts the small pleasures God gives each day. Chapter 3, a famous passage, is sometimes read at funerals and has become well known as the text of a popular folk song.

∞

Genesis
1–3

1

When God began to create heaven and earth—the earth being unformed and void, with darkness over the surface of the deep and a wind from God sweeping over the water—God said, "Let there be light"; and there was light. God saw that the light was good, and God separated the light from the darkness. God called the light Day, and the darkness He called Night. And there was evening and there was morning, a first day.

God said, "Let there be an expanse in the midst of the water, that it may separate water from water." God made the expanse, and it separated the water which was below the expanse from the water which was above the expanse. And it was so. God called the expanse Sky. And there was evening and there was morning, a second day.

God said, "Let the water below the sky be gathered into one area, that the dry land may appear." And it was so. God called the dry land Earth, and the gathering of waters He called Seas. And God saw that this was good. And God said, "Let the earth sprout vegetation: seed-bearing plants, fruit trees of every kind on earth that bear fruit with the seed in it." And it was so. The earth brought forth vegetation: seed-bearing plants of every kind, and trees of every kind bearing fruit with the seed in it. And God saw that this was good. And there was evening and there was morning, a third day.

God said, "Let there be lights in the expanse of the sky to separate day from night; they shall serve as signs for the set times—the days and the years; and they shall serve as lights in the expanse of the sky to shine upon the earth." And it was so. God made the two great lights, the greater light to dominate the day and the lesser light to dominate the night, and the stars. And God set them in the expanse of the sky to shine upon the earth, to dominate the day and the night, and to separate light from darkness. And God saw that this was good. And there was evening and there was morning, a fourth day.

God said, "Let the waters bring forth swarms of living creatures, and birds that fly above the earth across the expanse of the sky." God created the great sea monsters, and all the living creatures of every kind that creep, which the waters brought forth in swarms, and all the winged birds of every kind. And God saw that this was good. God blessed them, saying, "Be fertile and increase, fill the waters in the seas, and let the birds increase on the earth." And there was evening and there was morning, a fifth day.

God said, "Let the earth bring forth every kind of living creature: cattle, creeping things, and wild beasts of every kind." And it was so. God made wild beasts of every kind and cattle of every kind, and all kinds of creeping things of the earth. And God saw that this was good. And God said, "Let us make man in our image, after our likeness. They shall rule the fish of the sea, the birds of the sky, the cattle, the whole earth, and all the creeping things that creep on earth." And God created man in His image, in the image of God He created him; male and female He created them. God blessed them and God said to them, "Be fertile and increase, fill the earth and master it; and rule the fish of the sea, the birds of the sky, and all the living things that creep on earth."

God said, "See, I give you every seed-bearing plant that is upon all the earth, and every tree that has seed-bearing fruit; they shall be yours for food. And to all the animals on land, to all the birds of the sky, and to everything that creeps on earth, in which there is the breath of life, [I give] all the green plants for food. And it was so. And God saw all that He had made, and found it very good. And there was evening and there was morning, the sixth day.

2

The heaven and the earth were finished, and all their array. On the seventh day God finished the work that He had been doing, and He ceased on the seventh day from all the work that He had done. And God blessed the seventh day and declared it holy, because on it God ceased from all the work of creation that He had done. Such is the story of heaven and earth when they were created.

When the Lord God made earth and heaven—when no shrub of the field was yet one earth and no grasses of the field had yet sprouted, because the Lord God had not sent rain upon the earth and there was no man to till the soil, but a flow would well up from the ground and water the whole surface of the earth—the Lord God formed man from the dust of the earth. He blew into his nostrils the breath of life, and man became a living being.

The Lord God planted a garden in Eden, in the east, and placed there the man whom He had formed. And from the ground the Lord God caused to grow every tree that was pleasing to the sight and good for food, with the tree of life in the middle of the garden, and the tree of knowledge of good and bad.

A river issues from Eden to water the garden, and it then divides and becomes four branches. The name of the first is Pishon, the one that winds through the whole land of Havilah, where the gold is. The gold of that land is good; bdellium is there, and lapis lazuli. The name of the second river is Gihon, the one that winds through the whole land of Cush. The name of the third river is Tigris, the one that flows east of Asshur. And the fourth river is the Euphrates.

The Lord God took the man and placed him in the garden of Eden, to till it and tend it. And the Lord God commanded the man, saying, "Of every tree of the garden you are free to eat; but as for the tree of knowledge of good and bad, you must not eat of it; for as soon as you eat of it, you shall die."

The Lord God said, "It is not good for man to be alone; I will make a fitting helper for him." And the Lord God formed out of the earth all the wild beasts and all the birds of the sky, and brought them to the man to see what he would call them; and whatever the man called each living creature, that would be its name. And the man gave names to all the cattle and to the birds of the sky and to all the wild beasts; but for Adam no fitting helper was found. So the Lord God cast a deep sleep upon the man; and, while he slept, He took one of his ribs and closed up the flesh at that spot. And the Lord God fashioned the rib that He had taken from the man into a woman; and He brought her to the man. Then the man said,

> "This one at last
> Is bone of my bones
> And flesh of my flesh.
> This one shall be called Woman,
> For from man was she taken."

Hence a man leaves his father and mother and clings to his wife, so that they become one flesh.

The two of them were naked, the man and his wife, yet they felt no shame.

3

Now the serpent was the shrewdest of all the wild beasts that the Lord God had made. He said to the woman, "Did God really say: You shall not eat of any tree of the garden?" The woman replied to the serpent, "We may eat of the fruit of the other trees of the garden. It is only about fruit of the tree in the middle of the garden that God said: 'You shall not eat of it or touch it, lest you die.'" And the serpent said to the woman, "You are not going to die, but God knows that as soon as you eat of it your eyes will be opened and you will be like divine beings who know good and bad." When the woman saw that the tree was good for eating and a delight to the eyes, and that the tree was desirable as a source of wisdom, she took of its fruit and ate. She also gave some to her husband, and he ate. Then the eyes of both of them were opened and they perceived that they were naked; and they sewed together fig leaves and made themselves loincloths.

They heard the sound of the Lord God moving about in the garden at the breezy time of day; and the man and his wife hid from the Lord God among the trees of the garden. The Lord God called out to the man and said to him, "Where are you?" He replied, "I heard the sound of You in the garden, and I was afraid because I was naked, so I hid." Then He asked, "Who told you that you were naked? Did you eat of the tree from which I had forbidden you to eat?" The man said, "The woman You put at my side—she gave me of the tree, and I ate." And the Lord God said to the woman, "What is this you have done!" The woman replied, "The serpent duped me, and I ate." Then the Lord God said to the serpent,

> "Because you did this,
> More cursed shall you be
> Than all cattle
> And all the wild beasts:
> On your belly shall you crawl
> And dirt shall you eat
> All the days of your life.
> I will put enmity
> Between you and the woman,
> And between your offspring and hers;
> They shall strike at your head,
> And you shall strike at their heel."

And to the woman He said,

> "I will make most severe
> Your pangs in childbearing;

In pain shall you bear children.
Yet your urge shall be for your husband,
And he shall rule over you."

To Adam He said, "Because you did as your wife said and ate of the tree about which I commanded you, 'You shall not eat of it,'

Cursed be the ground because of you;
By toil shall you eat of it
All the days of your life:
Thorns and thistles shall it sprout for you.
But your food shall be the grasses of the field;
By the sweat of your brow
Shall you get bread to eat,

Until you return to the ground—
For from it you were taken.
For dust you are,
And to dust you shall return."

The man named his wife Eve, because she was the mother of all the living. And the LORD God made garments of skins for Adam and his wife, and clothed them.

And the LORD God said, "Now that the man has become like one of us, knowing good and bad, what if he should stretch out his hand and take also from the tree of life and eat, and live forever!" So the LORD God banished him from the garden of Eden, to till the soil from which he was taken. He drove the man out, and stationed east of the garden of Eden the cherubim and the fiery ever-turning sword, to guard the way to the tree of life.

Genesis 6—8

6

And it came to pass, when men began to multiply on the face of the earth, and daughters were born unto them, that the sons of God saw the daughters of men that they were fair; and they took them wives, whomsoever they chose. And the LORD said: "My spirit shall not abide in man for ever, for that he also is flesh; therefore shall his days be a hundred and twenty years." The Nephilim[1] were in the earth in those days, and also after that, when the sons of God came in unto the daughters of men, and they bore children to them; the same were the mighty men that were of old, the men of renown.

And the LORD saw that the wickedness of man was great in the earth, and that every imagination of the thoughts of his heart was only evil continually. And it repented the LORD that He had made man on the earth, and it grieved Him at His heart. And the LORD said: "I will blot out man whom I have created from the face of the earth; both man, and beast, and creeping thing, and fowl of the air; for it repenteth Me that I have made them." But Noah found grace in the eyes of the LORD.

These are the generations of Noah. Noah was in his generations a man righteous and whole-hearted; Noah walked with God. And Noah begot three sons, Shem, Ham, and Japheth. And the earth was corrupt before God, and the earth was filled with violence. And God saw the earth, and, behold, it was corrupt; for all flesh had corrupted their way upon the earth.

And God said unto Noah: "The end of all flesh is come before Me; for the earth is filled with violence through them; and, behold, I will destroy them with the earth. Make thee an ark of gopher wood; with rooms shalt thou make the ark, and shalt pitch it within and without with pitch. And this is how thou shalt make it: the length of the ark three hundred cubits, the breadth of it fifty cubits, and the height of it thirty cubits. A light shalt thou make to the ark, and to a cubit shalt thou finish it upward; and the door of the ark shalt thou set in the side thereof; with lower, second, and third stories shalt thou make it. And I, behold, I do bring the flood of waters upon the earth, to destroy all flesh, wherein is the breath of life, from under heaven; every thing that is in the earth shall perish. But I will establish My covenant with thee; and thou shalt come into the ark, thou, and thy sons, and thy wife, and thy sons' wives with thee. And of every living thing of all flesh, two of every sort shalt thou bring into the ark, to keep them alive with thee; they shall be male and female. Of the fowl after their kind, and of the cattle after their kind, of every creeping thing of the ground after its kind, two of every sort shall come unto thee, to keep them alive. And take thou unto thee of all food that is eaten, and gather it to thee; and it shall be for food for thee, and for them." Thus did Noah; according to all that God commanded him, so did he.

7

And the LORD said unto Noah: "Come thou and all thy house into the ark; for thee have I seen righteous before Me in this generation. Of every clean beast thou shalt take to thee seven and seven, each with his mate; and of the beasts that are not clean two [and two], each with his

---

[1] **Nephilim** The word, in Hebrew, means to fall; thus, probably, the fallen ones. Who they were is not certain. They are mentioned twice in the Holy Scriptures, and their fate seemed to be to die in some catastrophic manner.

mate; of the fowl also of the air, seven and seven, male and female; to keep seed alive upon the face of all the earth. For yet seven days, and I will cause it to rain upon the earth forty days and forty nights; and every living substance that I have made will I blot out from off the face of the earth." And Noah did according unto all that the LORD commanded him.

And Noah was six hundred years old when the flood of waters was upon the earth. And Noah went in, and his sons, and his wife, and his sons' wives with him, into the ark, because of the waters of the flood. Of clean beasts, and of beasts that are not clean, and of fowls, and of every thing that creepeth upon the ground, there went in two and two unto Noah into the ark, male and female, as God commanded Noah. And it came to pass after the seven days, that the waters of the flood were upon the earth. In the six hundredth year of Noah's life, in the second month, on the seventeenth day of the month, on the same day were all the fountains of the great deep broken up, and the windows of heaven were opened. And the rain was upon the earth forty days and forty nights.

In the selfsame day entered Noah, and Shem, and Ham, and Japheth, the sons of Noah, and Noah's wife, and the three wives of his sons with them, into the ark; they, and every beast after its kind, and all the cattle after their kind, and every creeping thing that creepeth upon the earth after its kind, and every fowl after its kind, every bird of every sort. And they went in unto Noah into the ark two and two of all flesh wherein is the breath of life. And they that went in, went in male and female of all flesh, as God commanded him; and the LORD shut him in. And the flood was forty days upon the earth; and the waters increased, and bore up the ark, and it was lifted up above the earth. And the waters prevailed, and increased greatly upon the earth; and the ark went upon the face of the waters. And the waters prevailed exceedingly upon the earth; and all the high mountains that were under the whole heaven were covered. Fifteen cubits upward did the waters prevail; and the mountains were covered. And all flesh perished that moved upon the earth, both fowl, and cattle, and beast, and every swarming thing that swarmeth upon the earth, and every man; all in whose nostrils was the breath of the spirit of life, whatsoever was in the dry land, died. And He blotted out every living substance which was upon the face of the ground, both man, and cattle, and creeping thing, and fowl of the heaven; and they were blotted out from the earth; and Noah only was left, and they that were with him in the ark. And the waters prevailed upon the earth a hundred and fifty days.

8

And God remembered Noah, and every living thing, and 1 all the cattle that were with him in the ark; and God

made a wind to pass over the earth, and the waters assuaged; the fountains also of the deep and the windows of heaven were stopped, and the rain from heaven was restrained. And the waters returned from off the earth continually; and after the end of a hundred and fifty days the waters decreased. And the ark rested in the seventh month, on the seventeenth day of the month, upon the mountains of Ararat. And the waters decreased continually until the tenth month; in the tenth month, on the first day of the month, were the tops of the mountains seen.

And it came to pass at the end of forty days, that Noah opened the window of the ark which he had made. And he sent forth a raven, and it went forth to and fro, until the waters were dried up from off the earth. And he sent forth a dove from him, to see if the waters were abated from off the face of the ground. But the dove found no rest for the sole of her foot, and she returned unto him to the ark, for the waters were on the face of the whole earth; and he put forth his hand, and took her, and brought her in unto him into the ark. And he stayed yet other seven days; and again he sent forth the dove out of the ark. And the dove came in to him at eventide; and lo in her mouth an olive-leaf freshly plucked; so Noah knew that the waters were abated from off the earth. And he stayed yet other seven days; and sent forth the dove; and she returned not again unto him any more.

And it came to pass in the six hundred and first year, in the first month, the first day of the month, the waters were dried up from off the earth; and Noah removed the covering of the ark, and looked, and, behold, the face of the ground was dried. And in the second month, on the seven and twentieth day of the month, was the earth dry.

And God spoke unto Noah, saying: "Go forth from the ark, thou, and thy wife, and thy sons, and thy sons' wives with thee. Bring forth with thee every living thing that is with thee of all flesh, both fowl, and cattle, and every creeping thing that creepeth upon the earth; that they may swarm in the earth, and be fruitful, and multiply upon the earth." And Noah went forth, and his sons, and his wife, and his sons' wives with him; every beast, every creeping thing, and every fowl, whatsoever moveth upon the earth, after their families, went forth out of the ark.

And Noah built an altar unto the LORD; and took 5 of every clean beast, and of every clean fowl, and offered burnt-offerings on the altar. And the LORD smelled the sweet savour; and the LORD said in His heart; "I will not again curse the ground any more for man's sake; for the imagination of man's heart is evil from his youth; neither will I again smite any more every thing living, as I have done. While the earth remaineth, seedtime and harvest, and cold and heat, and summer and winter, and day and night shall not cease."

Exodus

20

20

God spoke all these words, saying: 1

I the LORD am your God who brought you out of the land of Egypt, the house of bondage: You shall have no other gods besides Me.

You shall not make for yourself a sculptured image, or any likeness of what is in the heavens above, or on the earth below, or in the waters under the earth. You shall not bow down to them or serve them. For I the LORD your God am an impassioned God, visiting the guilt of the parents upon the children, upon the third and upon the fourth generations of those who reject Me, but showing kindness to the thousandth generation of those who love Me and keep My commandments.

You shall not swear falsely by the name of the LORD your God; for the LORD will not clear one who swears falsely by His name.

Remember the sabbath day and keep it holy. Six days 5 you shall labor and do all your work, but the seventh day is a sabbath of the LORD your God: you shall not do any work—you, your son or daughter, your male or female slave, or your cattle, or the stranger who is within your settlements. For in six days the LORD made heaven and earth and sea, and all that is in them, and He rested on the seventh day; therefore the LORD blessed the sabbath day and hallowed it.

Honor your father and your mother, that you may long endure on the land that the LORD your God is assigning to you.

You shall not murder.

You shall not commit adultery.

You shall not steal.

You shall not bear false witness against your neighbor. 10

You shall not covet your neighbor's house: you shall not covet your neighbor's wife, or his male or female slave, or his ox or his ass, or anything that is your neighbor's.

All the people witnessed the thunder and lightning, the blare of the horn and the mountain smoking; and when the people saw it, they fell back and stood at a distance. "You speak to us," they said to Moses, "and we will obey; but let not God speak to us, lest we die." Moses answered the people, "Be not afraid; for God has come only in order to test you, and in order that the fear of Him may be ever with you, so that you do not go astray." So the people remained at a distance, while Moses approached the thick cloud where God was.

The LORD said to Moses:

Thus shall you say to the Israelites: You yourselves saw that I spoke to you from the very heavens: With Me, therefore, you shall not make any gods of silver, nor shall you make for yourselves any gods of gold. Make for Me an alter of earth and sacrifice on it your burnt offerings and your sacrifices of well-being, your sheep and your oxen; in every place where I cause My name to be mentioned I will come to you and bless you. And if you make for Me an altar of stones, do not build it of hewn stones; for by wielding your tool upon them you have profaned them. Do not ascend My altar by steps, that your nakedness may not be exposed upon it.

Amos

5

5

Hear this word which I intone 1
As a dirge over you, O House of Israel:
Fallen, not to rise again,
Is Maiden Israel;
Abandoned on her soil
With none to lift her up.
For thus said my LORD God
About the House of Israel:

The town that marches out a thousand strong
Shall have a hundred left, 10
And the one that marches out a hundred strong
Shall have but ten left.

Thus said the LORD
To the House of Israel:
Seek Me, and you will live.
Do not seek Bethel,
Nor go to Gilgal,

Nor cross over to Beer-sheba[1];
For Gilgal shall go into exile,
And Bethel shall become a delusion.   20
Seek the LORD, and you will live,
Else He will rush like fire upon the House of Joseph[2]
And consume Bethel with none to quench it.

[Ah,] you who turn justice into wormwood
And hurl righteousness to the ground!
[Seek the LORD,]
Who made the Pleiades and Orion,[3]
Who turns deep darkness into dawn
And darkens day into night,
Who summons the waters of the sea   30
And pours them out upon the earth—
His name is the LORD!
It is He who hurls destruction upon strongholds,
So that ruin comes upon fortresses!

They hate the arbiter in the gate,
And detest him whose plea is just.
Assuredly,
Because you impose a tax on the poor
And exact from him a levy of grain,
You have built houses of hewn stone,   40
But you shall not live in them;
You have planted delightful vineyards,
But shall not drink their wine.
For I have noted how many are your crimes,
And how countless your sins—
You enemies of the righteous,
You takers of bribes,
You who subvert in the gate
The cause of the needy!
Assuredly,   50
At such a time the prudent man keeps silent,
For it is an evil time.

Seek good and not evil,
That you may live,
And that the LORD, the God of Hosts,
May truly be with you,
As you think.
Hate evil and love good,
And establish justice in the gate;
Perhaps the LORD, the God of Hosts,   60
Will be gracious to the remnant of Joseph.

Assuredly,

---

[1] **Bethel, Gilgal, Beer-sheba** Places of worship or towns in Israel.
[2] **House of Joseph** The descendants of Joseph through his "house" or line who now lived in Israel.
[3] **Pleiades and Orion** Two constellations.

Thus said the LORD,
My Lord, the God of Hosts:
In every square there shall be lamenting,
In every street cries of "Ah, woe!"
And the farm hand shall be
Called to mourn,
And those skilled in wailing
To lament;   70
For there shall be lamenting
In every vineyard, too,
When I pass through your midst
                       —said the LORD.

Ah, you who wish
For the day of the LORD!
Why should you want
The day of the LORD?
It shall be darkness, not light!
—As if a man should run from a lion   80
And be attacked by a bear;
Or if he got indoors,
Should lean his hand on the wall
And be bitten by a snake!
Surely the day of the LORD shall be
Not light, but darkness,
Blackest night without a glimmer.

I loathe, I spurn your festivals,
I am not appeased by your solemn assemblies.
If you offer Me burnt offerings—or your meal offerings— 90
I will not accept them;
I will pay no heed
To your gifts of fatlings.
Spare Me the sound of your hymns,
And let Me not hear the music of your lutes.
But let justice well up like water,
Righteousness like an unfailing stream.
Did you offer sacrifice and oblation to Me
Those forty years in the wilderness,
O House of Israel?   100

And you shall carry off your "king"—
Sikkuth and Kiyyun,[4]
The images you have made for yourselves
Of your astral deity—
As I drive you into exile beyond Damascus[5]
—Said the LORD, whose name is God of Hosts.

---

[4] **Sikkuth and Kiyyun** A king and a star god, both which have been made into images or idols.
[5] **Damascus** The powerful city to the northeast of Israel that was often at war with the Hebrews, and, in Amos's time, a threat. The Lord, says Amos, will drive the Israelites into exile even beyond Damascus—thus far from their homeland.

∽

Psalms

22

My God, my God,
  why have You abandoned me;
  why so far from delivering me
  and from my anguished roaring?
My God,
  I cry by day—You answer not;
  by night, and have no respite.

But You are the Holy One,
  enthroned,
  the Praise of Israel.
In You our fathers trusted;
  they trusted, and You rescued them.
To You they cried out
  and they escaped;
  in You they trusted
  and were not disappointed.

But I am a worm, less than human;
  scorned by men, despised by people.
All who see me mock me;
  they curl their lips,
  they shake their heads.
"Let him commit himself to the LORD;
  let Him rescue him,
  let Him save him,
  for He is pleased with him."
You drew me from the womb,
  made me secure at my mother's breast.
I became Your charge at birth;
  from my mother's womb You have been my God.
Do not be far from me,
  for trouble is near,
  and there is none to help.
Many bulls surround me,
  mighty ones of Bashan encircle me.
They open their mouths at me
  like tearing, roaring lions.
My life ebbs away:
  all my bones are disjointed;
  my heart is like wax,
  melting within me;
  my vigor dries up like a shard;
  my tongue cleaves to my palate;

You commit me to the dust of death.
Dogs surround me;
  a pack of evil ones closes in on me,
  like lions [they maul] my hands and feet.
I take the count of all my bones
  while they look on and gloat.
They divide my clothes among themselves,
  casting lots for my garments.

But You, O LORD, be not far off;
  my strength, hasten to my aid.
Save my life from the sword,
  my precious life from the clutches of a dog.
Deliver me from a lion's mouth;
  from the horns of wild oxen rescue me.
Then will I proclaim Your fame to my brethren,
  praise You in the congregation.
You who fear the LORD, praise Him!
All you offspring of Jacob, honor Him!
Be in dread of Him, all you offspring of Israel!
For He did not scorn, He did not spurn
  the plea of the lowly;
  He did not hide His face from him;
  when he cried out to Him, He listened.
  Because of You I offer praise in the great congregation;
  I pay my vows in the presence of His worshipers.
Let the lowly eat and be satisfied;
  let all who seek the LORD praise Him.
Always be of good cheer!
Let all the ends of the earth pay heed and turn to the LORD,
  and the peoples of all nations prostrate themselves
    before You;
  for kingship is the LORD's
  and He rules the nations.
All those in full vigor shall eat and prostrate themselves;
  all those at death's door, whose spirits flag,
  shall bend the knee before Him.
Offspring shall serve Him;
  the LORD's fame shall be proclaimed to the generation
    to come;
  they shall tell of His beneficence
  to people yet to be born,
  for He has acted.

23

The LORD is my shepherd; 1
    I lack nothing.
He makes me lie down in green pastures;
    He leads me to water in places of repose;
    He renews my life;
    He guides me in right paths
    as befits His name.

Though I walk through a valley of deepest darkness,
    I fear no harm, for You are with me;

Your rod and Your staff—they comfort me. 10
You spread a table for me in full view of my enemies;
    You anoint my head with oil;
    my drink is abundant.
Only goodness and steadfast love shall pursue me
    all the days of my life,
    and I shall dwell in the house of the LORD
    for many long years.

104

Bless the LORD, O my soul; 1
O LORD, my God, You are very great;
    You are clothed in glory and majesty,
    wrapped in a robe of light;
    You spread the heavens like a tent cloth.
He sets the rafters of His lofts in the waters,
    makes the clouds His chariot,
    moves on the wings of the wind.
He makes the winds His messengers,
    fiery flames His servants. 10
He established the earth on its foundations,
    so that it shall never totter.
You made the deep cover it as a garment;
    the waters stood above the mountains.
They fled at Your blast,
    rushed away at the sound of Your thunder,
    —mountains rising, valleys sinking—
    to the place You established for them.
You set bounds they must not pass
    so that they never again cover the earth. 20

You make springs gush forth in torrents;
    they make their way between the hills,
    giving drink to all the wild beasts;
    the wild asses slake their thirst.
The birds of the sky dwell beside them
    and sing among the foliage.
You water the mountains from Your lofts;
    the earth is sated from the fruit of Your work.
You make the grass grow for the cattle,
    and herbage for man's labor 30
    that he may get food out of the earth—
    wine that cheers the hearts of men
    oil that make the face shine,
    and bread that sustains man's life.
The trees of the LORD drink their fill,
    the cedars of Lebanon, His own planting,
    where birds make their nests;
    the stork has her home in the junipers.
The high mountains are for wild goats;
    the crags are a refuge for rock-badgers. 40

He made the moon to mark the seasons; 1
    the sun knows when to set.
You bring on darkness and it is night,
    when all the beasts of the forests stir.
The lions roar for prey,
    seeking their food from God.
When the sun rises, they come home
    and couch in their dens.
Man then goes out to his work,
    to his labor until the evening. 50

How many are the things You have made, O LORD;
    You have made them all with wisdom;
    the earth is full of Your creations.
There is the sea, vast and wide,
    with its creatures beyond number,
    living things, small and great.
There go the ships,
    and Leviathan that You formed to sport with.
All of them look to You
    to give them their food when it is due. 60
Give it to them, they gather it up;
    open Your hand, they are well satisfied;
    hide Your face, they are terrified;
    take away their breath, they perish
    and turn again into dust;
    send back Your breath, they are created,
    and You renew the face of the earth.
May the glory of the LORD endure forever;
    may the LORD rejoice in His works!
He looks at the earth and it trembles; 70
    He touches the mountains and they smoke.
I will sing to the LORD as long as I live;
    all my life I will chant hymns to my God.
May my prayer be pleasing to Him;
    I will rejoice in the LORD,
May sinners disappear from the earth,
    and the wicked be no more.
Bless the LORD, O my soul.
    Hallelujah.

∽

Job
1—3

1

There was a man in the land of Uz named Job. That man ₁ was blameless and upright; he feared God and shunned evil. Seven sons and three daughters were born to him; his possessions were seven thousand sheep, three thousand camels, five hundred yoke of oxen and five hundred she-asses, and a very large household. That man was wealthier than anyone in the East.

It was the custom of his sons to hold feasts, each on his set day in his own home. They would invite their three sisters to eat and drink with them. When a round of feast days was over, Job would send word to them to sanctify themselves, and, rising early in the morning, he would make burnt offerings, one for each of them; for Job thought, "Perhaps my children have sinned and blasphemed God in their thoughts." This is what Job always used to do.

One day the divine beings presented themselves before the LORD, and the Adversary[1] came along with them. The LORD said to the Adversary, "Where have you been?" The Adversary answered the LORD, "I have been roaming all over the earth." The LORD said to the Adversary, "Have you noticed My servant Job? There is no one like him on earth, a blameless and upright man who fears God and shuns evil!" The Adversary answered the LORD, "Does Job not have good reason to fear God? Why, it is You who have fenced him round, him and his household and all that he has. You have blessed his efforts so that his possessions spread out in the land. But lay Your hand upon all that he has and he will surely blaspheme You to Your face." The LORD replied to the Adversary, "See, all that he has is in your power; only do not lay a hand on him." The Adversary departed from the presence of the LORD.

One day, as his sons and daughters were eating and drinking wine in the house of their eldest brother, a messenger came to Job and said, "The oxen were plowing and the she-asses were grazing alongside them when Sabeans[2] attacked them and carried them off, and put the boys to the sword; I alone have escaped to tell you." This one was still speaking when another came and said, "God's fire fell from heaven, took hold of the sheep and the boys, and burned them up; I alone have escaped to tell you." This one was still speaking when another came and said, "A

Chaldean[3] formation of three columns made a raid on the camels and carried them off and put the boys to the sword; I alone have escaped to tell you." This one was still speaking when another came and said, "Your sons and daughters were eating and drinking wine in the house of their eldest brother when suddenly a mighty wind came from the wilderness. It struck the four corners of the house so that it collapsed upon the young people and they died; I alone have escaped to tell you."

Then Job arose, tore his robe, cut off his hair, and ₅ threw himself on the ground and worshiped. He said, "Naked came I out of my mother's womb, and naked shall I return there; the LORD has given, and the LORD has taken away; blessed be the name of the LORD."

For all that, Job did not sin nor did he cast reproach on God.

2

One day the divine beings presented themselves before ₁ the LORD. The Adversary came along with them to present himself before the LORD. The LORD said to the Adversary, "Where have you been?" The Adversary answered the LORD, "I have been roaming all over the earth." The LORD said to the Adversary, "Have you noticed My servant Job? There is no one like him on earth, a blameless and upright man who fears God and shuns evil. He still keeps his integrity; so you have incited Me against him to destroy him for no good reason." The Adversary answered the LORD, "Skin for skin—all that a man has he will give up for his life. But lay a hand on his bones and his flesh, and he will surely blaspheme You to Your face." So the LORD said to the Adversary, "See, he is in your power; only spare his life." The Adversary departed from the presence of the LORD and inflicted a severe inflammation on Job from the sole of his foot to the crown of his head. He took a potsherd to scratch himself as he sat in ashes. His wife said to him, "You still keep your integrity! Blaspheme God and die!" But he said to her, "You talk as any shameless woman might talk! Should we accept only good from God and not accept evil?" For all that, Job said nothing sinful.

When Job's three friends heard about all these calamities that had befallen him, each came from his home— Eliphaz the Temanite, Bildad the Shuhite, and Zophar the Naamathite. They met together to go and console and

---

[1] **Adversary** The Lord's opponent or enemy; translated in the Christian Holy Bible as Satan.
[2] **Sabeans** Inhabitants of Sheba, a kingdom in southwest Arabia. It was known for its wealth. Job, an Israelite, supposedly lived not in Israel but in north Arabia, which makes a raid by the Sabeans more plausible.

---

[3] **Chaldean** The Chaldeans lived along the Euphrates River in Mesopotomia. They could have been on a raiding party into Job's homeland.

comfort him. When they saw him from a distance, they could not recognize him, and they broke into loud weeping; each one tore his robe and threw dust into the air onto his head. They sat with him on the ground seven days and seven nights. None spoke a word to him for they saw how very great was his suffering.

3

Afterward, Job began to speak and cursed the day of his birth. Job spoke up and said: 1

> Perish the day on which I was born,
> And the night it was announced,
> "A male has been conceived!"
> May that day be darkness;
> May God above have no concern for it;
> May light not shine on it;
> May darkness and deep gloom reclaim it;
> May a pall lie over it;
> May what blackens the day terrify it.   10
> May obscurity carry off that night;
> May it not be counted among the days of the year;
> May it not appear in any of its months;
> May that night be desolate;
> May no sound of joy be heard in it;
> May those who cast spells upon the day damn it,
> Those prepared to disable Leviathan;
> May its twilight stars remain dark;
> May it hope for light and have none;
> May it not see the glimmerings of the dawn—   20
> Because it did not block my mother's womb,
> And hide trouble from my eyes.

> Why did I not die at birth,
> Expire as I came forth from the womb?
> Why were there knees to receive me,
> Or breasts for me to suck?
> For now would I be lying in repose, asleep and at rest,
> With the world's kings and counselors who rebuild
>   ruins for themselves,
> Or with nobles who possess gold and who fill their
>   houses with silver.
> Or why was I not like a buried stillbirth,   30
> Like babies who never saw the light?
> There the wicked cease from troubling;
> There rest those whose strength is spent.
> Prisoners are wholly at ease;
> They do not hear the taskmaster's voice.
> Small and great alike are there,
> And the slave is free of his master.

> Why does He give light to the sufferer
> And life to the bitter in spirit;
> To those who wait for death but it does not come,   40
> Who search for it more than for treasure,
> Who rejoice to exultation,
> And are glad to reach the grave;
> To the man who has lost his way,
> Whom God has hedged about?

> My groaning serves as my bread;
> My roaring pours forth as water.
> For what I feared has overtaken me;
> What I dreaded has come upon me.
> I had no repose, no quiet, no rest,   50
> And trouble came.

∞

19

19

Job said in reply: 1

> How long will you grieve my spirit,
> And crush me with words?
> Time and again you humiliate me,
> And are not ashamed to abuse me.
> If indeed I have erred,
> My error remains with me.
> Though you are overbearing toward me,
> Reproaching me with my disgrace,
> Yet know that God has wronged me;   10
> He has thrown up siege works around me.
> I cry, "Violence!" but am not answered;
> I shout, but can get no justice.
> He has barred my way; I cannot pass;

> He has laid darkness upon my path.
> He has stripped me of my glory,
> Removed the crown from my head.
> He tears down every part of me; I perish;
> He uproots my hope like a tree.
> He kindless His anger against me;   20
> He regards me as one of His foes.
> His troops advance together;
> They build their road toward me
> And encamp around my tent.
> He alienated my kin from me;
> My acquaintances disown me.
> My relatives are gone;
> My friends have forgotten me.
> My dependents and maidservants regard me as a
>   stranger;
> I am an outsider to them.   30

I summon my servant but he does not respond;
I must myself entreat him.
My odor is repulsive to my wife;
I am loathsome to my children.
Even youngsters disdain me;
When I rise, they speak against me.
All my bosom friends detest me;
Those I love have turned against me.
My bones stick to my skin and flesh;
I escape with the skin of my teeth.   40

Pity me, pity me! You are my friends;
For the hand of God has struck me!
Why do you pursue me like God,
Maligning me insatiably?
O that my words were written down;

Would they were inscribed in a record,
Incised on a rock forever
With iron stylus and lead!
But I know that my Vindicator lives;
In the end He will testify on earth—   50
This, after my skin will have been peeled off.
But I would behold God while still in my flesh,
I myself, not another, would behold Him;
Would see with my own eyes:
My heart pines within me.
You say, "How do we persecute him?
The root of the matter is in him."
Be in fear of the sword,
For [your] fury is iniquity worthy of the sword;
Know there is a judgment!   60

∞

38–42

38

Then the LORD replied to Job out of the tempest and said: 1

Who is this who darkens counsel,
Speaking without knowledge?
Gird your loins like a man;
I will ask and you will inform Me.

Where were you when I laid the earth's foundations?
Speak if you have understanding.
Do you know who fixed its dimensions
Or who measured it with a line?
Onto what were its bases sunk?   10
Who set its cornerstone
When the morning stars sang together
And all the divine beings shouted for joy?

Who closed the sea behind doors
When it gushed forth out of the womb,
When I clothed it in clouds,
Swaddled it in dense clouds,
When I made breakers My limit for it,
And set up its bar and doors,
And said, "You may come so far and no farther;   20
Here your surging waves will stop"?

Have you ever commanded the day to break,
Assigned the dawn its place,
So that it seizes the corners of the earth
And shakes the wicked out of it?
It changes like clay under the seal
Till [its hues] are fixed like those of a garment.
Their light is withheld from the wicked,
And the upraised arm is broken.

Have you penetrated to the sources of the sea,   30
Or walked in the recesses of the deep?
Have the gates of death been disclosed to you?
Have you seen the gates of deep darkness?
Have you surveyed the expanses of the earth?
If you know of these—tell Me.

Which path leads to where light dwells,
And where is the place of darkness,
That you may take it to its domain
And know the way to its home?
Surely you know, for you were born then,   40
And the number of your years is many!

Have you penetrated the vaults of snow,
Seen the vaults of hail,
Which I have put aside for a time of adversity,
For a day of war and battle?
By what path is the west wind dispersed,
The east wind scattered over the earth?
Who cut a channel for the torrents
And a path for the thunderstorms,
To rain down on uninhabited land,   50
On the wilderness where no man is,
To saturate the desolate wasteland,
And make the crop of grass sprout forth?
Does the rain have a father?
Who begot the dewdrops?
From whose belly came forth the ice?
Who gave birth to the frost of heaven?
Water congeals like stone,
And the surface of the deep compacts.

Can you tie cords to Pleiades   60
Or undo the reins of Orion?

Can you lead out Mazzaroth in its season,
Conduct the Bear with her sons[4]?
Do you know the laws of heaven
Or impose its authority on earth?

Can you send up an order to the clouds
For an abundance of water to cover you?
Can you dispatch the lightning on a mission
And have it answer you, "I am ready"?
Who put wisdom in the hidden parts?   70
Who gave understanding to the mind?
Who is wise enough to give an account of the
      heavens?
Who can tilt the bottles of the sky,
Whereupon the earth melts into a mass,
And its clods stick together.

Can you hunt prey for the lion,
And satisfy the appetite of the king of beasts?
They crouch in their dens,
Lie in ambush in their lairs.
Who provides food for the raven   80
When his young cry out to God
And wander about without food?

39

Do you know the season when the mountain goats   1
      give birth?
Can you mark the time when the hinds calve?
Can you count the months they must complete?
Do you know the season they give birth,
When they couch to bring forth their offspring,
To deliver their young?
Their young are healthy; they grow up in the open;
They leave and return no more.

Who sets the wild ass free?
Who loosens the bonds of the onager,   10
Whose home I have made the wilderness,
The salt land his dwelling-place?
He scoffs at the tumult of the city,
Does not hear the shouts of the driver.
He roams the hills for his pasture;
He searches for any green thing.

Would the wild ox agree to serve you?
Would he spend the night at your crib?
Can you hold the wild ox by ropes to the furrow?
Would he plow up the valleys behind you?   20
Would you rely on his great strength
And leave your toil to him?

Would you trust him to bring in the seed
And gather it in from your threshing floor?

The wing of the ostrich beats joyously;
Are her pinions and plumage like the stork's?
She leaves her eggs on the ground,
Letting them warm in the dirt,
Forgetting they may be crushed underfoot,
Or trampled by a wild beast.   30
Her young are cruelly abandoned as if they were
      not hers;
Her labor is in vain for lack of concern.
For God deprived her of wisdom,
Gave her no share of understanding,
Else she would soar on high,
Scoffing at the horse and its rider.

Do you give the horse his strength?
Do you clothe his neck with a mane?
Do you make him quiver like locusts,
His majestic snorting [spreading] terror?   40
He paws with force, he runs with vigor,
Charging into battle.
He scoffs at fear; he cannot be frightened;
He does not recoil from the sword.
A quiverful of arrows whizzes by him,
And the flashing spear and the javelin.
Trembling with excitement, he swallows the land;
He does not turn aside at the blast of the trumpet.
As the trumpet sounds, he says, "Aha!"
From afar he smells the battle,   50
The roaring and shouting of the officers.

Is it by your wisdom that the hawk grows pinions,
Spreads his wings to the south?
Does the eagle soar at your command,
Building his nest high,
Dwelling in the rock,
Lodging upon the fastness of a jutting rock?
From there he spies out his food;
From afar his eyes see it.
His young gulp blood;   60
Where the slain are, there is he.

40

The Lord said in reply to Job.   1

Shall one who should be disciplined complain
against Shaddai?
He who arraigns God must respond.

Job said in reply to the Lord:

See, I am of small worth; what can I answer You?
I clap my hand to my mouth.

---

[4] **Pleiades, Orion, Mazzaroth, Bear with her sons** All are references
to constellations or images in the sky. Pleiades, Orion, and the Bear
and her sons (Ursa major and Ursa minor) are constellations. *Mazzaroth* is the Hebrew word for the Zodiac.

I have spoken once, and will not reply;
Twice, and will do so no more.

Then the LORD replied to Job out of the tempest and said: 10

Gird your loins like a man;
I will ask, and you will inform Me.
Would you impugn My justice?
Would you condemn Me that you may be right?
Have you an arm like God's?
Can you thunder with a voice like His?
Deck yourself now with grandeur and eminence;
Clothe yourself in glory and majesty.
Scatter wide your raging anger
See every proud man and bring him low.   20
See every proud man and humble him,
And bring them down where they stand.
Bury them all in the earth;
Hide their faces in obscurity.
Then even I would praise you
For the triumph your right hand won you.

Take now behemoth,[5] whom I made as I did you;
He eats grass, like the cattle.
His strength is in his loins,
His might in the muscles of his belly.   30
He makes his tail stand up like a cedar;
The sinews of his thighs are knit together.
His bones are like tubes of bronze,
His limbs like iron rods.
He is the first of God's works;
Only his Maker can draw the sword against him.
The mountains yield him produce,
Where all the beasts of the field play.
He lies down beneath the lotuses,
In the cover of the swamp reeds.   40
The lotuses embower him with shade;
The willows of the brook surround him.
He can restrain the river from its rushing;
He is confident the stream will gush at his command.
Can he be taken by his eyes?
Can his nose be pierced by hooks?
Can you draw out Leviathan by a fishhook?
Can you press down his tongue by a rope?
Can you put a ring through his nose,
Or pierce his jaw with a barb?   50
Will he plead with you at length?
Will he speak soft words to you?
Will he make an agreement with you
To be taken as your lifelong slave?
Will you play with him like a bird,
And tie him down for your girls?
Shall traders traffic in him?
Will he be divided up among merchants?

---

[5] **behemoth** A monstrous-sized animal. In this context, it is probably the hippopotamus.

Can you fill his skin with darts
Or his head with fish-spears?   60
Lay a hand on him,
And you will never think of battle again.

41

See, any hope [of capturing] him must be
      disappointed;   1
One is prostrated by the very sight of him.
There is no one so fierce as to rouse him;
Who then can stand up to Me?
Whoever confronts Me I will requite,
For everything under the heavens is Mine.
I will not be silent concerning him
Or the praise of his martial exploits.
Who can uncover his outer garment?
Who can penetrate the folds of his jowls?   10
Who can pry open the doors of his face?
His bared teeth strike terror.
His protective scales are his pride,
Locked with a binding seal.
One scale touches the other;
Not even a breath can enter between them.
Each clings to each;
They are interlocked so they cannot be parted.
His sneezings flash lightning,
And his eyes are like the glimmerings of dawn.   20
Firebrands stream from his mouth;
Fiery sparks escape.
Out of his nostrils comes smoke
As from a steaming, boiling cauldron.
His breath ignites coals;
Flames blaze from his mouth.
Strength resides in his neck;
Power leaps before him.
The layers of his flesh stick together;
He is as though cast hard; he does not totter.   30
His heart is cast hard as a stone,
Hard as the nether millstone.
Divine beings are in dread as he rears up;
As he crashes down, they cringe.
No sword that overtakes him can prevail,
Nor spear, nor missile, nor lance.
He regards iron as straw,
Bronze, as rotted wood.
No arrow can put him to flight;
Slingstones turn into stubble for him.   40
Clubs are regarded as stubble;
He scoffs at the quivering javelin.
His underpart is jagged shards;
It spreads a threshing-sledge on the mud.
He makes the depths seethe like a cauldron;
He makes the sea [boil] like an ointment-pot.
His wake is a luminous path;
He makes the deep seem white-haired.
There is no one on land who can dominate him,
Made as he is without fear.   50

He sees all that is haughty;
He is king over all proud beasts.

42

Job said in reply to the Lord: 1

> I know that You can do everything,
> That nothing you propose is impossible for You.
> Who is this who obscures counsel without
>   knowledge?
> Indeed, I spoke without understanding
> Of things beyond me, which I did not know.
> Hear now, and I will speak;
> I will ask, and You will inform me.
> I had heard You with my ears,
> But now I see You with my eyes;   10
> Therefore, I recant and relent,
> Being but dust and ashes.

After the Lord had spoken these words to Job, the Lord said to Eliphaz the Temanite, "I am incensed at you and your two friends, for you have not spoken the truth about Me as did My servant Job. Now take seven bulls and seven rams and go to My servant Job and sacrifice a burnt offering for yourselves. And let Job, My servant, pray for you; for to him I will show favor and not treat you vilely, since you have not spoken the truth about Me as did My servant Job." Eliphaz the Temanite and Bildad the Shuhite and Zophar the Naamathite[6] went and did as the Lord had told them, and the Lord showed favor to Job. The Lord restored Job's fortunes when he prayed on behalf of his friends, and the Lord gave Job twice what he had before.

All his brothers and sisters and all his former friends came to him and had a meal with him in his house. They consoled and comforted him for all the misfortune that the Lord had brought upon him. Each gave him one *kesitah* and each one gold ring. Thus the Lord blessed the latter years of Job's life more than the former. He had fourteen thousand sheep, six thousand camels, one thousand yoke of oxen, and one thousand she-asses. He also had seven sons and three daughters. The first he named Jemimah, the second Keziah, and the third Keren-happuch. Nowhere in the land were women as beautiful as Job's daughters to be found. Their father gave them estates together with their brothers. Afterward, Job lived one hundred and forty years to see four generations of sons and grandsons. So Job died old and contented.

---

[6] **Eliphaz the Tenanite, Bildad the Shuhite, and Zophar the Naamathite** Job's three friends who came to counsel him and offer him their advice. Their speeches and Job's responses explore many issues regarding relationships between humans and God.

∽

Ecclesiastes

3

3

A season is set for everything, a time for every   1
    experience under heaven:
A time for being born and a time for dying,
A time for planting and a time for uprooting the
    planted;
A time for slaying and a time for healing,
A time for tearing down and a time for building up;
A time for weeping and a time for laughing,
A time for wailing and a time for dancing;
A time for throwing stones and a time for gathering
    stones,
A time for embracing and a time for shunning
    embraces;
A time for seeking and a time for losing,   10
A time for keeping and a time for discarding;
A time for ripping and a time for sewing,
A time for silence and a time for speaking;

A time for loving and a time for hating;
A time for war and a time for peace.

What value, then, can the man of affairs get from what he earns? I have observed the business that God gave man to be concerned with: He brings everything to pass precisely at its time; He also puts eternity in their mind, but without man ever guessing, from first to last, all the things that God brings to pass. Thus I realized that the only worthwhile thing there is for them is to enjoy themselves and do what is good in their lifetime; also, that whenever a man does eat and drink and get enjoyment out of all his wealth, it is a gift of God.

I realized, too, that whatever God has brought to pass will recur evermore:
    Nothing can be added to it
    And nothing taken from it—
and God has brought to pass that men revere Him
    What is occurring occurred long since,   20

And what is to occur occurred long since: and God seeks the pursued. And, indeed, I have observed under the sun:

Alongside justice there is wickedness,

Alongside righteousness there is wickedness. I mused: "God will doom both righteous and wicked, for there is a time for every experience and for every happening." So I decided, as regards men, to dissociate them [from] the divine beings and to face the fact that they are beasts. For in respect of the fate of man and the fate of beast, they have one and the same fate; as the one dies so dies the other, and both have the same lifebreath; man has no superiority over beast, since both amount to nothing. Both go to the same place; both came from dust and both return to dust. Who knows if a man's lifebreath does rise upward and if a beast's breath does sink down into the earth?

I saw that there is nothing better for man than to enjoy his possessions, since that is his portion. For who can enable him to see what will happen afterward?

Selections from *The Revised Standard Version of the Holy Bible*

Christians adopted the Jewish Bible, *The Holy Scriptures,* renaming it the Old Testament and rearranging its thirty-nine books into the Pentateuch, the Historical Books, the Wisdom Books, and the Prophetical Books. Christians also developed the New Testament—twenty-seven books about Jesus, grouped into the Gospels, the Acts of the Apostles, Epistles, and Apocalypse. The Christian Bible thus numbers sixty-six books. The books in the New Testament, written between A.D. 50 and 100, were brought together around A.D. 150 as the sacred text for the new religion of Christianity. Greek, the New Testament's language, enabled it to circulate freely in Rome's Greek-speaking eastern provinces. When Christianity triumphed in Rome around A.D. 400, the saintly Jerome rewrote the entire Bible into the ordinary, or common, Latin of that era; thereafter, his work was known as the Vulgate version (from Latin *vulgatus,* "common"). Since then, the Vulgate has been the church's official text, although the Protestants composed vernacular versions after 1500.

From the fall of Rome until recent times, the Holy Bible has been the West's most significant book, touching the lives of everyone in all walks of life. This privileged status rose not simply because the Bible contained God's holy words for Christian and Jewish believers, but most important, because it was the all-encompassing glue that bound the culture together. It influenced every aspect of culture, most notably in the arts, language, and personal behavior. The Bible offered an alternative body of writing to that of Greece and Rome and, as such, inspired artists, writers, and musicians. Its words and rhetoric enriched spoken and written language, and its parables and poems served as a handbook for moral guidance. Even in today's secular world, biblical knowledge is still indispensable for interpreting Western culture and history.

Reading the Selections

The selections from Matthew's Gospel include key scenes from the life of Jesus, including the virgin birth, the baptism by John the Baptist, the temptation by the devil, and the Sermon on the Mount. Most notably, the Sermon on the Mount presents Jesus's moral teachings. He begins this sermon with the beatitudes—a list of blessings on those who often are at odds with earthly society, such as the poor and the downtrodden. He next reinterprets the Jewish law, pointing out that obedience of rules is never enough; instead, he asks his followers to practice forgiveness even to the extent of loving one's enemies. Jesus expresses his law of love in what Christians later call the Golden Rule: "So whatever you wish that men would do to you, do so to them . . ." (Matthew 7:12). He also describes the correct way to worship God, giving the Lord's Prayer as the best model. Jesus concludes with a caution against false prophets—those who call on the Lord but refuse to obey his will.

The final selection is from the Epistles—the letters written by early Christian leaders to new congregations needing further knowledge of Christ and his teachings, advice on church organization, and help with understanding the rituals and beliefs of the emerging religion. The letters of Paul, the first Christian missionary, make up the largest number of the Epistles—fourteen out of twenty-one. Chapter 13 from Paul's First Letter to the Corinthians [the church in Corinth, Greece] is an exemplary summary of Christian love, which forgives others and asks nothing in return. This expression of unconditional love, so often read at wedding ceremonies, is more an ideal than a reality.

∞

The Gospel According to Matthew
1:18–25; 2–4
The Coming of Christ

Now the birth of Jesus Christ took place in this way. When his mother Mary had been betrothed to Joseph, before they came together she was found to be with child of the Holy Spirit; and her husband Joseph, being a just man and unwilling to put her to shame, resolved to divorce her quietly. But as he considered this, behold, an angel of the Lord appeared to him in a dream, saying, "Joseph, son of David, do not fear to take Mary your wife, for that which is conceived in her is of the Holy Spirit; she will bear a son, and you shall call his name Jesus, for he will save his people from their sins." All this took place to fulfill what the Lord had spoken by the prophet:

"Behold, a virgin shall conceive and bear a son,
and his name shall be called Emman'u-el"
(which means, God with us).

When Joseph woke from sleep, he did as the angel of the Lord commanded him; he took his wife, but knew her not until she had borne a son; and he called his name Jesus.

2

Now when Jesus was born in Bethlehem of Judea in the days of Herod the king, behold, wise men from the East came to Jerusalem, saying, "Where is he who has been born king of the Jews? For we have seen his star in the East, and have come to worship him." When Herod the king heard this, he was troubled, and all Jerusalem with him; and assembling all the chief priests and scribes of the people, he inquired of them where the Christ was to be born. They told him, "In Bethlehem of Judea; for so it is written by the prophet:

'And you, O Bethlehem, in the land of Judah,
are by no means least among the rulers of Judah;

for from you shall come a ruler
who will govern my people Israel.' "

Then Herod summoned the wise men secretly and ascertained from them what time the star appeared; and he sent them to Bethlehem, saying, "Go and search diligently for the child, and when you have found him bring me word, that I too may come and worship him." When they had heard the king they went their way; and lo, the star which they had seen in the East went before them, till it came to rest over the place where the child was. When they saw the star, they rejoiced exceedingly with great joy; and going into the house they saw the child with Mary his mother, and they fell down and worshiped him. Then, opening their treasures, they offered him gifts, gold and frankincense and myrrh. And being warned in a dream not to return to Herod, they departed to their own country by another way.

Now when they had departed, behold, an angel of the Lord appeared to Joseph in a dream and said, "Rise, take the child and his mother, and flee to Egypt, and remain there till I tell you; for Herod is about to search for the child, to destroy him." And he rose and took the child and his mother by night, and departed to Egypt, and remained there until the death of Herod. This was to fulfil what the Lord had spoken by the prophet, "Out of Egypt have I called my son."

Then Herod, when he saw that he had been tricked by the wise men, was in a furious rage, and he sent and killed all the male children in Bethlehem and in all that region who were two years old or under, according to the time which he had ascertained from the wise men. Then was fulfilled what was spoken by the prophet Jeremiah:

"A voice was heard in Ramah,
wailing and loud lamentation,
Rachel weeping for her children;

she refused to be consoled,
because they were no more."

But when Herod died, behold, an angel of the Lord appeared in a dream to Joseph in Egypt, saying, "Rise, take the child and his mother, and go to the land of Israel, for those who sought the child's life are dead." And he rose and took the child and his mother, and went to the land of Israel. But when he heard that Archela'us reigned over Judea in place of his father Herod, he was afraid to go there, and being warned in a dream he withdrew to the district of Galilee. And he went and dwelt in a city called Nazareth, that what was spoken by the prophets might be fulfilled, "He shall be called a Nazarene."

3

In those days came John the Baptist, preaching in the wilderness of Judea, "Repent, for the kingdom of heaven is at hand." For this is he who was spoken of by the prophet Isaiah when he said,

"The voice of one crying in the wilderness:
Prepare the way of the Lord,
make his paths straight."

Now John wore a garment of camel's hair, and a leather girdle around his waist; and his food was locusts and wild honey. Then went out to him Jerusalem and all Judea and all the region about the Jordan, and they were baptized by him in the river Jordan, confessing their sins.

But when he saw many of the Pharisees and Sad'-ducees[1] coming for baptism, he said to them, "You brood of vipers! Who warned you to flee from the wrath to come? Bear fruit that befits repentance, and do not presume to say to yourselves, 'We have Abraham as our father'; for I tell you, God is able from these stones to raise up children to Abraham. Even now the ax is laid to the root of the trees; every tree therefore that does not bear good fruit is cut down and thrown into the fire.

"I baptize you with water for repentance, but he who is coming after me is mightier than I, whose sandals I am not worthy to carry; he will baptize you with the Holy Spirit and with fire. His winnowing fork is in his hand, and he will clear his threshing floor and gather his wheat into the granary, but the chaff he will burn with unquenchable fire."

Then Jesus came from Galilee to the Jordan to John, to be baptized by him. John would have prevented him, saying, "I need to be baptized by you, and do you come to me?" But Jesus answered him, "Let it be so now; for thus it is fitting for us to fulfil all righteousness." Then he consented. And when Jesus was baptized, he went up imme-

diately from the water, and behold, the heavens were opened and he saw the Spirit of God descending like a dove, and alighting on him; and lo, a voice from heaven, saying, "This is my beloved Son, with whom I am well pleased."

4

Then Jesus was led up by the Spirit into the wilderness to be tempted by the devil. And he fasted forty days and forty nights, and afterward he was hungry. And the tempter came and said to him, "If you are the Son of God, command these stones to become loaves of bread." But he answered, "It is written,

'Man shall not live by bread alone,
but by every word that proceeds from the mouth of God.'"

Then the devil took him to the holy city, and set him on the pinnacle of the temple, and said to him, "If you are the Son of God, throw yourself down; for it is written,

'He will give his angels charge you,'

and

'On their hands they will bear you up,
lest you strike your foot against a stone.'"

Jesus said to him, "Again it is written, 'You shall not tempt the Lord your God.'" Again, the devil took him to a very high mountain, and showed him all the kingdoms of the world and the glory of them; and he said to him, "All these I will give you, if you will fall down and worship me." Then Jesus said to him, "Begone, Satan! for it is written,

'You shall worship the Lord your God
and him only shall you serve.'"

Then the devil left him, and behold, angels came and ministered to him.

Now when he heard that John had been arrested, he withdrew into Galilee; and leaving Nazareth he went and dwelt in Caper'na-um by the sea, in the territory of Zeb'ulun and Naph'tali, that what was spoken by the prophet Isaiah might be fulfilled:

"The land of Zeb'ulun and the land of Naph'tali,
toward the sea, across the Jordan,
Galilee of the Gentiles—
the people who sat in darkness
have seen a great light,
and for those who sat in the region and shadow of death
light has dawned."

From that time Jesus began to preach, saying, "Repent, for the kingdom of heaven is at hand."

As he walked by the Sea of Galilee, he saw two brothers, Simon who is called Peter and Andrew his brother,

---

[1] **Pharisees and Sad'ducees** Two factions or parties in Israel who often held opposing views on many Jewish beliefs and practices. Both groups questioned Jesus and never supported him or his followers. The early Christians saw the Pharisees and the Sad'ducees as their major critics and opponents.

casting a net into the sea; for they were fishermen. And he said to them, "Follow me, and I will make you fishers of men." Immediately they left their nets and followed him. And going on from there he saw two other brothers, James the son of Zeb'edee and John his brother, in the boat with Zeb'edee their father, mending their nets, and he called them. Immediately they left the boat and their father, and followed him.

And he went about all Galilee, teaching in their synagogues and preaching the gospel of the kingdom and healing every disease and every infirmity among the people. So his fame spread throughout all Syria, and they brought him all the sick, those afflicted with various diseases and pains, demoniacs, epileptics, and paralytics, and he healed them. And great crowds followed him from Galilee and the Decap'olis and Jerusalem and Judea and from beyond the Jordan.

5–7

Sermon on the Mount

5

Seeing the crowds, he went up on the mountain, and 1 when he sat down his disciples came to him. And he opened his mouth and taught them, saying:

"Blessed are the poor in spirit, for theirs is the kingdom of heaven.

"Blessed are those who mourn, for they shall be comforted.

"Blessed are the meek, for they shall inherit the earth.

"Blessed are those who hunger and thirst for righteousness, for they shall be satisfied. 5

"Blessed are the merciful, for they shall obtain mercy.

"Blessed are the pure in heart, for they shall see God.

"Blessed are the peacemakers, for they shall be called sons of God.

"Blessed are those who are persecuted for righteousness' sake, for theirs is the kingdom of heaven.

"Blessed are you when men revile you and persecute 10 you and utter all kinds of evil against you falsely on my account. Rejoice and be glad, for your reward is great in heaven, for so men persecuted the prophets who were before you.

"You are the salt of the earth; but if salt has lost its taste, how shall its saltness be restored? It is no longer good for anything except to be thrown out and trodden under foot by men.

"You are the light of the world. A city set on a hill cannot be hid. Nor do men light a lamp and put it under a bushel, but on a stand, and it gives light to all in the house. Let your light so shine before men, that they may see your good works and give glory to your Father who is in heaven.

"Think not that I have come to abolish the law and the prophets; I have come not to abolish them but to fulfil them. For truly, I say to you, till heaven and earth pass away, not an iota, not a dot, will pass from the law until all is accomplished. Whoever then relaxes one of the least of these commandments and teaches men so, shall be called least in the kingdom of heaven; but he who does them and teaches them shall be called great in the kingdom of heaven. For I tell you, unless your righteousness exceeds

that of the scribes and Pharisees, you will never enter the kingdom of heaven.

"You have heard that it was said to the men of old, 'You shall not kill; and whoever kills shall be liable to judgment.' But I say to you that every one who is angry with his brother shall be liable to judgment; whoever insults his brother shall be liable to the council, and whoever says, 'You fool!' shall be liable to the hell of fire. So if you are offering your gift at the altar, and there remember that your brother has something against you, leave your gift there before the altar and go; first be reconciled to your brother, and then come and offer your gift. Make friends quickly with your accuser, while you are going with him to court, lest your accuser hand you over to the judge, and the judge to the guard, and you be put in prison; truly, I say to you, you will never get out till you have paid the last penny.

"You have heard that it was said, 'You shall not commit adultery.' But I say to you that every one who looks at 15 a woman lustfully has already committed adultery with her in his heart. If your right eye causes you to sin, pluck it out and throw it away; it is better that you lose one of your members than that your whole body be thrown into hell. And if your right hand causes you to sin, cut it off and throw it away; it is better that you lose one of your members than that your whole body go into hell.

"It was also said, 'Whoever divorces his wife, let him give her a certificate of divorce.' But I say to you that every one who divorces his wife, except on the ground of unchastity, makes her an adulteress; and whoever marries a divorced woman commits adultery.

"Again you have heard that it was said to the men of old, 'You shall not swear falsely, but shall perform to the Lord what you have sworn.' But I say to you, Do not swear at all, either by heaven, for it is the throne of God, or by the earth, for it is his footstool, or by Jerusalem, for it is the city of the great King. And do not swear by your head, for you cannot make one hair white or black. Let what you say be simply 'Yes' or 'No'; anything more than this comes from evil.

"You have heard that it was said, 'An eye for an eye and a tooth for a tooth.' But I say to you, Do not resist one who is evil. But if any one strikes you on the right cheek, turn to him the other also; and if any one would sue you and take your coat, let him have your cloak as well; and if any one forces you to go one mile, go with him two miles. Give to him who begs from you, and do not refuse him who would borrow from you.

"You have heard that it was said, 'You shall love your neighbor and hate your enemy.' But I say to you, Love your enemies and pray for those who persecute you, so that you may be sons of your Father who is in heaven; for he makes his sun rise on the evil and on the good, and sends rain on the just and on the unjust. For if you love those who love you, what reward have you? Do not even the tax collectors do the same? And if you salute only your brethren, what more are you doing than others? Do not even the Gentiles do the same? You, therefore, must be perfect, as your heavenly Father is perfect.

6

"Beware of practicing your piety before men in order to be seen by them; for then you will have no reward from your Father who is in heaven.

"Thus, when you give alms, sound no trumpet before you, as the hypocrites do in the synagogues and in the streets, that they may be praised by men. Truly, I say to you, they have their reward. But when you give alms, do not let your left hand know what your right hand is doing, so that your alms may be in secret; and your Father who sees in secret will reward you.

"And when you pray, you must not be like the hypocrites; for they love to stand and pray in the synagogues and at the street corners, that they may be seen by men. Truly, I say to you, they have their reward. But when you pray, go into your room and shut the door and pray to your Father who is in secret; and your Father who sees in secret will reward you.

"And in praying do not heap up empty phrases as the Gentiles do; for they think that they will be heard for their many words. Do not be like them, for your Father knows what you need before you ask him. Pray then like this:

Our Father who art in heaven,
Hallowed be thy name.
Thy kingdom come,
Thy will be done,
   On earth as it is in heaven.
Give us this day our daily bread;
And forgive us our debts,
   As we also have forgiven our debtors;
And lead us not into temptation
   But deliver us from evil.

For if you forgive men their trespasses, your heavenly Father also will forgive you; but if you do not forgive men their trespasses, neither will your Father forgive your trespasses.

"And when you fast, do not look dismal, like the hypocrites, for they disfigure their faces that their fasting may be seen by men. Truly, I say to you, they have their reward.

But when you fast, anoint your head and wash your face, that your fasting may not be seen by men but by your Father who is in secret; and your Father who sees in secret will reward you.

"Do not lay up for yourselves treasures on earth, where moth and rust consume and where thieves break in and steal, but lay up for yourselves treasures in heaven, where neither moth nor rust consumes and where thieves do not break in and steal. For where your treasure is, there will your heart be also.

"The eye is the lamp of the body. So, if your eye is sound, your whole body will be full of light; but if your eye is not sound, your whole body will be full of darkness. If then the light in you is darkness, how great is the darkness!

"No one can serve two masters; for either he will hate the one and love the other, or he will be devoted to the one and despise the other. You cannot serve God and mammon.

"Therefore I tell you, do not be anxious about your life, what you shall eat or what you shall drink, nor about your body, what you shall put on. Is not life more than food, and the body more than clothing? Look at the birds of the air: they neither sow nor reap nor gather into barns, and yet your heavenly Father feeds them. Are you not of more value than they? And which of you by being anxious can add one cubit to his span of life? And why are you anxious about clothing? Consider the lilies of the field, how they grow; they neither toil nor spin; yet I tell you, even Solomon in all his glory was not arrayed like one of these. But if God so clothes the grass of the field, which today is alive and tomorrow is thrown into the oven, will he not much more clothe you, O men of little faith? Therefore do not be anxious, saying, 'What shall we eat?' or 'What shall we drink?' or 'What shall we wear?' For the Gentiles seek all these things; and your heavenly Father knows that you need them all. But seek first his kingdom and his righteousness, and all these things shall be yours as well.

"Therefore do not be anxious about tomorrow, for tomorrow will be anxious for itself. Let the day's own trouble be sufficient for the day.

7

"Judge not, that you be not judged. For with the judgment you pronounce you will be judged, and the measure you give will be the measure you get. Why do you see the speck that is in your brother's eye, but do not notice the log that is in your own eye? Or how can you say to your brother, 'Let me take the speck out of your eye,' when there is the log in your own eye? You hypocrite, first take the log out of your own eye, and then you will see clearly to take the speck out of your brother's eye.

"Do not give dogs what is holy; and do not throw your pearls before swine, lest they trample them underfoot and turn to attack you.

"Ask, and it will be given you; seek and you will find; knock, and it will be opened to you. For every one who asks receives, and he who seeks finds, and to him who knocks it will be opened. Or what man of you, if his son asks him for a loaf, will give him a stone? Or if he asks for a fish, will give him a serpent? If you then, who are evil, know how to give good gifts to your children, how much more will your Father who is in heaven give good things to those who ask him? So whatever you wish that men would do to you, do so to them; for this is the law and the prophets.

"Enter by the narrow gate; for the gate is wide and the way is easy, that leads to destruction, and those who enter by it are many. For the gate is narrow and the way is hard, that leads to life, and those who find it are few.

"Beware of false prophets, who come to you in sheep's 5 clothing but inwardly are ravenous wolves. You will know them by their fruits. Are grapes gathered from thorns, or figs from thistles? So, every sound tree bears good fruit, but the bad tree bears evil fruit. A sound tree cannot bear evil fruit, nor can a bad tree bear good fruit. Every tree that does not bear good fruit is cut down and thrown into the fire. Thus you will know them by their fruits.

"Not every one who says to me, 'Lord, Lord,' shall enter the kingdom of heaven, but he who does the will of my Father who is in heaven. On that day many will say to me, 'Lord, Lord, did we not prophesy in your name, and cast out demons in your name, and do many mighty works in your name?' And then will I declare to them, 'I never knew you; depart from me, you evildoers.'

"Every one then who hears these words of mine and does them will be like a wise man who built his house upon the rock; and the rain fell, and the floods came, and the winds blew and beat upon that house, but it did not fall, because it had been founded on the rock. And every one who hears these words of mine and does not do them will be like a foolish man who built his house upon the sand; and the rain fell, and the floods came, and the winds blew and beat against that house, and it fell; and great was the fall of it."

And when Jesus finished these sayings, the crowds were astonished at his teaching, for he taught them as one who had authority, and not as their scribes.

1 Corinthians

13

13

If I speak in the tongues of men and of angels, but have 1 not love, I am a noisy gong or a clanging cymbal. And if I have prophetic powers, and understand all mysteries and all knowledge, and if I have all faith, so as to remove mountains, but have not love, I am nothing. If I give away all I have, and if I deliver my body to be burned, but have not love, I gain nothing.

Love is patient and kind; love is not jealous or boastful; it is not arrogant or rude. Love does not insist on its own way; it is not irritable or resentful; it does not rejoice at wrong, but rejoices in the right. Love bears all things, believes all things, hopes all things, endures all things.

Love never ends; as for prophecy, it will pass away; as for tongues, they will cease; as for knowledge, it will pass away. For our knowledge is imperfect and our prophecy is imperfect; but when the perfect comes, the imperfect will pass away. When I was a child, I spoke like a child, I thought like a child, I reasoned like a child; when I became a man, I gave up childish ways. For now we see in a mirror dimly, but then face to face. Now I know in part; then I shall understand fully, even as I have been fully understood. So faith, hope, love abide, these three; but the greatest of these is love.

TERTULLIAN

Selections from *The Apparel of Women*

Tertullian (ca. A.D. 160–ca. A.D. 230), one of the earliest writers of the Christian era, helped formulate the new religion's beliefs within the broader pagan humanistic traditions and learning. He received a Classical education that aided him in relating his Christian faith to Greco-Roman thought, but any attempts to bridge the gap between these conflicting views ultimately failed, because once Tertullian converted to Christianity, he became a "true believer." Although his fundamentalist attitudes made him an inflexible polemicist and moralist and his invective writing style left little room for compromise, Tertullian addressed many important issues confronting the early church that would influence later thought and policies.

Little is known of his life. Evidence indicates that he was born into a pagan family living in Carthage, one of the major intellectual centers of the empire outside of Rome. He studied literature, philosophy, and law before going to Rome, where he probably pursued a career in law and was first exposed to Christianity. He returned to Carthage and converted to the new faith, which was winning many followers as a result of its dedicated leaders and zealous supporters. He quickly became a strong voice in the North African church as a teacher and a writer. Some years after accepting Christianity, Tertullian joined a splinter Christian group, Montanism. He was attracted to the movement's rigorous moral code and demanding personal habits. However, finding Montanism to be too lax for his high standards, he established his own following, which removed him even further from the Christian community. He apparently died as an embittered and disappointed old man who demanded too much from others and sought a perfection unattainable by humans.

However, Tertullian's contributions were not as a leader or sect founder but as a writer. His works, written in Latin, defined and defended many early Christian beliefs and practices that became part of the religion's tradition. Yet he was more of a propagandist than a theologian, as he attacked his enemies and called for strict adherence to Christian morals and behavior. He not only explained his faith and railed against the pagans, he also wrote on moral and practical choices that Christians new to the faith confronted every day in a society that either ridiculed or persecuted them. He gave Christians advice on whether to serve in the army, on what to do when facing the prospects of persecution, on marriage, on personal habits and use of leisure time, and on dress and behavior in public. Underlying all of his writings was the call for Christians never to give in to their enemies or the alien cultures that he saw as threats to their religion. When he asked, "What has Athens to do with Jerusalem?" Tertullian was merely reconfirming his Christian convictions that the old must give way to the new, that the Classical world would have to yield to the Age of Faith. By the end of his life his vehement denunciations of the secular world and his strident criticisms of the Christian church as an institution and organization made him an outsider, and, consequently, his contributions to Christianity were ignored for several centuries.

Reading the Selections

Tertullian's three earliest works deal with the one single issue: How should Christians live their lives in a pagan society? In the first publication he discusses the temptations of the theater, sporting events, and public celebrations, and, in the second, the worship of pagan idols and the emperor and the seductiveness of everyday activities confronting Christians. In the third work Tertullian considers the dress and behavior of women.

The Apparel of Women, written as two separate books, is addressed to women who have recently converted to Christianity and who, in Tertullian's opinion, need guidance and advice on how to dress modestly and how to avoid the fashions and fads of the day. Echoing the central thesis of many of his other works, these two books assert that a true Christian must renounce the pagan world and surrender to the teachings of Christ. Specifically, this means that women should not wear jewelry or expensive clothes, should not use cosmetics or body creams, and should not dye their hair or be concerned with hairstyles. He also warns men that they should not succumb to vanity or be concerned with their personal appearance. The first excerpt, Chapter 1 of Book One, blames Eve for all subsequent sins, and Tertullian quotes Genesis 3:16 to support his argument: "In sorrow and anxiety, you will bring forth, O woman, and you are subject to your husband, and he is your master." The next excerpts, from Book Two, detail how women displease God by using make-up, dyeing their hair, and wearing fancy clothes. In the final excerpt Tertullian exhorts his female readers to prepare for a better world to come by living modest and simple lives.

Book One

Chapter 1

If there existed upon earth a faith in proportion to the reward that faith will receive in heaven, no one of you, my beloved sisters, from the time when you came to know the living God and recognized your own state, that is, the condition of being a woman, would have desired a too attractive garb, and much less anything that seemed too ostentatious. I think, rather, that you would have dressed in mourning garments and even neglected your exterior, acting the part of mourning and repentant Eve in order to expiate more fully by all sorts of penitential garb that which woman derives from Eve—the ignominy, I mean, of original sin and the odium of being the cause of the fall of the human race. "In sorrow and anxiety, you will bring forth, O woman, and you are subject to your husband, and he is your master." Do you not believe that you are [each] an Eve?

The sentence of God on this sex of yours lives on even in our times and so it is necessary that the guilt should live on, also. You are the one who opened the door to the Devil, you are the one who first plucked the fruit of the forbidden tree, you are the first who deserted the divine law; you are the one who persuaded him whom the Devil was not strong enough to attack. All too easily you destroyed the image of God, man. Because of your desert, that is, death, even the Son of God had to die. And you still think of putting adornments over the skins of animals that cover you? Well, now—if, in the very beginning of the world, the Milesians had invented wool by shearing sheep, and if the Chinese had woven the strands of silk, and the Tyrians had invented dye and the Phrygians embroidery and the Babylonians weaving, if pearls had gleamed and rubies flashed with light, if gold itself had already been brought forth from the bowels of earth by man's greed, and finally, if a mirror had already been capable of giving forth its lying image, do you think that Eve, after she had been expelled from Paradise and was already dead, would have longed for all of these fineries? She would not. Therefore, she ought not to crave them or even to know them now, if she desires to be restored to life again. Those things which she did not have or know when she lived in God, all those things are the trappings appropriate to a woman who was condemned and is dead, arrayed as if to lend splendor to her funeral.

Book Two

Chapter 4

Holy women, let none of you, if she is naturally beautiful, be an occasion of sin; certainly, if even she be so, she must not increase beauty, but try to subdue it. If I were speaking to Gentiles, I would give you a Gentile precept and one that is common to all: you are bound to please no one except your own husbands. And, you will please your husbands in the proportion that you take no pains to please anyone else. Be unconcerned, blessed sisters: no wife is really ugly to her own husband. She was certainly pleasing to him when he chose to marry her, whether it was for her beauty or for her character. Let none of you think that she will necessarily incur the hatred and aversion of her husband if she spends less time in the adornment of her person.

Every husband demands that his wife be chaste; but beauty a Christian husband certainly does not demand, because we Christians are not fascinated by the same things that the Gentiles think to be good. If, on the other hand, the husband be an infidel, he will be suspicious of beauty precisely because of the unfavorable opinion the Gentiles have of us. For whose sake, then, are you cultivating your beauty? If for a Christian, he does not demand it, and if for an infidel, he does not believe it unless it is art-less. Why, then, are you so eager to please either one who is suspicious or one who does not desire it?

Chapter 6

I see some women dye their hair blonde by using saffron. They are even ashamed of their country, sorry that they were not born in Germany or in Gaul! Thus, as far as their hair is concerned, they give up their country. It is hardly a good omen for them that they wish their hair to be flame-colored and mistake for beauty something which merely stains them. As a matter of fact, the strength of these bleaches really does harm to the hair, and the constant application of even any natural moist substance will bring ruin to the head itself, just as the warmth of the sun, while desirable for giving life and dryness to the hair, if overdone is hurtful. How can they achieve beauty when they are doing themselves harm; how can they make something attractive by means of filth? Shall a Christian woman heap saffron on her hair as upon an altar? For, surely, anything that is normally burned in honor of an unclean spirit, may be considered as a sacrifice to idols, unless it is applied for honest and necessary and wholesome uses for which all of God's creatures were provided. But the Lord has said: "Which of you can make a white hair black or out of a black a white?" Thus do they refute the word of the Lord. "Behold," they say, "out of white or black we make it blonde, which is surely more attractive." Why, you will even find people who are ashamed of having lived to old age and try to make their hair black when it is white. Are you not ashamed of such folly? Trying to keep it a secret that you have reached that age for which you longed and prayed, sighing for youth which was a time of sin, missing the chance to show some true maturity! I hope that the daughters of Wisdom will avoid such foolishness. The harder we work to conceal our age the more we reveal it. Or does your eternal life depend on the youthful appearance of your hair? Is that the incorruptibility which we have to put on for the reign that is to come—the incorruptibility promised by the kingdom that will be free from sin? Well, indeed, you speed toward the Lord, well you make haste to be free from this most wicked world, you who find it unpleasant to approach your own end!

Chapter 8

Of course, I am now merely talking as a man and, jealous of women, I try to deprive them of what is their own! But are there not certain things that are forbidden to us, too, out of regard for the sobriety we should maintain out of fear we owe to God? Now, since, by a defect of nature, there is inborn in men because of women (just as in women because of men) the desire to please, the male sex also has its own peculiar trickeries for enhancing their appearance: for instance, cutting the beard a bit too sharply, trimming it too neatly, shaving around the mouth, arranging and dyeing our hair, darkening the first signs of gray hair, disguising the down on the whole body with some female ointments, smoothing off the rest of the body by means of some gritty powder, then always taking occasion to look in a mirror, gazing anxiously into it. Are not all of these things quite idle and hostile to modesty once we have known God, have put aside the desire to please others and foresworn all lasciviousness? For, where God is there is modesty, where modesty is there is dignity, its assistant and companion. How shall we ever practise modesty if we do not make use of its normal means, that is, dignity? How shall we ever be able to make use of dignity in practising modesty unless we bear a certain seriousness in our countenance, in our dress, and in the appearance of the entire man?

Chapter 10

Of course, it was God who taught men how to dye wool with the juice of herbs and the slime of shells; it had escaped Him, when He bade all things to come into existence, to issue a command for the production of purple and scarlet sheep! It was God, too, who devised the manufacture of those very garments which, light and thin in themselves, are heavy only in their price; God it was who produced such a great amount of gold for the careful setting and fitting of jewels; and it was God, too, to be sure, who caused the puncturing of ears and was so interested in tormenting his own creatures as to order suffering to infants with their first breath; and this, in order that from these scars on the body—it seems as if the latter was born to be cut—there might hang some sort of precious stones which, as is well known, the Parthians insert in their shoes in place of studs! As a matter of fact, this gold whose glitter you find so attractive is used by some nations for chains, as pagan literature tells us. And so, it is not because of intrinsic value that these things are good, but merely because they happen to be rare. After artistic skills, however, had been introduced by the fallen angels, who had also discovered the materials themselves, elaborate workmanship, combined with the rareness of these things, brought about the idea of their being precious and stimulated the desire on the part of the women to possess them because of their precious character.

Now, if these very angels who discovered the material substances of this kind as well as their charms—I mean gold and precious stones—and passed on the techniques of working them and taught, among other things, the use of eyelid-powder and the dyeing of cloth, if these angels, I say, are condemned by God, as Henoch[1] tells us, how are we ever going to please God by taking pleasure in things developed by those who because of those acts provoked the wrath and punishment of God?

· · ·

Chapter 13

· · ·

Therefore, my blessed sisters, let us think of the hardships to come, and we will not feel them. Let us abandon luxuries and we will never miss them. Let us stand ready to endure every violence, having nothing which we would be afraid to leave behind. For, these things are really the bonds that hold down the wings of our hope. Let us cast away the ornaments of this world if we truly desire those of heaven. Do not love gold—that substance which caused the very first sins of the people of Israel to be branded with infamy. You should hate that which ruined your fathers, that gold which they adored when they abandoned God, for even then gold was food for the fire.

But the lives of Christians are never spent in gold, and now less than ever, but in iron. The stoles of martyrdom are being prepared, and the angels who are to carry us [to heaven] are being awaited. Go forth to meet those angels, adorned with the cosmetics and ornaments of the

---

[1] **Henoch** Another spelling for Enoch. There are two Enochs: one is the son of Cain, who was the son of Adam; the second Enoch, father of Methuselah, was, according to the *Holy Scriptures,* taken by God to be with him. This biblical story became the basis of the legends surrounding Enoch and the origins of the books of Enoch. The books of Enoch consist of a collection of apocalyptic stories, legends, and parables that Tertullian probably read or of which he had some knowledge.

7

LATE ROMAN CIVILIZATION
The Civilizations of Late Rome, Byzantium, and the Early Medieval West

ST. AUGUSTINE
Selections from *Confessions* and *The City of God*

St. Augustine (A.D. 354–430) is one of the West's great bridge figures who appear at disjunctures in time and whose mission seems to be to culminate one phase of civilization and point history on a new path. St. Augustine, who lived in the final days of the western Roman Empire (A.D. 476 is the traditional date of its fall), functioned as a bridge between the dying Classical era and the embryonic Christian world. Born in North Africa to a Christian mother (Monica) and pagan father, he was a pagan himself until he joined Christianity at age thirty-three. Later, he became Bishop of Hippo, an ancient city near his birthplace; from that post, through his vast writings, he dominated the Roman world for almost thirty-five years. Fusing his knowledge of Greco-Roman philosophy, especially Platonism (see *The Republic, Phaedo*) and Neo-Platonism, with his understanding of Christian beliefs, he developed a theology now called Augustinianism. This theology provided a justification for a religious-centered world—the intellectual framework in which the Christian church operated until about 1300. A controversialist who wrote on every major Christian topic of his day, including original sin, salvation, and God and history, he became an authoritative voice whose influence is still active in Catholic theology.

St. Augustine was possessed of a ferocious vision that saw life on earth as a vale of tears through which humanity must travel. The true meaning of existence would be unveiled in a heavenly future. Within this vale of tears, St. Augustine did not sit idly on the sidelines; he actively engaged in the intellectual wars that consumed this age. Reflecting his self-ascribed natural combativeness, he had, before turning Christian, subscribed for nine years to Manicheanism, a religion that viewed the world as locked in a gigantic struggle between the forces of good and the forces of evil. He relished acrimonious quarrels, notably with fellow churchmen who differed from him on difficult points in theology. A prolific author, he wrote many pamphlets, letters, and essays that belong to Christian theology, as well as two classics of world literature: the *Confessions* (ca. 390s), his personal memoirs; and *The City of God* (ca. 420s), his Christian-inspired philosophy of history.

Reading the Selection from Confessions

Prior to Book VIII of the *Confessions,* St. Augustine recounted his youth, education, and above all, his search for a final truth, whether philosophical or religious. What fueled his personal search was his longing to feel moral, to gain relief from the guilt that had dogged him since youth, stemming from such sins as stealing pears and, in the main, consorting with mistresses. He often found solutions to his quest in, for example, the writings of Cicero (see *On the Republic*) or the dualistic religion of the Manichees; however, none of these could finally quench his restless spirit.

Book VIII of the *Confessions* concludes Augustine's quest with his conversion to Christianity. The heart of his conversion story occurs in Chapter 12: He hears a child's voice urging him to "Take it and read," a message he interprets as being from God, encouraging him to read at random in the Bible. He follows this mystical advice, and the first passage to greet his eyes is from a letter of Paul's. While reading the passage, St. Augustine feels flooded with light, and his earlier darkness falls away. Now, as a Christian convert, he hurries to tell his mother, who is overjoyed to learn that God has answered her prayers.

Reading the Selections from **The City of God**

In A.D. 410 the Visigoths, a tribe of German invaders, sacked Rome, a calamity that had happened only once before (ca. 400 B.C.) in the city's eleven-hundred-year history. Pagans blamed this most recent calamity on, in their eyes, the weak Christian God. To counter this pagan charge, Augustine wrote *The City of God*, and in the process also fleshed out a philosophy of history that was highly influential throughout the Middle Ages.

The City of God numbers about a thousand pages, divided into twenty-two books. Books I–X recount Rome's history and summarize pagan philosophical and religious arguments against Christian beliefs. In Books XI–XXII, Augustine sets forth his main theme about the City of Man and the City of God, which constitutes a belief in predestination: The citizens of the City of Man are doomed to hell, and the citizens of the City of God are destined for heaven.

In Book XIV, Augustine asserts that the two cities may be distinguished from one another by their origins, the City of Man being born of self-love and the City of God from God's love. In Chapter 17 of Book XIX, Augustine points out that the two cities may coexist, except in regard to religious laws. Perhaps fearing a pagan resurgence, which might overthrow Christian dominance of Rome, Augustine maintained that the City of Man and the City of God should *not* have the same religious laws. Here, Augustine laid down the principle of separation of church and state, an issue that became a battleground in medieval Europe and about which skirmishes are still being fought.

∽

Confessions

Book VIII

10

There are many abroad[1] who talk of their own fantasies and lead men's minds astray. They assert that because they have observed that there are two wills at odds with each other when we try to reach a decision, we must therefore have two minds of different natures, one good, the other evil. *Let them vanish at God's presence as the smoke vanishes.* As long as they hold these evil beliefs they are evil themselves, but even they will be good if they see the truth and accept it, so that your apostle may say to them *Once you were all darkness; now, in the Lord you are all daylight.* These people want to be light, not in the Lord, but in themselves, because they think that the nature of the soul is the same as God. In this way their darkness becomes denser still, because in their abominable arrogance they have separated themselves still further from you, who are *the true Light which enlightens every soul born into the world.* I say to them, "Take care what you say, and blush for shame. Enter God's presence, and find their enlightenment; *here is no room for downcast looks.*"

When I was trying to reach a decision about serving the Lord my God, as I had long intended to do, it was I who willed to take this course and again it was I who willed not to take it. It was I and I alone. But I neither willed to do it nor refused to do it with my full will. So I was at odds with myself. I was throwing myself into con-

---

[1] **many abroad** The Manichees, followers of Manichaeism, a dualistic religion, based on the beliefs that matter is evil and the soul is good. They taught that salvation came from knowledge of the soul's oneness with God; ethically, they abstained from the things of the flesh; founded in Persia by the prophet Mani (d. 274/277). Augustine, before becoming Christian, was a Manichaean.

fusion. All this happened to me although I did not want it, but it did not prove that there was some second mind in me besides my own. It only meant that my mind was being punished. *My action did not come from me, but from the sinful principle that dwells in me.*[2] It was part of the punishment of a sin freely committed by Adam, my first father.

If there were as many different natures in us as there are conflicting wills, we should have a great many more natures than merely two. Suppose that someone is trying to decide whether to go to the theatre or to the Manichees' meeting-house. The Manichees will say, "Clearly he has two natures, the good one bringing him here to us and the bad one leading him away. Otherwise, how can you explain this dilemma of two opposing wills?" I say that the will to attend their meetings is just as bad as the will to go off to the theatre,[3] but in their opinion it can only be a good will that leads a man to come to them. Suppose then that one of us is wavering between two conflicting wills and cannot make up his mind whether to go to the theatre or to our church. Will not the Manichees be embarrassed to know what to say? Either they must admit—which they will not do—that it is a good will which brings a man to our church, just as in their opinion it is a good will which brings their own communicants and adherents to their church; or they must presume that there are two evil natures and two evil minds in conflict in one man. If they think this, they will disprove their own theory that there is one good and one evil will in man. The only alternative is for them to be converted to the truth and to cease to deny that when a man tries to make a decision, he has one soul which is torn between conflicting wills.

So let us hear no more of their assertion, when they observe two wills in conflict in one man, that there are two opposing minds in him, one good and the other bad, and that they are in conflict because they spring from two opposing substances and two opposing principles. For you, O God of truth, prove that they are utterly wrong. You demolish their arguments and confound them completely. It may be that both the wills are bad. For instance, a man may be trying to decide whether to commit murder by poison or by stabbing; whether he should swindle another man out of one part of his property or another, that is, if he cannot obtain both; whether he should spend his money extravagantly on pleasure or hoard it like a miser; or whether he should go to the games in the circus or to the theatre, when there is a performance at both places on the same day. In this case there may be a third possibility, that he should go and rob another person's house, if he has the chance. There may even be a fourth choice open to him, because he may wonder whether to go and commit adultery, if the occasion arises at the same time. These possibilities may all occur at the same moment and all may seem equally desirable. The man cannot do all these things at once, and his mind is torn between four wills which cannot be reconciled—perhaps more than four, because there are a great many things that he might wish to do. But the Manichees do not claim that there are as many different substances in us as this.

It is just the same when the wills are good. If I question the Manichees whether it is good to find pleasure in reading Paul's Epistles or in the tranquil enjoyment of a Psalm or in a discussion of the Gospel, they will reply in each case that it is good. Supposing, then, that a man finds all these things equally attractive and the chance to do all of them occurs at the same time, is it not true that as long as he cannot make up his mind which of them he most wants to do his heart is torn between several different desires? All these different desires are good, yet they are in conflict with each other until he chooses a single course to which the will may apply itself as a single whole, so that it is no longer split into several different wills.

The same is true when the higher part of our nature aspires after eternal bliss while our lower self is held back by the love of temporal pleasure. It is the same soul that wills both, but it wills neither of them with the full force of the will. So it is wrenched in two and suffers great trials, because while truth teaches it to prefer one course, habit prevents it from relinquishing the other.

11

This was the nature of my sickness. I was in torment, reproaching myself more bitterly than ever as I twisted and turned in my chain. I hoped that my chain might be broken once and for all, because it was only a small thing that held me now. All the same it held me. And you, O Lord, never ceased to watch over my secret heart. In your stern mercy you lashed me with the twin scourge of fear and shame in case I should give way once more and the worn and slender remnant of my chain should not be broken but gain new strength and bind me all the faster. In my heart I kept saying "Let it be now, let it be now!", and merely by saying this I was on the point of making the resolution. I was on the point of making it, but I did not succeed. Yet I did not fall back into my old state. I stood on the brink of resolution, waiting to take fresh breath. I tried again and came a little nearer to my goal, and then a little nearer still, so that I could almost reach out and grasp it. But I did not reach it. I could not reach out to it or grasp it, because I held back from the step by which I should die to death and become alive to life. My lower instincts, which had taken firm hold of me, were stronger than the higher, which were untried. And the closer I came to the moment which was to mark the great change in me, the more I shrank from its horror. But it did not drive me back or turn me from my purpose: it merely left me hanging in suspense.

I was held back by mere trifles, the most paltry inanities, all my old attachments. They plucked at my garment of flesh and whispered, "Are you going to dismiss us? From this moment we shall never be with you again, for ever and ever. From this moment you will never again be allowed to do this thing or that, for evermore." What was it, my God, that they meant when they whispered "this

---

[2] *My action ... dwells in me.* Romans 7:17.
[3] **the theatre** The early Christian Church considered the theatre to be evil.

thing or that"? Things so sordid and so shameful that I beg you in your mercy to keep the soul of your servant free from them! These voices, as I heard them, seemed less than half as loud as they had been before. They no longer barred my way, blatantly contradictory, but their mutterings seemed to reach me from behind, as though they were stealthily plucking at my back, trying to make me turn my head when I wanted to go forward. Yet, in my state of indecision, they kept me from tearing myself away, from shaking myself free of them and leaping across the barrier to the other side, where you were calling me. Habit was too strong for me when it asked "Do you think you can live without these things?"

But by now the voice of habit was very faint. I had turned my eyes elsewhere, and while I stood trembling at the barrier, on the other side I could see the chaste beauty of Continence[4] in all her serene, unsullied joy, as she modestly beckoned me to cross over and to hesitate no more. She stretched out loving hands to welcome and embrace me, holding up a host of good examples to my sight. With her were countless boys and girls, great numbers of the young and people of all ages, staid widows and women still virgins in old age. And in their midst was Continence herself, not barren but a fruitful mother of children, of joys born of you, O Lord, her Spouse. She smiled at me to give me courage, as though she were saying, "Can you not do what these men and these women do? Do you think they find the strength to do it in themselves and not in the Lord their God? It was the Lord their God who gave me to them. Why do you try to stand in your own strength and fail? Cast yourself upon God and have no fear. He will not shrink away and let you fall. Cast yourself upon him without fear, for he will welcome you and cure you of your ills. "I was overcome with shame, because I was still listening to the futile mutterings of my lower self and I was still hanging in suspense. And again Continence seemed to say, "Close your eyes to the unclean whispers of your body, so that it may be mortified. It tells you of things that delight you, but not such things as the law of the Lord your God has to tell."

In this way I wrangled with myself, in my own heart, about my own self. And all the while Alypius[5] stayed at my side, silently awaiting the outcome of this agitation that was new in me.

12

I probed the hidden depths of my soul and wrung its pitiful secrets from it, and when I mustered them all before the eyes of my heart, a great storm broke within me, bringing with it a great deluge of tears. I stood up and left Alypius so that I might weep and cry to my heart's content, for it occurred to me that tears were best shed in solitude. I moved away far enough to avoid being embarrassed even by his presence. He must have realized what my feelings were, for I suppose I had said something and he had known from the sound of my voice that I was ready to burst into tears. So I stood up and left him where we had

been sitting, utterly bewildered. Somehow I flung myself down beneath a fig tree and gave way to the tears which now streamed from my eyes, the sacrifice that is acceptable to you. I had much to say to you, my God, not in these very words but in this strain: *Lord, will you never be content? Must we always taste your vengeance? Forget the long record of our sins.* For I felt that I was still the captive of my sins, and in my misery I kept crying "How long shall I go on saying 'tomorrow, tomorrow'? Why not now? Why not make an end of my ugly sins at this moment?"

I was asking myself these questions, weeping all the while with the most bitter sorrow in my heart, when all at once I heard the sing-song voice of a child in a nearby house. Whether it was the voice of a boy or a girl I cannot say, but again and again it repeated the refrain "Take it and read, take it and read." At this I looked up, thinking hard whether there was any kind of game in which children used to chant words like these, but I could not remember ever hearing them before. I stemmed my flood of tears and stood up, telling myself that this could only be a divine command to open my book of Scripture and read the first passage on which my eyes should fall. For I had heard the story of Antony,[6] and I remembered how he had happened to go into a church while the Gospel was being read and had taken it as a counsel addressed to himself when he heard the words *Go home and sell all that belongs to you. Give it to the poor, and so the treasure you have shall be in heaven; then come back and follow me.*[7] By this divine pronouncement he had at once been converted to you.

So I hurried back to the place where Alypius was sitting, for when I stood up to move away I had put down the book containing Paul's Epistles. I seized it and opened it, and in silence I read the first passage on which my eyes fell: *Not in revelling and drunkenness, not in lust and wantonness, not in quarrels and rivalries. Rather, arm yourselves with the Lord Jesus Christ; spend no more thought on nature and nature's appetites.*[8] I had no wish to read more and no need to do so. For in an instant, as I came to the end of the sentence, it was as though the light of confidence flooded into my heart and all the darkness of doubt was dispelled.

I marked the place with my finger or by some other sign and closed the book. My looks now were quite calm as I told Alypius what had happened to me. He too told me what he had been feeling, which of course I did not know. He asked to see what I had read. I showed it to him and he read on beyond the text which I had read. I did not know what followed, but it was this: *Find room among you for a man of over-delicate conscience.*[9] Alypius applied this to himself and told me so. This admonition was enough to give him strength, and without suffering the distress of hesitation he made his resolution and took this good purpose to himself. And it very well suited his moral character, which had long been far, far better than my own.

Then we went in and told my mother,[10] who was overjoyed. And when we went on to describe how it had

---

[4] **Continence** Self-restraint, especially the ability to control bodily desires.
[5] **Alypius** A friend of Augustine.

[6] **Antony** St. Antony of Egypt (d. 356), patron saint of monks.
[7] *Go home . . . and follow me.* Matthew 19:21.
[8] *Not in revelling . . . nature's appetites.* Romans 13:13–14.
[9] *Find room . . . over-delicate conscience.* Romans 14:1.
[10] **mother** Monica (333–387), later St. Monica; born in Tagaste (modern Souk-Ahras, Algeria).

all happened, she was jubilant with triumph and glorified you, *who are powerful enough, and more than powerful enough, to carry out your purpose beyond all our hopes and dreams.* For she saw that you had granted her far more than she used to ask in her tearful prayers and plaintive lamentations. You converted me to yourself, so that I no longer desired a wife or placed any hope in this world but stood firmly upon the rule of faith, where you had shown me to her in a dream so many years before. And you *turned her sadness into rejoicing,* into joy far fuller than her dearest wish, far sweeter and more chaste than any she had hoped to find in children begotten of my flesh.

The City of God
Book XIV

Chapter 28
The Character of the Two Cities

We see then that the two cities were created by two kinds of love: the earthly city was created by self-love reaching the point of contempt for God, the Heavenly City by the love of God carried as far as contempt of self. In fact, the earthly city glories in itself, the Heavenly City glories in the Lord. The former looks for glory from men, the latter finds its highest glory in God, the witness of a good conscience. The earthly lifts up its head in its own glory, the Heavenly City says to its God: "My glory; you lift up my head."[1] In the former, the lust for domination lords it over its princes as over the nations it subjugates; in the other both those put in authority and those subject to them serve one another in love, the rulers by their counsel, the subjects by obedience. The one city loves its own strength shown in its powerful leaders; the other says to its God, "I will love you, my Lord, my strength."[2]

Consequently, in the earthly city its wise men who live by men's standards have pursued the goods of the body or of their own mind, or of both. Or those of them who were able to know God "did not honour him as God, nor did they give thanks to him, but they dwindled into futility in their thoughts, and their senseless heart was darkened: in asserting their wisdom"—that is, exalting themselves in their wisdom, under the domination of pride—"they became foolish, and changed the glory of the imperishable God into an image representing a perishable man, or birds or beasts or reptiles"—for in the adoration of idols of this kind they were either leaders or followers of the general public—"and they worshipped and served created things instead of the Creator, who is blessed for ever."[3] In the Heavenly City, on the other hand, man's only wisdom is the devotion which rightly worships the true God, and looks for its reward in the fellowship of the saints, not only holy men but also holy angels, "so that God may be all in all."[4]

---

[1] **My glory . . . my head.** Psalm 3:3.
[2] **I will . . . my strength.** Psalm 18:1.

[3] **did not honour . . . who is blessed for ever.** Romans 1:21ff.
[4] **so that God may be all in all.** 1 Corinthians 15:29.

Book XV

Chapter 4
Conflict and Peace in the Earthly City

The earthly city will not be everlasting; for when it is condemned to the final punishment it will no longer be a city. It has its good in this world, and rejoices to participate in it with such gladness as can be derived from things of such a kind. And since this is not the kind of good that causes no frustrations to those enamoured of it, the earthly city is generally divided against itself by litigation, by wars, by battles, by the pursuit of victories that bring death with them or at best are doomed to death. For if any section of that city has risen up in war against another part, it seeks to be victorious over other nations, though it is itself the slave of base passions; and if, when victorious, it is exalted in its arrogance, that victory brings death in its train. Whereas if it considers the human condition and the changes and chances common to mankind, and is more tormented by possible misfortunes than puffed up by its present success, then its victory is only doomed to death. For it will not be able to lord it permanently over those whom it has been able to subdue victoriously.

However, it would be incorrect to say that the goods which this city desires are not goods, since even that city is better, in its own human way, by their possession. For example, that city desires an earthly peace, for the sake of the lowest goods; and it is that peace which it longs to attain by making war. For if it wins the war and no one survives to resist, then there will be peace, which the warring sections did not enjoy when they contended in their unhappy poverty for the things which they could not both possess at the same time. This peace is the aim of wars, with all their hardships; it is this peace that glorious victory (so called) achieves.

Now when the victory goes to those who were fighting for the juster cause, can anyone doubt that the victory is a matter for rejoicing and the resulting peace is something to be desired? These things are goods and undoubtedly they are gifts of God. But if the higher goods are neglected, which belong to the City on high, where victory will be serene in the enjoyment of eternal and perfect peace—if these goods are neglected and those other goods are so desired as to be considered the only goods, or are loved more than the goods which are believed to be higher, the inevitable consequence is fresh misery, and an increase of the wretchedness already there.

Book XIX

Chapter 17
The Origin of Peace Between the Heavenly Society and the Earthly City, and of Discord Between Them

But a household of human beings whose life is not based on faith is in pursuit of an earthly peace based on the things belonging to this temporal life, and on its advantages, whereas a household of human beings whose life is based on faith looks forward to the blessings which are promised as eternal in the future, making use of earthly and temporal things like a pilgrim in a foreign land, who does not let himself be taken in by them or distracted from his course towards God, but rather treats them as supports which help him more easily to bear the burdens of "the corruptible body which weighs heavy on the soul"[5]; they must on no account be allowed to increase the load. Thus both kinds of men and both kinds of households alike make use of the things essential for this mortal life; but each has its own very different end in making use of them. So also the earthly city, whose life is not based on faith, aims at an earthly peace, and it limits the harmonious agreement of citizens concerning the giving and obeying of orders to the establishment of a kind of compromise between human wills about the things relevant to mortal life. In contrast, the Heavenly City—or rather that part of it which is on pilgrimage in this condition of mortality, and which lives on the basis of faith—must needs make use of this peace also, until this mortal state, for which this kind of peace is essential, passes away. And therefore, it leads what we may call a life of captivity in this earthly city as in a foreign land, although it has already received the promise of redemption, and the gift of the Spirit as a kind of pledge of it; and yet it does not hesitate to obey the laws of the earthly city by which those things which are designed for the support of this mortal life are regulated; and the purpose of this obedience is that, since this mortal condition is shared by both cities, a harmony may be preserved between them in things that are relevant to this condition.

But this earthly city has had some philosophers belonging to it whose theories are rejected by the teaching inspired by God. Either led astray by their own speculation or deluded by demons, these thinkers reached the belief that there are many gods who must be won over to serve human ends, and also that they have, as it were, different departments with different responsibilities attached. Thus the body is the department of one god, the mind that of another; and within the body itself, one god is in charge of the head, another of the neck and so on with each of the separate members. Similarly, within the mind, one is responsible for natural ability, another for learning, another for anger, another for lust; and in the accessories of life there are separate gods over the departments of flocks, grain, wine, oil, forests, coinage, navigation, war and victory, marriage, birth, fertility, and so on. The Heavenly City, in contrast, knows only one God as the object of worship, and decrees, with faithful devotion, that he only is to be served with that service which the Greeks call *latreia*,[6] which is due to God alone. And the result of this difference has been that the Heavenly City could not have laws of religion common with the earthly city, and in defence of her religious laws she was bound to dissent from those who thought differently and to prove a burdensome nuisance to them. Thus she had to endure their anger and hatred, and the assaults of persecution; until at length that City shattered the morale of her adversaries by the terror inspired by her numbers, and by the help she continually received from God.

While this Heavenly City, therefore, is on pilgrimage in this world, she calls out citizens from all nations and so collects a society of aliens, speaking all languages. She takes on account of any difference in customs, laws, and institutions, by which earthly peace is achieved and preserved—not that she annuls or abolishes any of those, rather, she maintains them and follows them (for whatever divergences there are among the diverse nations, those institutions have one single aim—earthly peace), provided that no hindrance is presented thereby to the religion which teaches that the one supreme and true God is to be worshipped. Thus even the Heavenly City in her pilgrimage here on earth makes use of the earthly peace and defends and seeks the compromise between human wills in respect of the provisions relevant to the mortal nature of man, so far as may be permitted without detriment to true religion and piety. In fact, that City relates the earthly peace to the heavenly peace, which is so truly peaceful that it should be regarded as the only peace deserving the name, at least in respect of the rational creation; for this peace is the perfectly ordered and completely harmonious fellowship in the enjoyment of God, and of each other in God. When we arrive at that state of peace, there will be no longer a life that ends in death, but a life that is life in sure and sober truth; there will be no ani-

---

[5] **the corruptible body . . . the soul** Wisdom 9:15.

[6] **latreia** *Latria*, in Greek, means the state of a hired servant; used here by Augustine to refer to divine service to God.

mal body to "weigh down the soul" in its process of corruption; there will be a spiritual body with no cravings, a body subdued in every part to the will. This peace the Heavenly City possesses in faith while on its pilgrimage, and it lives a life of righteousness, based on this faith, having the attainment of that peace in view in every good action it performs in relation to God, and in relation to a neighbour, since the life of a city is inevitably a social life.

EUSEBIUS

Selections from *The History of the Church*

Eusebius of Caesarea (ca. 260–340) wrote a history of the Christian church that covered events from its founding by Christ to the time of Constantine (r. 306–337), the first Christian Roman emperor. Since Eusebius believed that God operated in human affairs and that the future belonged to the Christians, he concluded that a history of the spread of Christianity would disseminate these beliefs to a wider audience. He meant this didactic book for fellow Christians, but he also had in mind Rome's educated elite, most of whom were pagan when he wrote. Recognized today as the "founder of ecclesiastical history," Eusebius set the standard for church history until the Renaissance, when modern research methods, with their human-centered outlook and concern for scientific accuracy, rendered his pious type of history obsolete. Still, his account remains a classic, for it is one of the main sources for events and historical figures in the first years of Christianity.

Eusebius was probably born in Caesarea, in Palestine, an early Christian center under Roman rule. As a young man, he was mentored by Pamphilus, a devout and classically trained Christian whose school awakened Eusebius to the challenge of reconciling Christian thought with Greco-Roman learning. With Pamphilus, he wrote several books—all since lost—with Christian themes. Because of his beliefs, he was imprisoned in 309 and 311 in Rome's empire-wide assault on Christianity and its leaders. But in 314 he was made Bishop of Caesarea, a step that reflected Rome's changed policy toward Christians coincident with Constantine's conversion in 312. As Bishop of Caesarea, Eusebius himself baptized the pagan emperor into the new faith. Favored by Constantine, Eusebius grew in reputation to become one of the era's outstanding Christians, playing important roles at the historic Council of Nicaea and other church gatherings.

The History of the Church, arranged in ten books, was written over a sixteen-year period, a time frame based on internal evidence, such as mentions of historic events datable from other sources. Begun during the Great Persecution in 309, this history was completed in 325, when Constantine was presiding over a Christianized imperial court and Eusebius was one of its ornaments. Eusebius's plan for the book embraced a wide range of topics: namely, tracing the "lines of succession" of the first apostles, telling the stories of early Christian leaders, exposing heretics, detailing the calamities suffered by the Jews because of their treatment of Jesus, setting forth Rome's final assault on the Christian faith, and paying homage to the martyrs whose blood was "the seed of the church," in the words of another early Christian writer, Tertullian (ca. 160–ca. 230).

Reading the Selections

These passages from Eusebius's work show his method of writing God-centered history. Focusing on a person or event as a framing device, he creates a historical snapshot and at the same time stresses his belief in God's presence everywhere. For example, the treatment of the executions of Peter and Paul dwells on both their martyrdom and the folly of the Emperor Nero, "the first to be heralded as a conspicuous fighter against God." Just so, the narrative of the Great

Persecution blends details of Roman atrocities with a moving account of Christians willingly facing martyrdom. Finally, Constantine's triumph is described, although Eusebius makes it clear that the result was because of God, "in fulfillment of His purpose."

The Neronian[1] Persecution, in Which Paul[2] and Peter[3] Died

When Nero's power was now firmly established he gave himself up to unholy practices and took up arms against the God of the universe. To describe the monster of depravity that he became lies outside the scope of the present work. Many writers have recorded the facts about him in minute detail, enabling anyone who wishes to get a complete picture of his perverse and extraordinary madness, which led him to the senseless destruction of innumerable lives, and drove him in the end to such a lust for blood that he did not spare even his nearest and dearest but employed a variety of methods to do away with mother,[4] brothers,[5] and wife[6] alike, to say nothing of countless other members of his family, as if they were personal and public enemies. All this left one crime still to be added to his account—he was the first of the emperors to be the declared enemy of the worship of Almighty God. To this the Roman Tertullian[7] refers in the following terms:

Study your records: there you will find that Nero was the first to persecute this teaching when, after subjugating the entire East, in Rome especially he treated everyone with savagery. That such a man was author of our chastisement fills us with pride. For anyone who knows him can understand that anything not supremely good would never have been condemned by Nero.

So it came about that this man, the first to be heralded as a conspicuous fighter against God, was led on to mur-

der the apostles. It is recorded that in his reign Paul was beheaded in Rome itself, and that Peter likewise was crucified, and the record is confirmed by the fact that the cemeteries there are still called by the names of Peter and Paul, and equally so by a churchman named Gaius,[8] who was living while Zephyrinus was Bishop of Rome.[9] In his published *Dialogue* with Proclus,[10] the leader of the Phrygian heretics, Gaius has this to say about the places where the mortal remains of the two apostles have been reverently laid:

I can point out the monuments of the victorious apostles. If you will go as far as the Vatican[11] or the Ostian Way,[12] you will find the monuments of those who founded this church.

That they were both martyred at the same time Bishop Dionysius of Corinth[13] informs us in a letter written to the Romans:

In this way by your impressive admonition you have bound together all that has grown from the seed which Peter and Paul sowed in Romans and Corinthians alike. For both of them sowed in our Corinth and taught us jointly: in Italy too they taught jointly in the same city, and were martyred at the same time.

These evidences make the truth of my account still more certain.

---

[1] **Neronian** Related to the reign of the Roman emperor **Nero** (r. A.D. 54–68).

[2] **Paul** Jewish name, **Saul.** On three missionary trips through Asia Minor and Greece, he founded churches and sent them letters (the "Pauline epistles" of the New Testament). Arrested in Jerusalem and held prisoner for two years. As a Roman citizen, he appealed to emperor, who transferred him to Rome. Martyred in Rome between 62 and 68.

[3] **Peter** One of Jesus's original twelve apostles. Head of Christian community in Jerusalem after Jesus's crucifixion. Imprisoned by Herod Agrippa I, but escaped. Founded church in Antioch. According to tradition, he went to Rome, where he was martyred about 64. Perhaps author of two epistles in the New Testament.

[4] **mother** Agrippina, **Nero's** mother, assassinated by **Nero's** order, in 59.

[5] **brothers** Nero poisoned his half-brother, Britannicus, in 55.

[6] **wife** Nero's first wife Octavia was murdered on his order, in 62, and he caused the death of his second wife, Poppaea Sabine, in 65.

[7] **Tertullian** (ca. 160–ca. 230) One of the Fathers of the Church (see *The Apparel of Women*).

[8] **Gaius** Also **Caius.** A third-century church leader (an elder) and author of the (now lost) *Dialogue with Proclus* (ca. 200). An orthodox Christian and anti-Montanist.

[9] **Zephyrinus . . . Bishop of Rome** Pope (r. 198–217) and saint. The **Bishops of Rome** gradually amassed power over the whole church, to become the popes, based in Rome.

[10] **Proclus** (fl. second century) Also **Proculus;** a leading Montanist, a group of Christian schismatics, who proclaimed the dawn of the Millenium and called for strict ascetic living. Based in Phrygia, in west central Asia Minor.

[11] **Vatican** One of Rome's original hills. **Vatican Hill** rises near the Tiber River, with a low-lying plain between. According to tradition, the remains of **Peter** and **Paul** were buried at the foot of the hill— thus rendering the area a sacred space for the church.

[12] **Ostian Way** A road from Rome to the port of Ostia, following the Tiber River.

[13] **Bishop Dionysius of Corinth** (d. ca. 180) Saint; several of his letters survive.

∽

The Destruction of the Churches

Everything indeed has been fulfilled in my time; I saw ₁
with my own eyes the places of worship thrown down
from top to bottom, to the very foundations, the inspired
holy Scriptures committed to the flames in the middle of
the public squares, and the pastors of the churches hiding
disgracefully in one place or another, while others suffered
the indignity of being held up to ridicule by their enemies—a reminder of another prophetic saying: for contempt was poured on rulers, and He made them wander
in a trackless land where there was no road.[14] But it is not
for me to describe their wretched misfortunes in the event:
nor is it my business to leave on record their quarrels and
inhumanity to each other before the persecutions, so I
have made up my mind to relate no more about them than
enough to justify the divine judgement. I am determined
therefore to say nothing even about those who have been
tempted by the persecution or have made complete shipwreck of their salvation and of their own accord flung
themselves into the depths of the stormy sea; I shall
include in my overall account only those things by which
first we ourselves, then later generations, may benefit. Let
me therefore proceed from this point to describe in outline
the hallowed ordeals of the martyrs of God's word.

---

[14] **for contempt . . . was no road** Psalm 107:40.

It was the nineteenth year of Diocletian's[15] reign and
the month Dystrus, called March[16] by the Romans, and
the festival of the Saviour's Passion[17] was approaching,
when an imperial decree[18] was published everywhere,
ordering the churches to be razed to the ground and the
Scriptures destroyed by fire, and giving notice that those
in places of honour would lose their places, and domestic staff, if they continued to profess Christianity, would
be deprived of their liberty. Such was the first edict
against us. Soon afterwards other decrees arrived in
rapid succession, ordering that the presidents of the
churches in every place should all be first committed to
prison and then coerced by every possible means into
offering sacrifice.[19]

---

[15] **Diocletian** Roman emperor (r. 284–305), who began the last and
most severe persecution of the Christian Church.
[16] **March** In reality, the first destruction of churches began in Febru-
ary 302.
[17] **Saviour's Passion** The Easter season.
[18] **decree** The 302 decree ordered the destruction of churches, the
burning of Holy Scriptures, and the degrading of those who held to
their Christian beliefs.
[19] **offering sacrifice** The three later edicts required that (1) bishops,
presbyters (elders), and deacons be imprisoned; (2) church officials be
tortured and forced to sacrifice to the emperor; and (3) clergy and
laity also be tortured and forced to sacrifice.

∽

Ordeals Endured in the Persecution: God's Glorious Martyrs

Then, then it was that many rulers of the churches bore up ₁
heroically under horrible torments, an object lesson in the
endurance of fearful ordeals; while countless others, their
souls already numbed with cowardice, promptly succumbed to the first onslaught. Of the rest, each was subjected to a series of different tortures, one flogged
unmercifully with the whip, another racked and scraped
beyond endurance, so that the lives of some came to a
most miserable end. But different people came through
the ordeal very differently: one man would be forcibly
propelled by others and brought to the disgusting, unholy
sacrifices, and dismissed as if he had sacrificed, even if he
had done no such thing; another, who had not even
approached any abomination, much less touched it, but
was said by others to have sacrificed, would go away
without attempting to repudiate the baseless charge.
Another would be picked up half dead, and thrown away
as if already a corpse; and again a man lying on the
ground might be dragged a long way by his feet, though
included among the willing sacrificers. One man would

announce at the top of his voice his determination not to
sacrifice, another would shout that he was a Christian,
exulting in the confession of the Saviour's Name, while
yet another insisted that he had never sacrificed and never
would. These were struck on the mouth and silenced by a
formidable body of soldiers lined up for the purpose: their
faces and cheeks were battered and they were forcibly
removed. It was the one object in life of the enemies of true
religion to gain credit for having finished the job.

But no such methods could enable them to dispose of
the holy martyrs. What could I say that would do full justice
to them? I could tell of thousands who showed magnificent
enthusiasm for the worship of the God of the universe, not
only from the beginning of the general persecution, but
much earlier when peace was still secure. For at long last
the one[20] who had received the authority was as it were
awaking from the deepest sleep, after making attempts—as

---

[20] **the one** Diocletian.

yet secret and surreptitious—against the churches, in the interval that followed Decius[21] and Valerian.[22] He did not make his preparations all at once for the war against us, but for the time being took action only against members of the legions.[23] In this way he thought that the rest would easily be mastered if he joined battle with these and emerged victorious. Now could be seen large numbers of serving soldiers most happy to embrace civil life, in order to avoid having to repudiate their loyalty to the Architect of the universe. The commander-in-chief, whoever he was, was now

first setting about persecuting the soldiery, classifying and sorting those serving in the legions, and allowing them to choose either to obey orders and retain their present rank, or alternatively to be stripped of it if they disobeyed the enactment. But a great many soldiers of Christ's kingdom without hesitation or question chose to confess Him rather than cling to the outward glory and prosperity they enjoyed. Already here and there one or two of them were suffering not only loss of position but even death as the reward of their unshakable devotion: or the time being the man behind the plot was acting cautiously and going as far as bloodshed in a few cases only; he was apparently afraid of the number of believers, and shrank from launching out into war with them all at once. But when he stripped more thoroughly for battle, words are inadequate to depict the host of God's noble martyrs whom the people of every city and every region were privileged to see with their own eyes.

---

[21] **Decius** Roman emperor (r. 249–251). **Decius's** attempt to revitalize Rome's pagan cults led him to begin a new round of persecutions (250–251) of the Christian Church.
[22] **Valerian** Roman emperor (r. 253–260). Faced with enemies at home and abroad, **Valerian** turned from toleration of Christians to a savage assault on the church (258–260), which ended with the emperor's capture and death at the hands of the Persians.
[23] **legions** Units of the Roman army, scattered across the empire.

Victory of Constantine[24]; the Benefits He Conferred on His Subjects

When Licinius[25] had rushed headlong to the limit of madness, this seemed no longer endurable to the emperor,[26] God's friend, who—reasoning along sound lines and tempering the rigidity of justice with humanity—determined to rescue the tyrant's victims, and by putting a few destroyers out of the way made haste to save the bulk of the human race. He had treated Licinius with nothing but kindness hitherto, and had shown mercy where no sympathy was deserved. But Licinius grew no better: his wickedness continued unabated, and he raged more and more madly against his subject peoples; while for his victims there remained no hope of escape, with a wild beast tyrannizing over them.

And so, his love of goodness blended with a hatred of evil, the champion of the good set out with his son Crispus,[27] that most humane emperor, by his side, holding out a saving hand to all who were perishing. Then, taking God the universal King, and God's Son the Saviour of all, as

Guide and Ally, father and son together divided their battle array against God's enemies on every side, and easily carried off the victory: every detail of the encounter was made easy for them by God, in fulfillment of His purpose. Suddenly in less time than it takes to say it, those who a day or two before had been breathing death and threats were no more, and even their name was forgotten; their portraits and tributes were swept into merited oblivion; and the very things that Licinius with his own eyes had seen befall the wicked tyrants who preceded him he underwent himself, because he did not allow himself to be disciplined or learn wisdom from the blows that fell on his neighbours; and having pursued the same path of wickedness as they, he deservedly toppled over the identical cliff.

His adversary thus finally thrown down, the mighty victor Constantine, pre-eminent in every virtue that true religion can confer, with his son Crispus, an emperor most dear to God and in every way resembling his father, won back their own eastern lands and reunited the Roman Empire into a single whole, bringing it all under their peaceful sway, in a wide circle embracing north and south alike from the east to the farthest west. Men had now lost all fear of their former oppressors; day after day they kept dazzling festival; light was everywhere, and men who once dared not look up greeted each other with smiling faces and shining eyes. They danced and sang in city and country alike, giving honour first of all to God our Sovereign Lord, as they had been instructed, and then to the pious emperor with his sons, so dear to God. Old troubles were forgotten, and all irreligion passed into oblivion; good things present were enjoyed, those yet to come eagerly awaited. In every city the victorious emperor pub-

---

[24] **Constantine** Roman emperor (r. 306–337). He won the battle of Milvian Bridge (near Rome) and became sole emperor in the West (312); out of gratitude to the Christian God for the victory, he converted to Christianity and issued with **Licinius,** the emperor of the East, the Edict of Toleration (313), thus ending the persecution of the church. He became sole emperor in 324, when he defeated and executed **Licinius.**
[25] **Licinius** Roman emperor (308–324). He became emperor in the East, in 308, and joined with **Constantine** in issuing the Edict of Toleration (313), ending persecution of Christians in the empire. He was defeated and killed by **Constantine** in 324.
[26] **the emperor** Constantine.
[27] **Crispus** (d. 326) Roman soldier and son of the emperor **Constantine.** His father gave him title of *Caesar* and made him ruler of Gaul (modern France) in 317.

lished decrees full of humanity and laws that gave proof of munificence and true piety. Thus all tyranny had been purged away, and the kingdom that was theirs was preserved securely and without question for Constantine and his sons alone. They, having made it their first task to wipe the world clean from hatred of God, rejoiced in the blessings that He had conferred upon them, and, by the things they did for all men to see, displayed love of virtue and love of God, devotion and thankfulness to the Almighty.

ANNA COMNENA
Selections from *The Alexiad*

The Alexiad, as the first known history written by a woman, is a milestone in world literature. The author was Anna Comnena (1083–1153), the daughter of the Byzantine emperor Alexius I, whose reign (1081–1118) is covered in her book. Ignored by the Byzantines, *The Alexiad* was absorbed into Western culture after being discovered by Renaissance scholars, who translated it from Greek into European languages. Today it is accepted as a valuable historical source, partly as an eyewitness account of Alexius's reign and, equally important, as a sound work of scholarship.

Alexius Comnenus, the subject of *The Alexiad,* ruled Byzantium during a crucial time in its history. His career began as the empire, wracked by internal chaos, faced probable extinction from all sides: Seljuk Turks were on the move through Asia Minor, Normans advanced against Adriatic outposts, and varied tribes from the north menaced Constantinople, the capital. A gifted general and master of intrigue, Alexius seized the throne and, as Alexius I, gave the empire a new lease on life. He conducted winning campaigns against both Turks and Normans and weathered the First Crusade. His political and army reforms allowed the empire to endure until 1204, when soldiers of the Fourth Crusade conquered Constantinople and divided up its lands among themselves.

Anna Comnena's account of Alexius's reign uses the methods of the Greek historian Thucydides (see *History of the Peloponnesian War*). Like him, she writes contemporary history based on personal knowledge, memories of credible witnesses, and study of archival documents and treaties. Unlike him, she concentrates on wars and uprisings, a narrow focus that undoubtedly reflects her troubled age. Told from an insider's point of view and instilled with Christian and Classical learning, hers is a highly readable, persuasive account of Alexius's reign.

The Alexiad is not without flaws. Foremost among these are Anna's biases: She glorifies her father and ignores her brother, John, probably because John succeeded Alexius to the throne (r. 1118–1143), thus ending her hopes of being empress. She was also a religious zealot, gloating over the deaths of heretics. Her love of country led her to overdramatize events. ("They descended on their enemies like lions.") But overall, the book's virtues outweigh these flaws.

Reading the Selections

Anna Comnena, writing in the Preface to *The Alexiad,* echoes Thucydides when she asserts that history is a "bulwark against the stream of Time," thus allowing humans to salvage what is important from "the depths of Oblivion." From this highminded ideal, she descends to the reality of her subject, Alexius's empire as it is simultaneously invaded by Turks and soldiers of the First Crusade (1097–1104), known variously as Franks, Latins, or Kelts. Books I–XIII of *The Alexiad* are filled with military campaigns and governmental crises. The selection taken from Book XIV, the next to last chapter, offers a uniquely non-Western view of the crusaders, both as individuals and as a group. Enlisted in Europe's holy war against Middle East Muslims, the crusaders, in Anna's eyes, are nothing but undisciplined and untrustworthy barbarians, greedy for gain. To her, they are no match for her father, despite his declining health.

The selection ends with Anna digressing about her critics. At first, she claims the high ground, arguing that she does not favor her father but is simply writing the truth. Soon, though, she slips into a defense of herself against those who have spread lies about her since she was a child. Passages such as this raise questions about her personal bias, despite the disclaimer.

∞

Preface

The stream of Time, irresistible, ever moving, carries off and bears away all things that come to birth and plunges them into utter darkness, both deeds of no account and deeds which are mighty and worthy of commemoration; as the playwright[1] says, it "brings to light that which was unseen and shrouds from us that which was manifest." Nevertheless, the science of History is a great bulwark against this stream of Time; in a way it checks this irresistible flood, it holds in a tight grasp whatever it can seize floating on the surface and will not allow it to slip away into the depths of Oblivion.

I, Anna, daughter of the Emperor Alexius[2] and the Empress Irene,[3] born and bred in the Purple,[4] not without some acquaintance with literature—having devoted the most earnest study to the Greek language, in fact, and being not unpractised in Rhetoric[5] and having read thoroughly the treatises of Aristotle and the dialogues of Plato, and having fortified my mind with the Quadrivium of sciences[6] (these things must be divulged, and it is not self-advertisement to recall what Nature[7] and my own zeal for knowledge have given me, nor what God has apportioned to me from above and what has been contributed by Opportunity); I, having realized the effects wrought by Time, desire now by means of my writings to give an account of my father's deeds, which do not deserve to be consigned to Forgetfulness nor to be swept away on the flood of Time into an ocean of Non-Remembrance; I wish to recall everything, the achievements before his elevation to the throne and his actions in the service of others before his coronation.

I approach the task with no intention of flaunting my skill as a writer; my concern is rather that a career so brilliant should not go unrecorded in the future, since even the greatest exploits, unless by some chance their memory is preserved and guarded in history, vanish in silent darkness. My father's actions themselves prove his ability as a ruler and show, too, that he was prepared to submit to authority, within just limits.

Now that I have decided to write the story of his life, I am fearful of an underlying suspicion: someone might conclude that in composing the history of my father I am glorifying myself; the history, wherever I express admiration for any act of his, may seem wholly false and mere panegyric.[8] On the other hand, if he himself should ever lead me, under the compulsion of events, to criticize some action taken by him, not because of what he decided but because of the circumstances, here again I fear the cavillers: in their all-embracing jealousy and refusal to accept what is right, because they are malicious and full of envy, they may cast in my teeth the story of Noah's son Ham[9] and, as Homer says, "blame the guiltless."[10]

Whenever one assumes the role of historian, friendship and enmities have to be forgotten; often one has to bestow on adversaries the highest commendation (where their deeds merit it); often, too, one's nearest relatives, if their pursuits are in error and suggest the desirability of reproach, have to be censured. The historian, therefore, must shirk neither remonstrance with his friends, nor praise of his enemies. For my part, I hope to satisfy both parties, both those who are offended by us and those who accept us, by appealing to the evidence of the actual events and of eye-witnesses. The fathers and grandfathers of some men living today saw these things.

---

[1] **the playwright** Sophocles.
[2] **Alexius** Reign name, **Alexius I Comnenus.** Byzantine emperor (r. 1081–1118); founded Comnenian dynasty.
[3] **Irene** Full name **Irene Ducas** (about 1066–1120). Byzantine empress; wife of **Alexius I Comnenus,** Byzantine emperor. Retired to a monastery in 1118.
[4] **bred in the Purple** Greek, *Porphyra.* The Purple was the imperial nursery, where the ruler's offspring were born. The children were called *porphyrogeniti,* prince or princess. In Byzantium, the color purple was reserved for imperial or high rank.
[5] **Rhetoric** The art of speaking and writing effectively. Together with grammar and logic, it comprises the trivium, or arts portion of the seven liberal arts.
[6] **Quadrivium of sciences** Four areas of study—arithmetic, music, geometry, and astronomy—that comprise the science portion of the seven liberal arts.
[7] **Nature** The natural gift of intellect.

[8] **panegyric** A formal declaration of praise.
[9] **Noah's son Ham** Genesis 9:21–27 describes a drunken Noah, after the flood, being seen naked by his son Ham, who tells his brothers, Shem and Japheth. Shem and Japheth cover Noah's nakedness, while averting their gaze. When Noah awakens, he blesses Shem and Japheth and curses Ham's son Canaan. (Why Ham is not cursed is not explained.) The episode is often interpreted as an allegory: The descendents of Shem are the Semitic people; the descendents of Japheth are the Gentiles; and the descendents of Ham, through Canaan, are slaves. Also, the curse on the descendents of Canaan offers a justification for the Hebrews' later conquest of the land of Canaan (Palestine).
[10] **"blame the guiltless"** From *Odyssey,* Book 20.

∾

Book XIV

One day he was exercising at polo, his partner being the Taticius I have often mentioned. Taticius[11] was carried away by his horse and fell on the emperor, whose knee-cap was injured by the impact (Taticius was a heavy man). The pain affected the whole of his foot and although he did not show that he was in distress—he was used to bearing pain—he did receive some minor treatment. Little by little the trouble wore off and disappeared, so that his normal habits were resumed. That was the prime origin of his gout, for the painful areas attracted rheumatism. There was a second, more obvious cause of all this illness. Everyone knows that countless multitudes of Kelts[12] came to the imperial city, having migrated from their own lands and hurried from all directions to us. It was then that the emperor was plunged into a vast ocean of worries. He had long been aware of their dream of Empire; he was aware too of their overwhelming numbers—more than the grains of sand on the sea-shore or all the stars of heaven; the sum total of Roman[13] forces would equal not one tiny part of their multitudes, even if they were concentrated in one place—much less when they were dissipated over wide areas, for some were on guard in the valleys of Serbia and in Dalmatia,[14] others keeping watch near the Danube against Cuman[15] and Dacian[16] incursions, and many had been entrusted with the task of saving Dyrrachium[17] from a second Keltic victory. Under the circumstances he devoted his whole attention now to these Kelts and all else was considered of secondary importance. The barbarian world on our borders, which was restless but had not yet broken out into open hostility, he kept in check by granting honours and presents, while the ambition of the Kelts was confined by all possible means. The rebellious spirit of his own subjects caused no less trouble—in fact he suspected them even more and hastened to protect himself as best he could. Their plots were skilfully averted. But no one could adequately describe the ferment of troubles which descended on him at this period. It compelled him to become all things to all men, to accommodate himself as far as he could to circumstances. Like a trained physician (following the rules of his craft) he had to apply himself to the most pressing need. At daybreak, as soon as the sun leapt up over the eastern horizon, he took his seat on the imperial throne and every day on his orders all Kelts were freely admitted to his presence. The purpose of this was

twofold: he liked them to make their own requests, and he strove by various arguments to reconcile them to his wishes. The Keltic counts are brazen-faced, violent men, money-grubbers and where their personal desires are concerned quite immoderate. These are natural characteristics of the race. They also surpass all other nations in loquacity. So when they came to the palace they did so in an undisciplined fashion, every count bringing with him as many comrades as he wished; after him, without interruption, came another and then a third—an endless queue. Once there they did not limit the conversation by the water-clock, like the orators of ancient times, but each, whoever he was, enjoyed as much time as he wanted for the interview with the emperor. Men of such character, talkers so exuberant, had neither respect for his feelings nor thought for the passing of time nor any idea of the by-standers' wrath; instead of giving way to those coming behind them, they talked on and on with an incessant stream of petitions. Every student of human customs will be acquainted with Frankish verbosity and their pettifogging love of detail; but the audience on these occasions learnt the lesson more thoroughly—from actual experience. When evening came, after remaining without food all through the day, the emperor would rise from his throne and retire to his private apartment, but even then he was not free from the importunities of the Kelts. They came one after another, not only those who had failed to obtain a hearing during the day, but those who had already been heard returned as well, putting forward this or that excuse for more talk. In the midst of them, calmly enduring their endless chatter stood the emperor. One could see them there, all asking questions, and him, alone and unchanging, giving them prompt replies. But there was no limit to their foolish babbling, and if a court official did try to cut them short, he was himself interrupted by Alexius. He knew the traditional pugnacity of the Franks and feared that from some trivial pretext a mighty blaze of trouble might spring up, resulting in serious harm to the prestige of Rome. It was really a most extraordinary sight. Like a statue wrought by the hammer, made perhaps of bronze or cold-forged iron, the emperor would sit through the night, often from evening till midnight, often till third cock-crow, sometimes almost until the sun was shining clearly. The attendants were all worn out, but by frequently retiring had a rest and then came back again—in bad humour. Thus not one of them would stay motionless as long as he did; all in one way or another kept changing position: one would sit down, another turned his head away and rested it on something, another propped himself against a wall. Only one man, the emperor, faced this tremendous task without weakening. His endurance was truly remarkable. Hundreds of people were talking, each one prattling on at length, "brawling away unbridled of tongue"[18] as Homer says. As one stood aside he passed

---

[11] **Taticius** One of the emperor's generals.
[12] **Kelts** Another name for the European Crusaders.
[13] **Roman** Byzantine. With Byzantium as the successor to the old Eastern Roman Empire, the Byzantine rulers considered themselves and their people to be Romans.
[14] **Dalmatia** The area along the Adriatic coast, of modern Yugoslavia, Bosnia and Herzegovina, and Croatia.
[15] **Cuman** Turkic people from the steppe zone, ranging from the Ukraine to Central Eurasia, from the eleventh to the fourteenth centuries.
[16] **Dacian** The people of Dacia, modern Romania.
[17] **Dyrrachium** Modern Durres, Albania; a seaport on the Adriatic Sea.

[18] **"brawling away unbridled of tongue"** *Iliad*, Book 2.

the conversation on to another, and he to the next, and so on and on. They stood only in these intervals but he all the time, up to first or even second cock-crow. After a brief rest, when the sun rose he was again seated on his throne and once more fresh labours and twofold troubles succeeded those of the night. It was for this reason, then, that the emperor was attacked by the pain in his feet. From that time to the end of his life the rheumatism came on at regular intervals and caused him dreadful pain. Despite this he bore it so well that not once did he murmur in complaint; all he said was, "I deserve to suffer. This happens to me justly because of the multitude of my sins." And if by chance a cross word did escape his lips he immediately made the sign of the Cross against the assault of the evil demon. "Flee from me, wicked one," he would say. "A curse on you and your tempting of Christians!" I will say no more now about the pain that afflicted him. Maybe there was someone who contributed to this malady of his and increased the sufferings he bore (and surely his cup of bitterness was already full). I will give a brief outline of the story, not the full details. The empress smeared the rim of the cup with honey, as it were, and contrived that he should avoid most of his troubles, for she unceasingly watched over him.

·   ·   ·

At this stage of my history the reader perhaps will say that I am naturally biased. My answer is this: I swear by the perils the emperor endured for the well-being of the Roman people, by his sorrows and the travails he suffered on behalf of the Christians, that I am not favouring him when I say or write such things. On the contrary, where I perceive that he was wrong I deliberately transgress the law of nature and stick to the truth. I regard him as dear, but truth as dearer still. As one of the philosophers somewhere remarked, "Both are dear, but it is best to honour truth more highly." I have followed the actual course of events, without additions of my own, without suppression, and so I speak and write. And the proof of this is

near to hand. I am not writing the history of things that happened 10,000 years ago, but there are men still alive today who knew my father and tell me of his deeds. They have in fact made a not inconsiderable contribution to the history, for one reported or recalled to the best of his ability one fact, while another told me something else—but there was no discrepancy in their accounts. Most of the time, moreover, we were ourselves present, for we accompanied our father and mother. Our lives by no means revolved round the home; we did not live a sheltered, pampered existence. From my very cradle—I swear it by God and His Mother—troubles, afflictions, continual misfortunes were my lot, some from without, some from within. As to my physical characteristics, I will not speak of them—the attendants in the gynaeconitis[19] can describe and talk of them. But if I write of the evils that befell me from without, the troubles I encountered even before I had completed my eighth year and the enemies raised up against me by the wickedness of men, I would need the Siren[20] of Isocrates,[21] the grandiloquence of Pindar,[22] Polemo's[23] vivacity, the Calliope[24] of Homer, Sappho's[25] lyre or some other power greater still. For no danger, great or small from near or far away, failed to attack us at once. I was truly overwhelmed by the flood and ever since, right up to the present time, even to this moment when I write these words, the sea of misfortunes advances upon me, wave after wave. But I must stop—I have inadvertently drifted away into my own troubles.

---

[19] **gynaeconitis** From Greek, the place set aside for the exclusive use of women.
[20] **Siren** A Siren, half-woman, half-bird, cast a spell of enchantment with her song.
[21] **Isocrates** (436–338 B.C.) Athenian orator and founder of a school of rhetoric.
[22] **Pindar** (ca. 522–ca. 438 B.C.) Greek lyric poet from Thebes.
[23] **Polemo** (A.D. ca. 88–145) Greek orator from Laodicea.
[24] **Calliope** The muse of epic poetry; one of the nine muses of Greek culture.
[25] **Sappho** (ca. 600 B.C.) Greek lyric poet from Lesbos.

BOETHIUS

Selection from *The Consolation of Philosophy*

Boethius (ca. 480–524), like St. Augustine (see *Confessions*), was a transitional figure who bridged the Classical and Christian worlds. Privileged as an aristocrat and traditionally educated in liberal studies, Boethius, at an early age, came to the attention of Theodoric, the Ostrogoth (German) general who had conquered Italy before 493 and made himself its king. With the king's favor, Boethius rose through the ranks at the royal court, finally becoming, in effect, prime minister. He was made consul in 510.

Despite his administrative duties, Boethius still found time for his studies, writing books on arithmetic, astronomy, and music, and making Latin translations of works by Aristotle and other Greek scholars. His translations of Aristotle laid the foundation for scholasticism and systematized late Classical/Christian philosophy—two of his major contributions to thought during the Middle Ages.

Even though Boethius received royal favor, the king had him arrested as the result of palace intrigue that in turn was part of a conflict between Theodoric and the Byzantine emperor over political and religious issues. While awaiting death, Boethius composed one of the masterpieces of Western thought, *The Consolation of Philosophy,* which reflected his Classical education. He was executed in 524, when his jailers beat him with clubs until he died.

Reading the Selection

Boethius's *The Consolation of Philosophy* is a hybrid work that alternates prose and poetry. The author's mouthpiece in the first three chapters is Dame Philosophy, a personification technique that influenced later medieval writers (see Christine de Pizan's *The Book of the City of Ladies*). Dame Philosophy addresses Boethius and, by extension, the reader, in the ways that philosophy can help mortals face terrible misfortunes. Overall, her advice seems to be one of Stoic resignation to the unaccountable whims of Fortune, an ancient idea of the randomness at work in the world. Dame Philosophy herself does not oppose Fortune. She points out to Boethius that Fortune has been good to him, providing him with a loyal wife, two sons, and true friends; now, however, Fortune's wheel has turned, and he is in prison facing inevitable death. Thus, he must learn to accept life's bitterness with the sweet.

In Book III, Dame Philosophy introduces a new note when she says that there is no true happiness except in union with God. She pledges that she (that is, philosophy) will guide Boethius (the reader) to true happiness, though he must seek help from God.

God, as defined and addressed in this work, is a philosophical concept: "Thou who dost by everlasting reason rule / Creator of the planets and the sky, who time / From timelessness didst bring, unchanging Mover." This language suggests the influence of Plato (see *The Republic* and *Phaedo*) and Aristotle (see *Poetics*). Thus, as Boethius, one of the last Romans but also one of the first medieval Christians, faced death, he expressed no hope in the Christian belief of personal immortality but placed his trust in the truths of Greek philosophy.

Another important point about this selection is the mode of reasoning, which relies on quotations from famous authors and the Bible (appeals to authority), definitions of terms, and summary of all sides to an argument. Because this work was one of the few that was continuously read after the fall of the western Roman Empire, the reasoning methods employed by Boethius were widely imitated until about 1500.

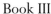

Book III

Chapter IX

. . .

"Even a blind man could see it," I[1] said, "and you[2] revealed it just now when you were trying to show the causes of false happiness. For unless I'm mistaken, true and perfect happiness is that which makes a man self-sufficient, strong, worthy of respect, glorious and joyful. And to show you that I have more than a superficial understanding, without a shadow of doubt I can see that happiness to be true happiness which, since they are all the same thing, can truly bestow any one of them."

"You are blessed in this belief, my child, provided you add one thing."

---

[1] **I** The narrator, Boethius himself.
[2] **you** Dame Philosophy.

"What is that?"

"Do you think there is anything among these mortal and degenerate things which could confer such a state?"

"No, I don't, and you have proved it as well as anyone could wish."

"Clearly, therefore, these things offer man only shadows of the true good,[3] or imperfect blessings, and cannot confer true and perfect good."

"Yes."

"Since then you have realized the nature of true happiness and seen its false imitations, what remains now is that you should see where to find this true happiness."

"Which is the very thing I have long and eagerly been waiting for."

"But since in the *Timaeus*[4] my servant Plato was pleased to ask for divine help even over small matters, what do you think we ought to do now in order to be worthy of discovering the source of that supreme good?"

"We ought to pray to the Father of all things. To omit to do so would not be laying a proper foundation."

"Right," she said, and immediately began the following hymn.

> *"O Thou who dost by everlasting reason rule,*
> *Creator of the planets and the sky, who time*
> *From timelessness didst bring, unchanging Mover,*
> *No cause drove Thee to mould unstable matter, but*
> *The form benign of highest good within Thee set.*
> *All things Thou bringest forth from Thy high archetype:*
> *Thou, height of beauty, in Thy mind the beauteous world*
> *Dost bear, and in that ideal likeness shaping it,*
> *Dost order perfect parts a perfect whole to frame.*
> *The elements[5] by harmony Thou dost constrain,*
> *That hot to cold and wet to dry[6] are equal made,*
> *That fire grow not too light, or earth too fraught with*
>   *weight.*
> *The bridge of threefold nature madest Thou soul, which*
>   *spreads*
> *Through nature's limbs harmonious and all things moves.*
> *The soul once cut, in circles two its motion joins,*
> *Goes round and to itself returns encircling mind,*
> *And turns in pattern similar the firmament.*
> *From causes like Thou bringst forth souls and lesser lives,*
> *Which from above in chariots swift Thou dost disperse*
> *Through sky and earth, and by Thy law benign they turn*
> *And back to Thee they come through fire that brings*
>   *them home.*
> *Grant, Father, that our minds Thy august seat may scan,*
> *Grant us the sight of true good's source, and grant us light*
> *That we may fix on Thee our mind's unblinded eye.*
> *Disperse the clouds of earthly matter's cloying weight;*
> *Shine out in all Thy glory; for Thou art rest and peace*

> *To those who worship Thee; to see Thee is our end,*
> *Who art our source and maker, lord and path and goal."*

Chapter X

"Since, then, you have seen the form both of imperfect and of perfect good, I think we now have to show where this perfect happiness is to be found.

"The first question to ask is, I think, whether any good of the kind I defined a moment ago can exist in the natural world. This will prevent our being led astray from the truth of the matter before us by false and ill-founded reasoning. But the existence of this good and its function as a kind of fountain-head of all good things cannot be denied; for everything that is said to be imperfect is held to be so by the absence of perfection. So that if a certain imperfection is visible in any class of things, it follows that there is also a proportion of perfection in it. For if you do away with perfection, it is impossible to imagine how that which is held to be imperfect could exist. The natural world did not take its origin from that which was impaired and incomplete, but issues from that which is unimpaired and perfect and then degenerates into this fallen and worn out condition. But we showed just now that there is a certain imperfect happiness in perishable good, so that there can be no doubt that a true and perfect happiness exists."

"Which is a very sound and true conclusion," I said.

"As to where it is to be found, then, you should think as follows. It is the universal understanding of the human mind that God, the author of all things, is good. Since nothing can be conceived better than God, everyone agrees that that which has no superior is good. Reason shows that God is so good that we are convinced that His goodness is perfect. Otherwise He couldn't be the author of creation. There would have to be something else possessing perfect goodness over and above God, which would seem to be superior to Him and of greater antiquity. For all perfect things are obviously superior to those that are imperfect. Therefore, to avoid an unending argument, it must be admitted that the supreme God is to the highest degree filled with supreme and perfect goodness. But we have agreed that perfect good is true happiness; so that it follows that true happiness is to be found in the supreme God."

"I accept that. There is nothing in any way open to contradiction."

"But," she said, "I must ask you to make sure that your approval of our statement that the supreme God is to the highest degree filled with supreme good is unqualified and final."

"How do you mean?" I asked.

"By avoiding the assumption that this Father of creation has received this supreme good with which He is said to be filled from outside Himself, or that He possesses it by nature but in such a way as would lead you to suppose that the substance of God the possessor was a separate thing from the substance of the happiness He possesses. If you thought that He received it from outside

---

[3] **shadows of the true good** An echo of Plato's argument in "The Allegory of the Cave."
[4] *Timaeus* Plato's book on cosmology, physics, and biology.
[5] **elements** Earth, air, fire, and water.
[6] **hot . . . cold . . . wet . . . dry** Qualities derived from the four **elements:** hot (fire); cold (earth); wet (water); and dry (air).

Himself, you would be able to count the giver superior to the receiver. But we are in agreement that it is right to consider God the most excellent of things.

"On the other hand, if goodness is a natural property of God, but something logically distinct from Him, whenever we speak of God as the author of creation, an able mind might be able to imagine the existence of a power responsible for bringing together the two that were separate.

"Finally, if one thing is distinct from another, it cannot be the thing from which it is perceived to be distinct. So that which by its own nature is something distinct from supreme good, cannot be supreme good; but this is something we may not hold about Him to whom we agree there is nothing superior. It is impossible for anything to be by nature better than that from which it is derived. I would therefore conclude with perfect logic that that which is the origin of all things is in its own substance supreme good."

"Perfectly right."

"But we have agreed that supreme good is the same as happiness."

"Yes."

"So that we have to agree that God is the essence of happiness."

"Your premises are incontestable and I see that this inference follows upon them."

"Then consider whether this, too, can be firmly accepted: that it is impossible for two supreme goods to exist separate from one another. For it is clear that if the two goods are separate, the one cannot be the other, so that neither could be perfect when each is lacking to the other. But that which is not perfect is obviously not supreme. It is therefore impossible for there to be two separate supreme goods. However, we deduced that both happiness and God are supreme goodness, so that it follows that supreme happiness is identical with supreme divinity."

"There could scarcely be a conclusion more true to reality, or more sure in its reasoning, or more worthy of God."

"I will add something to it. Just as in geometry some additional inference may be drawn from a theorem that has been proved, called in technical language, in Greek a *porisma* and in Latin a corollary, I too will give you a kind of corollary. Since it is through the possession of happiness that people become happy, and since happiness is in fact divinity, it is clear that it is through the possession of divinity that they become happy. But by the same logic as men become just through the possession of justice, or wise through the possession of wisdom, so those who possess divinity necessarily become divine. Each happy individual is therefore divine. While only God is so by nature, as many as you like may become so by participation."

"What you say is beautiful and valuable, whether you give it the Greek or the Latin name."

"But the most beautiful thing is what logic leads us to add to all this."

"What is that?"

"Are all the many things we see included under the word happiness like parts combining to form a single body, yet separate in their variety, or is there any one of them which can fully supply the essence of happiness and under which the others may be classed?"

"Could you clarify the question by being more specific?"

"Well, we consider happiness something good, don't we?"

"Yes, the supreme good."

"You could say the same of all of them. Absolute sufficiency is judged to be the same as happiness, and so too are power, reverence, glory and pleasure. Well, the question is this, all these things—sufficiency, power and the others—are they good as if happiness were a body of which they were members, or is goodness a kind of heading to which they belong?"

"I understand the question which you are proposing we should ask, but I should like to hear what your answer would be."

"This is how I would resolve it. If all these were related to happiness like limbs to a body, they would differ from one another, because it is the nature of parts that the body is one, but the parts that make it up are diverse. But all these things have been proved to be identical. So that they are not like limbs. Moreover it would appear that happiness was a body made up of a single limb, which is impossible."

"There is no doubt of that; but I am eager for what is to come."

"It is clear that the other properties are classed under good. It is just because sufficiency is judged a good that people want it, and it is just because it too is believed to be a good that power is sought after. And exactly the same conclusion may be reached about reverence, glory and pleasure.

"The chief point and reason, therefore, for seeking all things is goodness. For it is quite impossible for that which contains no good in itself whether real or apparent, to be an object of desire. On the other hand, things which are not good by nature are sought after if they nevertheless seem as if they were truly good.

"The result is, therefore, that there is justice in the belief that goodness is the chief point upon which the pursuit of everything hinges and by which it is motivated. What seems most to be desired is the thing that motivates the pursuit of something, as, for example, if a man wants to go riding for the sake of health; it is not so much the motion of horse-riding he desires as the resultant good health. Since, therefore, all things are desired for the sake of the good in them, no one desires them as much as the good itself. But we are agreed that the reason for desiring things is happiness. So that it is patently obvious that the good itself and happiness are identical."

"I can see no reason for anyone to disagree."

"But we have shown that God and happiness are one and the same thing."

"Yes."

"We may safely conclude, then, that God is to be found in goodness itself and nowhere else.

"Come hither now all you who captive are,
Whom false desire enchains in wicked bonds,
Desire that makes her home in earthly minds;
Here will you find release from grievous toil,
Here find a haven blessed with peaceful calm,

An ever open refuge from distress.
Not all the gold that Tagus'[7] sands bestow,
That Hermus[8] from his glittering banks casts up,
Or Indus,[9] on whose torrid shores are strewn

[7] **Tagus** A river in Spain and Portugal that empties into the Atlantic Ocean at Lisbon.
[8] **Hermus** Also Gediz. A river in modern western Turkey, emptying into the Gulf of Izmir.
[9] **Indus** An Asian river running from Tibet, through China, Kashmir, and Pakistan, to the Arabian Sea.

Green emeralds intermixed with dazzling pearls,
May sharpen and make bright the intellect,
But wealth in its own darkness clouds the thoughts.
For all that thus excites and charms the mind
Dim earth has fostered in her caverns deep;
While that bright light which rules and animates
The sky, will shun such dark and ruined souls:
Whoever once shall see this shining light
Will say the sun's own rays are not so bright."

EINHARD

Selection from *The Life of Charlemagne*

The Life of Charlemagne is a precious relic from one of Western civilization's darkest periods, when the fate of culture itself was in doubt. It dates from the Early Middle Ages (500–1000), as Europe, phoenixlike, struggled to rise from the ashes of Rome. Rome's empire in the West had disappeared, its regime wrecked by Germanic invaders, leaving people to either huddle in wooden huts beside armed fortresses or flee to monasteries. For such a masterly work to appear at this time was a sign that Europe's dark night was almost over.

This book is a brief and simple biography of Charlemagne (French, "Charles the Great") (r. 768–814), the ruler of the Germanic Franks; he originated the idea of Europe in his vast multiethnic empire, the first since Rome. In style, the book breaks no new ground but illustrates that this was a timid age, still in the shadow of Rome. Written in Latin and divided into five books, it is modeled on the Roman writer Suetonius's *Lives of the Caesars*, in terms of length and order of material. Passages are even taken from Suetonius and applied to Charlemagne.

The author, Einhard (ca. 770–840), was a noble-born Frank educated at the monastic school of Fulda, near Frankfurt. From 791 to 814, he served Charlemagne at the Palace School near the imperial court at Aachen, in modern Germany; here he helped train gifted boys of all social ranks for careers in public life. He was among a handful of scholars who made this school the driving force of the Carolingian Renaissance, the cultural rebirth led by Charlemagne, which blended Classical learning and Christian ideals. Einhard became the ruler's trusted adviser, a position that gave him intimate knowledge of the man whose biography he later wrote.

Written between 829 and 836, this biography is essentially a work of praise. At one point Einhard says his purpose was "to describe the life and the day-to-day habits of Charlemagne . . . and to write the public history of this . . . most famous king." He indeed achieves this limited goal, but when the topic touches on dangerous subjects, the text is either silent or veiled. For instance, he writes shyly of scandals involving the imperial daughters: "[Charlemagne] shut his eyes to all that happened, as if no suspicion of any immoral conduct had ever reached him, or as if the rumour was without foundation."

The lasting value of Einhard's work is that it is the fullest eyewitness account of Charlemagne. More than eighty copies of this work survive, attesting to its popularity. Even though Charlemagne's empire fell to pieces after a generation (843), his dream lived on. Today the European Union is a realization of his vision.

Reading the Selection

Book III of Einhard's biography is concerned with Charlemagne's private life, though of necessity it touches on affairs of state in this age when power was so personal and immediate. It covers varied aspects of the emperor's life, including family, guests, appearance, sports, dining habits, learning, and efforts at legal reform.

The most astonishing fact to be gleaned from this life is that Charlemagne was illiterate. "Although he tried very hard [to write], he had begun too late in life and he made little progress." He nevertheless was awed by the written word, as his liberal patronage of scholars proves. He spoke Latin well and understood a little Greek. His own tongue was Frankish, an early form of French. In this chaotic age, literacy was for monastic scholars, such as Einhard; everyone else, like Charlemagne, was illiterate.

Book III

The Emperor's Private Life

. . .

§19. Charlemagne was determined to give his children, his daughters just as much as his sons, a proper training in the liberal arts[1] which had formed the subject of his own studies. As soon as they were old enough he had his sons taught to ride in the Frankish fashion, to use arms and to hunt. He made his daughters learn to spin and weave wool, use the distaff[2] and spindle,[3] and acquire every womanly accomplishment, rather than fritter away their time in sheer idleness. . . .

When the death of Hadrian, the Pope of Rome[4] and his close friend, was announced to him, he wept as if he had lost a brother or a dearly loved son. He was firm and steady in his human relationships, developing friendship easily, keeping it up with care and doing everything he possibly could for anyone whom he had admitted to this degree of intimacy.

He paid such attention to the upbringing of his sons and daughters that he never sat down to table without them when he was at home, and never set out on a journey without taking them with him. His sons rode at his side and his daughters followed along behind. Hand-picked guards watched over them as they closed the line of march. These girls were extraordinarily beautiful and greatly loved by their father. It is a remarkable fact that, as a result of this, he kept them with him in his household until the very day of his death, instead of giving them in marriage to his own men or to foreigners, maintaining that

he could not live without them. The consequence was that he had a number of unfortunate experiences,[5] he who had been so lucky in all else that he undertook. However, he shut his eyes to all that happened, as if no suspicion of any immoral conduct had ever reached him, or as if the rumour was without foundation.

§20. I did not mention with the others a son called Pepin[6] who was born to Charlemagne by a concubine.[7] He was handsome enough, but a hunchback. At a moment when his father was wintering in Bavaria, soon after the beginning of his campaign against the Huns,[8] this Pepin pretended to be ill and conspired with certain of the Frankish leaders who had won him over to their cause by pretending to offer him the kingship.[9] The plot was discovered and the conspirators were duly punished. Pepin was tonsured[10] and permitted to take up, in the monastery of Prüm,[11] the life of a religious[12] for which he had already expressed a vocation.

Earlier on there had been another dangerous conspiracy against Charlemagne in Germany.[13] All the plotters

---

[1] **liberal arts** Greek educational ideal comprised of the arts (grammar, rhetoric, logic) and the sciences (arithmetic, music, astronomy, and geometry).

[2] **distaff** Staff for holding the flax, tow, or wool for spinning; ancient term for "women's work."

[3] **spindle** Round stick with tapered ends used to form and twist yarn in hand spinning.

[4] **Hadrian, the Pope of Rome** Hadrian I (r. 772–795).

[5] **unfortunate experiences** Charlemagne's daughters, Rotrude, gave birth to the illegitimate Lewis, who became Abbot of Saint Denis; another daughter, Bertha, had several illegitimate children, including the historian Nithard.

[6] **Pepin** Illegitimate son of Charlemagne.

[7] **concubine** Himiltrude.

[8] **the Huns** The Avars, an indeterminate people, perhaps Slavic nomads, who established an empire in eastern Europe, centered in Pannonia (modern Hungary), in the 550s; they fought periodic wars with Charlemagne until conquered by him in 805.

[9] **the kingship** In 792.

[10] **tonsured** The clipping or shaving of the crown of the head; a medieval ritual for admission to a Roman Catholic monastic vocation.

[11] **Prüm** A Benedictine abbey, near Trier, in modern Germany; founded in 720.

[12] **a religious** A member of a Roman Catholic order.

[13] **in Germany** The conspiracy of Hadrad, in 785–786.

were exiled, some having their eyes put out first, but the others were not maltreated physically. Only three of them were killed. These resisted arrest, drew their swords and started to defend themselves. They slaughtered a few men in the process and had to be destroyed themselves, as there was no other way of dealing with them.

The cruelty of Queen Fastrada[14] is thought to have been the cause of both these conspiracies, since it was under her influence that Charlemagne seemed to have taken actions which were fundamentally opposed to his normal kindliness and good nature. Throughout the remainder of his life he so won the love and favour of all his fellow human beings, both at home and abroad, that no one ever levelled against him the slightest charge of cruelty or injustice.

§21. He loved foreigners and took great pains to make them welcome. So many visited him as a result that they were rightly held to be a burden not only to the palace, but to the entire realm. In his magnanimity he took no notice at all of this criticism, for he considered that his reputation for hospitality and the advantage of the good name which he acquired more than compensated for the great nuisance of their being there.

§22. The Emperor was strong and well built. He was tall in stature, but not excessively so, for his height was just seven times the length of his own feet. The top of his head was round, and his eyes were piercing and unusually large. His nose was slightly longer than normal, he had a fine head of white hair and his expression was gay and good-humoured. As a result, whether he was seated or standing, he always appeared masterful and dignified. His neck was short and rather thick, and his stomach a trifle too heavy, but the proportions of the rest of his body prevented one from noticing these blemishes. His step was firm and he was manly in all his movements. He spoke distinctly, but his voice was thin for a man of his physique. His health was good, except that he suffered from frequent attacks of fever during the last four years of his life, and towards the end he was lame in one foot. Even then he continued to do exactly as he wished, instead of following the advice of his doctors, whom he came positively to dislike after they advised him to stop eating the roast meat to which he was accustomed and to live on stewed dishes.

He spent much of his time on horseback and out hunting, which came naturally to him, for it would be difficult to find another race on earth who could equal the Franks in this activity. He took delight in steam-baths at the thermal springs, and loved to exercise himself in the water whenever he could. He was an extremely strong swimmer and in this sport no one could surpass him. It was for this reason that he built his palace at Aachen[15] and remained continuously in residence there during the last years of his life and indeed until the moment of his death. He would invite not only his sons to bathe with him, but his nobles and friends as well, and occasionally even a crowd of his attendants and bodyguards, so that sometimes a hundred men or more would be in the water together.

§23. He wore the national dress of the Franks. Next to his skin he had a linen shirt and linen drawers; and then long hose and a tunic edged with silk. He wore shoes on his feet and bands of cloth wound round his legs. In winter he protected his chest and shoulders with a jerkin[16] made of otter skins or ermine. He wrapped himself in a blue cloak and always had a sword strapped to his side, with a hilt and belt of gold or silver. Sometimes he would use a jewelled sword, but this was only on great feast days or when ambassadors came from foreign peoples. He hated the clothes of other countries, no matter how becoming they might be, and he would never consent to wear them. The only exception to this was one day in Rome when Pope Hadrian entreated him to put on a long tunic and a Greek mantle, and to wear shoes made in the Roman fashion; and then a second time, when Leo,[17] Hadrian's successor, persuaded him to do the same thing. On feast days he walked in procession in a suit of cloth of gold, with jewelled shoes, his cloak fastened with a golden brooch and with a crown of gold and precious stones on his head. On ordinary days his dress differed hardly at all from that of the common people.

§24. He was moderate in his eating and drinking, and especially so in drinking; for he hated to see drunkenness in any man, and even more so in himself and his friends. All the same, he could not go long without food, and he often used to complain that fasting made him feel ill. He rarely gave banquets and these only on high feast days, but then he would invite a great number of guests. His main meal of the day was served in four courses, in addition to the roast meat which his hunters used to bring in on spits and which he enjoyed more than any other food. During his meal he would listen to a public reading or some other entertainment. Stories would be recited for him, or the doings of the ancients told again. He took great pleasure in the books of Saint Augustine[18] and especially in those which are called *The City of God.* . . .

§25. He spoke easily and fluently, and could express with great clarity whatever he had to say. He was not content with his own mother tongue, but took the trouble to learn foreign languages. He learnt Latin so well that he spoke it as fluently as his own tongue; but he understood Greek better than he could speak it. He was eloquent to the point of sometimes seeming almost garrulous.

He paid the greatest attention to the liberal arts; and he had great respect for men who taught them, bestowing

---

[14] **Queen Fastrada** The third wife of Charlemagne, the mother of two of his daughters.
[15] **Aachen** French, **Aix-la-Chapelle.** Capital of Charlemagne; site of Roman baths.

[16] **jerkin** Sleeveless, knee-length jacket.
[17] **Leo** Pope Leo III (795–816). Crowned Charlemagne emperor of the West (800).
[18] **Saint Augustine** (A.D. 354–430). One of the Fathers of the Church (see *The City of God*).

high honours upon them. When he was learning the rules of grammar he received tuition from Peter the Deacon of Pisa,[19] who by then was an old man, but for all other subjects he was taught by Alcuin,[20] surnamed Albinus, another Deacon, a man of the Saxon[21] race who came from Britain and was the most learned man anywhere to be found. Under him the Emperor spent much time and effort in studying rhetoric, dialectic and especially astrology. He applied himself to mathematics and traced the course of the stars with great attention and care. He also tried to learn to write. With this object in view he used to

keep writing-tablets and notebooks under the pillows on his bed, so that he could try his hand at forming letters during his leisure moments; but, although he tried very hard, he had begun too late in life and he made little progress. . . .

§29. Now that he was Emperor, he discovered that there were many defects in the legal system of his own people, for the Franks have two separate codes of law which differ from each other in many points. He gave much thought to how he could best fill the gaps, reconcile the discrepancies, correct the errors and rewrite the laws which were ill-expressed. None of this was ever finished; he added a few sections, but even these remained incomplete. What he did do was to have collected together and committed to writing the laws of all the nations under his jurisdiction which still remained unrecorded.

At the same time he directed that the age-old narra-   15
tive poems, barbarous enough, it is true, in which were celebrated the warlike deeds of the kings of ancient times, should be written out and so preserved. He also began a grammar of his native tongue. . . .

---

[19] **Peter the Deacon of Pisa** A scholar attached to Charlemagne's Palace School; taught grammar to Charlemagne.
[20] **Alcuin** Also **Albinus; Saxon** scholar, head of cathedral school of York, England; at Charlemagne's invitation, he became head of Palace School in **Aachen** in 781.
[21] **Saxon** A member of a Germanic people, who invaded England with the Angles and Jutes in A.D. fifth century, merging with them to become the Anglo-Saxons.

Selection from *Beowulf*

Beowulf is the first great poem in the English tradition. Its language was Anglo-Saxon, or Old English. It was composed orally, probably in England in the eighth century, and is preserved, presumably in complete form, in a single manuscript dating from about 1000. Like *The Epic of Gilgamesh* and Homer's *Iliad*, it is an epic, meant originally to be recited rather than read. Composed anonymously, *Beowulf* gives voice to the creative Anglo-Saxon imagination as it peopled the dark with primordial monsters.

The poem focuses on Beowulf, prince of the Geats (a tribe in Sweden). In the first part Beowulf sails to Denmark to rescue King Hrothgar from Grendel and Grendel's mother, two monsters. Swamp-dwellers, the monsters have been attacking Hrothgar's great hall by night and devouring his people. Beowulf kills the monsters. Back home, he is made king of the Geats and reigns for fifty years. In the second half of the poem, Beowulf faces a dragon. With his comrade Wiglaf's help, Beowulf defeats the dragon, only to die of his wounds.

Woven into *Beowulf* is a chilling theme: the never-ceasing battle of good against evil. The poem shows that evil never sleeps and comes in many forms, demonic and human, and that good, however vigilant, does not always win. Like Greek drama (see Sophocles' *Oedipus the King*), it offers the gloomy message that life is tragic and nothing is guaranteed.

Beowulf was written in alliterative verse, a rhymeless verse characterized by the repetition of consonant sounds, usually at the beginning of words, as in this example from a modern translation:

> *Down off the moorlands' misting fells came*
> *Grendel stalking; God's brand was on him.*

*The spoiler meant to snatch away
from the high hall some of human race.*

Alliterative verse was typical of Anglo-Saxon poetry and remained an essential feature of English poetry until the Late Middle Ages.

The setting in which Beowulf fights Grendel may be primitive and chaotic, but the society that spawned the poem was not. Modern scholars describe eighth-century England as Christian, law-abiding, and aristocratic. The Anglo-Saxons of the period were civilized, much altered from their pagan ancestors who settled England on the heels of the Roman withdrawal in about A.D. 400.

Reading the Selection

This brief selection from *Beowulf* deals with the defeat of the half-human Grendel. Among other things, it offers some insight into the poet's religious faith. The poet's world is decidedly Christian. It is claimed that [nothing can happen] "without God's willing it." Grendel is "God's enemy"; he is "feuding with God"; he (in a passage not included here) is said to be descended from Cain, the first murderer. Still, the older, primitive world of Anglo-Saxon myth keeps breaking through, in Beowulf's savagery and later in the primordial, nonhuman dragon. This seeming contradiction may be resolved by recognizing that the poem was composed when the Anglo-Saxon conversion to Christianity was only about one century old.

Beowulf's love of fame, or glory, also comes from the pre-Christian, Anglo-Saxon world. Not Christian salvation but desire for glory was his prime motive for living. "To Beowulf the glory of this fight was granted." At the epic's end (not included here), his epitaph reads: "The gentlest and most gracious of men, the kindest to his people and the most desirous of renown."

∞

. . .

Gliding through the shadows came
the walker in the night,[1] the warriors[2] slept
whose task was to hold the horned building,[3]
all except one.[4] It was well-known to men
that the demon could not drag them to the shades
without God's willing it; yet the one man kept
unblinking watch. He awaited, heart swelling
with anger against his foe, the ordeal of battle.
Down off the moorlands' misting fells came
Grendel stalking; God's brand was on him.   10
The spoiler meant to snatch away
from the high hall some of human race.
He came on under the clouds, clearly saw at last
the gold-hall of men, the mead[5]-drinking place
nailed with gold plates. That was not the first visit

he had paid to the hall of Hrothgar the Dane:[6]
he never before and never after
harder luck nor hall-guards found.

Walking to the hall came this warlike creature
condemned to agony. The door gave way,   20
toughed with iron, at the touch of those hands.
Rage-inflamed, wreckage-bent, he ripped open
the jaws of the hall. Hastening on,
the foe then stepped onto the unstained floor,
angrily advanced: out of his eyes stood
an unlovely light like that of fire.
He saw then in the hall a host of young soldiers,
a company of kinsmen caught away in sleep,
a whole warrior-band. In his heart he laughed then,
horrible monster, his hopes swelling   30
to a gluttonous meal. He meant to wrench
the life from each body that lay in the place
before night was done. It was not to be;
he was no longer to feast on the flesh of mankind
after that night.
    Narrowly the powerful

---

[1] **the walker in the night** The monster **Grendel.**
[2] **the warriors** The troop of soldiers who fight alongside **Beowulf.**
[3] **the horned building Heorot,** the banqueting hall, built by **Hrothgar.**
[4] **one Beowulf.**
[5] **mead** A fermented beverage made from honey, malt, yeast, and water.

---

[6] **Hrothgar the Dane** King of the **Danes.**

kinsman of Hygelac[7] kept watch how the ravager
set to work with his sudden catches;
nor did the monster mean to hang back.
As a first step he set his hands on   40
a sleeping soldier, savagely tore at him,
gnashed at his bone-joints, bolted huge gobbets,
sucked at his veins, and had soon eaten
all of the dead man, even down to his
hands and feet.
　　　　　　　Forward he stepped,
stretched out his hands to seize the warrior
calmly at rest there, reached out for him with his
unfriendly fingers: but the faster man
forestalling, sat up, sent back his arm.   50
The upholder of evils at once knew
he had not met, on middle earth's
extremest acres, with any man
of harder hand-grip: his heart panicked.
He was quit of the place no more quickly for that.
Eager to be away, he ailed[8] for his darkness
and the company of devils; the dealings he had there
were like nothing he had come across in his lifetime.
Then Hygelac's brave kinsman called to mind
that evening's utterance, upright he stood,   60
fastened his hold till fingers were bursting.
The monster strained away: the man stepped closer.
The monster's desire was for darkness between them,
direction regardless, to get out and run
for his fen[9]-bordered lair; he felt his grip's strength
crushed by his enemy. It was an ill journey
the rough marauder had made to Heorot.[10]

The crash in the banqueting-hall came to the Danes,
the men of the guard that remained in the building,
with the taste of death. The deepening rage   70
of the claimants to Heorot caused it to resound.
It was indeed wonderful that the wine-supper-hall
withstood the wrestling pair, that the world's palace
fell not to the ground. But it was girt firmly,
both inside and out, by iron braces
of skilled manufacture. Many a figured
gold-worked wine-bench, as we heard it,
started from the floor at the struggles of that pair.
The men of the Danes had not imagined that
any of mankind by what method soever   80
might undo that intricate, antlered hall,
sunder it by strength—unless it were swallowed up in
the embraces of fire.
　　　　　　　Fear entered into
the listening North Danes, as that noise rose up again
strange and strident. It shrilled terror
to the ears that heard it through the hall's side-wall,
the grisly plaint of God's enemy,
his song of ill-success, the sobs of the damned one
bewailing his pain. He was pinioned there   90

by the man of all mankind living
in this world's estate the strongest of his hands.

Not for anything would the earls'[11] guardian
let his deadly guest go living:
he did not count his continued existence
of the least use to anyone. The earls ran
to defend the person of their famous prince;
they drew their ancestral swords to bring
what aid they could to their captain, Beowulf.[12]
They were ignorant of this, when they entered the fight,   100
boldly-intentioned battle-friends,
to hew at Grendel, hunt his life
on every side—that no sword on earth,
not the truest steel, could touch their assailant;
for by a spell he had dispossessed all
blades of their bite on him.
　　　　　　　A bitter parting
from life was that day destined for him;
the eldritch[13] spirit was sent off on his
far faring into the fiends' domain.   110
It was then that this monster, who, moved by spite
against human kind, had caused so much harm
—so feuding with God—found at last
that flesh and bone were to fail him in the end;
for Hygelac's great-hearted kinsman
had him by the hand; and hateful to each
was the breath of the other.
　　　　　　　A breach in the giant
flesh-frame showed then, shoulder-muscles
sprang apart, there was a snapping of tendons,   120
bone-locks burst.[14] To Beowulf the glory
of this fight was granted; Grendel's lot
to flee the slopes fen-ward with flagging heart,
to a den where he knew there could be no relief,
no refuge for a life at its very last stage,
whose surrender-day had dawned. The Danish hopes
in this fatal fight had found their answer.

He had cleansed Heorot. He who had come from afar,
deep-minded, strong-hearted, had saved the hall
from persecution. He was pleased with his night's work,   130
the deed he had done. Before the Danish people
the Great captain had made good his boast,
had taken away all their unhappiness,
the evil menace under which they had lived,
enduring it by dire constraint,
no slight affliction. As a signal to all
the hero hung up the hand, the arm
and torn-off shoulder, the entire limb,
Grendel's whole grip, below the gable of the roof.

There was, as I heard it, at hall next morning   140
a great gathering in the gift-hall yard
to see the wonder. Along the wide highroads

---

[7] **kinsman of Hygelac Beowulf. Hygelac** was king of the **Geats,** a Swedish tribe, and **Beowulf** was his relative.
[8] **ailed** Yearned.
[9] **fen** Marshland.
[10] **Heorot** The banqueting hall, built by **Hrothgar.**

[11] **the earls** Noble warlords, companions of **Beowulf.**
[12] **Beowulf** Prince of the **Geats;** adviser to king **Hrothgar.**
[13] **eldritch** Weird.
[14] **bone-locks burst Beowulf** has torn off one of **Grendel's** massive arms.

the chiefs of the clans came from near and far
to see the foe's footprints. It may fairly be said
that his parting from life aroused no pity in any
who tracked the spoor-blood[15] of his blind flight
for the monster's mere-pool,[16] with mood flagging

and strength crushed, he had staggered onwards;
each step evidenced his ebbing life's blood.
The tarn was troubled; a terrible wave-thrash   150
brimmed it, bubbling; black-mingled,
the warm wound-blood welled upwards.
He had dived to his doom, he had died miserably;
here in his fen-lair he had laid aside
his heathen soul. Hell welcomed it.

---

[15] **spoor-blood** Blood droppings left by **Grendel** during his flight to
his lair.
[16] **mere-pool** Pool of lake water.

HROSVITHA

Selection from *Abraham*

Hrosvitha (ca. 935–1000), spelled variously as Hrotsvitha, Hrotsvit, and Roswitha, is the first
known German woman writer. She lived during the Old High German period, the first phase of
German literature, which lasted from 800 to 1050. German literature was still in its infancy, and
most writers were clerics who composed in Latin rather than the German tongue. Hrosvitha
was thus typical of the period's writers, for she was a nun writing exclusively in Latin.

As a woman writer, however, Hrosvitha was anything but typical, because most women
then had few educational opportunities. What educational opportunity existed was mainly for
women from culturally privileged social positions, such as Hrosvitha. A member of the nobly
born class of religious women, she was encouraged to study the classical liberal arts. At an
early age, she entered the Benedictine abbey at Gandersheim, a convent catering to aristocratic
women, which was under the patronage of the counts of Saxony, vassals of the Holy Roman
Emperor. This imperial abbey, founded in 852, was renowned as a center of service and learning
with a library rich in classical and medieval manuscripts. As a novice nun, she mastered Christian and Classical learning, especially the poets of pagan Rome, and learned to write fluent
Latin. This training, coupled with her own gifts, enabled Hrosvitha to leave a legacy of eight
verse legends, six plays, two epics, and a short poem.

Of Hrosvitha's works, the plays, all composed in rhymed, rhythmic prose, are considered
her finest creations. In the preface to the plays, she describes her literary style as imitating that
of the Roman playwright Terence, but she dissociates herself from what she deems his indecent
focus on the "shameless acts of lascivious women." Offering a Christian alternative to Terence's
pagan indecency, Hrosvitha's plays tend to emphasize assaults against women, especially vir-
ginal women, who strive to protect their virtue from any stain and, with God's grace, thereby to
earn eternal life in heaven. Her sources belong to the hagiography, or lives of the Christian
saints, that circulated in Europe and the Byzantine empire.

From the perspective of the history of Western theater, these works should be viewed as a
postscript to Roman drama and not as a harbinger of a new tradition. The plays were probably
never performed but were intended as edifying reading for the Gandersheim sisters. When
modern drama developed, it began not out of the imitations of Terence but from the mystery
plays of the church, blended with the spectacles of jugglers and mimes.

Hrosvitha's reputation has fluctuated over the centuries. After her death, her name and her
works soon lapsed into obscurity. In the Renaissance, her plays, discovered in an early
eleventh-century manuscript, were printed in book form (1501). In the Gothic Revival (1800s)
she became a source of interest to scholars exploring the Germanic heritage. Today, Hrosvitha
has become a feminist icon, especially in her identification of the female body as a battle zone in
the ongoing war between the sexes.

Reading the Selection

Abraham, the best known of Hrosvitha's dramas, is concerned with the themes of fall and redemption. The plot is based on a Christian legend preserved by a Byzantine author. Abraham, a Christian monk, leaves his ascetic life to become the spiritual father of his orphaned niece, Mary. Ignoring Abraham's moral warnings, Mary elopes with a monk who seduces her. Quickly abandoned, she becomes a prostitute in a brothel where Abraham rescues her three years later.

This selection from *Abraham,* the so-called recognition scene, is greatly admired by scholars for its drama and emotional impact. Abraham disguises himself to gain access to Mary in the brothel. Mary, deceived by the disguise, kisses the stranger and is suddenly reminded "of the fragrance of chastity I once practiced." The pair withdraw to a bedroom where Abraham reveals his true identity. Overcome with shame, Mary repudiates her sins and decides to become a Christian hermit, as a way of performing penance.

∽

*

ABRAHAM: Greetings, good host!   1

INNKEEPER: Who calls?
Greetings!

ABR.: Do you have a nice place for a traveler to stay overnight?

INN.: Indeed we do; our hospitality extends to all who alight.

ABR.: Good!

INN.: Come in, so that dinner can be prepared for you.

ABR.: I owe you much for this merry welcome, but I ask for even more from you.

INN.: Tell me what you desire, so that I may fulfill it.

ABR.: Here, take this little gold for the deal;
and arrange for the most beautiful girl who, as I hear,   10
stays with you, to share our meal.

INN.: Why do you wish to see her?

ABR.: I would delight in getting to know her whose beauty I have heard praised by so many and so often.

INN.: Whoever praised her beauty did not tell a lie, for in the loveliness of her face she outshines all other women.

ABR.: That is why I yearn for her love.

INN.: I wonder that in your old age you desire the love of a young woman.

ABR.: For sure, I come for no other purpose but to see her.

INN.: Come, Mary, come along. Show your beauty to our newcomer.

MARY: Here I am.

ABR.: What boldness, what constancy of mind I must muster as I see her whom I raised in my hidden hermitage[1] decked out in a harlot's garb.

But this is not the time to show in my face what is in   20
my heart;

---
[1] **hermitage** Monastery.

I must be on guard:
I will bravely suppress my tears gushing forth, like a man. With feigned cheerfulness of countenance I will veil the bitterness of my internal grief.

INN.: Lucky Mary, be merry,
because now not only men your age flock hither, as before, but even men of ripe old age seek your favors. It is you whom they querry.

MARY: I will not only give you a taste of sweet kisses but will caress your ancient neck with close embraces.

ABR.: That is what I am after.

MARY: What is it I feel? What is this spell?
What is this rare and wonderful odor I smell?
Oh, the smell of this fragrance reminds me of the   30
fragrance of chastity I once practiced!

ABR.: Now, now I must pretend, now I must persist, now I must be lustful in the manner of lewd young men and play the game
so that I am not recognized by my seriousness or else she might leave and hide for shame.

MARY: Woe is me, wretched woman! How I sank, how I fell into perdition's pit!

ABR.: This is not a fit place for complaints, where jolly guests sit.

INN.: Lady Mary, why do you sigh? Why do you cry? In the two years you have lived here, I never heard such grieving, not even a trace.

MARY: Oh, I wish I could have died three years ago!
Then I would not have sunk into such disgrace!

ABR.: I didn't come all this way
to join you in lamenting your sins, but to be joined to   40
you making love and being gay.

MARY: I was moved by a slight regret to utter such words;
but let us now dine and be merry
because, as you admonished me,
this is certainly not the time to bewail one's sins.

ABR.: Abundantly we have wined,

abundantly we have dined,
and are now tipsy, good host, with generous portions
you served. Give us now leave to rise from the table
so that I might be able   50
to lay down and refresh my weary body by sweet
rest.

INN.: I'll do as you request.

MARY: Rise, my lord, rise up. I shall accompany you to
your bedroom.

ABR.: That pleases me. In fact, I could not have been
forced to go, were I not going with you.

. . .

MARY: Here is a bedroom for us to stay in. Here is the bed,
decked with rich and lovely coverlets. Sit down, so
that I may take off your shoes and then you won't   60
have to tire yourself removing them.

ABR.: First, lock the door so that no one may enter.

MARY: Don't worry on that account. I will make sure
that the bolt is secure,
and that no one finds easy access to disturb us.

ABR.: Now the time has come to remove my hat and
reveal who I am. Oh my adoptive daughter, oh part of
my soul, Mary,
don't you recognize me,
the old man who raised you like a father and who   70
pledged you with a ring
to the only begotten Son of the Heavenly King?

MARY: Woe is me! It is my father and teacher Abraham
who speaks!

ABR.: What happened to you, my daughter Mary?

MARY: Tremendous misery.

ABR: Who deceived you?
Who seduced you?

MARY: He who overthrew our first parents too.[2]

ABR.: Where is that angelic life that already here on earth   80
you led?

MARY: Destroyed, it fled.

ABR.: Where is the modesty of your virginity? Where
your admirable countenance?

MARY: Lost and gone from hence.

ABR.: What reward for the efforts of your fasting,
prayers, and vigils can you hope for unless you
return to your senses, you who fell
from the height of Heaven and have sunk into the
depths of Hell?   90

MARY: Woe is me, alas!

ABR.: Why did you disdain me?
Why did you desert me?
Why did you not tell me of your wretched sin, so that
I and my beloved friend Effrem could perform wor-
thy penance for you?

MARY: After I first sinned, and sank into perfidy,
I did not dare, polluted as I was, to even approach
your sanctity.

ABR.: Who ever has lived free from sin except for the
Virgin's Son?   100

MARY: No one.

ABR.: It is human to err but evil to persist in sin; he who
fell suddenly is not the one to be blamed,
only he who fails to rise promptly again.

MARY: Woe is me, wretched woman.

ABR.: Why do you fall down?
Why do you stay immobile lying on the ground?
Arise and hear what I have to say!

MARY: I fell, shaken with fear, because I could not bear the
force of your fatherly admonitions' sway.   110

ABR.: Consider my love for you and put aside your fears.

MARY: I cannot; I cannot cease my tears.

ABR.: Did I not relinquish my accustomed hermitage on
your behalf, and did I not leave aside all observance
of our regular rule,[3]
so much so, that I who am an old hermit, have turned
into a pleasure-seeking lewd fool,
and I, who for so long practiced silence, made jokes
and spoke merry words so that I wouldn't be recognized? Why do you still stare at the ground with   120
lowered face? Why do you refuse to speak with me?

MARY: I am troubled by my grave offense;
this is why I don't dare to presume to lift my eyes to
Heaven or have the confidence
to speak with you.

ABR.: Don't lose faith, my daughter, but abandon the
abyss of dejection and place your hope in God.

MARY: The enormity of my sins has cast me into the
depths of despair.

ABR.: Your sins are grave, I admit,   130
but heavenly pity is greater than any sin we may
commit.
Therefore cast off your despair and beware of leaving
unused this short time given to you for penitence.
Know that Divine Grace abounds even where the
abomination of sins prevails.

MARY: If I had any hope of receiving forgiveness, my
eagerness to do penance would burst forth.

ABR.: Have mercy on my exhaustion, which I incurred on
your account, cast off this dangerous and sinful de-   140
spair, which we know to be a graver offense than all
other sins. For whoever despairs, thinking that God
would not come to the aid of sinners, that person sins
irremediably. Because just as the spark from a flint
stone one cannot set the sea on fire,
so the bitter taste of our sins cannot likewise aspire
to alter the sweetness of Divine goodwill.

MARY: It is not the magnificence of Heavenly Grace which
I doubt, but when I consider the enormity of my own
sin, then I fear that the performance of even a worthy   150
penance will not suffice.

ABR.: I take your sins upon myself; only come back to the
place which you deserted

---

[2] **He who overthrew our first parents too** Satan, who coerced Adam and Eve to eat the forbidden fruit, thereby provoking God to exile them from the Garden of Eden.

[3] **regular rule** From Latin *regula*, "rule." Regular clergy follow an ascetic rule, such as the Rule of Benedict, which typically requires vows of poverty, chastity, and obedience.

and take up again the life which you subverted.

MARY: I will never go against any of your wishes but will embrace obediently all your commandments.

ABR.: Now, I believe that you are my child, whom I raised; now I feel that you are the one to be loved above all others.

MARY: I possess some clothes and a little gold;   160
I wait to be told
how to dispose of them.

ABR.: What you acquired through sin
must be cast off together with the sins.

MARY: I thought, perhaps, they could be offered to the sacred altar or be given to the poor.

ABR.: It is neither sanctioned nor acceptable that gifts be given to God which were acquired through sin and are impure.

MARY: Beyond this, I have no concern.   170

ABR.: Dawn arrives; the day breaks. Let us return!

MARY: You, beloved father, must lead the way
as the good shepherd leads the sheep gone astray;
and I, advancing in your footsteps, will follow your lead.

ABR.: Not so; I will proceed on foot but you will ride on my horse so that the sharp rocks of the road will not hurt your tender little feet.

MARY: What shall I say? How shall I ever repay your kindness? You do not force me, miserable wretch, with   180
threats, but exhort me to do penance with kindness.

ABR.: I ask nothing of you, except that you remain intent upon spending the rest of your life in God's service.

MARY: Out of my own free will I shall remain contrite,
I shall persist in my penance with all my might,

and even if I lose the ability to perform the act,
the will to do it shall never lack.

ABR.: It is important that you serve the Divine will as eagerly as you served worldly vanities.   190

MARY: The will of the Lord be done in me, because of your merits.

ABR.: Let us return and hurry on our way.

MARY: Let us hurry, I am weary of delay.

·   ·   ·

MARY: With what speed we have traveled over this difficult and rugged road!

ABR.: Whatever is done with devotion is accomplished with ease. Behold, here is your deserted abode.

MARY: Woe is me, this cell is witness to my sin; therefore I fear to enter.   200

ABR.: That's understandable. Any place where the ancient enemy has won a triumph is to be avoided forever.

MARY: And where to you intend me to stay and perform my penance?

ABR.: Go into the small interior room[4] so that the ancient serpent will not find another opportunity to deceive you.

MARY: I will not contradict you but embrace eagerly what you command.

ABR.: I shall go to Effrem, my friend, so that he, who   210
alone mourned with me over your loss, may rejoice with me over your return.

MARY: A worthy concern!

---

[4] **the small interior room** A cloistered room, or cell, within the monastery.

8

THE WORLD OF ISLAM

Selections from the *Qur'an*

The *Qur'an* (from Arabic, "recitation," "reading," or "discourse") is the sacred book of Islam, the religion founded by Muhammad (ca. 570–632) in the early seventh century. The *Qur'an* is the heart and soul of Islamic culture. Its pages record Muhammad's words, which were dictated to secretaries and preserved as fragments on leaves and stones and in his followers' memories. After his death, Muhammad's words were compiled into a book. Islamic tradition holds that every word in the *Qur'an* is divinely inspired, being a direct revelation from God to his prophet, and is inimitable; that is, it cannot be imitated. Muhammad's work is the supreme manifestation of Islam's two central beliefs: There is but one God (Allah), and Muhammad is his prophet.

The work consists of 114 *suras* (chapters) arranged not in order of their original composition, which was unknown to its compilers, but in order of their descending length. The shorter and more poetic suras, which are the earliest words of the Prophet, appear at the end of the *Qur'an*. These suras, known as the Meccan suras since they are believed to have been revealed to Muhammad before he fled to Medina, focus on personal issues and speak more directly to the individual than do the other suras. They are the ones Muslims quote and recite, since these prophetic and revelatory passages offer guidance and advice on how to live a just and rewarding life. The so-called later Meccan suras, also revealed to Muhammad while still in Mecca, trace the origins and history of the prophets, including the biblical prophets, from Adam, the first prophet in Islam, to Muhammad. The Medinan suras concentrate on legal, historical, and religious issues, often in a polemic tone. Their content reflects the challenges facing Muhammad in Medina after he had established his religion, controlled the city, and confronted secular political, social, and economic issues.

As a book, the *Qur'an* has no narrative or chronological structure, nor does it tell stories in a linear format. For example, the lives of the other prophets, such as Abraham, Moses, and Jesus are scattered through the Meccan suras. Like other religious writings, the *Qur'an* utilizes metaphors, similes, and illustrations. Its lyrical character and repetitive words and phrases enhance the *Qur'an*'s poetic sense and makes the public reciting of the suras both inspiring and appealing.

The *Qur'an* grew out of the experiences and traditions of the Arab world, but its ideas owed much to Judaism and somewhat less to Christianity. Recognizing Jews and Christians as "People of the Book," it claimed to replace their "books" with God's final word. Like the Jewish and Christian Bibles, the *Qur'an* teaches monotheism, God's total power and knowledge; his divine mercy and forgiveness; human weaknesses and sins (but not original sin); and faith. Like the Talmud—Jewish writings on the Bible—it stresses the last judgment, resurrection, heaven, and hell. Like the New Testament, the *Qur'an* accepts Jesus as a prophet, though denies that he is the son of God.

The *Qur'an* must be approached and understood on its own terms. Its meaning or structure cannot be grasped in a total sense. Each sura stands alone, and many are a particular response to a specific problem or historic situation or event. Nearly all take the form of discourse by Allah or the angel Gabriel to Muhammad, his followers, or his enemies. The discourses typically announce a doctrine, tell a story, call for Holy War *(jihad)*, urge charitable giving, regulate trade and finance, or prescribe rituals. Because of its organization, the *Qur'an* should not be read from start to finish but should be sampled and browsed in order to appreciate and enjoy the richness of its diversity.

Reading the Selections

The following suras are arranged by topic, not by their appearance in the *Qur'an*. This arrangement introduces a number of topics and themes that might otherwise be difficult to understand if they were reprinted in the order they appear in the *Qur'an*.

The first selection is the first sura in the *Qur'an*. Known as the *Fatihah*, which means "The Opening," this passage has been described as the *Qur'an* in brief because of its profound truths, its summative affirmations, and its invocation to commune with God. Allah is described as being both compassionate—that is, the provider and giver of everything humans need—and merciful—that is, the guide humans need to lead righteous lives and to do good deeds. Like all suras, it begins with the prayer "In the Name of God, the Compassionate, the Merciful."

Sura 96, entitled "Clots of Blood" or "The Embryo," is believed to be the first revelation from Allah to Muhammad. The passage's first line is interpreted to be Allah's original command to Muhammad for him to recite what he, Allah, will now reveal to Muhammad, his chosen Prophet. The second line, which contains the title of the sura, probably refers to the origins of humans—from a clot of blood or an embryo. The pen reference, found in another sura, may be a metaphor for Allah's divine intellect. The next part of the sura warns humans to behave or suffer the consequences—a visit from the "guards of hell." The last lines admonish the reader not to follow the individual who disobeys Allah and tells him to prostrate himself in prayer, which is one of the five pillars of faith.

Sura 5 ("The Table"), verses 42–50, addresses the historical roles and importance of the Torah and its messages and of Jesus and the gospel. The *Qur'an* is the final word, the "Book with the truth" that confirms what is in the earlier books. God has, in his wisdom, formed not one but three communities that compete with one another to do good works, and, in the end, he will resolve their differences. Be warned, however, notes the sura, that one should not be misled by other believers who, since they do not follow the Islamic faith, will be punished for their sins.

Sura 21 ("The Prophets") is a discourse by Allah, speaking as the divine "We." This is only one of the many ways the *Qur'an* refers to Allah. By referring to him in different persons, such as "I," "him," or "your Lord," Allah does not take on anthropomorphic qualities—unlike the Jewish and Christian deity. To those who question the last judgment ("the day of Reckoning"), God says he will indeed punish doubters of his word ('blasphemers"), as he as done in the past. To show that he is merciful and not vengeful, he offers a line of prophets (Jews, Christians, and Arabs) who prospered because they submitted to him. One who has submitted, is, of course, a muslim—a person who has accepted submission or islam.

Sura 24 ("Light"), verses 35–46, defines God's nature, linking his essence to light, as in "His light is found in temples which God has sanctioned." The theme—God is light—derives from ancient sun worship (see *The Great Hymn to the Aten*) and was a prominent idea in early Christianity. This sura recognizes that such metaphors—as calling God "Light"—are proper for symbolizing Allah. As a result, Islamic mosques were outfitted with ritual lamps. Concerning religious paintings and statues, however, the *Qur'an,* like the Jewish *Holy Scriptures,* condemned such objects as idolatrous.

❦

The Opening

*In the Name of God
the Compassionate
the Merciful*

1

Praise be to God, Lord of the Universe,
The Compassionate, the Merciful,
Sovereign of the Day of Judgement!
You alone we worship, and to You alone

we turn for help.
Guide us to the straight path,
The path of those whom You have favoured,
Not of those who have incurred Your wrath,
Nor of those who have gone astray.

❦

Clots of Blood

*In the Name of God,
the Compassionate, the Merciful*

96

Recite in the name of your Lord who created—created man from clots of blood.

Recite! Your Lord is the Most Bountiful One, who by the pen taught man what he did not know.

Indeed, man transgresses in thinking himself his own master: for to your Lord all things return.

Observe the man who rebukes Our servant when he prays. Think: does he follow the right guidance or enjoin true piety?

Think: if he denies the Truth and pays no heed, does he not realize that God observes all?

No. Let him desist, or We will drag him by the forelock, his lying, sinful forelock.

Then let him call his helpmates. We will call the guards of Hell.

No, never obey him! Prostrate yourself and come nearer.

❦

The Table

5

They listen to falsehoods and practise what is unlawful. If they come to you, give them your judgement or avoid them. If you avoid them, they can in no way harm you; but if you do act as their judge, judge them with fairness. God loves those that deal justly.

But how will they come to you for judgement when they already have the Torah which enshrines God's own judgement? Soon after, they will turn their backs: they are no true believers.

We have revealed the Torah, in which there is guidance and light. By it the prophets who submitted to God judged the Jews, and so did the rabbis and the divines, according to God's Book which had been committed to their keeping and to which they themselves were witnesses.

Have no fear of man; fear Me, and do not sell My revelations for a paltry sum. Unbelievers are those who do not judge according to God's revelations.

Therein We decreed for them a life for a life, an eye for 5 an eye, a nose for a nose, an ear for an ear, a tooth for a tooth, and a wound for a wound. But if a man charitably forbears from retaliation, his remission shall atone for him. Transgressors are those that do not judge according to God's revelations.

After them We sent forth Jesus son of Mary, confirming the Torah already revealed, and gave him the Gospel, in which there is guidance and light, corroborating what was revealed before it in the Torah: a guide and an admonition to the righteous. Therefore let those who follow the Gospel judge according to what God has revealed therein. Evil-doers are those that do not judge according to God's revelations.

And to you We have revealed the Book with the truth. It confirms the Scriptures which came before it and stands as a guardian over them. Therefore give judgement among men according to God's revelations and do not yield to their whims or swerve from the truth made known to you.

We have ordained a law and assigned a path for each of you. Had God pleased, He could have made of you one community: but it is His wish to prove you by that which He has bestowed upon you. Vie with each other in good works, for to God shall you all return and He will resolve your differences for you.

Pronounce judgement among them according to God's revelations and do not be led by their desires. Take heed lest they turn you away from a part of that which God has revealed to you. If they reject your judgement, know that it is God's wish to scourge them for their sins. A great many of mankind are evil-doers.

Is it pagan laws that they wish to be judged by? Who 10 is a better judge than God for men whose faith is firm?

∞

The Prophets

In the Name of God, the Compassionate, the Merciful

21

The Day of Reckoning for mankind is drawing near, yet 1 they blithely persist in unbelief. They listen with ridicule to each fresh warning that their Lord gives them: their hearts are set on pleasure.

In private the wrongdoers say to each other: "Is this man not a mortal like yourselves? Would you follow witchcraft with your eyes open?"

Say: "My Lord has knowledge of whatever is said in heaven and earth. He hears all and knows all."

Some say: "It is but a medley of dreams." Others: "He has invented it himself." And yet others: "He is a poet: let him show us some sign, as did the apostles in days gone by."

Yet though We showed them signs, the nations whom 5 We destroyed before them did not believe either. Will *they* believe?

The apostles We sent before you were but men whom We inspired. Ask the People of the Book if you do not know this. The bodies We gave them could not dispense with food, nor were they immortal. Then We fulfilled Our promise: We delivered them and those We willed, and utterly destroyed the transgressors.

And now We have revealed a Book for your admonishment. Will you not give heed?

We have destroyed many a sinful nation and replaced them by other men. And when they felt Our might they took to their heels and fled. They were told: "Do not run away. Return to your comforts and to your dwellings. You shall be questioned all."

"Woe to us, we have done wrong!" was their reply. And this they kept repeating until We mowed them down and put out their light.

It was not in sport that We created the heavens and the 10 earth and all that lies between them. Had it been Our will to find a pastime, We could have found one near at hand.

We will hurl Truth at Falsehood, until Truth shall triumph and Falsehood be no more. Woe shall befall you, for all the falsehoods you have uttered.

His are all who dwell in the heavens and on earth. Those who stand in His presence do not disdain to worship Him, nor are they ever wearied. They praise Him day and night, unflaggingly.

Have they chosen earthly deities? And can these deities restore the dead to life? Were there other gods in heaven or earth besides God, both heaven and earth would be ruined. Exalted be God, Lord of the Throne, above their falsehoods!

None shall question Him about His works, but they shall be questioned. Have they chosen other gods besides Him?

Say: "Show us your proofs. Here are the Scriptures of 15 today and those of long ago." But most of them do not know the Truth, and this is why they give no heed.

We inspired all the apostles whom We sent before you, saying: "There is no god but Me. Therefore serve Me."

They say: "The Merciful has begotten children." God forbid! They are but His honoured servants. They do not speak till He has spoken: they act by His command. He knows what is before them and behind them. They intercede for none save those whom He accepts, and tremble for awe of Him. Whoever of them declares: "I am a god besides Him," shall be requited with Hell. Thus shall We reward the wrongdoers.

Are the disbelievers unaware that the heavens and the earth were but one solid mass which We tore asunder, and that We made every living thing of water? Will they not have faith?

We set firm mountains upon the earth lest it should move away with them, and hewed out highways in the rock so that they might be rightly guided.

We spread the heaven like a canopy and provided it with strong support: yet of its signs they are heedless. 20

It was He who created the night and the day, and the sun and the moon: each moves swiftly in an orbit of its own.

No man before you have We made immortal. If you yourself are doomed to die, will they live for ever?

Every soul shall taste death. We will prove you all with good and evil. To Us you shall return.

When the unbelievers see you, they scoff at you, saying: "Is this the man who fulminates against your gods?" And they deny all mention of the Merciful.

Impatience is the very stuff man is made of. You shall before long see My signs: you need not ask Me to hasten them. 25

They say: "When will this promise be fulfilled, if what you say be true?"

If only the unbelievers knew the day when they shall strive in vain to shield their faces and their backs from the fire of Hell; the day when none shall help them! It will overtake them unawares and stupefy them. They shall have no power to ward it off, nor shall they be reprieved.

Other apostles have been mocked before you; but those who scoffed at them were smitten by the very scourge they mocked.

Say: "Who will protect you, by night and by day, from the Lord of Mercy?" Yet are they unmindful of their Lord's remembrance.

Have they other gods to defend them? Their idols shall be powerless over their own salvation, nor shall they be protected from Our scourge. 30

We have bestowed good things upon these men and upon their fathers, and made their lives too long. Can they not see how We invade their land and curtail its borders? Is it they who will triumph?

Say: "I warn you only by that with which I am inspired." But the deaf can hear nothing when they are warned.

Yet if the lightest whiff from the vengeance of your Lord touched them, they would say: "Woe to us: we have done wrong!"

We shall set up just scales on the Day of Resurrection, so that no man shall in the least be wronged. Actions as small as a grain of mustard seed shall be weighed out. Our reckoning shall suffice.

We showed Moses and Aaron the distinction between right and wrong, and gave them a light and an admonition for righteous men: those who truly fear their Lord and dread the terrors of Judgement-day. 35

And in this We have revealed a blessed counsel. Will you then reject it?

We bestowed guidance on Abraham, for We knew him well. He said to his father and to his people: "What are these images to which you are so devoted?"

They replied: "They are the gods our fathers worshipped."

He said: "Then you and your fathers are in the grossest error."

"Is it the truth that you are preaching," they asked, "or is this but a jest?" 40

"Indeed," he answered, "your Lord is the Lord of the heavens and the earth. It was He that made them: to this I bear witness. By the Lord, I will overthrow your idols as soon as you have turned your backs."

He broke them all in pieces, except their supreme god, so that they might return to Him.

"Who has done this to our deities?" asked some. "He must surely be a wicked man."

Others replied: "We have heard a youth called Abraham speak of them."

They said: "Then bring him here in sight of all the people, that they may act as witnesses." 45

"Abraham," they said, "was it you who did this to our deities?"

"No," he replied. "It was their chief who smote them. Ask *them*, if they can speak."

Thereupon they turned their thoughts upon themselves and said to each other: "Surely you are the ones who have done wrong."

Confounded as they were, they said to Abraham: "You know they cannot speak."

He answered: "Would you then worship that, instead of God, which can neither help nor harm you? Shame on you and on your idols! Have you no sense?" 50

They cried: "Burn him and avenge your gods, if you must punish him!"

"Fire," We said, "be cool to Abraham and keep him safe."

They sought to lay a snare for him, but they themselves were ruined. We delivered him and Lot, and brought them to the land which We had blessed for all mankind.

We gave him Isaac, and then Jacob for a grandson; and We made each a righteous man. We ordained them leaders to guide mankind at Our behest, and enjoined on them charity, prayer, and almsgiving. They served none but Ourself.

To Lot We gave wisdom and knowledge and delivered him from the Wicked City; for its inhabitants were men of iniquity and evil. We admitted him to Our mercy: he was a righteous man. 55

Before him Noah invoked Us, and We heard his prayer. We saved him and all his kinsfolk from the great calamity, and delivered him from those who had denied Our revelations. Evil men they were; We drowned them all.

And tell of David and Solomon: how they passed judgement regarding the cornfield in which strayed lambs had grazed by night. We gave Solomon insight into the case and bore witness to both their judgements.

We bestowed on them wisdom and knowledge, and caused the birds and mountains to join with David in Our praise. All this We have done.

We taught him the armourer's craft, so that you might have protection in your wars. Will you then give thanks?

To Solomon We subjected the raging wind: it sped at his bidding to the land which We had blessed. We have knowledge of all things.

We assigned him devils who dived for him into the sea and who performed other tasks besides. Over them We kept a watchful eye.

And tell of Job: how he called on his Lord, saying: "I am sorely afflicted: but of all those that show mercy You are the most merciful."

We heard his prayer and relieved his affliction. We restored to him his family and as many more with them: a blessing from Ourself and an admonition to worshippers.

And you shall also tell of Ishmael, Idis, and Dhūl-Kifl,[1] who all endured with patience. To Our mercy We admitted them, for they were upright men.

And of Dhūl-Nūn:[2] how he went away in anger, thinking We had no power over him. But in the darkness he cried: "There is no god but You. Glory be to You! I have done wrong."

We answered his prayer and delivered him from distress. Thus shall We save the true believers.

And of Zacharias, who invoked his Lord, saying: "Lord, let me not remain childless, though of all heirs You are the best."

We answered his prayer and gave him John, curing his wife of sterility. They vied with each other in good works and called on Us with piety, fear, and submission.

And of the woman who kept her chastity. We breathed into her of Our spirit, and made her and her son a sign to all men.

Your religion is but one religion, and I am Your only Lord. Therefore serve Me. Men have divided themselves into factions, but to Us they shall all return. He that does good works in the fullness of his faith, his endeavours shall not be lost: We record them all.

It is ordained that no nation We have destroyed shall ever rise again. But when Gog and Magog[3] are let loose and rush headlong down every hill; when the true promise nears its fulfilment; the unbelievers shall stare in amazement, crying: "Woe to us! Of this we have been heedless. We have done wrong."

You and your idols shall be the fuel of Hell; therein you shall all go down. Were they true gods, your idols would not go there: but there they shall abide for ever. They shall groan with anguish and be bereft of hearing.

But those to whom We have long since shown Our favour shall be far removed from Hell. They shall not hear its roar, but shall delight for ever in what their souls desire.

The Supreme Terror shall not grieve them, and the angels will receive them, saying: "This is the day you have been promised."

On that day We shall roll up the heaven like a scroll of parchment. As We first created man, so will We bring him back to life. This is a promise We shall assuredly fulfill.

We wrote in the Psalms after the Torah was revealed: "The righteous among My servants shall inherit the earth." That is an admonition to those who serve Us.

We have sent you forth but as a blessing to mankind. Say: "It is revealed to me that your God is one God. Will you submit to Him?"

If they give no heed say: "I have warned you all alike, though I cannot tell whether the scourge you are threatened with is imminent or far off. He knows your spoken words and hidden thoughts. This may be a test for you and a short reprieve."

Say: "Lord, judge with fairness. Our Lord is the Merciful, whose help We seek against your blasphemies."

---

[1] **Ishmael, Idis, and Dhūl-Kifl** Ishmael was the son of Abraham and Hagar. By tradition, Muslims trace their origins back to Abraham through Ishmael. Idis is Enoch, an early legendary figure in the Holy Scriptures and a favorite of God. Dhūl-Kifl is probably the prophet Ezekiel.

[2] **Dhūl-Nūn** Dhūl-Nūn is Jonah, a prophet who at first resisted the call of God.

[3] **Gog and Magog** In the *Holy Scriptures*, enemies of Israel whom God lets loose on the Israelites but then destroys before they can conquer Israel. In the *Holy Bible* they are connected to some type of Satanic invasion after the thousand-year reign of the Messiah.

Light
24:35–46

24

God is the light of the heavens and the earth. His light may be compared to a niche that enshrines a lamp, the lamp within a crystal of star-like brilliance. It is lit from a blessed olive tree neither eastern nor western. Its very oil would almost shine forth, though no fire touched it. Light upon light; God guides to His light whom He will.

God speaks in metaphors to men. God has knowledge of all things.

His light is found in temples which God has sanctioned to be built for the remembrance of His name. In them, morning and evening, His praise is sung by men whom neither trade nor profit can divert from remembering Him, from offering prayers, or from giving alms; who dread the day when men's hearts and eyes shall writhe with anguish; who hope that God will requite them for their noblest deeds and lavish His grace upon them. God gives without measure to whom He will.

As for the unbelievers, their works are like a mirage in a desert. The thirsty traveller thinks it is water, but when he comes near he finds that it is nothing. He finds God there, who pays him back in full. Swift is God's reckoning.

Or like darkness on a bottomless ocean spread with clashing billows and overcast with clouds: darkness upon darkness. If he stretches out his hand he can scarcely see it. Indeed the man from whom God withholds His light shall find no light at all.

Do you not see how God is praised by those in heaven and those on earth? The very birds praise Him as they wing their flight. He notes the prayers and praises of all His creatures, and has knowledge of all their actions.

It is God who has sovereignty over the heavens and the earth. To Him shall all things return.

Do you not see how God drives the clouds, then gathers and piles them up in masses which pour down torrents of rain? From heaven's mountains He sends down the hail, pelting with it whom He will and turning it away from whom He pleases. The flash of His lightning almost snatches off men's eyes.

He makes the night succeed the day: surely in this there is a lesson for clear-sighted men.

God created every beast from water. Some creep upon their bellies, others walk on two legs, and others yet on four. God creates what He pleases. He has power over all things.

We have sent down revelations demonstrating the Truth. God guides whom He will to a straight path. . . .

IBN KHALDUN

Selections from the *Muqaddimah*

Ibn Khaldun (1332–1406), statesman, jurist, and scholar, wrote the most famous historical work in Islamic literature. Today's scholars consider his multivolume *Universal History* and the *Muqaddimah* or *Prolegomena* to be pioneering studies in history and sociology. Although his *Universal History* provides valuable information on the Muslim world, and, in particular North Africa, his *Muqaddimah* or *Prolegomena*—an introductory essay or discussion to explain and interpret a longer work—is the one usually read. The *Muqaddimah* ranges over many topics, including the theories, principles, and techniques of writing history (historiography), explanations of how and why civilizations rise and fall, and descriptions and analyses of the socioeconomic structures of societies.

Ibn Khaldun witnessed and participated in some of the most tumultuous events in Islamic history. His ancestors had served the Moorish (Muslim) rules in Spain before the Christians started to conquer southern Spain. The family fled to Tunis, in North Africa, where Ibn Khaldun was born. His education, for a young man from the upper class, consisted of studies of the *Qur'an*, which he memorized, grammar, poetry, philosophy, and jurisprudence. At age twenty he entered government service in Tunis but soon left for Fez, another North African city. A victim of political turmoils and intrigues, Ibn Khaldun escaped to Spain in 1362. In 1365 he returned to North Africa and again found himself caught in power struggles among the regional rulers. He survived by his wits and bravery, often changing sides and, on one occasion, raising an army of desert Arabs for a local sultan. Ibn Khaldun and his family, in 1375, under the protection of a tribal chief, found refuge in a rural retreat. During this time he worked on his *Universal History* and *Muqaddimah*. However, he eventually became bored, and three years later he was back in Tunis.

His life took another turn in 1382 when, on his way to Mecca, he stopped in Cairo. The Mameluke Sultan of Egypt brought him into his court, and Ibn Khaldun quickly rose to be chief justice of the judicial system that he proceeded to reform. While combating those unhappy with his changes, he suffered a shattering personal loss when his family was drowned in a shipwreck. Crushed by this tragedy, he resigned his office and made a pilgrimage to Mecca. Upon his return to Egypt, he held some academic posts and resumed his judgeship position, which continued to be an unsettling experience. In 1400 he met and negotiated with Tamerlane (1336–1405), the Tatar warrior and conqueror of much of the Middle East, over the siege of Damascus. Tamerlane eventually sacked Damascus, but Ibn Khaldun successfully saved some of its leading citizens. Ibn Khaldun came back to Cairo and resumed his judgeship until his death in 1406.

The *Muqaddimah* or *Prolegomena* includes the author's original Preface and Book I of his *Universal History*. After noting the wrong and right ways to study history, Ibn Khaldun defines the nature of civilization and notes what is necessary to create a civilization, the types of government identified with civilizations, and the economic structure and social systems found in a civilized society. In the concluding chapters, he surveys the various fields of learning and discusses the uniqueness and importance of the human thinking process.

Ibn Khaldun, influenced by earlier Muslim scholars who had read the Greek philosophers, and, in particular, Aristotle, recognized that individuals could only survive in some form of a social organization—be it a city-state, a desert tribe, or an urban complex. The community was held together by what Ibn Khaldun termed "solidarity," "group feeling," or "social solidarity." From this sense of belonging sprang the desires not only to form a civilization but also to conquer others. And, from such conquests and strife came larger civilizations—and dynasties. The sense of cooperation, however, was subject to change, and as the dynasty lost its sense of "solidarity," the society started to decay. Ultimately, a more vigorous civilization, characterized by a strong "solidarity," would rise and conquer the weakened civilization, thus explaining the cyclical nature of history. Within these larger themes of history, Ibn Khaldun explored, in detail and by example, the economic, religious, and social structures and functions of civilizations. Although the focus of his works is clearly on humans and their ways of living together or being engaged in conflict, the author never forgets that Allah is responsible for all and that he must be praised for what he has bestowed on humans.

Reading the Selections

These selections from the *Muqaddimah* represent the breadth of Ibn Khaldun's learning and interest. They range across many topics he discusses in his work: his understanding of the historical process, his definition of civilization, his recognition of how nature and humans are related, his insight into political power and leadership, his grasp of economic relationships, and his respect for the human intellect. These topics, however, constitute only a fraction of the total number of issues and subjects Ibn Khaldun examines in his historical study.

The first selections set the tone and provide the framework for the discussions that follow. Ibn Khaldun is especially concerned with establishing his definitions of good history and what is needed to write accurate and fair accounts of the past. He devotes much of his writing to describing civilizations and comments on their origins, characteristics, and fate, because he believes that this is the highest form of human endeavor. As he dissects the workings of a civilization, he reveals his knowledge of how societies function, and he shares his wisdom on why humans behave the way they do in a social setting. Finally, he notes what separates humans from other animals and asserts that humans should develop their minds to the highest levels they can achieve.

The Introduction

The excellence of historiography. An appreciation of the various approaches to history. A glimpse of the different kinds of errors to which historians are liable. Why these errors occur.

It should be known that history is a discipline that has a great number of approaches. Its useful aspects are very many. Its goal is distinguished.

History makes us acquainted with the conditions of past nations as they are reflected in their national charac-

ter. It makes us acquainted with the biographies of the prophets and with the dynasties and policies of rulers. Whoever so desires may thus achieve the useful result of being able to imitate historical examples in religious and worldly matters.

The (writing of history) requires numerous sources and much varied knowledge. It also requires a good speculative mind and thoroughness, which lead the historian to the truth and keep him from slips and errors. If he trusts historical information in its plain transmitted form and has no clear knowledge of the principles resulting from custom, the fundamental facts of politics, the nature of civilization, or the conditions governing human social organization, and if, furthermore, he does not evaluate remote or ancient material through comparison with near or contemporary material, he often cannot avoid stumbling and slipping and deviating from the path of truth. Historians, Qur'ân commentators and leading transmitters have committed frequent errors in the stories and events they reported. They accepted them in the plain transmitted form, without regard for its value. They did not check them with the principles underlying such historical situations, nor did they compare them with similar material. Also, they did not probe with the yardstick of philosophy, with the help of knowledge of the nature of things, or with the help of speculation and historical insight. Therefore, they strayed from the truth and found themselves lost in the desert of baseless assumptions and errors.

This is especially the case with figures, either of sums of money or of soldiers, whenever they occur in stories. They offer a good opportunity for false information and constitute a vehicle for nonsensical statements. They must be controlled and checked with the help of known fundamental facts. . . .

There are many such stories. They are always crop- 5 ping up in the works of the historians. The incentive for inventing and reporting them shows a tendency to forbidden pleasures and for smearing the reputation of others. People justify their own subservience to pleasure by citing the supposed doings of men and women of the past. Therefore, they often appear very eager for such information and are alert to find it when they go through the pages of published works.

I once criticized a royal prince for being so eager to learn to sing and play the strings. I told him it was not a matter that should concern him and that it did not befit his position. He referred me to Ibrâhîm b. al-Mahdî[1] who was the leading musician and best singer of his time. I replied: "For heaven's sake, why do you not rather follow the example of his father or his brother? Do you not see how that pursuit prevented Ibrâhîm from attaining their position?" The prince, however, was deaf to my criticism and turned away.

Further silly information is accepted by many historians. They do not care to consider the factual proofs and circumstantial evidence that require us to recognize that the contrary is true. . . .

Dynasty and government serve as the world's market-place, attracting to it the products of scholarship and craftsmanship alike. Wayward wisdom and forgotten lore turn up there. In this market stories are told and items of historical information are delivered. Whatever is in demand on this market is in general demand everywhere else. Now, whenever the established dynasty avoids injustice, prejudice, weakness, and double-dealing, with determination keeping to the right path and never swerving

from it, the wares on its market are as pure silver and fine gold. However, when it is influenced by selfish interests and rivalries, or swayed by vendors of tyranny and dishonesty, the wares of its market-place become as dross and debased metals. The intelligent critic must judge for himself as he looks around, examining this, admiring that, and choosing the other. . . .

Lengthy discussion of these mistakes has taken us rather far from the purpose of this work. However, many competent persons and expert historians slipped in connection with such stories and assertions, and they stuck in their minds. Many weak-minded and uncritical men learned these things from them, and even (competent historians) accepted them without critical investigation, and thus (strange stories) crept into their material. In consequence, historiography became nonsensical and confused, and its students fumbled around. Historiography came to be considered a domain of the common people. Therefore, today, the scholar in this field needs to know the principles of politics, the nature of things, and the differences among nations, places, and periods with regard to ways of life, character qualities, customs, sects, schools, and everything else. He further needs a comprehensive knowledge of present conditions in all these respects. He must compare similarities or differences between present and past conditions. He must know the causes of the similarities in certain cases and of the differences in others. He must be aware of the differing origins and beginnings of dynasties and religious groups, as well as of the reasons and incentives that brought them into being and the circumstances and history of the persons who supported them. His goal must be to have complete knowledge of the reasons for every happening, and to be acquainted with the origin of every event. Then, he must check transmitted information with the basic principles he knows. If it fulfils their requirements, it is sound. Otherwise, the historian must consider it as spurious and dispense with it. It was for this reason alone that historiography was highly esteemed by the ancients, so much so that aṭ-Ṭabarî, al-Bukhârî, and, before them, Ibn Isḥâq and other Muslim religious scholars, chose to occupy themselves with it. Most scholars, however, forgot this, the secret of historiography, with the result that it became a stupid occupation. Ordinary people as well as scholars who had no firm foundation of knowledge, considered it a simple matter to study and know history, to delve into it and sponge on it. Strays got into the flock, bits of shell were mixed with the nut, truth was adulterated with lies.

"The final outcome of things is up to God."[2] 10

A hidden pitfall in historiography is disregard for the fact that conditions within nations and races change with the change of periods and the passage of time. This is a sore affliction and is deeply hidden, becoming noticeable only after a long time, so that rarely do more than a few individuals become aware of it.

This is as follows. The condition of the world and of nations, their customs and sects, does not persist in the same form or in a constant manner. There are differences according to days and periods, and changes from one con-

---

[1] **Ibrâhîm b. al-Mahdî** The son of the caliph al-Mahdî, whom some considered, for a short time, to be the caliph. He lived 162–224 (Muslim calendar) or A.D. 779–839.

[2] *Qur'an* Sura 31.22.

dition to another. Such is the case with individuals, times, and cities, and it likewise happens in connection with regions and districts, periods and dynasties.

The old Persian nations, the Syrians, the Nabataeans, the Tubba's, the Israelites, and the Copts, all once existed. They all had their own particular institutions in respect of dynastic and territorial arrangements, their own politics, crafts, languages, technical terminologies, as well as their own ways of dealing with their fellow men and handling their cultural institutions. Their historical relics testify to that. They were succeeded by the later Persians, the Byzantines, and the Arabs. The old institutions changed and former customs were transformed, either into something very similar, or into something distinct and altogether different. Then, there came Islam. Again, all institutions underwent another change, and for the most part assumed the forms that are still familiar at the present time as the result of their transmission from one generation to the next.

Then, the days of Arab rule were over. The early generations who had cemented Arab might and founded the realm of the Arabs were gone. Power was seized by others, by non-Arabs like the Turks in the east, the Berbers in the west, and the European Christians in the north. With their passing, entire nations ceased to exist, and institutions and customs changed. Their glory was forgotten, and their power no longer heeded.

The widely accepted reason for changes in institutions and customs is the fact that the customs of each race depend on the customs of its ruler. As the proverb says: "The common people follow the religion of the ruler."[3]

---

[3] **religion of the ruler** The word for religion, *din*, is used here in the sense of the "way of doing things."

⧜

Chapter I

Human civilization in general

First Prefatory Discussion

Human social organization is something necessary. The philosophers expressed this fact by saying: "Man is 'political' by nature." That is, he cannot do without the social organization for which the philosophers use the technical term "town" *(polis)*.

This is what civilization means. (The necessary character of human social organization or civilization) is explained by the fact that God created and fashioned man in a form that can live and subsist only with the help of food. He guided man to a natural desire for food and instilled in him the power that enables him to obtain it.

However, the power of the individual human being is not sufficient for him to obtain (the food) he needs, and does not provide him with as much food as he requires to live. Even if we assume an absolute minimum of food—that is, food enough for one day, (a little) wheat, for instance—that amount of food could be obtained only after much preparation such as grinding, kneading, and baking. Each of these three operations requires utensils and tools that can be provided only with the help of several crafts, such as the crafts of the blacksmith, the carpenter, and the potter. Assuming that a man could eat unprepared grain, an even greater number of operations would be necessary in order to obtain the grain: sowing and reaping, and threshing to separate it from the husks of the ear. Each of these operations requires a number of tools and many more crafts than those just mentioned. It is beyond the power of one man alone to do all that, or part of it, by himself. Thus, he cannot do without a combination of many powers from among his fellow beings, if he is to obtain food for himself and for them. Through co-operation, the needs of a number of persons, many times greater than their own number, can be satisfied.

Likewise, each individual needs the help of his fellow beings for his defence. When God fashioned the natures of all living beings and divided the various powers among them, many dumb animals were given more perfect powers than God gave to man. The power of a horse, for instance, is much greater than the power of a man, and so is the power of a donkey or an ox. The power of a lion or an elephant is many times greater than the power of man.

Aggressiveness is natural in living beings. Therefore, God gave each of them a special limb for defence against aggression. To man, instead, He gave the ability to think, and the hand. With the help of the ability to think, the hand is able to prepare the ground for the crafts. The crafts, in turn, procure for man the instruments that serve him instead of limbs, which other animals possess for their defence. Lances, for instance, take the place of horns for goring, swords the place of claws to inflict wounds, shields the place of thick skins, and so on. There are other such things. They were all mentioned by Galen in *De usu partium*.[4]

The power of one individual human being cannot withstand the power of any one dumb animal, especially the power of the predatory animals. Man is generally unable to defend himself against them by himself. Nor is his unaided power sufficient to make use of the existing instruments of defence, because there are so many of them and they require so many crafts and things. It is absolutely necessary for man to have the co-operation of his fellow

---

[4] *De usu partium* Translated as "At the Beginning of the Work."

men. As long as there is no such co-operation, he cannot obtain any food or nourishment, and life cannot materialize for him, because God fashioned him so that he must have food if he is to live. Nor, lacking weapons, can he defend himself. Thus, he falls prey to animals and dies much before his time. Under such circumstances, the human species would vanish. When, however, mutual co-operation exists, man obtains food for his nourishment and weapons for his defence. God's wise plan that mankind should subsist and the human species be preserved will be fulfilled.

Consequently, social organization is necessary to the human species. Without it, the existence of human beings would be incomplete. God's desire to settle the world with human beings and to leave them as His representatives on earth[5] would not materialize. This is the meaning of civilization, the object of the science under discussion.

The aforementioned remarks have been in the nature of establishing the existence of the object in this particular field. A scholar in a particular discipline is not obliged to do this, since it is accepted in logic that a scholar in a particular science does not have to establish the existence of the object in that science.[6] . . .

(THE REAL MEANING OF PROPHECY)

This world with all the created things in it has a certain order and solid construction. It shows nexuses between causes and things caused, combinations of some parts of creation with others, and transformations of some existent things into others, in a pattern that is both remarkable and endless. Beginning with the world of the body and sensual perception, and therein first with the world of the visible elements, one notices how these elements are arranged gradually and continually in an ascending order, from earth to water, to air, and to fire. Each one of the elements is prepared to be transformed into the next higher or lower one, and sometimes is transformed. The higher one is always finer than the one preceding it. Eventually, the world of the spheres is reached. They are finer than anything else. They are in layers which are interconnected, in a shape which the senses are able to perceive only through the existence of motions. These motions provide some people with knowledge of the measurements and positions of the spheres, and also with knowledge of the existence of the essences beyond, the influence of which is noticeable in the spheres through the fact that they have motion.

One should then look at the world of creation. It 10
started out from the minerals and progressed, in an ingenious, gradual manner, to plants and animals. The last stage of minerals is connected with the first stage of plants, such as herbs and seedless plants. The last stage of plants, such as palms and vines, is connected with the first stage of animals, such as snails and shellfish which have only the power of touch. The word "connection" with regard to these created things means that the last stage of each

group is fully prepared to become the first stage of the next group.

The animal world then widens, its species become numerous, and, in a gradual process of creation, it finally leads to man, who is able to think and to reflect. The higher stage of man is reached from the world of the monkeys, in which both sagacity and perception are found, but which has not reached the stage of actual reflection and thinking. At this point we come to the first stage of man. This is as far as our (physical) observation extends.

Human civilization requires political leadership for its organization

We have mentioned before in more than one place that 1
human social organization is something necessary. It is the thing that is meant by "the civilization" which we have been discussing. (People) in any social organization must have someone who exercises a restraining influence and rules them and to whom recourse may be had. His rule over them is sometimes based upon a divinely revealed religious law. They are obliged to submit to it in view of their belief in reward and punishment in the other world. Sometimes, (his rule is based) upon rational politics. People are obliged to submit to it in view of the reward they expect from the ruler after he has become acquainted with what is good for them.

The first (type of rule) is useful for this world and for the other world, because the lawgiver knows the ultimate interest of the people and is concerned with the salvation of man in the other world. The second is useful only for this world.

We do not mean here that which is known as "political utopianism." By that, the philosophers mean the disposition of soul and character which each member of a social organization must have, if, eventually, people are completely to dispense with rulers. They call the social organization that fulfills these requirements the "ideal city." The norms observed in this connection are called "political utopias." They do not mean the kind of politics that the members of a social organization are led to adopt through laws for the common interest. That is something different. The "ideal city" (of the philosophers) is something rare and remote. They discuss it as a hypothesis.

Now, the aforementioned rational politics may be of two types. The first type of rational politics may concern itself with the general interest, and with the ruler's interest in connection with the administration of his realm, in particular. This was the politics of the Persians. It is something related to philosophy. God made this type of politics superfluous for us in Islam at the time of the caliphate. The religious laws take its place in connection with both general and (particular) interests, for they also include the maxims (of the philosophers) and the rules of royal authority.

The second type (of rational politics) is the one con- 5
cerned with the interest of the ruler and how he can maintain his rule through the forceful use of power. The general interest is, here, secondary. This is the type of politics practised by all rulers, whether they are Muslims or unbelievers. Muslim rulers, however, practise this type of politics in accordance with the requirements of the Muslim reli-

---

[5] *Qur'an* Sura 2.30.
[6] **object in that science** Ibn Khaldun is asserting that the "object" of a science or study is the fundamental elements at its basis that can be measured, such as numbers in mathematics or substances in physics. His new "science" is human organization or civilization.

gious law, as much as they are able to. Therefore, the political norms here are a mixture of religious laws and ethical rules, norms that are natural in social organization together with a certain necessary concern for strength and group feeling. . . .

With regard to the amount of prosperity and business activity in them, cities and towns differ in accordance with the different size of their population

The reason for this is that the individual human being cannot by himself obtain all the necessities of life. All human beings must co-operate to that end in their civilization. But what is obtained through the co-operation of a group of human beings satisfies the need of a number many times greater than themselves. For instance, no one, by himself, can obtain the share of the wheat he needs for food. But when six or ten persons, including a smith and a carpenter to make the tools, and others who are in charge of the oxen, the ploughing of the soil, the harvesting of the ripe grain, and all the other agricultural activities, undertake to obtain their food and work toward that purpose either separately or collectively and thus obtain through their labour a certain amount of food, (that amount) will be food for a number of people many times their own. The combined labour produces more than the needs and necessities of the workers.

If the labour of the inhabitants of a town or city is distributed in accordance with the necessities and needs of those inhabitants, a minimum of that labour will suffice. The labour (available) is more than is needed. Consequently, it is spent to provide the conditions and customs of luxury and to satisfy the needs of the inhabitants of other cities. They import (the things they need) from (people who have a surplus) through exchange or purchase. Thus, the (people who have a surplus) get a good deal of wealth.

It will become clear in the fifth chapter, which deals with profit and sustenance, that profit is the value realized from labour. When there is more labour, the value realized from it increases among the (people). Thus, their profit of necessity increases. The prosperity and wealth they enjoy leads them to luxury and the things that go with it, such as splendid houses and clothes, fine vessels and utensils, and the use of servants and mounts. All these involve activities that require their price and skillful people must be chosen to do them and be in charge of them. As a consequence, industry and the crafts thrive. The income and the expenditure of the city increase. Affluence comes to those who work and produce these things by their labour.

When population increases, the available labour again increases. In turn, luxury again increases in correspondence with the increasing profit, and the customs and needs of luxury increase. Crafts are created to obtain (luxury products). The value realized from them increases, and, as a result, profits are again multiplied in the town. Production there is thriving even more than before. And so it goes with the second and third increases. All the additional labour serves luxury and wealth, in contrast to the original labour that served (the necessities of) life. The city that is superior to another in (population) becomes superior to it also by its increased profit and prosperity and by its customs of luxury which are not found in the other city. The more numerous and the more abundant the population in a city, the more luxurious is the life of its inhabitants. This applies equally to all levels of the population. . . .

∞

Chapter 6
The various kinds of sciences. The methods of instruction. The conditions that obtain in these connections

Prefatory Discussion

On man's ability to think, which distinguishes human beings from animals and which enables them to obtain their livelihood, to co-operate to this end with their fellow men, and to study the Master whom they worship, and the revelations that the Messengers transmitted from Him. God thus caused all animals to obey man and to be in the grasp of his power. Through his ability to think, God gave man superiority over many of His creatures

I MAN'S ABILITY TO THINK

God distinguished man from all the other animals by an ability to think which He made the beginning of human perfection and the end of man's noble superiority over existing things.

This comes about as follows. Perception—that is, consciousness on the part of the person who perceives—is something peculiar to living beings to the exclusion of all other possible and existent things. Living beings may obtain consciousness of things that are outside their essence through the external senses God has given them, that is, the senses of hearing, vision, smell, taste, and touch. Man has this advantage over other beings: he can perceive things outside his essence through his ability to think, which is something beyond his senses. It is the result of (special) powers placed in the cavities of his brain. With the help of these powers, man takes the pictures of the *sensibilia*, applies his mind to them, and thus abstracts from them other pictures. The ability to think is the occupation with pictures that are beyond sense perception, and the application of the mind to them for analysis and synthesis. This is the meaning of the term.

The ability to think has several degrees. The first degree is man's intellectual understanding of the things that exist in the outside world in a natural or arbitrary order, so that he may try to arrange them with the help of his own power. This kind of thinking mostly consists of perceptions. It is the discerning intellect, with the help of which man obtains the things that are useful for him and his livelihood, and repels the things that are harmful to him.

The second degree is the ability to think which provides man with the ideas and the behaviour needed in dealing with his fellow men and in leading them. It mostly conveys apperceptions, which are obtained one by one through experience, until they have become really useful. This is called the experimental intellect.

The third degree is the ability to think which provides ₅ the knowledge, or hypothetical knowledge, of an object

beyond sense perception without any practical activity (going with it). This is the speculative intellect. It consists of both perceptions and apperceptions. They are arranged according to a special order, following special conditions, and thus provide some other knowledge of the same kind, that is, either perceptive or apperceptive. Then, they are again combined with something else, and again provide some other knowledge. The end of the process is to be provided with the perception of existence as it is, with its various genera, differences, reasons and causes. By thinking about these things, man achieves perfection in his reality and becomes pure intellect and perceptive soul. This is the meaning of human reality.

Selections from *The Arabian Nights*

The Arabian Nights is the most famous literary work produced by Islamic culture. Europeans first became acquainted with it through a French translation in the early 1700s, and later versions, rendered into most of the world's languages, made it a classic of world literature. Starting in the 1900s, with the rise of the mass media, the audience for *The Arabian Nights* expanded greatly, when many of the book's stories and characters, such as Ali Baba and the Forty Thieves and Aladdin and his Magic Lamp, became staples of popular culture, featured in comic strips, animated cartoons, and feature-length films.

Ironically, the world of Islam has been slow to appreciate the book's literary value. Only recently, in 1984, did there appear a definitive edition, by a Muslim scholar, of the fourteenth-century Syrian manuscript of *The Arabian Nights* in the Bibliothèque Nationale in Paris, which is one of the oldest versions and thus is thought to be close to the original form of the work. In the past, Islam's literary elite, although finding the work entertaining, disdained its colloquial language and grammatical errors and thought it only suitable for unsophisticated readers. Most important, Islam has a strong didactic element, so that literature, as all other elements of serious culture, is expected to serve a religious end, which is clearly not the case with the lighthearted stories in *The Arabian Nights*.

The stories in *The Arabian Nights* began circulating orally in the Muslim world, starting in the Golden Age, 800–1300, especially under the influence of Persian culture. Islam had initially been hostile to the story genre, because it was an offense against the religion's aesthetic code. A story "represented" reality and, thus, not being real, had no claim to truth. As Persians took leading roles in politics and society, they introduced elements of their tradition, such as the story form, into the fabric of Islamic life.

The earliest fragment from *The Arabian Nights* dates from the ninth century. The first reference to *The Arabian Nights* occurred in a tenth-century Arabic history, in a discussion of an Arabic work entitled *The Thousand Tales* or *The Thousand Nights,* which was a translation of a Persian work called *Hazar Afsana* ("A Thousand Legends"). Neither work has survived, but the *Hazar Afsana* inspired the alternative title, *A Thousand and One Nights,* by which *The Arabian Nights* is known. *Hazar Afsana* also supplied the framing tale, imported from an Indian source, which tells of the woman, Shahrazad, who develops a storytelling plan to keep King Shahrayar from his crazed plan of murdering a wife a day because of an earlier wife's infidelity. At first, fewer than a thousand tales existed, but over time, new ones were added to make the number exact.

The sources for the tales reflect Islam's ethnic diversity, including mainly Indian, Persian, and Arabic origins, but a few come from Iraq, Egypt, and Turkey. Many genres are represented:

fairy tales, romances, legends, fables, parables, anecdotes, and realistic adventures. The stories, though often ancient, were modified when they were written down to bring them into harmony with the conditions of Islamic society and culture.

The literary style is typical of Islamic writing, which has been compared to the intricate weaving of a hand-loomed carpet: highly colored, filled with details, scenes, and figures, both animal and human, each interesting in its own way but not readily related to one another, yet with an allover pattern that gives a general coherence. Especially appealing is the style's bold blend of the colloquial and the lofty, the tragic and the comic, the supernatural and the natural. In many stories, sex functions as a great equalizer, for example, reducing the arrogant king and the abject peasant to the same level—both characters bewitched and betrayed by the mysterious power of sexuality.

Reading the Selections

The book's setting is imaginary: the court of King (Caliph) Shahrayar, ruler of India and Indochina. Betrayed by a wife, he kills her and vows to kill a new wife each day, after their wedding night. The vizier, the highest official serving the king, has the unhappy duty of putting the women to death. As the selection begins, Shahrazad, the vizier's daughter, has devised a strategy both to save her life and end the senseless killings.

Divided into nights, the book develops two plot lines simultaneously, one telling a portion of a tale each night, often ending with a cliff-hanging incident, the other consisting of bits of dialogue among the King, Shahrazad, and Dinarzad, Shahrazad's sister. The work is made more intricate by the periodic insertion of poetic passages, either borrowed from existing collections or supplied by the anonymous author—a reflection of the deep respect given to poetry in the Muslim world.

The selection contains eight nights, during which Shahrazad tells three stories: "The Story of the Merchant and the Demon," "The First Old Man's Tale," and "The Second Old Man's Tale." Filled with magic, spells, and demons, each tale is a parable, offering a moral lesson that echoes the book's overall message: Victims can overcome their demon and human enemies if they keep their wits about them and rely on their storytelling gifts.

∽

Tired and exhausted, the vizier went to King Shahrayar and, kissing the ground before him, told him about his daughter, adding that he would give her to him that very night. The king was astonished and said to him, "Vizier, how is it that you have found it possible to give me your daughter, knowing that I will, by God, the Creator of heaven, ask you to put her to death the next morning and that if you refuse, I will have you put to death too?" He replied, "My King and Lord, I have told her everything and explained all this to her, but she refuses and insists on being with you tonight." The king was delighted and said, "Go to her, prepare her, and bring her to me early in the evening."

The vizier went down, repeated the king's message to his daughter, and said, "May God not deprive me of you." She was very happy and, after preparing herself and packing what she needed, went to her younger sister, Dinarzad, and said, "Sister, listen well to what I am telling you. When I go to the king, I will send for you, and when you come and see that the king has finished with me, say,

'Sister, if you are not sleepy, tell us a story.' Then I will begin to tell a story, and it will cause the king to stop his practice, save myself, and deliver the people." Dinarzad replied, "Very well."

At nightfall the vizier took Shahrazad and went with her to the great King Shahrayar. But when Shahrayar took her to bed and began to fondle her, she wept, and when he asked her, "Why are you crying?" she replied, "I have a sister, and I wish to bid her good-bye before daybreak." Then the king sent for the sister, who came and went to sleep under the bed. When the night wore on, she woke up and waited until the king had satisfied himself with her sister Shahrazad and they were by now all fully awake. Then Dinarzad cleared her throat and said, "Sister, if you are not sleepy, tell us one of your lovely little tales to while away the night, before I bid you good-bye at daybreak, for I don't know what will happen to you tomorrow." Shahrazad turned to King Shahrayar and said, "May I have your permission to tell a story?" He replied, "Yes," and Shahrazad was very happy and said, "Listen":

⧜

The First Night

The Story of the Merchant and the Demon

It is said, O wise and happy King, that once there was a prosperous merchant who had abundant wealth and investments and commitments in every country. He had many women and children and kept many servants and slaves. One day, having resolved to visit another country, he took provisions, filling his saddlebag with loaves of bread and with dates, mounted his horse, and set out on his journey. For many days and nights, he journeyed under God's care until he reached his destination. When he finished his business, he turned back to his home and family. He journeyed for three days, and on the fourth day, chancing to come to an orchard, went in to avoid the heat and shade himself from the sun of the open country. He came to a spring under a walnut tree and, tying his horse, sat by the spring, pulled out from the saddlebag some loaves of bread and a handful of dates, and began to eat, throwing the date pits right and left until he had had enough. Then he got up, performed his ablutions,[1] and performed his prayers.

But hardly had he finished when he saw an old demon, with sword in hand, standing with his feet on the ground and his head in the clouds. The demon approached until he stood before him and screamed, saying, "Get up, so that I may kill you with this sword, just as you have killed my son." When the merchant saw and heard the demon, he was terrified and awestricken. He asked, "Master, for what crime do you wish to kill me?" The demon replied, "I wish to kill you because you have killed my son." The merchant asked, "Who has killed your son?" The demon replied, "You have killed my son." The merchant said, "By God, I did not kill your son. When and how could that have been?" The demon said, "Didn't you sit down, take out some dates from your saddlebag, and eat, throwing the pits right and left?" The merchant replied, "Yes, I did." The demon said, "You killed my son, for as you were throwing the stones right and left, my son happened to be walking by and was struck and killed by one of them, and I must now kill you." The merchant said, "O my lord, please don't kill me." The demon replied, "I must kill you as you killed him—blood for blood." The merchant said, "To God we belong and to God we return. There is no power or strength, save in God the Almighty, the Magnificent. If I killed him, I did it by mistake. Please

forgive me." The demon replied, "By God, I must kill you, as you killed my son." Then he seized him and, throwing him to the ground, raised the sword to strike him. The merchant began to weep and mourn his family and his wife and children. Again, the demon raised his sword to strike, while the merchant cried until he was drenched with tears, saying, "There is no power or strength, save in God the Almighty, the Magnificent." Then he began to recite the following verses:

> Life has two days: one peace, one wariness,
> And has two sides: worry and happiness.
> Ask him who taunts us with adversity,   5
> "Does fate, save those worthy of note, oppress?
> Don't you see that the blowing, raging storms
> Only the tallest of the trees beset,
> And of earth's many green and barren lots,
> Only the ones with fruits with stones are hit,   10
> And of the countless stars in heaven's vault
> None is eclipsed except the moon and sun?
> You thought well of the days, when they were good,
> Oblivious to the ills destined for one.
> You were deluded by the peaceful nights,   15
> Yet in the peace of night does sorrow stun."

When the merchant finished and stopped weeping, the demon said, "By God, I must kill you, as you killed my son, even if you weep blood." The merchant asked, "Must you?" The demon replied, "I must," and raised his sword to strike.

But morning overtook Shahrazad, and she lapsed into silence, leaving King Shahrayar burning with curiosity to hear the rest of the story. Then Dinarzad said to her sister Shahrazad, "What a strange and lovely story!" Shahrazad replied, "What is this compared with what I shall tell you tomorrow night if the king spares me and lets me live? It will be even better and more entertaining." The king thought to himself, "I will spare her until I hear the rest of the story; then I will have her put to death the next day." When morning broke, the day dawned, and the sun rose; the king left to attend to the affairs of the kingdom, and the vizier, Shahrazad's father, was amazed and delighted. King Shahrayar governed all day and returned home at night to his quarters and got into bed with Shahrazad. Then Dinarzad said to her sister Shahrazad, "Please, sister, if you are not sleepy, tell us one of your lovely little tales to while away the night." The king added, "Let it be the conclusion of the story of the demon and the merchant, for I would like to hear it." Shahrazad replied, "With the greatest pleasure, dear, happy King":

---

[1] **ablutions** Ritual washing.

∞

The Second Night

It is related, O wise and happy King, that when the demon raised his sword, the merchant asked the demon again, "Must you kill me?" and the demon replied, "Yes." Then the merchant said, "Please give me time to say good-bye to my family and my wife and children, divide my property among them, and appoint guardians. Then I shall come back, so that you may kill me." The demon replied, "I am afraid that if I release you and grant you time, you will go and do what you wish, but will not come back." The merchant said, "I swear to keep my pledge to come back, as the God of Heaven and earth is my witness." The demon asked, "How much time do you need?" The merchant replied, "One year, so that I may see enough of my children, bid my wife good-bye, discharge my obligations to people, and come back on New Year's Day."[2] The demon asked, "Do you swear to God that if I let you go, you will come back on New Year's Day?" The merchant replied, "Yes, I swear to God."

After the merchant swore, the demon released him, and he mounted his horse sadly and went on his way. He journeyed until he reached his home and came to his wife and children. When he saw them, he wept bitterly, and when his family saw his sorrow and grief, they began to reproach him for his behavior, and his wife said, "Husband, what is the matter with you? Why do you mourn, when we are happy, celebrating your return?" He replied, "Why not mourn when I have only one year to live?" Then he told her of his encounter with the demon and informed her that he had sworn to return on New Year's Day, so that the demon might kill him.

When they heard what he said, everyone began to cry. His wife struck her face in lamentation and cut her hair, his daughters wailed, and his little children cried. It was a day of mourning, as all the children gathered around their

father to weep and exchange good-byes. The next day he wrote his will, dividing his property, discharged his obligations to people, left bequests and gifts, distributed alms, and engaged reciters to read portions of the *Qur'an* in his house. Then he summoned legal witnesses and in their presence freed his slaves and slave-girls, divided among his elder children their shares of the property, appointed guardians for his little ones, and gave his wife her share, according to her marriage contract. He spent the rest of the time with his family, and when the year came to an end, save for the time needed for the journey, he performed his ablutions, performed his prayers, and, carrying his burial shroud, began to bid his family good-bye. His sons hung around his neck, his daughters wept, and his wife wailed. Their mourning scared him, and he began to weep, as he embraced and kissed his children good-bye. He said to them, "Children, this is God's will and decree, for man was created to die." Then he turned away and, mounting his horse, journeyed day and night until he reached the orchard on New Year's Day.

He sat at the place where he had eaten the dates, waiting for the demon, with a heavy heart and tearful eyes. As he waited, an old man, leading a deer on a leash, approached and greeted him, and he returned the greeting. The old man inquired, "Friend, why do you sit here in this place of demons and devils? For in this haunted orchard none come to good." The merchant replied by telling him what had happened to him and the demon, from beginning to end. The old man was amazed at the merchant's fidelity and said, "Yours is a magnificent pledge," adding, "By God, I shall not leave until I see what will happen to you with the demon." Then he sat down beside him and chatted with him. As they talked. . . .

But morning overtook Shahrazad, and she lapsed into silence. 5
As the day dawned, and it was light, her sister Dinarzad said, "What a strange and wonderful story!" Shahrazad replied, "Tomorrow night I shall tell something even stranger and more wonderful than this."

---

[2] **New Year's Day** In the Arabic calendar, the first day of *Muharram*, which commemorates the *Hijra*, Muhammad's flight from Mecca to Medina; the actual day varies with the lunar calendar.

∞

The Third Night

When it was night and Shahrazad was in bed with the king, 1
Dinarzad said to her sister Shahrazad, "Please, if you are not sleepy, tell us one of your lovely little tales to while away the night." The king added, "Let it be the conclusion of the merchant's story." Shahrazad replied, "As you wish":

I heard, O happy King, that as the merchant and the man with the deer sat talking, another old man approached,

with two black hounds, and when he reached them, he greeted them, and they returned his greeting. Then he asked them about themselves, and the man with the deer told him the story of the merchant and the demon, how the merchant had sworn to return on New Year's Day, and how the demon was waiting to kill him. He added that when he himself heard the story, he swore never to leave until he saw what would happen between the merchant and the demon. When the man with the two dogs heard the story, he was amazed, and he too swore never to leave them until he saw what would happen between them. Then he questioned the merchant, and the merchant repeated to him what had happened to him with the demon.

While they were engaged in conversation, a third old man approached and greeted them, and they returned his greeting. He asked, "Why do I see the two of you sitting here, with this merchant between you, looking abject, sad, and dejected?" They told him the merchant's story and explained that they were sitting and waiting to see what would happen to him with the demon. When he heard the story, he sat down with them, saying, "By God, I too like you will not leave, until I see what happens to this man with the demon." As they sat, conversing with one another, they suddenly saw the dust rising from the open country, and when it cleared, they saw the demon approaching, with a drawn steel sword in his hand. He stood before them without greeting them, yanked the merchant with his left hand, and, holding him fast before him,

said, "Get ready to die." The merchant and the three old men began to weep and wail.

But dawn broke and morning overtook Shahrazad, and she lapsed into silence. Then Dinarzad said, "Sister, what a lovely story!" Shahrazad replied, "What is this compared with what I shall tell you tomorrow night? It will be even better; it will be more wonderful, delightful, entertaining, and delectable if the king spares me and lets me live." The king was all curiosity to hear the rest of the story and said to himself, "By God, I will not have her put to death until I hear the rest of the story and find out what happened to the merchant with the demon. Then I will have her put to death the next morning, as I did with the others." Then he went out to attend to the affairs of his kingdom, and when he saw Shahrazad's father, he treated him kindly and showed him favors, and the vizier was amazed. When night came, the king went home, and when he was in bed with Shahrazad, Dinarzad said, "Sister, if you are not sleepy, tell us one of your lovely little tales to while away the night." Shahrazad replied, "With the greatest pleasure":

⸎

The Fourth Night

It is related, O happy King, that the first old man with the deer approached the demon and, kissing his hands and feet, said, "Fiend and King of the demon kings, if I tell you what happened to me and that deer, and you find it strange and amazing, indeed stranger and more amazing than what happened to you and the merchant, will you grant me a third of your claim on him for his crime and guilt?" The demon replied, "I will." The old man said:

The First Old Man's Tale

Demon, this deer is my cousin, my flesh and blood. I married her when I was very young, and she a girl of twelve, who reached womanhood only afterward. For thirty years we lived together, but I was not blessed with children, for she bore neither boy nor girl. Yet I continued to be kind to her, to care for her, and to treat her generously. Then I took a mistress, and she bore me a son, who grew up to look like a slice of the moon. Meanwhile, my wife grew jealous of my mistress and my son. One day, when he was ten, I had to go on a journey. I entrusted my wife, this one here, with my mistress and son, bade her take good care of them, and was gone for a whole year. In my absence my wife, this cousin of mine, learned soothsaying and magic and cast a spell on my son and turned him into a young bull. Then she summoned my shepherd, gave my son to him, and said, "Tend this bull with the rest of the cattle." The shepherd took him and tended him for a while. Then

she cast a spell on the mother, turning her into a cow, and gave her also to the shepherd.

When I came back, after all this was done, and inquired about my mistress and my son, she answered, "Your mistress died, and your son ran away two months ago, and I have had no news from him ever since." When I heard her, I grieved for my mistress, and with an anguished heart I mourned for my son for nearly a year. When the Great Feast of the Immolation[3] drew near, I summoned the shepherd and ordered him to bring me a fat cow for the sacrifice. The cow he brought me was in reality my enchanted mistress. When I bound her and pressed against her to cut her throat, she wept and cried, as if saying, "My son, my son," and her tears coursed down her cheeks. Astonished and seized with pity, I turned away and asked the shepherd to bring me a different cow. But my wife shouted, "Go on. Butcher her, for he has none better or fatter. Let us enjoy her meat at feast time." I approached the cow to cut her throat, and again she cried, as if saying, "My son, my son." Then I turned away from her and said to the shepherd, "Butcher her for me." The shepherd butchered her, and when he skinned her, he found neither meat nor fat but only skin and bone. I regretted having her butchered and said to the shepherd, "Take her all for yourself, or give her as alms to whomever you wish, and find me a fat young bull from among the

---

[3] **Immolation** A Muslim festival, celebrated over four days, with the slaughter of sheep and cattle as offerings to Allah, that commemorates the pilgrimage to Mecca.

flock." The shepherd took her away and disappeared, and I never knew what he did with her.

Then he brought me my son, my heartblood, in the guise of a fat young bull. When my son saw me, he shook his head loose from the rope, ran toward me, and, throwing himself at my feet, kept rubbing his head against me. I was astonished and touched with sympathy, pity, and mercy, for the blood hearkened to the blood and the divine bond, and my heart throbbed within me when I saw the tears coursing over the cheeks of my son the young bull, as he dug the earth with his hoofs. I turned away and said to the shepherd, "Let him go with the rest of the flock, and be kind to him, for I have decided to spare him. Bring me another one instead of him." My wife, this very deer, shouted, "You shall sacrifice none but this bull." I got angry and replied, "I listened to you and butchered the cow uselessly. I will not listen to you and kill this bull, for I have decided to spare him." But she pressed me, saying, "You must butcher this bull," and I bound him and took the knife. . . .

But dawn broke, and morning overtook Shahrazad, and she 5 *lapsed into silence, leaving the king all curiosity for the rest of the story. Then her sister Dinarzad said, "What an entertaining story!" Shahrazad replied, "Tomorrow night I shall tell you something even stranger, more wonderful, and more entertaining if the king spares me and lets me live."*

The Fifth Night

The following night, Dinarzad said to her sister Shahrazad, 1 *"Please, sister, if you are not sleepy, tell us one of your little tales." Shahrazad replied, "With the greatest pleasure":*

I heard, dear King, that the old man with the deer said to the demon and to his companions:

I took the knife and as I turned to slaughter my son, he wept, bellowed, rolled at my feet, and motioned toward me with his tongue. I suspected something, began to waver with trepidation and pity, and finally released him, saying to my wife, "I have decided to spare him, and I commit him to your care." Then I tried to appease and please my wife, this very deer, by slaughtering another bull, promising her to slaughter this one next season. We slept that night, and when God's dawn broke, the shepherd came to me without letting my wife know, and said, "Give me credit for bringing you good news." I replied, "Tell me, and the credit is yours." He said, "Master, I have a daughter who is fond of soothsaying and magic and who is adept at the art of oaths and spells. Yesterday I took home with me the bull you had spared, to let him graze with the cattle, and when my daughter saw him, she laughed and cried at the same time. When I asked her why she laughed and cried, she answered that she laughed because the bull was in reality the son of our master the cattle owner, put under a spell by his stepmother, and that she cried because his father had slaughtered the son's mother. I could hardly wait till daybreak to bring you the good news about your son."

Demon, when I heard that, I uttered a cry and fainted, and when I came to myself, I accompanied the shepherd to his home, went to my son, and threw myself at him, kissing him and crying. He turned his head toward me, his tears coursing over his cheeks, and dangled his tongue, as if to say, "Look at my plight." Then I turned to the shepherd's daughter and asked, "Can you release him from the spell? If you do, I will give you all my cattle and all my possessions." She smiled and replied, "Master, I have no desire for your wealth, cattle, or possessions. I will deliver him, but on two conditions: first, that you let me marry him; second, that you let me cast a spell on her who had cast a spell on him, in order to control her and guard against her evil power." I replied, "Do whatever you wish and more. My possessions are for you and my son. As for my wife, who has done this to my son and made me slaughter his mother, her life is forfeit to you." She said, "No, but I will let her taste what she has inflicted on others." Then the shepherd's daughter filled a bowl with water, uttered an incantation and an oath, and said to my son, "Bull, if you have been created in this image by the All-Conquering, Almighty Lord, stay as you are, but if you have been treacherously put under a spell, change back to your human form, by the will of God, Creator of the wide world." Then she sprinkled him with the water, and he shook himself and changed from a bull back to his human form.

As I rushed to him, I fainted, and when I came to 5 myself, he told me what my wife, this very deer, had done to him and to his mother. I said to him, "Son, God has sent us someone who will pay her back for what you and your mother and I have suffered at her hands." Then, O demon, I gave my son in marriage to the shepherd's daughter, who turned my wife into this very deer, saying to me, "To me this is a pretty form, for she will be with us day and night, and it is better to turn her into a pretty deer than to suffer her sinister looks." Thus she stayed with us, while the days and nights followed one another, and the months and years went by. Then one day the shepherd's daughter died, and my son went to the country of this very man with whom you have had your encounter. Some time later I took my wife, this very deer, with me, set out to find out what had happened to my son, and chanced to stop here. This is my story, my strange and amazing story.

The demon assented, saying, "I grant you one-third of this man's life."

Then, O King Shahrayar, the second old man with the two black dogs approached the demon and said, "I too shall tell you what happened to me and to these two dogs, and if I tell it to you and you find it stranger and more amazing than this man's story will you grant me one-third

of this man's life?" The demon replied, "I will." Then the old man began to tell his story, saying . . .

But dawn broke, and morning overtook Shahrazad, and she lapsed into silence. Then Dinarzad said, "This is an amazing story," and Shahrazad replied, "What is this compared with what I shall tell you tomorrow night if the king spares me and lets me live!" The king said to himself, "By God, I will not have her put to death until I find out what happened to the man with the two black dogs. Then I will have her put to death, God the Almighty willing."

∞

The Sixth Night

When the following night arrived and Shahrazad was in bed ₁ *with King Shahrayar, her sister Dinarzad said, "Sister, if you are not sleepy, tell us a little tale. Finish the one you started." Shahrazad replied, "With the greatest pleasure":*

I heard, O happy King, that the second old man with the two dogs said:

The Second Old Man's Tale

Demon, as for my story, these are the details. These two dogs are my brothers. When our father died, he left behind three sons, and left us three thousand dinars, [4] with which each of us opened a shop and became a shopkeeper. Soon my older brother, one of these very dogs, went and sold the contents of his shop for a thousand dinars, bought trading goods, and, having prepared himself for his trading trip, left us. A full year went by, when one day, as I sat in my shop, a beggar stopped by to beg. When I refused him, he tearfully asked, "Don't you recognize me?" and when I looked at him closely, I recognized my brother. I embraced him and took him into the shop, and when I asked him about his plight, he replied, "The money is gone, and the situation is bad." Then I took him to the public bath, clothed him in one of my robes, and took him home with me. Then I examined my books and checked my balance, and found out that I had made a thousand dinars and that my net worth was two thousand dinars. I divided the amount between my brother and myself, and said to him, "Think as if you have never been away." He gladly took the money and opened another shop.

Soon afterward my second brother, this other dog, went and sold his merchandise and collected his money,

intending to go on a trading trip. We tried to dissuade him, but he did not listen. Instead, he bought merchandise and trading goods, joined a group of travelers, and was gone for a full year. Then he came back, just like his older brother. I said to him, "Brother, didn't I advise you not to go?" He replied tearfully, "Brother, it was foreordained. Now I am poor and penniless, without even a shirt on my back." Demon, I took him to the public bath, clothed him in one of my new robes, and took him back to the shop. After we had something to eat, I said to him, "Brother, I shall do my business accounts, calculate my net worth for the year, and after subtracting the capital, whatever the profit happens to be, I shall divide it equally between you and myself. When I examined my books and subtracted the capital, I found out that my profit was two thousand dinars, and I thanked God and felt very happy. Then I divided the money, giving him a thousand dinars and keeping a thousand for myself. With that money he opened another shop, and the three of us stayed together for a while. Then my two brothers asked me to go on a trading journey with them, but I refused, saying, "What did you gain from your ventures that I can gain?"

They dropped the matter, and for six years we ₅ worked in our stores, buying and selling. Yet every year they asked me to go on a trading journey with them, but I refused, until I finally gave in. I said, "Brothers, I am ready to go with you. How much money do you have?" I found out that they had eaten and drunk and squandered everything they had, but I said nothing to them and did not reproach them. Then I took inventory, gathered all I had together, and sold everything. I was pleased to discover that the sale netted six thousand dinars. Then I divided the money into two parts, and said to my brothers, "The sum of three thousand dinars is for you and myself to use on our trading journey. The other three thousand I shall bury in the ground, in case what happened to you happens to me, so that when we return, we will find three thousand dinars to reopen our shops." They replied, "This is an excellent idea." Then, demon, I divided my money and buried three thousand dinars. Of the remaining three I

---

[4] **dinars** Gold coins; the basic form of Muslim money.

gave each of my brothers a thousand and kept a thousand for myself. After I closed my shop, we bought merchandise and trading goods, rented a large seafaring boat, and after loading it with our goods and provisions, sailed day and night, for a month.

But morning overtook Shahrazad, and she lapsed into silence. Then her sister Dinarzad said, "Sister, what a lovely story!" Shahrazad replied, "Tomorrow night I shall tell you something even lovelier, stranger, and more wonderful if I live, the Almighty God willing."

∽

The Seventh Night

The following night Dinarzad said to her sister Shahrazad, "For God's sake, sister, if you are not sleepy, tell us a little tale." The king added, "Let it be the completion of the story of the merchant and the demon." Shahrazad replied, "With the greatest pleasure":

I heard, O happy King, that the second old man said to the demon:

For a month my brothers, these very dogs, and I sailed the salty sea, until we came to a port city. We entered the city and sold our goods, earning ten dinars for every dinar. Then we bought other goods, and when we got to the seashore to embark, I met a girl who was dressed in tatters. She kissed my hands and said, "O my lord, be charitable and do me a favor, and I believe that I shall be able to reward you for it." I replied, "I am willing to do you a favor regardless of any reward." She said, "O my lord, marry me, clothe me, and take me home with you on this boat, as your wife, for I wish to give myself to you. I, in turn, will reward you for your kindness and charity, the Almighty God willing. Don't be misled by my poverty and present condition." When I heard her words, I felt pity for her, and guided by what God the Most High had intended for me, I consented. I clothed her with an expensive dress and married her. Then I took her to the boat, spread the bed for her, and consummated our marriage. We sailed many days and nights, and I, feeling love for her, stayed with her day and night, neglecting my brothers. In the meantime they, these very dogs, grew jealous of me, envied me for my increasing merchandise and wealth, and coveted all our possessions. At last they decided to betray me and, tempted by the Devil, plotted to kill me. One night they waited until I was asleep beside my wife; then they carried the two of us and threw us into the sea.

When we awoke, my wife turned into a she-demon and carried me out of the sea to an island. When it was morning, she said, "Husband, I have rewarded you by saving you from drowning, for I am one of the demons who believe in God. When I saw you by the seashore, I felt love for you and came to you in the guise in which you saw me, and when I expressed my love for you, you accepted me. Now I must kill your brothers." When I heard what she said, I was amazed and I thanked her and said, "As for destroying my brothers, this I do not wish, for I will not behave like them." Then I related to her what had happened to me and them, from beginning to end. When she heard my story, she got very angry at them, and said, "I shall fly to them now, drown their boat, and let them all perish." I entreated her, saying, "For God's sake, don't. The proverb advises 'Be kind to those who hurt you.' No matter what, they are my brothers after all." In this manner, I entreated her and pacified her. Afterward, she took me and flew away with me until she brought me home and put me down on the roof of my house. I climbed down, threw the doors open, and dug up the money I had buried. Then I went out and, greeting the people in the market, reopened my shop. When I came home in the evening, I found these two dogs tied up, and when they saw me, they came to me, wept, and rubbed themselves against me. I started, when I suddenly heard my wife say, "O my lord, these are your brothers." I asked, "Who has done this to them?" She replied, "I sent to my sister and asked her to do it. They will stay in this condition for ten years, after which they may be delivered." Then she told me where to find her and departed. The ten years have passed, and I was with my brothers on my way to her to have the spell lifted, when I met this man, together with this old man with the deer. When I asked him about himself, he told me about his encounter with you, and I resolved not to leave until I found out what would happen between you and him. This is my story. Isn't it amazing?

The demon replied, "By God, it is strange and amazing. I grant you one-third of my claim on him for his crime."

Then the third old man said, "Demon, don't disappoint me. If I told you a story that is stranger and more amazing than the first two would you grant me one-third of your claim on him for his crime?" The demon replied, "I will." Then the old man said, "Demon, listen":

But morning overtook Shahrazad, and she lapsed into silence. Then her sister said, "What an amazing story!" Shahrazad replied, "The rest is even more amazing." The king said to himself, "I will not have her put to death until I hear what happened to the old man and the demon; then I will have her put to death, as is my custom with the others."

The Eighth Night

The following night Dinarzad said to her sister Shahrazad, "For ₁
God's sake, sister, if you are not sleepy, tell us one of your lovely
little tales to while away the night." Shahrazad replied, "With
the greatest pleasure":

I heard, O happy King, that the third old man told the
demon a story that was even stranger and more amazing
than the first two. The demon was very much amazed
and, swaying with delight, said, "I grant you one-third of
my claim on him for his crime." Then the demon released
the merchant and departed. The merchant turned to the
three old men and thanked them, and they congratulated
him on his deliverance and bade him good-bye. Then they
separated, and each of them went on his way. The merchant himself went back home to his family, his wife, and
his children, and he lived with them until the day he died.
But this story is not as strange or as amazing as the story
of the fisherman.

Dinarzad asked, "Please, sister, what is the story of the fisher-
man?"

. . .

RUMI

Selections from the *Masnavi*

Rumi (1207–1273), the Persian poet and Sufi mystic, was one of the most original figures in
medieval Islam. His life and poetry helped define Sufism, the mystical tradition that played a
creative role in Muslim society, by educating the masses, stressing spiritual values rather than
the strict legalism of orthodox religious leaders, and inspiring missionary efforts around the
globe. The greatest Persian poet, Rumi created two major works that had a profound impact on
Muslim mysticism and literature: the *Diwan-e Shams,* lyrical verses, and the *Masnavi-ye Ma'navi*
("Spiritual Couplets"), a compendium of mystical thought. After his death, disciples in Anatolia (modern Turkey) founded a Sufi ascetic order, the Whirling Dervishes (in Persian, the Sufis
were known as *darvish,* "the poor"), who used singing, chanting, and a whirling dance to
achieve union with God. Rumi's *Masnavi* has been widely translated, with many commentaries
written on it; Persian-speaking Sufis consider it second only to the *Qur'an* as a spiritual guide.

   The son of an eminent mystic, writer, and thinker, Rumi readily followed in his father's
footsteps. Born in the Persian Empire, in the city of Balkh (in modern Afghanistan), where he
was called Jalal ad-Din Balkhi, he and the rest of his family fled from invading Mongols in 1218.
After wandering the Middle East, the family settled in Anatolia, known as Rum, meaning
"Roman Anatolia," which then enjoyed peace under a Seljuk Turkish dynasty. There, living in
Konya, the capital, he became known as *Rumi,* that is, "the one from the country of Rum." On
his father's death, in 1231, Rumi replaced him as a prominent teacher in the local religious
schools, or *madrasas.*

   Having become a fixture in the civic life of Konya, Rumi had his quiet existence shattered
by a meeting, in 1244, with the wandering dervish, Shams ad-Din ("Sun of Religion"), formerly
of Tabriz (in modern Iran), an encounter that forever transformed Rumi's life. Instantly finding
Shams's simple faith seductive, Rumi made the dervish his lifelong passion in a Platonic friendship. The two friends grew inseparable, spending days together in mystic conversation.
Through friendship the men deepened their sense of communion with God, but it provoked
turmoil in Rumi's family and among his students, who felt neglected. Seeking to avoid conflict,
Shams abruptly disappeared, fleeing to Damascus, only to be discovered and summoned back
to Konya. After another dramatic meeting, the pair renewed their friendship, with Shams's

moving into Rumi's house and marrying a young girl of the household. This arrangement once again caused murmuring among Rumi's family and students. In 1248, Shams disappeared again, perhaps murdered by one of Rumi's sons—according to rumors of the period.

In response to his lost friend, Rumi composed the *Diwan-e Shams* ("The Poetry of Shams"), which he wrote in an ecstatic state, after listening to music, singing, and whirling about hour after hour. Using the themes of love and loss, Rumi speaks through the voice of Shams, thus symbolizing their union, a model of the Sufi goal of union with God. The operative word here is *fana,* Persian for "annihilation in God." In later years, Rumi developed similar friendships, as part of the Sufi search for mystical union with God.

Rumi's friendship with his student Husam ad-Din Chelebi sparked the poet's last work, the *Masnavi-ye Ma'navi,* a monumental collection of about 26,000 couplets, or poetic units of two successive rhyming lines. Dictated by Rumi as he went about his daily tasks and recorded by Husam, this work teaches the Sufi way, by indirection, using vivid and folksy examples, drawn from stories, anecdotes, proverbs, fables, and folktales.

Reading the Selection

The seven poems are from the *Masnavi,* in a free verse version by an American poet, who manages to capture the liveliness, earthiness, and surprise of the original poems. In several poems, the lover converses with or about the beloved, a symbol of the soul's ongoing love affair with God. Each piece teaches a similar moral lesson, usually involving the annihilation of the self *(fana),* so that the soul may be united with God.

The sources for four of the poems are proverbs: "The Food Sack," "The Grasses," "Zikr (Remembering)," and "The Core of Masculinity." In these poems, many short, pithy expressions embodying folk wisdom are used, as, for example, in "The Food Sack," "A nursing baby does not know the taste of roasted meat," and in "The Grasses," "Never brag of being strong." Two poems are meditations based on conversations, one called "I Have Five Things to Say," in which a lover addresses the beloved, and the other called "A Man and a Woman Arguing." In both, seemingly banal words become vehicles for the poet's thoughts about God. In the last poem, "Put This Design in Your Carpet," the poet interprets "spiritual experience" as a dense tapestry woven from everyday life—in many ways, a summary of Rumi's teachings about ultimate reality.

∞

I Have Five Things to Say

The wakened lover speaks directly to the beloved,   1
"You are the sky my spirit circles in,
the love inside love, the resurrection-place.

Let this window be your ear.
I have lost consciousness many times
with longing for your listening silence,
and your life-quickening smile.

You give attention to the smallest matters,
my suspicious doubts, and to the greatest.

You know my coins are counterfeit,   10
but you accept them anyway,
my impudence and my pretending!

I have five things to say,

five fingers to give
into your grace.

First, when I was apart from you,
    this world did not exist,
    nor any other.

Second, whatever I was looking for
    was always you.   20

Third, why did I ever learn to count to three?

Fourth, my cornfield is burning!

Fifth, this finger stands for Rabia,[1]
    and this is for someone else.

---

[1] **Rabia** (d. 801) An Islamic woman mystic from Basra.

Is there a difference?

Are these words or tears?
Is weeping speech?
What shall I do, my love?"

So he speaks, and everyone around
begins to cry with him, laughing crazily,
moaning in the spreading union
of lover and beloved.

This is the true religion. All others
are thrown-away bandages beside it.

This is the *sema*[2] of slavery and mastery
dancing together. This is not-being.

_____

[2] *sema* The whirling dance of the Sufis.

Neither words, nor any natural fact
can express this.

I know these dancers.
Day and night I sing their songs
in this phenomenal cage.

My soul, don't try to answer now!
Find a friend, and hide.

But what can stay hidden?
Love's secret is always lifting its head
out from under the covers,
"Here I am!"

The Food Sack

One day a sufi sees an empty food sack hanging on a nail.
He begins to turn[3] and tear his shirt, saying,
Food for what needs no food!
A cure for hunger!

His burning grows and others join him,
shouting and moaning in the love-fire.

An idle passerby comments, "It's only an empty sack."

The sufi says, *Leave. You want what we do not want.*
You are not a lover.

A lover's food is the love of bread,
not the bread. No one who really loves,

loves existence.

Lovers have nothing to do with existence.
They collect the interest without the capital.

No wings, yet they fly all over the world. No hands,
but they carry the polo ball from the field.

That dervish got a sniff of reality.
Now he weaves baskets of pure vision.

Lovers pitch tents on a field of nowhere.
They are all one color like that field.

A nursing baby does not know the taste of roasted meat.
To a spirit the foodless scent is food.

To an Egyptian, the Nile looks bloody.
To an Israelite, clear.
What is a highway to one is disaster to the other.

_____

[3] **turn** Whirl, the characteristic dance of the Whirling Dervishes.

The Grasses

The same wind that uproots trees
makes the grasses shine.

The lordly wind loves the weakness
and the lowness of grasses.

Never brag of being strong.

The axe doesn't worry how thick the branches are.
It cuts them to pieces. But not the leaves.
It leaves the leaves alone.

A flame doesn't consider the size of the woodpile.
A butcher doesn't run from a flock of sheep.   10

What is form in the presence of reality?
Very feeble. Reality keeps the sky turned over
like a cup above us, revolving. Who turns
the sky wheel? The universal intelligence.

And the motion of the body comes
from the spirit like a waterwheel
that's held in a stream.

The inhaling-exhaling is from spirit,
now angry, now peaceful.

Wind destroys, and wind protects.   20

There is no reality but God,

says the completely surrendered sheikh,[4]
who is an ocean for all beings.

The levels of creation are straws in that ocean.
The movement of the straws comes from an agitation
in the water. When the ocean wants the straws calm,
it sends them close to shore. When it wants them
back in the deep surge, it does with them
as the wind does with the grasses.
                              This never ends.[5]   30

————————
[4] **sheikh** In Sufism, a religious leader held in deep respect.
[5] **This never ends.** A metaphor, like the whirling dance of the Sufis, for the universal motion in Nature and the cosmos. Only God doesn't move.

∞

A Man and a Woman Arguing

One night in the desert   1
a poor Bedouin woman has this to say
to her husband,
                    "Everyone is happy
and prosperous, except us! We have no bread.
We have no spices. We have no water jug.
We barely have any clothes. No blankets

for the night. We fantasize that the full moon
is a cake. We reach for it! We're an embarrassment
even to the beggars. Everyone avoids us.   10

Arab men are supposed to be generous warriors,
but look at you, stumbling around! If some guest
were to come to us, we'd steal his rags
when he fell asleep. Who is your guide
that leads you to this? We can't even get
a handful of lentils! Ten years' worth
of nothing, that's what we are!"
                              She went on and on.
"If God is abundant, we must be following
an imposter. Who's leading us? Some fake,   20
that always says, *Tomorrow, illumination
will bring you treasure, tomorrow.*

As everyone knows, that never comes.
Though I guess, it happens very rarely, sometimes,
that a disciple following an imposter can somehow
surpass the pretender. But still I want to know
what this deprivation says about us."

The husband replied, finally,
                    "How long will you complain
about money and our prospects for money? The torrent   30

of our life has mostly gone by. Don't worry about
transient things. Think how the animals live.

The dove on the branch giving thanks.
The glorious singing of the nightingale.
The gnat. The elephant. Every living thing
trusts in God for its nourishment.

These pains that you feel are messengers.
Listen to them. Turn them to sweetness. The night
is almost over. You were young once, and content.
Now you think about money all the time.   40

You used to *be* that money. You were a healthy vine.
Now you're a rotten fruit. You ought to be growing
sweeter and sweeter, but you've gone bad.
As my wife, you should be equal to me.
Like a pair of boots, if one is too tight,
the pair is of no use.

Like two folding doors, we can't be mismatched.
A lion does not mate with a wolf."

So this man who was happily poor
scolded his wife until daybreak,   50
when she responded,
                    "Don't talk to me
about your high station! Look how you act!
Spiritual arrogance is the ugliest of all things.
It's like a day that's cold and snowy,
and your clothes are wet too!

It's too much to bear!
And don't call me your mate, you fraud!

You scramble after scraps of bone
with the dogs.

You're not as satisfied as you pretend!
You're the snake and the snake charmer
at the same time, but you don't know it.
You're charming a snake for money,
and the snake is charming you.

You talk about God a lot, and you make me feel guilty
by using that word. You better watch out!
That word will poison you, if you use it
to have power over me."

So the rough volume of her talking   70
fell on the husband, and he fought back,
                                        "Woman,
this poverty is my deepest joy.
This bare way of life is honest and beautiful.
We can hide nothing when we're like this.
You say I'm really arrogant and greedy,

and you say I'm a snake charmer and a snake,   60
but those nicknames are for you.

In your anger and your wantings
you see those qualities in me.   80
I want nothing from this world.

You're like a child that has turned round and round,
and now you think the house is turning.

It's your eyes that see wrong. Be patient,
and you'll see the blessings and the lord's light
in how we live."
                        This argument continued[6]
throughout the day, and even longer.

_____

[6] **This argument continued** A metaphor, like the whirling dance of
the Sufis, for the universal motion in Nature and the cosmos. Only
God doesn't move.

∽

Zikr[7]

A naked man jumps in the river, hornets swarming
above him. The water is the *zikr*, remembering,
There is no reality but God. There is only God.

The hornets are his sexual remembering, this woman,
that woman. Or if a woman, this man, that.
The head comes up. They sting.

Breathe water. Become river head to foot.
Hornets leave you alone then. Even if you're far
from the river, they pay no attention.

No one looks for stars when the sun's out.   10
A person blended into God does not disappear.
   He, or she,
is just completely soaked in God's qualities.
Do you need a quote from the *Qur'an*?

All shall be brought into our Presence.

_____

[7] **Zikr** Persian, "remembering."

Join those travelers. The lamps we burn go out,   1
some quickly. Some last till daybreak.
Some are dim, some intense, all fed with fuel.

If a light goes out in one house, that doesn't affect
the next house. This is the story of the animal soul,
not the divine soul. The sun shines on every house.
When it goes down, all houses get dark.   20

Light is the image of your teacher. Your enemies
love the dark. A spider weaves a web over a light,
out of himself, or herself, makes a veil.

Don't try to control a wild horse by grabbing its leg.
Take hold the neck. Use a bridle. Be sensible.
Then ride! There is a need for self-denial.

Don't be contemptuous of old obediences. They help.

The Core of Masculinity

The core of masculinity   1
does not derive from being male,
nor friendliness from those who console.

Your old grandmother says, "Maybe you shouldn't
go to school. You look a little pale."

Run when you hear that.
A father's stern slaps are better.

Your bodily soul wants comforting.
The severe father wants spiritual clarity.

He scolds but eventually   10
leads you into the open.

Pray for a tough instructor
to hear and act and stay within you.

We have been busy accumulating solace.
Make us afraid of how we were.

Put This Design in Your Carpet

Spiritual experience is a modest woman   1
who looks lovingly at only one man.

It's a great river where ducks
live happily, and crows drown.

The visible bowl of form contains food
that is both nourishing and a source of heartburn.

There is an unseen presence we honor
that gives the gifts.

You're water. We're the millstone.
You're wind. We're dust blown up into shapes.   10
You're spirit. We're the opening and closing
of our hands. You're the clarity.
We're this language that tries to say it.
You're joy. We're all the different kinds of laughing.

Any movement or sound is a profession of faith,
as the millstone grinding is explaining how it believes

in the river! No metaphor can say this,
but I can't stop pointing
to the beauty.

Every moment and place says,   20
"Put this design in your carpet!"

Like the shepherd . . .
who wanted to pick the lice off God's robe,
and stitch up God's shoes, I want to be
in such a passionate adoration
that my tent gets pitched against the sky!

Let the beloved come
and sit like a guard dog
in front of the tent.

When the ocean surges,   30
don't let me just hear it.
Let it splash inside my chest!

9

THE HIGH MIDDLE AGES
The Christian Centuries

Selections from *Song of Roland*

The anonymous poem *Song of Roland* belongs to the literary genre known as *chanson de geste* (from French, "song of deeds"), which dominated medieval literature in the first half of the twelfth century. Based on historical events, it tells of Count Roland, a vassal and knight of Charlemagne, the King of the Franks who ruled the then largest and most centralized state since the fall of Rome. According to medieval records, Roland governed the Breton march (modern Brittany) in the name of Charlemagne and died fighting in Spain in 778. Einhard (see *The Life of Charlemagne*) names Roland as a leader of Charlemagne's rear guard, who was killed by Christian Basques in an ambush in northern Spain while protecting the king and his forward army.

Only a distant echo of these actual events survives in the *Song of Roland,* which glorifies the knight and his sacrificial death. The poem was written down in about 1100, having circulated orally in songs performed by bards (singing poets) for several centuries. By the time it received its final form, what had been a minor skirmish had been transformed by poetic art into a battle of vast proportions. Why Roland, who was only one of the many "brave knights" sung about in the Middle Ages, should have become the focus of so much attention is a mystery. Whatever the cause, he became the central figure in a rousing tale of bravery, treachery, and pride.

The world described in the *Song of Roland* reflects more the time it was finally set in writing (the twelfth century) than the period when Roland lived (the eighth century). Medieval Europe had launched the Crusades (the first began in 1095) against the Muslim world; hence, in the poem, Charlemagne's enemies are changed from Christian Basques to Spanish Saracens (Muslims). France was also in the early stages of becoming a unified state; thus, in the poem, the farflung Frankish kingdom is transformed into France—a sign of embryonic nationalism that French kings wanted to nurture. Finally, the twelfth-century church was more powerful than in Charlemagne's day, and in the poem, this increased power is expressed in the pivotal role played by the warrior Archbishop Turpin.

The *Song of Roland* is typical of *chansons de geste* in that it celebrates a defeat. In an elaborately complicated story set at Charlemagne's court, Roland instigates a possibly deadly mission for his rival, Ganelon. But he suddenly finds the tables turned and himself a victim when Ganelon plots an ambush with the Spanish Saracens. Ultimately, Roland falls prey to his own pride, losing his own life and the lives of the rest of Charlemagne's rear guard.

Reading the Selection

These thirteen verses *(laisses)*, 79–87 and 129–132, depict the doomed Franks as they fall into the trap laid by the Saracens. The turning point of the poem, these verses also set forth the work's theme and moral. Roland, in verse 79, gives voice to the anonymous author's chivalric and self-consciously literary theme:

> *We know our duty: to stand here for our King . . .*
> *let them not sing a bad song about us!*

The work's moral message emerges in the angry verbal exchanges between Roland and his companion Oliver. Ignoring Oliver's well-considered advice, Roland three times refuses to sound the oliphant (a horn), which would bring Charlemagne to the rescue of his fellow Franks. When Roland does blow the horn, it is too late; the outnumbered Franks are soon overwhelmed (not included here). Faced with certain death, the cautious Oliver offers this lesson to Roland (and to readers):

> *I will tell you what makes a vassal good:*
> *it is judgment, it is never madness.*

∽

79.

They arm themselves in Saracen hauberks,[1]
all but a few are lined with triple mail;
they lace on their good helms[2] of Saragossa,
gird on their swords, the steel forged in Vienne;
they have rich shields, spears of Valencia,
and gonfanons[3] of white and blue and red.
They leave the mules and riding horses now,
mount their war horses and ride in close array.
The day was fair, the sun was shining bright,
all their armor was aflame with the light;   10
a thousand trumpets blow: that was to make it finer.
That made a great noise, and the men of France heard.
Said Oliver: "Companion, I believe
we may yet have a battle with the pagans."
Roland replies: "Now may God grant us that.
We know our duty: to stand here for our King.
A man must bear some hardships for his lord,
stand everything, the great heat, the great cold,
lose the hide and hair on him for his good lord.
Now let each man make sure to strike hard here: 20
let them not sing a bad song about us!
Pagans are wrong and Christians are right!

---

[1] **hauberks** Coats of mail or tunics of chained mail to cover the body.
[2] **helms** Helmets.
[3] **gonfanons** Standards or battle flags, often decorated with pendants or small flags.

They'll make no bad example of me this day!"

80.

Oliver climbs to the top of a hill,
looks to his right, across a grassy vale,
sees the pagan army on its way there;
and called down to Roland, his companion:
"That way, toward Spain: the uproar I see coming!
All their hauberks, all blazing, helmets like flames!
It will be a bitter thing for our French.
Ganelon knew, that criminal, that traitor,   30
when he marked us out before the Emperor."
"Be still, Oliver," Roland the Count replies.
"He is my stepfather—my stepfather.
I won't have you speak one word against him."

81.

Oliver has gone up upon a hill,
sees clearly now: the kingdom of Spain,
and the Saracens assembled in such numbers:
helmets blazing, bedecked with gems in gold,
those shields of theirs, those hauberks sewn with brass,   40
and all their spears, the gonfanons affixed;
cannot begin to count their battle corps,
thre are too many, he cannot take their number.

And he is deeply troubled by what he sees.
He made his way quickly down from the hill,
came to the French, told them all he had seen.

82.

Said Oliver: "I saw the Saracens,
no man on earth ever saw more of them—
one hundred thousand, with their shields, up in front,
helmets laced on, hauberks blazing on them,   50
the shafts straight up, the iron heads[4] like flames—
you'll get a battle, nothing like it before.
My lords, my French, may God give you the strength.
Hold your ground now! Let them not defeat us!"
And the French say: "God hate the man who runs!
We may die here, but no man will fail you."

83.

Said Oliver: "The pagan force is great;
from what I see, our French here are too few.
Roland, my companion, sound your horn then,
Charles will hear it, the army will come back."   60
Roland replies: "I'd be a fool to do it.
I would lose my good name all through sweet France.
I will strike now, I'll strike with Durendal,[5]
the blade will be bloody to the gold from striking!
These pagan traitors came to these passes doomed!
I promise you, they are marked men, they'll die."

84.

"Roland, Companion, now sound the olifant,[6]
Charles will hear it, he will bring the army back,
the King will come with all his barons to help us."
Roland replies: "May it never please God   70
that my kin should be shamed because of me,
or that sweet France should fall into disgrace.
Never! Never! I'll strike with Durendal,
I'll strike with this good sword strapped to my side,
you'll see this blade running its whole length with blood.
These pagan traitors have gathered here to die.
I promise you, they are all bound for death."

85.

"Roland, Companion, sound your olifant now,
Charles will hear it, marching through those passes.
I promise you, the Franks will come at once."   80
Roland replies: "May it never please God
that any man alive should come to say

---

[4] **iron heads** Wooden shafts with iron spikes or heads on them.
[5] **Durendal** Roland's sword.
[6] **olifant** Roland's ivory horn.

that pagans—pagans!—once made me sound this horn:
no kin of mine will ever bear that shame.
Once I enter this great battle coming
and strike my thousand seven hundred blows,
you'll see the bloody steel of Durendal.
These French are good—they will strike like brave men.
Nothing can save the men of Spain from death."

86.

Said Oliver: "I see no blame in it—   90
I watched the Saracens coming from Spain,
the valleys and mountains covered with them,
every hillside and every plain all covered,
hosts and hosts everywhere of those strange men—
and here we have a little company."
Roland replies: "That whets my appetite.
May it not please God and his angels and saints
to let France lose its glory because of me—
let me not end in shame, let me die first.
The Emperor loves us when we fight well."   100

87.

Roland is good, and Oliver is wise,
both these vassals men of amazing courage:
once they are armed and mounted on their horses,
they will not run, though they die for it, from battle.
Good men, these Counts, and their words full of spirit.
Traitor pagans are riding up in fury.
Said Oliver: "Roland, look—the first one,
on top of us—and Charles is far away.
You did not think it right to sound your olifant:
if the King were here, we'd come out without losses.   110
Now look up there, toward the passes of Aspre—
you can see the rear-guard: it will suffer.
No man in that detail will be in another."
Roland replies: "Don't speak such foolishness—
shame on the heart gone coward in the chest.
We'll hold our ground, we'll stand firm—we're the ones!
We'll fight with spears, we'll fight them hand to hand!"

.   .   .

129.

And Roland said: "I'll sound the olifant,
Charles will hear it, drawing through the passes,
I promise you, the Franks will return at once."   120
Said Oliver: "That would be a great disgrace,
a dishonor and reproach to all your kin,
the shame of it would last them all their lives.
When I urged it, you would not hear of it;
you will not do it now with my consent.
It is not acting bravely to sound it now—
look at your arms, they are covered with blood."
The Count replies: "I've fought here like a lord."

130.

And Roland says: "We are in a rough battle.
I'll sound the olifant, Charles will hear it."
Said Oliver: "No good vassal would do it.
When I urged it, friend, you did not think it right.
If Charles were here, we'd come out with no losses.
Those men down there—no blame can fall on them."
Oliver said: "Now by this beard of mine,
If I can see my noble sister, Aude,
once more, you will never lie in her arms!"

131.

And Roland said: "Why are you angry at me?"
Oliver answers: "Companion, it is your doing.
I will tell you what makes a vassal good: 140
    it is judgment, it is never madness;
restraint is worth more than the raw nerve of a fool.
Frenchmen are dead because of your wildness.
And what service will Charles ever have from us?
If you had trusted me, my lord would be here,
we would have fought this battle through to the end,
Marsilion would be dead, or our prisoner.
Roland, your prowess—had we never seen it!
    And now, dear friend, we've seen the last of it.
No more aid from us now for Charlemagne,   150

a man without equal till Judgment Day,
you will die here, and your death will shame France.
We kept faith, you and I, we were companions;   130
    and everything we were will end today.
We part before evening, and it will be hard."

132.

Turpin the Archbishop hears their bitter words,
digs hard into his horse with golden spurs
and rides to them; begins to set them right:
"You, Lord Roland, and you, Lord Oliver,
I beg you in God's name do not quarrel.   160
To sound the horn could not help us now, true,
but still it is far better that you do it:
let the King come, he can avenge us then—
these men of Spain must not go home exulting!
Our French will come, they'll get down on their feet,
and find us here—we'll be dead, cut to pieces.
They will lift us into coffins on the backs of mules,
and weep for us, in rage and pain and grief,
and bury us in the courts of churches;
and we will not be eaten by wolves or pigs or dogs."   170
Roland replies, "Lord, you have spoken well."

. . .

CHRÈTIEN DE TROYES

Selection from *Arthurian Romances*

Lancelot belongs to the legendary world of King Arthur and his knights, which gripped the imagination of writers and public alike in the twelfth and thirteenth centuries. Chrètien de Troyes's *Lancelot, or the Knight of the Cart,* was one of the works that put the Arthurian tradition on the map. This tradition has lived on in the popular consciousness for centuries, as evidenced by modern films and fiction on Arthurian themes.

The Arthurian legends sprang from the history of the Celts, ancient peoples (Gauls and Britons) who dominated western and central Europe until Germanic invaders pushed them to the continent's fringes of Ireland, Scotland, Wales, and Brittany. The historic Arthur ruled probably in sixth-century Wales, where his wars against both Romans and Germans made him a figure larger than life. Over the next six hundred years, the historic Arthur gave way to the Arthur of legend; in 1125 a writer could comment on the "idle fictions" and "wild tales" then circulating about the Welsh king. Little remains of these works, which were recited by wandering storytellers; but they form the background for Chrètien's writing.

Chrètien places the spotlight not on Arthur but on the court and the knights. The Arthurian court is depicted as the epitome of civilization. To be received there is joy; banishment is misery. The stories of the knights express the ideals of courtly love, the code that made duty to women a higher good than personal honor.

Chrètien de Troyes (fl. 1170) composed works for the feudal courts of northern France. Chrètien credits one patron, Countess Marie of Champagne, as inspiring *Lancelot.* Written in

French, these poems are long narratives of fantastic adventures of knights and ladies. They are the first romances, the genre that replaced the *chansons de geste* (see the *Song of Roland*) in popularity after 1150. The romances, with their ideal of love as an ennobling passion, helped raise women's status, especially among the feudal elite.

Reading the Selection

The plot of *Lancelot* is typical of Chrètien's romances. It is organized around a quest—Lancelot's search for Guinevere, Arthur's queen, who is abducted by the evil Meleagant, Prince of Gorre. The plot is complicated by Lancelot's initial and almost unforgivable sin: He hesitates for two steps to mount into the shameful cart. Lancelot's "sin" against the courtly code is that he chose even for an instant personal honor before love.

To redeem himself, Lancelot goes through a series of tests meant to teach him to serve women unhesitatingly. This selection includes four of these episodes. In the first, he shows ignorance when he disobeys a damsel and is wounded for his pride. Next, when a subdued Lancelot says to a second damsel that "without hesitation he will promise her anything she desires," he is soon rewarded. Meeting a third damsel, he instantly obeys her though it means going back on his word. In the last episode, confronted by still another damsel, he has not yet learned his lesson: "The knight hesitated at the door, and thought: 'God, what can I do?'"

Only in the poem's climax (not included here) does Lancelot reach the courtly ideal: He obeys the queen's every whim, even shaming himself in public. The final meaning of the two lovers' passion is hotly debated today. Was it meant to glorify adultery, or was it a traitorous love to be condemned by a courtly audience?

∽

Lancelot

· · ·

Late in the afternoon they arrive at a town, which, you must know, was very rich and beautiful. All three entered through the gate; the people are greatly amazed to see the knight borne upon the cart, and they take no pains to conceal their feelings, but small and great and old and young shout taunts at him in the streets, so that the knight hears many vile and scornful words at his expense. They all inquire: "To what punishment is this knight to be consigned? Is he to be flayed, or hanged, or drowned, or burned upon a fire of thorns? Tell us, thou dwarf, who art driving him, in what crime was he caught? Is he convicted of robbery? Is he a murderer, or a criminal?" And to all this the dwarf made no response, vouchsafing to them no reply. He conducts the knight to a lodging-place; and Gawain[1] follows the dwarf closely to a tower, which stood on the same level over against the town. Beyond there stretched a meadow, and the tower was built close by, upon a lofty eminence of rock, whose face formed a sharp precipice. Following the horse and cart, Gawain entered the tower. In the hall they met a damsel elegantly attired, than whom there was none fairer in the land, and with her they saw coming two fair and charming maidens. As soon

as they saw my lord Gawain, they received him joyously and saluted him, and then asked news about the other knight: "Dwarf, of what crime is this knight guilty, whom thou dost drive like a lame man?" He would not answer her question, but he made the knight get out of the cart, and then he withdrew, without their knowing whither he went. Then my lord Gawain dismounts, and valets come forward to relieve the two knights of their armour. The damsel ordered two green mantles to be brought, which they put on. When the hour for supper came, a sumptuous repast was set. The damsel sat at table beside my lord Gawain. They would not have changed their lodging-place to seek any other, for all that evening the damsel showed them great honour, and provided them with fair and pleasant company.

Vv. 463–538—When they had sat up long enough, two long, high beds were prepared in the middle of the hall; and there was another bed alongside, fairer and more splendid than the rest; for, as the story testifies, it possessed all the excellence that one could think of in a bed. When the time came to retire, the damsel took both the guests to whom she had offered her hospitality; she shows them the two fine, long, wide beds, and says: "These two beds are set up here for the accommodation of your bodies; but in that one yonder no one ever lay who did not

---

[1] **Gawain** A knight in the service of King Arthur.

merit it: it was not set up to be used by you." The knight who came riding on the cart replies at once: "Tell me," he says, "for what cause this bed is inaccessible." Being thoroughly informed of this, she answers unhesitatingly: "It is not your place to ask or make such an inquiry. Any knight is disgraced in the land after being in a cart, and it is not fitting that he should concern himself with the matter upon which you have questioned me; and most of all it is not right that he should lie upon the bed, for he would soon pay dearly for his act. So rich a couch has not been prepared for you, and you would pay dearly for ever harbouring such a thought." He replies: "You will see about that presently." . . . "Am I to see it?" . . . "Yes." . . . "It will soon appear." . . . "By my head," the knight replies, "I know not who is to pay the penalty. But whoever may object or disapprove, I intend to lie upon this bed and repose there at my ease." Then he at once disrobed in the bed, which was long and raised half an ell above the other two, and was covered with a yellow cloth of silk and a coverlet with gilded stars. The furs were not of skinned vair but of sable; the covering he had on him would have been fitting for a king. The mattress was not made of straw or rushes or of old mats. At midnight there descended from the rafters suddenly a lance, as with the intention of pinning the knight through the flanks to the coverlet and the white sheets where he lay. To the lance there was attached a pennon all ablaze. The coverlet, the bedclothes, and the bed itself all caught fire at once. And the tip of the lance passed so close to the knight's side that it cut the skin a little, without seriously wounding him. Then the knight got up, put out the fire and, taking the lance, swung it in the middle of the hall, all this without leaving his bed; rather did he lie down again and slept as securely as at first.

Vv. 539–982.—In the morning, at daybreak, the damsel of the tower had Mass celebrated on their account, and had them rise and dress. When Mass had been celebrated for them, the knight who had ridden in the cart sat down pensively at a window, which looked out upon the meadow, and he gazed upon the fields below. The damsel came to another window close by, and there my lord Gawain conversed with her privately for a while about something, I know not what. I do not know what words were uttered, but while they were leaning on the window-sill they saw carried along the river through the fields a bier, upon which there lay a knight, and alongside three damsels walked, mourning bitterly. Behind the bier they saw a crowd approaching, with a tall knight in front, leading a fair lady by the horse's rein. The knight at the window knew that it was the Queen. He continued to gaze at her attentively and with delight as long as she was visible. And when he could no longer see her, he was minded to throw himself out and break his body down below. And he would have let himself fall out had not my lord Gawain seen him, and drawn him back, saying: "I beg you, sire, be quiet now. For God's sake, never think again of committing such a mad deed. It is wrong for you to despise your life." "He is perfectly right," the damsel says; "for will not the news of his disgrace be known everywhere? Since he has been upon the cart, he has good reason to wish to die, for he would be better dead than alive. His life henceforth

is sure to be one of shame, vexation, and unhappiness." Then the knights asked for their armour, and armed themselves, the damsel treating them courteously, with distinction and generosity; for when she had joked with the knight and ridiculed him enough, she presented him with a horse and lance as a token of her goodwill. The knights then courteously and politely took leave of the damsel, first saluting her, and then going off in the direction taken by the crowd they had seen. Thus they rode out from the town without addressing them. They proceeded quickly in the direction they had seen taken by the Queen, but they did not overtake the procession, which had advanced rapidly. After leaving the fields, the knights enter an enclosed place, and find a beaten road. They advanced through the woods until it might be six o'clock, and then at a crossroads they met a damsel, whom they both saluted, each asking and requesting her to tell them, if she knows, whither the Queen has been taken. Replying intelligently, she said to them: "If you would pledge me your word, I could set you on the right road and path, and I would tell you the name of the country and of the knight who is conducting her; but whoever would essay to enter that country must endure sore trials, for before he could reach there he must suffer much." Then my lord Gawain replies: "Damsel, so help me God, I promise to place all my strength at your disposal and service, whenever you please, if you will tell me now the truth." And he who had been on the cart did not say that he would pledge her all his strength; but he proclaims, like one whom love makes rich, powerful and bold for any enterprise, that at once and without hesitation he will promise her anything she desires, and he puts himself altogether at her disposal. "Then I will tell you the truth," says she. Then the damsel relates to them the following story: "In truth, my lords, Meleagant, a tall and powerful knight, son of the King of Gorre, has taken her off into the kingdom whence no foreigner returns, but where he must perforce remain in servitude and banishment." Then they ask her: "Damsel, where is this country? Where can we find the way thither?" She replies: "That you shall quickly learn; but you may be sure that you will meet with many obstacles and difficult passages, for it is not easy to enter there except with the permission of the king, whose name is Bademagu; however, it is possible to enter by two very perilous paths and by two very difficult passage-ways. One is called 'the water-bridge,' because the bridge is under water, and there is the same amount of water beneath it as above it, so that the bridge is exactly in the middle; and it is only a foot and a half in width and in thickness. This choice is certainly to be avoided, and yet it is the less dangerous of the two. In addition there are a number of other obstacles of which I will say nothing. The other bridge is still more impracticable and much more perilous, never having been crossed by man. It is just like a sharp sword, and therefore all the people call it 'the sword-bridge.' Now I have told you all the truth I know." But they ask of her once again: "Damsel, deign to show us these two passages." To which the damsel makes reply: "This road here is the most direct to the water-bridge, and that one yonder leads straight to the sword-bridge." Then the knight, who had been on the cart, says: "Sire, I am ready to share with you without prejudice: take one of these two routes, and leave the other one to me; take whichever you prefer." "In truth," my lord Gawain replies, "both of them are hard and dangerous: I am not skilled in making such a choice, and hardly know which of them to take; but it is not right for me to hesitate when you have left the choice to me: I will choose the water-bridge." The other answers: "Then I must go uncomplainingly to the sword-bridge, which I agree to do." Thereupon, they all three part, each one commending the others very courteously to God. And when she sees them departing, she says: "Each one of you owes me a favour of my choosing, whenever I may choose to ask it. Take care not to forget that." "We shall surely not forget it, sweet friend," both the knights call out. Then each one goes his own way, and he of the cart is occupied with deep reflections, like one who has no strength or defence against love which holds him in its sway. His thoughts are such that he totally forgets himself, and he knows not whether he is alive or dead, forgetting even his own name, not knowing whether he is armed or not, or whither he is going or whence he came. Only one creature he has in mind, and for her his thought is so occupied that he neither sees nor hears aught else. And his horse bears him along rapidly, following no crooked road, but the best and the most direct; and thus proceeding unguided, he brings him into an open plain. In this plain there was a ford, on the other side of which a knight stood armed, who guarded it, and in his company there was a damsel who had come on a palfrey.[2] By this time the afternoon was well advanced, and yet the knight, unchanged and unwearied, pursued his thoughts. The horse, being very thirsty, sees clearly the ford, and as soon as he sees it, hastens toward it. Then he on the other side cries out: "Knight, I am guarding the ford, and forbid you to cross." He neither gives him heed, nor hears his words, being still deep in thought. In the meantime, his horse advanced rapidly toward the water. The knight calls out to him that he will do wisely to keep at a distance from the ford, for there is no passage that way; and he swears by the heart within his breast that he will smite him if he enters the water. But his threats are not heard, and he calls out to him a third time: "Knight, do not enter the ford against my will and prohibition; for, by my head, I shall strike you as soon as I see you in the ford." But he is so deep in thought that he does not hear him. And the horse, quickly leaving the bank, leaps into the ford and greedily begins to drink. And the knight says he shall pay for this, that his shield and the hauberk he wears upon his back shall afford him no protection. First, he puts his horse at a gallop, and from a gallop he urges him to a run, and he strikes the knight so hard that he knocks him down flat in the ford which he had forbidden him to cross. His lance flew from his hand and the shield from his neck. When he feels the water, he shivers, and though stunned, he jumps to his feet, like one aroused from sleep, listening and looking about him with astonishment, to see who it can be who has struck him. Then face to face with the

other knight, he said: "Vassal, tell me why you have struck me, when I was not aware of your presence, and when I had done you no harm." "Upon my word, you had wronged me," the other says; "did you not treat me disdainfully when I forbade you three times to cross the ford, shouting at you as loudly as I could? You surely heard me challenge you at least two or three times, and you entered in spite of me, though I told you I should strike you as soon as I saw you in the ford." Then the knight replies to him: "Whoever heard you or saw you, let him be damned, so far as I am concerned. I was probably deep in thought when you forbade me to cross the ford. But be assured that I would make you regret it, if I could just lay one of my hands on your bridle." And the other replies: "Why, what of that? If you dare, you may seize my bridle here and now. I do not esteem your proud threats so much as a handful of ashes." And he replies: "That suits me perfectly. However the affair may turn out, I should like to lay my hands on you." Then the other knight advances to the middle of the ford, where the other lays his left hand upon his bridle, and his right hand upon his leg, pulling, dragging and pressing him so roughly that he remonstrates, thinking that he would pull his leg out of his body. Then he begs him to let go, saying: "Knight, if it please thee to fight me on even terms, take thy shield and horse and lance, and joust with me." He answers: "That will I not do, upon my word; for I suppose thou wouldst run away as soon as thou hadst escaped my grip." Hearing this, he was much ashamed, and said: "Knight, mount thy horse, in confidence for I will pledge thee loyally my word that I shall not flinch or run away." Then once again he answers him: "First, thou wilt have to swear to that, and I insist upon receiving thy oath that thou wilt neither run away nor flinch, nor touch me, nor come near me until thou shalt see me on my horse; I shall be treating thee very generously, if, when thou art in my hands, I let thee go." He can do nothing but give his oath; and when the other hears him swear, he gathers up his shield and lance which were floating in the ford and by this time had drifted well down-stream; then he returns and takes his horse. After catching and mounting him, he seizes the shield by the shoulder-straps and lays his lance in rest. Then each spurs toward the other as fast as their horses can carry them. And he who had to defend the ford first attacks the other, striking him so hard that his lance is completely splintered. The other strikes him in return so that he throws him prostrate into the ford, and the water closes over him. Having accomplished that, he draws back and dismounts, thinking he could drive and chase away a hundred such. While he draws from the scabbard his sword of steel, the other jumps up and draws his excellent flashing blade. Then they clash again, advancing and covering themselves with the shields which gleam with gold. Ceaselessly and without repose they wield their swords; they have the courage to deal so many blows that the battle finally is so protracted that the Knight of the Cart is greatly ashamed in his heart, thinking that he is making a sorry start in the way he has undertaken, when he has spent so much time in defeating a single knight. If he had met yesterday a hundred such, he does not think or

---

[2] **palfrey** A small saddle horse suited for a woman to ride.

believe that they could have withstood him; so now he is much grieved and wroth to be in such an exhausted state that he is missing his strokes and losing time. Then he runs at him and presses him so hard that the other knight gives way and flees. However reluctant he may be, he leaves the ford and crossing free. But the other follows him in pursuit until he falls forward upon his hands; then he of the cart runs up to him, swearing by all he sees that he shall rue the day when he upset him in the ford and disturbed his revery. The damsel, whom the knight had with him, upon hearing the threats, is in great fear, and begs him for her sake to forbear from killing him; but he tells her that he must do so, and can show him no mercy for her sake, in view of the shameful wrong that he has done him. Then, with sword drawn, he approaches the knight who cries in sore dismay: "For God's sake and for my own, show me the mercy I ask of you." And he replies: "As God may save me, no one ever sinned so against me that I would not show him mercy once, for God's sake as is right, if he asked it of me in God's name. And so on thee I will have mercy; for I ought not to refuse thee when thou hast besought me. But first, thou shalt give me thy word to constitute thyself my prisoner whenever I may wish to summon thee." Though it was hard to do so, he promised him. At once the damsel said: "O knight, since thou hast granted the mercy he asked of thee, if ever thou hast broken any bonds, for my sake now be merciful and release this prisoner from his parole. Set him free at my request, upon condition that when the time comes, I shall do my utmost to repay thee in any way that thou shalt choose." Then he declares himself satisfied with the promise she has made, and sets the knight at liberty. Then she is ashamed and anxious, thinking that he will recognise her, which she did not wish. But he goes away at once, the knight and the damsel commending him to God, and taking leave of him. He grants them leave to go, while he himself pursues his way, until late in the afternoon he met a damsel coming, who was very fair and charming, well attired and richly dressed. The damsel greets him prudently and courteously, and he replies: "Damsel, God grant you health and happiness." Then the damsel said to him: "Sire, my house is prepared for you, if you will accept my hospitality; but you shall find shelter there only on condition that you will lie with me; upon these terms I propose and make the offer." Not a few there are who would have thanked her five hundred times for such a gift; but he is much displeased, and made a very different answer: "Damsel, I thank you for the offer of your house, and esteem it highly; but, if you please, I should be very sorry to lie with you." "By my eyes," the damsel says, "then I retract my offer." And he, since it is unavoidable, lets her have her way, though his heart grieves to give consent. He feels only reluctance now; but greater distress will be his when it is time to go to bed. The damsel, too, who leads him away, will pass through sorrow and heaviness. For it is possible that she will love him so that she will not wish to part with him. As soon as he had granted her wish and desire, she escorts him to a fortified place, than which there was none fairer in Thessaly; for it was entirely enclosed by a high wall and a deep moat, and

there was no man within except him whom she brought with her.

Vv. 983–1042.—Here she had constructed for her residence a quantity of handsome rooms, and a large and roomy hall. Riding along a river bank, they approached their lodging-place, and a drawbridge was lowered to allow them to pass. Crossing the bridge, they entered in, and found the hall open with its roof of tiles. Through the open door they pass, and see a table laid with a broad white cloth, upon which the dishes were set, and the candles burning in their stands, and the gilded silver drinking-cups, and two pots of wine, one red and one white. Standing beside the table, at the end of a bench, they found two basins of warm water in which to wash their hands, with a richly embroidered towel, all white and clean, with which to dry their hands. No valets, servants, or squires were to be found or seen. The knight, removing his shield from about his neck, hangs it upon a hook, and, taking his lance, lays it above upon a rack. Then he dismounts from his horse, as does the damsel from hers. The knight, for his part, was pleased that she did not care to wait for him to help her to dismount. Having dismounted, she runs directly to a room and brings him a short mantle of scarlet cloth which she puts on him. The hall was by no means dark; for beside the light from the stars, there were many large twisted candles lighted there, so that the illumination was very bright. When she had thrown the mantle about his shoulders, she said to him: "Friend, here is the water and the towel; there is no one to present or offer it to you except me whom you see. Wash your hands, and then sit down, when you feel like doing so. The hour and the meal, as you can see, demand that you should do so." He washes, and then gladly and readily takes his seat, and she sits down beside him, and they eat and drink together, until the time comes to leave the table.

Vv. 1043–1206.—When they had risen from the table, the damsel said to the knight: "Sire, if you do not object, go outside and amuse yourself; but, if you please, do not stay after you think I must be in bed. Feel no concern or embarrassment; for then you may come to me at once, if you will keep the promise you have made." And he replies: "I will keep my word, and will return when I think the time has come." Then he went out, and stayed in the courtyard until he thought it was time to return and keep the promise he had made. Going back into the hall, he sees nothing of her who would be his mistress; for she was not there. Not finding or seeing her, he said: "Wherever she may be, I shall look for her until I find her." He makes no delay in his search, being bound by the promise he had made her. Entering one of the rooms, he hears a damsel cry aloud, and it was the very one with whom he was about to lie. At the same time, he sees the door of another room standing open, and stepping toward it, he sees right before his eyes a knight who had thrown her down, and was holding her naked and prostrate upon the bed. She, thinking that he had come of course to help her, cried aloud: "Help, help, thou knight, who art my guest. If thou dost not take this man away from me, I shall find no one to do so; if thou dost not succour me speedily, he will wrong me before thy eyes. Thou art the one to lie with me, in accordance with thy promise; and shall this man by force accomplish his wish before thy eyes? Gentle knight, exert thyself, and make haste to bear me aid." He sees that the other man held the damsel brutally uncovered to the waist, and he is ashamed and angered to see him assault her so; yet it is not jealousy he feels, nor will he be made a cuckold by him. At the door there stood as guards two knights completely armed and with swords drawn. Behind them there stood four men-at-arms, each armed with an axe—the sort with which you could split a cow down the back as easily as a root of juniper or broom. The knight hesitated at the door, and thought: "God, what can I do? I am engaged in no less an affair than the quest of Queen Guinevere. I ought not to have the heart of a hare, when for her sake I have engaged in such a quest. If cowardice puts its heart in me, and if I follow its dictates, I shall never attain what I seek. I am disgraced, if I stand here; indeed, I am ashamed even to have thought of holding back. My heart is very sad and oppressed: now I am so ashamed and distressed that I would gladly die for having hesitated here so long. I say it not in pride: but may God have mercy on me if I do not prefer to die honourably rather than live a life of shame! If my path were unobstructed, and if these men gave me leave to pass through without restraint, what honour would I gain? Truly, in that case the greatest coward alive would pass through; and all the while I hear this poor creature calling for help constantly, and reminding me of my promise, and reproaching me with bitter taunts." Then he steps to the door, thrusting in his head and shoulders; glancing up, he sees two swords descending. He draws back, and the knights could not check their strokes: they had wielded them with such force that the swords struck the floor, and both were broken in pieces. When he sees that the swords are broken,

he pays less attention to the axes, fearing and dreading them much less. Rushing in among them, he strikes first one guard in the side and then another. The two who are nearest him he jostles and thrusts aside, throwing them both down flat; the third missed his stroke at him, but the fourth, who attacked him, strikes him so that he cuts his mantle and shirt, and slices the white flesh on his shoulder so that the blood trickles down from the wound. But he, without delay, and without complaining of his wound, presses on more rapidly, until he strikes between the temples him who was assaulting his hostess. Before he departs, he will try to keep his pledge to her. He makes him stand up reluctantly. Meanwhile, he who had missed striking him comes at him as fast as he can, and, raising his arm again, expects to split his head to the teeth with the axe. But the other, alert to defend himself, thrusts the knight toward him in such a way that he receives the axe just where the shoulder joins the neck, so that they are cleaved apart. Then the knight seizes the axe, wresting it quickly from him who holds it; then he lets go the knight whom he still held, and looks to his own defence; for the knights from the door, and the three men with axes are all attacking him fiercely. So he leaped quickly between the bed and the wall, and called to them: "Come on now, all of you. If there were thirty-seven of you, you would have all the fight you wish, with me so favourably placed; I shall never be overcome by you." And the damsel watching him, exclaimed: "By my eyes, you need have no thought of that henceforth where I am." Then at once she dismisses the knights and the men-at-arms, who retire from there at once, without delay or objection. And the damsel continues: "Sire you have well defended me against the men of my household. Come now, and I'll lead you on." . . .

MARIE DE FRANCE

Lanval

After 1150, Marie de France originated the narrative lay, a short poem telling a story and meant to be sung to the accompaniment of a musical instrument, such as a harp. (Lyrical lays were begun somewhat later [early thirteenth century] by a French poet and have a history different from that of narrative lays.) Like the romance (see Chrètien de Troyes's *Arthurian Romances*), with which it was contemporary, the narrative lay tells a courtly love tale based on Celtic sources. The narrative lay had a short life and vanished around 1300. After 1600 the term "lay" came to denote any simple song or narrative of adventure. The lay genre enjoyed a brief comeback in the Neo-Gothic revival of the 1800s.

Marie de France wrote in Old French; she was part of the so-called twelfth-century renaissance, centered in France, which produced scholastic philosophy (Abelard), the Gothic church (Suger), the universities (Bologna and Paris), polyphonic music, liturgical drama, and most especially, vernacular literature, including the *chansons de geste*, Arthurian romances, and love lyrics. Marie contributed to this movement by being the first known European woman to write successfully in the vernacular.

Of Marie de France (fl. 1160–1190) very little is known for certain. She was probably French, working as a professional writer at the English royal court. It was only after 1880 that scholars firmly linked de France with these lays. Even so, one expert claims her name is used "since [it is] convenient and attractive."

The mystery surrounding Marie extends to her works. Her lays are preserved in five manuscripts, the earliest dating from about fifty years after she wrote. Each of these contains several lays in varied groupings, with a few appearing in only one manuscript and most found in two or more, such as *Lanval*.

The general Prologue (not included here) to the manuscript containing *Lanval* offers insight into Marie's literary habits. In it she speaks of not being bullied into giving up her work because of gossip and threats. Whatever provoked these remarks, it seems that Marie valued her reputation and literary gifts. She dedicated these short tales to a "noble king," probably Henry II (1133–1189), the husband of Eleanor of Aquitaine (ca. 1122–1204), herself reputedly the founder of courtly love.

Marie also described her intense dedication to writing the lays:

"To put them into word and rhyme
I've often stayed awake."

Reading the Selection

Lanval, probably the most admired of Marie de France's lays, is set in Brittany, a setting that points to its origin perhaps in one of the French courts. Typical of her lays, it offers a moral message along with being a love story with a happy ending. The moral lesson is that true love may only be glimpsed on earth, because earthly love, even in its noblest form, the Arthurian court, is always at risk from the base motives of envious people.

The hero Lanval, the son of a foreign king, joins Arthur's Round Table for the express purpose of advancing his career. As the lay opens, Lanval sees all of his hopes dashed. He has served Arthur well, giving him military and financial support, but he has been repaid with royal neglect. The king overlooks him when he distributes wives and lands, and the rest of the knights envy him for his generosity and bravery. Lanval, in despair, goes off alone and, for the first time, experiences true love with a woman, perhaps a figment of his imagination but certainly an allegorical figure, who gives him everything that his heart desired. The sole condition for her love is that he must keep their relationship secret from the world.

Lanval, rejuvenated in spirit and purse, thanks to the magical powers of his unearthly love, returns to Arthur's court, where he is welcomed with open arms. Things soon fall apart, however. Marie depicts the court filled with intrigue and impressed with superficial things, such as gold; Arthur himself is hindered in his public duties by his obedience to an immoral and vindictive wife. Lanval even betrays his true love by making their affair public. The plot is sorted out with the unexpected arrival of Lanval's true love who reveals herself to all. Lanval leaves Arthur's court and joins his true love in Avalun, an allegorical land where pure love is sufficient unto itself.

⚭

Lanval

I shall tell you the adventure of another *lai*, just as it happened:	it was composed about a very noble vassal; in Breton, they call him Lanval.

1

Arthur, the brave and the courtly king,
was staying at Cardoel,[1]
because the Scots and the Picts
were destroying the land.
They invaded Logres[2]
and laid it waste.   10
At Pentecost,[3] in summer,
the king stayed there.
He gave out many rich gifts:
to counts and barons,
members of the Round Table—
such a company had no equal in all the world—
he distributed wives and lands,
to all but one who had served him.
That was Lanval; Arthur forgot him,
and none of his men favored him either.   20
For his valor, for his generosity,
his beauty and his bravery,
most men envied him;
some feigned the appearance of love
who, if something unpleasant happened to him,
would not have been at all disturbed.
He was the son of a king of high degree
but he was far from his heritage.
He was of the king's household
but he had spent all his wealth,   30
for the king gave him nothing
nor did Lanval ask.
Now Lanval was in difficulty,
depressed and very worried.
My lords, don't be surprised:
a strange man, without friends,
is very sad in another land,
when he doesn't know where to look for help.
The knight of whom I speak,
who had served the king so long,   40
one day mounted his horse
and went off to amuse himself.
He left the city
and came, all alone, to a field;
he dismounted by a running stream
but his horse trembled badly.
He removed the saddle and went off,
leaving the horse to roll around in the meadow.
He folded his cloak beneath his head
and lay down.   50
He worried about his difficulty,
he could see nothing that pleased him.
As he lay there
he looked down along the bank
and saw two girls approaching;
he had never seen any lovelier.

They were richly dressed,
tightly laced,
in tunics of dark purple;
their faces were very lovely.   60
The older one carried basins,
golden, well made, and fine;
I shall tell you the truth about it, without fail.
The other carried a towel.
They went straight
to where the knight was lying.
Lanval, who was very well bred,
got up to meet them.
They greeted him first
and gave him their message: 70
"Sir Lanval, my lady,
who is worthy and wise and beautiful,
sent us for you.
Come with us now.
We shall guide you there safely.
See, her pavilion is nearby!"
The knight went with them;
giving no thought to his horse
who was feeding before him in the meadow.
They led him up to the tent,   80
which was quite beautiful and well placed.
Queen Semiramis,[4]
however much more wealth,
power, or knowledge she had,
or the emperor Octavian[5]
could not have paid for one of the flaps.
There was a golden eagle on top of it,
whose value I could not tell,
nor could I judge the value of the cords or the poles
that held up the sides of the tent;   90
there is no king on earth who could buy it,
no matter what wealth he offered.
The girl was inside the tent:
the lily and the young rose
when they appear in the summer
are surpassed by her beauty.
She lay on a beautiful bed—
the bedclothes were worth a castle—
dressed only in her shift.
Her body was well shaped and elegant;   100
for the heat, she had thrown over herself,
a precious cloak of white ermine,
covered with purple alexandrine,[6]
but her whole side was uncovered,
her face, her neck and her bosom;
she was whiter than the hawthorn flower.
The knight went forward
and the girl addressed him.
He sat before the bed.
"Lanval," she said, "sweet love,   110

---

[1] **Cardoel** Also known as "Carlion," the legendary place where King Arthur was crowned and held court. Modern-day Caerleon is in southeast Wales.
[2] **Logres** England.
[3] **Pentecost** A Christian feast or celebration on the seventh Sunday after Easter, commemorating the Holy Spirit descending on the Apostles. Before the advent of numerical yearly calendars, dating was kept by events Christians believed were associated with Christ.

[4] **Queen Semiramis** Legendary queen who was very wealthy and powerful and was reputed to have built Babylon.
[5] **Octavian** Caesar Augustus, first emperor of the Roman Empire (31 B.C.–A.D. 14).
[6] **Alexandrine** A type of semiprecious stone.

because of you I have come from my land;
I came to seek you from far away.
If you are brave and courtly,
no emperor or count or king
will ever have known such joy or good;
for I love you more than anything."
He looked at her and saw that she was beautiful;
Love stung him with a spark
that burned and set fire to his heart.
He answered her in a suitable way.   120
"Lovely one," he said, "if it pleased you,
if such joy might be mine
that you would love me,
there is nothing you might command,
within my power, that I would not do,
whether foolish or wise.
I shall obey your command;
for you, I shall abandon everyone.
I want never to leave you.
That is what I most desire."   130
When the girl heard the words
of the man who could love her so,
she granted him her love and her body.
Now Lanval was on the right road!
Afterward, she gave him a gift:
he would never again want anything,
he would receive as he desired;
however generously he might give and spend,
she would provide what he needed.
Now Lanval is well cared for.   140
The more lavishly he spends,
the more gold and silver he will have.
"Love," she said, "I admonish you now,
I command and beg you,
do not let any man know about this.
I shall tell you why:
you would lose me for good
if this love were known;
you would never see me again
or possess my body."   150
He answered that he would do
exactly as she commanded.
He lay beside her on the bed;
now Lanval is well cared for.
He remained with her
that afternoon, until evening
and would have stayed longer, if he could,
and if his love had consented.
"Love," she said, "get up.
You cannot stay any longer.   160
Go away now; I shall remain
but I will tell you one thing:
when you want to talk to me
there is no place you can think of
where a man might have his mistress
without reproach or shame,
that I shall not be there with you
to satisfy all your desires.
No man but you will see me
or hear my words."   170

When he heard her, he was very happy,
he kissed her, and then got up.
The girls who had brought him to the tent
dressed him in rich clothes;
when he was dressed anew,
there wasn't a more handsome youth in all the world;
he was not fool, no boor.
They gave him water for his hands
and a towel to dry them,
and they brought him food.   180
He took supper with his love;
it was not to be refused.
He was served with great courtesy,
he received it with great joy.
There was an entrement
that vastly pleased the knight
for he kissed his lady often
and held her close.
When they finished dinner,
his horse was brought to him.   190
The horse had been well saddled;
Lanval was very richly served.
The knight took his leave, mounted,
and rode toward the city,
often looking behind him.
Lanval was very disturbed;
he wondered about his adventure
and was doubtful in his heart;
he was amazed, not knowing what to believe;
he didn't expect ever to see her again.   200
He came to his lodging
and found his men well dressed.
That night, his accommodations were rich
but no one knew where it came from.
There was no knight in the city
who really needed a place to stay
whom he didn't invite to join him
to be well and richly served.
Lanval gave rich gifts,
Lanval released prisoners,   210
Lanval dressed jongleurs [performers],
Lanval offered great honors.
There was no stranger or friend
to whom Lanval didn't give.
Lanval's joy and pleasure were intense;
in the daytime or at night,
he could see his love often;
she was completely at his command.

In that same year, it seems to me,
after the feast of St. John,[7]   220
about thirty knights
were amusing themselves
in an orchard beneath the tower
where the queen was staying.
Gawain was with them

———————

[7] **feast of St. John** Christian feast honoring John the Baptist; June 24 by modern calendars and close to the date of midsummer festivals.

and his cousin, the handsome Yvain;
Gawain, the noble, the brave,
who was so loved by all, said:
"By God, my lords, we wronged
our companion Lanval,   230
who is so generous and courtly,
and whose father is a rich king,
when we didn't bring him with us."
They immediately turned back,
went to his lodging
and prevailed on Lanval to come along with them.
At a sculpted window
the queen was looking out;
she had three ladies with her.
She saw the king's retinue,   240
recognized Lanval and looked at him.
Then she told one of her ladies
to send for her maidens,
the loveliest and the most refined;
together they went to amuse themselves
in the orchard where the others were.
She brought thirty or more with her;
they descended the steps.
The knights came to meet them,
because they were delighted to see them.   250
The knights took them by the hand;
their conversation was in no way vulgar.
Lanval went off to one side,
far from the others; he was impatient
to hold his love,
to kiss and embrace and touch her;
he thought little of others' joys
if he could not have his pleasure.
When the queen saw him alone,
she went straight to the knight.   260
She sat beside him and spoke,
revealing her whole heart:
"Lanval, I have shown you much honor,
I have cherished you, and loved you.
You may have all my love;
just tell me your desire.
I promise you my affection.
You should be very happy with me."
"My lady," he said, "let me be!
I have no desire to love you.   270
I've served the king a long time;
I don't want to betray my faith to him.
Never, for you or for your love,
will I do anything to harm my lord."
The queen got angry;
in her wrath, she insulted him:
"Lanval," she said, "I am sure
you don't care for such pleasure;
people have often told me
that you have no interest in women.   280
You have fine-looking boys
with whom you enjoy yourself.
Base coward, lousy cripple,
my lord made a bad mistake
when he let you stay with him.
For all I know, he'll lose God because of it."

When Lanval heard her, he was quite disturbed;
he was not slow to answer.
He said something out of spite
that he would later regret.   290
"Lady," he said, "of that activity
I know nothing,
but I love and I am loved
by one who should have the prize
over all the women I know.
And I shall tell you one thing;
you might as well know all:
any one of those who serve her,
the poorest girl of all,
is better than you, my lady queen,   300
in body, face, and beauty,
in breeding and in goodness."
The queen left him
and went, weeping, to her chamber.
She was upset and angry
because he had insulted her.
She went to bed sick;
never, she said, would she get up
unless the king gave her satisfaction
for the offense against her.   310
The king returned from the woods,
he'd had a very good day.
He entered the queen's chambers.
When she saw him, she began to complain.
She fell at his feet, asked his mercy,
saying that Lanval had dishonored her;
he had asked for her love,
and because she refused him
he insulted and offended her:
he boasted of a love   320
who was so refined and noble and proud
that her chambermaid,
the poorest one who served her,
was better than the queen.
The king got very angry;
he swore an oath:
if Lanval could not defend himself in court
he would have him burned or hanged.
The king left her chamber
and called for three of his barons;   330
he sent them for Lanval
who was feeling great sorrow and distress.
He had come back to his dwelling,
knowing very well
that he'd lost his love,
he had betrayed their affair.
He was all alone in a room,
disturbed and troubled;
he called on his love, again and again,
but it did him no good.   340
He complained and sighed,
from time to time he fainted;
then he cried a hundred times for her to have mercy
and speak to her love.
He cursed his heart and his mouth;
it's a wonder he didn't kill himself.
No matter how much he cried and shouted,

ranted and raged,
she would not have mercy on him,
not even let him see her. 350
How will he ever contain himself?
The men the king sent
arrived and told him
to appear in court without delay:
the king had summoned him
because the queen had accused him.
Lanval went with his great sorrow;
they could have killed him, for all he cared.
He came before the king;
he was very sad, thoughtful, silent; 360
his face revealed great suffering.
In anger the king told him:
"Vassal, you have done me a great wrong!
This was a base undertaking,
to shame and disgrace me
and to insult the queen.
You have made a foolish boast:
your love is much too noble
if her maid is more beautiful,
more worthy, than the queen." 370
Lanval denied that he'd dishonored
or shamed his lord,
word for word, as the king spoke:
he had not made advances to the queen;
but of what he had said,
he acknowledged the truth,
about the love he had boasted of,
that now made him sad because he'd lost her.
About that he said he would do
whatever the court decided. 380
The king was very angry with him;
he sent for all his men
to determine exactly what he ought to do
so that no one could find fault with his decision.
They did as he commanded,
whether they liked it or not.
They assembled,
judged, and decided,
than Lanval should have his day;
but he must find pledges for his lord 390
to guarantee that he would await the judgment,
return, and be present at it.
Then the court would be increased,
for now there were none but the king's household.
The barons came back to the king
and announced their decision.
The king demanded pledges.
Lanval was alone and forlorn,
he had no relative, no friend.
Gawain went and pledged himself for him, 400
and all his companions followed.
The king addressed them: "I release him to you
on forfeit of whatever you hold from me,
lands and fiefs, each one for himself."
When Lanval was pledged, there was nothing else to do.
He returned to his lodging.
The knights accompanied him,
they reproached and admonished him

that he give up his great sorrow;
they cursed his foolish love. 410
Each day they went to see him,
because they wanted to know
whether he was drinking and eating;
they were afraid that he'd kill himself.
On the day that they had named,
the barons assembled.
The king and queen were there
and the pledges brought Lanval back.
They were all very sad for him:
I think there were a hundred 420
who would have done all they could
to set him free without a trial
where he would be wrongly accused.
The king demanded a verdict
according to the charge and rebuttal.
Now it all fell to the barons.
They went to the judgment,
worried and distressed
for the noble man from another land
who'd gotten into such trouble in their midst. 430
Many wanted to condemn him
in order to satisfy their lord.
The Duke of Cornwall said:
"No one can blame us;
whether it makes you weep or sing
justice must be carried out.
The king spoke against his vassal
whom I have heard named Lanval;
he accused him of felony,
charged him with a misdeed— 440
a love that he had boasted of,
which made the queen angry.
No one but the king accused him:
by the faith I owe you,
if one were to speak the truth,
there should have been no need for defense,
except that a man owes his lord honor
in every circumstance.
He will be bound by his oath,
and the king will forgive us our pledges 450
if he can produce proof;
if his love would come forward,
if what he said,
what upset the queen, is true,
then he will be acquitted,
because he did not say it out of malice.
But if he cannot get his proof,
we must make it clear to him
that he will forfeit his service to the king;
he must take his leave." 460
They sent to the knight,
told and announced to him
that he should have his love come
to defend and stand surety for him.
He told them that he could not do it:
he would never receive help from her.
They went back to the judges,
not expecting any help from Lanval.
The king pressed them hard

because of the queen who was waiting.
When they were ready to give their verdict
they saw two girls approaching,
riding handsome palfreys.[8]
They were very attractive,
dressed in purple taffeta,
over their bare skin.
The men looked at them with pleasure.
Gawain, taking three knights with him,
went to Lanval and told him;
he pointed out the two girls.   480
Gawain was extremely happy, and begged him
to tell if his love were one of them.
Lanval said he didn't know who they were,
where they came from or where they were going.
The girls proceeded
still on horseback;
they dismounted before the high table
at which Arthur, the king, sat.
They were of great beauty,
and spoke in a courtly manner: 490
"King, clear your chambers,
have them hung with silk
where my lady may dismount;
she wishes to take shelter with you."
He promised it willingly
and called two knights
to guide them up to the chambers.
On that subject no more was said.
The king asked his barons
for their judgment and decision;   500
he said they had angered him very much
with their long delay.
"Sire," they said, "we have decided.
Because of the ladies we have just seen
we have made no judgment.
Let us reconvene the trial."
Then they assembled, everyone was worried;
there was much noise and strife.
While they were in that confusion,
two girls in noble array,   510
dressed in Phrygian silks[9]
and riding Spanish mules,
were seen coming down the street.
This gave the vassals great joy;
to each other they said that now
Lanval, the brave and bold, was saved.
Gawain went up to him,
bringing his companions along.
"Sire," he said, "take heart.
For the love of God, speak to us.   520
Here come two maidens,
well adorned and very beautiful;
one must certainly be your love."
Lanval answered quickly
that he did not recognize them,
he didn't know them or love them.
Meanwhile they'd arrived,

and dismounted before the king.   470
Most of those who saw them praised them
for their bodies, their faces, their coloring;   530
each was more impressive
than the queen had ever been.
The older one was courtly and wise,
she spoke her message fittingly:
"King, have chambers prepared for us
to lodge my lady according to her need
she is coming here to speak with you."
He ordered them to be taken
to the others who had preceded them.
There was no problem with the mules.   540
When he had seen to the girls,
he summoned all his barons
to render their judgment;
it had already dragged out too much.
The queen was getting angry
because she had fasted so long.
They were about to give their judgment
when through the city came riding
a girl on horseback:
there was none more beautiful in the world.   550
She rode a white palfrey,
who carried her handsomely and smoothly:
he was well apportioned in the neck and head,
no finer beast in the world.
The palfrey's trappings were rich;
under heaven there was no count or king
who could have afforded them all
without selling or mortgaging lands.
She was dressed in this fashion:
in a white linen shift   560
that revealed both her sides
since the lacing was along the side.
Her body was elegant, her hips slim,
her neck whiter than snow on a branch,
her eyes bright, her face white,
a beautiful mouth, a well-set nose,
dark eyebrows and an elegant forehead,
her hair curly and rather blond;
golden wire does not shine
like her hair in the light.   570
Her cloak, which she had wrapped around her,
was dark purple.
On her wrist she held a sparrow hawk,
a greyhound followed her.
In the town, no one, small or big,
old man or child,
failed to come look.
As they watched her pass,
there was no joking about her beauty.
She proceeded at a slow pace.   580
The judges who saw her
marveled at the sight;
no one who looked at her
was not warmed with joy.
Those who loved the knight
came to him and told him
of the girl who was approaching,
if God pleased, to rescue him.
"Sir companion, here comes one

---

[8] **palfreys** Saddle horses for young women.
[9] **Phrygian silks** Reference to the far-off land of Phrygia in Asia Minor; hence expensive clothes from an exotic place.

neither tawny nor dark;
this is, of all who exist,
the most beautiful woman in the world."
Lanval heard them and lifted his head;
he recognized her and sighed.
The blood rose to his face;
he was quick to speak.
"By my faith," he said, "that is my love.
Now I don't care if I am killed,
if only she forgives me.
For I am restored, now that I see her."   600
The lady entered the palace;
no one so beautiful had ever been there.
She dismounted before the king
so that she was well seen by all.
And she let her cloak fall
so they could see her better.
The king, who was well bred,
rose and went to meet her;
all the others honored her
and offered to serve her.   610
When they had looked at her well,
when they had greatly praised her beauty,
she spoke in this way,
she didn't want to wait:
"I have loved one of your vassals:
you see him before you—Lanval.
He has been accused in your court—
I don't want him to suffer
for what he said; you should know
that the queen was in the wrong.   620

590   He never made advances to her.
And for the boast that he made,
if he can be acquitted through me,
let him be set free by your barons."
Whatever the barons judged by law
the king promised would prevail.
To the last man they agreed
that Lanval had successfully answered the charge.
He was set free by their decision
and the girl departed.   630
The king could not detain her,
though there were enough people to serve her.
Outside the hall stood
a great stone of dark marble
where heavy men mounted
when they left the king's court;
Lanval climbed on it.
When the girl came through the gate
Lanval leapt, in one bound,
onto the palfrey, behind her.   640
With her he went to Avalun,[10]
so the Bretons tell us,
to a very beautiful island;
there the youth was carried off.
No man heard of him again,
and I have no more to tell.

————

[10] **Avalun** Also spelled Avalon. The paradise place in Arthurian legends; where King Arthur went upon his death.

—————— ⧢ ——————

ST. THOMAS AQUINAS

Selection from *Summa theologica*

Thomas Aquinas's (1226–1274) theology, called Thomism, is the climax of the key intellectual trend that characterized the High Middle Ages (1000–1300). Thomism uniquely embodies the age's spirit, which tried to harmonize the opposing domains of philosophy and theology, reason and faith. Thomas performed this feat with two vast *summas* (from Latin, a comprehensive treatise), namely the *Summa theologica* and the *Summa contra gentiles.* In these works, he founded a rational theology that aligned Aristotle's thought with Christian principles. Some of Thomas's ideas (on, for example, the Trinity) were called into question after his death, but his reputation steadily grew; in 1874 the papacy declared Thomism to be the official basis of Roman Catholic beliefs.

In order to develop a rational theology along the lines laid down by Aristotle, Thomas had to come to terms with the pessimistic thought of Augustine (see *Confessions*), which had dominated Christian discourse since the fifth century. To Augustine, reason is helpless because it cannot operate apart from the human will, which has lost its freedom because of original sin. In reply, Thomas held that the will is free, and reason, while spoiled by sin, is yet able to discover much about the world; reason, even if limited, must be obeyed as far as it goes. Augustine further claimed that true knowledge can arise only if God implants it in the mind, either slowly or all at once. In contrast, Thomas was more hopeful, saying that all knowledge begins in the senses, even of things that lie beyond the senses. Finally, Augustine thought that not only was human nature impaired, but so was the world of nature. Thomas's opposing view was that the natural world, though necessarily incomplete because it is created, is nonetheless good since it reflects God as its creator. Thus, Thomism ranged widely over human concerns, covering topics such as justice, fair prices, usury, and good government.

Reading the Selection

This selection from the *Summa theologica* deals with faith, or belief. Faith, to Thomas, is one of the three theological virtues—the others are hope and charity—which have God as their object and bring eternal life to those who obey them. In discussing the theological, or spiritual, virtues, St. Thomas was inspired by the Greek thinker Aristotle, who had identified the four cardinal virtues of secular life: wisdom, courage, justice, and temperance. Thomist thought eventually embraced both the theological and the cardinal virtues, maintaining that both were essential to a Christian.

The Fifth Article from the *Summa theologica* deals with the question, Should matters of faith be tested by the rules of science? After a full discussion, Thomas concludes that faith and science (reason) are two separate domains and should not be intermingled: "[T]he object of science is something seen, whereas the object of faith is the unseen."

Thomas's argument is typical of the medieval style of reasoning, which included a question, discussion, and resolution. The opening question is followed by a series of arguments, pro and con, drawn from the Bible *(1 Timothy, 2 Corinthians)*, the church fathers (Gregory), Aristotle ("the Philosopher"), and logic. Thomas gives the resolution in the first person ("I answer that"), though his presence is ever felt, shaping the argument as he replies to both the pro and con sides of the debate. Because of its give-and-take format, this method is believed to have begun in the classroom practices of schools and universities, hence the name *scholasticism*.

∞

Fifth Article

Whether Those Things That Are of Faith Can Be an Object of Science?

We proceed thus to the Fifth Article:—Objection 1. It would seem that those things that are of faith can be an object of science. For where science is lacking there is ignorance, since ignorance is the opposite of science. Now we are not in ignorance of those things we have to believe, since ignorance of such things savors of unbelief, according to 1 Tim. i. 13: *I did it ignorantly in unbelief.* Therefore things that are of faith can be an object of science.

Obj. 2. Further, science is acquired by reasons. Now sacred writers employ reasons to inculcate things that are of faith. Therefore such things can be an object of science.

Obj. 3. Further, things which are demonstrated are an object of science, since a *demonstration is a syllogism that produces science.* Now certain matters of faith have been demonstrated by the philosophers, such as the Existence and Unity of God, and so forth. Therefore things that are of faith can be an object of science.

Obj. 4. Further, opinion is further from science than faith is, since faith is said to stand between opinion and science. Now opinion and science can, in a way, be about the same object, as stated in *Poster.* i. Therefore faith and science can be about the same object also.

On the contrary, Gregory[1] says (*Hom.* xxvi *in Ev.*) that *when a thing is manifest, it is the object, not of faith, but of perception.* Therefore things that are of faith are not the object of perception, whereas what is an object of science is the object of perception. Therefore there can be no faith about things which are an object of science.

I answer that, All science is derived from self-evident and therefore *seen* principles; wherefore all objects of science must needs be, in a fashion, seen.

---

[1] **Gregory** St. Gregory or Gregory the Great, sixth-century pope who expanded the church, wrote many theological works, and supposedly arranged the Gregorian chant.

Now as stated above (A. 4) it is impossible that one and the same thing should be believed and seen by the same person. Hence it is equally impossible for one and the same thing to be an object of science and of belief for the same person. It may happen, however, that a thing which is an object of vision or science for one, is believed by another: since we hope to see some day what we now believe about the Trinity, according to 1 Cor. xiii. 12: *We see now through a glass in a dark manner; but then face to face:* which vision the angels possess already; so that what we believe, they see. In like manner it may happen that what is an object of vision or scientific knowledge for one man, even in the state of a wayfarer, is, for another man, an object of faith, because he does not know it by demonstration.

Nevertheless, that which is proposed to be believed equally by all, is equally unknown by all as an object of science: such are the things which are of faith simply. Consequently faith and science are not about the same things.

Reply Obj. 1. Unbelievers are in ignorance of things that are of faith, for neither do they see or know them in themselves, nor do they know them to be credible. The faithful, on the other hand, know them, not as by demonstration, but by the light of faith which makes them see that they ought to believe them, as stated above (A. 4, *ad* 2, 3).

Reply Obj. 2. The reasons employed by holy men to prove things that are of faith, are not demonstrations; they are either persuasive arguments showing that what is proposed to our faith is not impossible, or else they are proofs drawn from the principles of faith, i.e. from the authority of Holy Writ, as Dionysius[2] declares (*Div. Nom.* ii). Whatever is based on these principles is as well proved in the eyes of

10

the faithful, as a conclusion drawn from self-evident principles is in the eyes of all. Hence again, theology is a science, as we stated at the outset of this work (P. I, Q. 1, A. 2).

Reply Obj. 3. Things which can be proved by demonstration are reckoned among the articles of faith, not because they are believed simply by all, but because they are a necessary presupposition to matters of faith, so that those who do not know them by demonstration must know them first of all by faith.

Reply Obj. 4. As the Philosopher[3] says *(loc. cit.), science and opinion about the same object can certainly be in different men,* as we have stated above about science and faith; yet it is possible for one and the same man to have science and faith about the same thing relatively, i.e. in relation to the object, but not in the same respect. For it is possible for the same person, about one and the same object, to know one thing and to think another: and, in like manner, one may know by demonstration the unity of the Godhead, and, by faith, the Trinity. On the other hand, in one and the same man, about the same object, and in the same respect, science is incompatible with either opinion or faith, yet for different reasons. Because science is incompatible with opinion about the same object simply, for the reason that science demands that its object should be deemed impossible to be otherwise, whereas it is essential to opinion, that its object should be deemed possible to be otherwise. Yet that which is the object of faith, on account of the certainty of faith, is also deemed impossible to be otherwise: and the reason why science and faith cannot be about the same object and in the same respect is because the object of science is something seen, whereas the object of faith is the unseen, as stated above.

[2] **Dionysius** Known as Dionysius the Areopagite, lived around A.D. 500 and was probably from Syria. Wrote many mystical and theological books that influenced medieval thinkers.

[3] **the Philosopher** Aristotle, the famous Greek thinker who lived in the fourth century B.C.

DANTE ALIGHIERI

Selections from *The Divine Comedy*

(The introduction to the cantos and footnotes accompanying *The Divine Comedy* written by John Ciardi.)

Few writers of any time have had such an impact on Western culture as the medieval writer Dante Alighieri (1265–1321) of Florence. So great were his gifts that the world was not the same after he wrote. His works in Italian had such broad appeal that the geographic focus of Europe's culture shifted from France to Italy, where it stayed until about 1600. His poetry affected all of Europe and changed the terms in which poets wrote. Dante, for example, composed lyrics celebrating his undying love for the beautiful Beatrice; later poets, enchanted by these poems, followed his lead, with Petrarch writing verses to Laura (see *Canzoniere*), Shakespeare to the Dark Lady, and so on. Scholars often link Dante to the Renaissance, but this surely is an exaggeration, given his religious views. He is better understood as the culmination of the medieval spirit, as he balances the secular and the spiritual, the ancient and the new.

Of Dante's works, *The Divine Comedy* (about 1314) is his enduring masterpiece. In form, this long narrative poem belongs to the epic genre with its hero of superhuman caliber, dangerous journey, misadventures, divine dimension, digressions, long speeches, vivid descriptions, and general lofty tone (see *The Epic of Gilgamesh,* Homer's *Iliad* and *Odyssey,* and Vergil's *Aeneid*). But *The Divine Comedy* is *much* more than an epic, because Dante worked into the poem anything he felt like including. It is an allegory of great complexity, meant by Dante to be interpreted on many levels, such as depicting the way to God or the way of the artist. It is a hymn to the Middle Ages, including scholastic reasoning, mysticism, numerology, Thomism (see St. Thomas Aquinas's *Summa theologica*), Aristotelianism, and Italian history. Above all, it is a vision of Christianity and Classicism reconciled.

The elaborate framework is built over a fairly simple plot. The hero, Dante himself, goes on a journey of self-discovery through hell, purgatory, and heaven, led first by Vergil, the Latin poet, and later by Beatrice, his human muse. The time is Easter 1300. The perennial appeal of this plot is that Dante becomes a stand-in for readers, virtually all of whom have been prey to self-doubts similar to those driving this hero on his life-or-death voyage.

Reading the Selections

The selections include four cantos (chapters) from the *Inferno* portion of *The Divine Comedy.* The Inferno, or hell, is the realm of sinners who suffer not because of predestined fate but because of their own bad choices. Here are found those who rejected spiritual values and yielded to animal appetites or violence, or perverted their human reason to fraud or malice against other human beings.

Canto I introduces Dante, who is tortured by self-doubts: "I went astray . . . and woke to find myself alone in a dark wood." He learns that two guides will lead him back to "the straight road."

Dante and Vergil enter hell in Canto III and are instantly greeted by the cries of the Opportunists, those sinners who chose to sit on the fence rather than side with evil or good. Dante begins to understand that God's justice reigns even in hell, as the Opportunists are punished in a manner appropriate to their sin; namely, they spend eternity chasing ever-shifting banners.

In Canto V, Dante and Vergil encounter the Carnal, those who succumbed to lust. Their eternal punishment is to be swept along in a whirlwind, just as their passions carried them to doom.

The *Inferno*'s last canto, XXXIV, describes the center of hell, where a mindless Satan (called Dis)—a three-faced fallen angel, representative of the anti-Trinity and characterized by impotence, ignorance, and hatred—sits enthroned in ice. Dis's three mouths chew eternally on those ultimate rebels who betrayed church and state.

∞

Inferno, Canto I

The Dark Wood of Error

Midway in his allotted threescore years and ten, Dante comes to himself with a start and realizes that he has strayed from the True Way into the Dark Wood of Error (Worldliness). As soon as he has realized his loss, Dante lifts his eyes and sees the first light of the sunrise (the Sun is the Symbol of Divine Illumination) lighting the shoulders of a little hill (The Mount of Joy). It is the Easter Season, the time of resurrection, and the sun is in its equinoctial rebirth. This juxtaposition of joyous symbols fills Dante with hope and he sets out at once to climb directly up the Mount of Joy, but almost

immediately his way is blocked by the Three Beasts of Worldliness: THE LEOPARD OF MALICE AND FRAUD, THE LION OF VIOLENCE AND AMBITION, and THE SHE-WOLF OF INCONTINENCE. These beasts, and especially the She-Wolf, drive him back despairing into the darkness of error. But just as all seems lost, a figure appears to him. It is the shade of VERGIL, Dante's symbol of HUMAN REASON.

Vergil explains that he has been sent to lead Dante from error. There can, however, be no direct ascent past the beasts: the man who would escape them must go a longer and harder way. First he must descend through Hell (The Recognition of Sin), then he must ascend

through Purgatory (The Renunciation of Sin), and only then may
he reach the pinnacle of joy and come to the Light of God. Vergil
offers to guide Dante, but only as far as Human Reason can go.
Another guide (BEATRICE, symbol of DIVINE LOVE) must take
over for the final ascent, for Human Reason is self-limited. Dante
submits himself joyously to Vergil's guidance and they move off.

Midway in our life's journey,[1] I went astray   1
   from the straight road and woke to find myself
   alone in a dark wood. How shall I say

what wood that was! I never saw so drear,
   so rank, so arduous a wilderness!
   Its very memory gives a shape to fear.

Death could scarce be more bitter than that place!
   But since it came to good, I will recount
   all that I found revealed there by God's grace.

How I came to it I cannot rightly say,   10
   so drugged and loose with sleep had I become
   when I first wandered there from the True Way.

But at the far end of that valley of evil
   whose maze had sapped my very heart with fear!
   I found myself before a little hill

and lifted up my eyes. Its shoulders glowed
   already with the sweet rays of that planet[2]
   whose virtue leads men straight on every road,

and the shining strengthened me against the fright
   whose agony had wracked the lake of my heart   20
   through all the terrors of that piteous night.

Just as a swimmer, who with his last breath
   flounders ashore from perilous seas, might turn
   to memorize the wide water of his death—

so did I turn, my soul still fugitive
   from death's surviving image, to stare down
   that pass that none had ever left alive.

And there I lay to rest from my heart's race

till calm and breath returned to me. Then rose
   and pushed up that dead slope at such a pace   30

each footfall rose above the last.[3] And lo!
   almost at the beginning of the rise
   I faced a spotted Leopard, all tremor and flow

and gaudy pelt. And it would not pass, but stood
   so blocking my every turn that time and again
   I was on the verge of turning back to the wood.

This fell at the first widening of the dawn
   as the sun was climbing Aries with those stars
   that rode with him to light the new creation.[4]

Thus the holy hour and the sweet season   40
   of commemoration did much to arm my fear
   of that bright murderous beast with their good omen.

Yet not so much but what I shook with dread
   at sight of a great Lion that broke upon me
   raging with hunger, its enormous head

held high as if to strike a mortal terror
   into the very air. And down his track,
   a She-Wolf drove upon me, a starved horror

ravening and wasted beyond all belief.
   She seemed a rack for avarice, gaunt and craving.   50

---

[3] **each footfall rose above the last** The literal rendering would be: "So that the fixed foot was ever the lower." "Fixed" has often been translated "right" and an ingenious reasoning can support that reading, but a simpler explanation offers itself and seems more competent: Dante is saying that he climbed with such zeal and haste that every footfall carried him above the last despite the steepness of the climb. At a slow pace, on the other hand, the rear foot might be brought up only as far as the forward foot. This device of selecting a minute but exactly-centered detail to convey the whole of a larger action is one of the central characteristics of Dante's style.

THE THREE BEASTS: Leopard, Lion, and She-Wolf. These three beasts undoubtedly are taken from *Jeremiah* v, 6. Many additional and incidental interpretations have been advanced for them, but the central interpretation must remain as noted. They foreshadow the three divisions of Hell (*incontinence, violence, and fraud*) which Vergil explains at length in Canto XI, 16–111.

[4] **Aries . . . that rode with him to light the new creation** The medieval tradition had it that the sun was in Aries at the time of the Creation. The significance of the astronomical and religious conjunction is an important part of Dante's intended allegory. It is just before dawn of Good Friday 1300 A.D. when he awakens in the Dark Wood. Thus his new life begins under Aries, the sign of creation, at dawn (rebirth) and in the Easter season (resurrection). Moreover the moon is full and the sun is in the equinox, conditions that did not fall together on any Friday of 1300. Dante is obviously constructing poetically the perfect Easter as a symbol of his new awakening.

---

[1] **midway in our life's journey** The Biblical life span is three-score years and ten. The action opens in Dante's thirty-fifth year, i.e., 1300 A.D.

[2] **that planet** The sun. Ptolemaic astronomers considered it a planet. It is also symbolic of God as He who lights man's way.

Oh many the souls she has brought to endless grief!

She brought such heaviness upon my spirit
　　at sight of her savagery and desperation,
　　I died from every hope of that high summit.

And like a miser—eager in acquisition
　　but desperate in self-reproach when Fortune's wheel
　　turns to the hour of his loss—all tears and attrition

I wavered back; and still the beast pursued,
　　forcing herself against me bit by bit
　　till I slid back into the sunless wood.　　　　60

And as I fell to my soul's ruin, a presence
　　gathered before me on the discolored air,
　　the figure of one who seemed hoarse from long silence.

At sight of him in that friendless waste I cried:
　　"Have pity on me, whatever thing you are,
　　whether shade or living man." And it replied:

"Not man, though man I once was, and my blood
　　was Lombard, both my parents Mantuan.
　　I was born, though late, *sub Julio*,[5] and bred

in Rome under Augustus in the noon　　　　70
　　of the false and lying gods. I was a poet
　　and sang of old Anchises' noble son

who came to Rome after the burning of Troy.
　　But you—why do *you* return to these distresses
　　instead of climbing that shining Mount of Joy.

which is the seat and first cause of man's bliss?"
　　"And are you then that Vergil and that fountain
　　of purest speech?" My voice grew tremulous:

"Glory and light of poets! now may that zeal
　　and love's apprenticeship that I poured out　　80
　　on your heroic verses serve me well!

For you are my true master and first author,
　　the sole maker from whom I drew the breath
　　of that sweet style whose measures have brought me
　　　　honor.

See there, immortal sage, the beast I flee.

For my soul's salvation, I beg you, guard me from her,
　　for she has struck a mortal tremor through me."

And he replied, seeing my soul in tears:
　　"He must go by another way who would escape
　　this wilderness, for that mad beast that fleers　　90

before you there, suffers no man to pass.
　　She tracks down all, kills all, and knows no glut,
　　but, feeding, she grows hungrier than she was.

She mates with any beast and will mate with more
　　before the Greyhound becomes to hunt her down.
　　He will not feed on lands nor loot, but honor

and love and wisdom will make straight his way.
　　He will rise between Feltro and Feltro,[6] and in him
　　shall be the resurrection and new day

of that sad Italy for which Nisus died,　　　　100
　　and Turnus, and Euryalus, and the maid Camilla.[7]
　　He shall hunt her through every nation of sick pride

till she is driven back forever to Hell
　　whence Envy first released her on the world.
　　Therefore, for your own good, I think it well

you follow me and I will be your guide
　　and lead you forth through an eternal place.
　　There you shall see the ancient spirits tried

in endless pain, and hear their lamentation
　　as each bemoans the second death[8] of souls　　110
　　Next you shall see upon a burning mountain

souls in fire and yet content in fire,
　　knowing that whensoever it may be
　　they yet will mount into the blessed choir.

To which, if it is still your wish to climb,

---

[6] **The Greyhound . . . Feltro and Feltro** Almost certainly refers to
Can Grande della Scala (1290-1329), great Italian leader born in
Verona, which lies between the towns of Feltre and Montefeltro.
[7] **Nisus, Turnus, Euryalus, Camilla** All were killed in the war
between the Trojans and the Latians when, according to legend,
Aeneas led the survivors of Troy into Italy. Nisus and Euryalus
(*Aeneid IX*) were Trojan comrades-in-arms who died together. Camilla
(*Aeneid XI*) was the daughter of the Latian king and one of the warrior women. She was killed in a horse charge against the Trojans after
displaying great gallantry. Turnus (*Aeneid XII*) was killed by Aeneas
in a duel.
[8] **the second death** Damnation. "This is the second death, even the
lake of fire." (*Revelation* xx, 14)

---

[5] *sub Julio* In the reign of Julius Caesar.

a worthier spirit shall be sent to guide you.
With her shall I leave you, for the King of Time,

who reigns on high, forbids me to come there
since, living, I rebelled against his law.[9]
He rules the waters and the land and air   120

and there holds court, his city and his throne.
Oh blessed are they he chooses!" And I to him:
"Poet, by that God to you unknown,

lead me this way. Beyond this present ill

---

[9] **forbids me to come there since, living, etc.** Salvation is only through Christ in Dante's theology. Virgil lived and died before the establishment of Christ's teachings in Rome, and cannot therefore enter Heaven.

and worse to dread, lead me to Peter's gate[10]
and be my guide through the sad halls of Hell."

And he then: "Follow." And he moved ahead
in silence, and I followed where he led.

---

[10] **Peter's gate** The gate of Purgatory. (See *Purgatorio* IX, 76 ff.) The gate is guarded by an angel with a gleaming sword. The angel is Peter's vicar (Peter, the first Pope, symbolized all Popes; i.e., Christ's vicar on earth) and is entrusted with the two great keys.

Some commentators argue that this is the gate of Paradise, but Dante mentions no gate beyond this one in his ascent to Heaven. It should be remembered, too, that those who pass the gate of Purgatory have effectively entered Heaven.

The three great gates that figure in the entire journey are: the gate of Hell (Canto III, 1–11), the gate of Dis (Canto VIII, 79–113, and Canto IX, 86–87), and the gate of Purgatory, as above.

Inferno, Canto III

The Vestibule of Hell

THE OPPORTUNISTS

The Poets pass the Gate of Hell and are immediately assailed by cries of anguish. Dante sees the first of the souls in torment. They are THE OPPORTUNISTS, those souls who in life were neither for good nor evil but only for themselves. Mixed with them are those outcasts who took no sides in the Rebellion of the Angels. They are neither in Hell nor out of it. Eternally unclassified, they race round and round pursuing a wavering banner that runs forever before them through the dirty air; and as they run they are pursued by swarms of wasps and hornets, who sting them and produce a constant flow of blood and putrid matter which trickles down the bodies of the sinners and is feasted upon by loathsome worms and maggots who coat the ground.

The law of Dante's Hell is the law of symbolic retribution. As they sinned so are they punished. They took no sides, therefore they are given no place. As they pursued the ever-shifting illusion of their own advantage, changing their courses with every changing wind, so they pursue eternally an elusive, ever-shifting banner. As their sin was a darkness, so they move in darkness. As their own guilty conscience pursued them, so they are pursued by swarms of wasps and hornets. And as their actions were a moral filth, so they run eternally through the filth of worms and maggots which they themselves feed.

Dante recognizes several, among them POPE CELESTINE V, but without delaying to speak to any of these souls, the Poets move on to ACHERON, the first of the rivers of Hell. Here the newly arrived souls of the damned gather and wait for monstrous CHARON to ferry them over to punishment. Charon recognizes Dante as a living man and angrily refuses him passage. Virgil forces Charon to serve them, but Dante swoons with terror, and does not reawaken until he is on the other side.

I AM THE WAY INTO THE CITY OF WOE.   1
I AM THE WAY TO A FORSAKEN PEOPLE.
I AM THE WAY INTO ETERNAL SORROW.
SACRED JUSTICE MOVED MY ARCHITECT.
I WAS RAISED HERE BY DIVINE OMNIPOTENCE,
PRIMORDIAL LOVE AND ULTIMATE INTELLECT.

ONLY THOSE ELEMENTS TIME CANNOT WEAR[1]
WERE MADE BEFORE ME, AND BEYOND TIME I
STAND.[2]

---

[1] **Only those elements time cannot wear** The Angels, the Empyrean, and the First Matter are the elements time cannot wear, for they will last to all time. Man, however, in his mortal state, is not eternal. The Gate of Hell, therefore, was created before man. The theological point is worth attention. The doctrine of Original Sin is, of course, one familiar to many creeds. Here, however, it would seem that the preparation for damnation predates Original Sin. True, in one interpretation, Hell was created for the punishment of the Rebellious Angels and not for man. Had man not sinned, he would never have known Hell. But on the other hand, Dante's God was one who knew all, and knew therefore that man would indeed sin. The theological problem is an extremely delicate one.

It is significant, however, that having sinned, man lives out his days on the rind of Hell, and that damnation is forever below his feet. This central concept of man's sinfulness, and, opposed to it, the doctrine of Christ's ever-abounding mercy, are central to all of Dante's theology. Only as man surrenders himself to Divine Love may he hope for salvation, and salvation is open to all who will surrender themselves.

[2] **and beyond time I stand** So odious is sin to God that there can be no end to its just punishment.

ABANDON ALL HOPE YE WHO ENTER HERE.[3]

These mysteries I read cut into stone 10
    above a gate. And turning I said: "Master,
    what is the meaning of this harsh inscription?"

And he then as initiate to novice:
    "Here must you put by all division of spirit
    and gather your soul against all cowardice.

This is the place I told you to expect.
    Here you shall pass among the fallen people,
    souls who have lost the good of intellect."

So saying, he put forth his hand to me,
    and with a gentle and encouraging smile 20
    he led me through the gate of mystery.

Here sighs and cries and wails coiled and recoiled
    on the starless air, spilling my soul to tears.
    A confusion of tongues and monstrous accents toiled

in pain and anger. Voices hoarse and shrill
    and sounds of blows, all intermingled, raised
    tumult and pandemonium that still

whirls on the air forever dirty with it
    as if a whirlwind sucked at sand. And I,
    holding my head in horror, cried: "Sweet Spirit, 30

what souls are these who run through this black haze?"
    And he to me: "These are the nearly soulless
    whose lives concluded neither blame nor praise.

They are mixed here with that despicable corps
    of angels who were neither for God nor Satan,
    but only for themselves. The High Creator

scourged them from Heaven for its perfect beauty,
    and Hell will not receive them since the wicked
    might feel some glory over them." And I:

"Master, what gnaws at them so hideously 40
    their lamentation stuns the very air?"
    "They have no hope of death," he answered me,

"and in their blind and unattaining state
    their miserable lives have sunk so low
    that they must envy every other fate.

No word of them survives their living season.
    Mercy and Justice deny them even a name.
    Let us not speak of them: look, and pass on."

I saw a banner there upon the mist.
    Circling and circling, it seemed to scorn all pause. 50
    So it ran on, and still behind it pressed

a never-ending rout of souls in pain.
    I had not thought death had undone so many
    as passed before me in that mournful train.

And some I knew among them; last of all
    I recognized the shadow of that soul
    who, in his cowardice, made the Great Denial.[4]

At once I understood for certain: these
    were of that retrograde and faithless crew
    hateful to God and to His enemies. 60

These wretches never born and never dead
    ran naked in a swarm of wasps and hornets
    that goaded them the more they fled,

and made their faces stream with bloody gouts
    of pus and tears that dribbled to their feet
    to be swallowed there by loathsome worms and
        maggots.

Then looking onward I made out a throng
    assembled on the beach of a wide river,
    whereupon I turned to him: "Master, I long

to know what souls these are, and what strange usage 70
    makes them as eager to cross as they seem to be
    in this infected light." At which the Sage:

---

[3] **Abandon all hope ye who enter here** The admonition, of course, is
to the damned and not to those who come on Heaven-sent errands.
The Harrowing of Hell (see Canto IV, note to 1. 53) provided the only
exemption from this decree, and that only through the direct interces-
sion of Christ.

[4] **who, in his cowardice, made the Great Denial** This is almost certainly intended to be Celestine V, who became Pope in 1294. He was a
man of saintly life, but allowed himself to be convinced by a priest
named Benedetto that his soul was in danger since no man could live
in the world without being damned. In fear for his soul he withdrew
from all worldly affairs and renounced the papacy. Benedetto
promptly assumed the mantle himself and became Boniface VIII, a
Pope who became for Dante a symbol of all the worst corruptions of
the church. Dante also blamed Boniface and his intrigues for many of
the evils that befell Florence. We shall learn in Canto XIX that the fires
of Hell are waiting for Boniface in the pit of the Simoniacs, and we
shall be given further evidence of his corruption in Canto XXVII.
Celestine's great guilt is that his cowardice (in selfish terror for his
own welfare) served as the door through which so much evil entered
the church.

"All this shall be made known to you when we stand
   on the joyless beach of Acheron." And I
   cast down my eyes, sensing a reprimand

in what he said, and so walked at his side
   in silence and ashamed until we came
   through the dead cavern to that sunless tide.

There, steering toward us in an ancient ferry
   came an old man[5] with a white bush of hair,   80
   bellowing: "Woe to you depraved souls! Bury

here and forever all hope of Paradise:
   I come to lead you to the other shore,
   into eternal dark, into fire and ice.

And you who are living yet, I say begone
   from these who are dead." But when he saw me stand
   against his violence he began again:

"By other windings[6] and by other steerage
   shall you cross to that other shore. Not here! Not here!
   A lighter craft than mine must give you passage."   90

And my Guide to him: "Charon, bite back your spleen:
   this has been willed where what is willed must be,
   and is not yours to ask what it may mean."

The steersman of that marsh of ruined souls,
   who wore a wheel of flame around each eye,
   stifled the rage that shook his woolly jowls.

But those unmanned and naked spirits there
   turned pale with fear and their teeth began to chatter
   at sound of his crude bellow. In despair

they blasphemed God,[7] their parents, their time on earth,   100
   the race of Adam, and the day and the hour
   and the place and the seed and the womb that gave
      them birth.

But all together they drew to that grim shore
   where all must come who lose the fear of God.
   Weeping and cursing they come for evermore,

and demon Charon with eyes like burning coals
   herds them in, and with a whistling oar
   flails on the stragglers to his wake of souls.

As leaves in autumn loosen and stream down
   until the branch stands bare above its tatters   110
   spread on the rustling ground, so one by one

the evil seed of Adam in its Fall
   cast themselves, at his signal, from the shore
   and streamed away like birds who hear their call.

So they are gone over that shadowy water,
   and always before they reach the other shore
   a new noise stirs on this, and new throngs gather.

"My son," the courteous Master said to me,
   "all who die in the shadow of God's wrath
   converge to this from every clime and country.   120

And all pass over eagerly, for here
   Divine Justice transforms and spurs them so
   their dread turns wish: they yearn for what they fear.[8]

No soul in Grace comes ever to this crossing;
   therefore if Charon rages at your presence
   you will understand the reason for his cursing."

When he had spoken, all the twilight country
   shook so violently, the terror of it
   bathes me with sweat even in memory:

the tear-soaked ground gave out a sigh of wind   130
   that spewed itself in flame on a red sky,
   and all my shattered senses left me. Blind,

like one whom sleep comes over in a swoon,[9]
   I stumbled into darkness and went down.

---

[5] **an old man** Charon. He is the ferryman of dead souls across the Acheron in all classical mythology.

[6] **By other windings** Charon recognizes Dante not only as a living man but as a soul in grace, and knows, therefore, that the Infernal Ferry was not intended for him. He is probably referring to the fact that souls destined for Purgatory and Heaven assemble not at his ferry point, but on the banks of the Tiber, from which they are transported by an Angel.

[7] **they blasphemed God** The souls of the damned are not permitted to repent, for repentance is a divine grace.

---

[8] **they yearn for what they fear** Hell (allegorically Sin) is what the souls of the damned really wish for. Hell is their actual and deliberate choice, for divine grace is denied to none who wish for it in their hearts. The damned must, in fact, deliberately harden their hearts to God in order to become damned. Christ's grace is sufficient to save all who wish for it.

[9] **DANTE'S SWOON** This device (repeated at the end of Canto V) serves a double purpose. The first is technical: Dante uses it to cover a transition. We are never told how he crossed Acheron, for that would involve certain narrative matters he can better deal with when he crosses Styx in Canto VII. The second is to provide a point of departure for a theme that is carried through the entire descent: the theme of Dante's emotional reaction to Hell. These two swoons early in the descent show him most susceptible to the grief about him. As he descends, pity leaves him, and he even goes so far as to add to the torments of one sinner. The allegory is clear: we must harden ourselves against every sympathy for sin.

∞

Inferno, Canto V

Circle Two

THE CARNAL

*The Poets leave Limbo and enter the SECOND CIRCLE. Here
begin the torments of Hell proper, and here, blocking the way, sits
MINOS, the dread and semi-bestial judge of the damned who
assigns to each soul its eternal torment. He orders the Poets back;
but Vergil silences him as he earlier silenced Charon, and the Poets
move on.*

*They find themselves on a dark ledge swept by a great whirl-
wind, which spins within it the souls of the CARNAL, those who
betrayed reason to their appetites. Their sin was to abandon themselves to the tempest of their passions: so they are swept forever in
the tempest of Hell, forever denied the light of reason and of God.
Vergil identifies many among them. SEMIRAMIS is there, and
DIDO, CLEOPATRA, HELEN, ACHILLES, PARIS, and TRIS-
TAN. Dante sees PAOLO and FRANCESCA swept together, and
in the name of love he calls to them to tell their sad story. They
pause from their eternal flight to come to him, and Francesca tells
their history while Paolo weeps at her side. Dante is so stricken by
compassion at their tragic tale that he swoons once again.*

So we went down to the second ledge alone;   1
    a smaller circle[1] of so much greater pain
    the voice of the damned rose in a bestial moan.

There Minos[2] sits, grinning, grotesque, and hale.
    He examines each lost soul as it arrives
    and delivers his verdict with his coiling tail.

That is to say, when the ill-fated soul
    appears before him it confesses all,[3]
    and that grim sorter of the dark and foul

decides which place in Hell shall be its end,   10
    then wraps his twitching tail about himself
    one coil for each degree it must descend.

The soul descends and others take its place:
    each crowds in its turn to judgment, each confesses,
    each hears its doom and falls away through space.

"O you who come into this camp of woe,"
    cried Minos when he saw me turn away
    without awaiting his judgment," watch where you go

once you have entered here, and to whom you turn!
    Do not be misled by that wide and easy passage!"   20
    And my Guide to him: "That is not your concern;

it is his fate to enter every door.
    This has been willed where what is willed must be,
    and is not yours to question. Say no more."

Now the choir of anguish, like a wound,
    strikes through the tortured air. Now I have come
    to Hell's full lamentation,[4] sound beyond sound.

I came to a place stripped bare of every light
    and roaring on the naked dark like seas
    wracked by a war of winds. Their hellish flight   30

of storm and counterstorm through time foregone,
    sweeps the souls of the damned before its charge.
    Whirling and battering it drives them on,

and when they pass the ruined gap of Hell[5]
    through which we had come, their shrieks begin anew.
    There they blaspheme the power of God eternal.

And this, I learned, was the never ending flight
    of those who sinned in the flesh, the carnal and lusty
    who betrayed reason to their appetite.

As the wings of wintering starlings bear them on   40
    in their great wheeling flights, just so the blast
    wherries these evil souls through time foregone.

---

[1] **a smaller circle** The pit of Hell tapers like a funnel. The circles of
ledges accordingly grow smaller as they descend.

[2] **Minos** Like all the monsters Dante assigns to the various offices of
Hell, Minos is drawn from classical mythology. He was the son of
Europa and of Zeus, who descended to her in the form of a bull.
Minos became a mythological king of Crete, so famous for his wisdom and justice that after death his soul was made judge of the dead.
Virgil presents him fulfilling the same office at Aeneas' descent to the
underworld. Dante, however, transforms him into an irate and
hideous monster with a tail. The transformation may have been suggested by the form Zeus assumed for the rape of Europa—the monster is certainly bullish enough here—but the obvious purpose of the
brutalization is to present a figure symbolic of the guilty conscience
of the wretches who come before it to make their confessions. Dante
freely reshapes his materials to his own purposes.

[3] **it confesses all** Just as the souls appeared eager to cross Acheron,
so they are eager to confess even while they dread. Dante is once
again making the point that sinners elect their Hell by an act of their
own will.

---

[4] **Hell's full lamentation** It is with the second circle that the real tortures of Hell begin.

[5] **the ruined gap of Hell** See note to Canto II, 53. At the time of the
Harrowing of Hell a great earthquake shook the underworld shattering rocks and cliffs. Ruins resulting from the same shock are noted in
Canto XII, 34, and Canto XXI, 112 ff. At the beginning of Canto XXIV,
the Poets leave the *bolgia* of the Hypocrites by climbing the ruined
slabs of a bridge that was shattered by this earthquake.

THE SINNERS OF THE SECOND CIRCLE (THE CARNAL): Here
begin the punishments for the various sins of Incontinence (The sins
of the She-Wolf). In the second circle are punished those who sinned
by excess of sexual passion. Since this is the most natural sin and the
sin most nearly associated with love, its punishment is the lightest of
all to be found in Hell proper. The Carnal are whirled and buffeted
endlessly through the murky air (symbolic of the beclouding of their
reason by passion) by a great gale (symbolic of their lust).

Here, there, up, down, they whirl and, whirling, strain
  with never a hope of hope to comfort them,
  not of release, but even of less pain.

As cranes go over sounding their harsh cry,
  leaving the long streak of their flight in air,
  so come these spirits, wailing as they fly.

And watching their shadows lashed by wind, I cried:
  "Master, what souls are these the very air   50
  lashes with its black whips from side to side?"

"The first of these whose history you would know,"
  he answered me, "was Empress of many tongues.[6]
  Mad sensuality corrupted her so

that to hide the guilt of her debauchery
  she licensed all depravity alike,
  and lust and law were one in her decree.

She is Semiramis of whom the tale is told
  how she married Ninus and succeeded him
  to the throne of that wide land the Sultans hold.   60

The other is Dido[7]; faithless to the ashes
  of Sichaeus, she killed herself for love.
  The next whom the eternal tempest lashes

is sense-drugged Cleopatra. See Helen there,
  from whom such ill arose. And great Achilles,[8]
  who fought at last with love in the house of prayer.

And Paris. And Tristan." As they whirled above
  he pointed out more than a thousand shades
  of those torn from the mortal life by love.

I stood there while my Teacher one by one   70
  named the great knights and ladies of dim time;
  and I was swept by pity and confusion.

At last I spoke: "Poet, I should be glad

to speak a word with those two swept together[9]
  so lightly on the wind and still so sad."

And he to me: "Watch them. When next they pass,
  call to them in the name of love that drives
  and damns them here. In that name they will pause."

Thus, as soon as the wind in its wild course
  brought them around, I called: "O wearied souls!   80
  if none forbid it, pause and speak to us."

As mating doves that love calls to their nest
  glide through the air with motionless raised wings,
  borne by the sweet desire that fills each breast—

Just so those spirits turned on the torn sky
  from the band where Dido whirls across the air;
  such was the power of pity in my cry.

"O living creature, gracious, kind, and good,
  going this pilgrimage through the sick night,
  visiting us who stained the earth with blood,   90

were the King of Time our friend, we would pray His
      peace
  on you who have pitied us. As long as the wind
  will let us pause, ask of us what you please.

The town where I was born lies by the shore
  where the Po descends into its ocean rest
  with its attendant streams in one long murmur.

Love, which in gentlest hearts will soonest bloom
  seized my lover with passion for that sweet body
  from which I was torn unshriven to my doom.

Love, which permits no loved one not to love,   100
  took me so strongly with delight in him

---

[6] **Empress of many tongues** Semiramis, a legendary queen of
Assyria who assumed full power at the death of her husband, Ninus.
[7] **Dido** Queen and founder of Carthage. She had vowed to remain
faithful to her husband, Sichaeus, but she fell in love with Aeneas.
When Aeneas abandoned her she stabbed herself on a funeral pyre
she had had prepared.
  According to Dante's own system of punishments, she should be
in the Seventh Circle (Canto XIII) with the suicides. The only clue
Dante gives to the tempering of her punishment is his statement that
"she killed herself for love." Dante always seems readiest to forgive
in that name.
[8] **Achilles** He is placed among this company because of his passion
for Polyxena, the daughter of Priam. For love of her, he agreed to
desert the Greeks and to join the Trojans, but when he went to the
temple for the wedding (according to the legend Dante has followed)
he was killed by Paris.

---

[9] **those two swept together** Paolo and Francesca (PAH-oe-loe: Frahn-
CHAY-ska).
  Dante's treatment of these two lovers is certainly the tenderest and
most sympathetic accorded any of the sinners in Hell, and legends
immediately began to grow about this pair.
  The facts are these. In 1275 Giovanni Malatesta (Djoe-VAH-nee
Mahl-ah-TEH-stah) of Rimini, called Giovanni the Lame, a somewhat
deformed but brave and powerful warrior, made a political marriage
with Francesca, daughter of Guido da Polenta of Ravenna. Francesca
came to Rimini and there an amour grew between her and Giovanni's younger brother Paolo. Despite the fact that Paolo had married in 1269 and had become the father of two daughters by 1275, his
affair with Francesca continued for many years. It was sometime
between 1283 and 1286 that Giovanni surprised them in Francesca's
bedroom and killed both of them.
  Around these facts the legend has grown that Paolo was sent by
Giovanni as his proxy to the marriage, that Francesca thought he was
her real bridegroom and accordingly gave him her heart irrevocably
at first sight. The legend obviously increases the pathos, but nothing
in Dante gives it support.

that we are one in Hell, as we were above.[10]

Love led us to one death. In the depths of Hell
    Caïna waits for him[11] who took our lives."
    This was the piteous tale they stopped to tell.

And when I had heard those world-offended lovers
    I bowed my head. At last the Poet spoke:
    "What painful thoughts are these your lowered brow
        covers?"

When at length I answered, I began: "Alas!
    What sweetest thoughts, what green and young desire   110
    led these two lovers to this sorry pass."

Then turning to those spirits once again,
    I said: "Francesca, what you suffer here
    melts me to tears of pity and of pain.

But tell me: in the time of your sweet sighs
    by what appearances found love the way
    to lure you to his perilous paradise?"

And she: "The double grief of a lost bliss
    is to recall its happy hour in pain.
    Your Guide and Teacher knows the truth of this.   120

But if there is indeed a soul in Hell
    to ask of the beginning of our love
    out of his pity, I will weep and tell:

On a day for dalliance we read the rhyme
    of Lancelot,[12] how love had mastered him.
    We were alone with innocence and dim time.[13]

Pause after pause that high old story drew
    our eyes together while we blushed and paled;
    but it was one soft passage overthrew

our caution and our hearts. For when we read   130
    how her fond smile was kissed by such a lover,
    he who is one with me alive and dead

breathed on my lips the tremor of his kiss.
    That book, and he who wrote it, was a pander.[14]
    That day we read no further." As she said this,

the other spirit, who stood by her, wept
    so piteously, I felt my senses reel
    and faint away with anguish. I was swept

by such a swoon as death is, and I fell,
    as a corpse might fall, to the dead floor of Hell.   140

---

[10] **that we are one in Hell, as we were above** At many points of *The Inferno*, Dante makes clear the principle that the souls of the damned are locked so blindly into their own guilt that none can feel sympathy for another, or find any pleasure in the presence of another. The temptation of many readers is to interpret this line romantically: *i.e.,* that the love of Paolo and Francesca survives Hell itself. The more Dantean interpretation, however, is that they add to one another's anguish (a) as mutual reminders of their sin, and (b) as insubstantial shades of the bodies for which they once felt such great passion.

[11] **Caïna waits for him** Giovanni Malatesta was still alive at the writing. His fate is already decided, however, and upon his death, his soul will fall to Caina, the first ring of the last circle (Canto XXXII), where lie those who performed acts of treachery against their kin.

[12] **the rhyme of Lancelot** The story exists in many forms. The details Dante makes use of are from an Old French version.

[13] **dim time** The original simply reads "We were alone, suspecting nothing." "Dim time" is rhyme-forced, but not wholly outside the legitimate implications of the original, I hope. The old courtly romance may well be thought of as happening in the dim ancient days. The apology, of course, comes after the fact: one does the possible, then argues for justification, and there probably is none.

[14] **that book, and he who wrote it, was a pander** "Galeotto," the Italian word for "pander," is also the Italian rendering of the name of Gallehault, who is the French Romance Dante refers to here, urged Lancelot and Guinevere on to love.

∞

Inferno, Canto XXXIV

NINTH CIRCLE: *Cocytus*   *Compound Fraud*
ROUND FOUR: *Judecca*   *The Treacherous to Their Masters*
THE CENTER   *Satan*

"On march the banners of the King," Vergil begins as the Poets face the last depth. He is quoting a medieval hymn, and to it he adds the distortion and perversion of all that lies about him. "On march the banners of the King—of Hell." And there before them, in an infernal parody of Godhead, they see Satan in the distance, his great wings beating like a windmill. It is their beating that is the source of the icy wind of Cocytus, the exhalation of all evil.

*   All about him in the ice are strewn the sinners of the last round, JUDECCA, named for Judas Iscariot. These are the TREACHEROUS TO THEIR MASTERS. They lie completely sealed in the ice, twisted and distorted into every conceivable posture. It is impossible to speak to them, and the Poets move on to observe Satan.*

*   He is fixed into the ice at the center to which flow all the rivers of guilt; and as he beats his great wings as if to escape, their icy wind only freezes him more surely into the polluted ice. In a grotesque parody of the Trinity, he has three faces, each a different color, and in each mouth he clamps a sinner whom he rips eternally with his teeth. JUDAS ISCARIOT is in the central mouth: BRUTUS and CASSIUS in the mouths on either side.*

*   Having seen all, the Poets now climb through the center, grappling hand over hand down the hairy flank of Satan himself—a last supremely symbolic action—and at last, when they have passed the center of all gravity, they emerge from Hell. A long climb from*

the earth's center to the Mount of Purgatory awaits them, and they push on without rest, ascending along the sides of the river Lethe, till they emerge once more to see the stars of Heaven, just before dawn on Easter Sunday.

"On march the banners of the King[1] of Hell,"
   my Master said. "Toward us. Look straight ahead:
   can you make him out at the core of the frozen shell?"

Like a whirling windmill seen afar at twilight,
   or when a mist has risen from the ground—
   just such an engine rose upon my sight

stirring up such a wild and bitter wind
   I cowered for shelter at my Master's back,
   there being no other windbreak I could find.

I stood now where the souls of the last class   10
   (with fear my verses tell it) were covered wholly;
   they shone below the ice like straws in glass.

Some lie stretched out; others are fixed in place
   upright, some on their heads, some on their soles;
   another, like a bow, bends foot to face.

When we had gone so far across the ice
   that it pleased my Guide to show me the foul creature[2]
   which once had worn the grace of Paradise,

he made me stop, and, stepping aside, he said:
   "Now see the face of Dis! This is the place   20
   where you must arm your soul against all dread."

Do not ask, Reader, how my blood ran cold
   and my voice choked up with fear. I cannot write it:
   this is a terror that cannot be told.

I did not die, and yet I lost life's breath:
   imagine for yourself what I became,
   deprived at once of both my life and death.

The Emperor of the Universe of Pain
   jutted his upper chest above the ice;
   and I am closer in size to the great mountain   30

the Titans make around the central pit,
   than they to his arms. Now, starting from this part,
   imagine the whole that corresponds to it!

If he was once as beautiful as now
   he is hideous, and still turned on his Maker,
   well may he be the source of every woe!

With what a sense of awe I saw his head

towering above me! for it had three faces:[3]
   one was in front, and it was fiery red;

the other two, as weirdly wonderful,   40
   merged with it from the middle of each shoulder
   to the point where all converged at the top of the skull;

the right was something between white and bile;
   the left was about the color that one finds
   on those who live along the banks of the Nile.

Under each head two wings rose terribly,
   their span proportioned to so gross a bird:
   I never saw such sails upon the sea.

They were not feathers—their texture and their form
   were like a bat's wings—and he beat them so   50
   that three winds blew from him in one great storm:

it is these winds that freeze all Cocytus.
   He wept from his six eyes, and down three chins
   the tears ran mixed with bloody froth and pus.[4]

In every mouth he worked a broken sinner
   between his rake-like teeth. Thus he kept three
   in eternal pain at his eternal dinner.

For the one in front the biting seemed to play
   no part at all compared to the ripping: at times
   the whole skin of his back was flayed away.   60

"That soul that suffers most," explained my Guide,
"is Judas[5] Iscariot, he who kicks his legs on the fiery chin
   and has his head inside.

Of the other two, who have their heads thrust forward,
   the one who dangles down from the black face
   is Brutus: note how he writhes without a word.

And there, with the huge and sinewy arms,[6] is the soul
   of Cassius.—But the night is coming on[7]
   and we must go, for we have seen the whole."

Then, as he bade, I clasped his neck, and he,
   watching for a moment when the wings   70
   were opened wide, reached over dexterously

and seized the shaggy coat of the king demon;

---

[1] **On march the banners of the King** The hymn (*Vexilla regis prodeunt*) was written in the sixth century by Venantius Fortunatus, Bishop of Poitiers. The original celebrates the Holy Cross, and is part of the service for Good Friday to be sung at the moment of uncovering the cross.
[2] **the foul creature** Satan.

[3] **three faces** Numerous interpretations of these three faces exist. What is essential to all explanation is that they be seen as perversions of the qualities of the Trinity.
[4] **bloody froth and pus** The gore of the sinners he chews which is mixed with his slaver.
[5] **Judas** Note how closely his punishment is patterned on that of the Simoniacs (Canto XIX).
[6] **huge and sinewy arms** The Cassius who betrayed Caesar was more generally described in terms of Shakespeare's "lean and hungry look." Another Cassius is described by Cicero (*Catiline* III) as huge and sinewy. Dante probably confused the two.
[7] **the night is coming on** It is now Saturday evening.

then grappling matted hair and frozen crusts
from one tuft to another, clambered down.

When we had reached the joint where the great thigh
merges into the swelling of the haunch,
my Guide and Master, straining terribly,

turned his head to where his feet had been
and began to grip the hair as if he were climbing;
so that I thought we moved toward Hell again. 80

"Hold fast!" my Guide said, and his breath came shrill[8]
with labor and exhaustion. "There is no way
but by such stairs to rise above such evil."

At last he climbed out through an opening
in the central rock, and he seated me on the rim;
then joined me with a nimble backward spring.

I looked up, thinking to see Lucifer
as I had left him, and I saw instead
his legs projecting high into the air.

Now let all those whose dull minds are still vexed 90
by failure to understand what point it was
I had passed through, judge if I was perplexed.

"Get up. Up on your feet," my Master said.
"The sun already mounts to middle tierce,[9]
and a long road and hard climbing lie ahead."

It was no hall of state we had found there,
but a natural animal pit hollowed from rock
with a broken floor and a close and sunless air.

"Before I tear myself from the Abyss,"
I said when I had risen, "O my Master, 100
explain to me my error in all this:

where is the ice? and Lucifer—how has he
been turned from top to bottom: and how can the sun
have gone from night to day so suddenly?"

And he to me: "You imagine you are still
on the other side of the center where I grasped
the shaggy flank of the Great Worm of Evil

which bores through the world—you *were* while I
climbed down,
but when I turned myself about, you passed

the point to which all gravities are drawn. 110

You are under the other hemisphere where you stand;
the sky above us is the half opposed
to that which canopies the great dry land.

Under the mid-point of that other sky
the Man who was born sinless and who lived
beyond all blemish, came to suffer and die.

You have your feet upon a little sphere
which forms the other face of the Judecca.
There it is evening when it is morning here.

And this gross Fiend and Image of all Evil 120
who made a stairway for us with his hide
is pinched and prisoned in the ice-pack still.

On this side he plunged down from heaven's height,
and the land that spread here once hid in the sea
and fled North to our hemisphere for fright;

and it may be that moved by that same fear,
the one peak[10] that still rises on this side
fled upward leaving this great cavern[11] here.

Down there, beginning at the further bound
of Beelzebub's dim tomb, there is a space 130
not known by sight, but only by the sound

of a little stream[12] descending through the hollow
it has eroded from the massive stone
in its endlessly entwining lazy flow."

My Guide and I crossed over and began
to mount that little known and lightless road
to ascend into the shining world again.

He first, I second, without thought of rest
we climbed the dark until we reached the point
where a round opening brought in sight the blest 140

and beauteous shining of the Heavenly cars.
And we walked out once more beneath the Stars.[13]

---

[8] **his breath came shrill** Cf. Canto XXIII, 85, where the fact that
Dante breathes indicates to the Hypocrites that he is alive. Vergil's
breathing is certainly a contradiction.

[9] **middle tierce** In the canonical day tierce is the period from about
six to nine A.M. Middle tierce, therefore, is seven-thirty. In going
through the center point, they have gone from night to day. They
have moved ahead twelve hours.

[10] **the one peak** The Mount of Purgatory.

[11] **this great cavern** The natural animal pit of line 97. It is also
"Beelzebub's dim tomb," line 130.

[12] **a little stream** Lethe. In classical mythology, the river of forgetfulness, from which souls drank before being born. In Dante's symbolism it flows down from the top of Purgatory, where it washes away
the memory of sin from the souls that have achieved purity. That
memory it delivers to Hell, which drawn all sin to itself.

[13] **Stars** As part of his total symbolism Dante ends each of the three
divisions of the *Commedia* with this word. Every conclusion of the
upward soul is toward the stars. God's shining symbols of hope and
virtue. It is just before dawn of Easter Sunday that the Poets
emerge—a further symbolism.

HILDEGARD OF BINGEN

Selections from *Scivias (Know the Ways of the Lord)*

Hildegard of Bingen (1098–1179) is a rare female voice from the Middle Ages. Indeed, in an era defined by a hierarchical male-dominated political, religious, and cultural system, she stands out as a remarkable individual. In particular, she expressed her most intimate feelings in books and participated in the period's major debates through public discourses and correspondence with leading figures. Today, as her reputation is on the rise, she has become a protean figure viewed from myriad angles, some contradictory, but all of them pioneering. Some admirers claim her as the first in a long line of visionary women who offers guidance to souls in distress. Others place her in the tradition of Christian thinkers who focus on Divine Wisdom, as evidenced by her stress on creation and redemption. Modern feminists salute her as a role model, for her managerial skills and willingness to confront patriarchal power. Traditionalists also admire her for her strong papalist politics, as a supporter of the church's hierarchy and the conservative reforms of Pope Gregory VII. Musicians and musicologists are now beginning to recognize her as an innovative composer of hymns and sacred songs. Historians study her letters for clues to the personalities of the period and for insight into medieval problems. Historians of science believe she broke new ground with her works on nature and medicine, especially regarding diagnosis and treatment of diseases. Finally, literary scholars identify her as a master of medieval prose with her prodigious and varied writings; they also marvel at the secret language she created, composed of nearly nine hundred words, to disguise her most confidential writing.

From the age of five to her last days, Hildegard experienced visions of God, in which she claimed she was directed to write down the details of her encounters as an aid to others. At first skeptical of her mystical writings, the church investigated but ultimately was satisfied and thereafter encouraged her in this path. Over the course of her life, she wrote three visionary books that are still considered classics of this genre. The first book dealt with religious beliefs, the second was concerned with virtue and vice, and the third summarized her theological ideas.

Scito vias Domini or *Know the Ways of the Lord,* better known by its shortened title, *Scivias,* was the first of Hildegard's three visionary and prophetic books. She worked on the book for ten years, from 1141 to 1151. Divided into three sections, it comprises a series of twenty-six visions, each accompanied by a commentary and an interpretation of the vision. Book One is on God the creator and what he has created; Book Two is on God the redeemer and his power of redemption; Book Three is a history of salvation as symbolized as a building with its towers, walls, and pillars representing various aspects of Christian salvation.

Hildegard explains each of the twenty-six visions by first describing the vision. She then interprets the vision with the aid of biblical texts and often in allegorical terms. Throughout she continually asks what is the meaning of each vision and concludes each vision with an admonition to the reader. By way of her visions, Hildegard addresses many topics of medieval Christian thought and doctrine, such as the power of God, the story of the creation, the various ways humans have fallen from grace, the Trinity, the role of the church, the devil, and the Day of Judgment.

Reading the Selections

The first selection is the "Declaration," which sets the pattern and tone for the remaining visions in *Scivias.* Hildegard describes her encounter with a "heavenly voice." In obedience to its urgings, she transcribes and interprets the mystical encounter. She concludes with an account of a mysterious illness, which probably accounts for her taking ten years to complete the book. Her final words recall the voice from heaven telling her that she must write about her visions.

"Confirmation," Vision Four in Book Two, begins, as do all the visions, with Hildegard's description of her vision or visual experience, followed by an explanation of the vision. In paragraph 1 she connects the first baptism with the power of confirmation for all Christians. Paragraphs 2, 3, and 4 offer further explanations of her vision. In paragraph 5 Hildegard turns to the scriptures to reinforce her argument, a device she often employed. In paragraph 14, the concluding passage, she quotes the prophet Ezekiel to underscore her argument that although the sacraments are necessary for salvation, repentance and good works are also mandatory for final salvation.

∞

Declaration
These Are True Visions Flowing from God

And behold! In the forty-third year of my earthly course, as I was gazing with great fear and trembling attention at a heavenly vision, I saw a great splendor in which resounded a voice from Heaven, saying to me,

"O fragile human, ashes of ashes, and filth of filth! Say and write what you see and hear. But since you are timid in speaking, and simple in expounding, and untaught in writing, speak and write these things not by a human mouth, and not by the understanding of human invention, and not by the requirements of human composition, but as you see and hear them on high in the heavenly places in the wonders of God. Explain these things in such a way that the hearer, receiving the words of his instructor, may expound them in those words, according to that will, vision and instruction. Thus therefore, O human, speak these things that you see and hear. And write them not by yourself or any other human being, but by the will of Him Who knows, sees and disposes all things in the secrets of His mysteries."

And again I heard the voice from Heaven saying to me, "Speak therefore of these wonders, and, being so taught, write them and speak."

It happened that, in the eleven hundred and forty-first year of the Incarnation of the Son of God, Jesus Christ, when I was forty-two years and seven months old, Heaven was opened and a fiery light of exceeding brilliance came and permeated my whole brain, and inflamed my whole heart and my whole breast, not like a burning but like a warming flame, as the sun warms anything its rays touch. And immediately I knew the meaning of the exposition of the Scriptures, namely the Psalter, the Gospel and the other catholic volumes of both the Old and the New Testaments, though I did not have the interpretation of the words of their texts or the division of the syllables or the knowledge of cases or tenses. But I had sensed in myself wonderfully the power and mystery of secret and admirable visions from my childhood—that is, from the age of five—up to that time, as I do now. This, however, I showed to no one except a few religious persons who were living in the same manner as I; but meanwhile, until the time when God by His grace wished it to be manifested, I concealed it in quiet silence. But the visions I saw I did not perceive in dreams, or sleep, or delirium, or by the eyes of the body, or by the ears of the outer self, or in hidden places; but I received them while awake and seeing with a pure mind and the eyes and ears of the inner self, in open places, as God willed it. How this might be is hard for mortal flesh to understand.

But when I had passed out of childhood and had reached the age of full maturity mentioned above, I heard a voice from Heaven saying, "I am the Living Light, Who illuminates the darkness. The person [Hildegard] whom I have chosen and whom I have miraculously stricken as I willed, I have placed among great wonders, beyond the measure of the ancient people who saw in Me many secrets; but I have laid her low on the earth, that she might not set herself up in arrogance of mind. The world has had in her no joy or lewdness or use in worldly things, for I have withdrawn her from impudent boldness, and she feels fear and is timid in her works. For she suffers in her inmost being and in the veins of her flesh; she is distressed in mind and sense and endures great pain of body, because no security has dwelt in her, but in all her undertakings she has judged herself guilty. For I have closed up the cracks in her heart that her mind may not exalt itself in pride or vainglory, but may feel fear and grief rather than joy and wantonness. Hence in My love she searched in her mind as to where she could find someone who would run in the path of salvation. And she found such a one and loved him [the monk Volmar of Disibodenberg], knowing that he was a faithful man, working like herself on another part of the work that leads to Me. And, holding fast to him, she worked with him in great zeal so that My hidden miracles might be revealed. And she did not seek to exalt herself above herself but with many sighs bowed to him whom she found in the ascent of humility and the intention of good will.

"O human, who receives these things meant to manifest what is hidden not in the disquiet of deception but in the purity of simplicity, write, therefore, the things you see and hear."

But I, though I saw and heard these things, refused to write for a long time through doubt and bad opinion and the diversity of human words, not with stubbornness but in the exercise of humility, until, laid low by the scourge of God, I fell upon a bed of sickness; then, compelled at last by many illnesses, and by the witness of a certain noble maiden of good conduct [the nun Richardis of Stade] and of that man whom I had secretly sought and found, as mentioned above, I set my hand to the writing. While I was doing it, I sensed, as I mentioned before, the deep profundity of scriptural exposition; and, raising myself from

illness by the strength I received, I brought this work to a close—though just barely—in ten years.

These visions took place and these words were written in the days of Henry, Archbishop of Mainz, and of Conrad, King of the Romans, and of Cuno, Abbot of Disibodenberg, under Pope Eugenius.

And I spoke and wrote these things not by the invention of my heart or that of any other person, but as by the secret mysteries of God I heard and received them in the heavenly places.

And again I heard a voice from Heaven saying to me, "Cry out therefore, and write thus!" 10

∽

Vision Four
Confirmation

And then I saw the image of an immense round tower, all made 1 *of a single white stone, with three windows in its summit from which shone so much brilliance that even the roof of the tower, which was constructed like a cone, showed very clearly in its light. These windows were adorned all round with beautiful emeralds. And the tower stood directly in back of the image of the woman described in the previous vision, just as a tower is placed in the wall of a city, so that because of its strength the image could not fall.*

And I saw those children who, as mentioned before, had passed through the womb of that image, shining with great brightness; some of them were adorned with gold color from their foreheads to their feet, but others lacked that color and had only the brightness. And some of these children were looking at a pure and brilliant splendor, but the rest at a turbulent red flash located in the East. Of those who were meditating on the pure and brilliant splendor, some had clear eyes and strong feet and were marching forward vigorously in the womb of the image; but others had weak eyes and crippled feet and were blown here and there by the wind. These, however, had a staff in their hands, and they flew in front of the image and touched it at times, though languidly. Still others had calm eyes but weak feet, and they moved back and forth in the air before the image; and others had weak eyes and strong feet, but they walked before the image languidly. But of the ones who were contemplating the turbulent red flash, some were well-ornamented and advanced into the image with vigor; but others tore themselves away from her and attacked her and broke her established rules. Among these, some by the fruit of penitence humbly returned to her, but others by obstinacy and neglect remained in the elation of the way of death. And again I heard the voice from Heaven saying to me:

1 Each baptized person should be anointed and confirmed by a bishop

After the illumination of baptism, which rose with the Sun of Justice Who sanctified the world by His own washing,

the new Bride of the Lamb was adorned and confirmed in the fire of the ardor of the Holy Spirit for the perfection of her beauty. So also each of the faithful who is regenerated by the Spirit and water should be decorated and confirmed by a bishop's anointing, so that he will be strengthened in all his members toward achieving beatitude and find himself most perfectly adorned with the full fruits of highest justice.

Therefore, *this tower that you see* represents the flaming forth of the gifts of the Holy Spirit, which the Father sent into the world for love of His Son, to enkindle the hearts of His disciples with fiery tongues and make them stronger in the name of the Holy and True Trinity. Before the coming upon them of the Holy Spirit in fire, they were sitting shut up in their house, protecting their bodies, for they were timid about speaking of God's justice and feeble in facing their enemies' persecutions. Because they had seen My Son in the flesh, their inner vision was unopened and they loved Him in the flesh, and thus did not yet see the bright teaching that afterward, when they were made strong in the Holy Spirit, they spread abroad in the world. But by Its coming they were so confirmed that they did not shrink from any penalty, but bravely endured it. And this is the strength of that tower, which strengthened the Church so much that the insane fury of the Devil can never overcome it.

2 Confirmation confers the immense sweetness of the Holy Spirit

You see the tower as immense and round, all made of a single 5 *white stone.* This means that the sweetness of the Holy Spirit is boundless and swift to encompass all creatures in grace, and no corruption can take away the fullness of its just integrity. Its path is a torrent, and streams of sanctity flow from it in its bright power, with never a stain of dirt in them; for the Holy Spirit Itself is a burning and shining serenity, which cannot be nullified, and which enkindles ardent virtue so as to put all darkness to flight.

3   In confirmation the Trinity manifests itself by verdant virtues

It has three windows in its summit from which shine so much brilliance that even the roof of the tower, which is constructed like a cone, shows very clearly in its light; for the ineffable Trinity is manifested in the outpouring of the gifts of the power of the Holy Spirit. And from the blessed Trinity so much clarity of justice emanates through the teaching of the apostles that in it the great power of Divinity, which in the height of its omnipotent majesty is incomprehensible, is shown more clearly to mortal creatures, that is, humans. But it can be grasped only as much as possible for the faith of a believing and faithful person.

Hence these windows are adorned all round with beautiful emeralds; for the Trinity is declared openly throughout the world by the verdant virtues and tribulations of the apostles, which are never greeted with arid apathy. How? Because it is known how ravening wolves sought to tear apart the apostles for their faith in the truth, and these various calamities strengthened them for the struggle, so that by fighting they constructed the Church and strengthened her with strong virtues to build up the faith and adorned her with many brilliancies. And because the Church, through the inspiration of the Holy Spirit, has been so strengthened by them, she desires and asks that her children also be adorned in this anointing by the Holy Spirit, Which penetrated the hearts of the faithful in that high and mystical mercy when by the will of God the Father It came into the world in fiery tongues. Therefore, the person who was baptized with the baptism of salvation must also be confirmed by the anointing of that excellent Teacher, as the Church is confirmed on the firm rock.

4   How the Church, fortified by the Holy Spirit, can never fall into error

Hence the tower stands directly in back of the image of the woman described in the previous vision, just as a tower is placed in the wall of a city, so that because of its strength the image cannot fall. For the Holy Spirit has worked marvels in the exceeding strength of Him Who is the true Bridegroom of the Church, and It shows the Church to be so strong in her defenses that, because of the fortitude she derives from Its fiery gift, she can never be thrown down by any error of wickedness. Under heavenly protection she will always rejoice, without spot or wrinkle, in the love of her Bridegroom, because My Only-Begotten was conceived nobly by the Holy Spirit and born without stain of the Virgin, as I said to Moses:

5   Words of Moses on this subject

"Behold, He said, there is a place with Me, and you shall stand upon the rock. And when My glory shall pass by, I will set you in a hole of the rock and protect you with My right hand, until I pass. And I will take away My hand, and you shall see My back parts" [Exodus 33:21–23]. What does this mean? The miracle is at hand that will be fulfilled in My will. But first you will fight with harsh legal precepts whose force is in their outward significance and where you will not find the sweetness and gentleness that will be revealed in My Son. And this harshness of the Law, which by My command you will write down, will stand in hard and stony hearts until you and your followers have shown all the glory that is to be rendered to Me until the coming of My Son. And when this is fulfilled in the Law you are writing, I will be glorified, and I will place you inside the pierced rock. How? I will place you in the hardness of the Law, appointing you to be over it as master of the old times, which will be pierced by My Son, when I send Him into the world at the right time and He expounds it farther than you have in His mystical words. So His strength will protect you, for He will bring words more acute than yours; and He will open the Law's commands that are now closed until He returns to Me. What does this mean?

He, taking on a body from the Virgin, will in that body give words of salvation to the world until in it He passes through death. Then I will take away My hand, when I lift Him up to Me above the stars and lay bare all His mysteries through the Holy Spirit; and thus you will see His Incarnation as a person is seen from the back and not the front, seeing Him when incarnate but not grasping His Divinity. For your children will see him when he returns to Me, more than they understood Him when He lived visibly among them.

6   The baptized are adorned when they are anointed by the bishop

And you see those children who, as mentioned before, had passed through the womb of that image, shining with great brightness. These are they who in the innocence of a clean and pure heart have gained a mother, the Church, in the font of regeneration, as was shown to you before, and are children of light, for their sins are washed away. *Some of them are adorned with gold color from their foreheads to their feet;* for from their beginning in good works to their end in sanctity, they are adorned with the shining gifts of the Holy Spirit by their anointing with chrism in the true faith at the hand of the bishop. How? Just as gold is adorned by having precious stones set into it, so baptism is adorned with the chrism given to those baptized in faith by the hand of the bishop, as it is written. . . .

14   Words of Ezekiel

"The King shall mourn, and the prince shall be clothed with sorrow, and the hands of the people of the land shall be troubled. I will do to them according to their way, and I will judge them according to their judgments, and they shall know that I am the Lord" [Ezekiel 7:27]. What does this mean? The soul in which Reason is king, feeling the pleasure of sin at hand, assents to it mournfully because it knows the evil of it. How? Because its reason, wisdom and knowledge are inspired by God; and thus, though the body consents, it finds the evil shameful, knowing that it is not good.

Therefore, when it is polluted with many crimes by the acts of the flesh, it heaves deep sighs and yearns for God. And when in the breath of pride the sinful deed is done, the body is clothed with confusion like an unworthy prince, having exercised its sovereignty in uncleanness; for as a person grieves when clothed in vile garments, so also he is sad when a shameful reputation originates, to his confusion, in himself. Therefore the bad deeds of those prostrate in their evils on the ground will be confounded by heavenly commands, for such do not have the garments of salvation, which is beatitude with God; and evil confusion will possess those who lack this happiness. And so I will deal with them in the road of iniquity in which they stand, honoring the path of sin and putting no justice into their hearts though warned by the Holy Spirit; I will grant them no mercy, because they do not know the good or fear Me, but disdain Me, the Creator of all, with raging wickedness, and do whatever they like.

Therefore I will judge them according to their own judgments, which are the works they desire and do; I will give them no rewards of happiness, but set the punishment of damnation in their way, since they show Me no honor; and they shall know that no one can free them from it except Me, the Lord of all.

But let the one who sees with watchful eyes and hears with attentive ears welcome with a kiss My mystical words, which proceed from Me Who am life.

10

THE LATE MIDDLE AGES
1300–1500

PETRARCH

Selections from the *Canzoniere* and "Letter to Posterity"

Francesco Petrarch (in Italian, "Petrarca") (1304–1374) is another of the West's great bridge figures (see St. Augustine's *Confessions*), whose careers straddle historical periods with opposing cultural tendencies. He lived in the Late Middle Ages, a period dominated by Gothic forms and ideals; yet, he was a founder of the Renaissance, for he was the first author to make his writing task the recovery and updating of the Classical literary tradition. He is particularly noted for his reintroduction of lost or neglected texts from antiquity into European culture. Inspired by Classicism, he placed the natural before the supernatural, thus reversing the judgment of his age; and he was the first European writer to defend secular culture and earthly fame. Despite his modern outlook, he saw some merit in the medieval view, as in the dialogue *Secretum* (or *My Secret*), in which he gives St. Augustine some of the best lines.

Despite being born in Italy and residing there, notably in Rome and Florence, for much of his life, Petrarch was a true European. Widely traveled, in part because of his studies and in part because his patrons required that he act as a diplomat, he spent months in France, Flanders, and the Rhineland. During these travels, he searched for and found old manuscripts (for example, some letters of Cicero), revised earlier works, and began new tasks. His most famous visit was to Avignon, a papal territory, where the worldliness of the papal court led him to coin the famous phrase "the Babylonian Captivity of the Papacy" to denote the seventy-year period when the popes lived in Avignon instead of Rome. His works, regardless of where written, reflect his impressions of daily life and his drive for self-understanding.

Reading the Selections

Besides being devoted to Classicism and Latin literature, Petrarch was equally famed as a master of Italian poetry, as shown in the *Canzoniere* (*Songbook* or *Rhymes*), his masterpiece in his native tongue. Drawing on Classical models and the ethos of the troubadour poets of southern France, these poems were inspired by the living woman he called Laura, whom he first saw in Avignon in 1327. Though she was married to someone else and completely uninterested in the poet's attentions, Laura personified beauty and truth for Petrarch. Nevertheless, in private life he wooed other women and fathered two children. When Laura was carried off by the Black Death in 1348, Petrarch turned to God, struggling with his sense of sin and the fate of his soul.

Three of the 366 poems in the *Canzoniere* are presented here. All were composed in the form of sonnets, the fourteen-line verse form that Petrarch inherited from Italian predecessors and brought to perfection. The Petrarchan sonnet is divided into two parts: The first eight lines usually rhyme *abbaabba;* the following six lines usually rhyme *cdecde.* This verse form was imported into England in the sixteenth century, where it enjoyed great vogue.

The three poems in the category of *in vita* (on life) recall Petrarch's introduction to Laura, who ignored him. They dwell on the pain of unrequited love.

Petrarch organized and edited most of the 550 letters he wrote during his lifetime. Some scholars believe that his letters provide the most accurate portrait of the man, as they reveal his personality and private thoughts and are less concerned with contemporary political and religious issues, which dominated much of his writing. His "Letter to Posterity" is usually considered to be quite different from his other letters. He probably meant it to be his autobiography, but it records his life only up to 1351, twenty-three years before his death in 1374. During that period Petrarch wrote many works, traveled on several diplomatic missions, and lived in Milan and Prague before settling in Padua and then Arquà, a small village outside Padua, where he spent his last years.

In this edited version of his Letter, Petrarch deprecates himself while, at the same time, implying that he has enjoyed his fame and reputation. On his education, he admits that the law, as a profession, did not appeal to him because the practice of law was "perverted by men's wickedness." His heart belonged to literature, and he dedicated the rest of his life to writing poems, essays, epics, histories, and his letters. Petrarch cherished friendships, one of the genuine pleasures of life, over material comforts; and he preferred small towns to large cities, which made Vaucluse, and later Arquà, so attractive to him.

3

It was the day the sun's ray had turned pale
with pity for the suffering of his Maker
when I was caught, and I put up no fight,
my lady, for your lovely eyes had bound me.

It seemed no time to be on guard against
Love's blows; therefore, I went my way
secure and fearless—so, all my misfortunes
began in midst of universal woe.

Love found me all disarmed and found the way
was clear to reach my heart down through the eyes
which have become the halls and doors of tears.

It seems to me it did him little honour
to wound me with his arrow in my state
and to you, armed, not show his bow at all.

132

If it's not love, then what is it I feel?
But if it's love, by God, what is this thing?
If good, why then the bitter mortal sting?
If bad, then why is every torment sweet?

If I burn willingly, why weep and grieve?
And if against my will, what good lamenting?
O living death, O pleasurable harm,
how can you rule me if I not consent?

And if I do consent, it's wrong to grieve.
Caught in contrasting winds in a frail boat
on the high seas I am without a helm,

so light of wisdom, so laden of error,
that I myself do not know what I want,
and shiver in midsummer, burn in winter.

∞

134

I find no peace, and I am not at war,   1
I fear and hope, and burn and I am ice;
I fly above the heavens, and lie on earth,
and I grasp nothing and embrace the world.

One keeps me jailed who neither locks nor opens,
nor keeps me for her own nor frees the noose;
Love does not kill, nor does he loose my chains;
he wants me lifeless but won't loosen me.

I see with no eyes, shout without a tongue;
I yearn to perish, and I beg for help;   10
I hate myself and love somebody else.

I thrive on pain and laugh with all my tears;
I dislike death as much as I do life:
because of you, lady, I am this way.

∞

"Letter to Posterity"

To posterity, an account of his background, conduct, and the development of his character and studies.

Francis Petrarch to posterity, greetings. Perhaps you will   1
have heard something about me, although this too is
doubtful, whether a petty, obscure name would reach far
into either space or time. And perhaps you will wish to
know what sort of man I was, or what were the results of
my labors, especially of those whose fame has reached
you or whose bare titles you have heard. On the first point
men's opinions will vary. For almost everyone speaks as
his pleasure, not the truth, impels, and there are no standards for either praise or blame. But I was one of your
troop, a poor mortal man, neither of too great nor of base
origin, but of an ancient family, as Augustus Caesar[1] says
of himself; by nature, anyhow, I was of neither foul nor
shameless temperament, had the habits caught from others not harmed it. Adolescence misled me, youth swept
me away, but old age set me right, and taught me by experience that truth I had read long before: that adolescence
and pleasure are vain; or rather, it was the Creator of all
ages and times who set me right. He sometimes allows
wretched mortals, puffed up with nothing, to go astray so
that, being aware of their sins, however late, they may
know themselves. In my youth my body was not very
strong, but quite supple. I do not boast of being especially
handsome, but enough to be pleasing in my greener
years—with a clear complexion, between light and dark,
lively eyes, and for a long time very keen vision, which
unexpectedly abandoned me after the sixtieth year, so
that, to my disgust I had to resort to glasses. Old age
invaded my body, which had been very healthy in every
age, and surrounded it with the usual array of ills.

I was born in exile in Arezzo in the year 1304 of this
last age, which began with Christ, at dawn on a Monday,
July [20], of honorable parents, Florentine in origin, of
modest fortune, and, to tell the truth, verging on poverty,
but driven from their homeland. I am a confirmed
despiser of riches, not because I would not wish for them,
but because I hated toil and worry, the inseparable companions of wealth—not that access to a fancy dinner
requires such worry! I have led a happier life with plain
living and ordinary fare than all the followers of Apicius,[2]
with their elaborate feasts. What are called banquets, since
they are revels, injurious to decency and good manners I
have always disliked. I considered it irksome and useless
to invite others for that purpose, and no less so to be
invited by others. But dining with friends is so delightful
that I have thought nothing more welcome than their
unexpected arrival, nor have I ever willingly taken a meal
without a companion. Nothing has displeased me more
than pomp, not only because it is evil and contrary to
humility, but because it is troublesome and distracting. I
struggled in my adolescence with the most intense but
constant and honorable love, and would have struggled
even longer, had not a premature but expedient death
extinguished the flame that was already cooling. I wish, of
course, I could say I was utterly free of lust, but, if I did, I
would be lying. This I shall say with confidence, that,
though carried away by the fervor of that age and of my
temperament, I have always cursed such vileness in my
heart. But as soon as I was approaching my fortieth year,
while I still had plenty of ardor and strength, I so completely threw off not only that obscene act, but the very
recollection of it, that it seemed I had never looked at a
woman. I count this among my greatest blessings, thanks
be to God who freed me, while still sound and vigorous,
from so vile and hateful a slavery.

---

[1] **Augustus Caesar** First Roman Emperor (31 B.C.–14 A.D.). Julius Caesar was his great uncle and adopted him as his son.

[2] **Apicius** Marcus Gavius Apicius, first-century A.D. Roman who supposedly spent much of his money to satisfy his desire for rare foods and delicacies.

But I turn to other matters. I have perceived pride in others, not in myself; and unimportant though I have been, in my own judgment I have always been even less important. My anger has very often hurt me, but never others. I have been a most eager and faithful devotee of honorable friendships. Fearlessly, because I know I speak the truth, I boast of being hot-tempered, but very forgetful of wrongs and ever mindful of kindnesses. I was fortunate to the point of envy in my associations with princes and kings, and in my friendships with nobles. But this is the penalty for growing old: to weep ever so often over the deaths of your dear ones. The greatest rulers of this age have loved and courted me; but I know not why—let them explain it. And I stayed with some of them in a way that they were, so to speak, my guests, so that I derived many advantages and no annoyances from their eminence. I fled, however, from many of those whom I loved a great deal; such love for freedom was implanted in me that I studiously avoided anyone whose very name seemed incompatible with it.

I had a well-balanced rather than a keen intellect, fit for all kinds of good and wholesome study, but especially inclined to moral philosophy and poetry. Yet in the course of time I abandoned the latter, when I found delight in sacred letters, in which I felt the hidden sweetness I once despised; for I limit poetry to embellishment only. I have dwelt single-mindedly on learning about antiquity, among other things because this age has always displeased me, so that, unless love for my dear ones pulled me the other way, I always wished to have been born in any other age whatever, and to forget this one, seeming always to graft myself in my mind onto other ages. I have therefore been charmed by the historians, though I was no less offended by their disagreements; and, when in doubt, I followed the version toward which either the verisimilitude of the content or the authority of the writers pulled me. My style, as some have said, was clear and powerful, but it seemed to me weak and obscure. In ordinary conversation with friends or relatives I have no concern for eloquence, and I marvel that Augustus Caesar did take such pains. But when the subject itself or the place or the listener seemed to demand otherwise, I have exerted myself a little, how successfully I do not know; let them judge in whose presence I spoke. As long as I lived well, I would care little how I had spoken; to seek fame merely from verbal elegance is but empty glory.

Either luck or my will has up to now divided my time in this fashion. The first year of my life I spent partially in Arezzo, where nature had brought me to light: the six following years in my father's country home in Incisa, fourteen miles above Florence, after my mother had been recalled from exile; my eighth year in Pisa, the ninth and thereafter in Transalpine Gaul, on the left bank of the Rhone in the city called Avignon, where the Roman Pontiff holds, and has long held, the Church of Christ in shameful exile, although a few years ago Urban V[3] seemed to have led her back to her own See. But it came to nothing, as is

obvious; and what I bear all the harder, it was even while he was alive, as if he repented of his good work. Had he lived a little longer, he would doubtless have learned how I felt about his retreat. My pen was already in hand, but that unhappy man abruptly deserted that glorious undertaking along with his life. How happily he could have died before the altar of Peter and in his own home! For had his successors remained in their See, he would have been the author of that fine achievement; or had they left, his virtue would have been all the nobler, the more obvious their fault. But this complaint is too long and not to the point.

There, then, on the bank of that very windy river, I spent my boyhood under my parents, and then my whole adolescence under my follies, but not without long absences. During this time I spent four whole years in the small city of Carpentras, a little to the east of Avignon; and in these two cities I learned as much of grammar, logic, and rhetoric as my age could, or rather, as is usually learned in school; and you, dear reader, know how little that is. Then I set out for Montpellier for the study of law, staying another four years there; then to Bologna where I spent three years and heard lectures on the whole body of civil law, and would have been a young man with a great future, as many thought, had I concentrated on the project. But I abandoned that subject altogether as soon as my parents abandoned me [because of their death]. Not that I did not like the dignity of the law, which is doubtless great and replete with Roman antiquity which delights me, but that practicing it is perverted by men's wickedness. It therefore irked me to master something I did not want to use dishonestly, and could scarcely use honestly; and had I wanted to, my good intentions would have been ascribed to inexperience.

So at the age of twenty-two I returned home. I call home that place of exile, Avignon, where I had been since my later childhood, for habit is like second nature. I already had begun to be known there, and my friendship sought by great men. Just why, I confess I do not now know, and marvel at it, though I did not marvel then, being of an age when I thought myself most worthy of every honor. I was sought primarily by the distinguished and generous Colonna family, which then frequented the Roman Curia, or rather, gave it luster. They summoned me and held me in great esteem which, however it may be now, I certainly did not deserve then; and that illustrious and incomparable man, Giacomo Colonna, then Bishop of Lombez, whose peer I know not whether I have ever seen or shall see, who took me to Gascony, where I spent a nearly heavenly summer in the foothills of the Pyrenees; my master and his retinue were so charming that I always sigh as I remember that time. Returning from there, for many years I was under his brother, Giovanni Cardinal Colonna, not as under a master but under a father, or rather, not even that, but with a most loving brother or with myself in my own home.

At that time a youthful craving drove me to travel through France and Germany; and although I invented other reasons to have my elders approve my journey, the real reason was my ardor and curiosity to see many things. On that journey I saw Paris for the first time and was delighted to inquire what was true and what was mythical in the stories told about that city. On my return, I went to

---

[3] **Urban V** Pope (1378–1389) who tried to return the papacy to Rome between 1367 and 1370. He failed, and the church remained in Avignon until 1377. Petrarch was a bitter critic of the Avignon exile.

Rome, which I had ardently longed to see since childhood. There I so waited upon Stefano Colonna, the noble head of the family, a man equal to any of the ancients, and I was so well received that you would say there was no distinction between me and any of his sons. The love and affection of that excellent man for me always remained constant until the last day of his life; and even now it lives in me, and will never end, unless I come to an end first.

When I again returned from there, since I cannot bear the nausea and hate for all cities implanted in my heart by nature, and above all for that most disgusting city [Avignon]. I sought some refuge as though it were a haven; and I discovered a tiny valley, secluded and delightful, called Vaucluse, about fifteen miles from Avignon, where the king of all springs, the Sorgue, rises. Taken by the charm of the place, I moved my books and myself there. It will be a long story if I go on to describe what I did there over many, many years. To be brief, almost all of the works I have let fall from my pen were either completed or begun or conceived there. . . .

Later on, the blazon of fame won me the good will of a fine man; I do not know whether among the lords of his time there has been anyone like him, or rather I know there has been none—I mean Giacomo da Carrara the Younger, through whose messengers and letters I was wearied with such earnest entreaties beyond the Alps when I was there, and wherever I was throughout Italy for many years. I was so urged into friendship with him that, though I hoped for nothing from the well-to-do. I decided at last to go to him and see what this insistence on the part of a great man, unknown to me, meant. Thus, I came, though late, to Padua, where I was received by that man of illustrious memory, not just kindly, but as the blessed souls are greeted in heaven, with such joy and such inestimable love and fondness, that, since I cannot hope to equal it with words, it is better to cover it with silence. Among many things, knowing that I had led a clerical life since childhood, he made me a canon of Padua in order to bind me more tightly not only to himself but to his city. In short, had his life been longer, it would have been the end of all my wandering and journeys. But alas, among mortals nothing is enduring; and if anything sweet appears, it soon ends in bitterness. In not quite two years, God, who had sent him to me, to his fatherland, and to the world, took him away; neither I nor his fatherland nor the world—I am not blinded by love—was worthy of him. And although he was succeeded by his son, a most prudent and eminent man who, following in his father's footsteps, always loved and honored me, still, after the loss of the one with whom I had been better matched, especially in age. I again returned to France, incapable of staying still, and not so much with a yearning to see again what I had seen a thousand times, as with an effort to cope with stiffness—as sick people do—by a shift of position.

10

GIOVANNI BOCCACCIO

Selections from *The Decameron*

The Decameron is one of the most important works of European literature. It was written by Giovanni Boccaccio (1313–1375), the contemporary of his fellow humanist and friend, Petrarch (see *Canzoniere* and "Letter to Posterity"), in turbulent fourteenth-century Italy. Like Petrarch, he was devoted to Classicism, especially to reading and translating the great works of Latin literature. Boccaccio, too, was attracted to the world's delights, recognizing that life was to be experienced and, for the most part, enjoyed. He also suffered the pangs of guilt for his sins and expressed regrets about his earlier life in his old age.

The illegitimate son of a successful Florentine financier, Boccaccio prepared for a banking career and studied law before turning to a life of letters. Awakened to the possibility of a literary career while attached to the court of the well-educated king of Naples, Robert the Wise (r. 1309–1343), he became enamored of a court lady whom he christened Fiammetta (Little Flame) and wrote sonnets to her in the style of Petrarch. Removed to Florence, where his literary fame and fortune soared, he lived an active life engaged in diplomatic missions that took him up and down the Italian peninsula. In Florence, he survived the devastation of the Black Death, which, by one estimate, killed nearly half the population in 1348.

Boccaccio's Classical scholarship, medieval romances in both poetry and prose, and Italian love lyrics would have ensured him an honored place in Western letters; however, *The Decameron* has made him one of the literary immortals. Composed between 1349 and 1353, *The Decameron* presents this chaotic age in microcosm, showing the good and evil therein. It contains a rich collection of folktales, parables, romances, and stories from Italian, French, Near Eastern, Classical, and biblical sources. The work's realism, secular spirit, and frank probing of the human heart had an immediate impact on European fiction, leading ultimately to the modern novel. In later years, Boccaccio expressed regret about his most famous work, deploring its lighthearted style.

Reading the Selections

The Decameron (from the Greek for "ten") is a tale within a tale, an old genre most famously realized in *The Arabian Nights* (see Chapter Eight). In Boccaccio's work, this structure unfolds as ten young Florentines—seven ladies and three gentlemen—escape the plague that is ravaging their city and take refuge in a country palace. There, they pass the time, each telling a story a day for ten days, hence one hundred tales total.

The first selection, taken from the author's introduction to *The Decameron,* opens with Boccaccio addressing female readers, the audience for vernacular literature in the Middle Ages because male readers supposedly were only interested in works in Latin. He advises these "fairest ladies" not to give up too soon on his book, though he knows that the details of the plague, which of necessity he must include in his story, may be unappetizing to them. After this warning, he describes the plague, showing how it disrupted Florentine life at every level—one of the most valuable aspects of this work for modern scholars. The details of the disease's symptoms and the victims' suffering—verified as accurate by medical historians—vividly portray the conditions under which people died or survived. He also discusses varied responses to the plague, ranging from self-imposed isolation to riotous living to even abandoning loved ones, including spouses and children.

The second selection (from First Day, Third Story) contains the philosophical tale known as "the legend of the three rings." In it, Melchisedech, a Jew, escapes a trap set by Saladin, a Muslim warrior whose deeds made him a hero to medieval Europeans even though his reputation came from fighting Christians during the Crusades. Saladin, needing money, invites the rich Melchisedech to dinner and asks which of the three faiths—Christianity, Judaism, or Islam—is best. Aware that this is a trick question, Melchisedech replies with an allegorical fable that artfully avoids calling one religion the best. Saladin, recognizing Melchisedech's wisdom, adopts him as a close friend. Such a tale suggests that Boccaccio was freer of religious bigotry than most Europeans of the time.

∽

Introduction

· · ·

Whenever, fairest ladies, I pause to consider how compassionate you all are by nature, I invariably become aware that the present work will seem to you to possess an irksome and ponderous opening. For it carries at its head the painful memory of the deadly havoc wrought by the recent plague, which brought so much heartache and misery to those who witnessed, or had experience of it. But I do not want you to be deterred, for this reason, from reading any further, on the assumption that you are to be subjected, as you read, to an endless torrent of tears and sobbing. You will be affected no differently by this grim beginning than walkers confronted by a steep and rugged hill, beyond which there lies a beautiful and delectable plain. The degree of pleasure they derive from the latter will correspond directly to the difficulty of the climb and the descent. And just as the end of mirth is heaviness, so sorrows are dispersed by the advent of joy.

This brief unpleasantness (I call it brief, inasmuch as it is contained within few words) is quickly followed by the sweetness and the pleasure which I have already promised you, and which, unless you were told in advance, you would not perhaps be expecting to find after such a beginning as this. Believe me, if I could decently have taken you whither I desire by some other route, rather than along a path so difficult as this, I would gladly have done so. But since it is impossible without this memoir to show the origin of the events you will read about later, I really have no alternative but to address myself to its composition.

I say, then, that the sum of thirteen hundred and forty-eight years had elapsed since the fruitful Incarnation of the Son of God, when the noble city of Florence, which for its great beauty excels all others in Italy, was visited by the deadly pestilence. Some say that it descended upon the human race through the influence of the heavenly bodies, others that it was a punishment signifying God's righteous anger at our iniquitous way of life. But whatever its cause, it had originated some years earlier in the East, where it had claimed countless lives before it unhappily spread westward, growing in strength as it swept relentlessly on from one place to the next.

In the face of its onrush, all the wisdom and ingenuity of man were unavailing. Large quantities of refuse were cleared out of the city by officials specially appointed for the purpose, all sick persons were forbidden entry, and numerous instructions were issued for safeguarding the people's health, but all to no avail. Nor were the countless petitions humbly directed to God by the pious, whether by means of formal processions or in any other guise, any less ineffectual. For in the early spring of the year we have mentioned, the plague began, in a terrifying and extraordinary manner, to make its disastrous effects apparent. It did not take the form it had assumed in the East, where if anyone bled from the nose it was an obvious portent of certain death. On the contrary, its earliest symptom, in men and women alike, was the appearance of certain swellings in the groin or the armpit, some of which were egg-shaped whilst others were roughly the size of the common apple. Sometimes the swellings were large, sometimes not so large, and they were referred to by the populace as *gavòccioli*. From the two areas already mentioned, this deadly *gavòcciolo* would begin to spread, and within a short time it would appear at random all over the body. Later on, the symptoms of the disease changed, and many people began to find dark blotches and bruises on their arms, thighs, and other parts of the body, sometimes large and few in number, at other times tiny and closely spaced. These, to anyone unfortunate enough to contract them, were just as infallible a sign that he would die as the *gavòcciolo* had been earlier, and as indeed it still was.

Against these maladies, it seemed that all the advice of physicians and all the power of medicine were profitless and unavailing. Perhaps the nature of the illness was such that it allowed no remedy: or perhaps those people who were treating the illness (whose numbers had increased enormously because the ranks of the qualified were invaded by people, both men and women, who had never received any training in medicine), being ignorant of its causes, were not prescribing the appropriate cure. At all events, few of those who caught it ever recovered, and in most cases death occurred within three days from the appearance of the symptoms we have described, some people dying more rapidly than others, the majority without any fever or other complications.

But what made this pestilence even more severe was that whenever those suffering from it mixed with people who were still unaffected, it would rush upon these with the speed of a fire racing through dry or oily substances that happened to be placed within its reach. Nor was this the full extent of its evil, for not only did it infect healthy persons who conversed or had any dealings with the sick, making them ill or visiting an equally horrible death upon

them, but it also seemed to transfer the sickness to anyone touching the clothes or other objects which had been handled or used by its victims.

It is a remarkable story that I have to relate. And were it not for the fact that I am one of many people who saw it with their own eyes, I would scarcely dare to believe it, let alone commit it to paper, even though I had heard it from a person whose word I could trust. The plague I have been describing was of so contagious a nature that very often it visibly did more than simply pass from one person to another. In other words, whenever an animal other than a human being touched anything belonging to a person who had been stricken or exterminated by the disease, it not only caught the sickness, but died from it almost at once. To all of this, as I have just said, my own eyes bore witness on more than one occasion. One day, for instance, the rags of a pauper who had died from the disease were thrown into the street, where they attracted the attention of two pigs. In their wonted fashion, the pigs first of all gave the rags a thorough mauling with their snouts after which they took them between their teeth and shook them against their cheeks. And within a short time they began to writhe as though they had been poisoned, then they both dropped dead to the ground, spreadeagled upon the rags that had brought about their undoing.

These things, and many others of a similar or even worse nature, caused various fears and fantasies to take root in the minds of those who were still alive and well. And almost without exception, they took a single and very inhuman precaution, namely to avoid or run away from the sick and their belongings, by which means they all thought that their own health would be preserved.

Some people were of the opinion that a sober and abstemious mode of living considerably reduced the risk of infection. They therefore formed themselves into groups and lived in isolation from everyone else. Having withdrawn to a comfortable abode where there were no sick persons, they locked themselves in and settled down to a peaceable existence, consuming modest quantities of delicate foods and precious wines and avoiding all excesses. They refrained from speaking to outsiders, refused to receive news of the dead or the sick, and entertained themselves with music and whatever other amusements they were able to devise.

Others took the opposite view, and maintained that an infallible way of warding off this appalling evil was to drink heavily, enjoy life to the full, go round singing and merrymaking, gratify all of one's cravings whenever the opportunity offered, and shrug the whole thing off as one enormous joke. Moreover, they practised what they preached to the best of their ability, for they would visit one tavern after another, drinking all day and night to immoderate excess; or alternatively (and this was their more frequent custom), they would do their drinking in various private houses, but only in the ones where the conversation was restricted to subjects that were pleasant or entertaining. Such places were easy to find, for people behaved as though their days were numbered, and treated their belongings and their own persons with equal abandon. Hence most houses had become common property, and any passing stranger could make himself at home as naturally as though he were the rightful owner. But for all their riotous manner of living, these people always took good care to avoid any contact with the sick.

In the face of so much affliction and misery, all respect for the laws of God and man had virtually broken down and been extinguished in our city. For like everybody else, those ministers and executors of the laws who were not either dead or ill were left with so few subordinates that they were unable to discharge any of their duties. Hence everyone was free to behave as he pleased.

There were many other people who steered a middle course between the two already mentioned, neither restricting their diet to the same degree as the first group, nor indulging so freely as the second in drinking and other forms of wantonness, but simply doing no more than satisfy their appetite. Instead of incarcerating themselves, these people moved about freely, holding in their hands a posy of flowers, or fragrant herbs, or one of a wide range of spices, which they applied at frequent intervals to their nostrils, thinking it an excellent idea to fortify the brain with smells of that particular sort; for the stench of dead bodies, sickness, and medicines seemed to fill and pollute the whole of the atmosphere.

Some people, pursuing what was possibly the safer alternative, callously maintained that there was no better or more efficacious remedy against a plague than to run away from it. Swayed by this argument, and sparing no thought for anyone but themselves, large numbers of men and women abandoned their city, their homes, their relatives, their estates and their belongings, and headed for the countryside, either in Florentine territory or, better still, abroad. It was as though they imagined that the wrath of God would not unleash this plague against men for their iniquities irrespective of where they happened to be, but would only be aroused against those who found themselves within the city walls; or possibly they assumed that the whole of the population would be exterminated and that the city's last hour had come.

Of the people who held these various opinions, not all of them died. Nor, however, did they all survive. On the contrary, many of each different persuasion fell ill here, there, and everywhere, and having themselves, when they were fit and well, set an example to those who were as yet unaffected, they languished away with virtually no one to nurse them. It was not merely a question of one citizen avoiding another, and of people almost invariably neglecting their neighbours and rarely or never visiting their relatives, addressing them only from a distance; this scourge had implanted so great a terror in the hearts of men and women that brothers abandoned brothers, uncles their nephews, sisters their brothers, and in many cases wives deserted their husbands. But even worse, and almost incredible, was the fact that fathers and mothers refused to nurse and assist their own children, as though they did not belong to them.

Hence the countless numbers of people who fell ill, both male and female, were entirely dependent upon either the charity of friends (who were few and far between) or the greed of servants, who remained in short supply despite the attraction of high wages out of all proportion to the services they performed. Furthermore, these latter were men and women of coarse intellect and the majority were unused to such duties, and they did little more than hand things to the invalid when asked to do so and watch over him when he was dying. And in performing this kind of service, they frequently lost their lives as well as their earnings.

As a result of this wholesale desertion of the sick by neighbours, relatives and friends, and in view of the scarcity of servants, there grew up a practice almost never previously heard of, whereby when a woman fell ill, no matter how gracious or beautiful or gently bred she might be, she raised no objection to being attended by a male servant, whether he was young or not. Nor did she have any scruples about showing him every part of her body as freely as she would have displayed it to a woman, provided that the nature of her infirmity required her to do so; and this explains why those women who recovered were possibly less chaste in the period that followed.

Moreover a great many people died who would perhaps have survived had they received some assistance. And hence, what with the lack of appropriate means for tending the sick, and the virulence of the plague, the number of deaths reported in the city whether by day or night was so enormous that it astonished all who heard tell of it, to say nothing of the people who actually witnessed the carnage. And it was perhaps inevitable that among the citizens who survived there arose certain customs that were quite contrary to established tradition.

It had once been customary, as it is again nowadays, for the women relatives and neighbours of a dead man to assemble in his house in order to mourn in the company of the women who had been closest to him; moreover his kinfolk would forgather in front of his house along with his neighbours and various other citizens, and there would be a contingent of priests, whose numbers varied according to the quality of the deceased; his body would be taken thence to the church in which he had wanted to be buried, being borne on the shoulders of his peers amidst the funeral pomp of candles and dirges. But as the ferocity of the plague began to mount, this practice all but disappeared entirely and was replaced by different customs. For not only did people die without having many women about them, but a great number departed this life without anyone at all to witness their going. Few indeed were those to whom the lamentations and bitter tears of their relatives were accorded; on the contrary, more often than not bereavement was the signal for laughter and witticisms and general jollification—the art of which the women, having for the most part suppressed their feminine concern for the salvation of the souls of the dead, had learned to perfection. Moreover it was rare for the bodies of the dead to be accompanied by more than ten or twelve neighbours to the church, nor were they borne on the shoulders of worthy and honest citizens, but by a kind of gravedigging fraternity, newly come into being and drawn from the lower orders of society. These people assumed the title of sexton, and demanded a fat fee for their services, which consisted in taking up the coffin and hauling it swiftly away, not to the church specified by the dead man in his will, but usually to the nearest at hand. They would be preceded by a group of four or six clerics, who between them carried one or two candles at most, and sometimes none at all. Nor did the priests go to the trouble of pronouncing solemn and lengthy funeral rites, but, with the aid of these so-called sextons, they hastily lowered the body into the nearest empty grave they could find.

As for the common people and a large proportion of the bourgeoisie, they presented a much more pathetic spectacle, for the majority of them were constrained, either by their poverty or the hope of survival, to remain in their houses. Being confined to their own parts of the city, they fell ill daily in their thousands, and since they had no one to assist them or attend to their needs, they inevitably perished almost without exception. Many dropped dead in the open streets, both by day and by night, whilst a great many others, though dying in their own houses, drew their neighbours' attention to the fact more by the smell of their rotting corpses than by any other means. And what with these, and the others who were dying all over the city, bodies were here, there and everywhere.

Whenever people died, their neighbours nearly always followed a single, set routine, prompted as much by their fear of being contaminated by the decaying corpse as by any charitable feelings they may have entertained towards the deceased. Either on their own, or with the assistance of bearers whenever these were to be had, they extracted the bodies of the dead from their houses and left them lying outside their front doors, where anyone going about the streets, especially in the early morning, could have observed countless numbers of them. Funeral biers would then be sent for, upon which the dead were taken away, though there were some who, for lack of biers, were carried off on plain boards. It was by no means rare for more than one of these biers to be seen with two or three bodies upon it at a time; on the contrary, many were seen to contain a husband and wife, two or three brothers and sisters, a father and son, or some other pair of close relatives. And times without number it happened that two priests would be on their way to bury someone, holding a cross before them, only to find that bearers carrying three or four additional biers would fall in behind them; so that whereas the priests had thought they had only one burial to attend to, they in fact had six or seven, and sometimes more. Even in these circumstances, however, there were no tears or candles or mourners to honour the dead; in fact, no more respect was accorded to dead people than would nowadays be shown towards dead goats. For it was quite apparent that the one thing which, in normal times, no wise man had ever learned to accept with patient resignation (even though it struck so seldom and unobtrusively), had now been brought home to the feeble-minded as well, but the scale of the calamity caused them to regard it with indifference.

Such was the multitude of corpses (of which further consignments were arriving every day and almost by the hour at each of the churches), that there was not sufficient consecrated ground for them to be buried in, especially if each was to have its own plot in accordance with long-established custom. So when all the graves were full, huge trenches were excavated in the churchyards, into which new arrivals were placed in their hundreds, stowed tier upon tier like ships' cargo, each layer of corpses being covered over with a thin layer of soil till the trench was filled to the top.

But rather than describe in elaborate detail the calamities . . . experienced in the city at that time, I must mention that, whilst an ill wind was blowing through Florence itself, the surrounding region was no less badly affected. In the fortified towns, conditions were similar to those in the city itself on a minor scale; but in the scattered hamlets and the countryside proper, the poor unfortunate peasants and their families had no physicians or servants whatever to assist them, and collapsed by the wayside, in their fields, and in their cottages at all hours of the day and night, dying more like animals than human beings. Like the townspeople, they too grew apathetic in their ways, disregarded their affairs, and neglected their possessions. Moreover they all behaved as though each day was to be their last, and far from making provision for the future by tilling their lands, tending their flocks, and adding to their previous labours, they tried in every way they could think of to squander the assets already in their possession. Thus it came about that oxen, asses, sheep, goats, pigs, chickens, and even dogs (for all their deep fidelity to man) were driven away and allowed to roam freely through the fields, where the crops lay abandoned and had not even been reaped, let alone gathered in. And after a whole day's feasting, many of these animals, as though possessing the power of reason, would return glutted in the evening to their own quarters, without any shepherd to guide them.

But let us leave the countryside and return to the city. What more remains to be said, except that the cruelty of heaven (and possibly, in some measure, also that of man) was so immense and so devastating that between March and July of the year in question, what with the fury of the pestilence and the fact that so many of the sick were inadequately cared for or abandoned in their hour of need because the healthy were too terrified to approach them, it is reliably thought that over a hundred thousand human lives were extinguished within the walls of the city of Florence? Yet before this lethal catastrophe fell upon the city, it is doubtful whether anyone would have guessed it contained so many inhabitants.

Ah, how great a number of splendid palaces, fine houses, and noble dwellings, once filled with retainers, with lords and with ladies, were bereft of all who had lived there, down to the tiniest child! How numerous were the famous families, the vast estates, the notable fortunes, that were seen to be left without a rightful successor! How many gallant gentlemen, fair ladies, and sprightly youths, who would have been judged hale and hearty by Galen, Hippocrates and Aesculapius[1] (to say nothing of others), having breakfasted in the morning with their kinsfolk, acquaintances and friends, supped that same evening with their ancestors in the next world! . . .

---

[1] **Galen, Hippocrates, and Aesculapius** Galen and Hippocrates were famous Greek physicians well known in the Middle Ages. Aesculapius was the Greek god of healing, who was also worshiped by the Romans.

∽

First Day, Third Story

Melchisedech, a Jew, by means of a short story about three rings, escapes from a trap set for him by Saladin.

Neifile's tale was praised by all, and when she had finished talking, at the queen's command, Filomena began to speak in this fashion.

The tale that Neifile told brings back to my memory a dangerous incident that once happened to a Jew; and since God and the truth of our faith have already been well dealt with by us, we should not be forbidden to descend to the acts of men from now on. Now, I shall tell you this story and when you have heard it, perhaps you will become more cautious when you reply to questions put to you.

You should know, my dear companions, that just as stupidity can often remove one from a state of happiness and place him in the greatest misery, so, too, intelligence can rescue the wise man from the gravest of dangers and restore him to his secure state. The fact that stupidity leads one from a state of happiness to one of misery is shown by many examples which, at present, I do not intend to relate, since thousands of clear illustrations of this appear every day; but, as I promised, I shall demonstrate briefly in a little story how intelligence may be the cause of some consolation.

Saladin, whose worth was such that from humble beginnings he became Sultan of Babylon and won many victories over Christian and Saracen kings, discovered one day that he had consumed, in his various wars and his displays of grandiose magnificence, all his treasury, while the occasion arose in which he needed a large amount of money. Not being able to envision a means of obtaining what he needed in a short time, he happened to recall a rich Jew, whose name was Melchisedech, who loaned money at usurious rates in Alexandria, and he thought that this man might be able to assist him, if only he would agree to. But this Jew was so avaricious that he would not do so of his own free will, and the Sultan did not wish to have recourse to force; therefore, as his need was pressing, he thought of nothing but finding a means of getting the Jew to help him, and he decided to use some colorful pretext to accomplish this. He had him summoned, and after welcoming him in a friendly manner, he had him sit beside him and said to him:

"Worthy man, I have heard from many people that you are very wise and most versed in the affairs of God; because of this, I should like to know from you which of the three Laws you believe to be the true one: the Jewish, the Saracen,[1] or the Christian."

The Jew, who really was a wise man, realized too well that Saladin was trying to catch him with his words in order to accuse him of something, and he understood that he could not praise any of the three Laws more than the other without Saladin achieving his goal; therefore, he sharpened his wits, like one who seems to need an answer

in order not to be entrapped, and knew well what he had to say before he had to, and said:

"My Lord, the question which you have put to me is a good one, and in order to give you an answer, I shall have to tell you a little story which you shall now hear. If I am not mistaken, I remember having heard many times that there once was a great and wealthy man who had a most beautiful and precious ring among the many precious jewels in his treasury. Because of its worth and its beauty, he wanted to honor it by bequeathing it to his descendants forever, and he ordered that whichever of his sons would be found in possession of this ring, which he would have left him, should be honored and revered as his true heir and head of the family by all the others. The man to whom he left the ring did the same as his predecessor had, having left behind the same instructions to his descendants; in short, this ring went from hand to hand through many generations, and finally it came into the hands of a man who had three handsome and virtuous sons, all of whom were obedient to their father, and for this reason, all three were equally loved by him. Since the father was growing old and they knew about the tradition of the ring, each of the three men was anxious to be the most honored among his sons, and each one, as best he knew how, begged the father to leave the ring to him when he died. The worthy man, who loved them all equally, did not know himself which of the three he would choose to leave the ring, and since he had promised it to each of them, he decided to try and satisfy all three: he had a good jeweler secretly make two more rings which were so much like the first one that he himself, who had had them made, hardly could tell which was the real one. When the father was dying, he gave a ring to each of his sons in secret, and after he died each son claimed the inheritance and position and one son denied the claims of the other, each bringing forth his ring to prove his case; when they discovered the rings were so much alike that they could not recognize the true one, they put aside the question of who the true heir was and left it undecided as it is to this day.

"And let me say the same thing to you, my lord, concerning the three Laws given the three peoples by God our Father which are the subject of the question you posed to me: each believes itself to be the true heir, to possess the true Law, and to follow the true commandments, but whoever is right, just as in the case of the rings, is still undecided."

Saladin realized how the man had most cleverly avoided the trap which he had set to snare him, and for that reason he decided to make his needs known openly to him and to see if he might wish to help him; and he did so, revealing to him what he had in mind to do if the Jew had not replied to his question as discreetly as he had. The Jew willingly gave Saladin as much money as he desired, and Saladin later repaid him in full; in fact, he more than repaid him: he gave him great gifts and always esteemed him as his friend and kept him near at court in a grand and honorable fashion.

---

[1] **Saracen** Islam.

GEOFFREY CHAUCER
Selections from *The Canterbury Tales*

The Canterbury Tales by Geoffrey Chaucer (ca. 1340–1400) is generally recognized as the earliest masterpiece in English. Its popularity helped assure the triumph of the native tongue over Anglo-Norman, the French spoken in England after the Norman conquest (1066). Recited perhaps as court entertainment and circulated privately in manuscript, it quickly established Chaucer as a master storyteller and a melodious poet, a judgment shared by generations of readers. Today, it is among the best loved works in English; its lively tales are enjoyed by children and adults alike, and its unique characters are a part of popular culture. For scholars, the poem is a treasure trove for the social attitudes of its day.

The literary form of *The Canterbury Tales* (ca. 1385–1400) is beautifully simple, a tale within a tale, a genre inspired by Boccaccio's *The Decameron.* For plot, Chaucer introduces himself as a traveler who joins a motley band of English men and women at the Tabard Inn in Southwark (south London); he rides horseback with them on their partly religious, partly diverting pilgrimage to the shrine of St. Thomas à Becket at Canterbury. On the journey, he put into their mouths the tales and learning that he had acquired during his lifetime. For reasons unknown, Chaucer left the work unfinished; he completed only twenty-three tales of the more than 120 projected.

For the modern reader, much of the interest of this work lies in the full-blooded description of the pilgrims. Together, the thirty-one pilgrims constitute a cross-section of Late Medieval English society. Especially in the "end-bits" linking the tales, he presents the pilgrims in their own words, as they joke, quarrel, and philosophize. The frank, sometimes obscene language spoken by a few low characters (e.g., the Miller) reflects the open speech of England before the advent of Puritanism in the late 1500s.

Reading the Selections

The Prologue—the opening section of the poem—introduces each pilgrim with a pithy description full of telling detail. Chaucer's method is to blend random data of physical traits, personal and work habits, clothing features, and speech patterns in order to create memorable characters. The unforgettable portrait of the Wife of Bath is one such character—a talented weaver in her native town, with her wide-spaced teeth, large hips, even larger hat, vulgar taste for red clothes, roving eye, and skill at "wandering by the way." Moral yet forgiving of the vices that he sees in church, state, and society, Chaucer unfailingly pokes fun at the foibles of his contemporaries. His insight into personality proves he was a keen psychologist, perhaps the finest in European letters prior to Machiavelli.

The Wife of Bath's Tale is typical of Chaucer's comical-moral tales. Originating the literary device that each tale should morally suit its teller, he presents the domineering Wife of Bath as she recounts a tale whose theme is that happy wives need henpecked husbands. Even more to the Wife's discredit, her tale is thoroughly immoral, as the knight-rapist in the story escapes death and wins true love by solving a riddle. The tale is a reworking of a common folk story ("The Loathly Lady"), which Chaucer embellishes with magnificently irrelevant references to Ovid (see *Metamorphoses*), Dante (see *The Divine Comedy*), Boethius (see *The Consolation of Philosophy*), and Juvenal (see *Satire III*). Beneath the sexual politics, however, Chaucer offers a revolutionary moral: Gentility comes from God alone, not from social breeding.

To illustrate Chaucer's language, the first thirty-four lines of the General Prologue are reprinted in the original Middle English. Modern English equivalents are provided in the right margin for certain words. Note especially variations in spelling and verb forms, and the frequency of the final *e*, which was pronounced with the "schwa" sound, as in so*fa* and *a*bout. Final *e* was not pronounced when it occurred before words beginning with vowels or weakly pronounced *h*s.

∽

The General Prologue
(in Middle English)

Whan that Aprill with his shoures sote°	*sweet showers* 1
The droghte° of Marche hath perced to	
the rote,°	*dryness/root*
And bathed every veyne° in swich	
licour,°	*vein / such moisture*
Of which vertu° engendred is the flour;	*By power of which*
Whan Zephirus° eek with his swete breeth	*the west wind*
Inspired° hath in every holt	
and heeth°	*Breathed into / wood / heath*
The tendre croppes,° and the yonge sonne	*sprouts*
Hath in the Ram his halfe cours y-ronne;	
And smale fowles° maken melodye,	*birds*
That slepen al the night with open yë°—	*eye(s)* 10
So priketh hem Nature in hir corages—	
Than longen° folk to goon° on pilgrimages,	*Then long / go*
And palmeres for to seken straunge strondes,	
To ferne halwes,° couthe° in sondry	
londes;	*far-off shires / known*
And specially, from every shires ende	
Of Engelond to Caunterbury they wende,	
The holy blisful martir for to seke,°	*seek*

That hem hath holpen,° whan that they	
were seke.°	*helped / sick*
Bifel° that, in that seson on a day,	*It befell*
In Southwerk at the Tabard° as I lay°	*(an inn)/lodged* 20
Redy to wenden° on my pilgrimage	*depart*
To Caunterbury with ful devout corage,°	*heart*
At night was come into that hostelrye°	*inn*
Wel nyne and twenty in a companye	
Of sondry folk, by aventure° y-falle°	*chance/fallen*
In felawshipe, and pilgrims were they alle,	
That toward Caunterbury wolden° ryde.	*wished to*
The chambres° and the stables weren	
wyde,°	*bedrooms/spacious*
And wel we weren esed°	
atte beste.°	*made comfortable / in the best (ways)*
And shortly, whan the sonne was to° reste,	*at* 30
So hadde I spoken with hem everichon°	*each and every one*
That I was of hir felawshipe anon,	
And made forward° erly for to ryse,	*agreement*
To take oure wey, ther as I yow devyse.°	*(will) tell*

∽

The Prologue

When in April the sweet showers fall 1
And pierce the drought of March to the root, and all
The veins are bathed in liquor of such power
As brings about the engendering of the flower,
When also Zephyrus with his sweet breath
Exhales an air in every grove and heath
Upon the tender shoots, and the young sun
His half-course in the sign of the *Ram* has run,[1]
And the small fowl are making melody
That sleep away the night with open eye 10
(So nature pricks them and their heart engages)
Then people long to go on pilgrimages
And palmers[2] long to seek the stranger strands

Of far-off saints, hallowed in sundry lands,
And specially, from every shire's end
Of England, down to Canterbury they wend
To seek the holy blissful martyr,[3] quick
To give his help to them when they were sick.
    It happened in that season that one day
In Southwark, at *The Tabard*, as I lay 20
Ready to go on pilgrimage and start
For Canterbury, most devout at heart,
At night there came into that hostelry
Some nine and twenty in a company
Of sundry folk happening then to fall
In fellowship, and they were pilgrims all
That towards Canterbury meant to ride.

---

[1] **His half-course in the sign of the *Ram* has run** The Ram or Aries in the Zodiac is the time between March 21 and April 20; thus it is early April.
[2] **palmers** Pilgrims who displayed crossed palm leaves as a sign that they were going to the Holy Land.

---

[3] **the holy blissful martyr** Thomas à Becket, the martyred Archbishop of Canterbury, murdered in the cathedral by men loyal to King Henry II of England, had become a saint by Chaucer's time. Becket supposedly had healing powers to help the sick.

The rooms and stables of the inn were wide;
They made us easy, all was of the best.
And, briefly, when the sun had gone to rest, 30
I'd spoken to them all upon the trip
And was soon one with them in fellowship,
Pledged to rise early and to take the way
To Canterbury, as you heard me say.

But none the less, while I have time and space,
Before my story takes a further pace,
It seems a reasonable thing to say
What their condition was, the full array
Of each of them, as it appeared to me,
According to profession and degree, 40
And what apparel they were riding in;
And at a Knight I therefore will begin.
There was a *Knight*, a most distinguished man,
Who from the day on which he first began
To ride abroad had followed chivalry,
Truth, honour, generousness and courtesy.
He had done nobly in his sovereign's war
And ridden into battle, no man more,
As well in Christian as in heathen places,
And ever honoured for his noble graces. 50

When we took Alexandria, he was there.
He often sat at table in the chair
Of honour, above all nations, when in Prussia.
In Lithuania he had ridden, and Russia,
No Christian man so often, of his rank.
When, in Granada, Algeciras sank
Under assault, he had been there, and in
North Africa, raiding Benamarin;
In Anatolia he had been as well
And fought when Ayas and Attalia fell, 60
For all along the Mediterranean coast
He had embarked with many a noble host.
In fifteen mortal battles he had been
And jousted for our faith at Tramissene
Thrice in the lists, and always killed his man.
This same distinguished knight had led the van
Once with the Bey of Balat, doing work
For him against another heathen Turk;
He was of sovereign value in all eyes.
And though so much distinguished, he was wise 70
And in his bearing modest as a maid.
He never yet a boorish thing had said
In all his life to any, come what might;
He was a true, a perfect gentle-knight.

Speaking of his equipment, he possessed
Fine horses, but he was not gaily dressed.
He wore a fustian tunic stained and dark
With smudges where his armour had left mark;
Just home from service, he had joined our ranks
To do his pilgrimage and render thanks. 80

He had his son with him, a fine young *Squire*,
A lover and cadet, a lad of fire
With locks as curly as if they had been pressed.
He was some twenty years of age, I guessed.
In stature he was of a moderate length,
With wonderful agility and strength.
He'd seen some service with the cavalry

In Flanders and Artois and Picardy
And had done valiantly in little space
Of time, in hope to win his lady's grace. 90
He was embroidered like a meadow bright
And full of freshest flowers, red and white.
Singing he was, or fluting all the day;
He was as fresh as is the month of May.
Short was his gown, the sleeves were long and wide;
He knew the way to sit a horse and ride.
He could make songs and poems and recite,
Knew how to joust and dance, to draw and write.
He loved so hotly that till dawn grew pale
He slept as little as a nightingale. 100
Courteous he was, lowly and serviceable,
And carved to serve his father at the table.

There was a *Yeoman*[4] with him at his side,
No other servant; so he chose to ride.
This Yeoman wore a coat and hood of green,
And peacock-feathered arrows, bright and keen
And neatly sheathed, hung at his belt the while
—For he could dress his gear in yeoman style,
His arrows never dropped their feathers low—
And in his hand he bore a mighty bow. 110
His head was like a nut, his face was brown.
He knew the whole of woodcraft up and down.
A saucy brace was on his arm to ward
It from the bow-string, and a shield and sword
Hung at one side, and at the other slipped
A jaunty dirk,[5] spear-sharp and well-equipped.
A medal of St Christopher he wore
Of shining silver on his breast, and bore
A hunting-horn, well slung and burnished clean,
That dangled from a baldrick of bright green. 120
He was a proper forester, I guess.

There also was a *Nun*, a Prioress,
Her way of smiling very simple and coy.
Her greatest oath was only "By St Loy!"
And she was known as Madam Eglantyne.
And well she sang a service, with a fine
Intoning through her nose, as was most seemly,
And she spoke daintily in French, extremely,
After the school of Stratford-atte-Bowe;
French in the Paris style she did not know. 130
At meat her manners were well taught withal;
No morsel from her lips did she let fall,
Nor dipped her fingers in the sauce too deep;
But she could carry a morsel up and keep
The smallest drop from falling on her breast.
For courtliness she had a special zest,
And she would wipe her upper lip so clean
That not a trace of grease was to be seen
Upon the cup when she had drunk; to eat,
She reached a hand sedately for the meat. 140
She certainly was very entertaining,

---

[4] *Yeoman* Can be an independent landholder who owns a small amount of land, or an attendant to a member of a noble or royal household. In this case, he seems to be both.
[5] **dirk** A long straight-bladed knife.

Pleasant and friendly in her ways, and straining
To counterfeit a courtly kind of grace,
A stately bearing fitting to her place,
And to seem dignified in all her dealings.
As for her sympathies and tender feelings,
She was so charitably solicitous
She used to weep if she but saw a mouse
Caught in a trap, if it were dead or bleeding.
And she had little dogs she would be feeding   150
With roasted flesh, or milk, or fine white bread.
And bitterly she wept if one were dead
Or someone took a stick and made it smart[6];
She was all sentiment and tender heart.
Her veil was gathered in a seemly way,
Her nose was elegant, her eyes glass-grey;
Her mouth was very small, but soft and red,
Her forehead, certainly, was fair of spread,
Almost a span across the brows, I own[7];
She was indeed by no means undergrown.   160
Her cloak, I noticed, had a graceful charm.
She wore a coral trinket on her arm,
A set of beads, the gaudies tricked in green,
Whence hung a golden brooch of brightest sheen
On which there first was graven a crowned A,
And lower, *Amor vincit omnia*.[8]
    Another *Nun*, the secretary at her cell,
Was riding with her, and *three Priests* as well.
    A *Monk* there was, one of the finest sort
Who rode the country; hunting was his sport.   170
A manly man, to be an Abbot able;
Many a dainty horse he had in stable.
His bridle, when he rode, a man might hear
Jingling in a whistling wind as clear,
Aye, and as loud as does the chapel bell
Where my lord Monk was Prior of the cell.
The Rule of good St Benet or St Maur[9]
As old and strict he tended to ignore;
He let go by the things of yesterday
And took the modern world's more spacious way.   180
He did not rate that text at a plucked hen
Which says that hunters are not holy men
And that a monk uncloistered is a mere
Fish out of water, flapping on the pier,
That is to say a monk out of his cloister.
That was a text he held not worth an oyster;
And I agreed and said his views were sound;
Was he to study till his head went round
Poring over books in cloisters? Must he toil
As Austin[10] bade and till the very soil?   190

Was he to leave the world upon the shelf?
Let Austin have his labour to himself.
    This Monk was therefore a good man to horse;
Greyhounds he had, as swift as birds, to course.
Hunting a hare or riding at a fence
Was all his fun, he spared for no expense.
I saw his sleeves were garnished at the hand
With fine grey fur, the finest in the land,
And on his hood, to fasten it at his chin
He had a wrought-gold cunningly fashioned pin;   200
Into a lover's knot it seemed to pass.
His head was bald and shone like looking-glass;
So did his face, as if it had been greased.
He was a fat and personable priest;
His prominent eyeballs never seemed to settle.
They glittered like the flames beneath a kettle;
Supple his boots, his horse in fine condition.
He was a prelate[11] fit for exhibition,
He was not pale like a tormented soul.
He liked a fat swan best, and roasted whole.   210
His palfrey was as brown as is a berry.
    There was a *Friar*, a wanton one and merry,
A Limiter,[12] a very festive fellow.
In all Four Orders there was none so mellow,
So glib with gallant phrase and well-turned speech.
He'd fixed up many a marriage, giving each
Of his young women what he could afford her.[13]
He was a noble pillar to his Order.
Highly beloved and intimate was he
With County folk within his boundary,   220
And city dames of honour and possessions;
For he was qualified to hear confessions,
Or so he said, with more than priestly scope;
He had a special licence from the Pope.
Sweetly he heard his penitents at shrift
With pleasant absolution, for a gift.
He was an easy man in penance-giving
Where he could hope to make a decent living;
It's a sure sign whenever gifts are given
To a poor Order that a man's well shriven,[14]   230
And should he give enough he knew in verity
The penitent repented in sincerity.
For many a fellow is so hard of heart
He cannot weep, for all his inward smart.
Therefore instead of weeping and of prayer
One should give silver for a poor Friar's care.
He kept his tippet stuffed with pins for curls,
And pocket-knives, to give to pretty girls.
And certainly his voice was gay and sturdy,
For he sang well and played the hurdy-gurdy.   240
At sing-songs he was champion of the hour.

---

[6] **smart** Sharp or pointed.
[7] **own** To acknowledge or to claim to be true.
[8] *Amor vincit omnia*. Latin, in English, "Love conquers all."
[9] **St Benet or St Maur** Both saints wrote rules and regulations for monastic orders. St. Benedict founded the Benedictine order in the sixth century, which was the first of many monastic orders.
[10] **Austin** St. Augustine, one of the early Church Fathers, who after his conversion to Christianity, spent his life working for the church, wrote many books on Christian thought and described how a holy man should live. He lived in the late fourth and early fifth centuries.

---

[11] **prelate** An official in the hierarchy of the church. Obviously Chaucer is giving the monk a title above his ranking to make the point that the monk, in his dress and tastes, lives like a prelate.
[12] **A Limiter** A member of an order who travels about begging for contributions to his order.
[13] **He'd fixed up many . . . afford her.** The reference is not to his officiating at weddings but to his impregnating young women.
[14] **shriven** To be free from guilt after having confessed one's sins.

His neck was whiter than a lily-flower
But strong enough to butt a bruiser down.
He knew the taverns well in every town
And every innkeeper and barmaid too
Better than lepers, beggars and that crew,
For in so eminent a man as he
It was not fitting with the dignity
Of his position, dealing with a scum
Of wretched lepers; nothing good can come 250
Of commerce with such slum-and-gutter dwellers,
But only with the rich and victual-sellers.
But anywhere a profit might accrue
Courteous he was and lowly of service too.
Natural gifts like his were hard to match.
He was the finest beggar of his batch,
And, for his begging-district, paid a rent;
His brethren did no poaching where he went.
For though a widow mightn't have a shoe,
So pleasant was his holy how-d'ye-do 260
He got his farthing from her just the same
Before he left, and so his income came
To more than he laid out. And how he romped,
Just like a puppy! He was ever prompt
To arbitrate disputes on settling days
(For a small fee) in many helpful ways,
Not then appearing as your cloistered scholar
With threadbare habit hardly worth a dollar,
But much more like a Doctor or a Pope.
Of double-worsted was the semi-cope 270
Upon his shoulders, and the swelling fold
About him, like a bell about its mould
When it is casting, rounded out his dress.
He lisped a little out of wantonness
To make his English sweet upon his tongue.
When he had played his harp, or having sung,
His eyes would twinkle in his head as bright
As any star upon a frosty night.
This worthy's name was Hubert, it appeared.
    There was a *Merchant* with a forking beard 280
And motley dress; high on his horse he sat,
Upon his head a Flemish beaver hat
And on his feet daintily buckled boots.
He told of his opinions and pursuits
In solemn tones, he harped on his increase
Of capital; there should be sea-police
(He thought) upon the Harwich-Holland ranges[15];
He was expert at dabbling in exchanges.
This estimable Merchant so had set
His wits to work, none knew he was in debt, 290
He was so stately in administration,
In loans and bargains and negotiation.
He was an excellent fellow all the same;
To tell the truth I do not know his name.
    An *Oxford Cleric,* still a student though,
One who had taken logic long ago,

Was there; his horse was thinner than a rake,
And he was not too fat, I undertake,
But had a hollow look, a sober stare;
The thread upon his overcoat was bare. 300
He had found no preferment in the church
And he was too unworldly to make search
For secular employment. By his bed
He preferred having twenty books in red
And black, of Aristotle's philosophy,
Than costly clothes, fiddle or psaltery.
Though a philosopher, as I have told,
He had not found the stone for making gold.
Whatever money from his friends he took
He spent on learning or another book 310
And prayed for them most earnestly, returning
Thanks to them thus for paying for his learning.
His only care was study, and indeed
He never spoke a word more than was need,
Formal at that, respectful in the extreme,
Short, to the point, and lofty in his theme.
A tone of moral virtue filled his speech
And gladly would he learn, and gladly teach.
    A *Serjeant at the Law*[16] who paid his calls,
Wary and wise, for clients at St Paul's 320
There also was, of noted excellence.
Discreet he was, a man to reverence,
Or so he seemed, his sayings were so wise.
He often had been Justice of Assize[17]
By letters patent, and in full commission.
His fame and learning and his high position
Had won him many a robe and many a fee.
There was no such conveyancer as he;
All was fee-simple to his strong digestion,
Not one conveyance could be called in question. 330
Though there was nowhere one so busy as he,
He was less busy than he seemed to be.
He knew of every judgment, case and crime
Ever recorded since King William's time.[18]
He could dictate defences or draft deeds;
No one could pinch a comma from his screeds[19]
And he knew every statute off by rote.
He wore a homely parti-coloured coat,
Girt with a silken belt of pin-stripe stuff;
Of his appearance I have said enough. 340
    There was a *Franklin*[20] with him, it appeared;
White as a daisy-petal was his beard.
A sanguine man, high-coloured and benign,
He loved a morning sop of cake in wine.
He lived for pleasure and had always done,

---

[15] **the Harwich-Holland ranges** The sea route between Harwich, an English port, and Holland.

[16] *Serjeant at the Law* Today, a special ranking for a barrister (one who practices before the bar or in a court in England) in the sovereign's court system. Chaucer describes him as a regular lawyer.
[17] **Justice of Assize** The district civil court.
[18] **King William's time** William the Conqueror (1066–1087).
[19] **screeds** A lengthy discourse or argument.
[20] *Franklin* A country landowner who was free or not indentured but not of noble birth.

For he was Epicurus,' very son,[21]
In whose opinion sensual delight
Was the one true felicity in sight.
As noted as St Julian[22] as for bounty
He made his household free to all the County.   350
His bread, his ale were finest of the fine
And no one had a better stock of wine.
His house was never short of bake-meat pies,
Of fish and flesh, and these in such supplies
It positively snowed with meat and drink
And all the dainties that a man could think.
According to the seasons of the year
Changes of dish were ordered to appear.
He kept fat partridges in coops, beyond,
Many a bream and pike were in his pond.   360
Woe to the cook unless the sauce was hot
And sharp, or if he wasn't on the spot!
And in his hall a table stood arrayed
And ready all day long, with places laid.
As Justice at the Sessions none stood higher;
He often had been Member for the Shire.[23]
A dagger and a little purse of silk
Hung at his girdle, white as morning milk.
As Sheriff he checked audit, every entry.
He was a model among landed gentry.   370

　　A *Haberdasher,* a *Dyer,* a *Carpenter,*
A *Weaver* and a *Carpet-maker* were
Among our ranks, all in the livery
Of one impressive guild-fraternity.[24]
They were so trim and fresh their gear would pass
For new. Their knives were not tricked out with brass
But wrought with purest silver, which avouches
A like display on girdles and on pouches.
Each seemed a worthy burgess, fit to grace
A guild-hall with a seat upon the dais.   380
Their wisdom would have justified a plan
To make each one of them an alderman;
They had the capital and revenue,
Besides their wives declared it was their due.
And if they did not think so, then they ought;
To be called "*Madam*" is a glorious thought,
And so is going to church and being seen
Having your mantle carried, like a queen.

　　They had a *Cook* with them who stood alone
For boiling chicken with a marrow-bone,   390
Sharp flavouring-powder and a spice for savour.
He could distinguish London ale by flavour,
And he could roast and seethe and broil and fry,
Make good thick soup and bake a tasty pie.
But what a pity—so it seemed to me,
That he should have an ulcer on his knee.

As for blancmange, he made it with the best.
　　There was a *Skipper* hailing from far west;
He came from Dartmouth, so I understood.
He rode a farmer's horse as best he could,   400
In a woollen gown that reached his knee.
A dagger on a lanyard falling free
Hung from his neck under his arm and down.
The summer heat had tanned his colour brown,
And certainly he was an excellent fellow.
Many a draught of vintage, red and yellow,
He'd drawn at Bordeaux, while the trader snored.
The nicer rules of conscience he ignored.[25]
If, when he fought, the enemy vessel sank,
He sent his prisoners home; they walked the plank.   410
As for his skill in reckoning his tides,
Currents and many another risk besides,
Moons, harbours, pilots, he had such dispatch
That none from Hull to Carthage was his match.
Hardy he was, prudent in undertaking;
His beard in many a tempest had its shaking,
And he knew all the heavens as they were
From Gottland to the Cape of Finisterre,
And every creek in Brittany and Spain;
The barge he owned was called *The Maudelayne.*   420

　　A *Doctor* too emerged as we proceeded;
No one alive could talk as well as he did
On points of medicine and of surgery,
For, being grounded in astronomy,
He watched his patient closely for the hours
When, by his horoscope, he knew the powers
Of favourable planets, then ascendent,
Worked on the images for his dependent.
The cause of every malady you'd got
He knew, and whether dry, cold, moist or hot;   430
He knew their seat, their humour and condition.
He was a perfect practising physician.
These causes being known for what they were,
He gave the man his medicine then and there.
All his apothecaries in a tribe
Were ready with the drugs he would prescribe
And each made money from the other's guile;
They had been friendly for a goodish while.
He was well-versed in Aesculapius too
And what Hippocrates and Rufus knew   440
And Dioscorides, now dead and gone,
Galen and Rhazes, Hali, Serapion,
Averroes, Avicenna, Constantine,
Scotch Bernard, John of Gaddesden, Gilbertine.[26]
In his own diet he observed some measure;
There were no superfluities for pleasure,
Only digestives, nutritives and such.

---

[21] **Epicurus' very son** The Franklin thought that Epicurus, the Greek philosopher, advocated a life of bodily pleasures, which was not what the thinker really believed.
[22] **St Julian** The patron saint of hospitality.
[23] **Member for the Shire** Representative of his district to Parliament.
[24] **guild-fraternity** The five pilgrims mentioned were members of their respective guilds and dressed in their livery or identifying clothing.

[25] **The nicer rules of conscience he ignored.** The "skipper" is really a pirate.
[26] **Aesculapius, Hippocrates, Rufus, Dioscorides, Galen, Rhazes, Hali, Serapion, Averroes, Avicenna, Constantine, Scotch Bernard, John of Gaddesden, Gilbertine** List of legendary, ancient, medieval, Muslim, and contemporary men of medicine. Many wrote medical books that would have been read and used by the doctor.

He did not read the Bible very much.
In blood-red garments, slashed with bluish grey
And lined with taffeta, he rode his way;   450
Yet he was rather close as to expenses
And kept the gold he won in pestilences.
Gold stimulates the heart, or so we're told.
He therefore had a special love of gold.

    A worthy *woman* from beside *Bath* city
Was with us, somewhat deaf, which was a pity.
In making cloth she showed so great a bent
She bettered those of Ypres and of Ghent.
In all the parish not a dame dared stir
Towards the altar steps in front of her,   460
And if indeed they did, so wrath was she
As to be quite put out of charity.
Her kerchiefs were of finely woven ground;
I dared have sworn they weighed a good ten pound,
The ones she wore on Sunday, on her head.
Her hose were of the finest scarlet red
And gartered tight; her shoes were soft and new.
Bold was her face, handsome, and red in hue.
A worthy woman all her life, what's more
She'd had five husbands, all at the church door,   470
Apart from other company in youth;
No need just now to speak of that, forsooth.
And she had thrice been to Jerusalem,
Seen many strange rivers and passed over them;
She'd been to Rome and also to Boulogne,
St James of Compostella and Cologne,
And she was skilled in wandering by the way.
She had gap-teeth, set widely, truth to say.
Easily on an ambling horse she sat
Well wimpled up,[27] and on her head a hat   480
As broad as is a buckler or a shield;
She had a flowing mantle that concealed
Large hips, her heels spurred sharply under that.
In company she liked to laugh and chat
And knew the remedies for love's mischances,
An art in which she knew the oldest dances.

    A holy-minded man of good renown
There was, and poor, the *Parson* to a town,
Yet he was rich in holy thought and work.
He also was a learned man, a clerk,   490
Who truly knew Christ's gospel and would preach it
Devoutly to parishioners, and teach it.
Benign and wonderfully diligent,
And patient when adversity was sent
(For so he proved in much adversity)
He hated cursing to extort a fee,[28]
Nay rather he preferred beyond a doubt
Giving to poor parishioners round about
Both from church offerings and his property;
He could in little find sufficiency.   500
Wide was his parish, with houses far asunder,

Yet he neglected not in rain or thunder,
In sickness or in grief, to pay a call
On the remotest, whether great or small,
Upon his feet, and in his hand a stave.
This noble example to his sheep he gave
That first he wrought, and afterwards he taught;
And it was from the Gospel he had caught
Those words, and he would add this figure too,
That if gold rust, what then will iron do?   510
For if a priest be foul in whom we trust
No wonder that a common man should rust;
And shame it is to see—let priests take stock—
A shitten shepherd and a snowy flock.
The true example that a priest should give
Is one of cleanness, how the sheep should live.[29]
He did not set his benefice to hire[30]
And leave his sheep encumbered in the mire
Or run to London to earn easy bread
By singing masses for the wealthy dead,   520
Or find some Brotherhood and get enrolled.
He stayed at home and watched over his fold
So that no wolf should make the sheep miscarry.
He was a shepherd and no mercenary.
Holy and virtuous he was, but then
Never contemptuous of sinful men,
Never disdainful, never too proud or fine,
But was discreet in teaching and benign.
His business was to show a fair behaviour
And draw men thus to Heaven and their Saviour,   530
Unless indeed a man were obstinate;
And such, whether of high or low estate,
He put to sharp rebuke, to say the least.
I think there never was a better priest.
He sought no pomp or glory in his dealings,
No scrupulosity had spiced his feelings.
Christ and His Twelve Apostles and their lore
He taught, but followed it himself before.

    There was a *Plowman*[31] with him there, his brother;
Many a load of dung one time or other   540
He must have carted through the morning dew.
He was an honest worker, good and true,
Living in peace and perfect charity,
And, as the gospel bade him, so did he,
Loving God best with all his heart and mind
And then his neighbour as himself, repined
At no misfortune, slacked for no content,
For steadily about his work he went
To thrash his corn, to dig or to manure
Or make a ditch; and he would help the poor   550
For love of Christ and never take a penny
If he could help it, and, as prompt as any,
He paid his tithes in full when they were due

---

[27] **Well wimpled up** Her head covered with a veil or a wimple, a cloth worn outdoors to cover the head, neck, and chin.

[28] **He hated cursing to extort a fee** The Parson refused to curse or to excommunicate a person who did not tithe or contribute a tenth of his income to the church, which was supposed to be the normal pattern of giving.

---

[29] **And shame it is to see . . . how the sheep should live.** The priest, like the shepherd, should not be dirty (shitten), but be clean and live an exemplary life in order to lead his flock.

[30] **He did not set his benefice to hire** Some priests would deliberately (set) hire or sell their benefice to other priests to make money. A *benefice* was an ecclesiastical office with a source of revenue—thus, a steady income.

[31] *Plowman* A peasant farmer or farm laborer.

On what he owned, and on his earnings too.
He wore a tabard smock and rode a mare.
    There was a *Reeve*, also a *Miller*, there,
A College *Manciple* from the Inns of Court,
A papal *Pardoner* and, in close consort,
A Church-Court *Summoner*, riding at a trot,[32]
And finally myself—that was the lot.
    The *Miller* was a chap of sixteen stone,
A great stout fellow big in brawn and bone.
He did well out of them, for he could go
And win the ram at any wrestling show.
Broad, knotty and short-shouldered, he would boast
He could heave any door off hinge and post,
Or take a run and break it with his head.
His beard, like any sow or fox, was red
And broad as well, as though it were a spade;
And, at its very tip, his nose displayed
A wart on which there stood a tuft of hair
Red as the bristles in an old sow's ear.
His nostrils were as black as they were wide.
He had a sword and buckler at his side,
His mighty mouth was like a furnace door.
A wrangler and buffoon, he had a store
Of tavern stories, filthy in the main.
His was a master-hand at stealing grain.
He felt it with his thumb and thus he knew
Its quality and took three times his due—
A thumb of gold, by God, to gauge an oat!
He wore a hood of blue and a white coat.
He liked to play his bagpipes up and down
And that was how he brought us out of town.
    The *Manciple* came from the Inner Temple;
All caterers might follow his example
In buying victuals; he was never rash
Whether he bought on credit or paid cash.
He used to watch the market most precisely
And got in first, and so he did quite nicely.
Now isn't it a marvel of God's grace
That an illiterate fellow can outpace
The wisdom of a heap of learned men?
His masters—he had more than thirty then—
All versed in the abstrusest legal knowledge,
Could have produced a dozen from their College
Fit to be stewards in land and rents and game
To any Peer in England you could name,
And show him how to live on what he had
Debt-free (unless of course the Peer were mad)
Or be as frugal as he might desire,
And make them fit to help about the Shire

In any legal case there was to try;
And yet this Manciple could wipe their eye.
    The *Reeve* was old and choleric and thin;
His beard was shaven closely to the skin,
His shorn hair came abruptly to a stop
Above his ears, and he was docked on top
Just like a priest in front; his legs were lean,
Like sticks they were, no calf was to be seen.
He kept his bins and garners[33] very trim;
No auditor could gain a point on him.
And he could judge by watching drought and rain
The yield he might expect from seed and grain.
His master's sheep, his animals and hens,
Pigs, horses, dairies, stores and cattle-pens
Were wholly trusted to his government.
He had been under contract to present
The accounts, right from his master's earliest years.
No one had ever caught him in arrears.
No bailiff, serf or herdsman dared to kick,
He knew their dodges, knew their every trick;
Feared like the plague he was, by those beneath.
He had a lovely dwelling on a heath,
Shadowed in green by trees above the sward.
A better hand at bargains than his lord,
He had grown rich and had a store of treasure
Well tucked away, yet out it came to pleasure
His lord with subtle loans or gifts of goods,
To earn his thanks and even coats and hoods.
When young he'd learnt a useful trade and still
He was a carpenter of first-rate skill.
The stallion-cob he rode at a slow trot
Was dapple-grey and bore the name of Scot.
He wore an overcoat of bluish shade
And rather long; he had a rusty blade
Slung at his side. He came, as I heard tell,
From Norfolk, near a place called Baldeswell.
His coat was tucked under his belt and splayed.
He rode the hindmost of our cavalcade.
    There was a *Summoner* with us at that Inn,
His face on fire, like a cherubin,
For he had carbuncles. His eyes were narrow,
He was as hot and lecherous as a sparrow.
Black scabby brows he had, and a thin beard.
Children were afraid when he appeared.
No quicksilver, lead ointment, tartar creams,
No brimstone, no boracic, so it seems,
Could make a salve that had the power to bite,
Clean up or cure his whelks of knobby white
Or purge the pimples sitting on his cheeks.
Garlic he loved, and onions too, and leeks,
And drinking strong red wine till all was hazy.
Then he would shout and jabber as if crazy,
And wouldn't speak a word except in Latin
When he was drunk, such tags[34] as he was pat in;
He had only a few, say two or three,
That he had mugged up out of some decree;
No wonder, for he heard them every day.

[32] *Reeve, Miller, Manciple, Pardoner, Summoner* All five are reprehensible characters—petty white-collar thieves who cheat their customers, take bribes, steal from their superiors, or play upon the fears of credulous Christians. A reeve was a manager or overseer of an estate. A miller, of course, was one who would grind grain or corn. A manciple was the financial manager of an educational institution. A summoner summoned people to a court that tried offenses against the church, similar to a process-server today. A pardoner sold holy relics and also pardons to those who confessed their sins and sought forgiveness—thus putting a cash price on a spiritual act or sacrament. By Chaucer's time such practices were scandalous ways for unscrupulous churchmen to make money.

[33] **garners** Granary or grain bins.
[34] **tags** Verbal expressions, sayings, or quotations.

And, as you know, a man can teach a jay
To call out "Walter" better than the Pope.
But had you tried to test his wits and grope
For more, you'd have found nothing in the bag.
Then *"Questio quid juris"*[35] was his tag.
He was a noble varlet[36] and a kind one,
You'd meet none better if you went to find one.
Why, he'd allow—just for a quart of wine—
Any good lad to keep a concubine
A twelvemonth and dispense him altogether!
And he had finches of his own to feather:[37]   670
And if he found some rascal with a maid
He would instruct him not to be afraid
In such a case of the Archdeacon's curse
(Unless the rascal's soul were in his purse)
For in his purse the punishment should be.
"Purse is the good Archdeacon's Hell," said he.
But well I know he lied in what he said;
A curse should put a guilty man in dread,
For curses kill, as shriving brings, salvation.
We should beware of excommunication.   680
Thus, as he pleased, the man could bring duress
On any young fellow in the diocese.
He knew their secrets, they did what he said.
He wore a garland set upon his head
Large as the holly-bush upon a stake
Outside an ale-house, and he had a cake,
A round one, which it was his joke to wield
As if it were intended for a shield.

　　He and a gentle *Pardoner* rode together,
A bird from Charing Cross of the same feather,   690
Just back from visiting the Court of Rome.
He loudly sang *"Come hither, love, come home!"*
The Summoner sang deep seconds to this song,
No trumpet ever sounded half so strong.
This Pardoner had hair as yellow as wax,
Hanging down smoothly like a hank of flax.
In driblets fell his locks behind his head
Down to his shoulders which they overspread;
Thinly they fell, like rat-tails, one by one.
He wore no hood upon his head, for fun;   700
The hood inside his wallet had been stowed,
He aimed at riding in the latest mode;
But for a little cap his head was bare
And he had bulging eye-balls, like a hare.
He'd sewed a holy relic on his cap;
His wallet lay before him on his lap,
Brimful of pardons come from Rome, all hot.
He had the same small voice a goat has got.
His chin no beard had harboured, nor would harbour,
Smoother than ever chin was left by barber.   710

I judge he was a gelding, or a mare.   660
As to his trade, from Berwick down to Ware[38]
There was no pardoner of equal grace,
For in his trunk he had a pillow-case
Which he asserted was Our Lady's veil.
He said he had a gobbet[39] of the sail
Saint Peter had the time when he made bold
To walk the waves, till Jesu Christ took hold.
He had a cross of metal set with stones
And, in a glass, a rubble of pigs' bones.   720
And with these relics, any time he found
Some poor up-country parson to astound,
In one short day, in money down, he drew
More than the parson in a month or two,
And by his flatteries and prevarication
Made monkeys of the priest and congregation.
But still to do him justice first and last
In church he was a noble ecclesiast.[40]
How well he read a lesson or told a story!
But best of all he sang an Offertory,   730
For well he knew that when that song was sung
He'd have to preach and tune his honey-tongue
And (well he could) win silver from the crowd.
That's why he sang so merrily and loud.
Now I have told you shortly, in a clause,
The rank, the array, the number and the cause
Of our assembly in this company
In Southwark, at that high-class hostelry
Known as *The Tabard*, close beside *The Bell*.
And now the time has come for me to tell   740
How we behaved that evening; I'll begin
After we had alighted at the Inn,
Then I'll report our journey, stage by stage,
All the remainder of our pilgrimage.
But first I beg of you, in courtesy,
Not to condemn me as unmannerly
If I speak plainly and with no concealings
And give account of all their words and dealings,
Using their very phrases as they fell.
For certainly, as you all know so well,   750
He who repeats a tale after a man
Is bound to say, as nearly as he can,
Each single word, if he remembers it,
However rudely spoken or unfit,
Or else the tale he tells will be untrue,
The things pretended and the phrases new.
He may not flinch although it were his brother,
He may as well say one word as another.
And Christ Himself spoke broad in Holy Writ,
Yet there is no scurrility in it,   760
And Plato says, for those with power to read,
"The word should be as cousin to the deed."
Further I beg you to forgive it me
If I neglect the order and degree
And what is due to rank in what I've planned.
I'm short of wit as you will understand. . . .

---

[35] *"Questio quid juris"* "What portion of the law applies in this case?" was a phrase the summoner would sometimes repeat in the court.
[36] **varlet** An unprincipled person.
[37] **And he had finches of his own to feather** The summoner had to make certain that he got his own share or reward. Similar to a saying of our times: "To feather one's nest."
[38] **Berwick, Ware** Berwick-upon-Tweed and Ware are two towns in England some distance apart; thus Chaucer is emphasizing the large territory over which the pardoner sells his relics.

---

[39] **gobbet** A small piece.
[40] **A noble ecclesiast** A very effective and talented preacher who could spellbind a congregation, sing the Offertory, and sell his relics.

∾

The Wife of Bath's Tale

When good King Arthur ruled in ancient days,   1
(A king that every Briton loves to praise.)
This was a land brim-full of fairy folk.
The Elf-Queen and her courtiers joined and broke
Their elfin dance on many a green mead,[1]
Or so was the opinion once, I read,
Hundreds of years ago, in days of yore.
But no one now sees fairies any more,
For now the saintly charity and prayer
Of holy friars seem to have purged the air;   10
They search the countryside through field and stream
As thick as motes that speckle a sun-beam,
Blessing the halls, the chambers, kitchens, bowers,
Cities and boroughs, castles, courts and towers,
Thorpes,[2] barns and stables, outhouses and dairies,
And that's the reason why there are no fairies.
Wherever there was wont to walk an elf
To-day there walks the holy friar himself
As evening falls or when the daylight springs,
Saying his mattins and his holy things,   20
Walking his limit round from town to town.
Women can now go safely up and down.
By every bush or under every tree;
There is no other incubus[3] but he,
So there is really no one else to hurt you
And he will do no more than take your virtue.

    Now it so happened, I began to say,
Long, long ago in good King Arthur's day,
There was a knight who was a lusty liver.
One day as he came riding from the river   30
He saw a maiden walking all forlorn
Ahead of him, alone as she was born.
And of that maiden, spite of all she said,
By very force he took her maidenhead.[4]

    This act of violence made such a stir,
So much petitioning of the king for her,
That he condemned the knight to lose his head
By course of law. He was as good as dead
(It seems that then the statues took that view)
But that the queen, and other ladies too,   40
Implored the king to exercise his grace
So ceaselessly, he gave the queen the case
And granted her his life, and she could choose
Whether to show him mercy or refuse.

    The queen returned him thanks with all her might,
And then she sent a summons to the knight
At her convenience, and expressed her will:
"You stand, for such is the position still,
In no way certain of your life," said she,
"Yet you shall live if you can answer me: 50
What is the thing that women most desire?

Beware the axe and say as I require.
    "If you can't answer on the moment, though,
I will concede you this: you are to go
A twelvemonth and a day to seek and learn
Sufficient answer then you shall return.
I shall take gages[5] from you to extort
Surrender of your body to the court."

    Sad was the knight and sorrowfully sighed,
But there! All other choices were denied,   60
And in the end he chose to go away
And to return after a year and day
Armed with such answer as there might be sent
To him by God. He took his leave and went.

    He knocked at every house, searched every place,
Yes, anywhere that offered hope of grace.
What could it be that women wanted most?
But all the same he never touched a coast,
Country or town in which there seemed to be
Any two people willing to agree.   70

    Some said that women wanted wealth and treasure,
"Honour," said some, some "Jollity and pleasure,"
Some "Gorgeous clothes" and others "Fun in bed,"
"To be oft widowed and remarried," said
Others again, and some that what most mattered
Was that we should be cosseted and flattered.
That's very near the truth, it seems to me;
A man can win us best with flattery.
To dance attendance on us, make a fuss,
Ensnares us all, the best and worst of us.   80

    Some say the things we most desire are these:
Freedom to do exactly as we please,
With no one to reprove our faults and lies,
Rather to have one call us good and wise.
Truly there's not a woman in ten score
Who has a fault, and someone rubs the sore,
But she will kick if what he says is true;
You try it out and you will find so too.
However vicious we may be within
We like to be thought wise and void of sin.   90

    Others assert we women find it sweet
When we are thought dependable, discreet
And secret, firm of purpose and controlled,
Never betraying things that we are told.
But that's not worth the handle of a rake;
Women conceal a thing? For Heaven's sake!
Remember Midas? Will you hear the tale?

    Among some other little things, now stale,
Ovid[6] relates that under his long hair
The unhappy Midas grew a splendid pair   100
Of ass's ears; as subtly as he might,
He kept his foul deformity from sight;

---

[1] **mead** Meadow.
[2] **Thorpes** Villages.
[3] **incubus** Evil spirit.
[4] **took her maidenhead** The knight raped the maiden.

[5] **gages** Pledges.
[6] **Ovid** The Roman author who wrote the story about Midas and his ears in *Metamorphoses II*. Ovid based his story on one of the ancient myths about King Midas of Phrygia.

Save for his wife, there was not one that knew.
He loved her best, and trusted in her too.
He begged her not to tell a living creature
That he possessed so horrible a feature.
And she—she swore, were all the world to win,
She would not do such villainy and sin
As saddle her husband with so foul a name;
Besides to speak would be to share the shame.   110
Nevertheless she thought she would have died
Keeping this secret bottled up inside;
It seemed to swell her heart and she, no doubt,
Thought it was on the point of bursting out.

　　Fearing to speak of it to woman or man,
Down to a reedy marsh she quickly ran
And reached the sedge.[7] Her heart was all on fire
And, as a bittern bumbles in the mire,[8]
She whispered to the water, near the ground,
"Betray me not, O water, with thy sound!   120
To thee alone I tell it: it appears
My husband has a pair of ass's ears!
Ah! My heart's well again, the secret's out!
I could no longer keep it, not a doubt."
And so you see, although we may hold fast
A little while, it must come out at last,
We can't keep secrets; as for Midas, well,
Read Ovid for his story; he will tell.

　　This knight that I am telling you about
Perceived at last he never would find out   130
What it could be that women loved the best.
Faint was the soul within his sorrowful breast
As home he went, he dared no longer stay;
His year was up and now it was the day.

　　As he rode home in a dejected mood,
Suddenly, at the margin of a wood,
He saw a dance upon the leafy floor
Of four and twenty ladies, nay, and more.
Eagerly he approached, in hope to learn
Some words of wisdom ere he should return;   140
But lo! Before he came to where they were,
Dancers and dance all vanished into air!
There wasn't a living creature to be seen
Save one old woman crouched upon the green.
A fouler-looking creature I suppose
Could scarcely be imagined. She arose
And said, "Sir knight, there's no way on from here.
Tell me what you are looking for, my dear,
For peradventure that were best for you;
We old, old women know a thing or two."   150

　　"Dear Mother," said the knight, "alack the day!
I am as good as dead if I can't say
What thing it is that women most desire;
If you could tell me I would pay your hire."
"Give me your hand," she said, "and swear to do
Whatever I shall next require of you
—If so to do should lie within your might—

_____
[7] **sedge** A type of tufted march plant.
[8] **And, as a bittern bumbles in the mire** The bittern is a bird that, according to popular lore, produced its cry by sticking its beak in the mud and bumbling or droning.

And you shall know the answer before night."
"Upon my honour," he answered, "I agree."
"Then," said the crone,[9] "I dare to guarantee   160
Your life is safe; I shall make good my claim.
Upon my life the queen will say the same.
Show me the very proudest of them all
In costly coverchief or jewelled caul
That dare say no to what I have to teach.
Let us go forward without further speech."
And then she crooned her gospel in his ear
And told him to be glad and not to fear.

　　They came to court. This knight, in full array,
Stood forth and said, "O Queen, I've kept my day   170
And kept my word and have my answer ready."

　　There sat the noble matrons and the heady
Young girls, and widows too, that have the grace
Of wisdom, all assembled in that place,
And there the queen herself was throned to hear
And judge his answer. Then the knight drew near
And silence was commanded through the hall.

　　The queen then bade the knight to tell them all
What thing it was that women wanted most.
He stood not silent like a beast or post,   180
But gave his answer with the ringing word
Of a man's voice and the assembly heard:

　　"My liege and lady, in general," said he,
"A woman wants the self-same sovereignty
Over her husband as over her lover,
And master him; he must not be above her.
That is your greatest wish, whether you kill
Or spare me; please yourself. I wait your will."

　　In all the court not one that shook her head
Or contradicted what the knight had said;   190
Maid, wife and widow cried, "He's saved his life!"

　　And on the word up started the old wife,
The one the knight saw sitting on the green,
And cried, "Your mercy, sovereign lady queen!
Before the court disperses, do me right!
'Twas I who taught this answer to the knight,
For which he swore, and pledged his honour to it,
That the first thing I asked of him he'd do it,
So far as it should lie within his might.
Before this court I ask you then, sir knight,   200
To keep your word and take me for your wife;
For well you know that I have saved your life.
If this be false, deny it on your sword!"

　　"Alas!" he said, "Old lady, by the Lord
I know indeed that such was my behest,
But for God's love think of a new request,
Take all my goods, but leave my body free."
"A curse on us," she said, "if I agree!
I may be foul, I may be poor and old,
Yet will not choose to be, for all the gold   210
That's bedded in the earth or lies above,
Less than your wife, nay, than your very love!"

　　"My love?" said he. "By Heaven, my damnation!
Alas that any of my race and station

_____
[9] **crone** Hag.

Should ever make so foul a misalliance!"
Yet in the end his pleading and defiance
All went for nothing, he was forced to wed.
He takes his ancient wife and goes to bed.

　　Now peradventure some may well suspect
A lack of care in me since I neglect
To tell of the rejoicings and display
Made at the feast upon their wedding-day.
I have but a short answer to let fall;
I say there was no joy or feast at all,
Nothing but heaviness of heart and sorrow.
He married her in private on the morrow
And all day long stayed hidden like an owl,
It was such torture that his wife looked foul.

　　Great was the anguish churning in his head
When he and she were piloted to bed;
He wallowed back and forth in desperate style.
His ancient wife lay smiling all the while;
At last she said "Bless us! Is this, my dear,
How knights and wives get on together here?
Are these the laws of good King Arthur's house?
Are knights of his all so contemptuous?
I am your own beloved and your wife,
And I am she, indeed, that saved your life;
And certainly I never did you wrong.
Then why, this first of nights, so sad a song?
You're carrying on as if you were half-witted!
Say, for God's love, what sin have I committed?
I'll put things right if you will tell me how."

　　"Put right?" he cried. "That never can be now!
Nothing can ever be put right again!
You're old, and so abominably plain,
So poor to start with, so low-bred to follow;
It's little wonder if I twist and wallow!
God, that my heart would burst within my breast!"

　　"Is that," said she, "the cause of your unrest?"

　　"Yes, certainly," he said, "and can you wonder?"

　　"I could set right what you suppose a blunder,
That's if I cared to, in a day or two,
If I were shown more courtesy by you.
Just now," she said, "you spoke of gentle birth,
Such as descends from ancient wealth and worth.
If that's the claim you make for gentlemen
Such arrogance is hardly worth a hen.
Whoever loves to work for virtuous ends,
Public and private, and who most intends
To do what deeds of gentleness he can,
Take him to be the greatest gentleman.
Christ wills we take our gentleness from Him,
Not from a wealth of ancestry long dim,
Though they bequeath their whole establishment
By which we claim to be of high descent.
Our fathers cannot make us a bequest
Of all those virtues that became them best
And earned for them the name of gentleman,
But bade us follow them as best we can.

　　"Thus the wise poet of the Florentines,
Dante by name, has written in these lines,
For such is the opinion Dante launches:
'Seldom arises by these slender branches

Prowess of men, for it is God, no less,
Wills us to claim of Him our gentleness.'
For of our parents nothing can we claim
Save temporal things, and these may hurt and maim.

　　"But everyone knows this as well as I;
For if gentility were implanted by
The natural course of lineage down the line,
Public or private, could it cease to shine
In doing the fair work of gentle deed?
No vice or villainy could then bear seed.

　　"Take fire and carry it to the darkest house
Between this kingdom and the Caucasus,
And shut the doors on it and leave it there,
It will burn on, and it will burn as fair
As if ten thousand men were there to see,
For fire will keep its nature and degree,
I can assure you, sir, until it dies.

　　"But gentleness, as you will recognize,
Is not annexed in nature to possessions,
Men fail in living up to their professions;
But fire never ceases to be fire.
God knows you'll often find, if you enquire,
Some lording full of villainy and shame.
If you would be esteemed for the mere name
Of having been by birth a gentleman
And stemming from some virtuous, noble clan,
And do not live yourself by gentle deed
Or take your father's noble code and creed,
You are no gentleman, though duke or earl.
Vice and bad manners are what make a churl.[10]

　　"Gentility is only the renown
For bounty that your fathers handed down,
Quite foreign to your person, not your own;
Gentility must come from God alone.
That we are gentle comes to us by grace
And by no means is it bequeathed with place.

　　"Reflect how noble (says Valerius)
Was Tullius surnamed Hostilius,
Who rose from poverty to nobleness.
And read Boethius, Seneca no less,[11]
Thus they express themselves and are agreed:
'Gentle is he that does a gentle deed.'
And therefore, my dear husband, I conclude
That even if my ancestors were rude,
Yet God on high—and so I hope He will—
Can grant me grace to live in virtue still,
A gentlewoman only when beginning
To live in virtue and to shrink from sinning.

　　"As for my poverty which you reprove,
Almighty God Himself in whom we move,
Believe and have our being, chose a life
Of poverty, and every man or wife
Nay, every child can see our Heavenly King

---

[10] **churl** A rude and ill-bred person.
[11] **Valerius, Tullius Hostilius, Boethius, Seneca** Valerius Maximus, a Roman author, wrote about Tullius Hostilius, a legendary king of Rome. Boethius was an early Christian philosopher, and Seneca was a Roman writer and playwright. The three authors wrote on the nature of human character and values.

Would never stoop to choose a shameful thing.
No shame in poverty if the heart is gay,
As Seneca and all the learned say.   330
He who accepts his poverty unhurt
I'd say is rich although he lacked a shirt.
But truly poor are they who whine and fret
And covet what they cannot hope to get.
And he that, having nothing, covets not,
Is rich, though you may think he is a sot.
    "True poverty can find a song to sing.
Juvenal[12] says a pleasant little thing:
'The poor can dance and sing in the relief
Of having nothing that will tempt a thief.'   340
Though it be hateful, poverty is good,
A great incentive to a livelihood,
And a great help to our capacity
For wisdom, if accepted patiently.
Poverty is, though wanting in estate,
A kind of wealth that none calumniate.
Poverty often, when the heart is lowly,
Brings one to God and teaches what is holy,
Gives knowledge of oneself and even lends
A glass by which to see one's truest friends.   350
And since it's no offence, let me be plain;
Do not rebuke my poverty again.
    "Lastly you taxed me, sir, with being old.
Yet even if you never had been told
By ancient books, you gentlemen engage
Yourselves in honour to respect old age.
To call an old man 'father' shows good breeding,
And this could be supported from my reading.
    "You say I'm old and fouler than a fen.[13]
You need not fear to be a cuckold, then.   360
Filth and old age, I'm sure you will agree,
Are powerful wardens upon chastity.
Nevertheless, well knowing your delights,
I shall fulfil your worldly appetites.
    "You have two choices; which one will you try?
To have me old and ugly till I die,

But still a loyal, true and humble wife
That never will displease you all her life,
Or would you rather I were young and pretty
And chance your arm what happens in a city   370
Where friends will visit you because of me,
Yes, and in other places too, maybe.
Which would you have? The choice is all your own."
    The knight thought long, and with a piteous groan
At last he said, with all the care in life,
"My lady and my love, my dearest wife,
I leave the matter to your wise decision.
You make the choice yourself, for the provision
Of what may be agreeable and rich
In honour to us both, I don't care which;   380
Whatever pleases you suffices me."
    "And have I won the mastery?" said she,
"Since I'm to choose and rule as I think fit?"
"Certainly, wife," he answered her, "that's it."
"Kiss me," she cried. "No quarrels! On my oath
And word of honour, you shall find me both,
That is, both fair and faithful as a wife;
May I go howling mad and take my life
Unless I prove to be as good and true
As ever wife was since the world was new!   390
And if to-morrow when the sun's above
I seem less fair than any lady-love,
Than any queen or empress east or west,
Do with my life and death as you think best.
Cast up the curtain, husband. Look at me!"
    And when indeed the knight had looked to see,
Lo, she was young and lovely, rich in charms.
In ecstasy he caught her in her arms,
His heart went bathing in a bath of blisses
And melted in a hundred thousand kisses,   400
And she responded in the fullest measure
With all that could delight or give him pleasure.
    So they lived ever after to the end
In perfect bliss; and may Christ Jesus send
Us husbands meek and young and fresh in bed,
And grace to overbid them when we wed.
And—Jesu hear my prayer!—cut short the lives
Of those who won't be governed by their wives;
And all old, angry niggards of their pence,
God send them soon a very pestilence!   410

---

[12] **Juvenal** The Roman poet and satirist.
[13] **fen** A marshy land or boggy area.

CHRISTINE DE PIZAN
Selections from *The Book of the City of Ladies*

History pretty much overlooked Christine de Pizan's *The Book of the City of Ladies* (1405) for almost 550 years, until the upsurge of feminism after World War II. Although the author was recognized as a minor poet, this book, existing in four manuscript copies, remained almost unknown. Recently, because of its topical theme—the problem of female authority—feminists have rescued the book from oblivion. Today, it is accepted as one of the earliest feminist texts, and its author is hailed as the first to identify the "woman question"—a central concern in the West's ongoing intellectual debate.

Christine's *City of Ladies* was a late medieval salvo fired in the perennial battle of the sexes. It was meant to counter the misogyny (hatred of women) of men who claimed that women were innately inferior because female frailty descended from Eve, the first mother. It avoided the thorny debate over Eve and, forecasting a modern view, assumed woman's basic morality and goodness. Although medieval in its reasoning style and antidemocratic ideas, this book is a seminal work of Western literature.

In form, the *City of Ladies* is an allegorical debate modeled on Boethius's *Consolation of Philosophy.* The debate members are Christine herself and the three Virtues who appear in a waking dream. Dressed as goddesses, the Virtues are Lady Reason, carrying a mirror, who shows viewers their true images; Lady Rectitude, carrying a ruler, who divides good from evil; and Lady Justice, holding a measuring cup, who sets limits to earthly things. They offer Christine moral guidance as she frames an ideal city where women will be safe for all time from misogynist attack.

The Book of the City of Ladies consists of three "books," or chapters. Lady Reason dominates the first book, praising women who founded cities and cultural institutions. Lady Rectitude holds forth in the second book, telling stories of female seers and offering insight into mother-child and husband-wife relations. The third book features Lady Justice's tales of saints' lives, mainly of martyrs.

Christine de Pizan's (1364–ca. 1430) sensitivity to women's issues sprang from her marginal status as an Italian at the French court. She was moved there by her Venetian father, who served as court astrologer, and she later wed a court secretary. Marginalized even more by her husband's death in 1389, she supported her family through writing, with patronage from the French kings and the dukes of Burgundy. She was France's first professional woman of letters.

Reading the Selections

These selections are taken from Books I and II of *City of Ladies.* In section I.1, Christine explains her book's purpose: to reject the misogynist's view that "women [are] inclined to and full of every vice." Whereas once sharing this view, she now abhors it, believing instead in the innate goodness of God and woman herself.

In section I.27, Lady Reason advances the radical notion that women and men, though unequal physically, are equal mentally, if given equal access to education and public careers. Sections I.30 and I.34 show Lady Reason detailing the cultural achievements of the Greek poet Sappho (see Chapter Two) and the Greek goddess Minerva (Athena).

In section II.36, Dame Rectitude argues that the sexes should have the same education, especially in morality. She reasons that such parity would make women virtuous as well as satisfy their natural bent toward learning.

∞

Book I

1. Here Begins the Book of the City of Ladies, Whose First Chapter Tells Why and for What Purpose This Book Was Written.

One day as I was sitting alone in my study surrounded by books on all kinds of subjects, devoting myself to literary studies, my usual habit, my mind dwelt at length on the weighty opinions of various authors whom I had studied for a long time. I looked up from my book, having decided to leave such subtle questions in peace and to relax by reading some light poetry. With this in mind, I searched for some small book. By chance a strange volume came into my hands, not one of my own, but one which had been given to me along with some others. When I held it open and saw from its title page that it was by Mathéolus,[1] I smiled, for though I had never seen it before, I had often heard that like other books it discussed respect for women. I thought I would browse through it to amuse myself. I had not been reading for very long when my good mother called me to refresh myself with some supper, for it was evening. Intending to look at it the next day, I put it down. The next morning, again seated in my study as was my habit, I remembered wanting to examine this book by Mathéolus. I started to read it and went on for a little while. Because the subject seemed to me not very pleasant for people who do not enjoy lies, and of no use in developing virtue or manners, given its lack of integrity in diction and theme, and after browsing here and there and reading the end, I put it down in order to turn my attention to more elevated and useful study. But just the sight of this book, even though it was of no authority, made me wonder how it happened that so many different men— and learned men among them—have been and are so inclined to express both in speaking and in their treatises and writings so many wicked insults about women and their behavior. Not only one or two and not even just this Mathéolus (for this book had a bad name anyway and was intended as a satire) but, more generally, judging from the treatises of all philosophers and poets and from all the orators—it would take too long to mention their names—it seems that they all speak from one and the same mouth. They all concur in one conclusion: that the behavior of women is inclined to and full of every vice. Thinking deeply about these matters, I began to examine my character and conduct as a natural woman and, similarly, I considered other women whose company I frequently kept, princesses, great ladies, women of the middle and lower classes, who had graciously told me of their most private and intimate thoughts, hoping that I could judge impar-

tially and in good conscience whether the testimony of so many notable men could be true. To the best of my knowledge, no matter how long I confronted or dissected the problem, I could not see or realize how their claims could be true when compared to the natural behavior and character of women. Yet I still argued vehemently against women, saying that it would be impossible that so many famous men—such solemn scholars, possessed of such deep and great understanding, so clear-sighted in all things, as it seemed—could have spoken falsely on so many occasions that I could hardly find a book on morals where, even before I had read it in its entirety, I did not find several chapters or certain sections attacking women, no matter who the author was. This reason alone, in short, made me conclude that, although my intellect did not perceive my own great faults and, likewise, those of other women because of its simpleness and ignorance, it was however truly fitting that such was the case. And so I relied more on the judgment of others than on what I myself felt and knew. I was so transfixed in this line of thinking for such a long time that it seemed as if I were in a stupor. Like a gushing fountain, a series of authorities, whom I recalled one after another, came to mind, along with their opinions on this topic. And I finally decided that God formed a vile creature when He made woman, and I wondered how such a worthy artisan could have deigned to make such an abominable work which, from what they say, is the vessel as well as the refuge and abode of every evil and vice. As I was thinking this, a great unhappiness and sadness welled up in my heart, for I detested myself and the entire feminine sex, as though we were monstrosities in nature. And in my lament I spoke these words:

"Oh, God, how can this be? For unless I stray from my faith, I must never doubt that Your infinite wisdom and most perfect goodness ever created anything which was not good. Did You yourself not create woman in a very special way and since that time did You not give her all those inclinations which it pleased You for her to have? And how could it be that You could go wrong in anything? Yet look at all these accusations which have been judged, decided, and concluded against women. I do not know how to understand this repugnance. If it is so, fair Lord God, that in fact so many abominations abound in the female sex, for You Yourself say that the testimony of two or three witnesses lends credence, why shall I not doubt that this is true? Alas, God, why did You not let me be born in the world as a man, so that all my inclinations would be to serve You better, and so that I would not stray in anything and would be as perfect as a man is said to be? But since Your kindness has not been extended to me, then forgive my negligence in Your service, most fair Lord God, and may it not displease You, for the servant who receives fewer gifts from his lord is less obliged in his service." I spoke these words to God in my lament and a great deal

---

[1] **Mathéolus** Mathieu of Boulongne or Mathéolus was the author of *The Lamentations of Mathéolus*, written about 1295. Mathéolus, a confirmed misogynist, or woman hater, advised his readers on all the ills and evils of women. Christine de Pizan uses his work as a foil to begin her defense and admiration for women.

more for a very long time in sad reflection, and in my folly I considered myself most unfortunate because God had made me inhabit a female body in this world. . . .

27. Christine Asks Reason Whether God Has Ever Wished to Ennoble the Mind of Woman With the Loftiness of the Sciences; and Reason's Answer.

After hearing these things, I replied to the lady who spoke infallibly: "My lady, truly has God revealed great wonders in the strength of these women whom you describe. But please enlighten me again, whether it has ever pleased this God, who has bestowed so many favors on women, to honor the feminine sex with the privilege of the virtue of high understanding and great learning, and whether women ever have a clever enough mind for this. I wish very much to know this because men maintain that the mind of women can learn only a little."

She answered, "My daughter, since I told you before, you know quite well that the opposite of their opinion is true, and to show you this even more clearly, I will give you proof through examples. I tell you again—and don't doubt the contrary—if it were customary to send daughters to school like sons, and if they were then taught the natural sciences, they would learn as thoroughly and understand the subtleties of all the arts and sciences as well as sons. And by chance there happen to be such women, for, as I touched on before, just as women have more delicate bodies than men, weaker and less able to perform many tasks, so do they have minds that are freer and sharper whenever they apply themselves."

"My lady, what are you saying? With all due respect, could you dwell longer on this point, please. Certainly men would never admit this answer is true, unless it is explained more plainly, for they believe that one normally sees that men know more than women do."

She answered, "Do you know why women know less?"

"Not unless you tell me, my lady."

"Without the slightest doubt, it is because they are not involved in many different things, but stay at home, where it is enough for them to run the household, and there is nothing which so instructs a reasonable creature as the exercise and experience of many different things."

"My lady, since they have minds skilled in conceptualizing and learning, just like men, why don't women learn more?"

She replied, "Because, my daughter, the public does not require them to get involved in the affairs which men are commissioned to execute, just as I told you before. It is enough for women to perform the usual duties to which they are ordained. As for judging from experience, since one sees that women usually know less than men, that therefore their capacity for understanding is less, look at men who farm the flatlands or who live in the mountains. You will find that in many countries they seem completely savage because they are so simple-minded. All the same,

there is no doubt that Nature provided them with the qualities of body and mind found in the wisest and most learned men. All of this stems from a failure to learn, though, just as I told you, among men and women, some possess better minds than others. Let me tell you about women who have possessed great learning and profound understanding and treat the question of the similarity of women's minds to men's."

30. Here She Speaks of Sappho, That Most Subtle Woman, Poet, and Philosopher.

"The wise Sappho, who was from the city of Mytilene, was no less learned than Proba. This Sappho had a beautiful body and face and was agreeable and pleasant in appearance, conduct, and speech. But the charm of her profound understanding surpassed all the other charms with which she was endowed, for she was expert and learned in several arts and sciences, and she was not only well-educated in the works and writings composed by others but also discovered many new things herself and wrote many books and poems. Concerning her, Boccaccio[2] has offered these fair words couched in the sweetness of poetic language: 'Sappho, possessed of sharp wit and burning desire for constant study in the midst of bestial and ignorant men, frequented the heights of Mount Parnassus, that is, of perfect study. Thanks to her fortunate boldness and daring, she kept company with the Muses, that is, the arts and sciences, without being turned away. She entered the forest of laurel trees filled with may boughs, greenery, and different colored flowers, soft fragrances and various aromatic spices, where Grammar, Logic, noble Rhetoric, Geometry, and Arithmetic live and take their leisure. She went on her way until she came to the deep grotto of Apollo, god of learning, and found the brook and conduit of the fountain of Castalia, and took up the plectrum and quill of the harp and played sweet melodies, with the nymphs all the while leading the dance, that is, following the rules of harmony and musical accord.' From what Boccaccio says about her, it should be inferred that the profundity of both her understanding and of her learned books could only be known and understood by men of great perception and learning, according to the testimony of the ancients. Her writings and poems have survived to this day, most remarkably constructed and composed, and they serve as illumination and models of consummate poetic craft and composition to those who have come afterward. She invented different genres of lyric and poetry, short narratives, tearful laments and strange lamentations about love and other emotions, and these were so well made and so well ordered that they were named 'Sapphic' after her. Horace recounts, concerning her poems, that when Plato, the great philosopher who was Aristotle's teacher, died, a book of Sappho's poems was found under his pillow.

---

[2] **Boccaccio** The renowned fourteenth-century Italian poet and author wrote *On Famous Women,* in which he planned to extol the virtues of many women. He finished chapters on only four women.

"In brief this lady was so outstanding in learning that in the city where she resided a statue of bronze in her image was dedicated in her name and erected in a prominent place so that she would be honored by all and be remembered forever. This lady was placed and counted among the greatest and most famous poets, and according to Boccaccio, the honors of the diadems and crowns of kings and the miters of bishops are not any greater, nor are the crowns of laurel and victor's palm.

"I could tell you a great deal about women of great learning. Leontium was a Greek woman and also such a great philosopher that she dared, for impartial and serious reasons, to correct and attack the philosopher Theophrastus,[3] who was quite famous in her time."

34. Here She Speaks of Minerva, Who Invented Many Sciences and the Technique of Making Armor from Iron and Steel.

"Minerva, just as you have written elsewhere, was a maiden of Greece and surnamed Pallas. This maiden was of such excellence of mind that the foolish people of that time, because they did not know who her parents were and saw her doing things which had never been done before, said she was a goddess descended from Heaven; for the less they knew about her ancestry, the more marvelous her great knowledge seemed to them, when compared to that of the women of her time. She had a subtle mind, of profound understanding, not only in one subject but also generally, in every subject. Through her ingenuity she invented a shorthand Greek script in which a long written narrative could be transcribed with far fewer letters, and which is still used by the Greeks today, a fine invention whose discovery demanded great subtlety. She invented numbers and a means of quickly counting and adding sums. Her mind was so enlightened with general knowledge that she devised various skills and designs which had never before been discovered. She developed the entire technique of gathering wool and making cloth and was the first who ever thought to shear sheep of their wool and then to pick, comb, and card it with iron spindles and finally to spin it with a distaff, and then she invented the tools needed to make the cloth and also the method by which the wool should finally be woven.

"Similarly she initiated the custom of extracting oil from different fruits of the earth, also from olives, and of squeezing and pressing juice from other fruits. At the same time she discovered how to make wagons and carts to transport things easily from one place to another.

"This lady, in a similar manner, did even more, and it seems all the more remarkable because it is far removed from a woman's nature to conceive of such things; for she invented the art and technique of making harnesses and armor from iron and steel, which knights and armed soldiers employ in battle and with which they cover their bodies, and which she first gave to the Athenians whom she taught how to deploy an army and battalions and how to fight in organized ranks.

"Similarly she was the first to invent flutes and fifes, trumpets and wind instruments. With her considerable force of mind, this lady remained a virgin her entire life. Because of her outstanding chastity, the poets claimed in their fictions that Vulcan, the god of fire, wrestled with her for a long time and that finally she won and overcame him, which is to say that she overcame the ardor and lusts of the flesh which so strongly assail the young. The Athenians held this maiden in such high reverence that they worshiped her as a goddess and called her the goddess of arms and chivalry because she was the first to devise their use, and they also called her the goddess of knowledge because of her learnedness.

"After her death they erected a temple in Athens dedicated to her, and there they placed a statue of her, portraying a maiden, as a representation of wisdom and chivalry. This statue had terrible and cruel eyes because chivalry has been instituted to carry out rigorous justice; they also signified that one seldom knows toward what end the meditation of the wise man tends. She wore a helmet on her head which signified that a knight must have strength, endurance, and constant courage in the deeds of arms, and further signified that the counsels of the wise are concealed, secret, and hidden. She was dressed in a coat of mail which stood for the power of the estate of chivalry and also taught that the wise man is always armed against the whims of Fortune, whether good or bad. She held some kind of spear or very long lance, which meant that the knight must be the rod of justice and also signified that the wise man casts his spears from great distances. A buckler or shield of crystal hung at her neck, which meant that the knight must always be alert and oversee everywhere the defense of his country and people and further signified that things are open and evident to the wise man. She had portrayed in the middle of this shield the head of a serpent called Gorgon, which teaches that the knight must always be wary and watchful over his enemies like the serpent, and furthermore, that the wise man is aware of all the malice which can hurt him. Next to this image they also placed a bird that flies by night, named the owl, as if to watch over her, which signified that the knight must be ready by night as well as by day for civil defense, when necessary, and also that the wise man should take care at all times to do what is profitable and fitting for him. For a long time this lady was held in such high regard and her great fame spread so far that in many places temples were founded to praise her. Even long afterward, when the Romans were at the height of their power, they included her image among their gods."

---

[3] **Theeophrastus** Greek philsopher and scientist, a disciple of Aristotle and his successor. Lived in fourth and third centuries B.C.

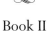

Book II

36. Against Those Men Who Claim It Is Not Good for Women to Be Educated.

Following these remarks, I, Christine, spoke, "My lady, I 1
realize that women have accomplished many good things
and that even if evil women have done evil, it seems to
me, nevertheless, that the benefits accrued and still accru-
ing because of good women—particularly the wise and literary ones and those educated in the natural sciences
whom I mentioned above—outweigh the evil. Therefore, I
am amazed by the opinion of some men who claim that
they do not want their daughters, wives, or kinswomen to
be educated because their mores would be ruined as a
result."

She responded, "Here you can clearly see that not all
opinions of men are based on reason and that these men
are wrong. For it must not be presumed that mores necessarily grow worse from knowing the moral sciences,
which teach the virtues, indeed, there is not the slightest
doubt that moral education amends and ennobles them.
How could anyone think or believe that whoever follows
good teaching or doctrine is the worse for it? Such an
opinion cannot be expressed or maintained. I do not
mean that it would be good for a man or a woman to
study the art of divination or those fields of learning
which are forbidden—for the holy Church did not
remove them from common use without good reason—
but it should not be believed that women are the worse
for knowing what is good.

"Quintus Hortensius, a great rhetorician and consu-
mately skilled orator in Rome, did not share this opinion.
He had a daughter, named Hortensia, whom he greatly
loved for the subtlety of her wit. He had her learn letters
and study the science of rhetoric, which she mastered so
thoroughly that she resembled her father Hortensius not
only in wit and lively memory but also in her excellent
delivery and order of speech—in fact, he surpassed her in
nothing. As for the subject discussed above, concerning
the good which comes about through women, the benefits
realized by this woman and her learning were, among others, exceptionally remarkable. That is, during the time
when Rome was governed by three men, this Hortensia
began to support the cause of women and to undertake

what no man dared to undertake. There was a question
whether certain taxes should be levied on women and on
their jewelry during a needy period in Rome. This
woman's eloquence was so compelling that she was listened to, no less readily than her father would have been,
and she won her case.

"Similarly, to speak of more recent times, without
searching for examples in ancient history, Giovanni
Andrea, a solemn law professor in Bologna not quite sixty
years ago, was not of the opinion that it was bad for women
to be educated. He had a fair and good daughter, named
Novella, who was educated in the law to such an advanced
degree that when he was occupied by some task and not at
leisure to present his lectures to his students, he would send
Novella, his daughter, in his place to lecture to the students
from his chair. And to prevent her beauty from distracting
the concentration of her audience, she had a little curtain
drawn in front of her. In this manner she could on occasion
supplement and lighten her father's occupation. He loved
her so much that, to commemorate her name, he wrote a
book of remarkable lectures on the law which he entitled
Novella super Decretalium, after his daughter's name.

"Thus, not all men (and especially the wisest) share 5
the opinion that it is bad for women to be educated. But it is
very true that many foolish men have claimed this because
it displeased them that women knew more than they did.
Your father, who was a great scientist and philosopher, did
not believe that women were worth less by knowing science; rather, as you know, he took great pleasure from seeing your inclination to learning. The feminine opinion of
your mother, however, who wished to keep you busy with
spinning and silly girlishness, following the common custom of women, was the major obstacle to your being more
involved in the sciences. But just as the proverb already
mentioned above says, 'No one can take away what Nature
has given,' your mother could not hinder in you the feeling
for the sciences which you, through natural inclination,
had nevertheless gathered together in little droplets. I am
sure that, on account of these things, you do not think you
are worth less but rather that you consider it a great treasure for yourself; and you doubtless have reason to."

And I, Christine, replied to all of this, "Indeed, my
lady, what you say is as true as the Lord's Prayer."

11

THE EARLY RENAISSANCE
Return to Classical Roots
1400–1494

GIOVANNI PICO DELLA MIRANDOLA

Selections from *On the Dignity of Man*

The Latin oration *On the Dignity of Man* is a tour de force by Pico (1463–1494), a son of the noble house of Mirandola (Italy). Written when Pico was twenty-four, the oration is a mixture of Aristotelian, Hebraic, Arabic, Persian, and Aramaic notions held together by Neo-Platonism—a blend of Plato's ideas and Christian beliefs. Its central Neo-Platonic motif is that love is the divine glue unifying the universe. Christian in structure, this heady synthesis of ideas breaks free of its frame to become a nonsectarian philosophy.

Pico's oration embodies the Renaissance spirit. In its appeal to wide-ranging sources, it expresses Renaissance zeal for the Classic texts of Greece and Rome as well as hitherto ignored ancient sources. Its theme is the Renaissance belief that the findings of reason and the truths of the Bible share a basic unity that is reflected in the history of thought. Most of all, its view that human nature has no limits is the prototype of the Renaissance idea of unlimited possibility. Today this idea, with its corollary of free expression, is a defining trait of Western culture.

The oration was composed to introduce a debate Pico scheduled for Rome in 1487. In this debate, Pico proposed to defend nine hundred theses gleaned from his vast readings; he even offered to pay his potential opponents' travel expenses. The debate, however, did not take place because Pope Innocent VIII forbade it. The pope also appointed a commission to examine the debate topics, with the result that seven theses were condemned as heretical, and six more were suspect. Threatened by church officials, Pico subsequently settled in Florence, where he was caught up in the anti-Renaissance crusade of the monk Savonarola. Pico's plan to wander as an evangelist was cut short in 1494, when he died suddenly at age thirty-one.

Reading the Selections

The first selection from the oration *On the Dignity of Man* begins with a greeting—"Most venerable fathers"—thus establishing that the work was meant to be recited orally, ostensibly before a group of clergy. The major insights to be gained from this selection are Pico's concept of human nature and his style of reasoning.

Pico's concept of human nature is his major contribution to Western thought. For him, human nature is not fixed, and the will is perfectly free. In a burst of lyricism he claimed that human beings are shape-shifting creatures who may be vegetative, bestial, rational, divine, or even co-equal with God: When humanity's quest ends, "We shall . . . not be ourselves, but He himself who made us." Brushing aside medieval ideas, Pico expresses the radiant faith of Renaissance humanism, that human beings are not flawed by original sin but are capable of becoming godlike.

Pico's style of reasoning reflects the Renaissance trend of treating old problems in new ways. To deal with the question of human nature, he takes the Platonic concept of the Great Chain of Being, which maintains that creation is a linked cord reaching step by step from the simplest life to God, and gives it a modern twist. Ancient thinkers had used the Great Chain of Being to argue that human potential is limited, since the place of human beings in the chain is fixed, and that change would destroy the whole creation. In contrast, Pico claimed that human beings may make of themselves anything they please, because as hybrids of the whole creation, they exist both outside and above the Great Chain of Being.

∾

Most venerable fathers, I have read in the records of the Arabians that Abdul the Saracen, on being asked what thing on, so to speak, the world's stage, he viewed as most greatly worthy of wonder, answered that he viewed nothing more wonderful than man. And Mercury's, "a great wonder, Asclepius, is man!" agrees with that opinion. On thinking over the reason for these sayings, I was not satisfied by the many assertions made by many men concerning the outstandingness of human nature: that man is the messenger between creatures, familiar with the upper and king of the lower; by the sharpsightedness of the senses, by the hunting-power of reason, and by the light of intelligence, the interpreter of nature; the part in between the standstill of eternity and the flow of time, and, as the Persians say, the bond tying the world together, nay, the nuptial bond; and, according to David,[1] "a little lower than the angels." These reasons are great but not the chief ones, that is, they are not reasons for a lawful claim to the highest wonder as to a prerogative. Why should we not wonder more at the angels themselves and at the very blessed heavenly choirs?

Finally, it seemed to me that I understood why man is the animal that is most happy, and is therefore worthy of all wonder; and lastly, what the state is that is allotted to man in the succession of things, and that is capable of arousing envy not only in the brutes but also in the stars and even in minds beyond the world. It is wonderful and beyond belief. For this is the reason why man is rightly said and thought to be a great marvel and the animal really worthy of wonder. Now hear what it is, fathers; and with kindly ears and for the sake of your humanity, give me your close attention:

Now the highest Father, God the master-builder, had, by the laws of his secret wisdom, fabricated this house, this world which we see, a very superb temple of divinity. He had adorned the super-celestial region with minds. He had animated the celestial globes with eternal souls; he had filled with a diverse throng of animals the cast-off and residual parts of the lower world. But, with the work finished, the Artisan desired that there be someone to reckon up the reason of such a big work, to love its beauty, and to wonder at its greatness. Accordingly, now that all things had been completed, as Moses and Timaeus[2] testify, He lastly considered creating man. But there was nothing in the archetypes from which He could mold a new sprout, nor anything in His storehouses which He could bestow as a heritage upon a new son, nor was there an empty judiciary seat where this contemplator of the universe could sit. Everything was filled up; all things had been laid out in the highest, the lowest, and the middle orders. But it did not belong to the paternal power to have failed in the final parturition, as though exhausted by childbearing; it did not belong to wisdom, in a case of necessity, to have been tossed back and forth through want of a plan; it did not belong to the loving-kindness which was going to praise divine liberality in others to be forced to condemn itself. Finally, the best of workmen decided that that to which nothing of its very own could be given should be, in composite fashion, whatsoever had belonged individually to each and every thing. Therefore He took up

---

[1] **Abdul the Saracen, Mercury, Asclepius, David** Pico is including various sources to show that man is a wonder in himself and worthy of study and praise. Abdul the Saracen is probably the famous Arabian physician, Abul Kassim, who wrote a medical textbook used for more than five hundred years in Europe. Mercury is the Roman god of merchants and traders who, by the Renaissance, was seen as a symbol of the human intellect and the mediator between the human mind and divine wisdom. Asclepius was the Greek god of healing; he became a Roman god in the third century B.C. after a plague. King David of the Old Testament was often referenced by writers and scholars for his wisdom as recorded in the Bible.

[2] **Moses and Timaeus** Moses, from the Old Testament, to whom God gave the Ten Commandments, and who led his people to the Promised Land, was considered a strong and wise leader. Timaeus was a Greek philosopher who was the major voice in Plato's work, *Timaeus*. The dialogue refers to the creation of the world that Christians later associated with God as the creator. The Neo-Platonists used Timaeus in their works against the Aristotelians and Scholasticism.

man, a work of indeterminate form; and, placing him at the midpoint of the world, He spoke to him as follows:

"We have given to thee, Adam, no fixed seat, no form of thy very own, no gift peculiarly thine, that thou mayest feel as thine own, have as thine own, possess as thine own the seat, the form, the gifts which thou thyself shalt desire. A limited nature in other creatures is confined within the laws written down by Us. In conformity with thy free judgment, in whose hand We have placed thee, thou art confined by no bounds; and thou wilt fix limits of nature for thyself. I have placed thee at the center of the world, that from there thou mayest more conveniently look around and see whatsoever is in the world. Neither heavenly nor earthly, neither mortal nor immortal have We made thee. Thou, like a judge appointed for being honorable, art the molder and maker of thyself; thou mayest sculpt thyself into whatever shape thou dost prefer. Thou canst grow downward into the lower natures which are brutes. Thou canst again grow upward from thy soul's reason into the higher natures which are divine."

O great liberality of God the Father! O great and wonderful happiness of man. It is given him to have that which he chooses and to be that which he wills. As soon as brutes are born, they bring with them, "from their dam's bag," as Lucilius[3] says, what they are going to possess. Highest spirits have been, either from the beginning or soon after, that which they are going to be throughout everlasting eternity. At man's birth the Father placed in him every sort of seed and sprouts of every kind of life. The seeds that each man cultivates will grow and bear their fruit in him. If he cultivates vegetable seeds, he will become a plant. If the seeds of sensation, he will grow into brute. If rational, he will come out a heavenly animal. If intellectual, he will be an angel, and a son of God. And if he is not contented with the lot of any creature but takes himself up into the center of his own unity, then, made one spirit with God and settled in the solitary darkness of the Father, who is above all things, he will stand ahead of all things. Who does not wonder at this chameleon which we are? Or who at all feels more wonder at anything else whatsoever? It was not unfittingly that Asclepius the Athenian said that man was symbolized by Prometheus in the secret rites, by reason of our nature sloughing its skin and transforming itself; hence metamorphoses were popular among the Jews and the Pythagoreans.[4] For the more secret Hebrew theology at one time reshapes holy Enoch[5] into an angel of divinity, whom they call *malach hashechina*, and at other times reshapes other men into other divinities. According to the Pythagoreans, wicked men are deformed into brutes and, if you believe Empedocles,[6] into plants too. And copying them, Maumeth [Moham-

med] often had it on his lips that he who draws back from divine law becomes a brute. And his saying so was reasonable: for it is not the rind which makes the plant, but a dull and non-sentient nature; not the hide which makes a beast of burden, but a brutal and sensual soul; not the spherical body which makes the heavens, but right reason; and not a separateness from the body but a spiritual intelligence which makes an angel. For example, if you see a man given over to his belly and crawling upon the ground, it is a bush not a man that you see. If you see anyone blinded by the illusions of his empty and Calypso-like[7] imagination, seized by the desire of scratching, and delivered over to the senses, it is a brute not a man that you see. If you come upon a philosopher winnowing out all things by right reason, he is a heavenly not an earthly animal. If you come upon a pure contemplator, ignorant of the body, banished to the innermost places of the mind, he is not an earthly, not a heavenly animal; he more superbly is a divinity clothed with human flesh.

Who is there that does not wonder at man? And it is not unreasonable that in the mosaic and Christian holy writ man is sometimes denoted by the name "all flesh" and at other times by that of "every creature"; and man fashions, fabricates, transforms himself into the shape of all flesh, into the character of every creature. Accordingly, where Evantes the Persian tells of the Chaldaean theology, he writes that man is not any inborn image of himself, but many images coming in from the outside: hence that saying of the Chaldaeans: *enosh hu shinuy vekamah tevaoth baal chayim*, that is, man is an animal of diverse, multiform, and destructible nature.

But why all this? In order for us to understand that, after having been born in this state so that we may be what we will to be, then, since we are held in honor, we ought to take particular care that no one may say against us that we do not know that we are made similar to brutes and mindless beasts of burden. But rather, as Asaph[8] the prophet says: "Ye are all gods, and sons of the most high," unless by abusing the very indulgent liberality of the Father, we make the free choice, which he gave to us, harmful to ourselves instead of helpful toward salvation. Let a certain holy ambition invade the mind, so that we may not be content with mean things but may aspire to the highest things and strive with all our forces to attain them: for if we will to, we can. Let us spurn earthly things; let us struggle toward the heavenly. Let us put in last place whatever is of the world; and let us fly beyond the chambers of the world to the chamber nearest the most lofty divinity. There, as the sacred mysteries reveal, the seraphim, cherubim, and thrones occupy the first places. Ignorant of how to yield to them and unable to endure the second places, let us compete with the angels in dignity and glory. When we have willed it, we shall be not at all below them. . . .

---

[3] **Lucilius** Roman poet, third and second century B.C., who supposedly originated the satirical form used by later Roman poets. Only fragments of his works remain.

[4] **Pythagoreans** Followers of the sixth-century B.C. Greek philosopher and mathematician Pythagoras. The Pythagoreans contributed to the study of mathematics and astronomy.

[5] **Enoch** Biblical figure who, according the Book of Genesis, did not die as a mortal because "God took him."

[6] **Empedocles** Fifth-century B.C. Greek philosopher who explained the physical world as composed of four elements controlled by Strife and Love.

---

[7] **Calypso-like** Calypso, the nymph who kept Odysseus on the island for seven years, was also associated with the "hidden"; thus, an illusion or one who creates illusions.

[8] **Asaph** Several Asaphs in the Old Testament. One was the Choirmaster during David's time; his name is connected to a small collection of psalms, and he is probably the one Pico is referencing in this passage.

... Not only the Mosaic or Christian mysteries but also the theology of the ancients show the advantages for us and the dignity of these liberal arts about which I have come here to dispute. For what else is meant by the degrees of initiation that are customary in the secret rites of the Greeks? First, to those who had been purified by moral and dialectic arts, which we have called, as it were, purgative, befell the reception of the mysteries. And what else can this reception be but the interpretation of more hidden nature by means of philosophy? Then lastly, to those who had been thus prepared, came that ϲποπτεία, that is, a vision of divine things by means of the light of theology. Who does not seek to be initiated into such rites? Who does not set all human things at a lower value and, contemning the goods of fortune and neglecting the body, does not desire, while still continuing on earth, to become the drinking-companion of the gods; and, drunken with the nectar of eternity, to bestow the gift of immortality upon the mortal animal? Who does not wish to have breathed into him the Socratic frenzies sung by Plato in the *Phaedrus,* that by the oarlike movement of wings and feet he may quickly escape from here, that is, from this world where he is laid down as in an evil place, and be carried in speediest flight to the heavenly Jerusalem. We shall be possessed, fathers, we shall be possessed by these Socratic frenzies, which will so place us outside of our minds that they will place our mind and ourselves in God. We shall be possessed by them if we have first done what is in us to do. For if through morality the forces of the passions will have been so stretched to the [proper] measure, through due proportions, that they sound together in fixed concord, and if through dialectic, reason will have moved, keeping time in her forward march, then, aroused by the frenzy of the muses, we shall drink in the heavenly harmony of our ears. Then Bacchus the leader of the muses, in his own mysteries, that is, in the visible signs of nature, will show the invisible things of God to us as we philosophize, and will make us drunk with the abundance of the house of God. In this house, if we are faithful like Moses, holiest theology will approach, and will inspire us with a twofold frenzy. We, raised up into the loftiest watchtower of theology, from which, measuring with indivisible eternity the things that are, will be, and shall have been, and looking at their primeval beauty, shall be prophets of Phoebus,[9] his winged lovers, and finally, aroused with ineffable charity as with fire, placed outside of ourselves like burning Seraphim,[10] filled with divinity, we shall now not be ourselves, but He himself who made us.

---

[9] **Phoebus** Another name for Apollo, the Greek god of prophecy, the patron of music and poetry; also connected with the sun and, thus, the "shining one," as Phoebus is likewise called.

[10] **Seraphim** In the Hebrew tradition and Bible, they are supernatural beings associated with the presence of God. Pico is using both Phoebus and the Seraphim as images of light to lift the reader to new heights of knowledge and wisdom.

LEON BATTISTA ALBERTI
Selection from *On Painting*

Alberti's *On Painting* helped ensure the triumph of the new Renaissance style over older medieval art. Published in Latin (1435) and Italian (1436) just as the Renaissance was picking up steam, this was the first modern treatise on the theory of painting. It became the era's authoritative guide for painters, both within and outside Florence, including Fra Angelico (ca. 1400–1455), Piero della Francesca (1420–1492), and perhaps Leonardo da Vinci (1452–1519). From 1600 until 1800, Alberti's treatise was invoked as an authority for painting practices approved by Europe's art academies. Today's historians still find this work invaluable, for it prepared the way for the art, the artist, and the patron of the Renaissance.

Alberti wrote his treatise "as a painter speaking to painters." The work is divided into three "books," or parts. Book I presents a mathematical method for creating perspective—the illusion of depth on a flat surface. Some perspectival ideas had long been used in Italy, but he was the first to codify them into an accessible work. Book II deals with painterly matters, such as color, drawing, and grace and beauty in poses and movements. Book III sets forth a type of humanist painting that uses Greco-Roman themes and depicts the soul's condition through bodily gestures and facial expressions.

Leon Battista Alberti (1404–1472) was the "universal man," the beau ideal of the age, and his achievements rivaled those of the later Leonardo da Vinci. Besides painting, Alberti also mastered music, mathematics, engineering, architecture, sculpture, poetry, drama, and civil and canon law and wrote books on most of these fields. A friend of Cosimo de' Medici (1389–1464), the merchant-banker who dominated Florence, Alberti was active in Cosimo's Platonic Academy, the club of artists and thinkers who studied Plato (see *Phaedo* and *The Republic*). Alberti's spirit had such force that his friends called him the complete genius, hence the authority attributed to his works.

Reading the Selection

This selection from Book II of *On Painting* shows Alberti as a Renaissance humanist, making the case for a radical new role for the age's painters. These painters are characterized by intellect, with the ascendancy of mind over hand visible in their art. Humanism is the theme: "[P]ainting contributes to the most honorable delights of the soul." This argument echoes the familiar rationale of humanists that studying and practicing grammar, rhetoric, logic, arithmetic, geometry, music, and astronomy—the seven liberal arts—are good exercises for the soul. What is radical in Alberti's claim is the ranking of painting with the liberal arts. In fact, in the Middle Ages, painting ranked low, on a par with crafts (shoemaking, weaving, and such). The favorable reception of this treatise encouraged the rise of independent artists, as evidenced around 1500 in the careers of Michelangelo, Leonardo da Vinci, and Raphael.

Alberti also argued that painting should be part of the core curriculum of the schools. To prove his case, he used examples from antiquity showing that the best families required that painting be taught to their sons and daughters. By 1513, Alberti's hope was realized in the well-rounded backgrounds of the idealized lady and gentleman of Castiglione's highly influential *The Book of the Courtier*.

Finally, Alberti was a pioneer in his claim for the sovereign power of painting: "Who can doubt that painting is the master art?" A generation later Leonardo gave voice to the identical claim.

∽

Book II

Because this [process of] learning may perhaps appear a fatiguing thing to young people, I ought to prove here that painting is not unworthy of consuming all our time and study.

Painting contains a divine force which not only makes absent men present, as friendship is said to do, but moreover makes the dead seem almost alive. Even after many centuries they are recognized with great pleasure and with great admiration for the painter. Plutarch[1] says that Cassander, one of the captains of Alexander, trembled through all his body because he saw a portrait of his King. Agesilaos, the Lacedaemonian, never permitted anyone to paint him or to represent him in sculpture; his own form so displeased him that he avoided being known by those who would come after him. Thus the face of a man who is already dead certainly lives a long life through painting. Some think that painting shaped the gods who were adored by the nations. It certainly was their greatest gift to mortals, for painting is most useful to that piety which joins us to the gods, and keeps our souls full of religion. They say that Phidias[2] made in Aulis a god Jove[3] so beautiful that it considerably strengthened the religion then current.

The extent to which painting contributes to the most honourable delights of the soul and to the dignified beauty of things can be clearly seen not only from other things but especially from this: you can conceive of almost nothing so precious which is not made far richer and much more beautiful by association with painting. Ivory,

---

[1] **Plutarch** Greek biographer who wrote *Parallel Lives,* which were character studies comparing famous Greeks and Romans who lived from antiquity to Plutarch's time in the first century A.D.

[2] **Phidias** Regarded as the most famous of all Greek sculptors. Lived in fifth-century Athens and produced many works, including sculptures for the Parthenon.

[3] **Jove** Another Latin name for Jupiter, who was the chief deity of the Roman system of gods and goddesses.

gems and similar expensive things become more precious when worked by the hand of the painter. Gold worked by the art of painting outweighs an equal amount of unworked gold. If figures were made by the hand of Phidias or Praxiteles[4] from lead itself—the lowest of metals—they would be valued more highly than silver. The painter, Zeuxis,[5] began to give away his things because, as he said, they could not be bought. He did not think it possible to come to a just price which would be satisfactory to the painter, for in painting animals he set himself up almost as a god.

Therefore, painting contains within itself this virtue that any master painter who sees his works adored will feel himself considered another god. Who can doubt that painting is the master art or at least not a small ornament of things? The architect, if I am not mistaken, takes from the painter architraves, bases, capitals, columns, façades and other similar things. All the smiths, sculptors, shops and guilds are governed by the rules and art of the painter. It is scarcely possible to find any superior art which is not concerned with painting, so that whatever beauty is found can be said to be born of painting. *But also this, a dignified painting is held in high honour by many so that among all artists some smiths are named, only this is not the rule among smiths.* For this reason, I say among my friends that Narcissus who was changed into a flower, according to the poets, was the inventor of painting. Since painting is already the flower of every art, the story of Narcissus[6] is most to the point. What else can you call painting but a similar embracing with art of what is presented on the surface of the water in the fountain?

Quintilian[7] said that the ancient painters used to circumscribe shadows cast by the sun, and from this our art has grown. There are those who say that a certain Philocles, an Egyptian, and a Cleantes were among the first inventors of this art. The Egyptians affirm that painting was in use among them a good 6000 years before it was carried into Greece. They say that painting was brought to us from Greece after the victory of Marcellus[8] over Sicily. But we are not interested in knowing who was the inventor of the art or the first painter, since we are not telling stories like Pliny.[9] We are, however, building anew an art of painting about which nothing, as I see it, has been written in this age. They say that Euphranor of Isthmus wrote something about measure and about colours, that Antigonos and Xenocrates exchanged something in their

letters about painting, and that Apelles wrote to Pelleus about painting. Diogenes Laertius recounts that Demetrius made commentaries on painting.[10] Since all the other arts were recommended in letters by our great men, and since painting was not neglected by our Latin writers, I believe that our ancient Tuscan [ancestors] were already most expert masters in painting.

Trismegistus,[11] an ancient writer, judged that painting and sculpture were born at the same time as religion, *for thus he answered Aesclepius: mankind portrays the gods in his own image from his memories of nature and his own origins.* Who can here deny that in all things public and private, profane and religious, painting has taken all the most honourable parts to itself so that nothing has ever been so esteemed by mortals?

The incredible prices of painted pictures have been recorded. Aristides the Theban sold a single picture for one hundred talents. They say that Rhodes was not burned by King Demetrius for fear that a painting of Protogenes' should perish. It could be said that the city of Rhodes was ransomed from the enemy by a single painting. Pliny collected many other such things in which you can see that good painters have always been greatly honoured by all. The most noble citizens, philosophers and quite a few kings not only enjoyed painted things but also painted with their own hands. Lucius Manilius, Roman citizen, and Fabius, a most noble man, were painters. Turpilius, a Roman knight, painted at Verona. Sitedius, praetor and proconsul, acquired renown as a painter. Pacuvius, tragic poet and nephew of the poet Ennius, painted Hercules in the Roman forum. Socrates, Plato, Metrodorus, Pyrrho were connoisseurs of painting. The emperors Nero, Valentinian, and Alexander Severus were most devoted to painting. It would be too long, however, to recount here how many princes and kings were pleased by painting. Nor does it seem necessary to me to recount all the throng of ancient painters. Their number is seen in the fact that 360 statues, part on horseback and part in chariots, were completed in four hundred days for Demetrius Phalerius,[12] son of Phanostratus. In a land in which there was such a great number of sculptors, can you believe that painters were lacking? I am certain that both these arts are related and nurtured by the same genius, painting with sculpture. But I always give higher rank to the genius of the painter because he works with more difficult things.

However, let us return to our work. Certainly the number of sculptors and painters was great in those times when princes and plebeians, learned and unlearned

5

---

[4] **Praxiteles** Greek sculptor of the fourth century B.C.; many of his works are extant.

[5] **Zeuxis** Fifth-century B.C. Greek painter whose paintings were very realistic. None of his works exist today.

[6] **Narcissus** A handsome youth who fell in love with his own image reflected in a fountain pool and died of frustration from being unable to fulfill his love.

[7] **Quintilian** First-century A.D. Roman lawyer, orator, and author of a book on Roman education.

[8] **Marcellus** Roman general who conquered Sicily in the third century B.C.

[9] **Pliny** Probably Pliny the Elder, not his son, the Younger. The Elder, who lived in the first century A.D., wrote extensively on many topics, including an existing encyclopedia of natural science.

---

[10] **Euphranor of Isthmus, Antigonos, Xenocrates, Apelles, Pelleus, Diogenes Laertius, Demetrius** All these men were ancient Greek sculptors, painters, or philosophers who lived in the fourth and third centuries B.C. Many of their works are lost; most are known only by name or secondary references.

[11] **Trismegistus** Alberti is probably referring to the author of a set of ancient books who was supposed to be Thoth, the Egyptian god of wisdom, and whom the Greeks called Hermes Trismegistus. The books were reputed to include information on every possible topic.

[12] **Demetrius Phalerius** Fourth- and third-century B.C. Athenian orator and statesman.

enjoyed painting, and when painted panels and portraits, considered the choicest booty from the provinces, were set up in the theatres. Finally L. Paulus Aemilius and not a few other Roman citizens taught their sons painting along with the fine arts and the art of living piously and well. This excellent custom was frequently observed among the Greeks who, because they wished their sons to be well educated, taught them painting along with geometry and music. It was also an honour among women to know how to paint. Martia, daughter of Varro,[13] is praised by the writers because she knew how to paint. Painting had such reputation and honour among the Greeks that laws and edicts were passed forbidding slaves to learn painting. It was certainly well that they did this, for the art of painting has always been most worthy of liberal minds and noble souls.

As for me, I certainly consider a great appreciation of painting to be the best indication of a most perfect mind, even though it happens that this art is pleasing to the uneducated as well as to the educated. It occurs rarely in any other art that what delights the experienced also moves the inexperienced. In the same way you will find that many greatly desire to be well versed in painting. Nature herself seems to delight in painting, for in the cut faces of

marble she often paints centaurs and faces of bearded and curly headed kings. It is said, moreover, that in a gem from Pyrrhus all nine Muses, each with her symbol, are to be found clearly painted by nature. Add to this that in no other art does it happen that both the experienced and the inexperienced of every age apply themselves so voluntarily to the learning and exercising of it. Allow me to speak of myself here. Whenever I turn to painting for my recreation, which I frequently do when I am tired of more pressing affairs, I apply myself to it with so much pleasure that I am surprised that three or four hours have passed. Thus this art gives pleasure and praise to whoever is skilled in it; riches and perpetual fame to one who is master of it. Since these things are so, since painting is the best and most ancient ornament of things, worthy of free men, pleasing to learned and unlearned, I greatly encourage our studious youth to exert themselves as much as possible in painting.

Therefore, I recommend that he who is devoted to painting should learn this art. The first great care of one who seeks to obtain eminence in painting is to acquire the fame and renown of the ancients. It is useful to remember that avarice is always the enemy of virtue. Rarely can anyone given to acquisition of wealth acquire renown. I have seen many in the first flower of learning suddenly sink to money-making. As a result they acquire neither riches nor praise. However, if they had increased their talent with study, they would have easily soared into great renown. Then they would have acquired much riches and pleasure. . . .

---

[13] **Varro** Probably Marcus Terentius Varro, second- and first-century B.C. Roman scholar and author of many books on law, customs, religion, and philosophy.

12

THE HIGH RENAISSANCE AND EARLY MANNERISM
1494–1564

GASPARA STAMPA

Poems

Gaspara Stampa (ca. 1524–1554) is generally regarded as the best woman poet of the Italian Renaissance and, quite probably, the greatest Italian woman poet ever. Although she created only a small body of work, the sonnets she wrote, based principally on intense love affairs, helped to redefine the genre of lyric poetry. Hers is a worthy name to place beside the other great figures of this period, such as the artists Michelangelo and Titian, the architect Palladio, the writer Vasari, and the composer Adrian Willaert. Yet, she is hardly known outside her native land.

Stampa and her literary achievement are inextricably linked to Renaissance Venice, which became her home in 1531, when her father died. Stampa's worldview and poetic vision were shaped by this city of stark contrasts, which offered both toleration and oppression, simplicity and luxury, duty and license. Sixteenth-century Venice was ruled by a merchant oligarchy who jealously guarded their privileges and developed a sedate, even puritanical society that focused on civic rituals, church groups, and charitable organizations. Paralleling and overlapping this elitist culture was a marginal world peopled by writers, musicians, artists, intellectuals, would-be intellectuals, and independent women, including aristocrats, soldiers, wealthy merchants, adventurers, and high officials of church and state, who were quite indifferent to Christian values. This mixed society assembled in the private homes of culturally privileged women who held salons or drawing rooms, known as *ridotti,* where the time was spent in intellectual conversation and gossip, musical concerts, dancing, parlor games, storytelling, and flirtation with the ladies. Stampa, born probably into the noble class though not a member of the Venetian elite, was drawn to this glittering, pleasure-loving, and corrupt marginal world.

This twilight world was an open society and entry was gained through many means, including breeding, money, connections, and most especially education or genius. Stampa's beauty and noble blood would probably have ensured her admission, absent other traits. However, in addition, she had pursued an exceptional education in the Classics, philosophy, and Italian letters, including training in music—the curriculum favored by progressive aristocratic families for their daughters during the Renaissance. Music and study not only paved the way for Stampa's entry into Venice's twilight world but empowered her to become one of its magnetic figures. In 1548, at the age of twenty-six, Stampa was idling her life away in these *ridotti,* when she met the Venetian aristocrat Count Collaltino di Collato, the man whose love caused her to find her poetic voice.

Most of her poems describe in vivid, poignant detail the all-consuming but ultimately unrequited love she experienced during a three-year liaison with the Count. Despite this, the precise nature of their relationship is highly disputed today. Some scholars portray Stampa as a courtesan, of which Venice had many: More than 11,000 were listed in the 1509 census, out of a population of about 300,000. Others insist on Stampa's chastity, explaining that readers should beware of the "biographical fallacy," that is, the tendency to confuse poetic events with a poet's biography. Whatever the case, Stampa's poetry attests to love's transforming power.

Reading the Selections

Lyric poetry in sixteenth-century Italy was dominated by the model of Petrarch (see *Canzoniere*), the great Tuscan poet. Virtually all the major writers composed lyric verses in the Petrarchan manner. Renaissance theory in general favored imitation and the vernacular poems of Pietro Bembo (1470–1547), who made direct imitations of Petrarch, became accepted as the standard approach to versification. It is not surprising, then, that Stampa adopted the Petrarchan sonnet as the preferred poetic form to express her unfettered feelings.

Constrained by the Petrarchan model, Stampa nevertheless made a significant innovation in her poetic works. Unlike Petrarch, who glorified a distant lover, Stampa made herself the focal point, claiming the high moral ground for the suffering lover, thus transforming the essentially male Petrarchan ideal into a female point of view. The theme in virtually all her poems is unresponsive love, though she was sufficiently gifted to show great originality in her variations.

Five of the 311 poems in the *Rima*, or *Poems*, are offered here. All are sonnets, the verse form that Petrarch made his own. In this translation there is no rhyme, though the line count and the argument are true to the original. Sonnet 3 sets forth the speaker's poetic mission: to use unrequited love as a means for "wak[ing] the sleeping talent in my soul"—the Platonic ideal that envisioned love as engendering a higher state of being. Sonnet 43 depicts the speaker happy in her humiliation before her beloved. In Sonnet 98 the speaker claims moral superiority for the abandoned lover, because the Count—a soldier—is off to fight in France. Sonnet 104 describes a sexual interlude and has been used by scholars to prove that Stampa was a courtesan. In sonnet 151, addressed to women readers, the speaker rakes over the dead coals of her love affair, contrasting her faithfulness with the heartless rejection of her once-beloved.

∞

3

If the Ascrean mountain[1] made a poet[2]   1
Of the rough shepherd with his flocks and herds,
Raising him up to such a peak of fame
As stole the praise from all the other writers,
What marvel is it if my high green hill

Much more than any planet or deep study
Has raised me, low and common as I am,
To write my story that will touch all hearts—
The hill whose sacred and resistless shade
Like a swift tempest, swept out of my heart   10
All ignorance and all baseness from my life.
This lifts me from my low position; this
Renews my style, whets my poetic vein,
And wakes the sleeping talent in my soul.

---

[1] **Ascrean mountain** Mount Helicon, the home of the muses, in Greek mythology; it was near the town of Ascra.
[2] **poet** Greek poet Hesiod (fl. ca. 800 B.C.), author of *Works and Days;* he claimed the muses appeared to him while he was tending his sheep.

∽

43

Harsh is my fortune, but still harder fate
Is dealt me by my lord[3]; he flees from me.
I follow him, while others pine for me,
But I cannot admire another's face.
I hate the one who loves, love him who scorns me.
Against the humble ones, my heart rebels,

────────

[3] **lord** Collaltino.

But I am humble toward the one who spurns me.
So my soul starves for such a harmful food!
He gives me cause for anger every day,
The others try to give comfort and peace.
Those I deny, but cling to my tormentor.
Thus, in your school, O Love, the scholars win
The opposite of that which they deserve:
The humble are despised, the proud are praised.

∽

98

My Count, your valor is so infinite
That it defeats the valor of all others,
But truly it's inferior to the pain
That I have suffered through my love for you.
Though nothing ever yet was read or heard
That could be greater than the infinite,
The miracles of Love are so immense

That they can vanquish the decrees of heaven.
There was a time when my deep joy in you
Could overcome by far the grief I felt,
For Hope still blossomed sweetly in my heart.
Now hope is gone and grief remains alone,
Since, owing to my bitter, evil star,
You, my dear lord, took flight from me to France.

∽

104

O night, more glorious and more blest to me
Than are the brightest and most blissful days!
Night, worthy to be praised by the most brilliant
Of human minds, not only by my words.
You only were the faithful minister
Of all my joys; and all the bitterness
That had oppressed me you made sweet and dear,
Bringing back to my arms him who had bound me.
I only lacked the gift that was bestowed

On fortunate Alcmena,[4] when you lingered
Far past the usual hour of dawn's return.
And yet I cannot say so much of you,
O shining night, but that this song of mine
Will not be overwhelmed by what it sings.

────────

[4] **Alcmena** In Greek mythology, wife of Amphitryon, king of Thebes.
Zeus, king of the gods, seduced her, and she gave birth to Hercules.
The last mortal woman to sleep with Zeus.

∽

151

Weep, Ladies, and let Love join in your grief.
He does not weep, who wounded me so sore
That soon my soul will take its final leave
From this tormented and afflicted body.
If ever a compassionate, gentle heart
Should grant a loving woman's dying wish,
When, dead and cold, I in my grave shall lie,

Write down the reasons for my early death:
"Loving too much, loved little in return,
She lived and died unhappy, who now lies
Here, the most loyal lover of all times.
Pray for her soul's repose, good passer-by,
And learn from her, who was so badly used,
Never to love one cruel and untrue."

BALDASSARE CASTIGLIONE

Selections from *The Book of the Courtier*

The Book of the Courtier (*courtier* being a "gentleman") belongs to the genre of etiquette books
that flourished in Renaissance Europe as a religious-based culture gave way to a more humanistic world. Books of this type were much in evidence, in response to this period's ideal that
secular life in the upper levels of society should be marked by reserved grace, especially
between the sexes. Court life, whether in the royal or aristocratic domain, already had well-
established rules of behavior derived from the medieval chivalric code; however, courts were
still dominated by a male ethos, manifested in rough speech, crude manners, and general lack
of refinement between men and women. Whereas most Renaissance etiquette books were
meant to correct crude behavior and speech, *The Courtier* took a broader view by offering an
idealized vision of court life in which courteous ladies became the arbiters of society. Published in 1528 and translated into most Western languages by 1600, this work became the bible
of politeness for Europe's upper classes, and its rules were formalized into strict expectations.
This Renaissance book is the source from which modern notions of "lady" and "gentleman"
descend.

The *Courtier*'s author, Baldassare Castiglione (1478–1529), was himself a polished courtier,
growing up among the Italian nobility and studying the Classics at the University of Milan.
Later, he was attached to various northern Italian ducal courts (Milan, Urbino, and Mantua), for
whose rulers he performed military and diplomatic missions. While serving as the Duke of
Mantua's ambassador to Rome, he was brought by his duties into the cultivated court of the
Medici pope, Leo X. A later pope, Clement VII, made Castiglione the papal representative to
Spain, a post he held until he died.

The Courtier, Castiglione's only publication, was his life's work. He was moved to write it
during his eleven years at the ducal court of Urbino, which was the center of an accomplished circle of artists, writers, and intellectuals presided over by the old duke and his
young wife, Elisabetta. This Urbino circle, with its witty talk, integrity, and grace, came to
embody Castiglione's social ideal. When he wrote *The Courtier,* he tried to capture the conver-
sational tone of this circle by making the work a dialogue, divided into four books, set during
an evening in the ducal palace. In his book, as in life, Duchess Elisabetta is the playful leader
of the group.

Reading the Selections

These selections from *The Book of the Courtier* are excerpts from Books I and III, dealing
respectively with the qualities that define a courtier and a lady. Not based on real life, these
attributes are ideals meant as a guide for correct deportment and had been gleaned from Castiglione's readings in medieval and Classical literature. Of the ideal courtier, the participants
agree that he should be both a soldier trained in the bearing of arms and a scholar skilled in
the liberal arts and social graces; however, they are of two minds as to which role should
dominate.

No such dispute divides Castiglione's participants over the ideal lady: All concur that she
should be the consummate hostess—charming, witty, graceful, physically attractive, and
utterly feminine. An innovative aspect of this idealized model is the insistence that a lady be
educated in the liberal arts in the same way as a gentleman. This idea swept away the barrier
that, since the Middle Ages, had excluded women from higher learning. However, women
remained barred from universities until the nineteenth century.

∽

Book I

. . .

"But to come to specific details, I[1] judge that the first and true profession of the courtier must be that of arms; and this above everything else I wish him to pursue vigorously. Let him also stand out from the rest as enterprising, bold, and loyal to whomever he serves. And he will win a good reputation by demonstrating these qualities whenever and wherever possible, since failure to do so always incurs the gravest censure. Just as once a woman's reputation for purity has been sullied it can never be restored, so once the reputation of a gentleman-at-arms has been stained through cowardice or some other reproachful behaviour, even if only once, it always remains defiled in the eyes of the world and covered with ignominy. The more our courtier excels in this art, therefore, the more praise he will deserve, although I do not think he needs to have the professional knowledge of such things and the other qualities appropriate to a military commander. However, since the subject of what constitutes a great captain takes us into very deep waters, we shall be content, as we said, for the courtier to show complete loyalty and an undaunted spirit, and for these to be always in evidence. For men demonstrate their courage far more often in little things than in great. Very often in the face of appalling danger but where there are numerous witnesses one will find those who, though ready to drop dead with fear, driven on by shame or the presence of others, will press forward, with their eyes closed, and do their duty; and only God knows how. But in things of trifling importance, when they believe they can avoid danger without its being noticed, they are only too willing to play for safety. As for those who, even when they are sure they are not being observed or seen or recognized by anyone, are full of ardour and avoid doing anything, no matter how trivial, for which they would incur reproach, they possess the temper and quality we are looking for in our courtier. All the same, we do not wish the courtier to make a show of being so fierce that he is always blustering and bragging, declaring that he is married to his cuirass,[2] and glowering with the haughty looks that we know only too well in Berto.[3] To these may very fairly be said what a worthy lady once remarked jokingly, in polite company, to a certain man (I don't want just now to mention him by name) whom she had honoured by asking him to dance and who not only refused but would not listen to music or take part in the many other entertainments offered, protesting all the while that such frivolities were not his business. And when at length the lady asked what his business was, he answered with a scowl: "Fighting . . ."

"'Well then,' the lady retorted, 'I should think that since you aren't at war at the moment and you are not engaged in fighting, it would be a good thing if you were to have yourself well greased and stowed away in a cupboard with all your fighting equipment, so that you avoid getting rustier than you are already.'

"And of course everyone burst out laughing at the way she showed her contempt for his stupid presumption.

"Therefore," Count Lodovico went on, "the man we are seeking should be fierce, rough and always to the fore, in the presence of the enemy; but anywhere else he should be kind, modest, reticent and anxious above all to avoid ostentation or the kind of outrageous self-glorification by which a man always arouses loathing and disgust among those who have to listen to him. . . .

"I should like our courtier to be a more than average scholar, at least in those studies which we call the humanities; and he should have a knowledge of Greek as well as Latin, because of the many different things that are so beautifully written in that language. He should be very well acquainted with the poets, and no less with the orators and historians, and also skilled at writing both verse and prose, especially in our own language; for in addition to the satisfaction this will give him personally, it will enable him to provide constant entertainment for the ladies, who are usually very fond of such things. But if because of his other activities or through lack of study he fails to achieve a commendable standard in his writing, then he should take pains to suppress his work, to avoid ridicule, and he should show it only to a friend he can trust. And the exercise of writing will be profitable for him at least to the extent that it will teach him how to judge the work of others. For it is very unusual for someone who is not a practised writer, however erudite he may be, to understand completely the demanding work done by writers, or appreciate their stylistic accomplishments and triumphs and those subtle details characteristic of the writers of the ancient world. Moreover, these studies will make our courtier well informed and eloquent and (as Aristippus[4] said to the tyrant) self-confident and assured no matter whom he is talking to. However, I should like our courtier to keep one precept firmly in mind: namely, that in what I have just discussed and in everything else he should always be diffident and reserved rather than forward, and he should be on his guard against assuming that he knows what he does not know. For we are instinctively all too greedy for praise, and there is no sound or

---

[1] **I** Count Lodovico da Canossa (1476–1532) is speaking. A noble from Verona, he was appointed papal ambassador to England and France by Pope Leo X (pope 1513–1521); made Bishop of Bayeux (in France) in 1520; appointed emissary to Venice by King Francis I of France; resident at Urbino at intervals after 1496. A relative of Castiglione.

[2] **cuirass** Breastplate armor covering the body from neck to waist.

[3] **Berto** Perhaps a papal buffoon, or fool, during the time of Pope Julius II (pope 1503–1513) or Leo X.

---

[4] **Aristippus** (ca. 435–366 B.C.) Greek philosopher who founded a hedonistic school of philosophy in Cyrene, North Africa.

song that comes sweeter to our ears; praise, like Sirens'[5] voices, is the kind of music that causes shipwreck to the man who does not stop his ears to its deceptive harmony. Recognizing this danger, some of the philosophers of the ancient world wrote books giving advice on how a man can tell the difference between a true friend and a flatterer. Even so, we may well ask what use is this, seeing that there are so many who realize perfectly well that they are listening to flattery, and yet love the flatterer and detest the one who tells them the truth. Indeed, very often, deciding that the one who praises them is not being fulsome enough, they lend him a hand themselves and say such things that even the most outrageous flatterer feels ashamed. Let us leave these blind fools to their errors and decide that our courtier should possess such good judgement that he will not be told that black is white or presume anything of himself unless he is certain that it is true, and especially in regard to those flaws which, if you remember, when he was suggesting his game for the evening Cesare[6] recalled we had often used to demonstrate the particular folly of this person or another. To make no mistake at all, the courtier should, on the contrary, when he knows the praises he receives are deserved, not assent to them too openly nor let them pass without some protest. Rather he should tend to disclaim them modestly, always giving the impression that arms are, as indeed they should be, his chief profession, and that all his other fine accomplishments serve merely as adornments; and this should especially be his attitude when he is in the company of soldiers, lest he behave like those who in the world of scholarship want to be taken for warriors and among warriors want to seem men of letters. In this way, as we have said, he will avoid affectation, and even his modest achievements will appear great."

At this point, Pietro Bembo[7] interrupted: "I cannot see, my dear Count, why you wish this courtier, who is so literate and so well endowed with other worthy qualities, to regard everything as serving to adorn the profession of arms, and not arms and the rest as serving to adorn the profession of letters, which, taken by themselves, are as superior in dignity to arms as is the soul to the body, since letters are a function of the soul, just as arms are of the body."

Then the Count answered: "On the contrary, the profession of arms pertains both to the soul and to the body. But I should not want you to be the judge of this, Pietro, because by one of the parties concerned it would be assumed that you were prejudiced. And as this is a controversy that the wisest men have already thrashed out, there

is no call to re-open it. As it is, I consider that it has been settled in favour of arms; and since I may form our courtier as I wish, I want him to be of the same opinion. If you think the contrary, wait until you hear of a contest in which the man who defends the cause of arms is allowed to use them, just as those who defend the cause of letters make use of letters in their defence; for if each one uses his own weapons, you will see that the men of letters will lose."

"Ah," said Pietro Bembo, "you were only too ready earlier on to damn the French for their scant appreciation of letters, and you mentioned the glory that they bring to men and the way they make a man immortal. And now you seem to have changed your mind. Do you not remember that:

Giunto Alessandro alla famosa tomba
del fero Achille, sospirando disse:
O fortunato, che sì chiara tromba
trovasti, e chi di te sì alto scrisse![8]

And if Alexander[9] was envious of Achilles[10] not because of what he had done himself but because of the way he was blessed by fortune in having his deeds celebrated by Homer, we must conclude that he put a higher value on the writings of Homer than on the arms of Achilles. What other judge do you want, or what other verdict on the relative worth of arms and letters than the one delivered by one of the greatest commanders that has ever lived?"

The Count replied: "I blame the French for believing that letters are harmful to the profession of arms, and I maintain myself that it is more fitting for a warrior to be educated than for anyone else; and I would have these two accomplishments, the one helping the other, as is most fitting, joined together in our courtier. I do not think that this means I have changed my opinion. But, as I said, I do not wish to argue which of them is more praiseworthy. Let it be enough that men of letters hardly ever choose to praise other than great men and glorious deeds, which deserve praise both on their own account and because, in addition, they provide writers with a truly noble theme. And this subject-matter embellishes what is written and, no doubt, is the reason why such writings endure, for otherwise, if they dealt not with noble deeds but with vain and trivial subjects, they would surely be read and appreciated less. And if Alexander was envious of Achilles because he was praised by Homer, it still does not necessary follow that he thought more of letters than of arms;

---

[5] **Sirens** In Homer's *Odyssey,* monstrous creatures, half-woman, half-bird, whose singing lured sailors onto destructive rocks at sea.
[6] **Cesare** Cesare Gonzaga (1475–1512), a famous warrior, from the illustrious Gonzaga family in Mantua; a cousin and friend of Castiglione.
[7] **Pietro Bembo** (1470–1547), a Venetian noble and Renaissance man; regarded as an authority on language, style, and Platonic love. Appointed papal secretary by Pope Leo X; made cardinal in 1539; resident at Urbino, 1506–1512.

[8] *. . . alto scrisse!* The first quatrain of a sonnet by Petrarch, literally: "When Alexander reached the famous tomb of fierce Achilles, he sighed and said: O happy man, who found so illustrious a trumpet, and one to write of you so nobly!"
[9] **Alexander** Alexander III, called Alexander the Great (r. 336–323 B.C.). Macedonian general and founder of a great empire, stretching from his homeland to the Indus River.
[10] **Achilles** Ancient Greek hero (see Homer's *Iliad*).

and if he had thought that he was as inferior to Achilles as a soldier as he believed that all those who would write about him were inferior to Homer as writers, he would, I[11] am sure, have far preferred brave exploits on his own part to brave talk from others. Therefore I believe that when he said what he did, Alexander was tacitly praising himself, and expressing a desire for what he thought he lacked, namely supreme ability as a writer, rather than for what he took for granted he already had, namely prowess as a warrior, in which he was far from acknowledging Achilles as his superior. So when he called Achilles fortunate he meant that if so far his own fame did not rival that of Achilles (which had been made bright and illustrious through so inspired a poem) this was not because his valour and merits were less notable or less deserving of the highest praise but because of the way fortune had granted Achilles a born genius to be his herald and to trumpet his deeds to the world. Moreover, perhaps Alexander wanted to encourage some gifted person to write about him, showing that his pleasure in this would be as great as his love and respect for the sacred monuments of literature. And now we have said enough about this subject."

"Indeed, far too much," remarked signor Lodovico, 10 "for I don't think that one could discover anywhere in the world a vessel big enough to hold all the things you want to put into our courtier." . . .

Book III

. . .

"Thus just as it is very fitting that a man should display a 1 certain robust and sturdy manliness, so it is well for a woman to have a certain soft and delicate tenderness, with an air of feminine sweetness in her every movement, which, in her going and staying and whatsoever she does, always makes her appear a woman, without any resemblance to a man. If this precept be added to the rules that these gentlemen have taught the courtier, then I think that she ought to be able to make use of many of them, and adorn herself with the finest accomplishments, as signor Gaspare[12] says. For I consider that many virtues of the mind are as necessary to a woman as to a man; as it is to be of good family; to shun affectation; to be naturally graceful; to be well mannered, clever and prudent; to be neither proud, envious or evil-tongued, nor vain, contentious or clumsy; to know how to gain and keep the favour of her mistress and of everyone else; to perform well and gracefully the sports suitable for women. It also seems to me that good looks are more important to her than to the courtier, for much is lacking to a woman who lacks beauty. She must also be more circumspect and at greater pains to avoid giving an excuse for someone to speak ill of her; she should not only be beyond reproach but also beyond even suspicion, for a woman lacks a man's resources when it comes to defending herself. And now, seeing that Count Lodovico has explained in great detail what should be the principal occupation of a courtier, namely, to his mind, the profession of arms, it seems right for me to say what I consider ought to be that of the lady at Court. And when I have done this, then I shall believe that most of my task has been carried out.

"Leaving aside, therefore, those virtues of the mind which she must have in common with the courtier, such as prudence, magnanimity, continence[13] and many others besides, and also the qualities that are common to all kinds of women, such as goodness and discretion, the ability to take good care, if she is married, of her husband's belongings and house and children, and the virtues belonging to a good mother, I say that the lady who is at Court should properly have, before all else, a certain pleasing affability whereby she will know how to entertain graciously every kind of man with charming and honest conversation, suited to the time and the place and the rank of the person with whom she is talking. And her serene and modest behaviour, and the candour that ought to inform all her actions, should be accompanied by a quick and vivacious spirit by which she shows her freedom from boorishness; but with such a virtuous manner that she makes herself thought no less chaste, prudent and benign than she is pleasing, witty and discreet. Thus she must observe a certain difficult mean,[14] composed as it were of contrasting qualities, and take care not to stray beyond certain fixed limits. . . .

"Now since signor Gaspare also asks what are the many things a lady at Court should know about, how she ought to converse, and whether her virtues should be such as to contribute to her conversation, I declare that I want her to understand what these gentlemen have said the

---

[11] **I** Giuliano de' Medici (1479–1516), of Florence; son of Lorenzo de' Medici and brother of Pope Leo X; during the exile of the Medici from Florence, 1494–1512, Giuliano lived in Urbino, where he was called the "Magnifico Giulaiano." See p. 292.
[12] **signor Gaspare** (1486–1511), of a distinguished Lombard family; friend of Castiglione.

[13] **continence** Self-restraint in matters of the flesh.
[14] **mean** An idea rooted in Aristotle's ethics.

courtier himself ought to know; and as for the activities we have said are unbecoming to her, I want her at least to have the understanding that people can have of things they do not practise themselves; and this so that she may know how to value and praise the gentlemen concerned in all fairness, according to their merits. And, to repeat in just a few words something of what has already been said, I want this lady to be knowledgeable about literature and painting, to know how to dance and play games, adding a discreet modesty and the ability to give a good impression of herself to the other principles that have been taught the courtier. And so when she is talking or laughing, playing or jesting, no matter what, she will always be most graceful, and she will converse in a suitable manner with whomever she happens to meet, making use of agreeable witticisms and jokes. And although continence, magnanimity, temperance, fortitude of spirit, prudence and the other virtues may not appear to be relevant in her social encounters with others, I want her to be adorned with these as well, not so much for the sake of good company, though they play a part in this too, as to make her truly virtuous, and so that her virtues, shining through everything she does, make her worthy of honour."

"I am quite surprised," said signor Gaspare with a laugh, "that since you endow women with letters, continence,

magnanimity and temperance, you do not want them to govern cities as well, and to make laws and lead armies, while the men stay at home to cook and spin."

The Magnifico replied, also laughing: "Perhaps that would not be so bad, either."

Then he added: "Do you not know that Plato, who was certainly no great friend of women, put them in charge of the city and gave all the military duties to the men[15]? Don't you think that we might find many women just as capable of governing cities and armies as men? But I have not imposed these duties on them, since I am fashioning a Court lady and not a queen. I'm fully aware that you would like by implication to repeat the slander that signor Ottaviano[16] made against women yesterday, namely, that they are most imperfect creatures, incapable of any virtuous act, worth very little and quite without dignity compared with men. But truly both you and he would be very much in error if you really thought this." . . .

----

[15] **Plato . . . to the men** Plato reasoned that in the ideal state both men and women philosophers should rule (see Plato, *The Republic*).
[16] **signor Ottaviano** Ottaviano Fregosa (d. 1524), a noble from Genoa; elected *doge*, or chief magistrate, of Genoa, in 1513; appointed governor of Genoa by King Francis I, of France.

NICCOLÒ MACHIAVELLI

Selections from *The Prince*

The Prince is a short and strikingly honest handbook on how to win power and keep it. Based on Niccolò Machiavelli's (1469–1527) personal experiences as diplomat and government employee (in the service of his beloved Florence), the book has become the foundation of modern political theory. In his other works, in particular his histories of Italy and Florence, Machiavelli drew upon his Classical education and personal experiences to develop this message: Learn from the past what works and what does not. But nowhere else does Machiavelli express his thesis so boldly and succinctly as in *The Prince:* "The end justifies any means."

The Prince's harsh and amoral attitude toward politics sparked controversies when first published. Many of Machiavelli's contemporaries, who were witnessing the end of the medieval Age of Faith and experiencing the dawn of a more secular time, were sharply divided over the meaning of his writings. Especially damaging to the book's reputation was its persistent low opinion of human nature. Succeeding generations have debated his analysis of human behavior and his consequent rationale for a strong government. In modern secular society, many readers have come to accept Machiavelli's view that political power, driven by personal or group interests, must be understood in utilitarian and practical terms.

The Prince, a treatise on the art of successful governing, is composed of three parts. The first part, comprising eleven chapters, categorizes and describes the various types of existing governments. The second part, which consists of fourteen chapters, offers advice and examples on winning and maintaining political power. In these fourteen chapters, Machiavelli instructs the ruler on how to raise and organize armies, how to keep subjects loyal, and how to avoid the pitfalls of overconfidence and flattery. Throughout *The Prince,* the author compares and contrasts key traits that make a ruler a success or a failure. He also addresses the issue of fortune—what is now called opportunity—and emphasizes how often it affects a ruler. In the third part—the concluding chapter—Machiavelli calls upon "the prince" to unite the Italians against foreign oppressors and drive them from Italy.

Reading the Selections

Chapters XV, XVI, and XVII appear in the second part of *The Prince,* in which Machiavelli discusses the most effective way for a ruler to govern his subjects. He points out that his discussion is rooted in practical politics, rather than based on imaginary regimes created by writers—a reference to the idealized commonwealths of Plato and medieval Christian authors. In Chapter XV, Machiavelli lists traits for which rulers are praised or blamed—such as being called stubborn or flexible, religious or skeptical—and notes that no ruler could continuously practice the best of these without damaging his ability to govern. Thus, in a crisis the ruler should not shrink from being blamed for vices if they are needed to safeguard the state, though most of the time, the prince should pretend to be what he is not in order to keep his subjects' loyalty.

In Chapter XVI, Machiavelli focuses on the traits of generosity and miserliness and shows, through ancient and current examples, the consequences for rulers who practiced one or the other of them. He concludes, given his dark view of human nature, that a ruler is better to be miserly than generous. In Chapter XVII, Machiavelli raises perhaps the most controversial question in the treatise: Is it better for the ruler to be loved or feared? Ideally, the ruler should be both loved and feared, but as this is nearly impossible, then the ruler should be feared. Machiavelli, realizing that fear has its limits, ends on a cautionary note: The "wise prince" must avoid being hated by his subjects, for hatred is the soil out of which rebellions grow.

∽

Chapter XV
The Things for Which Men, and Especially Princes, Are Praised or Blamed

It now remains for us to see how a prince should govern his conduct towards his subjects or his friends. I know that this has often been written about before, and so I hope it will not be thought presumptuous for me to do so, as, especially in discussing this subject, I draw up an original set of rules. But since my intention is to say something that will prove of practical use to the inquirer, I have thought it proper to represent things as they are in real truth, rather than as they are imagined. Many have dreamed up republics and principalities which have never in truth been known to exist; the gulf between how one should live and how one does live is so wide that a man who neglects what is actually done for what should be done learns the way to self-destruction rather than self-preservation. The fact is that a man who wants to act virtuously in every way necessarily comes to grief among so many who are not virtuous. Therefore if a prince wants to maintain his rule he must learn how not to be virtuous, and to make use of this or not according to need.

So leaving aside imaginary things, and referring only to those which truly exist, I say that whenever men are discussed (and especially princes, who are more exposed to view), they are noted for various qualities which earn them either praise or condemnation. Some, for example, are held to be generous, and others miserly (I use the Tuscan[1] word rather than the word avaricious: we call a man who is mean with what he possesses, miserly, and a man who wants to plunder others, avaricious). Some are held to be benefactors, others are called grasping; some cruel, some compassionate; one man faithless, another faithful; one man effeminate and cowardly, another fierce and courageous; one man courteous, another proud; one man lascivious, another pure; one guileless, another crafty; one stubborn, another flexible; one grave, another frivolous; one religious, another sceptical; and so forth. I know everyone will agree that it would be most laudable if a prince possessed all the qualities deemed to be good among those I have enumerated. But, human nature being what it is, princes cannot possess those qualities, or rather

---

[1] **Tuscan** Having to do with Tuscany, the Italian region, whose capital is Florence, Machiavelli's home.

they cannot always exhibit them. So a prince should be so prudent that he knows how to escape the evil reputation attached to those vices which could lose him his state, and how to avoid those vices which are not so dangerous, if he possibly can; but, if he cannot, he need not worry so much about the latter. And then, he must not flinch from being blamed for vices which are necessary for safeguarding the state. This is because, taking everything into account, he will find that some of the things that appear to be virtues will, if he practises them, ruin him, and some of the things that appear to be wicked will bring him security and prosperity.

⧉

Chapter XVI
Generosity and Parsimony

So, starting with the first of the qualities I enumerated above, I say it would be splendid if one had a reputation for generosity; nonetheless if your actions are influenced by the desire for such a reputation you will come to grief. This is because if your generosity is good and sincere it may pass unnoticed and it will not save you from being reproached for its opposite. If you want to acquire a reputation for generosity, therefore, you have to be ostentatiously lavish; and a prince acting in that fashion will soon squander all his resources, only to be forced in the end, if he wants to maintain his reputation, to lay excessive burdens on the people, to impose extortionate taxes, and to do everything else he can to raise money. This will start to make his subjects hate him, and, since he will have impoverished himself, he will be generally despised. As a result, because of this generosity of his, having injured many and rewarded few, he will be vulnerable to the first minor setback, and the first real danger he encounters will bring him to grief. When he realizes this and tries to retrace his path he will immediately be reputed a miser.

So as a prince cannot practise the virtue of generosity in such a way that he is noted for it, except to his cost, he should if he is prudent not mind being called a miser. In time he will be recognized as being essentially a generous man, seeing that because of his parsimony his existing revenues are enough for him, he can defend himself against an aggressor, and he can embark on enterprises without burdening the people. So he proves himself generous to all those from whom he takes nothing, and they are innumerable, and miserly towards all those to whom he gives nothing, and they are few. In our own times great things have been accomplished only by those who have been held miserly, and the others have met disaster. Pope Julius II[2] made use of a reputation for generosity to win the papacy, but subsequently he made no effort to maintain this reputation, because he wanted to be able to finance his wars. The present king of France[3] has been able to wage so many wars without taxing his subjects excessively only because his long-standing parsimony enabled him to meet the additional expenses involved. Were the present king of Spain[4] renowned for his generosity he would not have started and successfully concluded so many enterprises.

So if a prince does not have to rob his subjects, if he can defend himself, if he is not plunged into poverty and shame, if he is not forced to become rapacious, he ought not to worry about being called a miser. Miserliness is one of those vices which sustain his rule. Someone may object: Caesar[5] came to power by virtue of his generosity, and many others, because they practised and were known for their generosity, have risen to the very highest positions. My answer to this is as follows. Either you are already a prince, or you are on the way to becoming one. In the first case, your generosity will be to your cost; in the second, it is certainly necessary to have a reputation for generosity. Caesar was one of those who wanted to establish his own rule over Rome; but if, after he had established it, he had remained alive and not moderated his expenditure he would have fallen from power.

Again, someone may retort: there have been many princes who have won great successes with their armies, and who have had the reputation of being extremely generous. My reply to this is: the prince gives away what is his own or his subjects', or else what belongs to others. In the first case he should be frugal; in the second, he should indulge his generosity to the full. The prince who campaigns with his armies, who lives by pillaging, sacking, and extortion, disposes of what belongs to aliens; and he must be open-handed, otherwise the soldiers would refuse to follow him. And you can be more liberal with what does not belong to you or your subjects, as Caesar, Cyrus,[6] and Alexander were. Giving away what belongs to strangers in no way affects your standing at home; rather it increases it. You hurt yourself only when you give away what is your own. There is nothing so self-defeating as generosity: in the act of practising it, you lose the ability to do so, and you become either poor and

---

[2] **Pope Julius II** (pope 1503–1513).
[3] **king of France** Louis XII (r. 1498–1515).

[4] **king of Spain** Ferdinand V (r. 1474–1504), joint ruler, with Isabella, of Castile; their marriage created the modern state of Spain; served as regent of Castile for his daughter, Joanna the Mad, 1506–1516. As Ferdinand II, he ruled Aragon, 1479–1516.
[5] **Caesar** Julius Caesar (100–44 B.C.). Roman general and statesman.
[6] **Cyrus** Cyrus II, known as the Great (ca. 585–ca. 529 B.C.). King of Persia and founder of the Achaemenian dynasty and empire.

despised or, seeking to escape poverty, rapacious and hated. A prince should try to avoid, above all else, being despised and hated; and generosity results in your being both. Therefore it is wiser to incur the reputation of being

a miser, which invites ignominy but not hatred, than to be forced by seeking a name for generosity to incur a reputation for rapacity, which brings you hatred as well as ignominy.

Chapter XVII
Cruelty and Compassion; and Whether It Is Better to Be Loved Than Feared, or the Reverse

Taking others of the qualities I enumerated above, I say that a prince should want to have a reputation for compassion rather than for cruelty: nonetheless, he should be careful that he does not make bad use of compassion. Cesare Borgia[7] was accounted cruel; nevertheless, this cruelty of his reformed the Romagna, brought it unity, and restored order and obedience. On reflection, it will be seen that there was more compassion in Cesare than in the Florentine people, who, to escape being called cruel, allowed Pistoia to be devastated.[8] So a prince should not worry if he incurs reproach for his cruelty so long as he keeps his subjects united and loyal. By making an example or two he will prove more compassionate than those who, being too compassionate, allow disorders which lead to murder and rapine. These nearly always harm the whole community, whereas executions ordered by a prince only affect individuals. A new prince, of all rulers, finds it impossible to avoid a reputation for cruelty, because of the abundant dangers inherent in a newly won state. Vergil,[9] through the mouth of Dido,[10] says:

Res dura, et regni novitas me talia cogunt
Moliri, et late fines custode tueri.[11]

Nonetheless, a prince should be slow to take action, and should watch that he does not come to be afraid of his own shadow; his behaviour should be tempered by humanity and prudence so that over-confidence does not make him rash or excessive distrust make him unbearable.

From this arises the following question: whether it is better to be loved than feared, or the reverse. The answer is that one would like to be both the one and the other; but because it is difficult to combine them, it is far better to be feared than loved if you cannot be both. One can make this generalization about men: they are ungrateful, fickle, liars, and deceivers, they shun danger and are greedy for profit; while you treat them well, they are yours. They would shed their blood for you, risk their property, their lives, their children, so long, as I said above, as danger is remote; but when you are in danger they turn against you. Any prince who has come to depend entirely on promises and has taken no other precautions ensures his own ruin; friendship which is bought with money and not with greatness and nobility of mind is paid for, but it does not last and it yields nothing. Men worry less about doing an injury to one who makes himself loved than to one who makes himself feared. The bond of love is one which men, wretched creatures that they are, break when it is to their advantage to do so; but fear is strengthened by a dread of punishment which is always effective.

The prince should nonetheless make himself feared in such a way that, if he is not loved, at least he escapes being hated. For fear is quite compatible with an absence of hatred; and the prince can always avoid hatred if he abstains from the property of his subjects and citizens and from their women. If, even so, it proves necessary to execute someone, this should be done only when there is proper justification and manifest reason for it. But above all a prince should abstain from the property of others; because men sooner forget the death of their father than the loss of their patrimony.[12] It is always possible to find pretexts for confiscating someone's property; and a prince who starts to live by rapine always finds pretexts for seizing what belongs to others. On the other hand, pretexts for executing someone are harder to find and they are less easily sustained.

However, when a prince is campaigning with his soldiers and is in command of a large army then he need not

---

[7] **Cesare Borgia** (1475/1476–1507) Member of an illustrious Italian family of Spanish origin. Son of Pope Alexander VI (d. 1503) by the Roman woman Vannozza Cattanei; appointed bishop of Pamplona in 1491, archbishop of Valencia in 1492, and cardinal in 1493; served as papal legate in 1497 and 1498; gave up cardinal's hat in 1498. Captain general of papal army in 1499; conquered, with French aid, Romagna and the Marches, 1499–1501; made duke by his father, 1501; seized Urbino in 1501; opposed by enemies, including Pope Julius II (elected 1503); imprisoned, 1504–1506; escaped and killed.
[8] **Pistoia . . . devastated** Pistoia was a subject-city of Florence, which forcibly restored order there when conflict broke out between two rival factions in 1501–1502. Machiavelli was concerned with this business at first hand.
[9] **Vergil** (70–19 B.C.) Roman poet (see *The Aeneid*).
[10] **Dido** Legendary Queen of Carthage. Originally a Phoenecian princess from Tyre, she fled to Africa and founded Carthage. Vergil made her tragic love affair with Aeneas, the founder of ancient Rome, the unifying theme for the first four books of the *Aeneid*.
[11] *Res . . . custode tueri.* "Harsh necessity, and the newness of my kingdom, force me to do such things and to guard my frontiers everywhere" *Aeneid* I, 563.

[12] **patrimony** An estate inherited from one's father.

worry about having a reputation for cruelty; because, without such a reputation, he can never keep his army united and disciplined. Among the admirable achievements of Hannibal[13] is included this: that although he led a huge army, made up of countless different races, on foreign campaigns, there was never any dissension, either among the troops themselves or against their leader, whether things were going well or badly. For this, his inhuman cruelty was wholly responsible. It was this, along with his countless other qualities, which made him feared and respected by his soldiers. If it had not been for his cruelty, his other qualities would not have been enough. The historians, having given little thought to this, on the one hand admire what Hannibal achieved, and on the other condemn what made his achievements possible.

That his other qualities would not have been enough by themselves can be proved by looking at Scipio,[14] a man unique in his own time and through all recorded history. His armies mutinied against him in Spain, and the only reason for this was his excessive leniency, which allowed his soldiers more licence than was good for military disci-pline. Fabius Maximus[15] reproached him for this in the Senate and called him a corrupter of the Roman legions.[16] Again, when the Locri[17] were plundered by one of Scipio's officers, he neither gave them satisfaction nor punished his officer's insubordination; and this was all because of his having too lenient a nature. By way of excuse for him some senators argued that many men were better at not making mistakes themselves than at correcting them in others. But in time Scipio's lenient nature would have spoilt his fame and glory had he continued to indulge it during his command; when he lived under orders from the Senate, however, this fatal characteristic of his was not only concealed but even brought him glory.

So, on this question of being loved or feared, I conclude that since some men love as they please but fear when the prince pleases, a wise prince should rely on what he controls, not on what he cannot control. He should only endeavour, as I said, to escape being hated.

---

[13] **Hannibal** (247–183 B.C.) Carthaginian general. In Second Punic War, led his troops from Spain, across the Alps, and into Italy, where he fought various battles and eventually marched on Rome, 218–211 B.C.; Romans held on and waited him out; recalled to Carthage in 203, and defeated at battle of Zama in 202 B.C.; headed Carthaginian government, 202–195 B.C.; fled to Asia Minor; committed suicide.
[14] **Scipio** Scipio Africanus (236–184/183 B.C.) Roman general. In Second Punic War, led army in Spain, 210–206 B.C.; led Roman invasion of Carthage; defeated **Hannibal** at battle of Zama in 202 B.C.

[15] **Fabius Maximus** (d. 203) Called *Cunctator*, the "Delayer." Roman general, famous for his delaying strategy against Hannibal in the Second Punic War. Fabius successfully made quick incursions against Hannibal's forces, while avoiding set battles. A group of English socialists in the late 1800s adopted the name Fabian in honor of this strategy.
[16] **legions** Roman army units, each composed of 3,000 to 6,000 foot soldiers with calvary.
[17] **Locri** Ancient city founded by the Greeks, located on the eastern side of the "toe" of Italy; Locri changed sides between Rome and its enemies until it was captured by **Scipio Africanus** and made Roman, in the Second Punic War.

CREDITS

AKHENATEN, "The Great Hymn to Aten" from *Wings of the Falcon: Life and Thought in Ancient Egypt*, translated by Joseph Kaster. Copyright © 1968 by Joseph Kaster. Reprinted with the permission of Henry Holt and Company, LLC.

LEON BATTISTA ALBERTI, from *On Painting*, translated by Cecil Grayson. Copyright © 1972 by Cecil Grayson. Reprinted with the permission of the Estate of Cecil Grayson.

Michael Alexander (trans.), excerpt from *Beowulf*. Copyright © 1973 by Michael Alexander. Reprinted with the permission of Penguin Books, Ltd.

ST. THOMAS AQUINAS, "Fifth Article" from *Summa Theologica, Volume II*, translated by the Fathers of the English Dominican Province. Copyright 1947 by Benzinger Publishing Company. Reprinted with the permission of the publisher.

ARISTOTLE, "A Description of Tragedy," "Reversal, Discovery, and Calamity," "Tragic Action," "Fear and Pity," and "The Characters of Tragedy" from *Classical Literary Criticism*, translated by T. S. Dorsch. Copyright © 1985 by T. S. Dorsch. Reprinted with the permission of Penguin Books Ltd. Book I from "Politics and Economics," translated by B. Jowett in *The Oxford Translation of Aristotle*, edited by W. D. Ross, Volume 10. Reprinted with the permission of Oxford University Press, Ltd.

ST. AUGUSTINE, from *Confessions*, translated by R.S. Pine-Coffin. Copyright © 1961 by R.S. Pine-Coffin. Reprinted with the permission of Penguin Books Ltd. from *Concerning The City of God: Against the Pagans*, translated by Henry Bettenson. Copyright © 1972 by Henry Bettenson. Reprinted with the permission of Penguin Books, Ltd.

MARCUS AURELIUS, excerpts from *Meditations*, translated by Gregory Hays. Copyright © 2002 by Random House, Inc. Reprinted with the permission of The Modern Library, a division of Random House, Inc.

Bible, excerpts from *The Holy Scriptures*. Copyright © 1985 by the Jewish Publication Society. Used by permission.

GIOVANNI BOCCACIO, "Introduction," and "First Day, Third Story" from *The Decameron*, translated by Mark Musa and Peter Bondanella. Copyright © 1982 by Mark Musa and Peter Bondanella. Reprinted with the permission of E. P. Dutton, a division of Penguin Group (USA) Inc.

BOETHIUS, from *The Consolation of Philosophy*, translated by V. E. Watts. Copyright © 1969 by V. E. Watts. Reprinted with the permission of Penguin Books, Ltd.

Baldassare Castiglione, from *The Book of the Courtier*, translated by George Bull. Copyright © 1967 by George Bull. Reprinted with the permission of Penguin Books, Ltd.

CATULLUS, 5, 22, 51, and 72 from *The Poems of Catullus*, translated by Peter Whigham. Copyright © 1966 by Peter Whigham. Reprinted with the permission of Penguin Books, Ltd.

GEOFFREY CHAUCER, "The General Prologue" from *The Canterbury Tales: Nine Tales and the General Prologue: A Norton Critical Edition*, edited by V.A. Kolve and Glending Olson. Copyright © 1989 by W. W. Norton & Company, Inc. Reprinted with the permission of W. W. Norton & Company, Inc. "The Prologue," and "The Wife of Bath's Tale" from *The Canterbury Tales*, translated by Nevil Coghill. Copyright © 1958, 1960, 1975, 1977 by Nevil Coghill. Reprinted with the permission of Penguin Books, Ltd.

CICERO, "The Dream of Scipio" from *On the Good Life*, translated by Michael Grant. Copyright © 1971 by Michael Grant. Reprinted with the permission of Penguin Books, Ltd.

ANNA COMNENA, excerpts from *The Alexiad of Anna Comnena*, translated by E.R.A. Sewter. Copyright © 1969 by E.R.A. Sewter. Reprinted with the permission of Penguin Books Ltd.

DANTE ALIGHERI, from *The Divine Comedy*, translated by John Ciardi. Copyright 1954, © 1957, 1959, 1960, 1961,

INDEX

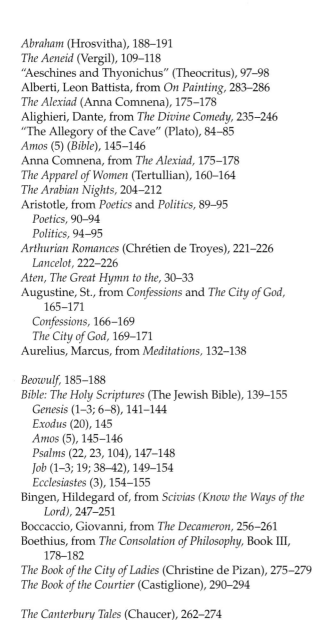